Fodor's
ESSENTIAL
CHINA

Welcome to China

China—old and new—is a feast for the senses. The vast, awe-inspiring landscapes run the gamut from river deltas, subtropical jungles, and deserts to pulsing megacities with space-age skylines. Tranquil palaces and fog-wrapped mountain peaks evoke the Taoist philosophers of yesteryear. Hong Kong's and Beijing's dizzying modernity exhilarates city culture vultures. Full of diverse peoples and traditions, this fast-changing country reveals its riches to travelers who seek them out, from foodies on a quest for the best dumplings to explorers trekking the Silk Road.

TOP REASONS TO GO

★ **Great Wall:** China's most iconic fortification delivers postcard-perfect views.

★ **Tiger Leaping Gorge:** Breathtaking mountain scenery rewards adventurous hikers.

★ **Architecture:** Futuristic skyscrapers vie with dynastic compounds to dazzle the eye.

★ **Food:** The vibrant flavors of authentic Chinese cuisine are a gourmand's delight.

★ **Imperial History:** Terracotta Warriors and ancient temples take you back 5,000 years.

★ **Cities:** Beijing's Olympic makeover, Hong Kong's harbor, Shanghai's Art Deco splendor.

Contents

Fodor's Features

MAPS

中国万向

Chapter 1

EXPERIENCE CHINA

25 ULTIMATE EXPERIENCES

China offers terrific experiences that should be on every traveler's list. Here are Fodor's top picks for a memorable trip.

1 Float Down the Li River

Relax in a bamboo armchair under an awning as your raft is paddled along the curve of the Li River, past the lush karst peaks on both sides. Or rent a kayak and explore the river on your own and in almost complete silence. *(Ch. 8)*

2 Visit the Temple of Heaven

The Temple of Heaven is not one structure but a 15th-century complex built inside a beautiful park. The anchor building is the wooden Hall of Prayer for Good Harvests. *(Ch. 3)*

3 See Giant Pandas

Pandas are supercute, and there's nowhere else in the world other than the Giant Panda Breeding Research Base where you'll see so many in one place. *(Ch. 9)*

4 Eat Dim Sum

Dim sum is a variety of bite-sized portions of food served in small bamboo steamers or on small plates. The more people in your party, the more dishes you can try. *(Ch. 7)*

5 Stroll through a Classical Garden

The Classical Gardens of Suzhou were built over nearly a thousand years, beginning in the 11th century. These set the standard for Classical Chinese garden design. *(Ch. 4)*

6 Visit Kashgar's Sunday Market

Kashgar's Sunday Market is actually two markets 6 miles apart. The Yengi Bazaar and Ulak Bazaar. Keen photographers won't be able to snap photos fast enough. *(Ch. 10)*

7 Eat Hotpot

Sichuan's cuisine owes its fiery flavor to the peppercorn of the same name. Hotpot broth is packed with heat so take care before slurping it down. *(Ch. 9)*

8 Go to the Top of Victoria Peak

Victoria Peak on Hong Kong Island reaches 1,811 feet. The Peak Tram is the world's steepest funicular railway, and riding it to the top is great fun. *(Ch. 7)*

9 Ogle the Longsheng Longji Rice Terraces

These rice terraces are cut into the hills, worked for generations by Yao, Dong, Zhuang, and Miao farmers, and look like undulating ribbons. They're mesmerizing. *(Ch. 8)*

10 See the Mogao Grottoes

Located outside Dunhuang on the Silk Road, these 700 caves are filled with ancient Buddhist art, including library caves dating from the 5th to early 11th centuries. *(Ch. 10)*

11 Tour Lijiang Old Town

Go off the town's few main streets and explore the quiet alleyways lined in traditional Naxi wooden houses. The Naxi have their own language and culture. *(Ch. 8)*

12 See the Forbidden City From Above

In Jingshan Park, walk up the winding staircase to the top of Jingshan Hill. On a clear day, it's the best view of the Forbidden City you'll ever have. *(Ch. 3)*

13 Eat an Egg Tart

Macau was a Portuguese colony and adopted delicious egg tarts. The shells are light and flaky, and the sweet custard interior has a crème brûlée consistency. *(Ch. 7)*

14 Go Hiking in the Yellow Mountains

This UNESCO Site is one of the most popular hiking spots in the country. Jagged mountaintops and unique rock formations peak in and out of a sea of clouds. *(Ch. 4)*

15 Hike Tiger Leaping Gorge

The world's deepest gorge offers intrepid travelers great treks. There are guesthouses scattered along the trail, or you can catch buses back to Lijiang. *(Ch. 8)*

16 Stroll Along the Bund

The colonial-era buildings on the Bund remain as iconic as ever. There are at least half-a-dozen architectural styles from the late 19th to early 20th centuries. *(Ch. 5)*

17 Take a Cable Car Ride Over the Big Buddha

Leave behind some of the chaos of Hong Kong and visit Tian Tian Buddha, or Big Buddha. It sits at the top of 268 steps and the cable car ride offers sweeping views. *(Ch. 7)*

18 Eat Xiaolongbao (Soup Dumplings)

The thin-skinned, soup-filled pork dumplings, are served with shredded ginger and Zhenjiang vinegar, a black rice vinegar made in Zhenjiang. *(Ch. 5)*

19 Visit the Giant Buddha in Leshan

The hand-carved Giant Buddha blissfully overlooks the swirling, choppy confluence of three rivers. It's 1,200 years old and is the world's largest Buddhist sculpture. *(Ch. 9)*

20 See the Neon Lights of Nathan Road

After dark in Kowloon, you can see the Hong Kong island skyline lit up, its lights reflected in Victoria Harbour, and the neon lights of Nathan Road are ablaze. *(Ch. 7)*

21 Eat Peking Duck

This former imperial court dish is now the specialty of a handful of restaurants around Beijing. It's carved tableside and served with hoisin sauce and thin pancakes. *(Ch. 3)*

22 Walk Around West Lake

Visitors come from across the country to see Hangzhou's West Lake. For thousands of years, it has inspired poems, stories, paintings, and sketches. *(Ch. 6)*

23 Get to the top of Emeishan

Ten-thousand-foot Emeishan is an important Buddhist pilgrimage site, one of China's Four Sacred Buddhist Mountains. The summit is a 25-mile trek up stone staircases. *(Ch. 9)*

24 Climb the Great Wall of China

If you only visit one historic site in the China, make it this. The Great Wall runs more than 13,000 miles—the distance by plane from New York to Beijing and back. *(Ch. 3)*

25 See the Terracotta Warriors

Three tombs house roughly 7,000 soldiers and hundreds of chariots and horses. The detail are incredible, each warrior has unique hair and facial features. *(Ch. 10)*

WHAT'S WHERE

1 Beijing. Beijing is in massive flux, and the construction never stops. Feel the ancient pulse beneath the current clamor.

2 Beijing to Shanghai: Hebei, Shandong, Anhui, Jiangsu. Discover a cultural and natural treasure trove—Huangshan peaks are islands in a sea of clouds, and canal-laced Suzhou is the Venice of the Orient.

3 Shanghai. In the 1920s Shanghai was known as the Whore of the Orient, but we like to think of her as a classy lady who knows how to have a good time. The party stopped for a few decades after the revolution, but now Shanghai is back in swing.

4 East Coast: Zhejiang, Fujian. Fujian's Xiamen is an undiscovered pearl, with all the history, culture, and infrastructure of more popular tourist magnets. Zhejiang's Hangzhou is known for scenic West Lake, immortalized in Chinese poetry.

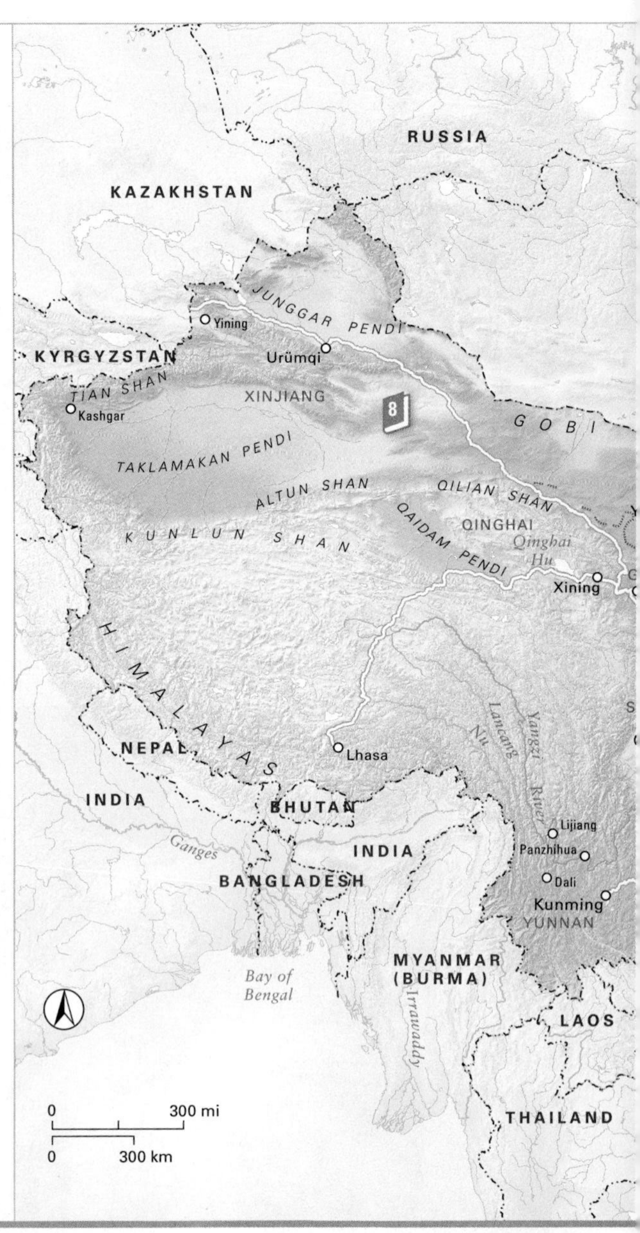

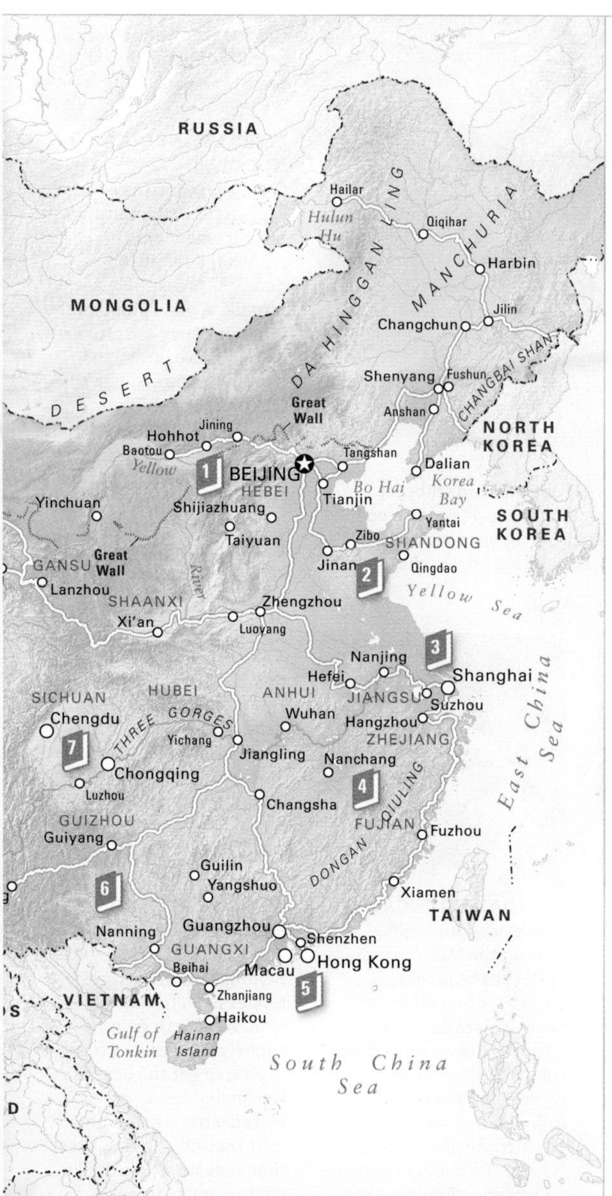

5 Hong Kong. A city of contrasts—east and west, old and new, work hard and play harder. Long nights of barhopping are offset by tai chi sessions at dawn.

6 Southwest: Guangxi, Guizhou, Yunnan. The mountains are high and the emperor is far away. If you're looking to take a walk on the wild tribal side, then any or all of these three regions should be high on your list.

7 Sichuan and Chongqing. China's latest industrial revolution is happening in faraway Sichuan and Chongqing, where the nearby Three Gorges Dam (in Hubei), while hotly debated, remains a stunning sight.

8 Xi'an and the Silk Road: Shaanxi, Gansu, Qinghai, Xinjiang. Distant and mysterious, this was ancient China's lifeline to the outside world. Visit the country's last remaining walled cities—Xi'an is fascinating for its cultural and its historical importance.

10 Things to Eat & Drink in China

CONGEE BREAKFAST
Cancel default morning munch options and embrace China's breakfast food of choice: congee. It's a long-cooked rice porridge, which comes spruced up with pickled vegetables and meat or tofu, depending on which region you're in.

SUCCULENT DONGPO PORK
This wonderfully fatty dish originates in Hangzhou, the pleasant city near Shanghai, with its famed West Lake. Named after the Song Dynasty scholar Su Dongpo, the pork is pan-fried then stewed before being served in small squares, and when prepared correctly, melts in the mouth.

HOLIDAY MOONCAKES
A wildly popular gift around the Mid-Autumn Festival, these round pastries, often with beautiful traditional patterns drawn onto their tops, are filled with increasingly varied ingredients but red bean paste is the most common. Häagen-Dazs now makes its own brand of mooncake.

WHITE RABBIT CANDIES
These milky soft candies are a taste of nostalgia for many Chinese and still available in pretty much every convenience store in the country. Take a handful home if only for their retro-cool packaging.

FIERY CHONGQING NOODLES
Chongqing cuisine isn't just known for its scorching hot pot—its *xiaomian*, translated to "little noodles," are equally as intense. A staple food in the huge city, they are often eaten for breakfast and usually feature hyper-spicy Sichuan pepper. If you don't make it to Chongqing you can try them at Pangmei Mianzhuang, a fantastic lane house restaurant in Beijing, which is usually rammed with locals slurping these supercheap noodle dishes.

XINJIANG LAMB SKEWERS
The lamb- and cumin-heavy cuisine of far-flung Xinjiang is loved across the land and these tasty grilled skewers are the perfect street food and available in every province.

THE ONE, THE ONLY: PEKING DUCK
The absolute must-try Beijing dish, from its juicy tender flesh to its crispy skin. It's worth going slightly high-end in the capital to get the best of the bird—the classy restaurants run by famed chef Da Dong have servers that slice up whole ducks next to your table.

Peking Duck

DIN TAI FUNG SOUP DUMPLINGS
Taiwanese restaurant chain Din Tai Fung might well serve the best soup dumplings, *xiao long bao*, in the world. Load up on the pork versions, dip them in ginger and vinegar, then either pop them in your mouth whole for a soupy burst or nibble an edge and suck out the liquid.

FLUFFY BAOZI
Steamed, fluffy, and ubiquitous across China, these doughy balls of joy are like oversized dumplings, but with marshmallow softness. They come stuffed with various ingredients, most commonly pork, and are often eaten as a breakfast snack but are delicious any time.

HAIRY CRAB
Every October the invasion of the hairy crabs begins in east China. They're most prized around the annual Golden Week national holiday, when the gooey orange roe matures. You'll see the funny little crabs strung up in every Chinese supermarket during this time.

BEGGAR'S CHICKEN
This is by far China's most fun dish: a whole chicken that comes served in a hard clay covering it's been cooked in, which the diner smashes with a hammer before tucking into the bird inside. Another meal with a legend, according to this one a beggar once wrapped a chicken in clay to cook it because he had no pots or pans, accidentally stumbling across a brilliant cooking technique.

DAINTY ZONGZI
These little parcels are one of China's most beloved traditional dishes. They typically feature glutinous rice stuffed with fillings that vary from meats to vegetables to nuts, wrapped in bamboo leaves and tied up with string. Eat them during the Dragon Boat Festival in late spring.

10 Things to Buy in China

FANS
China's ubiquitous folding paper fans actually originated in Japan. There are hundreds of other varieties, including the famous sandalwood fans from Jiangsu, the ink-sketched "fire-painting" fans from Guangdong region, and the Zhejiang silk fans.

SILK AND THE CHINESE KNOT
Handwoven chinese knots are all the rage with designers keen to incorporate aspects of their cultural heritage into their modern designs. China has been producing silk for over 5,000 years and the knots first gained popularity during the Qing dynasty but the craft was almost lost during the Cultural Revolution.

CHILI SAUCE
China is home to some of the hottest dishes out there, and while your mind might jump instantly to the hot and numbing spicy Sichuan pepper, don't overlook Chongqing's spicy hotpot, Hubei's hot and dry noodles, and Hunan's fiery red chili sauce. Chili fans will love dipping into the spice shops, and sampling the varieties of chili sauce, from peanut-loaded to black bean–infused.

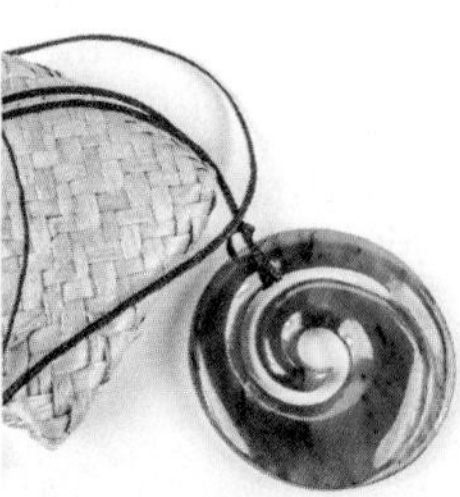

JADE
Jade is the equivalent of gold in China, and it can be far more valuable. It has long symbolized virtue, loyalty, and longevity. The stone's luck-bearing and health-bringing qualities make it one of the most sought-after gems in the world. Serious shoppers interested in purchasing authentic (and expensive) jade jewelry should visit Canton Road—colloquially known as Jade Street—in Hong Kong.

PEARLS

Pearls have been farmed in China since the 3rd century AD and for the last three decades, the country has been the world's largest producer of cultured pearls. The town of Zhuji, just outside of Shanghai, is where modern pearl cultivation began and is one of the best places to buy these real but farmed pearls.

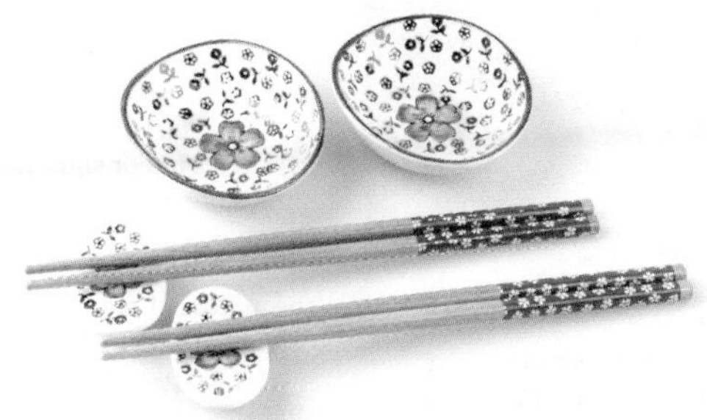

CHOPSTICKS

Traditional chopsticks were first popularized during the Ming Dynasty (1368-1644). They are made of anything from the common plastic to elegant lacquered bamboo. Learner chopsticks, with rubber tops connecting the chopsticks together, are great for kids.

OPERA MASKS

Beijing's famous opera was born in the Anhui and Hubei provinces to honor the birthday of the Qianlong Emperor in 1790. Mask colors represent different character traits: the red mask is usually the hero, while the yellow, green, and white masks denote different degrees of villainy.

TEA

Tea has a long history in China and it's cultivated across the country. Yunnan province is home to the famous Pu'er black tea, while Guizhou province is known for its light and fragrant green and white teas. Visiting a tea plantation is a great experience, as is partaking in a tea ceremony. Some places allow you to sample teas before you buy.

FAKES

From Louis Vuitton bags to Prada sunglasses to Montblanc pens, China's is rich in knock-off designer goods, but they're not all created equal. Try to find the real fakes, which are actually legitimate designer products that have been rejected from the factories because of quantity controls.

CUSTOM ARTWORK

The Dafen Artist Village in Shenzen used to produce 60% of the world's oil paintings, and this is still one of the best places in the world to get custom artwork produced. These skilled painters can reproduce incredible works for a fraction of the price, in a matter of hours.

8 Natural Wonders of China

HUANGGUOSHU WATERFALL NATIONAL PARK, GUIZHOU

Guizhou reveals even more of its natural splendor with China's biggest cluster of waterfalls. The park has 17 other waterfalls, but at 255 feet, Huangguoshu is the highest waterfall in the park and the tallest in East Asia.

TIGER LEAPING GORGE, YUNNAN

The jewel of southwest China is also one of the best hikes in the entire country. It's possible to spend several days exploring the well-marked trails along the northern side. Tiger Leaping Gorge is the deepest gorge of its kind in the world, with the Jinsha River winding its way through the bottom.

SHILIN STONE FOREST, YUNNAN

A huge national park that's home to limestone rock formations which date back over two hundred million years. The shape of these pointy karst peaks is the result of wind and water erosion over the years. The entire site is over 185 square miles.

SHUANGHE CAVE, GUIZHOU

Recently crowned the longest cave in Asia and the sixth in the world, Shuanghe stretches over 145 miles. There are over 200 entrances with connecting cave chambers, waterfalls, and underground rivers, some of which are home to cave shrimp and blind fish. Guizhou province is one of the most ethnically diverse provinces in the country.

QINGHAI LAKE, QINGHAI

Located over 10,000 feet above sea level, Qinghai Hu, also known as "Blue Lake," is China's largest saltwater lake. It's a major sight in its namesake province of Qinghai, in northwest China. This lake is also in the middle of many of the continent's main bird migration paths. Some species of rare birds are still sighted here, along with the Przhevalsky horse, which is the only living subspecies of wild horse left in the world. Traditionally, Tibetan Buddhists from the surrounding regions of Mongolia have circled the entirety of Qinghai Lake as a form of pilgrimage. The most popular time for this was during the year of the horse—and the journey was done either on horse or sometimes on foot.

HUANGSHAN, ANHUI

Above a sea of clouds is Huangshan, or Mount Huang, in eastern China. Also known as the Yellow Mountain, it's a designated UNESCO World Heritage Site and one of the most popular hiking spots in the country. The vistas of Huangshan are reminiscent

Huangshan, Anhui

of classic Chinese landscape paintings and have inspired poets and artists for centuries. The unique-looking granite peaks date back to the Mesozoic era and the mountain's particular pine trees, named Huangshan pine, have survived by growing directly out of these spectacular rock formations—it's a wonderful example of nature's strength and agility. Huangshan is known for being one of the best places in the country for green tea farming. Be sure to pick up some to bring back home.

LIMESTONE KARSTS OF YANGSHUO, GUANGXI

The ancient village town of Yangshuo is home to a sea of green peaks that rise almost vertically from the earth and give the entire area a dreamy, moonscape quality. Yangshuo's West Street offers great view of the fang-like peaks that surround the town.

BAILI AZALEA FOREST PARK , GUIZHOU PROVINCE

Covering a sprawling area of over 80 square miles is this park dedicated to white, pink, and red azalea blossoms. Located in the city of Bijie in southern China's Guizhou province, the Baili Azalea Forest Park's been recently renamed the One Hundred Mile Azalea Forest by officials. There are more than 20 types of rhododendron blooms in existence here, and this flower park is the largest natural Azalea forest in the world. The bloom lasts for about three weeks, and some of the azaleas have been sighted blooming together on the same shrub.

JIUZHAIGOU NATIONAL PARK, SICHUAN

Jiu means nine in Chinese, and the name literally translates as the "Valley of Nine Villages," the nine Tibetan villages in the area. This UNESCO Heritage Site is a scene of turquoise lakes and waterfalls contrasted with layers of red, orange and yellow foliage.

10 Best UNESCO Sites of China

THE GREAT WALL OF CHINA, BEIJING
The Great wall dates back more than 2,000 years and was built to defend against the invading hordes (notice the various watchtowers and barracks for soldiers), but also provided a way to collect taxes on goods being transferred along the Silk Road.

TEMPLE OF HEAVEN, BEIJING
Set in a huge, serene, mushroom-shaped park southeast of the Forbidden City, the Temple of Heaven is surrounded by splendid examples of Ming Dynasty architecture. Construction began in the early 15th century under Yongle, whom many call the "architect of Beijing."

TERRACOTTA WARRIORS, XI'AN
Local farmers stumbled upon this massive ancient treasure in 1974, and more continues to be unearthed to this day. Each statue has a unique expression, armor, and clothing. Archeologists soon realized that the soldiers were actually standing in order of their rank.

FORBIDDEN CITY, BEIJING
Once the Ming and Qing Dynasty's palace complex, the modern city of Beijing has grown around this majestic and sprawling series of buildings. This is the largest collection of preserved ancient wooden structures on the planet, according to UNESCO, and now houses the Palace Museum that draws thousands of tourists daily to see its collection of Ming and Qing Dynasty art.

LINGYIN TEMPLE, HANGZHOU
This is one of the largest Buddhist temples in China and it contains a working monastery with numerous grottoes and gardens dotted with statues and pagodas. At the Feilai Feng scenic area and grottoes, look for the expansive rock reliefs depicting various scenes of Buddha. The double-eaved Hall of Heavenly Kings is the main entrance to the temple.

OLD CITY WALL, XI'AN
This defensive barrier wraps around the old city of Xi'an for nearly nine miles and marks the original city center, which was one of the ending points of the Silk Road. It is one of the best preserved original fortification walls in the country and undergoes regular refurbishment.

GIANT BUDDHA, LESHAN
Standing at 233 feet tall, this massive statue is carved into the sandstone cliff facing a point where several rivers meet each other. Its imposing structure is framed by lush greenery. Look closely at the impressive carved details, like the more than 1,000 coiled buns in the hair.

CLASSICAL GARDENS, SUZHOU
The city of Suzhou is known for its famous gardens, the most important and the city's largest being the Humble Administrator's Garden. It has pavilions and bridges that cross over atmospheric ponds shaded by crape myrtle branches hanging low toward the water.

OLD TOWN OF LIJIANG, LIJIANG
Located at the base of majestic Jade Dragon Snow Mountain, visiting Old Town is like stepping back more than 1,000 years in time. Pedestrians stroll along the canal-side pathways that wind through town and are crisscrossed by the most charming arched bridges. Lijiang is home to the Naxi people, who are related to Tibetans but have their own language and culture.

MOGAO CAVES, DUNHUANG
Also known as the Caves of the Thousand Buddhas, the hand-carved Mogao Caves are located along the historic Silk Road, where Buddhism is said to have entered China. With more than 1,000 paintings and sculptures of Buddha, this is the world's largest collection of Buddhist artwork. A massive cache of historic documents dating back more than 1,700 years is also housed here.

CHINA BEST BETS

Fodor's writers and editors have chosen our favorites to help you plan. Search individual chapters for more recommendations.

RESTAURANTS

BEST FOR ROMANCE

Hutong, *$$$$, Ch. 7*
Inakaya, *$$$$, Ch. 7*
Lost Heaven, *$$, Ch. 5*
Mercato $$$$, *Ch. 5*
Restaurante Espaço Lisboa, *$$, Ch. 7*
Together, *$$$, Ch. 5*

BEST HAND-PULLED NOODLES

Ma Zilu Beef Noodles, *$, Ch. 9*
Made in China, *$$$, Ch. 3*
Old Beijing Noodle King, *$, Ch. 3*
Yau Yuan Xiao Jui, *$, Ch. 9*

BEST FOR FAMILIES

Bellagio, *$, Ch. 5*
Bellini, *$$, Ch. 3*
Brooklyn Pizzeria, *$$, Ch. 7*
De Fa Chang Restaurant, *$$, Ch. 9*
Deng Qiang, *$$, Ch. 8*
Goldfinch Restaurant, *$$, Ch. 6*

BEST WESTERN CUISINE

8½ Otto e Mezzo Bombana, *$$$$, Ch. 7*
A Lorcha, *$$, Ch. 7*
Aux Beaux Arts, *$$$, Ch. 7*
Bellini, *$$, Ch. 5*
Bottega, *$$, Ch. 3*
Brooklyn Pizzeria, *$$, Ch. 7*
Café Gray Deluxe, *$$$$, Ch. 7*
Ginger by the Park, *$, Ch. 5*

BEST YUNNAN CUISINE

1910 La Gare du Sud, *$$, Ch. 7*
Dali Courtyard, *$$, Ch. 7 and Ch. 3*
Hani Geju, *$$, Ch. 3*

BEST SICHUAN CUISINE

Golden Maurya, *$$, Ch. 5*
Hong Xing, *$$, Ch. 8*
Huang Cheng Lao Ma, *$$$, Ch. 8*
Little Swan Hot Pot, *$$$, Ch. 8*
Transit, *$$$, Ch. 3*
Yu Xin Chuan Cai, *$, Ch. 5*

BEST DUMPLINGS IN SHANGHAI

Bai Wei Jiaozi Cheng, *$$, Ch. 5*
Da Hu Chun, *$, Ch. 5*
Fuchun Xiaolong, *$, Ch. 5*
Lu Bo Lang, *$$, Ch. 5*
Jia Jia Tang Bao, *$, Ch. 5*
Paradise Dynasty, *$, Ch. 5*
Sui Tang Li, *$$$, Ch. 5*

BEST PEKING DUCK IN BEIJING

Da Dong Roast Duck, *$$$, Ch. 3*
Deyuan Roast Duck, *$, Ch. 3*
Duck de Chine, *$$$$, Ch. 3*
Made in China, *$$$, Ch. 3*
Jingzun Roast Duck Restaurant, *$, Ch. 3*

BEST DIM SUM IN HONG KONG

Yung Kee, *$, Ch. 7*
Wing Lei, *$$$$, Ch. 7*
Dynasty 8, *$$, Ch. 7*

★FODOR'S CHOICE BEIJING

Dali Courtyard, *$$, Ch. 3*
King's Joy, *$$$$, Ch. 3*
Made In China, *$$$, Ch. 3*
Temple Restaurant Beijing, *$$$$, Ch. 3*
Da Dong Roast Duck, *$$$, Ch. 3*
Din Tai Fung, *$$, Ch. 3*
Migas, *$$, Ch. 3*
Sake Manzo, *$$, Ch. 3*
Yotsuba, *$$$, Ch. 3*

★FODOR'S CHOICE HONG KONG

Tim's Kitchen, *$$$, Ch. 7*
Café Gray Deluxe, *$$$$, Ch. 7*
The Chairman, *$$$, Ch. 7*
8½ Otto e Mezzo Bombana, *$$$$, Ch. 7*
Fa Zu Jie, *$$$$, Ch. 7*
Little Bao, *$, Ch. 7*
Lung King Heen, *$$$$, Ch. 7*
Liu Yuan Pavilion, *$$, Ch. 7*
Samsen, *$$, Ch. 7*
Tung Po, *$$, Ch. 7*
Hutong, *$$$$, Ch. 7*
Yau Yuan Xiao Jui, *$, Ch. 7*

★FODOR'S CHOICE SHANGHAI

Lost Heaven, *$$, Ch. 7*
Sui Tang Li, *$$$, Ch. 7*
Yong Yi Ting, *$$$$, Ch. 7*

HOTELS

BEST FOR FAMILIES

Andaz Hotel Shanghai Xintiandi, *$$, Ch. 5*

Butterfly on Morrison, *$, Ch. 3*

Grand Coloane Resort, *$$, Ch. 7*

Grand Hyatt Beijing, *$$$$, Ch. 3*

The Giggling Tree, *$, Ch. 7*

Huiquan Dynasty Hotel, *$, Ch. 9*

InterContinental Shanghai Ruijin, *$, Ch. 5*

BEST VALUE

Bishop Lei International House, *$, Ch. 7*

Crown Hotel, *$, Ch. 8*

Ibis Xian, *$, Ch. 9*

Melia Shanghai Hongqiao, *$, Ch. 5*

Minshan Fandian, *$, Ch. 7*

New Century Grand Hotel Shaoxing, *Ch. 5*

New Era Hotel, *$, Ch. 7*

Suzhou Garden View Hotel, *$, Ch. 3*

Tibet Hotel, *$, Ch. 8*

BEST SPLURGE

Aman at Summer Palace, *$$$$, Ch. 3*

Amanfayun Resort, *$$$$, Ch. 5*

Four Seasons Hotel Hangzhou at West Lake, *$$$$, Ch. 5*

The Landmark Mandarin Oriental, *$$$$, Ch. 7*

Mandarin Oriental Hong Kong, *$$$$, Ch. 7*

The Peninsula Hong Kong, *$$$$, Ch. 7*

The Peninsula Shanghai, *$$$$, Ch. 4*

The Regent, *$$$$, Ch. 3*

The Ritz-Carlton, Hong Kong, *$$$$, Ch. 7*

Wynn Palace Cotai, *$$$$, Ch. 7*

BEST HISTORICAL HOTELS

Aman at Summer Palace, *$$$$, Ch. 3*

Amanfayun Resort, *$$$$, Ch. 5*

Capella Shanghai Jian Ye Li, *$$$$, Ch. 5*

Donghu Hotel, *$, Ch 5*

Fairmont Peace Hotel, *$$$, Ch. 4*

Hotel Lisboa, *$, Ch 6*

Mandarin Oriental Hong Kong, *$$$$, Ch. 7*

Pig's Inn, *$, Ch. 3*

Qi Wang Lou, *$$, Ch. 3*

Shangri-La Hotel Hangzhou

★FODOR'S CHOICE BEIJING

Beijing Hotel NUO, *$$, Ch. 3*

Grand Hyatt Beijing, *$$$$, Ch. 3*

Hilton Beijing Wangfujing, *$$$, Ch. 3*

Holiday Inn Express Beijing Dongzhimen, *$, Ch. 3*

Lüsongyuan, *$, Ch. 3*

The Orchid, *$, Ch. 3*

The Regent, *$$, Ch. 3*

Temple Hotel Beijing, *$$$$, Ch. 3*

3+1 Bedrooms, *$$, Ch. 3*

Waldorf Astoria Beijing, *$$$$, Ch. 3*

EAST, *Beijing, $$, Ch. 3*

Four Seasons Hotel Beijing, *$$$, Ch. 3*

The Opposite House, *$$$, Ch. 3*

Park Hyatt Beijing, *$$$$, Ch. 3*

St. Regis, *$$, Ch. 3*

Aman at Summer Palace, *$$$$, Ch. 3*

★FODOR'S CHOICE HONG KONG

Bishop Lei International House, *$, Ch. 7*

Four Seasons Hotel Hong Kong, *$$$$, Ch. 7*

The Landmark Mandarin Oriental, *$$$$, Ch. 7*

Mandarin Oriental Hong Kong, *$$$$, Ch. 7*

The Upper House, *$$$$, Ch. 7*

Little Tai Hang, *$$, Ch. 7*

Hop Inn Carnarvon, *$, Ch. 7*

Hotel ICON, *$$$, Ch. 7*

InterContinental Hong Kong, *$$, Ch. 7*

The Peninsula Hong Kong, *$$$$, Ch. 7*

The Ritz-Carlton, Hong Kong, *$$$$, Ch. 7*

W Hong Kong, *$$$$, Ch. 7*

★FODOR'S CHOICE SHANGHAI

The Peninsula Shanghai, *$$$$, Ch. 7*

The Middle House, *$$$$, Ch. 7*

The PuLi Hotel & Spa, *$$$, Ch. 7*

URBN, *$$, Ch. 7*

Mandarin Oriental Pudong, *Shanghai, $$$$, Ch. 7*

Pudong Shangri-La, *East Shanghai, $$$$, Ch. 7*

China Today

GOVERNMENT

Mao Zedong's announcement of the establishment of the People's Republic of China on October 1, 1949, finished one turbulent chapter in Chinese history and began another. The fall of the Qing, growing incursion by foreign countries, and the devastation of World War II sandwiched between two periods of bloody civil war gave way to purges of the country's artists and intellectuals, increasing isolationism, the colossal failure of the Great Leap Forward, and the tragic chaos of the Cultural Revolution.

The last quarter century has been characterized by relative stability and growth. Since the late 1970s the sole power holder in the People's Republic of China, the Chinese Communist Party, has brought hundreds of millions out of poverty and significantly relaxed its iron grip on personal freedoms. Diplomatically, Beijing has also become an increasingly savvy power broker on the global stage, while Western powers have been distracted by war and economic woes.

The party has no shortage of challenges that threaten its mandate to rule, including widespread corruption, an increasingly vocal and media-savvy populace, environmental disasters, and a widening wealth gap. In 2014, thousands of pro-democracy advocates shut down city streets in Hong Kong protesting reforms to Hong Kong's political system that would allow direct elections, but only from cherry-picked candidates that meet Beijing's approval.

ECONOMY

China is undergoing the greatest economic expansion the world has ever seen, with the country now the world's most important producer and consumer of just about everything. Since the launch of Paramount Leader Deng Xiaoping's reform and open policy in 1978, the Middle Kingdom has experienced roughly 10% annual GDP growth and has become the world's second-largest economy, trailing only that of the United States (for now).

China's coastal region was the early beneficiary of economic reforms, with cities such as Shanghai, Beijing, Shenzhen, and Guangzhou powering an export-focused economic model. Today the story is the awakening of markets in second- and third-tier cities as the country moves toward a consumption-driven economy.

MEDIA

The media in China has primarily served as a government mouthpiece since 1949. Since 1999 the Internet has not only provided Chinese people with greater access to information, it has also given rise to "Netizens," Chinese who use the Internet to voice their concerns and displeasures with modern society.

Beijing's attempts to manage the Internet have drawn much criticism beyond China's borders, but that hasn't stopped the Internet from becoming a part of daily life for more and more Chinese. With more than 772 million people regularly going online, China is the world's largest Internet market.

Government attempts to control the Internet have caused some of the world's biggest companies to pull out of the country or be blocked. Google shut down services 2010, rerouting traffic to Hong Kong, but has attempted to reenter mainland China in recent years with proposed censored changes to its search engine. Sites including Facebook and Twitter were blocked in 2009, presumably owing to government concerns about the potential for social media to be used in organizing anti-government activities.

RELIGION

Officially an atheist country, China is home to large numbers of Buddhists, Muslims, Christians, and Taoists. Until recently, practicing any religion could lead to detention or worse, but now the country's temples, mosques, and churches are active once more—although the watchful eye of the government is never far away.

Despite its general increasing tolerance toward religion, the Chinese government has taken strong measures against groups that it considers a threat to its rule, most notably the Falun Gong, which it considered a cult and banned in 2000. Buddhists in Tibet and Uighur Muslims in Xinjiang frequently clash with police and soldiers, leading to heightened tension in those regions.

SPORTS

Despite its Olympic success, China has not been able to develop popular homegrown sports leagues. Men's soccer is seen as one of the country's biggest disappointments—China's national team has only once qualified for the World Cup. The national soccer league is riddled with corruption and empty seats, with most Chinese preferring to watch European matches.

Basketball is also extremely popular in China—even remote mountaintop villages have a court or two. In the late 1990s NBA games began to be broadcast on the mainland, to the delight of sports fans. Yao Ming, now retired from the Houston Rockets, was one of China's most successful athletes to play internationally. Everyone from kids to grandparents seemed to have a Chicago Bulls cap, and Michael Jordan was as recognizable as Bill Clinton. Today Kobe Bryant and a new generation of stars are being emulated by Chinese streetballers, and many former NBA players are finding second careers in the Chinese Basketball Association.

SEXUAL MORES

China is often thought of as a sexually conservative country, but you don't get to be the world's most populous country by being a bunch of prudes. Over the centuries Chinese society has seen it all, from polygamy to prostitutes, from eunuchs to transvestite actors.

Premarital sex in China may be discouraged, but young Chinese all over the country are engaging in sex, whether it be with a steady boyfriend or girlfriend or a drunken one-night stand. Public displays of affection in broad daylight aren't commonplace, but also not unheard-of.

Part and parcel with China's economic development has been the return of prostitution. More often than not, Chinese hotels will have on-site prostitution, and the odd international five-star occasionally gets busted for offering "special services" to guests.

Homosexuality was officially considered a mental illness in China until 2001—since then the country has become considerably more accepting of gays, lesbians, and transgendered individuals. These days nearly every major city has a few gay bars, and even straight Chinese take fashion cues from their LGBTQ "comrades."

Sexual relations between Chinese and foreigners are generally accepted, but there is occasional friction or unpleasantness. On the short end of China's gender-imbalance stick, some Chinese men resent foreign men and the Chinese women who date them. On the flip side of that coin, a Chinese man who is dating a foreign woman is often hailed as a stud.

What to Read and Watch Before Your Trip

With almost six thousand years of intrigue and plot twists, China is often touted as the oldest surviving civilization. The empire has ebbed and flowed over the centuries, and the language, dress, and customs have changed beyond recognition, but China remains, as it did in Marco Polo's day, one of the most fascinating places on earth. Start your trip with a little armchair travel and check out these recommended works from some of the county's most interesting contemporary artists.

BOOKS

TO LIVE BY YU HUA

Though initially banned in China, Yu Hua's 1993 novel is now considered a classic of Chinese literature. It tells the story of Xu Fugoi who starts out as a privileged young man who gambles away all of his family's money. Over the course of his life he and his family endure a string of hardships and Fugoi transforms from the spoiled son of a rich landlord into a kind peasant. By the end of his life, he has only an ox for company, but still he perseveres.

RAISE THE RED LANTERN BY SU TONG

This collection of three novellas explores how China's old ways continued to prevail in the early 20th century. The first of the novellas is *Raise the Red Lantern,* which was adapted into a widely acclaimed film starring Gong Li, tells the story of a young woman who leaves college after her father dies by suicide. She becomes the fourth concubine of a wealthy merchant only to find herself enmeshed in the cruelty and dysfunction of the household. *Nineteen Thirty-Four Escapes* follows the story of a family over the course of a year as they endure sickness, poverty, and uncertainty. The third novella, *Opium Family,* tells of a wealthy landowning family of opium growers who are brought low by their own corruption and greed.

FRONTIER BY CAN XUE

This surreal novel from Can Xue (a pseudonym that means "dirty snow, leftover snow") takes place in the small community of Pebble Town, at the base of Snow Mountain. Each chapter is told from the point of view of a different resident. Though translated into English in simple, precise language, the effect of this experimental text is purposefully hazy and mystifying. For readers, it can be challenging and intoxicating all at once.

RED SORGHUM BY MO YAN

The novel (which contains five volumes entitled "Red Sorghum," "Sorghum Wine," "Dog Ways," "Sorghum Funeral," and "Strange Death") tells the story of three generations of a family caught up in the turbulent years that gripped rural China in the 1920s and 30s, with threats from without (Japanese invaders) and from within (clashing warlords). Though frequently brutal and violent this vividly rendered novel is as haunting and lyrical as it is unforgettable.

NO ENEMIES, NO HATRED BY LIU XIABO

When writer and human rights activist Liu Xiabobo was awarded the Nobel Prize in 2010 he was unable to accept the honor as he was serving an 11-year sentence for "incitement to subvert state power." In 2017, Liu died of an unspecified illness when Beijing refused to release him so that he could seek medical treatment abroad, despite the insistence of family, medical experts, and foreign governments. This collection of selected essays and poems (chosen by Liu's wife) challenges China's government and champions the dignity of those targeted by its tyranny, as only the country's most famous dissident could.

MOVIES

CROUCHING TIGER, HIDDEN DRAGON

Ang Lee's *wuxia* (fiction genre about martial artists of ancient China) epic tells the story of a 19th-century martial arts master who, having decided to retire, entrusts his legendary sword to a fellow warrior and subject of his unspoken love. But when the sword is stolen from the house of a nobleman by a mysterious thief he finds that the past isn't so easy to leave behind. It's a film that balances stunning action set pieces—staged everywhere from crowded teahouses to the remote reaches of the Gobi desert—with beautifully rendered themes of duty, love, and regret.

A TOUCH OF SIN

This stark drama from Jia Zhangke is loosely based on actual news stories, telling the tales of four different people—a man pushed to his breaking point by the corrupt oligarchs that control his town, a killer, a woman navigating an affair with a married man, and a young man who leaves a factory to work in a host club that caters to wealthy women—and how their lives overlap, if only for the briefest of moments. It is a bleak, violent, and unflinching examination on China in its modern, capitalist age.

AI WEIWEI: NEVER SORRY

This documentary examines the life and work of artist and activist Ai Weiwei. It follows him as he prepared a piece in which he gathers the names of 5,000 students killed in the 2008 Sichuan earthquake—deaths he believes were caused due to corrupt local officials' negligence in the construction of the collapsed schools.

IN THE HEAT OF THE SUN

Set during the Cultural Revolution, *In the Heat of the Sun* is a coming of age story about a teenage boy nicknamed Monkey. With their parents distracted and school out of session, Monkey and his friends are free to roam the streets of Beijing. The dreamlike quality of the film allows it to play with and comment on the elusive nature of memory.

YELLOW EARTH

This period piece, set in the 1930s, follows the story of a young communist soldier who travels to Yan'nan, a city in the Shaanxi province that was the epicenter of the Chinese Communist revolution. He's been tasked by the propaganda department to collect happy folk songs, only to find that the people in Yan'nan have only known hardship, so all of their songs are sad. Director Chen Kaige's debut marked the rise of Chinese cinema's Fifth Generation.

People of China

People often think of China as an ancient, monolithic culture comprised of a single, massive group of genetically similar people. In actuality, China contains a rich mosaic of different cultures and ethnicities, and officially recognizes 56 distinct ethnic groups. Ranging from populations of a few thousand to 1.3 billion, each group has made a unique contribution to China's cultural diversity with its language, costume, cuisine, philosophies, and traditions.

THE HAN

The largest of China's ethnic groups is the **Han** people, who make up more than 90% of China's total population and around one-fifth of all humanity. They trace their origins to the Yellow River region, and take their name from the Han Dynasty, which was established in 206 BC. The Han have had the biggest impact on China's history, and every major dynasty but two—the Yuan and the Qing—has been Han.

THE ZHUANG

Outside of China, few people know of the **Zhuang** people, but they are China's second-largest ethnic group. The Zhuang speak a language related to Thai, and are primarily found in Guangxi, which is officially an "autonomous region" and ruled by the Zhuang, at least in theory.

THE TIBETANS

Tibetans—known for their unique brand of Buddhism—are the best-known ethnic group inhabiting China's more rugged geography.

THE PEOPLES OF YUNNAN PROVINCE

Mountainous Yunnan Province in the country's southwest is home to the largest variety of ethnic groups, with some like the **Jinuo** and **Pumi** found nowhere else. **Tibetans, Naxi, Bai, Yi,** and **Lisu** are major ethnic groups found in the highlands of northwest Yunnan. In southern Yunnan, near the borders with Laos and Vietnam, there are ethnic **Dai, Hani,** and **Miao,** who have more in common with Southeast Asia than northern China. The Miao people are spread across Southern China, and are typically found in mountain villages.

THE MONGOLS AND MANCHUS

The **Mongols** and **Manchus** are the two Chinese ethnic groups that can claim to have ruled the Han. Kublai Khan founded the Yuan Dynasty in 1271, but keeping control over China and other territories proved too much for the Mongols, and the dynasty was finished just under a century later. Today Mongols in China are primarily found in Inner Mongolia in the country's north, where many still live nomadic lives on the grasslands.

The Qing Dynasty of the Manchus had more staying power, running from 1644 to 1912 and producing several notable emperors. Under Qing rule Han Chinese adopted some Manchu customs, including the long braids worn by men and the binding of women's feet. Most Manchus in China live in the northeastern provinces of Jilin, Liaoning, and Heilongjiang.

THE UIGHURS AND THE HUI

The Muslim **Uighurs** of Xinjiang in northwest China are more numerous than Tibetans, and are related to modern-day Turks—some Uighurs have blonde hair and green eyes. The **Hui** are China's largest Muslim group, and are known for being skilled businesspeople—not a big surprise, considering that they are descended from Silk Road traders. Of China's minorities, the Hui are the most widely dispersed—Hui-run Muslim restaurants can be found in virtually every city or large town.

Terracotta warriors

THE AGE OF EMPIRES

When asked his opinion on the historical impact of the French Revolution, Zhou Enlai, the first Premier of Communist China, quipped, "It's too early to tell." Though a bit tongue in cheek, China does measure its history in millennia, and in its grand timeline, interactions with the West have been mere blips.

According to historical records, Chinese civilization stretches back to the 15th century BC—markings found on turtle shells carbon dated to around 1500 BC bear some similarity to modern Chinese script. China then resembled city-states rather than a unified nation. Iconic figures such as Laozi (the father of Taoism), Sun Tzu (author of the Art of War), and Confucius lived during this period. Generally, 221 BC is accepted as the beginning of Imperial China, when the city-states united under various banners.

Over the next 2,200 years (give or take a few), China alternated between periods of harmony and political upheaval. Its armies conquered new territory and were in turn conquered by external invaders (most of whom wound up themselves being assimilated).

By the early 18th century, the long, slow decline of the Qing—the last of China's Imperial dynasties—was already in progress, making the ancient nation ripe for exploitation by rising European powers. The Imperial era ended with the forced abdication of child Emperor Puyi (whose life is chronicled in Bernardo Bertolucci's The Last Emperor), and it's here that the history of modern China, first with the founding of the republic under Dr. Sun Yat-sen and then with the establishment of the People's Republic under Mao Zedong, truly begins.

Writing Appears

1500 BC | 1200 BC | 900 BC

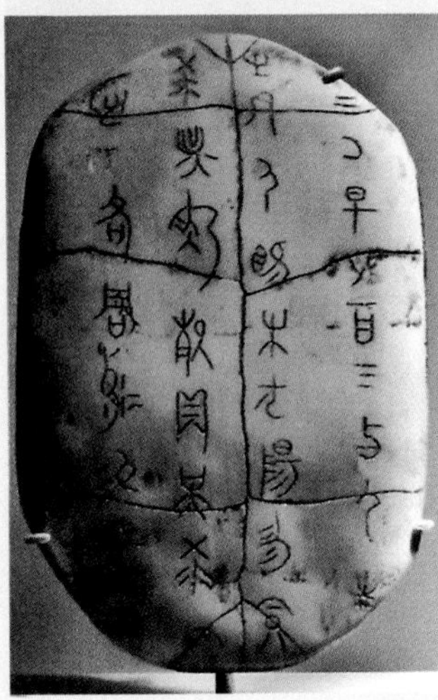

(left) Oracle shell with early Chinese characters. (top, right) The Great Wall stretches 4,163 miles from east to west. (bottom, right) Confucius, Lao-tzu, and a Buddhist Arhat.

CIRCA 1500 BC

Writing Appears

The earliest accounts of Chinese history are still shrouded in myth and legend, and it wasn't until 1959 that stories were verified by archaeological findings. For millennia, people formed communities in the fertile lands of what is now central China. The first recorded Chinese characters are said to have been developed 3,500 years ago. Though sometimes referred to as the Shang Dynasty, this period was more of a precursor to modern Chinese dynasties than a truly unified kingdom.

722–475 BC

The Warring States Period

China was so far from unified that these centuries are collectively remembered as the Warring States Period. As befitting such a contentious time, military science progressed, iron replaced bronze, and weapons material improved. Some of China's greatest luminaries lived during this period, including the father of Taoism, Lao-tzu, Confucius, and Sun-Tzu, one of the greatest military tacticians and the author of the infamous *Art of War*, which is still studied in military academies around the world.

221–207 BC

The First Dynasty

The Qin Dynasty eventually defeated all of the other warring factions thanks to their cutting-edge military technology, namely the cavalry. The Qin were also called Ch'in, which may be where the word China first originated. The first Emperor, Qin Shi Huang, unified much of the lands and established a legal code and vast bureaucracy to hold it together. The Qin dynasty also standardized the written and spoken language and introduced a common currency.

(left) Terracotta warrior. (top right) Temple of Xichan in Fuzhou

In order to protect his newly unified country, Qin Shi Huang ordered the creation of the massive Great Wall of China, which was built and rebuilt over the next 1,000 years. He was also a sculpture enthusiast and commissioned a massive army of stone soldiers to follow him into the afterlife. Buried with him, these terra-cotta warriors would remain hidden from the eyes of the world for two thousand years, until they were found by a farmer digging in a field just outside of Xian. These warriors are among the most important archaeological finds of the 20th century.

Buddhism Arrives

220–265 AD

Emperor Qin's dreams of a unified China fell apart, and eventually the kingdom split into three warring factions. But what was bad for stability turned out to be good for literature. The Three Kingdoms Period is still remembered in song and story. The Romance of the Three Kingdoms is as popular among Asian bookworms as the Legend of King Arthur is among Western readers. It's still widely read and has been translated into almost every language. Variations of the story have been adapted for manga, television series, and video games.

The Three Kingdoms period was filled with court intrigue, murder, and massive battles that, while exciting to read about centuries later, weren't much fun at the time. Armies ravaged the countryside, and most people lived and died in misery. Perhaps it was the carnage and disunity of the time that turned the country into a magnet for forces of harmony; it was during this period that Buddhism took hold in China, traveling over the Himalayas from India, via the Silk Road.

Religion Diversifies

600 800 1000

(left) Statue of Genghis Khan. (top right) Dong-guan Mosque in Xining, Qinghai. (bottom right) Empress Shengshen

618–845 Religion Diversifies

Chinese spiritual life continued to diversify. Nestorian Monks from Asia Minor arrived bearing news of Christianity, and Saad ibn Abi Waqqas (a companion of the Prophet Muhammad) supposedly visited the Middle Kingdom to spread the word of Islam. During this era, Wu Zetian, onetime concubine, seized power from the Tang Dynasty and became the first (and only) woman to assume the title of emperor. She ruled for 25 years through puppet emperors and finally, for 15 years, as Emperor Shengshen.

1271–1368 Ghengis Invades

In Xanadu did Kublai Khan a stately pleasure dome decree . . .

Or so goes the famed Coleridge poem. But Kublai's grandfather Temujin (better known as Ghengis Khan) had bigger things in mind. One of the greatest war tacticians in history, he united the restive nomads of Mongolia's grassy plains and eventually sacked, looted, and pillaged much of the known west and most of the Chinese landmass. By the time Ghengis died in 1227, his grandson was well-tutored and ready to take on the rest of China. By 1271, Kublai had established a capital in a landlocked city that would only much later become known as Beijing. This marks the beginning of the first (but not last) non-Han dynasty. Kublai Khan kept fighting southward and by 1279, Guangzhou fell to the Mongols, and Khan became the ultimate monarch of China. Though barbarians at heart, the Mongols must be credited for encouraging the arts and a number of early public works projects, including extending the highways and grand canals.

(left) Emperor Chengzu of the Ming Dynasty. (top right) Forbidden City in Beijing (bottom right) Child emperor Puyi.

1368–1644 Ming Dynasty

Many scholars believe that the Mongols' inability to relate with the Han is what ultimately pushed the Han to rise up and overthrow them. The reign of the Ming Dynasty was the last ethnically Han Dynasty to rule over a unified China. At its apex, the Bright Empire encompassed a landmass easily recognized as China, even by today's mapmakers. The Ming Emperors built a huge army and navy, refurbished the agricultural system, and printed many books using movable type long before Gutenberg. In the 15th century, Emperor Yongle began construction of the famous Forbidden City in Beijing, a veritable icon of China.

Also during the Ming Dynasty, China's best known explorer, Zheng He, plied the seven seas in massive treasure fleets that dwarfed in size and range the ships of Christopher Columbus. A giant both in stature and persona, Admiral Zheng (who was also a eunuch) spent two decades expanding China's knowledge of the world outside of its already impressive borders. He traveled as far as India, Africa, and (some say) even the coast of the New World.

1644–1911 Qing Dynasty

The final dynasty represented a serious case of minority rule. They were Manchus from the northeast. The early Qing dynasty was a brutal period as forces loyal to the new emperor crushed those loyal to the old. The Qing Dynasty peaked in the mid-to-late 18th century but soon after, its military powers began to wane. In the 19th century, Qing control weakened and prosperity diminished. By 1910 China was fractured, a baby sat on the Imperial throne, and the Qing Dynasty was on its deathbed.

(top left) A depiction of the Second Opium War. (bottom left) Chiang Kai-shek (top, right) Mao Zedong on December 6, 1944. (bottom, right) Dr. Sun Yat-sen.

1834–1860 The Opium Wars

European powers were hungry to open new territories up for trade, but the Qing weren't buying. The British East India Company, strapped for cash, realized they could sell opium in China at huge profits. The Chinese government quickly banned the nefarious trade and in response, a technologically superior Britain declared war. After a humiliating defeat in the first Opium War, China was forced to cede Hong Kong. Other foreign powers soon followed with territorial demands of their own.

1912–1949 Republican Era

China's Republican period was chaotic and unstable. The revolutionary Dr. Sun Yat-sen—revered by most Chinese as the father of modern China—was unable to build a cohesive government without the aid of regional warlords and urban gangsters. When he died of cancer in 1925, power passed to Chiang Kai-shek, who set about unifying China under the Kuomintang. What began as a unified group of both left- and right-wingers quickly deteriorated, and by the mid-1920s, civil war between the Communists and Nationalists was brewing.

The '30s and '40s were bleak decades for the Chinese people, caught between a vicious war with Japan and periodic clashes between Kuomintang and Communist forces. After Japan's defeat in 1945, China's civil war kicked into high gear. Though the Kuomintang were armed with superior weapons and backed by American money, the majority of Chinese people rallied behind the Com-munists. Within four years, the Kuomintang were driven off the mainland to Taiwan, where the Republic of China exists to the present day.

(top left) 1950s Chinese stamp with Mao and Stalin.
(top right) Shenzhen
(bottom left) Poster of Mao's slogans.

1949–Present

The People's Republic

On October 1, 1949, Mao Zedong declared from atop Beijing's Gate of Heavenly Peace that "The Chinese People have stood up." And so the People's Republic of China was born. The Communist party set out to overhaul China's ancient feudal system, emphasizing class struggle, redistribution of wealth, and elimination of foreign dominance. The next three decades would see a massive, often painful transformation of Chinese society from feudalism into the modern age.

The Great Leap Forward was a disaster—Chinese peasants were encouraged to cram 100 years of industrial development into as many weeks. Untenable decisions led to industrial and agricultural ruin, widespread famine, and an estimated 30 million deaths. The trauma of this period, however, pales in comparison to The Great Proletarian Cultural Revolution. From 1966–1976, fear and zealotry gripped the nation as young revolutionaries heeded Chairman Mao's call to root out class enemies. During this decade, millions died, millions were imprisoned, and much of China's accumulated religious, historical, and cultural heritage literally went up in smoke.

Like a phoenix rising from its own ashes, China rose from its own self-inflicted destruction. In the early 1980s, Deng Xiao-ping took the first steps in reforming China's stagnant economy. With the maxim "To Get Rich is Glorious," Deng loosened central control on the economy and declared Special Economic Zones where the seeds of capitalism could be incubated. Three decades later, the nation is one of the world's most vibrant economic engines. Though China's history is measured in millennia, her brightest years may well have only just begun.

Did You Know?

Beijing's Lama Temple (Yonghe Temple) is one of the largest and most important Tibetan Buddhist monasteries in the world. The temple houses a 55-foot-high golden statue of Maitreya Buddha.

Chapter 2

TRAVEL SMART CHINA

Updated by
Julie Grundvig

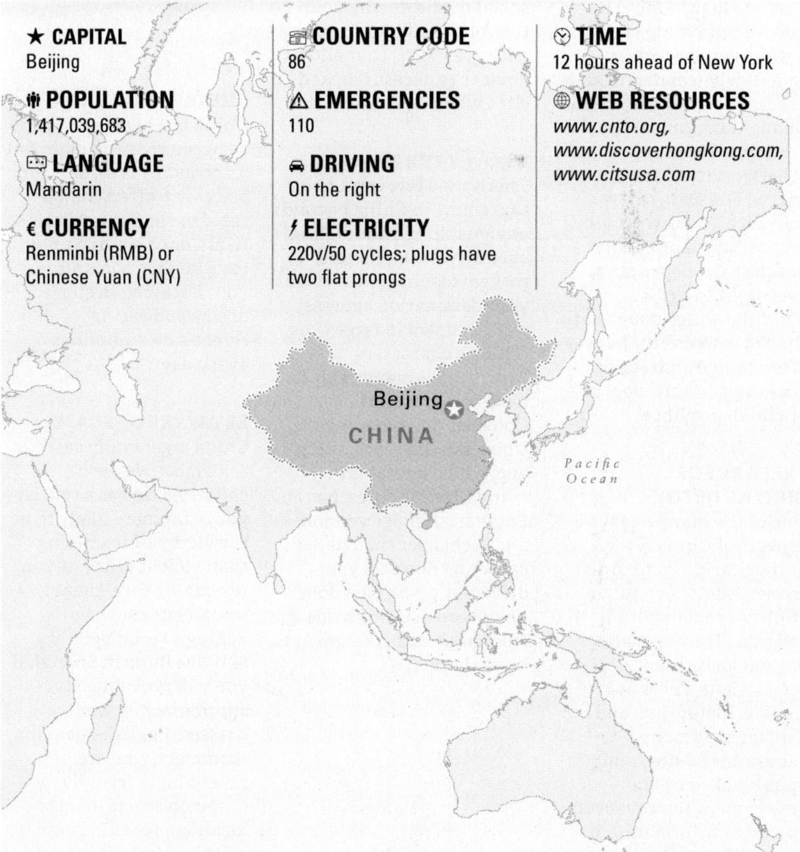

★ **CAPITAL**
Beijing

POPULATION
1,417,039,683

LANGUAGE
Mandarin

€ **CURRENCY**
Renminbi (RMB) or Chinese Yuan (CNY)

COUNTRY CODE
86

⚠ **EMERGENCIES**
110

DRIVING
On the right

ELECTRICITY
220v/50 cycles; plugs have two flat prongs

TIME
12 hours ahead of New York

WEB RESOURCES
www.cnto.org, www.discoverhongkong.com, www.citsusa.com

10 Things to Know Before You Visit China

From the neon-blast urban intensity of Shanghai to the history-soaked residential lanes of Beijing to the sweeping mountains of Yangshuo, China is a vast and varied country and home to some 1.35 billion people. Choose where to travel, and then making the most of your time on the ground, is a daunting task. Here are some things you need to know before booking your trip.

THERE ARE MORE THAN SKYSCRAPERS
China brings to mind its famous sprawling cities, but the countryside is completely wonderful and exotic. Yangshuo, in the Guangxi region, offers stunning views on otherworldly limestone karsts, and Dali, in the southern Yunnan province is charming. For a truly unique experience stay overnight in a *tulou* building—huge doughnut-shaped community houses often built hundreds of years ago—in the depths of Fujian province.

PREPARE FOR DIGITAL DETOX
One of the many negative aspects of China's authoritarian communist government, beyond chilling crackdowns on religious freedoms and dissent, is Internet restrictions. Facebook, Google, Instagram, and Twitter are among thousands of sites and apps blocked by the government to prevent the spread of information it can't control. Embrace the chance to escape Western social media during your trip, or get a virtual proxy network (VPN) that allows devices to access blocked sites when in China.

KNOW YOUR TAXIS
There are a few ways to be taxi smart in China beyond obvious things like making sure drivers use meters rather than haggling. Have your destination address written down in large type Chinese characters (worryingly, many cabbies have bad eyesight). Consider downloading the Uber-like DiDi car hailing app, which operates in many Chinese cities, has an English language version, and is cheaper than hailed cabs. And don't tip your driver—tipping isn't done anywhere in China aside from high-end, foreign-brand hotels.

WECHAT, WECHAT, WECHAT
The messaging and social media app WeChat (pronounced "Way-shin" locally) is ubiquitous in China, where most of the app's billion-plus users live. It easily allows you to swap contact details with other users by typing in their username, phone number, or scanning a QR code on their screen. "Can I have your WeChat?" is the new "Can I have your number?". You can download an English-language version of WeChat for your phone but be warned, even private messages on the app are censored by the government.

CHINA IS NOT CHEAP
China has big wealth gaps between rich and poor, but its economy is strong and prices are often comparable to the United States. In major cities, don't plan for a budget trip unless you're staying in shared dorms and eating street-side dumplings every day.

BE AWARE OF SCAMS
China is generally safer than most Western countries, and as a tourist you're far more likely to be the victim of scamming than violent crime. If you resemble a foreigner at tourist sites such as Beijing's Forbidden City and The Bund in Shanghai you will probably be approached by well-dressed, English-speaking scammers, who are disarmingly friendly. Common scams involve locals approaching you

spontaneously, sometimes to practise English or pose for a photo. Next, you're invited to an overpriced teahouse and then presented with an extortionate bill, or a gallery where you're pressured to buy worthless art. On a seedier side, touts approach foreign men, offering them reasonably priced massages from ladies—until they get slapped with a big room charge. Avoiding scams are easy: when someone approaches you on the street, firmly refuse to go anywhere with them.

TAKE TRAINS, NOT PLANES

China is enormous, so it's tempting to save travel time and book flights around the country. However, domestic flights are frequently delayed and cancelled, so booking them is a gamble. In contrast, China's trains are wonderfully reliable and usually cost about two-thirds of the price of flights. The Chinese high-speed train network is the largest in the world, and it's comfortable and efficient. Long distance trains have decent beds in cabins (a soft sleeper ticket). Train tickets often sell out in advance, so book from the excellent English-language Trip.com site and have them delivered to your hotel.

PREPARE FOR BUREAUCRACY OVERLOAD

Most Western visitors require a tourist visa, which is a hassle to apply for so begin at least a month in advance. The visa is also expensive compared to other Asian countries. For a fee, visa agencies have an express service if you're late. You're legally required to present your passport when you check into hotels in China, and some will make you register it at a local police station. If using Airbnb ask your host if they can help with this. Regular hosts may be able to take your passport and go to the police station for you. It's best to carry your passport with you at all times in China as many attractions, even minor ones, require ID to enter. You'll need to show your passport when you collect or buy plane and train tickets, and then show it again when boarding.

KNOW HOW TO AVOID POLLUTION

Since the Chinese government announced a war on pollution in 2014, levels of harmful airborne particles in Beijing are slowly decreasing but the capital and many other cities are still often enveloped in apocalyptic smog. In Beijing, the smog starts getting bad in November, when the city switches on its heating units, and continues for a couple of months depending on wind levels. Spring and fall are the best times to visit most cities, when smog levels are usually low and the weather is pleasant. Xiamen, a breezy island city in southern Fujian province, and Kunming, the gateway to the rural areas of Yunnan province, tend to have good air.

DON'T GO DURING A CHINESE HOLIDAY

Do not travel during the country's main vacation periods unless you're prepared to battle elbow-shunting armies of domestic tourists at every turn. The two periods to avoid are Chinese New Year, which usually takes place in January or February, and the National Day holidays, also known as Golden Week, which is usually in October.

Getting Here and Around

Air Travel

Beijing, Shanghai, and Hong Kong are China's three major international hubs. You can catch nonstop or one-stop flights to Beijing from New York (13¾ hours), Chicago (13–14 hours), San Francisco (11½–12½ hours), Los Angeles (11½–13 hours), London (10½–11½ hours), and Sydney (14–16 hours). Though most airlines say that reconfirming your return flight is unnecessary, some local airlines cancel your seat if you don't reconfirm.

AIR PASSES

If you are flying to China on a SkyTeam airline (Delta, for example), consider the Go Greater China Pass, which covers 150 destinations in China, including Hong Kong, Macao, and Taiwan. After you purchase your international ticket to mainland China or Taiwan on a SkyTeam member airline, you can take between 3 and 16 flights within China on China Airlines, China Southern, China Eastern, or Xiamen Airlines. If you are a member of a frequent-flier program, these flights will count toward miles. The price of the pass is between $270 and $1,300, depending upon the distance you plan to fly.

FLIGHTS

TO AND FROM CHINA

Air China is China's flagship carrier. It operates nonstop flights from Beijing and Shanghai to various North American and European cities. Although it once had a sketchy safety record, the situation has improved dramatically, and it is now part of the Star Alliance of airlines worldwide. Don't confuse it with the similarly named China Airlines, which is operated out of Taiwan.

WITHIN CHINA

The service on most Chinese airlines is on a par with low-cost American airlines—be prepared for limited legroom, iffy food, and possibly no personal TV. Always arrive at least two hours before departure, as chronic overbooking means latecomers just don't get on. In southern China typhoons often ground airplanes, so be prepared for delays if you are traveling between July and October.

Travel Times from Beijing

TO	BY AIR	BY TRAIN
Shanghai	2¼ hours	5–20 hours
Xi'an	2 hours	5–15 hours
Guangzhou	3 hours	8–29 hours
Hong Kong	3¾ hours	24 hours
Guilin	3¼ hours	11–30 hours
Kunming	3¼ hours	13–44 hours
Nanjing	1¾ hours	4 hours
Lhasa	6 hours	40 hours
Ürümqi	4 hours	32–40 hours
Chengdu	3¾ hours	8–29 hours

Bike Travel

Bicycles are still the primary form of transport for millions of Chinese people, although the proliferation of cars and smog make biking in the cities a chore. Large cities like Beijing, Chengdu, Xi'an, Shanghai, and Guilin have well-defined bike lanes, often separated from other traffic. Travel by bike is common in the countryside around places like Guilin, for locals and tourists alike. Locals don't use gears much—take your cue from them and just roll along at a leisurely pace. Note that bikes have to give way to motorized vehicles at intersections. If a flat tire or sudden brake failure strikes, seek out the nearest street-side mechanic (they're everywhere), easily identified by their bike parts and pumps.

In major cities, some lower-end hotels and hostels rent bikes. Street-side bike rental stations are also proliferating. Otherwise, inquire at bike shops, hotels, or even corner shops.

Boat Travel

Trains and planes are fast replacing China's boat and ferry services. The China-Japan International Ferry Company operates the Shanghai Ferry Boat that has a weekly ferry every Tuesday to Kobe or Osaka. The company maintains an English-language website with timetables.

Four- to seven-day cruises along the Yangtze River are the most popular, and thus the most touristy of the domestic boat rides. Both local and international companies run these tours, but shop around, as prices vary drastically. *See Chapter 9 for detailed information on Yangtze River cruises.*

Bus Travel

China has some reasonably comfortable long-distance buses running between most major cities. These luxury coaches are equipped with air-conditioning, soft seats, and screens playing nonstop movies, usually at deafening levels. Bring earplugs if you can't stand the noise.

Car Travel

Driving yourself is not permitted in mainland China, as the only valid driver's licenses are Chinese ones. However, this restriction should be cause for relief, as city traffic is terrible, drivers manic and maniacal, and getting lost inevitable for first-timers. Conditions in Hong Kong aren't much better, but you can drive there using a U.S. or international license.

The quickest way to arrange for a car and driver is to flag down a taxi. If you're happy with a driver you've used for trips around town, ask if you can hire him for the day. After some negotiating, expect to pay between Y350 and Y600, depending on the type of car. Most hotels can make arrangements for you, though they often charge you double that rate.

Another alternative is American car-rental agency Avis, which includes mandatory chauffeurs as part of all rental packages.

Train Travel

China's enormous rail network is one of the world's busiest. Though crowded, trains are usually safe, efficient, and run strictly to schedule. The high-speed rail system makes getting around the country very easy. In 2012, the Beijing–Guangzhou line opened, cutting travel time between the two cities from 30 hours to about 8–9 hours. At 1,428 miles, the line is the longest in the world.

There are certain intricacies to buying tickets, which usually have to be purchased in your departure city. You can buy most tickets up to 18 days in advance; 3 to 4 days ahead is usually enough time, except during the three national holidays—Chinese New Year (two days in mid-January–February), Labor Day (May 1), and National Day (October 1).

You can find out just about everything about Chinese train travel at Seat 61's comprehensive website. China Highlights has a searchable online timetable for major train routes.

Before You Go

Passport

All U.S. citizens, even infants, need a valid passport with a tourist visa stamped in it to enter China (except for Hong Kong, where you only need a valid passport). It's always best to have at least six months' validity on your passport before traveling to Asia.

Visa

Getting a tourist visa to China in the United States is straightforward. Standard visas are for single-entry stays of up to 30 days, and are valid for 90 days from the day of issue (not the day of entry), so don't get your visa too far in advance.

Foreign visitors to Tibet must have a Tibet Travel Permit and travel with an organized tour approved by the Tibet Tourism Bureau. Travel agencies in China can arrange this.

Children traveling with only one parent do not need a notarized letter of permission to enter China, but policies can change, being overprepared isn't a bad idea.

General Requirements for Mainland China	
Passport	Must be valid for six months after date of arrival
Visa	Required for U.S. citizens ($140)
Required Vaccinations	None
Recommended Vaccinations	Hepatitis A and B, typhoid, influenza, booster for tetanus-diphtheria
Driving	Chinese driver's license required

Immunizations

No immunizations are required for entry into China, but it's a good idea to be immunized against typhoid and Hepatitis A and B before traveling, as well as to get routine tetanus-diphtheria and measles boosters. In summer months malaria is a risk in tropical and rural areas, especially Hainan and Yunnan provinces—consult your doctor four to six weeks before your trip.

US Embassy/Consulate

The U.S. Embassy is in Beijing and the U.S. Consulates General are in Chengdu, Guangzhou, Shanghai, Shenyang, and Wuhan.

When to Go

HIGH SEASON $$$$
China is massive with varied weather. In general, the best time to visit is spring (late March to May) and fall (September to early-November), when temperatures are in the 50s–70s°F.

LOW SEASON $
Mid-November to early March is frigid in northern and western China and cold and damp around Shanghai, but this can be a good time to visit Beijing. Avoid Chinese New Year, in late January or early February.

VALUE SEASON $$
June, July, and August are sweltering and humid in and around Shanghai; it's slightly cooler in Beijing and drier. In far northwest China, it's hot but dry. Hotel prices are moderate.

What to Pack for China

BREATHABLE CLOTHING
The climate is hot and humid so you will want to pack clothes made of breathable fabrics like light cotton or linen. Drip-dry clothing is an especially good idea, because the tropical sun and high humidity encourage frequent changes of clothing. Lightweight but long sleeve shirts and long pants will come in handy for visiting temples and also provide protection against insect bites.

WATERPROOF GEAR
If traveling in the rainy season a lightweight rain jacket or waterproof poncho is essential. If you plan to partake of water activites or just to spend a lot of time on the beach, bring a waterproof bag to keep your camera, phone, and wallet dry; it will also come in handy during the rainy season. A waterproof phone case is a good idea, too, if you plan to use your phone's camera when you travel.

LAYERS
A fleece sweater is welcome on cool evenings or in notoriously over-air-conditioned restaurants, cafes, buses, and trains.

PRACTICAL SHOES
The paths leading to temples can be rough, so bring sturdy walking shoes. Slip-ons are preferable to lace-up shoes, as they must be removed before you enter shrines and temples.

SUNSCREEN AND HAT
The tropical sun is powerful, and its effects long-lasting (and painful) so bring a hat and UV-protection sunglasses and sunscreen. Don't let a rainy season forecast fool you; you will still need to be protected from the sun.

A SARONG
Out of respect for the Buddhist culture, women are expected to cover up in temples. Pack a sarong to tie over shorts in such situations. It will also come in handy on the beach and as a head cover during tropical heat.

INSECT REPELLENT
As with most hot and humid countries, you will find a lot of mosquitoes in China. DEET-based insect repellent is preferable to avoid being bitten.

ANTI-DIARRHEAL PILLS
To be safe, pack "Bangkok Belly" busters such as Imodium (known generically as Loperamide) and soothers such as Pepto Bismol, as well as rehydration salts or solution such as Gastrolyte. Activated charcoal can also be helpful.

TRAVEL ADAPTER
Thai power outlets most commonly feature two-prong round or flat sockets; pack a universal travel power adapter to avoid complications.

LUGGAGE LOCK
If you plan to travel throughout China, particularly if you plan to travel by bus, pack luggage locks to prevent tampering with your luggage.

VPN
If you're planning to work or stay connected while you travel, a portable VPN will ensure you won't get blocked from accessing certain sites. It also protects your passwords, credit cards, and identity while you travel.

Essentials

Lodging

Location is the first thing you should consider. Chinese cities are sprawling so you want to be close to what interests you. Locally owned hotels with four stars or fewer have erratic standards both inside and outside big cities However, air-conditioning, color TVs, and private bathrooms are the norm for three to four stars, and even lone-star hotels have private bathrooms, albeit with a squatter toilet.

APARTMENT AND HOUSE RENTALS

There's an abundance of furnished properties for short- and long-term rentals in Beijing, Guangzhou, Hong Kong, Shanghai, and some other cities. What you get for your money fluctuates, so shop around.

HOTELS

When checking into a hotel, you need to show your passport—the desk clerk records the number before you're given a room. In smaller hotels outside of the big cities, unmarried couples may occasionally have problems staying together in the same room, but simply wearing a wedding band is one way to avoid this complication. Friends or couples of the same sex, especially women, shouldn't have a problem getting a room together.

What it Costs in Yuan

$	$$	$$$	$$$$
under Y1,100	Y1,100–Y1,400	Y1,401–Y1,800	over Y1,800

Prices are for two people in a standard double room in high season.

Dining

The standard eating procedure is to hold the bowl close to your mouth and shovel in the contents without any qualms. Place bones or seeds in a small dish or on the table beside your bowl. Do not point or play with your chopsticks, or place them on top of your rice bowl when you're finished eating (place the chopsticks horizontally on the table or plate). Avoid leaving your chopsticks standing up in a bowl of rice—they look like the two incense sticks burned at funerals.

MEALS AND MEALTIMES

Meals in China are served early: breakfast until 9 am, lunch between 11 and 2, and dinner from 5 to 9.

Unless otherwise noted, the restaurants listed in this guide are open daily for lunch and dinner.

What it Costs in Yuan

$	$$	$$$	$$$$
under Y100	Y100–Y150	Y151–Y200	over Y200

Prices are the average cost of a main dish at dinner or, if dinner isn't served, at lunch.

PAYING

At most restaurants you ask for the bill (*mai dan*) at the end of the meal, as you do back home. At cheap noodle bars and street stands you often pay up front. Only very upmarket restaurants accept credit cards.

RESERVATIONS AND DRESS

Regardless of where you are, it's a good idea to make a reservation if you can. For popular restaurants, book as far ahead as you can and reconfirm when you arrive. (Large parties should always call ahead to check the reservations policy.) We mention dress only when men are required to wear a jacket or a jacket and tie.

Health/Safety

Drink only bottled, boiled, or purified water and drinks; don't drink from public fountains or ask for beverages with ice. You should even consider using bottled or boiled water to brush your teeth. Make sure food has been thoroughly cooked and is served to you fresh and hot; avoid vegetables and fruits that you haven't washed (in bottled or purified water) or peeled yourself. If you have problems, mild cases of traveler's diarrhea may respond to Imodium (known generically as loperamide) or Pepto-Bismol. Be sure to drink plenty of fluids; if you can't keep fluids down, seek medical help immediately. Make sure the water bottle is sealed when you buy it.

SPECIFIC ISSUES IN CHINA

At China's public hospitals, foreigners need to pay fees to register, to see a doctor, and then for all tests and medication. Most doctors at public hospitals don't speak English, and hygiene standards outside of the major cities can be low.

The best place to start looking for a suitable doctor is through your hotel concierge. If you become seriously ill or are injured, it is best to fly home, or at least to Hong Kong, as quickly as possible. In Hong Kong, English-speaking doctors are widely available.

If you need to buy prescription drugs, try to go to the pharmacies of reputable private hospitals or to bigger chain stores like Watsons.

OVER-THE-COUNTER REMEDIES

Most pharmacies in big Chinese cities carry over-the-counter Western medicines and traditional Chinese medicines. You usually need to ask for the generic name of the drug you're looking for, not a brand name. Acetaminophen—or Tylenol—is often known as paracetomol in Hong Kong. In big cities reputable pharmacies like Watsons are always a better bet than no-name ones.

Money

With the exception of major cities, China is a cheap destination by most North Americans' standards. In mainland China, the best places to convert your dollars into yuan are your hotel's front desk or a branch of a major bank, such as Bank of China, CITIC, or HSBC. Although credit cards are gaining ground in China, for day-to-day transactions cash is definitely king.

Tipping

Tipping is a tricky issue in China. It's officially forbidden by the government, and locals simply don't do it. In general, follow their lead without qualms. Nevertheless, the practice is beginning to catch on, especially among tour guides, who often expect Y10 a day. You don't need to tip in restaurants or in taxis.

Packing

Most Chinese people dress for comfort, so you can plan to do the same. There's little risk of offending people with your dress: Westerners tend to attract attention regardless of their attire. Fashion capitals Hong Kong and Shanghai are the exceptions so opt for your smarter jeans or pants for sightseeing there.

Keep packets of tissues and antibacterial hand wipes in your day pack. The brands in Chinese pharmacies are limited, so take adequate stocks of your potions and lotions, feminine-hygiene products (tampons are especially hard to find), and birth control.

Great Itineraries

Stretching over 3,100 miles from east to west, China is an enormous country with wildly varied geography, ranging from the mist-wrapped peaks of Huangshan in the east to the dusty Tarim Basin in the northwest, one of the lowest points on earth. To get around this vast country you'll need plenty of patience and a good sense of humor. With the development of high-speed trains, it's now easy to zip between major cities like Beijing and Shanghai, but travel to more distant destinations is generally slower and more unpredictable. Domestic flights can get you almost anywhere, though they are often more expensive than other options. Whether traveling by plane, train, or bus, it's good to book ahead, especially during Chinese New Year, when you are competing for tickets with 1.3 billion people on the move.

LAY OF THE LAND

Beijing

Like China itself, Beijing is a study in contrasts: old versus new, tradition versus innovation, Chinese versus Western. These juxtapositions make this sprawling city a fascinating and vibrant place, but given its size (more than 21 million inhabitants) and history (three millennia and counting), Beijing can seem like an overwhelming destination to visit. Still, every city has its superlatives, so we've handpicked the best of Beijing for you to consider for your next trip. Spectacular palaces, historic temples, beautiful parks, bargain shopping, addictive cuisine, and so much more await you in the Chinese capital.

Beijing to Shanghai

Once home to emperors, China's capital city of Beijing presides over the heavily industrialized northeast. Hypermodern Shanghai is halfway down China's prosperous east coast and is iconic for its architecture and fashion. Suzhou lies within an arm's reach from Shanghai and is famous for its classical gardens and unique stone bridges. Upriver from Shanghai on the banks of the Yangtze, you'll find the ancient city of Nanjing, once China's southern capital. The lofty peaks of Huangshan, only a few hours by train from Nanjing, are a wonderful place to take refuge from the summer heat.

East Coast

Zhejiang is China's wealthiest province. Hangzhou, surrounded by forested hills and tea plantations, is most famous for its lovely West Lake and is a wonderful place for a biking excursion. Nestled within the Yangtze Delta, the province also has a number of charming restored waterways and villages waiting to be explored. Rugged, mountainous Fujian boasts verdant tea fields, ancient Hakka roundhouses, and unspoiled beaches. On the coast, prosperous Xiamen is worth exploring for its colonial architecture.

Hong Kong

"A New York minute is a Hong Kong second" is a saying you'll hear from expats who live in this thrilling, idiosyncratic city of 7 million residents, and it's not hard to see why. Hong Kong teems with energy from the moment you arrive, and it never lets up. Shopping is on the list, as are dim sum, sightseeing, and the latest, hippest crop of restaurants and bars. Landmarks and skylines need to be photographed, there are countless street markets to explore or get lost in, and ferries and boat rides are waiting. Needless to say, it's impossible to do everything, but there are some experiences that simply shouldn't be missed.

The Southwest

The dramatic karst peaks and winding rivers of Guilin and Yangshuo in Guangxi Province grace so many postcards of China. Lush mountains dotted with

villages surround Guiyang, Guizhou's capital. Kunming, the capital of Yunnan, is also home to many of China's ethnic groups and boasts some of the most stunning topography in China, ranging from the sweltering jungles of the Mekong Delta in the south to the dramatic snowcapped mountains of the Tibetan Plateau in the west. The province shares road connections with neighboring Myanmar and Laos and is linked by rail to Vietnam.

Sichuan and Chongqing

Southwestern Sichuan Province, known as the "rice bowl" of China, includes the fertile Sichuan basin and is considered the country's agricultural heartland. Its capital, Chengdu, is the financial hub of the southwest, and its many rail and bus connections link eastern and western China. Outside of Chengdu is the Buddhist holy mountain of Emei Shan, famous not only for its temples but also its unruly golden monkeys. In the very center of China sits hilly Chongqing, or "Mountain City," and the best place to hop on a Three Gorges cruise along the Yangtze.

The Silk Road

In northwest China is Xi'an, long-ago capital of the Tang Dynasty. Once the most cosmopolitan city in the world, Xi'an was the terminus of the eastern Silk Road. The emblematic Terracotta Warriors are now its most famous attraction. The Mogao Caves of Gansu offer a glimpse into the most important Buddhist pilgrimage site along the Silk Road. Sweeping deserts and plains make up the Xinjiang Autonomous Region, China's largest province. Xinjiang is home to the Uyghurs, a large Muslim minority. Its capital city, Ürümqi, is an excellent place to launch explorations into the desert or westwards to the ancient Silk Road city of Kashgar.

TIMING

Because China is so vast, the best time to visit depends on where you are traveling. In general, the most comfortable times of year are in spring or fall to avoid extreme temperatures. Summers can be unbearably hot and humid, with drenching rain and flooding. Winters in the north are bitterly cold.

PEAK SEASON: OCTOBER AND MAY

Whatever season you go, don't travel during the rush of peak holiday times, especially the first week of October and May and during Chinese New Year.

Great Itineraries

The Classic First Trip

BEIJING, THE SILK ROAD, SICHUAN, AND SHANGHAI, 12 DAYS

This journey covers many of China's most iconic destinations. Begin in Beijing, exploring the former glory of Beijing's imperial palaces and climb the Great Wall before embarking westward to Xi'an, once the capital of the Tang Dynasty and home to China's famous Terracotta Warriors. Head southwest to Chengdu to see the world's largest Buddha before ending your visit in the bustling megacity of Shanghai, once dubbed the "Paris of the East."

DAY 1: BEIJING

Beijing is the cultural heart of China and the nation's top travel destination. Stay at **The Orchid,** a snug boutique hotel tucked away in one of the few remaining hutong areas (alleyways) of Beijing near the Drum Tower. It's a short taxi ride to the Forbidden City. It's also close to **Tiananmen Square,** where you can watch the daily flag-raising ceremony at dawn. After the flag raising, take a stroll around the square and soak in the atmosphere. And of course, a tour of the **Forbidden City** is an essential Beijing experience. Finish your day with a traditional feast at the **Li Qun Roast Duck Restaurant,** Beijing's most popular spot for Peking duck.

DAY 2: THE GREAT WALL

(Excursion will take approximately 8 hours, either by private car or tour bus)

China's greatest monument is still a must-see. Avoid the more commercial Badaling and head farther afield to the less-crowded sections of the **Great Wall** at Mutianyu, Simatai, or Jinshaling. Pack a picnic lunch and enjoy the spectacular views from the top. Tour buses leaving for the Great Wall congregate around Tiananmen Square, or you could book a private tour or hire a car and driver.

DAY 3: SUMMER PALACE AND THE TEMPLE OF HEAVEN

(Summer Palace is 45 minutes by car from Tiananmen Square, Temple of Heaven is 12 minutes by car from Tiananmen Square)

Beijing is dotted with numerous imperial palaces and pleasure gardens. Take a taxi to the city's northwestern reaches to visit the lovely **Summer Palace,** which has come to symbolize the decadence that brought about the fall of the Qing Dynasty. The **Temple of Heaven** is considered to be the perfect example of Ming Dynasty architecture, and is a great place to take a break from the frenetic pace of the capital. For dinner, try a savory bowl of traditional hand-pulled noodles at **Old Beijing Noodle King,** a short walk from the Temple of Heaven. Later in the evening, take in the colorful theatrics at the nearby Tianqiao Acrobatic Theatre.

DAY 4: SHOPPING AND ART

Beijing teems with cultural performances, fabulous restaurants, and sprawling outdoor markets. Spend the morning hunting for souvenirs at **Beijing Curio City** or the **Silk Alley Market** in the Chaoyang District. In the afternoon explore the **798 Art District,** a popular place to see Chinese contemporary art. For dinner, tuck into a bowl of steaming pork or vegetable dumplings at **Baoyuan Dumpling.**

DAYS 5–7: XI'AN, CHINA'S ANCIENT CAPITAL

(2 hours by plane from Beijing; 4½ hours by high-speed train from Beijing's West Rail Station)

Xi'an was the most important city in China until the 9th century AD. Once the eastern gateway to the Silk Road, the region is a gold mine of historical treasures, most of which can be covered in just a few days. For convenience, head to Xi'an's Old City and check yourself

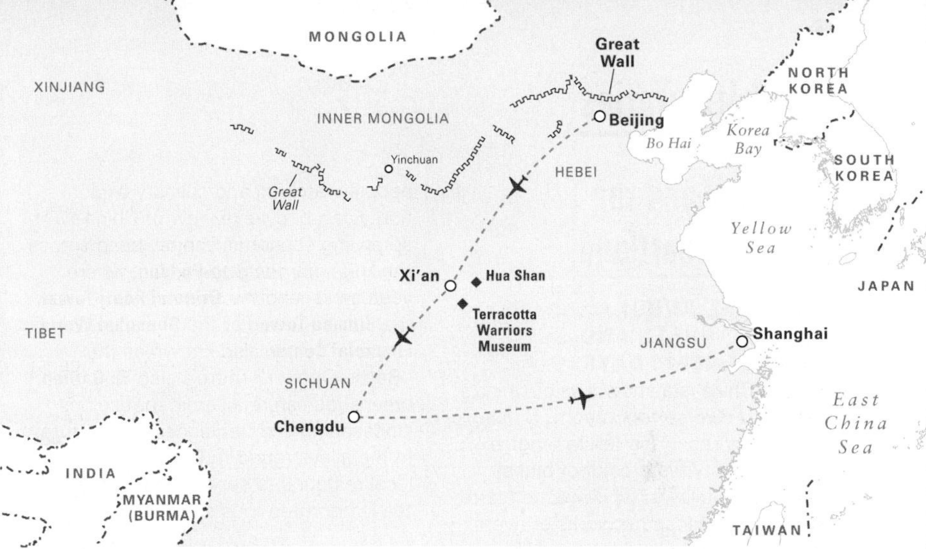

into the **Ibis Xi'an,** which has clean and comfortable rooms. Your first day should be spent visiting Xi'an's most popular attractions, including the **Bell Tower** in the city center and the impressive **Big Wild Goose Pagoda.** Make sure to attend the Tang Dynasty dinner theater, which serves imperial cuisine and acrobatic shows every evening.

Devote your next day to visiting the **Terracotta Warriors Museum,** east of Xi'an. The life-size warriors and horses, built to protect China's first emperor in the afterlife, are part of a huge necropolis that stretches for miles. If you have the time, we also recommend a day trip to the spectacular peaks of **Hua Shan.** To get to either of these sites, book a tour or catch a public bus.

DAYS 8–10: CHENGDU

(1½ hours by plane from Xi'an; 4½ hours by high-speed train from Xi'an)

See days 15–18 of the Southern China itinerary.

DAYS 10–12: SHANGHAI

(2½ hours by plane from Chengdu; 14 hours by train from Chengdu)

See days 1–2 of the Shanghai and the Chinese Heartland itinerary.

TIPS

- Temples and royal buildings, such as Bangkok's Grand Palace, require modest dress (no shorts or tank tops).
- Take a taxi to the Grand Palace or an express boat to nearby Tha Chang Pier. Wat Po is a 10-minute walk south. Hire a longtail boat to get to the canals and back at Tha Chang Pier. Khao San Road is a short taxi ride from the pier.
- Bangkok Airways owns the airport at Koh Samui, and flights there are relatively expensive due to taxes. Bangkok Airways runs most of the many daily flights, and these are slightly lower in price than Thai Airways. Nok Air, AirAsia, and Thai Lion also offer cheap flights to nearby Surat Thani or Nakhon Si Thammarat, from which you can take a ferry to the island.
- Late November through April is the best time to explore the Andaman Coast. For the Gulf Coast there's good weather from late November until August.
- Hotels in the south are frequently packed during high season and Thai holidays, so book in advance.

Great Itineraries

Shanghai and the Chinese Heartland

SHANGHAI, ANHUI, JIANGSU, HUBEI, AND SICHUAN, 11–14 DAYS

Eastern China is a showcase of China's amazingly diverse topography. Much of this area lies in the fertile Yangtze basin—a misty watercolor of blues, greens and yellows, whitewashed farmhouses, and dense networks of rivers, waterways, and canals. Journey from the glittering skyscrapers of Shanghai to the wilds of Huangshan and the Yangtze River. Because of the distances covered, it's suggested to fly some legs of this trip to save time.

DAY 1: SHANGHAI

Shanghai is all about the country's future, not its past. Catch the ultrafast train from the airport to the city center. The most convenient place for hotels is the neighborhood of Puxi, which includes the **Former French Concession,** close to most of Shanghai's most popular attractions. Stay in the delightful **Magnolia Bed and Breakfast,** a small boutique hotel south of Jing'an Park. After checking in, explore some of Shanghai's fascinating colonial history by foot or taxi. Walk through **Xintiandi,** where restored traditional houses mix with bars, boutiques, and galleries. Spend some time searching for the perfect souvenir on **Nanjing Road.** Alternatively, you could time travel through 3,000 years of Chinese art and antiquities at the **Shanghai Museum.** For dinner, head to longtime favorite **Grape** for home-style Chinese food in a friendly atmosphere.

DAY 2: PARIS OF THE EAST

The next day explore **The Bund** by foot, taxi, or subway. This waterfront boulevard is the city's best spot for people-watching and culinary exploration. For a bird's-eye view of China's sprawling economic capital, head across the Huangpu River to **Pudong,** where you can ascend the **Oriental Pearl Tower,** the **Jinmao Tower,** or the **Shanghai World Financial Center,** also known as the "Bottle Opener." There's also **Yu Garden,** where you can relax amid meticulous landscaping and traditional architecture. In the alleys round Yu Garden are many local restaurants serving terrific food and tea in unpretentious surroundings.

DAYS 3–4: SUZHOU AND TONGLI

(Suzhou is 35 minutes by high-speed train from Shanghai; Tongli is 90 minutes by taxi from Shanghai)

Regarded in ancient times as heaven on earth, **Suzhou** retains many of its charms despite the encroaching forces of modernization. Stroll through elegant gardens and temples along the gently flowing branches of the Grand Canal.

Suzhou is close enough to work well as a day trip from Shanghai but it's highly recommended to spend the night and catch a bus the next day to **Tongli,** a restored water village. If you're staying in Suzhou, book a room at the **Pan Pacific Suzhou,** situated in a lovely garden complex. A quick walk or taxi will take you to the **Master of the Nets Gardens,** which holds Chinese opera performances on summer evenings. Also make sure to visit the iconic **Suzhou Museum,** designed by I.M. Pei. For a memorable meal, try the fragrant soup-filled dumpling at **Xichengyuan Wonton** near the Master of the Nets Gardens. After two days spent exploring Suzhou and Tongli, take the train back to Shanghai where you can catch a plane to Huangshan.

DAYS 5–8: HUANGSHAN

(1 hour by plane from Shanghai to Tunxi)

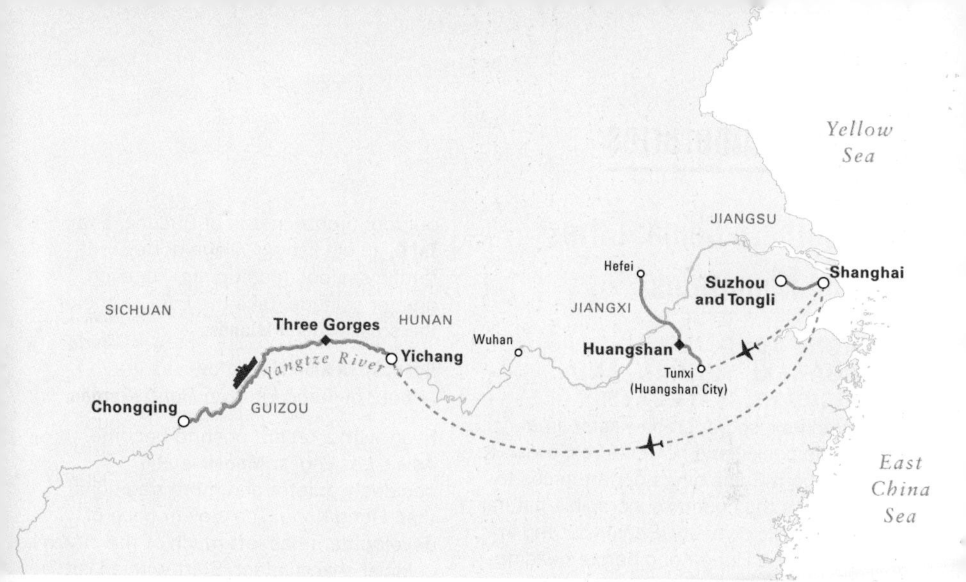

One of China's best-known natural wonders, **Huangshan** (Yellow Mountain) is a breathtaking range of 72 jagged peaks punctuated by fantastically twisted pine trees and unusual rock formations. **Tunxi,** or Huangshan City, is about 40 miles from Huangshan. After landing in Tunxi, hire a taxi or take a minibus to **Tangkou** at the base of the mountain. There are numerous ways to the top, either on foot or by cable car. Spend a night at the **Baiyun Hotel,** one of the mountaintop guesthouses, before waking at dawn to watch the sun rise over an eerie sea of fog.

After visiting Huangshan, the quickest way to continue on to the Three Gorges is to return to Shanghai where you can catch a flight onwards to Yichang, in Hubei Province.

DAYS 9–13: YICHANG AND THE THREE GORGES

(2 hours by plane from Shanghai to Yichang)

A cruise along the **Yangtze River** through the **Three Gorges** is an unforgettable experience. Along the way you'll pass over abandoned metropolises that were humming with life only a few years ago, as well as their modern counterparts that were built on higher ground. One recommended cruise line is Victoria Cruises, which offers a range of excursions up and down the Yangtze.

The town of **Yichang** sits at the eastern entrance of the Three Gorges. Cruises will sail through the Gezhou Dam and offer excursions to the Three Gorges Dam site, Fengdu, or "Ghost City," and the Little Three Gorges before disembarking at **Chongqing.**

DAY 14: CHONGQING

(5 days by boat from Yichang)

After finishing a cruise along the Yangtze, **Chongqing** has enough to recommend a day or two of exploration. Built into the side of a hill, the city is a maze of steep stairways, hills, and tunnels. Most of the main tourist sites and hotels are located around the Jiefang Bei area. The convenient **Howard Johnson ITC Plaza** offers plush rooms and an excellent restaurant. After settling in, walk to **18 Steps,** one of the most curious attractions in Chongqing. Not to be missed is a ride in a cable car, where you are treated to a bird's-eye view of the Yangtze and the sprawling city below. For traditional Sichuan cuisine, head to **Xiaotian'e Sichuan Restaurant** on the banks of the Yangtze to indulge in hotpot and other fiery specialties.

Great Itineraries

Southern China: Cities and Mountains

HONG KONG, MACAU, GUANGXI, YUNNAN, AND SICHUAN, 15–18 DAYS

With its lush geography, karst limestone peaks, and rich cultures, a visit to southern China offers opportunities to witness the country's incredible natural and ethnic diversity. Begin your trip in fast-paced Hong Kong before heading farther south to the gorgeous backcountry of Guangxi, Guizhou, and Yunnan.

DAY 1: HONG KONG

Despite the city's return to Chinese rule in 1997, **Hong Kong** still feels a world away from the mainland. Get settled in at the **Lan Kwai Fong Hotel** with its amazing harbor views. When you're rested, take a ride on the Star Ferry connecting Hong Kong Island with **Kowloon.** Try dim sum at the legendary **Tim Ho Wan** in Kowloon—the coconut cream buns and shrimp dumplings are superb. Back on Hong Kong Island, don't miss the smoke-filled **Man Mo Temple** and Hong Kong's famous assortment of antiques shops and art galleries. Ride the very steep tram to the summit of **Victoria Peak,** with views of the entire harbor.

DAY 2: GET OUT OF THE CITY

(30 minutes by express ferry to Lantau)

While the business districts clustered around the harbor feature some of the world's densest urban jungle, Hong Kong also has a relaxed natural side. **Lantau Island** is a favorite of visitors for its beaches and hiking trails. Board the ferry at the Outlying Islands Ferry Pier on Hong Kong Island. Arriving at the town of **Mui Wo,** you can catch a bus to the island's top two attractions: **Po Lin Monastery,** featuring the world's tallest outdoor bronze statue of Buddha, and **Tai O,** an old fishing village dotted with terrific seafood restaurants. For even greater solitude, take the ferry to one of the smaller **Outer Islands.**

DAY 3: MACAU

(1 hour by TurboJet from Hong Kong)

Even with a recent push to become Asia's Las Vegas, **Macau** is still decidedly quieter and more traditional than Hong Kong. The slower pace of development has left much of the city's colonial charm intact. Start with a visit to **Largo do Senado** (Senate Square), paved with Portuguese-style tiles and surrounded by brightly colored colonial buildings. The city is home to two beautiful churches, **São Domingos** and **São Paulo,** the latter featuring exhibits on the early history of Asian Christianity. If you plan to stay overnight, the **Altira Macau** has breathtaking ocean views. For flavorful Macanese dishes like steamed crab and clams stewed in beer, **A Lorcha** restaurant is highly recommended.

DAYS 4–8: YANGSHUO AND LONGSHENG

(1½-hour flight from Hong Kong to Guilin; 90-minute bus ride or 4-hour boat ride from Guilin to Yangshuo; 3 hours by bus from Guilin to Longsheng)

The scenery in northern Guangxi is some of the most beautiful in all of China. Enchanted by dramatic groupings of sheer limestone karst mountains, visitors often find themselves loath to leave. To get to **Yangshuo,** you'll first head to Guilin, where you'll have a choice of taking the bus or the more scenic four-hour Li River Cruise. Once in Yangshuo, the **Giggling Tree** is an excellent base for exploring natural sites like **Green Lotus Peak** and **Moon Hill.** For meals, join the backpackers at **Kelly's Place** for beer and

dumplings. Head back through Guilin to the town of **Longsheng,** home to the famously photogenic **Dragon's Backbone Rice Terraces** before returning to Guilin.

DAYS 9–14: NORTHWEST YUNNAN

(2- to 2½-hour flight from Guilin to Dali or Lijiang with connection in Kunming)

Sandwiched between the Tibetan Plateau and Myanmar, this area has long attracted foreigners with its mix of minority cultures and stunning natural beauty. **Dali,** beside the waters of Erhai Lake, is home to the Bai people, who settled here 4,000 years ago; the elegant **Three Pagodas** north of town is one of China's most iconic images. For a unique experience, book a room at the **Yunnan Inn,** owned by Chinese artist Fang Lijun. Pancakes and decent coffee at **Café de Jack** will fill you up before heading out to explore Dali's scenic **Old Town.** A three-hour bus ride north of Dali lies **Lijiang,** home of the Naxi people. The **East River Hotel** offers a tranquil location and is close to **Mishi** for grilled yak meat and beer. The highlight of the region is **Tiger Leaping Gorge,** one of the deepest river gorges in the world and a popular two-day hike.

DAY 15–18: CHENGDU

(1½-hour flight from Dali to Chengdu)

As the capital of Sichuan Province, **Chengdu** has long been one of China's great cultural centers. Famous for its spicy cuisine, the city also manages to maintain a pleasant atmosphere of yesteryear. Stay at the elegant **Minshan Fandian** in the center of town near People's Park. A quick taxi ride away is the remarkable **Buddhist Wenshu Monastery,** known for its peaceful tea gardens. For animal lovers, take a bus 45 minutes out of town to the **Giant Panda Breeding Research Base.** If you crave authentic Sichuan hotpot, **Shijing Shenghuo** brings the fire. No matter how little time you have available, make the three-hour bus trip south to **Leshan** to see the world's largest stone-carved Buddha. With toes the size of a small bus, the seated **Grand Buddha** is impressive, to say the least.

On The Calendar

Most of China's holidays and festivals are calculated according to the lunar calendar and can vary by as much as a few weeks from year to year. Check online for the most accurate dates.

January

New Years Weekend. The day following January 1 is a public holiday and a day off for the general population, and schools and most businesses are closed.

February

Chinese New Year. China's most celebrated and important holiday, follows the lunar calendar and falls between mid-January and mid-February. It gives the Chinese an official week-long holiday to visit their relatives, eat special meals, and set off firecrackers to celebrate the New Year and its respective Chinese zodiac animal. Avoid visiting during Spring Festival as the city tends to shut down and many of the things you'll want to see may be shut.

Miao Bullfight Festival. Among the Miao people who live in Yunnan and Guizhou, a "bullfight" is a contest between the bulls themselves. This festival traditionally takes place on the 25th day of the first lunar month (in February or March) between the planting of rice seedlings and their harvest a few months later. Owners of bulls meet beforehand to size up the competition prior to agreeing to the fight. The atmosphere on fight day is lively, with drinking, music, and exchanging of gifts. Fireworks entice the bulls into combat until one falls down or runs away.

March

Spring Lantern Festival. The Spring Lantern Festival marks the end of the Chinese New Year, and is celebrated on the 15th day of the first lunar month (sometime in February or March, depending on the year). Residents flock to local parks for a display of Chinese lanterns and fireworks.

April

Qing Ming. Not so much a holiday as a day of worship, Qing Ming (literally, "clean and bright"), or Tomb Sweeping Day, gathers relatives at the graves of the deceased on the 15th day from the spring equinox—April 4th, 5th, or 6th, depending on the year—to clean the surfaces and leave fresh flowers. In 1997, the staunchly atheist Communist party passed a law stating that cremation is compulsory in cities and other densely populated areas. As such, this festival has since lost much of its original meaning.

May

Labor Day. Always on May 1, this is another busy travel time. In 2008, the government reduced the length of this holiday from five days to two, but the length of the celebration now changes from year to year.

Sister's Meal Festival. Unmarried women harvest rice from the terraced fields and prepare a special dish of sticky rice colored blue, pink, and yellow. Men arrive to serenade the women, and the women offer gifts of rice wine and small packets of rice. In the evening, women dress up for a night of dancing. Traditionally, it takes place in the middle of the third lunar month, between April and June.

Siyueba. Similar to Mardi Gras (but without the drinking or bawdy behavior), Siyueba, which translates as Eighth Day of the Fourth Month (May, give or take a month), is a major holiday in the region. During it the Miao, Buyi, Dong, Yao, Zhuang, Yi, and others in the Southwest celebrate spring. Guiyang is a great place to check it out—the area around the fountain in the city center erupts with music, dancing, and general merrymaking.

June

Dragon Boat Festival. On the fifth day of the fifth moon (usually falling in June), the Dragon Boat Festival celebrates the national hero Qu Yuan, an honest politician who drowned himself during the Warring States Period of ancient China in despair over his inability to save his state (it was a time of great corruption). Legend has it that the fishermen who unsuccessfully attempted to rescue Qu by boat tried to distract fish from eating his body by throwing rice dumplings wrapped in bamboo leaves into the river. Today, crews in narrow dragon boats race to the beat of heavy drums, while balls of rice wrapped in bamboo leaves (*zongzi*) are consumed by the population en masse.

July

Liuyueliu. Named the Sixth Day of the Sixth Month, this midsummer holiday is an important festival for Guizhou's Buyi population. According to legend, a beautiful Buyi maiden embroidered an image of the mountains and rivers. A villain plotted to steal it and sent his minions to take it by force. The maiden cast her embroidery into the air, where it was transformed into the mountains and rivers of the province.

August

Ghost Festival. On the fifteenth day of the seventh month in the lunar calendar, living descendants pay homage to their deceased ancestors by burning fake paper money and making offerings to the dead to comfort them in the afterlife and keep them from troubling the living.

September

Mid-Autumn Festival. Mid-Autumn Festival is celebrated on the 15th day of the eighth moon, which generally falls between mid-September and early October. The Chinese spend this time (trying to) gaze at the full moon and exchanging edible "mooncakes": moon-shaped pastries filled with meat, red-bean paste, lotus paste, salted egg, date paste, and other delectable surprises.

October

National Day. Every October 1, China celebrates National Day, in honor of the founding of the People's Republic of China back in 1949. Tiananmen Square fills up with a hefty crowd of visitors on this official holiday, with people granted the entire week off work and school. Domestic tourists from around the country flock to the capital during this time. Steer clear of Beijing during national week if you don't want to battle endless crowds at all the main sights.

December

Laba Festival. On the eighth day of the the twelfth lunar month, the Buddha attained enlightenment. On this day sometime in December, People eat Laba congee, which is made of mixed grains and fruits.

Contacts

Air Travel

Airline and Airport Links.com. *www.airlineandairportlinks.com.*

AIRLINE SECURITY
Transportation Security Administration. *www.tsa.gov.*

AIR PASS INFO
Go Greater China Pass. *800/221–1212* *www.skyteam.com/en/flights-and-destinations/travel-passes/go-greater-china/.* **Visit Asia Pass.** *800/233–2742* *www.oneworld.com/flights/single-continent-fares/visit-asia.*

AIRPORT INFORMATION
Beijing Capital International Airport. *010/6454–1100 wen.bcia.com.cn.* **Chengdu Shuangliu International Airport.** *028/8520–5555* *www.cdairport.com/en.* **Guangzhou Baiyun International Airport.** *P020/3606–6999* *www.guangzhouairportonline.com.* **Guilin Liangjiang International Airport.** *P0773/284–5359.* **Hong Kong International Airport.** *P852/2181–8888* *www.hongkongairport.com.* **Kunming Changshui International Airport.** *P871/96566* *www.kmcsia.com.* **Shanghai Hongqiao International Airport.** *021/96990* *www.shanghaiairport.com.* **Shanghai Pudong International Airport.** *021/96990* *wen.shairport.com/pudongair.html.* **Shenzhen Bao'an International Airport.** *0755/2777–2000* *eng.szairport.com.* **Xiamen Gaoqi International Airport.** *0592/570–6078.* **Xi'an Xianyang International Airport.** *029/96788* *www.xxia.com.*

AIRLINE CONTACTS
Air China. *800/882–8122* *www.airchina.com.* **China Eastern.** *0086–21–95530 hotline* *http://ca.ceair.com/en/.* **China Southern.** *888/338–8988* *www.csair.com/en/.*

Boat Travel

China-Japan International Ferry Company. *908 Dongdaming Lu, Shanghai* *021/6325–7642* *www.shinganjin.com/index_e.php.*

Car Travel

Avis. *021/6229–1118* *www.avis.com/en.*

Train Travel

China Highlights. *www.chinahighlights.com.* **Seat 61.** *www.seat61.com/china.htm.* **Travel China Guide.** *www.travelchinaguide.com/china-trains.*

Visa

HONG KONG TRAVEL AGENTS
China Travel Service. *78–83 Connaught Rd., Hong Kong* *852/2998–7888* *ct-shk.com/english/index.htm.*

Chinese Consulate. *212/244–9456* *newyork.china-consulate.org/eng/.* **Chinese Embassy Visa Office.** *202/495–2266* *www.china-embassy.org/eng.*

HEALTH WARNINGS
National Centers for Disease Control & Prevention (CDC). *800/232–4636 International Travelers' Health Line* *wwwnc.cdc.gov/travel.* **World Health Organization (WHO).** *www.who.int.*

U.S. Embassy and Consulate
United States Consulate. *Citizen Services, Westgate Mall, 1038 West Nanjing Rd., 8th fl., Jing'an* *021/3271–4650, 021/8531–4000 after-hrs emergencies* *shanghai.usembassy-china.org.cn.* **United States Embassy.** *55 Anjialou Lu, Chaoyang P010/8531–3000, 010/8531–4000 emergencies* *beijing.usembassy-china.org.cn.* **United States Citizens Services.** *4 Ling Shiguan Rd., Chengdu* *028/8558–3992, 010/8531–4000 after-hrs emergencies* *chengdu.usembassy-china.org.cn/service.html b43 Hua Jiu Rd., Zhujiang New Town, Tianhe* *020/3814–5775 in Guangzhou, 010/8531–4000 after-hrs emergencies in Guangzhou.*

Chapter 3

BEIJING

3

Updated by
Amy Hawkins

Sights ★★★★★

Restaurants ★★★★☆

Hotels ★★★★☆

Shopping ★★★☆☆

Nightlife ★★★☆☆

WELCOME TO BEIJING

TOP REASONS TO GO

★ **The Forbidden City:** Built by more than 200,000 workers, it's the largest palace in the world and has the best-preserved and most complete collection of imperial architecture in China.

★ **Tiananmen Square:** The political heart of modern China, the square covers 100 acres, making it the largest public square in the world.

★ **Temple of Heaven:** One of the best examples of religious architecture in China, the sprawling, tree-filled complex is a pleasant place for wandering. Watch locals practice martial arts, play traditional instruments, and enjoy ballroom dancing on the grass.

★ **Magnificent Markets:** So much to bargain for, so little time! Visit outdoor Panjiayuan Antiques Market, the Silk Alley Market, or the Pearl Market.

★ **Summer Palace:** This garden complex dates back eight centuries, to when the first emperor of the Jin Dynasty built the Gold Mountain Palace on Longevity Hill.

1 Dongcheng District. Dongcheng (East District) encompasses the Forbidden City, Tiananmen Square, Wangfujing (a major shopping street), the Lama Temple, and many other historical sights dating back to imperial times.

2 Xicheng District. Xicheng (West District), west of Dongcheng, includes Beihai Park, former playground of the imperial family, and a series of connected lakes bordered by willow trees, courtyard-lined *hutong*, and pleasant local restaurants.

3 Chaoyang District. Chaoyang is the biggest and busiest district, occupying the areas north, east, and south of the eastern Second Ring Road. It's home to foreign embassies, multinational companies, the Central Business District, and the Olympic Park.

4 Haidian District. Haidian is the technology and university district. It's northwest of the Third Ring Road and packed with shops selling electronics and students cramming for the next exam.

TO BEIJING AIRPORT
XINJIEKOU
DONGCHENG
DI'ANMEN
DONGSI
XISI
DONGZHIMEN
DONGDAN
CHAOYANG
XIDAN
FUXINGMEN
XUAN-WU
QIANMEN
CHONGWEN
Liuyin Park
Ditan Park
Beihai Park
Forbidden City
Tiananmen Square
Beijing Train Station
Ritan Park
Temple of Heaven
Tiantan Park
Taoranting Park
Longtan Park
Xihai
Houhai
Qianhai
Beihai
Zhonghai
Nanhai
Xinjiekouwai Dajie
Deshengmenwei Dajie
Gulouwai Dajie
Andingmenwai
Hepingli Xijie
Hepingli Dongjie
Hepingli Beijie
Beisanhuandong Lu
Zuojiazhuang Dongjie
Zuojiazhuang
Xibahe Nanlu
Ande Lu
Deshengmendong Dajie
(2nd Ring Rd.)
Andingmendong Dajie
Gulouxi Dajie
Jiugulou Dajie
Beiluogu Xiang
Yonghegong Dajie
Dongzhimenbei Dajie
Xianheyuan Lu
Dongzhimenwaixie Jie
Xindong Lu
Xinyunnan Lu
Xinjiekoubei Dajie
Jiaodaokou Dongdajie
Dongzhimennei Dajie
Dongzhimenwai Dajie
Nan Luogu Xiang
Dongzhimen nan Dajie
Xindong Lu
Sanlitun Lu
Di'anmenxi Dajie
Zhangzizhong Lu
Dongsi Tiao
Gongrentiyuchangbei Lu
Xisibei Dajie
Xishiku Dajie
Nansanlitun Lu
Xi'anmen Dajie
Wenjin Jie
Dongsibei Dajie
Chaoyangmennei Dajie
Chaoyangmenwai Dajie
Xisinan Dajie
Fuyou Jie
Beichizi Dajie
Dongsinan Dajie
Chaoyangmenbei Dajie
Jinyu
Wangfujing Dajie
Nanchizi Dajie
Dongdanbei Dajie
Beijingzhan
Dongdaqiao Lu
Guanghua Lu
Xidanbei Dajie
Fuxingmennei Dajie
Chang'an Jie
Jianguomennei Dajie
Jianguomenwai Dajie
Jianguo Lu
Beixinhua Jie
Xuanwumendong Dajie
Qianmenxi Dajie
Chongwenmenxi Dajie
Tonghui River
Nanxinhua Jie
Qianmen Dajie
Zushikoudong Dajie
Guanqumenwai Lu
Luomashi Dajie
Zhushikouxi Dajie
Guangqumennanbinhe (2nd Ring Rd.)
City Moat
Tiantan Lu
Hufan Lu
Nanheng Xijie
Beiwei Lu
Tiyuguan Lu
Guangming Lu
Jinsong Lu
Taoranting Lu
Taiping Lu
Tianqiaonan Dajie
Tiantandong Lu
nen Dongbinhe Lu
0 1 mile
0 1 kilometer
1
3

There's nowhere else in the world quite like Beijing. It's a modern-day megalopolis at the very core of the world's second-greatest economy, but it's also a gateway into China's imperial past and 5,000 years of history. This is a city where you can stand at the crossroads of time.

In Beijing the march to modernity may seem unrelenting at times, but the city still clings to parts of the past, including a heritage perhaps best encapsulated by the extraordinary Forbidden City. Once home to the emperors of old, it still dominates the city's center. And then, just an hour or two from downtown, stands one of the great wonders of the world: the Great Wall. Built during the Ming Dynasty to keep out the world, it's a telling contrast to the China of today.

Despite the proliferation of shiny office towers, high-rise residences, and shopping centers, there are still plenty of world-class historic sites to be discovered, including the famous rapidly disappearing *hutong*, neighborhoods formed from alleyways. Scores of the city's imperial palaces, mansions, and temples built under the Mongols during the Yuan Dynasty (1271–1368) were rebuilt during the later Ming and Qing dynasties. Despite the ravages of time and the Cultural Revolution, many of these refurbished sites are still in excellent condition.

Planning

When to Go

The best time to visit Beijing is spring or early fall, when the weather is pleasant and crowds are a bit smaller. Book at least one month in advance for travel during these two times of year. In winter Beijing's Forbidden City and Summer Palace can look fantastical and majestic, when the traditional tiled roofs are covered with a light dusting of snow and the venues are devoid of tourists.

Avoid the two long national holidays: Chinese New Year, which ranges from mid-January to mid-February; and National Day holiday, the first week of October, when Chinese normally get a lengthy holiday. Millions of Chinese travel during these weeks, making it difficult to book hotels, tours, and transportation.

The weather in Beijing is at its best in September and October, with a good chance of sunny days and mild temperatures. Winters are cold, but it seldom snows. Late April through June is lovely, but come July the days are hot and excruciatingly humid with a greater chance of rain. Spring is also the time of year for Beijing's famous dust storms.

Getting Around

ON FOOT

Though traffic and modernization have put a bit of a cramp in Beijing's walking style, meandering remains one of the best ways to experience the capital—especially the old hutong that are rich with culture and sights.

BIKE TRAVEL

The proliferation of cars (some 1,000 new automobiles take to the streets of the capital every day, bringing the total to more than 5 million vehicles) has made biking less pleasant and more dangerous here. Fortunately, most streets have wide, well-defined bike lanes often separated from other traffic by an island. If a flat tire or sudden brake failure strikes, seek out the nearest street-side mechanic, easily identified by the bike parts and pumps. Bikes can be rented at many hotels and next to some subway stations; the city is now also awash with thousands of brightly colored yellow and orange share bikes, which don't need to be docked in stations. Although this leads to bikes being left in incongruous places, they're nevertheless a convenient, nifty way to get around. If you have your phone, get a Chinese SIM card, create an account with Mobike or Ofo (the two main share-bike companies), and ride around the city at your leisure.

SUBWAY TRAVEL

The subway is the best way to avoid Beijing's frequent traffic jams. With the opening of new lines, Beijing's subway service is increasingly convenient. The metropolitan area is currently served by 14 lines as well as an express line to the airport. A new tram line, connected to the subway, now takes you to the Summer Palace and Fragrant Hills quickly and conveniently. The subway runs from about 5 am to midnight daily, depending on the station. Fares are Y2 per ride for any distance and transfers are free. Stations are marked in both Chinese and English, and stops are also announced in both languages. Subways are best avoided during rush hours, when severe overcrowding is unavoidable.

TAXI TRAVEL

The taxi experience in Beijing has improved significantly as the city's taxi companies gradually shift to cleaner, more comfortable new cars. In the daytime, flag-fall for taxis is Y13 for the first 3 km (2 miles) and Y2 per kilometer thereafter. The rate rises to Y3 per kilometer on trips over 15 km (8 miles) and after 11 pm, when the flag-fall also increases to Y14. At present, there's also a Y1 gas surcharge for any rides exceeding 3 km (2 miles). ■ **TIP→ Be sure to check that the meter has been engaged to avoid fare negotiations at your destination.** Taxis are easy to hail during the day, but can be difficult during evening rush hour, especially when it's raining. If you're having difficulty, go to the closest hotel and wait in line there. Few taxi drivers speak English, so ask your hotel concierge to write down your destination in Chinese.

Restaurants

Since imperial times, Beijing has drawn citizens from all corners of China, and the country's economic boom has only accelerated the culinary diversity of the capital. These days, diners can find food from the myriad cuisines of far-flung regions of China, as well as just about every kind of international food.

Highlights include rare fungi and flowers from Yunnan, chili-strewn Hunan cooking from Mao's home province, Tibetan yak and *tsampa* (barley flour), mutton kebabs and grilled flatbreads from Xinjiang, numbingly spicy Sichuan cuisine, and chewy noodles from Shaanxi. And then there are ethnic foods from all over, with some—notably Italian, Japanese, and Korean—in abundance.

You can spend as little as $5 per person for a decent meal or $100 and up on a lavish banquet. The variety of venues is also part of the fun, with five-star hotel dining rooms, holes-in-the-wall, and refurbished courtyard houses all represented. Reservations are always a good idea, especially for higher-end places, so ask your hotel to book you a table.

Beijingers tend to eat dinner around 6 pm, and many local restaurants will have closed their kitchens by 9 pm, though places that stay open until the wee hours aren't hard to find. Tipping is not the custom although some larger, international restaurants will add a 15% service charge to the bill, as do five-star hotel restaurants. Be aware before you go out that small and medium venues only take cash payments or local bank cards; more established restaurants usually accept credit cards.

What it Costs in Yuan

	$	$$	$$$	$$$$
RESTAURANTS	under Y100	Y100–Y150	Y151–Y200	over Y200

Hotels

The first real wave of tourists to visit China in the early 1980s had little need for guidebooks—foreigners were only allowed to stay in ugly, state-run, Stalinist-style blocks. But times have changed. Now Beijing has it all: a glorious glut of the world's best hotel brands; cheap and breezy places to make your base; intimate boutique beauties; and historical courtyard conversions.

The main hubs for hotels are around Wangfujing (Beijing's famous shopping strip), in the vicinity of the northeast Third Ring Road, and along Chang'an/Jianguomen, one of the city's main thoroughfares that connect the Central Business District (CBD) to Tiananmen Square. This is where you'll find the city's most recognizable and reputable hotels, all of which offer luxurious rooms, international-standard facilities, and attentive service. Don't despair if you're on a budget: there are plenty of decent dwellings next to the tourist trail at a fraction of the cost.

"Location, location, location" should be your mantra when booking a Beijing hotel, especially if you're only in town for a few days. It's a big city: there's no point schlepping halfway across it for one particular hotel when a similar option is available in a more convenient area. Consider where you'll be going (Summer Palace? Forbidden City? Great Wall?), then pick your bed. Busy execs should choose wisely in order to avoid getting snarled up in Beijing's horrific traffic, which most likely means staying a little farther west near Financial Street or in the other commercial hub of Guomao (the CBD) in the east. Those in search of nightlife will want to be by Sanlitun, home to the capital's best bars and restaurants. If you're after a one-of-a-kind Beijing experience, check out the city's courtyard hotels. These distinctive lodgings are often converted *siheyuan*—traditional homes built as residential quadrangles among the hutongs.

What it Costs in Yuan

	$	$$	$$$	$$$$
HOTELS	under Y1,100	Y1,100–Y1,400	Y1,401–Y1,800	over Y1,800

Nightlife

With intimate bars, world-class cocktail lounges, happening dance halls, sports bars, and even English-style pubs, Beijing has just about every kind of experience you can imagine. Keep in mind, though, that establishments seemingly rise up overnight, and can disappear just as quickly in the breakneck pace of development that is endemic to Beijing.

Performing Arts

The performing arts in China took a long time to recover from the Cultural Revolution (1966–76), and political works are still generally banned or avoided. In recent years, names such as Kevin Spacey and the Royal Shakespeare Company have alighted on Beijing, reinforcing the capital's reputation as an arts destination. For culture vultures, there are avant-garde plays, chamber music, traditional Peking opera, acrobatics shows, and lots more.

As most of the stage is inaccessible to non-Chinese speakers, visitors to Beijing are more likely to hunt out the big visual spectacles, such as Beijing opera or kung fu displays. These long-running shows are tailored for travelers: your hotel will be able to recommend performances and venues and will likely be able to help you book tickets.

Shopping

Shopping is an integral part of any trip to Beijing. Between the hutongs, the markets, the malls, and the shopping streets, it sometimes seems like you can buy anything here.

Large markets and malls are the lifeblood of Beijing, and they're generally open from 9 am to 9 pm, though hours vary from shop to shop. If a stall looks closed (perhaps the lights are out or the owner is resting), don't give up. Many merchants conserve electricity or take catnaps when business is slack. Just knock or offer the greeting *ni hao* and, more often than not, the lights will flip on and you'll be invited to come in. Shops in malls have more regular hours and will only be closed on a few occasions throughout the year, such as Chunjie (Chinese New Year) and October's National Day Golden Week.

Major credit cards are accepted in pricier venues but cash is the driving force here. ATMs abound, however it's worth noting that before accepting any Mao-faced Y100 notes, most vendors will hold them up to the light, tug at the corners, and rub their fingers along the surface. Counterfeiting is becoming increasingly sophisticated in China, and banks are reluctant to accept responsibility for ATMs that dispense fake notes.

The official currency unit of China is the yuan or *renminbi* (literally, "the people's currency"). Informally, though, the main unit of currency is called *kuai* (using "kuai" is the equivalent of saying a "buck" in the United States). On price tags, renminbi is usually written in its abbreviated form, RMB, and yuan is abbreviated as ¥. 1 RMB = 1 Renminbi = 1 Yuan = 1 Kuai = 10 Jiao = 10 Mao = 100 Fen.

If you're looking to bargain, head to the markets; Western-style shops generally go by the price tags. Stalls frequented by foreigners often have at least one employee with some degree of fluency in English. In many situations—whether or not there's a common tongue—the shop assistant will whip out a calculator, look at you to see what they think you'll cough up, then type in a starting price. You're then expected to punch in your offer (start at one third of their valuation). The clerk will usually come down a surprisingly large amount, and so on and so on. A good tip to note is that there's a common superstition in Chinese markets that if you don't make a sale with your first customer of the day, the rest of the day will go badly—so set out early, and if you know you're the first customer of the day, bargain relentlessly.

Tours

Taking a tour will make it easier to sightsee without the hassle. However, if you're adventurous, you can easily explore the city on your own, even if you don't speak Chinese. You can't rely on taxi drivers to know the English names of the major tourist sites, but armed with the names in Chinese in this guide, you should have few or no problems getting around. If you do opt for an organized tour, keep in mind that a little research pays off.

GENERAL CULTURAL AND SPECIAL INTEREST TOURS

Local guides are often creative when it comes to showing you history and culture, so having an expert with you can make a big difference. Learning is the focus of Smithsonian Journeys' small-group tours, which are led by university professors. China experts also lead National Geographic's trips, but all that knowledge doesn't come cheap. Wild-China is a local company with unusual trips: one of their cultural trips explores China's little-known Jewish history. The Hutong and the China Culture Center are also wonderful local resources for tours, classes, lectures, and other events in Beijing. The China Guide is a Beijing-based, American-managed travel agency offering tours that do *not* make shopping detours. Bespoke Beijing and Stretch-a-Leg Travel, and WildChina specialize in taking visitors to off-the-beaten-track locations and can offer personalized tours.

CONTACTS Bespoke Beijing ✉ *07A110, 7th fl., 10 Jintong Xi Lu, Chaoyang* ☎ *151/0167–9082* 🌐 *www.bespoke-beijing.com.* **China Culture Center** ✉ *The Victoria Gardens D4, Chaoyang Park West Rd., Chaoyang* ☎ *010/6432–9341, 010/8420–0671 weekends* 🌐 *www.chinaculture-center.org.* **The China Guide** ✉ *Bldg. 7–1, Jianguomenwai Waijiaogongyu Diplomatic Compound, 8th fl., Room 81, Chaoyang* ☎ *010/8532–1860* 🌐 *www.thechinaguide.com.* **National Geographic Expeditions** ☎ *888/966–8687* 🌐 *www.nationalgeographicexpeditions.com.* **Smithsonian Journeys** ☎ *855/330–1542 in U.S.* 🌐 *www.smithsonianjourneys.org.* **Stretch-A-Leg Travel** ✉ *2 Qian'gulouyuan, Jiaodaokou, Dongcheng District* 🌐 *beijing.stretchalegtravel.com.*

BIKING

Cycle China offers plenty of cycling trips in and around Beijing and beyond, such as the Great Wall. You can hire bikes from them, or take your own. Bike China Adventures organizes trips of varying length and difficulty all over China.

CONTACTS Bike China Adventures 🌐 *www.bikechina.com.* **Cycle China** ✉ *12–1 Jingshan Dong Jie, Dongcheng District* ✢ *Opposite east gate of Jingshan Park* ☎ *139/1188–6524* 🌐 *www.cyclechina.com.*

CULINARY

Intrepid Travel is an Australian company offering a China Gourmet Traveler tour with market visits, cooking demonstrations, and plenty of good eats. Imperial Tours Culinary Tour combines sightseeing with cooking lectures and demonstrations, and lots of five-star dining.

CONTACTS Imperial Tours ✉ *Dangdai Moma 10–906 Bei Qu, 1 Xiangheyuan Lu, Dongcheng District* ☎ *10/8440–7162, 010/8440–7162* 🌐 *www.imperialtours.net* **Intrepid Travel** ☎ *707/296–7011* 🌐 *www.intrepidtravel.com.*

HIKING

Beijing Hikers offer multiple hikes and camping stays on and around the Great Wall and always make sure that they leave no rubbish behind, unlike many other companies.

CONTACTS Beijing Hikers ✉ *Potevio Industrial Innovation Park, 5 Jiangtai Lu, Bldg. B1, 2nd fl., Room 221, Chaoyang* ☎ *010/6432–2786* 🌐 *www.beijinghikers.com.*

PEDICAB TOURS

Pedicabs (basically large tricycles with room for passengers behind a pedaling driver) were once the vehicles of choice for Beijingers laden with a week's worth of groceries or tourists eager for a street's-eye city tour. Today many residents are wealthy enough to bundle their purchases into taxis or their own cars, and the tourist trade has moved on to the tight schedules of air-conditioned buses. But pedicabs have made a big comeback in Beijing in recent years and can now be hired near major tourist sites. A ride through the hutong near Houhai is the most popular pedicab journey. ■ **TIP→ Be absolutely sure to negotiate the fare in advance, clarifying which currency will be used (yuan or dollars), whether the fare is considered a one-way or round-trip (some drivers will demand payment for a round-trip whether or not you use the pedicab for the return journey), and whether it is for one person or two.** Beginning in 2008, government-approved pedicab tours were supposed to be fixed at Y35 per hour, though the actual price is often higher. Feel free to tip your driver for good service on longer tours. Independent pedicabs for hutong tours can be found in the small plaza between the Drum Tower and the Bell Tower.

Visitor Information

For general information, including advice on tours, insurance, and safety, call, or visit China National Tourist Office's website, as well as the website run by the Beijing Tourism Administration (BTA). ■ **TIP→ The BTA maintains a 24-hour hotline for tourist inquiries and complaints, with operators fluent in English. BTA also runs Beijing Tourist Information Centers, whose staff can help you with free maps and directions in Beijing.**

BEIJING TOURIST INFORMATION Beijing Tourism Administration ☏ *010/8353–1111* ✉ *visitbeijingeng@163.com* 🌐 *english.visitbeijing.com.cn.*

Dongcheng District

Feeling the weight and the power of China's history is inevitable as you stand on the Avenue of Eternal Peace, Chang'an Jie, at the crossroads of ancient and modern China. The pale expanse of Tiananmen Square, built by Mao Zedong to fit up to a million revolutionary souls, leaves even mobs of tourists looking tiny and scattered. An iconic portrait of Mao sits upon the scarlet wall of Tiananmen Gate, the serenity of his gaze belying the tumult of his reign. And beyond, the splendors of the Forbidden City await.

The soul of old Beijing lives on throughout Dongcheng District, where you'll find the city's top historic sites and idyllic hutong worth getting lost in. A day or two exploring the district will leave you feeling as if you've been introduced to the complicated character of the capital. Dongcheng is also one of the smaller districts in the city, which makes it ideal for tackling on foot or by bicycle. ■ **TIP→ Note that indoor photography in many temples and sites like the Forbidden City is not permitted.**

GETTING HERE AND AROUND

Dongcheng is easily accessible by subway, with stops along most of its perimeter: Tiananmen East station to Jianguomen on Line 1 forms the south side of this district; Jianguomen to Gulou Dajie on Line 2 forms the district's north and east sides. Line 2 stops at the Lama Temple, the Ancient Observatory, Wangfujing, and Tiananmen Square. Taxi travel during peak hours (7 to 9 am and 5 to 8 pm) is difficult. At other times traveling by taxi is affordable, convenient, and the fastest option (especially at noon, when much of the city is at lunch, and after 10 pm). Renting a bike to see the sites is also a good option. Bus travel within the city is only Y1 for shorter distances and can be very convenient, but requires reading knowledge of Chinese to find the correct bus to take. Once on the bus, stops are announced in Chinese and English.

Beijing's Subway

Although Beijing's subway system has grown to 22 lines, the original 2 lines provide access to the most popular areas of the capital. **Line 1** runs east and west along Chang'an Jie past the China World Trade Center, Jianguomen (one of the embassy districts), the Wangfujing shopping area, Tiananmen Square and the Forbidden City, Xidan (another major shopping location), and the Military Museum, before heading out to the far western suburbs. **Line 2** (the inner loop line) runs along a sort of circular route around the center of the city shadowing the Second Ring Road. Important destinations include the Drum and Bell towers, Lama Temple, Dongzhimen (with a connection to the airport express), Dongsishitiao (near Sanlitun and the Workers' Stadium), Beijing Train Station, and Qianmen (Front Gate), south of Tiananmen Square. Free transfers between Lines 1 and 2 can be made at either Fuxingmen or Jianguomen stations. Line 10, which forms a rough loop following the Third Ring Road, runs through the Central Business District at Guomao station (where a transfer is possible to Line 1), up toward the Sanlitun area at Tuanjiehu, and connects with the airport express line at Sanyuanqiao.

If both you and your final destination are near the Second Ring Road, on Chang'an Jie, or on the northern or eastern sides of the Third Ring Road, the best way to get there is probably by subway. It stops just about every kilometer (half mile), and you'll easily spot the entrances (with blue subway logos) dotting the streets. Each stop is announced in both English and Chinese, and there are clearly marked signs in English or pinyin at each station. Transferring between lines is easy and free, with the standard Y2 ticket including travel between any two destinations.

Subway tickets can be purchased from electronic kiosks and ticket windows in every station. Start off by finding the button that says "English," insert your money, and press another button to print. Single-ride tickets cost Y2, and you'll want to pay with exact change; the machines don't accept Y1 bills, only Y1 coins. It's also possible to buy a stored-value subway card with a Y20 deposit and a purchase of Y10–Y100.

In the middle of each subway platform you'll find a map of the Beijing subway system along with a local map showing the position of exits. Subway cars also have a simplified diagram of the line you're riding above the doors.

Trains can be very crowded, especially during rush hour, and it's not uncommon for people to push onto the train before exiting passengers can get off. Prepare to get off by making your way to the door before you arrive at your station. Be especially wary of pickpockets.

■ TIP→ Unfortunately, the subway system is not convenient for disabled people. In some stations there are no escalators, and sometimes the only entrance or exit is via steep steps.

MAKING THE MOST OF YOUR TIME

Most of Dongcheng can be seen in a day, but it's best to set aside two, because the **Forbidden City** and **Tiananmen Square** will likely take the better part of one day. The climb up Coal Hill (also called Prospect Hill) in **Jingshan Park** will take about 30 minutes for an average walker. From there, take a taxi to the **Lama Temple,** which is worth a good two hours, then visit the nearby **Confucius Temple.**

Sights

★ **Confucius Temple** (孔庙 *Kǒngmiào*)
MEMORIAL | This tranquil temple to China's great sage has endured close to eight centuries of additions and restorations. The Hall of Great Accomplishment in the temple houses Confucius's funeral tablet and shrine, flanked by copper-colored statues depicting China's wisest Confucian scholars. As in Buddhist and Taoist temples, worshippers can offer sacrifices (in this case to a mortal, not a deity). The 198 tablets lining the courtyard outside the Hall of Great Accomplishment contain 51,624 names belonging to advanced Confucian scholars from the Yuan, Ming, and Qing dynasties. Flanking the Gate of Great Accomplishment are two carved stone drums dating to the Qianlong period (1735–96). In the Hall of Great Perfection you'll find the central shrine to Confucius. Check out the huge collection of ancient musical instruments.

In the front and main courtyards of the temple you'll find a cemetery of stone tablets. These tablets, or stelae, stand like rows of crypts. On the front stelae you can barely make out the names of thousands of scholars who passed imperial exams. Another batch of stelae, carved in the mid-1700s to record the *Thirteen Classics,* which are philosophical works attributed to Confucius, line the west side of the grounds.

■ TIP→ We recommend combining a tour of the Confucius Temple with the nearby Lama Temple. Access to both is convenient from the Yonghegong subway stop at the intersection of Line 2 and Line 5. You can also easily get to the Temple of Heaven by taking Line 5 south to Tiantandongmen.

The complex is now combined with the Imperial Academy next door, once the highest educational institution in the country. Established in 1306 as a rigorous training ground for high-level government officials, the academy was notorious, especially during the early Ming Dynasty era, for the harsh discipline imposed on scholars perfecting their knowledge of the Confucian classics. The Riyong Emperors Lecture Hall is surrounded by a circular moat (although the building is rectangular in shape). Emperors would come here to lecture on the classics. This ancient campus would be a glorious place to study today with its washed red walls, gold-tiled roofs, and towering cypresses (some as old as 700 years). ⊠ *15 Guozijian Jie, off Yonghegong Dajie near Lama Temple, Dongcheng District* ☎ *010/6405–7214* 🌐 *www.kmgzj.com* 🎫 *Y30* Ⓜ *Yonghegong.*

Ditan Park (地坛公园 *Dìtán gōngyuán*)
ARCHAEOLOGICAL SITE | In "Temple of Earth Park," 105 acres of 16th-century green space, are the square altar where emperors once made sacrifices to the earth god, and the Hall of Deities. This is a lovely place for a stroll, especially if you're already near the Drum Tower or Lama Temple. ⊠ *Andingmen Wai Dajie, just north of Second Ring Rd., Dongcheng District* ☎ *010/6421–4657* 🎫 *Y2.*

★ **The Forbidden City** (故宫 *Gùgōng*)
CASTLE/PALACE | Undeniably sumptuous, the Forbidden City, once home to a long line of emperors, is Beijing's most enduring emblem. Magnificent halls, winding lanes, and stately courtyards await you. At 180 acres, this is the world's largest palace complex. The sheer grandeur of

Continued on page 82

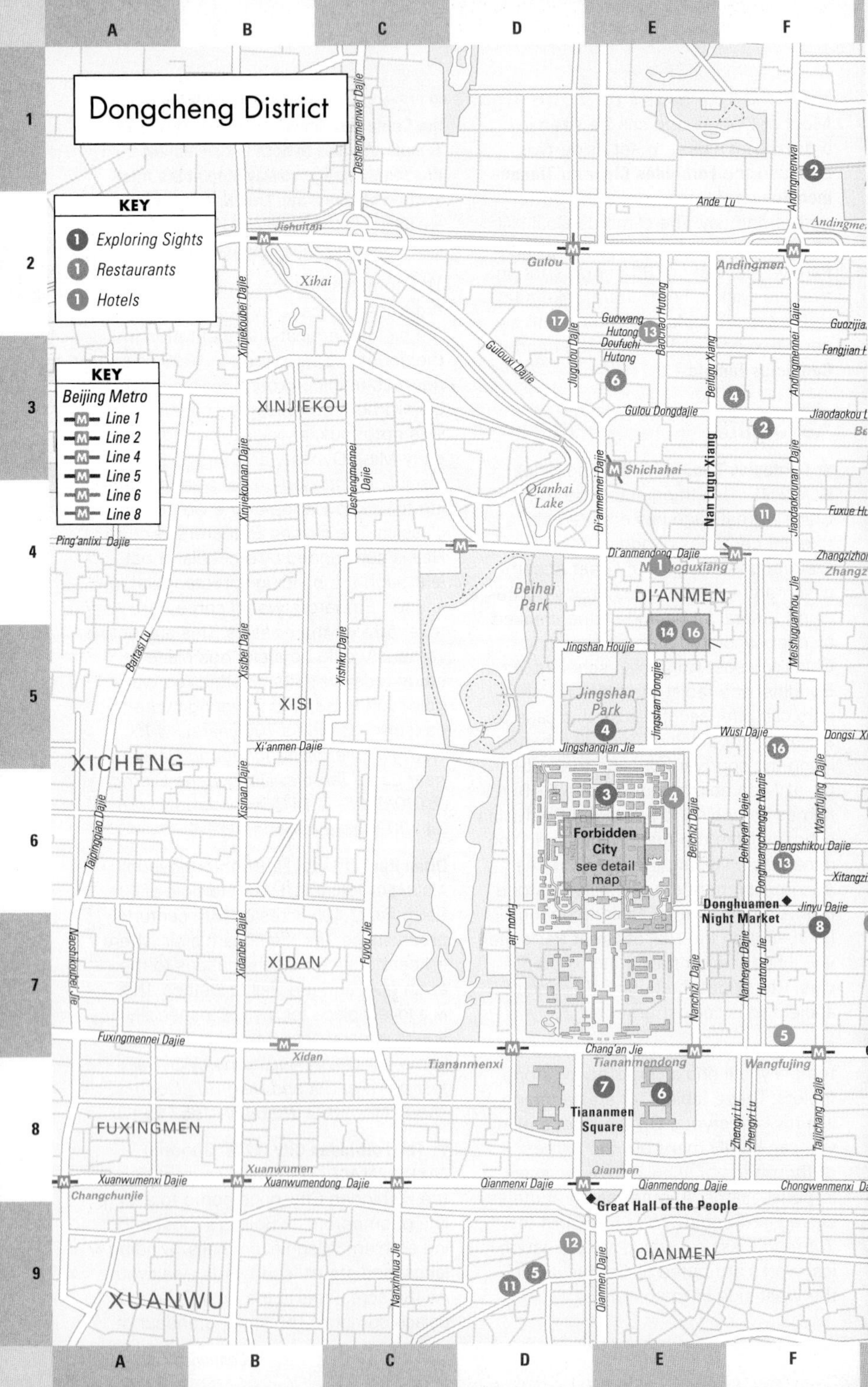
Dongcheng District
KEY
Exploring Sights
Restaurants
Hotels
KEY
Beijing Metro
Line 1
Line 2
Line 4
Line 5
Line 6
Line 8
XINJIEKOU
XISI
XICHENG
XIDAN
FUXINGMEN
XUANWU
DI'ANMEN
QIANMEN
Beihai Park
Jingshan Park
Forbidden City
see detail map
Tiananmen Square
Donghuamen Night Market
Great Hall of the People
Qianhai Lake
Xihai
Jishuitan
Gulou
Andingmen
Shichahai
Xidan
Tiananmenxi
Tiananmendong
Wangfujing
Xuanwumen
Qianmen
Changchunjie
Deshengmenwei Dajie
Ande Lu
Andingmenwai
Gulouxi Dajie
Guowang Hutong
Doufuchi Hutong
Baochao Hutong
Jiugulou Dajie
Beilugu Xiang
Andingmennei Dajie
Gulou Dongdajie
Nan Luogu Xiang
Jiaodaokou Dajie
Jiaodaokounan Dajie
Fuxue Hutong
Di'anmennei Dajie
Di'anmendong Dajie
Zhangzizhong Lu
Xinjiekoubei Dajie
Xinjiekounan Dajie
Deshengmennei Dajie
Ping'anlixi Dajie
Baitasi Lu
Xisibei Dajie
Xishiku Dajie
Jingshan Houjie
Jingshan Dongjie
Meishuguanhou Jie
Wusi Dajie
Dongsi Xi
Jingshanqian Jie
Xi'anmen Dajie
Xisinan Dajie
Taipingqiao Dajie
Beichizi Dajie
Beiheyan Dajie
Donghuangchengge Nanjie
Wangfujing Dajie
Dengshikou Dajie
Xitangzi
Jinyu Dajie
Naoshikoubei Jie
Xidanbei Dajie
Fuyou Jie
Nanchizi Dajie
Nanheyan Dajie
Huatong Jie
Fuxingmennei Dajie
Chang'an Jie
Zhengyi Lu
Taijichang Dajie
Xuanwumenxi Dajie
Xuanwumendong Dajie
Qianmenxi Dajie
Qianmendong Dajie
Chongwenmenxi Dajie
Nanxinhua Jie
Qianmen Dajie
Guozijian
Fangjian Hutong
A
B
C
D
E
F
1
2
3
4
5
6
7
8
9

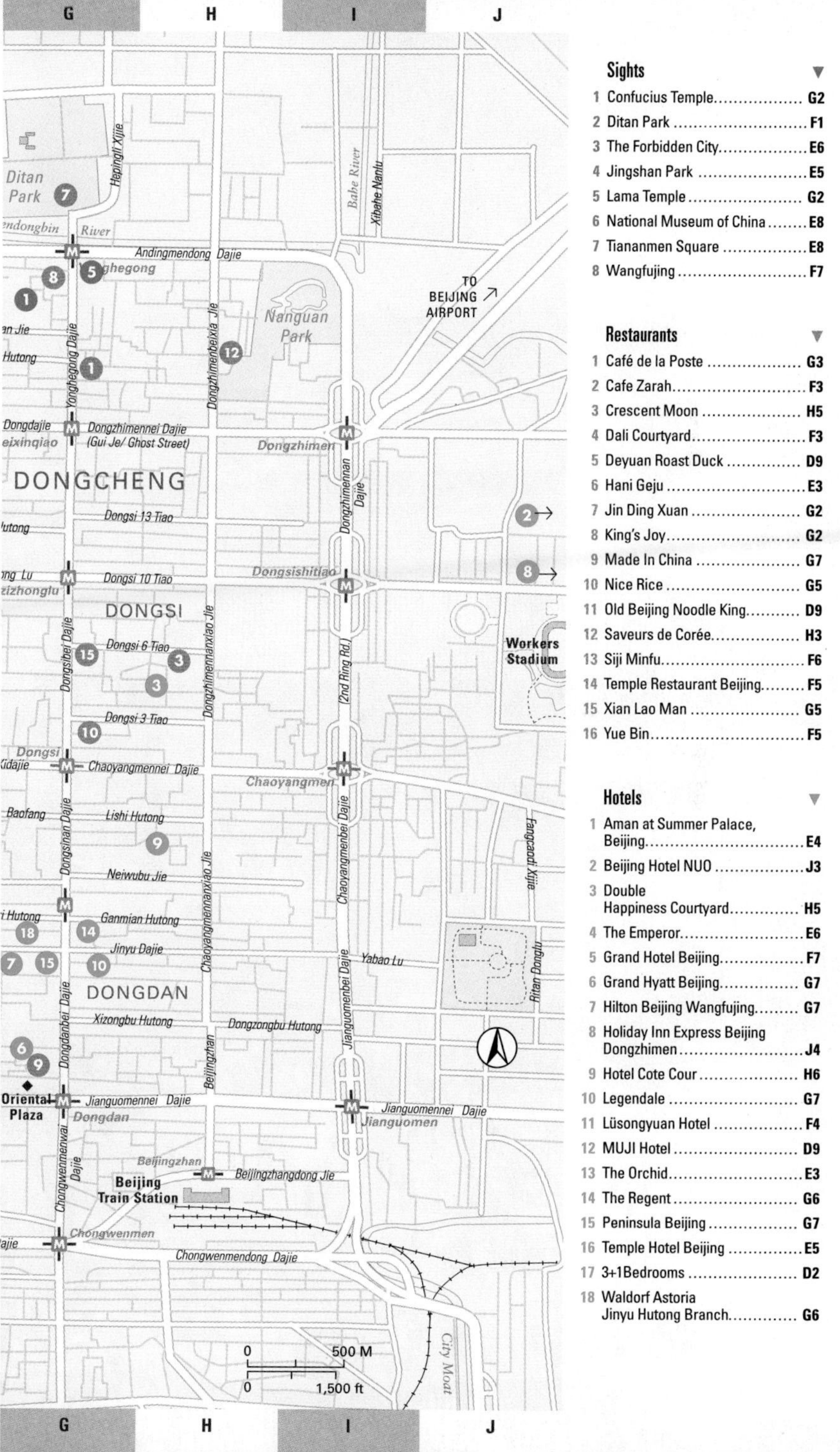

Sights

1 Confucius Temple G2
2 Ditan Park F1
3 The Forbidden City E6
4 Jingshan Park E5
5 Lama Temple G2
6 National Museum of China E8
7 Tiananmen Square E8
8 Wangfujing F7

Restaurants

1 Café de la Poste G3
2 Cafe Zarah F3
3 Crescent Moon H5
4 Dali Courtyard F3
5 Deyuan Roast Duck D9
6 Hani Geju E3
7 Jin Ding Xuan G2
8 King's Joy G2
9 Made In China G7
10 Nice Rice G5
11 Old Beijing Noodle King D9
12 Saveurs de Corée H3
13 Siji Minfu F6
14 Temple Restaurant Beijing F5
15 Xian Lao Man G5
16 Yue Bin F5

Hotels

1 Aman at Summer Palace, Beijing E4
2 Beijing Hotel NUO J3
3 Double Happiness Courtyard H5
4 The Emperor E6
5 Grand Hotel Beijing F7
6 Grand Hyatt Beijing G7
7 Hilton Beijing Wangfujing G7
8 Holiday Inn Express Beijing Dongzhimen J4
9 Hotel Cote Cour H6
10 Legendale G7
11 Lüsongyuan Hotel F4
12 MUJI Hotel D9
13 The Orchid E3
14 The Regent G6
15 Peninsula Beijing G7
16 Temple Hotel Beijing E5
17 3+1Bedrooms D2
18 Waldorf Astoria Jinyu Hutong Branch G6

故宫博物院

THE FORBIDDEN CITY

Undeniably sumptuous, the Forbidden City, once home to a long line of emperors, is Beijing's most enduring emblem. Magnificent halls, winding lanes, and stately courtyards await you—welcome to the world's largest palace complex.

As you gaze up at roofs of glazed-yellow tiles—a symbol of royalty—try to imagine a time when only the emperor ("the son of God") was permitted to enter this palace, accompanied by select family members, concubines, and eunuch-servants. Now, with its doors flung open, the Forbidden City's mysteries beckon.

The sheer grandeur of the site—with 800 buildings and more than 8,000 rooms—conveys the pomp and circumstance of Imperial China. The shady palaces, musty with age, recall life at court, where corrupt eunuchs and palace officials schemed and bored concubines gossiped.

BUILDING TO GLORY

Under the third Ming emperor, Yongle, 200,000 laborers built this complex over the course of 14 years, finishing in 1420. Yongle relocated the Ming capital to Beijing (from Nanjing in the south) to strengthen China's northern frontier. After Yongle, the palace was home to 23 Ming and Qing emperors, until the dynastic system crumbled in 1911.

In imperial times, no buildings were allowed to exceed the height of the palace. Moats and massive timber doors protected the emperor. Gleaming yellow roof tiles marked the vast complex as the royal court's exclusive dominion. Ornate interiors displayed China's most exquisite artisanship, including ceilings covered with turquoise-and-blue dragons, walls draped with priceless scrolls, intricate cloisonné screens, sandalwood thrones padded in delicate silks, and floors of golden-hued bricks. Miraculously, the palace survived fire, war, and imperial China's collapse.

MORE THAN FENG SHUI

The Forbidden City embodies Feng Shui, architectural principles used for thousands of years throughout China. Each main hall faces south, opening to a courtyard flanked by lesser buildings. This symmetry repeats itself along a north–south axis that bisects the imperial palace, with a broad walkway paved in marble. This path was reserved exclusively for the emperor's sedan chair.

The entire complex follows the principles of Feng Shui.

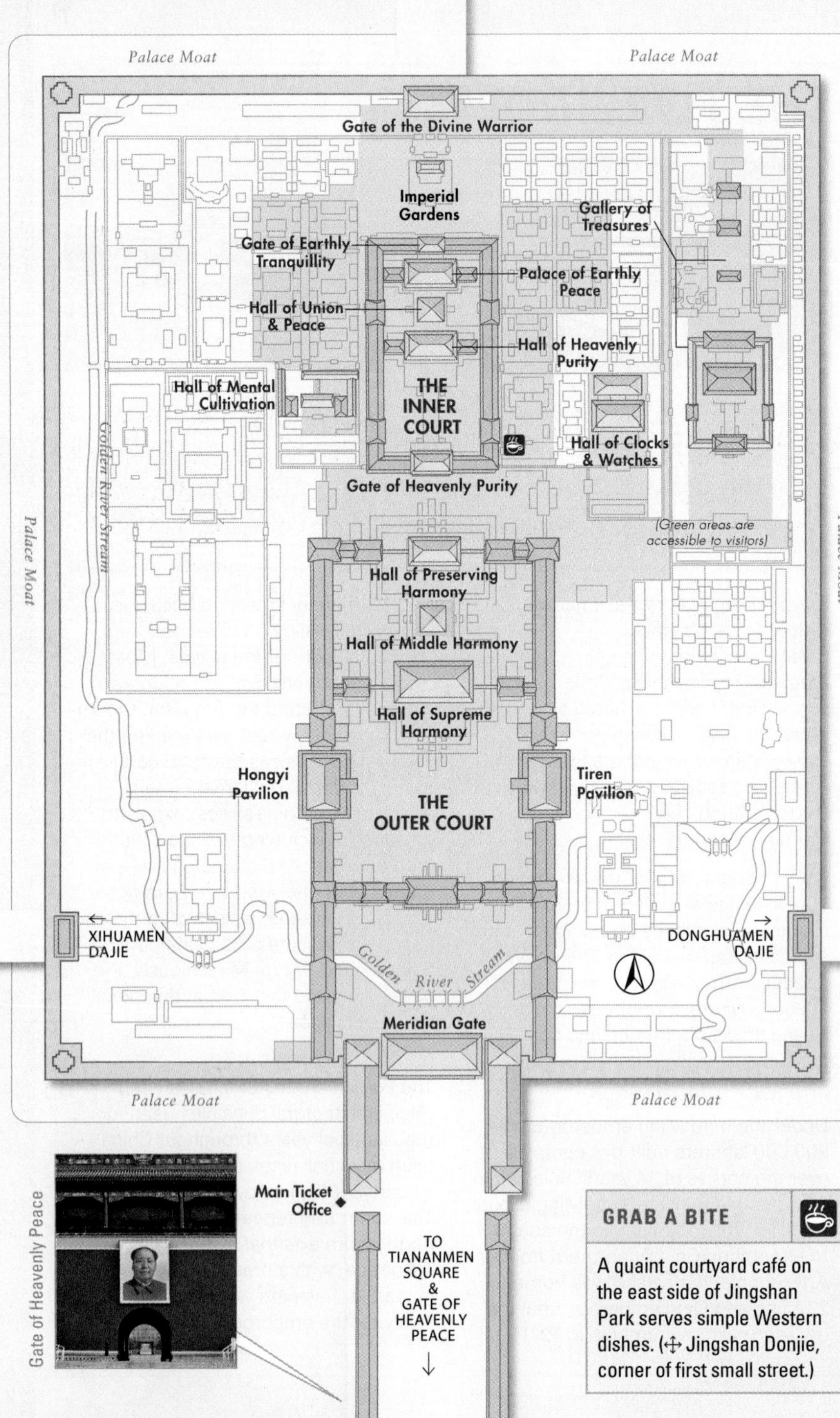

GRAB A BITE

A quaint courtyard café on the east side of Jingshan Park serves simple Western dishes. (✣ Jingshan Donjie, corner of first small street.)

WHAT TO SEE

The most impressive way to reach the Forbidden City is through the **Gate of Heavenly Peace** (Tiananmen), connected to Tiananmen Square. The Great Helmsman himself stood here to establish the People's Republic of China on October 1, 1949.

The **Meridian Gate** (Wumen), sometimes called Five Phoenix Tower, is the main southern entrance to the palace. Here, the emperor announced yearly planting schedules according to the lunar calendar; it's also where errant officials were flogged. The main ticket office and audio-guide rentals are just west of this gate.

THE OUTER COURT

The **Hall of Supreme Harmony** (Taihedian) was used for coronations, royal birthdays, and weddings. Bronze vats, once kept brimming with water to fight fires, ring this vast expanse. The hall sits atop three stone tiers with an elaborate drainage system with 1,000 carved dragons. On the top tier, bronze cranes symbolize longevity. Inside, cloisonné cranes flank the imperial throne, above which hangs a heavy bronze ball—placed there to crush any pretender to the throne.

Emperors greeted audiences in the **Hall of Middle Harmony** (Zhonghedian). It also housed the royal plow, with which the emperor would turn a furrow to commence spring planting.

The highest civil service examinations, which were personally conducted by the emperor, were once administered in the **Hall of Preserving Harmony** (Baohedian). Behind the hall, a 200-ton marble relief of dragons, the palace's most treasured stone carving, adorns the staircase.

A short jaunt to the right is **Hall of Clocks and Watches** (Zhongbiaoguan), where you'll find a collection of early timepieces. It's pure opulence, with jeweled, enameled, and lacquered timepieces (some astride elephants, others implanted in ceramic trees). Our favorites? Those crafted from red sandalwood. *(additional admission cost)*

You'll see that lions in the palace live in pairs. A female lion playing with a cub symbolizes imperial fertility. A male lion, sitting majestically with a sphere beneath his paw, represents power.

The central entrance of the Meridian was reserved for the emperor. The one day the empress was allowed to walk through it was her wedding day.

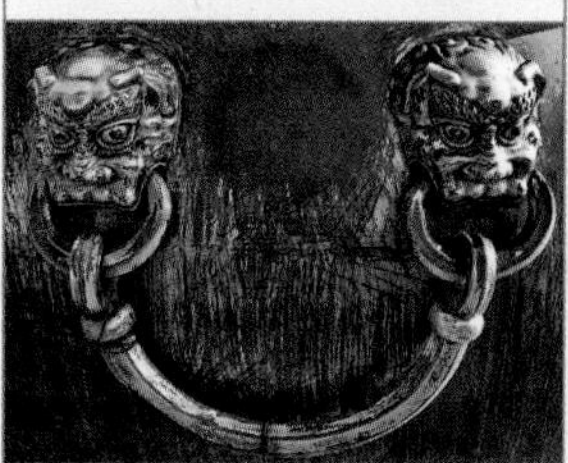

Take a close look at the bronze vats and you'll see the telltale scratch marks of greedy foreign soldiers who scraped the gold with their bayonets.

The Hall of Supreme Harmony was the site of many imperial weddings.

Marble dragons will greet you behind the Hall of Preserving Harmony.

DID YOU KNOW?

- 24 emperors and two dynasties ruled from within these labyrinthine halls.
- The emperor was the only non-castrated male allowed in the eastern and western palaces. This served as proof that any pregnant concubine was carrying the royal one's baby.
- If you prepared for your trip by watching Bertolucci's The Last Emperor, you may recognize the passage outside the Hall of Mental Cultivation: this is where young Puyi rode his bike in the film.
- Women can enter the Forbidden City for half price on March 8, International Women's Day.
- When it was first built in the 15th century, the palace was called the Purple Forbidden City; today, its official name is the Ancient Palace Museum (Gugong Bowuguan); often it's shortened simply to Gugong.

Emperors Throne in the Palace of Heavenly Purity

THE INNER COURT

Now you're approaching the very core of the palace. Several emperors chose to live in the Inner Palace with their families. The **Hall of Heavenly Purity** (Qianqinggong) holds another imperial throne; the **Hall of Union and Peace** (Jiaotaidian) was the venue for the empress's annual birthday party; and the **Palace of Earthly Peace** (Kunninggong) was where royal couples consummated their marriages. The banner above the throne bizarrely reads DOING NOTHING.

On either side of the Inner Palace are six western and six eastern palaces—the former living quarters of con-cubines, eunuchs, and servants. The last building on the western side, the **Hall of Mental Cultivation** (Yangxin-dian), is the most important of these; starting with Emperor Yongzheng, all Qing Dynasty emperors attended to daily state business in this hall.

AN EMPEROR CHEAT SHEET

JIAJING (1507–1567)

Ming Emperor Jiajing was obsessed with Taoism, which he hoped would give him longevity, but which also led him to ignore state affairs for 25 years. His other fixation was the pursuit of girls: his 18 concubines conspired to strangle him in his sleep, but their plot was uncovered. Nearly all of the girls, and their families, were killed.

YONGZHENG (1678–1735)

The third emperor of the Qing Dynasty, Yongzheng was tyrannical but efficient. He became emperor amid rumors that he had forged his father's will. He appeased his brothers by promoting them, but then proceeded to murder and imprison anyone who posed a challenge, including his own brothers, two of whom died in prison.

Pagoda in the Imperial Garden

The Gallery of Treasures (Zhenbaoguan), actually a series of halls, has breathtaking examples of imperial ornamentation. The first room displays candleholders, wine vessels, tea sets, and a golden pagoda commissioned by Qing emperor Qian Long in honor of his mother. A cabinet on one wall contains the 25 imperial seals. Jade bracelets, golden hair pins, and coral fill the second hall; carved jade landscapes a third. *(Admission: Y10)*

HEAD FOR THE GREEN

North of the Forbidden City's private palaces, beyond the **Gate of Earthly Tranquillity**, lie the most pleasant parts of the Forbidden City: the **Imperial Gardens** (Yuhuayuan), composed of ancient cypress trees and stone mosaic pathways. During festivals, palace inhabitants climbed the Hill of Accumulated Elegance. You can exit the palace at the back of the gardens through the park's **Gate of the Divine Warrior** (Shenwumen).

FAST FACTS

Address: The main entrance is just north of the Gate of Heavenly Peace, which faces Tiananmen Square on Chang'an Jie.

Web site: www.dpm.org.cn

Open: Tues.–Sun.

UNESCO Status: Declared a World Heritage Site in 1987. You must check your bags prior to entry and also pass through a metal detector.

- The palace is always packed with visitors, but it's impossibly crowded on national holidays.
- Allow 2–4 hours to explore the palace. There are souvenir shops and restaurants inside.
- You can rent audio guides at the Meridian Gate.

CIXI (1835–1908)

The Empress Dowager served as de facto ruler of China from 1861 until 1908. She was a concubine at 16 and soon became Emperor Xianfeng's favorite. She gave birth to his only son to survive: the heir apparent. Ruthless and ambitious, she learned the workings of the imperial court and used every means to gain power.

PUYI (1906–1967)

Puyi, whose life was depicted in Bertolucci's classic *The Last Emperor,* took the throne at age two. The Qing dynasty's last emperor, he was forced to abdicate after the dynasty fell. During an attempted restoration in 1917, he held the throne for 12 days. Puyi was forced out of the Imperial City in 1924 by a warlord.

the site—with 800 buildings and a rumored 9,999 rooms—conveys the pomp of Imperial China. The shady palaces, musty with age, recall the tedium of life at court was relieved by gossip and scheming. ✉ *Facing Tiananmen Square on Chang'an Jie, Dongcheng District* ☎ *010/6404–4071* 🌐 *www.dpm.org.cn* 🎟 *Apr. 1– Oct. 31 Y60; Nov. 1–Mar 31 Y40; entry to the Hall of Clocks and Watches and to the Gallery of Treasures are an additional Y10.*

★ **Jingshan Park** (景山公园 *Jǐngshān gōngyuán*)
NATIONAL/STATE PARK | This park, also known as Coal Hill Park, was built around a small peak formed from earth excavated for the Forbidden City's moats. Ming rulers ordered the hill's construction to improve the feng shui of their new palace to the south. You can climb a winding stone staircase past peach and apple trees to Wanchun Pavilion, the park's highest point. On a clear day it offers unparalleled views of the Forbidden City and the Bell and Drum towers. Chongzhen, the last Ming emperor, is said to have hanged himself at the foot of Coal Hill as his dynasty collapsed in 1644. As the park is on Beijing's central axis, you can access it from the west gate in Xicheng District or the east gate in Dongcheng. ✉ *Jingshan Qian Dajie, opposite north gate of Forbidden City, Xicheng District* ☎ *010/6403–8098* 🎟 *Y2.*

Lama Temple (雍和宫 *Yōnghégōng*)
RELIGIOUS SITE | One of the most important functioning Buddhist temples in Beijing, this much-visited Tibetan Buddhist masterpiece has five main halls and numerous galleries hung with finely detailed *thangkhas* (Tibetan religious scroll paintings). The entire temple is decorated with Buddha images—all guarded by somber lamas dressed in brown robes. Originally a palace for Prince Yongzheng, it was transformed into a temple once he became the Qing's third emperor in 1723. The temple flourished under Emperor Qianlong, housing some 500 resident monks. This was once the official "embassy" of Tibetan Buddhism in Beijing, but today only about two dozen monks live in this complex.

Don't miss the **The Hall of Heavenly Kings,** with statues of Maitreya, the future Buddha, and Weitou, China's guardian of Buddhism. This hall is worth a slow stroll. In the courtyard beyond, a pond with a bronze mandala represents paradise. The Statues of Buddhas of the Past, Present, and Future hold court in **The Hall of Harmony.** Look on the west wall where an exquisite silk thangkha of White Tara—the embodiment of compassion—hangs. Images of the Medicine and Longevity Buddhas line **The Hall of Eternal Blessing.** In **The Pavilion of Ten Thousand Fortunes** you see the breathtaking 26-meter (85-foot) Maitreya Buddha carved from a single block of sandalwood. ■ **TIP→ Combine a visit to the Lama Temple with the Confucius Temple and the Imperial Academy, which are a five-minute walk away, within the hutong neighborhood opposite the main entrance.** ✉ *28 Yonghegong Dajie, Beixinqiao, Dongcheng District* ☎ *010/8419–1919* 🎟 *Y25* Ⓜ *Yonghegong, Line 2.*

National Museum of China (中国国家博物馆 *Zhōngguó guójiā bówùguǎn*)
MUSEUM | This monumental edifice on the eastern side of Tiananmen Square showcases 5,000 years of history in immaculate surroundings. With 2 million square feet of exhibition space, it's impossible to see everything. The propaganda-heavy history sections can be safely skipped; focus instead on the ancient China section on the lower level, which houses magnificent displays of bronzes and jade artifacts. The museum also features strong shows of visiting works from abroad, such as Renaissance art from Florence and ceramics from the British Museum and the Victoria and Albert Museum. ✉ *16 Dong Chang An*

Jie, Dongcheng District ☎ *010/6511–6400* 🌐 *en.chnmuseum.cn* 🎫 *Free with passport* Ⓜ *Tiananmen East.*

★ **Tiananmen Square** (天安门广场 *Tiānānmén guǎngchǎng*)
PLAZA | The world's largest public square, and the very heart of modern China, Tiananmen Square owes little to grand imperial designs and everything to Mao Zedong. At the height of the Cultural Revolution, hundreds of thousands of Red Guards crowded the square; in June 1989 the square was the scene of tragedy when student demonstrators were killed.

Today the square is packed with sightseers, families, and undercover policemen. Although formidable, the square is a little bleak, with no shade, benches, or trees. Come here at night for an eerie experience—it's a little like being on a film set. Beijing's ancient central axis runs right through the center of Mao's mausoleum, the Forbidden City, the Drum and Bell towers, and the Olympic Green. The square is sandwiched between two grand gates: the Gate of Heavenly Peace (Tiananmen) to the north and the Front Gate (Qianmen) in the south. Along the western edge is the Great Hall of the People. The National Museum of China lies along the eastern side. The 125-foot granite obelisk you see is the Monument to the People's Heroes; it commemorates those who died for the revolutionary cause of the Chinese people. ✉ *Bounded by Chang'an Jie to north and Qianmen Dajie to south, Dongcheng District* 🎫 *Free* Ⓜ *Qianmen.*

Wangfujing (王府井 *Wángfǔjǐng*)
HISTORIC SITE | Wangfujing, one of the city's oldest and busiest shopping districts, is still lined with a handful of *laozihao*, old brand-name shops, some dating back a century, and 1950s-era state-run stores. This short walking street is a pleasant place for window-shopping. Also on Wangfujing is the gleaming Oriental Plaza, with its expensive high-end shops (Tiffany's, Burberry, Ermenegildo Zegna, and Audi among them), interspersed with Levi's Jeans, Esprit, Starbucks, Pizza Hut, KFC, Häagen-Dazs, and a modern movie multiplex. ✉ *Wangfujing, Dongcheng District.*

Did You Know? 

A network of tunnels lies beneath Tiananmen Square. Mao Zedong is said to have ordered them dug in the late 1960s after Sino-Soviet relations soured. They extend across Beijing and many have been sealed up or fallen into disrepair, though migrant workers inhabit some.

Restaurants

Café de la Poste (云游驿 *Yúnyóu yì*)
$$ | **FRENCH** | Although good, the French food at this cozy bistro seems beside the point: people come for the nighttime revelry. The bar doesn't close till the last person leaves (even if it's 5 am)! **Known for:** popular with expats; summer terrace; cheap beer. 💲 *Average main: Y100* ✉ *58 Yonghegong Dajie, Dongcheng District* ☎ *010/6402–7047* 🌐 *none* 💳 *No credit cards* Ⓜ *Yonghegong.*

Cafe Zarah
$ | **EUROPEAN** | An old oak tree grows up through both levels of this gorgeous courtyard restaurant. The setting is traditional Chinese, but the menu offerings include good coffee, sandwiches, salads, and other Western comfort foods. **Known for:** stylish hipster hangout; great cocktails; popular buffet brunch. 💲 *Average main: Y60* ✉ *46 Gulou Dong Dajie, Dongcheng District* ☎ *010/8403–9807* 🌐 *www.cafezarah.com* 💳 *No credit cards* Ⓜ *Beixinqiao.*

Crescent Moon (弯弯的月亮 *Wānwānde yuèliàng*)
$ | **CHINESE** | Heaping platters of grilled-lamb skewers, house-made flatbreads, and other hearty fare feature greatly on the menu here. It's also less flashy than some of Beijing's other Xinjiang establishments. **Known for:** authentic atmosphere; good value; Xinjiang black beer. *Average main: Y60* ✉ *16 Dongsi Liutiao, Dongcheng District* ☎ *010/6400–5281* *No credit cards* Ⓜ *Zhangzizhonglu.*

★ **Dali Courtyard** (大理 *Dàlǐ*)
$$ | **YUNNAN** | This beautiful courtyard restaurant serves refined Yunnan food. What's more, the menu is fixed, so this is an excellent choice for those who don't want to misfire on the ordering. **Known for:** tranquil atmosphere; fresh ingredients; authentic cuisine. *Average main: Y150* ✉ *67 Xiaojingchang Hutong, Gulou Dong Dajie, Dongcheng District* ☎ *010/8404–1430* Ⓜ *Guloudajie.*

Deyuan Roast Duck (德缘烤鸭店 *Dé yuán kǎoyā diàn)*
$ | **NORTHERN CHINESE** | Just because this restaurant offers excellent value for the money, doesn't mean you'll have to forego the celebratory experience of having your Peking duck carved tableside. The service is a bit brusque, but that's all part of its authentic Beijing charm. **Known for:** you can only order a whole duck—easily enough to feed four people; historic location; fast service. *Average main: Y80* ✉ *57 Dashilan Xijie, Xicheng District* ☎ *010/6308–5371* Ⓜ *Qianmen.*

Hani Geju (哈尼个旧餐厅 *Hāní gèjiù cāntīng*)
$$ | **YUNNAN** | More familial than fancy, this cozy restaurant serves Yunnan staples such as Bai-minority goat cheese with bacon (smoked in-house), potato balls (fluffy inside, addictively crisp outside), zingy mint salads, and delicate rice noodle dishes. It's also just a stone's throw from the Bell Tower. **Known for:** no MSG; Yunnan hotpot; hard to find but worth the hunt. *Average main: Y110* ✉ *48 Zhonglouwan Hutong, Southeast of Bell Tower, Dongcheng District* ☎ *010/6401–3318* Ⓜ *Guloudajie.*

Jin Ding Xuan (金鼎轩酒楼 *jīndǐngxuān jiǔlóu*)
$ | **CANTONESE** | A gloriously gaudy atmosphere is the main draw of this 24-hour dim sum restaurant. It serves all the classics as well as a "pollution menu" featuring dishes that supposedly counteract the effects of Beijing's smog. **Known for:** you can't go wrong with the shrimp dumplings; prices are reasonable; long lines. *Average main: Y70* ✉ *77 Hepingli Xijie, Dongcheng District* ☎ *010/6429–6699* Ⓜ *Yonghegong.*

★ **King's Joy** (京兆尹 *Jīng zhào yǐn*)
$$$$ | **VEGETARIAN** | The miracle-worker chef transforms tofu, wheat gluten, mushrooms, and other vegetarian ingredients into delectable "fake meat" dishes at this upscale courtyard restaurant. The views of the Lama Temple across the street seem equally miraculous. **Known for:** appeals even to meat-lovers; heavenly harp music; elegant, inspirational setting. *Average main: Y250* ✉ *2 Wudaoying Hutong, Yonghegong, Dongcheng District* ☎ *010/8404–9191* Ⓜ *Yonghegong.*

★ **Made In China** (长安壹号 *Cháng'ān yīhào*)
$$$ | **NORTHERN CHINESE** | Inside the glassed-in kitchen of this Grand Hyatt restaurant, white-robed chefs artfully twirl floury noodles and efficiently hook beautifully bronzed Peking ducks on poles outside tall brick ovens. Although pricey, it's Chinese dining at its finest. **Known for:** sumptuous setting; theatrical preparation; stellar service. *Average main: Y200* ✉ *Grand Hyatt, 1 Dong Chang An Jie, Dongcheng District* ☎ *010/8518–1234* 🌐 *beijing.grand.hyatt.com/en/hotel/dining/MadeinChina.html* Ⓜ *Wangfujing.*

A portrait of the Great Helmsman gazes down on Tiananmen Square.

Nice Rice (百米粒 *Bǎi Mǐlì)*
$ | **HUNAN** | A peaceful hutong is the setting for this welcoming Hunan restaurant, whose signature dish is Chairman Mao's favorite: *hong shao rou* (braised pork belly). The food is almost unrelentingly spicy; if you can handle the heat, though, it's worth it. **Known for:** lovely rooftop dining area; great craft beer; friendly service. *Average main: Y80* *23 Dongsi Er Tiao, Dongcheng District* *010/8408–4345* *No credit cards* *Dongsi Shitiao.*

Old Beijing Noodle King (老北京炸酱面大王 *Lǎo Běijīng zhájiàngmiàn dàwáng)*
$ | **NORTHERN CHINESE** | A lively, old-time atmosphere and hand-pulled noodles are the hallmarks of this chain. Try the classic *zhajiang* noodle, served in a ground-meat sauce with accompaniments of celery, bean sprouts, green beans, soybeans, slivers of cucumber, and red radish. **Known for:** raucous atmosphere; traditional dishes; popular with locals. *Average main: Y30* *56 Dong Xinglong Jie, Dongcheng District* *010/6701–9393* *No credit cards* *Chongwenmen.*

Saveurs de Corée (韩香馆 *Hán xiāng guǎn)*
$$ | **KOREAN** | Don't let the French name fool you: this well-established restaurant serves thoroughly delicious Korean food. The beef stew is a particular hit, as are the kimchi pancakes. **Known for:** friendly owner; North Korean beer; Korean-inspired cocktails. *Average main: Y120* *2nd fl., Rum Coabana Hotel, 22 Dongzhimen Bei Xiaojie, Dongcheng District* *010/5741–5753* *Dongsi Shitiao.*

Siji Minfu (四季民福烤鸭店 *Sìjì mín fú kǎoyā diàn)*
$ | **NORTHERN CHINESE** | This excellent restaurant, part of a local chain, says "yes" to seasonality and no to "MSG." Folks line up for over an hour to get a taste of its famous Peking duck. **Known for:** the zhajiangmian (traditional Beijing noodles); long waits (groups must book more than a week in advance); buzzing atmosphere. *Average main: Y90* *Donghua Hotel, 32 Dengshikou Xijie, Wangfujing Dajie, Dongcheng District* *010/6513–5141* *Dengshikou.*

★ **Temple Restaurant Beijing**
$$$$ | **MODERN EUROPEAN** | Worship at the altar of Epicureanism, and surround yourself with serenity at the city's best international fine-dining restaurant, nestled in the heart of Old Beijing. TRB (as it's also known) serves high-end European cuisine in a spacious, minimalist dining room within a fabulously restored Ming Dynasty Buddhist temple complex. **Known for:** excellent wine list; impeccable service; four-course tasting menu. *$ Average main: Y250 ✉ 23 Songzhusi, Shatan Beijie, Dongcheng District ☎ 010/8400–2232 🌐 www.temple-restaurant.com Ⓜ National Art Museum.*

Xian Lao Man (馅老满 *Xiàn Lǎo Mǎn*)
$ | **VEGETARIAN** | You can (unofficially) bring your own booze to this airy Buddhist restaurant, but the main reason to come is to explore the weird, wonderful world of "fake meat" vegetarian dishes. Here, some of them seem utterly improbable (almost laughable); many are totally convincing; most are truly delicious. **Known for:** "spare ribs" made from lotus root; great dumplings; popular with locals. *$ Average main: Y40 ✉ 316 Dongsi Bei Dajie, Dongcheng District ☎ 010/8402–5779 💳 No credit cards Ⓜ Dongsi.*

Yue Bin (悦宾饭馆 *Yuèbīn fànguǎn*)
$ | **CHINESE** | Yue Bin was the first private restaurant to open in Beijing after the Cultural Revolution era, and its home-style cooking remains popular. The tiny, no-frills dining room is just big enough for half a dozen tables, where you'll see families chowing down on specialities such as *suanni zhouzi,* garlic-marinated braised pork shoulder. **Known for:** historical significance; sour plum juice, a traditional Beijing drink; hearty local fare. *$ Average main: Y50 ✉ 43 Cuihua Hutong, Dongcheng District ☎ 010/6524–5322 💳 No credit cards Ⓜ National Art Museum.*

Hotels

★ **Beijing Hotel NUO** (北京饭店NUO *Běijīng fàndiàn NUO*)
$$ | **HOTEL** | An iconic 1901 residence houses the original lobby and historic rooms, and a newer addition offers rooms with amenities for business travelers at this hotel, formerly part of the Raffles brand; it's now overseen by the luxury NUO group, which has ensured that the standards for service remain high. For dining, choose between classic French and international, while the Writer's Bar is replete with large leather armchairs and a polished wooden dance floor dating back to the 1920s. **Pros:** nifty location for sightseeing; switched-on staff; spacious rooms. **Cons:** pricey restaurants; despite having business amenities, not in the right part of town for business travelers; occasional problems with the pool. *$ Rooms from: Y1200 ✉ 33 Dongchang'an Jie, off Wangfujing Dajie, Dongcheng District ☎ 010/6526–3388 🌐 www.nuohotel.com/beijingchangan ⇄ 164 rooms 🍽 No meals Ⓜ Wangfujing.*

Double Happiness Courtyard (北京阅微庄四合院酒店 *Běijīng yuè wēi zhuāng sìhéyuàn jiǔdiàn*)
$ | **HOTEL** | The rooms in this atmospheric warren of wooden corridors, courtyards, and rickety staircases are fairly spacious, with Chinese-style beds, wooden furniture, and small bathrooms, but it's the friendly, English-speaking service, central location, and good rates that make it so popular. **Pros:** traditional architecture; hutong location; good for families. **Cons:** dingy entrance; old-fashioned facilities; can be chilly in winter. *$ Rooms from: Y780 ✉ 37 Dongsi Sitiao, Dongcheng District ☎ 010/6400–7762 🌐 www.hotel37.com ⇄ 32 rooms 🍽 No meals Ⓜ Dongsi, Line 5.*

Street food is ubiquitous in Beijing; kebabs, from China's northwest, are local favorites.

The Emperor (皇家驿栈 *Huángjiā yìzhàn*) $ | **HOTEL** | Lauded for its lovely rooftop bar with views over the Forbidden City, the Emperor's has a traditional exterior that belies guest rooms seemingly inspired by the film *2001: A Space Odyssey*: minimalist white decor, sunken beds with tube pillows, lozenge-like sofas, and minibars that rise up from concealed cabinets. **Pros:** popular rooftop bar; unbeatable views; rooftop swimming pool. **Cons:** small rooms; limited gym facilities; far from the subway. *Rooms from: Y1000* *33 Qihelou Jie, Dongcheng District* *www.theemperor.com.cn* *55 rooms* *No meals.*

Grand Hotel Beijing (北京贵宾楼饭店 *Běijīng Guìbīnlóu fàndiàn*) $$ | **HOTEL** | On the north side of Chang'an Avenue, and adjoining the ritzier Raffles, the Grand offers a decent blend of luxury and comfort without the international brand price tag. **Pros:** good location; classic decor; great rooftop views. **Cons:** some rooms in need of renovation; confusing layout; little atmosphere. *Rooms from: Y1200* *35 Dongchang'an Jie, Dongcheng District* *010/6513–7788, 010/6513–0048* *www.grandhotelbeijing.com* *217 rooms* *No meals* *Wangfujing.*

★ **Grand Hyatt Beijing** (北京东方君悦酒店 *Běijīng Dōngfāngjūnyuè jiǔdiàn*) $$$$ | **HOTEL** | **FAMILY** | The wow factor at this top-notch hotel—close to Tiananmen Square and the Forbidden City—comes from its huge glass facade and extraordinary lagoon-like swimming area: above its lush vegetation, waterfalls, and statues, a "virtual sky" ceiling imitates different weather patterns. **Pros:** great dining; plenty of shopping; very impressive pool and gym. **Cons:** dull rooms; overpriced bar; Internet is extra. *Rooms from: Y2200* *1 Dongchang'an Jie, corner of Wangfujing, Dongcheng District* *010/8518–1234* *www.beijing.grand.hyatt.com* *825 rooms* *No meals* *Wangfujing.*

★ **Hilton Beijing Wangfujing** (北京王府井希尔顿酒店 *Běijīng wángfǔ jǐng xī'ěrdùn jiǔdiàn*)
$$$ | **HOTEL** | Even the smallest rooms at this big-brand boutique-style hotel come with walk-in wardrobes, freestanding tubs, and six-head showers, and if you can stand the very bachelor-pad brown and slate interiors, you'll reap the benefits of being just a stroll from the Forbidden City and Tiananmen Square. **Pros:** central location; quiet; huge guest rooms. **Cons:** not easy to get cabs; service can be strained; other comparably priced hotels are more luxurious. *Rooms from: Y1800 ✉ 8 Wangfujing Dong Jie, Dongcheng District ☎ 010/5812–8888 ⊕ www3.hilton.com 197 rooms No meals Ⓜ Wangfujing.*

★ **Holiday Inn Express Beijing Dongzhimen** (北京东直门智选假日酒店 *Běijīng dōngzhīmēn zhìxu jiǔdiàn*)
$ | **HOTEL** | **FAMILY** | Cheap and cheerful does it at this value chain close to Sanlitun (Beijing's lively nightlife center)—yes, it lacks a pool and gym, and guest rooms are somewhat small, but the lobby gleams, the beds are surprisingly comfortable, and the free-to-use Macs next to the front desk and a games console are thoughtful touches. **Pros:** cheap yet extremely modern and clean; tour operator next door; close to great nightlife and dining. **Cons:** breakfast can be crowded (and no lunch or dinner options); small rooms; subway is a long walk away. *Rooms from: Y558 ✉ 1 Chunxiu Rd., Dongcheng District ☎ 010/6416–9999 ⊕ www.holidayinnexpress.com 350 rooms Breakfast.*

Hotel Cote Cour (北京演乐70号 *Běijīng yǎn lè 70 hào*)
$$ | **HOTEL** | This boutique courtyard hideaway claims to have once served as a rehearsal space for Imperial musicians during the Ming Dynasty; renovated rooms wrap around an attractive old courtyard and feature antique pieces, comfy beds with feather duvets, and the usual Western comforts. **Pros:** central location; boutique atmosphere; English spoken. **Cons:** standard rooms a little small; expensive; cramped building. *Rooms from: Y1300 ✉ 70 Yanyue Hutong, Dongcheng District ☎ 010/6523–9598 ⊕ www.hotelcotecourbj.com 14 rooms No meals Ⓜ Dongsi.*

Legendale (励骏酒店 *Lìjùn jiǔdiàn*)
$$$ | **HOTEL** | The faux European spectacle that is the Legendale screams nouveau riche, but this château-like hotel, with its sparkling chandeliers, gilded staircase, and Parisian fireplace in the lobby, is genuinely comfortable and luxurious. **Pros:** plenty of pampering; in a great neighborhood; luxurious rooms. **Cons:** high prices; vast size can make it feel empty; no traditional Chinese elements. *Rooms from: Y1410 ✉ 90–92 Jinbao St., Dongcheng District ☎ 010/8511–3388 ⊕ www.legendalehotel.com 390 rooms Breakfast Ⓜ Dengshikou.*

★ **Lüsongyuan** (侣松园宾馆 *Lǚsōngyuán bīnguǎn*)
$ | **HOTEL** | The wooden entrance to this delightful courtyard hotel, on the site of an old Mandarin residence, is guarded by two *menshi* (stone lions), an indicator that this hotel offers a classic old-Beijing experience: good, affordable accommodations with few modern updates and little in the way of fancy design. **Pros:** convenient location; near restaurants; unfussy courtyard conversion. **Cons:** a lack of luxury; can be hard to find; carpets are in need of a clean. *Rooms from: Y768 ✉ 22 Banchang Hutong, Kuanjie, Dongcheng District ☎ 010/6401–1116 55 rooms No meals Ⓜ Zhangzizhonglu.*

MUJI Hotel (酒店 *MUJI jiǔdiàn*)
$ | **HOTEL** | This hotel is exactly what you would except from the chic minimalists at Muji: a stylish, industrial, exposed-brick interior—in this case, one that starkly contrasts with the classic architecture of a gorgeous hutong locale—and rooms that don't skimp on comfort. **Pros:**

great location; terrace with beautiful Tiananmen views; rental bikes available. **Cons:** smallest rooms are teeny; can feel austere; no gym. *Rooms from: Y500 Bldg. 1, 21 Langfang Toutiao, Meishi Jie, Dongcheng District 010/6316–9199 hotel.muji.com/beijing/en/ 42 rooms Qianmen.*

★ The Orchid

$ | **HOTEL** | A firm favorite among travelers looking for somewhere hip but still down-to-earth, The Orchid is a serene spot in the heart of Beijing's most vibrant hutong district, with two tiers of flower-strewn terraces, ludicrously comfy beds, a complimentary à la carte breakfast menu, and friendly staff who have an infectious love for their gentrifying neighborhood. **Pros:** great hutong location; cool interiors; some rooms with gardens. **Cons:** reservations a must; can be hard to find; restaurant gets busy with nonguests. *Rooms from: Y800 65 Baochao Hutong, Gulou Dong Dajie, Gulou, Dongcheng District 010/8404–4818 www.theorchid-beijing.com 10 rooms Breakfast Guloudajie.*

★ Peninsula Beijing (王府半岛酒店 *Wángfǔ Bàndǎo jiǔdiàn*)

$$$ | **HOTEL** | Guests enjoy an impressive combination of modern facilities and traditional luxury, and though rooms are a little small for this sort of hotel, they're superlatively appointed, with teak and rosewood flooring, colorful rugs, and high-tech touches like custom bedside control panels to adjust lighting, temperature, and the flat-screen TVs. **Pros:** impeccable rooms; close to restaurants and shops; near the Forbidden City. **Cons:** lobby is squeezed by the surrounding luxury shopping mall; hectic; rooms could be bigger. *Rooms from: Y1800 8 Jinyu Hutong, Wangfujing, Dongcheng District 010/8516–2888 beijing.peninsula.com 230 rooms No meals Dengshikou.*

★ The Regent (北京丽晶酒店 *Běijīng Lìjīng jiǔdiàn*)

$$ | **HOTEL** | Luxurious (if businesslike) rooms, a prestigious location on the corner of ritzy Jinbao Jie close to Wangfujing, and a spectacularly soaring glass-walled lobby are reasons why the Regent is a top choice for high rollers. **Pros:** convenient location; close to the subway; spacious rooms. **Cons:** unimpressive breakfast; occasional blemishes in some rooms; check-in can be slow. *Rooms from: Y1250 99 Jinbao St., Dongcheng District 010/8522–1888 www.regenthotels.com 500 rooms No meals Dengshikou.*

★ Temple Hotel Beijing (东景缘 *Dōng jǐng yuán*)

$$$$ | **HOTEL** | Five hundred years in the making, this beguiling combination of boutique luxury and heritage architecture is one of Beijing's most romantic hotel experiences. **Pros:** historic buildings in hutong location; great for art lovers; exceptional. **Cons:** no gym, pool, or spa; expensive; bad location for business travelers. *Rooms from: Y2400 23 Shatan Beilu, Dongcheng District 010/8401–5680 www.thetemplehotel.com 8 rooms No meals.*

★ 3+1 Bedrooms

$$ | **HOTEL** | Modern, minimalist design—pure white interiors, freestanding bathtubs, individual courtyards—meets old Beijing at this intimate four-bedroom boutique hotel within the quaint alleyways (hutong) near the historic Drum and Bell towers. **Pros:** spacious rooms; free in-room Wi-Fi and minibar; private terraces. **Cons:** no health club; no restaurants; occasionally absent service. *Rooms from: Y1200 17 Zhangwang Hutong, Jiu Gulou Dajie, Drum Tower, Dongcheng District 010/6404–7030 www.3plus1bedrooms.com 3 rooms, 1 suite Breakfast Gulou Dajie.*

★ **Waldorf Astoria Beijing** (**北京华尔道夫酒店** *Běijīng huá ěr dàofū jiǔdiàn*)
$$$$ | **HOTEL** | No expense has been spared on this stunning, boutique-inspired hotel in central Wangfujing; the public areas have walls of Suzhou silk, staircases of gold-flecked Italian marble, and countless pieces of art, while guest rooms strike a delightful balance of contemporary style and high-tech luxury, with Apple TVs, Bose sound systems, Nespresso machines, Japanese toilets, heated bathroom floors, and a Samsung tablet beside the bed to control the lights, TV, and curtains, and also order various services. **Pros:** has the relaxed yet refined Brasserie 1893 restaurant; modern furnishings; central location. **Cons:** expensive; not much nightlife in the immediate area; can feel a bit stuffy. *Rooms from: Y2500* ✉ *5–15 Jinyu Hutong, Dongcheng District* ☎ *010/8520-8989* 🌐 *waldorfastoria3.hilton.com* *176 rooms* *No meals* Ⓜ *Dengshikou.*

Nightlife

BARS

★ **Great Leap Brewing #6** (**大跃啤酒** *Dàyuèpíjiǔ*)
BARS/PUBS | At Beijing's first proper microbrewery, the beers are made with ingredients such as tea and Sichuan peppercorns. Don't miss the bar peanuts—spicy and salty, they'll keep you going back to the bar for just one more brew. This place has been so successful, in fact, that the owners have since opened a much-larger flagship in Liangmaqiao, which also serves food. ✉ *6 Doujiao Hutong, Dongcheng District* ☎ *010/5717–1399* 🌐 *www.greatleapbrewing.com.*

Mao Mao Chong (**毛毛虫** *Máomáochóng*)
BARS/PUBS | This bar is known for top-quality infused cocktails, including a chili-infused vodka Bloody Mary and a Sichuan peppercorn Moscow Mule. Another standout is the owners' own Bangkok Hilton: Thai tea–infused Scotch, crème de cassis, bitters, syrup made from *pandanus* (screw pine) leaves, and an orange twist. The pizzas and artwork are an added reason to stop in. ✉ *12 Banchang Hutong, Jiaodaokounan, Dongcheng District* ☎ *010/6405–5718* 🌐 *www.maomaochongbeijing.com* *Closed Mon.*

★ **Nina**
BARS/PUBS | Specializing in all things spritzy, from Americano cocktails to Negronis, this place is relaxed and intimate on weekdays and often packed during weekend DJ events. Feel the need to line your stomach? The excellent-value platters of *arancini* (Italian, deep-fried risotto balls) are just the ticket. ✉ *66 Beiluoguxiang, Dongcheng District* Ⓜ *Nanluoguxiang.*

Yin (**饮 (皇家驿栈屋顶)** *Huángjiā Yìzhàn*)
BARS/PUBS | The Emperor Hotel's rooftop terrace bar certainly has the "wow" factor when it comes to the view of the Forbidden City; there's even a hot tub on hand if you need to relax. Unsurprisingly, drink prices are high, and it tends to be too empty for real fun but, befitting the hotel's design focus, red lanterns and fashionably outfitted staff add to the classiness of the experience. If only it had a bit more buzz. ✉ *The Emperor Hotel, 33 Qihelou Dajie, top floor, Dongcheng District* ☎ *010/6526–5566* Ⓜ *Tiananmen East.*

Performing Arts

ACROBATICS AND KUNG FU

★ **The Red Theatre** (**红剧场** *Hóng jùchǎng*)
THEATER | If it's Vegas-style stage antics you're after, the *Legend of Kung Fu* show is what you want. Extravagant martial arts—performed by dancers, not martial artists—are complemented by neon, fog, and heavy-handed sound effects. Shows are garish but also sometimes glorious. ✉ *44 Xingfu Dajie, Dongcheng District* ☎ *010/5165–1914, 135/5252–7373* 🌐 *www.redtheatre.cn* Ⓜ *Tiantan Dong Men.*

BEIJING OPERA

Chang'an Grand Theater (**长安大戏院** *Cháng'ān dàxìyuàn*)

OPERA | In this theater specializing in Chinese opera, spectators can choose to sit either in the traditional seats or at cabaret-style tables. Besides Peking-style opera, the theater also puts on performances of other regional styles, such as *yueju* (from Guangdong) and *chuanju* (from Sichuan). ✉ *7 Jianguomennei Dajie, Dongcheng District* ☎ *010/6510–1309* 🌐 *www.changantheater.com* Ⓜ *Jianguomen.*

MUSIC

Poly Theater (**保利剧院** *Bǎolì jùyuàn*)

MUSIC | This is a modern shopping-center-like complex on top of Dongsishitiao subway station. One of Beijing's better-known theaters, the Poly hosts Chinese and international concerts, ballets, and musicals. **■ TIP→ If you're seeking a performance in English, this is one of your best bets.** ✉ *1/F Poly Plaza, 14 Dongzhimen Nandajie, Dongcheng District* ☎ *010/6500–1188* 🌐 *www.polytheatre.com* Ⓜ *Dongsishitiao.*

Shopping

Strolling the old hutong (alleyways) of Dongcheng is one of the simplest pleasures to be found in Beijing. This area is rife with them and, despite a local council that's itching to modernize, many remain relatively unscathed—and filled with households that have lived there for generations. Efforts to reinvigorate some of the hutongs have resulted in a thriving boutique culture, with Nanluoguxiang the first to receive the attentions of tourist dollars. Its bohemian mix of hipster-chic stores, silk shops, and Old China wares attracts huge interest. Next to bask in the limelight was the quieter, but no less hip, Wudaoying Hutong, opposite Lama Temple. Today both command high rents and almost as much attention as nearby Houhai. For some truly unusual finds, try exploring some of the lesser-trod tributaries off Gulou Dongdajie, such as Baochao, Fangjia, and Beiluoguxiang instead.

ART AND ANTIQUES

Beijing Postcards (**北京卡片** *Běijīng Kǎpiàn*)

ANTIQUES/COLLECTIBLES | Run by historians, this small gallery near bustling Nanluoguxiang showcases a small collection of hundred-year-old Beijing maps and photos of the Drum and Bell Tower. As well as selling postcards, reprints, and calendars, the company also runs town walks and historical talks—some of the best you'll find in the city. Check the website for upcoming events as well as a list of other stores selling its products. To visit the gallery, email or phone for an appointment. ✉ *97 Yangmeizhu Xiejie, Xuanwu District* ☎ *156/1145–3992* 🌐 *www.bjpostcards.com* Ⓜ *Qianmen.*

The Bulk House

HOUSEHOLD ITEMS/FURNITURE | This petite Gulou boutique has a big mission: encourage Beijingers to reduce waste, no small task in a country where plastic and other excess packaging is ubiquitous. Founded by a British-Chinese couple, Bulk House sells stylish, reusable wares such as hemp shopping bags and aluminum water bottles. It's a good spot to pick up locally sourced travel essentials, too, and the English-speaking staff will happily chat about the changing face of Chinese environmentalism. ✉ *24–2 Gulou Dong Dajie, Dongcheng District* ☎ *186/0000–0000* 🌐 *www.thebulkhouse.com.*

Lost & Found (**失物招领** *Shīwù zhāolǐng*)

ANTIQUES/COLLECTIBLES | Stylish and sensitive to Beijing's past, American designer Paul Gelinas and Chinese partner Xiao Miao salvage objects—whether they're chipped enamel street signs from a long-demolished hutong, a barbershop chair, or a 1950s Shanghai fan—and lovingly remove the dirt before offering them on sale in their treasure trove of a store. This branch is tucked down a tree-lined hutong where imperial exams once took place, and there's another a few doors down. ✉ *42 Guozijian, Dongcheng District* ☎ *010/6401–1855* Ⓜ *Yonghegong* ✉ *57 Guozijian, Dongcheng District* ☎ *010/6400–1174* Ⓜ *Yonghegong.*

CLOTHING

Mega Mega Vintage

CLOTHING | In Gulou, the only real currency is "vintage." Fresh-from-the-factory retro T-shirts have their place, but nothing can replace leafing through the racks at Mega Mega Vintage in search of gold. Distressed denim, classic tees, leather bags, and old-style dresses crown a collection that rises high above the "frumpery" peddled by countless copycat boutiques. ✉ *241 Gulou Dong Dajie, Dongcheng District* ☎ *010/8404–5637* 🌐 *www.douban.com/group/mmvintage* Ⓜ *Beixinqiao.*

★ **Plastered T-Shirts** (创可贴 *Chuàngkětiē*)

CLOTHING | This is a must-visit shop for the rarest of Beijing souvenirs: something that you'll actually use when home. T-shirt designs capture the nostalgic days of Old Peking; posters, notebooks, thermoses, and other retro items take you back to the 1980s. It's fun and kitschy, and everything costs around Y100. ✉ *61 Nanluoguxiang Hutong, Dongcheng District* ☎ *136/8339–4452* 🌐 *www.plasteredtshirts.com* Ⓜ *Nanluoguxiang.*

Woo (妩 *Wǔ*)

CLOTHING | The gorgeous scarves displayed in the windows here lure in passersby with their bright colors and luxurious fabrics. In contrast to those of the vendors in the markets, the cashmere, silk, and bamboo used here are 100% natural. The design and construction are comparable to top Italian designers, while the prices are much more affordable. ✉ *110/1 Nanluoguxiang, Dongcheng District* ☎ *010/6400–5395* Ⓜ *Nanluoguxiang.*

MALLS

Malls at Oriental Plaza (东方广场购物中心 *Dōngfāng guǎngchǎng*)

DEPARTMENT STORES | This enormous shopping complex originates at the southern end of Wangfujing, where it meets Chang'an Jie, and stretches a city block east to Dongdan Dajie. It's a true city within a city and certainly geared toward higher budgets. Some of the more upscale shops include Kenzo and Armani Exchange; ladies should check out the boutique from iconic Chinese-American designer Anna Sui for clothes, accessories, and makeup. ✉ *1 Dongchang'an Jie, Dongcheng District* ☎ *010/8518–6363* Ⓜ *Wangfujing.*

MARKET

Hongqiao Market (红桥市场 *Hóngqiaó shìchǎng*)

OUTDOOR/FLEA/GREEN MARKETS | **FAMILY** | Hongqiao, or Pearl Market, is full of kitschy goods, knockoff handbags, and cheap watches, but it's best known for its namesake pearls. Freshwater, seawater, black, pink, white: the quantity is overwhelming, and quality varies by stall. Prices also range wildly, though the cheapest items are often fakes. Fanghua Pearls (4th floor, No. 4318) sells quality necklaces and earrings—with photos of Hillary Clinton and Margaret Thatcher shopping there to prove it—and has a second store devoted to fine jade and precious stones. Throughout the market, stallholders can be pushy; try to accept their haggling in the gamelike spirit it's intended. Or wear headphones and drown them out. ✉ *9 Tiantan Lu, east of northern entrance to Temple of Heaven, Dongcheng District* ☎ *010/6711–7630* Ⓜ *Tiantan Dongmen.*

SILK AND FABRICS

Daxin Textiles Co. (大新纺织 *Dàxīn fǎngzhī*)

TEXTILES/SEWING | For a wide selection of all types of fabrics, from worsted wools to sensuous silks, head to this shop. It's best to buy the material here and find a tailor elsewhere, as sewing standards can be shoddy. ✉ *Northeast corner of Dongsi, Dongcheng District* ☎ *010/6403–2378* Ⓜ *Dongsi.*

Xicheng District

Xicheng District is home to a charming combination of some of the most distinctive things that the city has to offer: cozy hutongs, palatial courtyard houses, charming lakes, and fine restaurants. For many visitors, this is one of the best areas in which to fall in love with Beijing.

The best way to do that is to take a walk or bicycle tour of the hutongs here: there's no better way to scratch the surface of this sprawling city (before it disappears) than by exploring these courtyard houses as you wander in and out of historic sites in the area.

This is also a great area for people-watching, especially along the shores of Houhai. As you wander, sample the local snacks sold from shop windows. Treats abound on Huguosi Jie (just west of Mei Lanfang's house). In the evening, relax at a restaurant or bar with a view of the lake. The lakes at Shichahai are hopping day and night.

GETTING HERE AND AROUND

Houhai and Beihai Park are conveniently reached by taxi. Line 1 subway stops include Tiananmen West, Xidan, and Fuxingmen. Line 2 makes stops from Fuxingmen to the Drum Tower (Gulou), following Xicheng's perimeter.

MAKING THE MOST OF YOUR TIME

Xicheng's must-see sites are few in number but all special. Walk around **Beihai Park** in the early afternoon. If you come to Beijing in the winter, **Qianhai** will be frozen and you can rent skates, runner-equipped bicycles, or the local favorite, a chair with runners welded to the bottom and a pair of metal sticks with which to propel yourself across the ice. Dinner along the shores of **Houhai** is a good option. Head toward the northern section for a more tranquil setting or join the crowds for a booming bar scene farther south. Plan to spend a few hours shopping at **Xidan**; this can be a great place to pick up funky, cheap gifts.

Sights

Beihai Park (北海 *Běihǎi*)
ARCHAEOLOGICAL SITE | A white stupa is perched on a small island just north of the south gate of this park. Also at the south entrance is **Round City,** which contains a white-jade Buddha and an enormous jade bowl given to Kublai Khan. Nearby, the well-restored **Temple of Eternal Peace** houses a variety of Buddhas. Climb to the stupa from Yongan Temple. Once there, you can pay an extra Y1 to ascend the Buddha-bedecked **Shanyin Hall.**

The lake is Beijing's largest and most beautiful public waterway. On summer weekends the lake teems with paddleboats. The **Five Dragon Pavilion,** on Beihai's northwest shore, was built in 1602 by a Ming Dynasty emperor who liked to fish under the moon. ✉ *1 Weijin Jie, Xicheng District* ☎ *010/6403–1102* 🌐 *www.beihaipark.com.cn* 🎫 *Y10; extra fees for some sites.*

Beijing Zoo (北京动物园 *Běijīng dòngwù yuán*)
ZOO | **FAMILY** | Though visitors usually go straight to see the giant pandas, don't miss the other interesting animals, like tigers from the northeast, yaks from Tibet, enormous sea turtles from China's seas, and red pandas from Sichuan. The zoo started out as a garden belonging to one of the sons of Shunzhi, the first emperor of the Qing dynasty. In 1747, the Qianlong emperor had it refurbished (along with other imperial properties, including the summer palaces) and turned it into a park in honor of his mother's 60th birthday. In 1901, the Empress

Dowager gave it another extensive facelift and used it to house a collection of animals given to her as a gift by a Chinese minister who had bought them during a trip to Germany. By the 1930s, most of the animals had died and were stuffed and put on display in a museum on the grounds. ✉ *137 Xizhimenwai Dajie, Xicheng District* ☎ *010/6839–0274* 🌐 *www.bjzoo.com* 🎫 *Apr.–Oct. Y15; Nov.–Mar. Y10; plus Y5 for the pandas* Ⓜ *Beijing Zoo.*

Capital Museum (首都博物馆 *Shǒudū bówùguǎn*)
MUSEUM | Moved to an architecturally striking new home west of Tiananmen Square in 2005, this is one of China's' finest cultural museums. Artifacts are housed in a multistoried bronze cylinder that dominates the building's facade, while paintings, calligraphy, and photographs of historic Beijing fill the remaining exhibition halls. The museum gets extra points for clear English descriptions and modern, informative displays. Entry is free, but tickets must be booked (via the website) in advance. ✉ *16 Fuxingmenwai Dajie, Xicheng District* ☎ *010/6337–0491* 🌐 *www.capitalmuseum.org.cn/en* 🎫 *Free.*

Drum Tower (鼓楼 *Gŭlóu*)
BUILDING | Until the late 1920s, the 24 drums once housed in this tower were Beijing's timepiece. Sadly, all but one of these huge drums have been destroyed. Kublai Khan built the first drum tower on this site in 1272. You can climb to the top of the present tower, which dates from the Ming Dynasty. Old photos of hutong neighborhoods line the walls beyond the drum; there's also a scale model of a traditional courtyard house. The nearby **Bell Tower,** renovated after a fire in 1747, offers fabulous views of the hutongs from the top of a long, narrow staircase. The huge 63-ton bronze bell, supported by lacquered wood stanchions, is also worth seeing. In recent years, the authorities have demolished a number of historical hutong in this area, so don't be surprised if you come across serious signs of reconstruction around here. ✉ *North end of Dianmen Dajie, Xicheng District* ☎ *010/6404–1710* 🎫 *From Y20* Ⓜ *Guloudajie.*

Prince Gong's Palace (恭王府 *Gōngwángfŭ*)
CASTLE/PALACE | This grand compound sits in a neighborhood once reserved for imperial relatives. Built in 1777 during the Qing Dynasty, it fell to Prince Gong—brother of Qing emperor Xianfeng and later an adviser to Empress Dowager Cixi—after the original inhabitant was executed for corruption. With nine courtyards joined by covered walkways, it was once one of Beijing's most lavish residences. The museum offers Beijing opera and tea to visitors who pay the higher ticket price. Some literary scholars believe this was the setting for *Dream of the Red Chamber,* one of China's best-known classical novels. ✉ *17 Qianhai Xijie, Xicheng District* ☎ *010/8328–8149* 🌐 *www.pgm.org.cn* 🎫 *From Y40.*

Qianhai and Houhai (前海后海 *Qiánhăi, Hòuhăi*)
BODY OF WATER | Most people come to these lakes, along with Xihai to the northwest, to stroll and enjoy the shoreside bars and restaurants. In summer you can boat or fish. In winter, sections of the frozen lakes are fenced off for skating. This day trip is easily combined with a visit to Beihai Park or the Bell and Drum towers. ✉ *North of Beihai Lake, Xicheng District* Ⓜ *Beihai North.*

Soong Ching-ling's Former Residence (宋庆龄故居 *Sòng Qìnglíng gùjū*)
HOUSE | Soong Ching-ling (1893–1981) was the youngest daughter of Charles Soong, a wealthy, American-educated bible publisher. At the age of 18, disregarding her family's strong opposition, she eloped to marry the much older Sun Yat-sen. When her husband founded the Republic of China in 1911, Soong

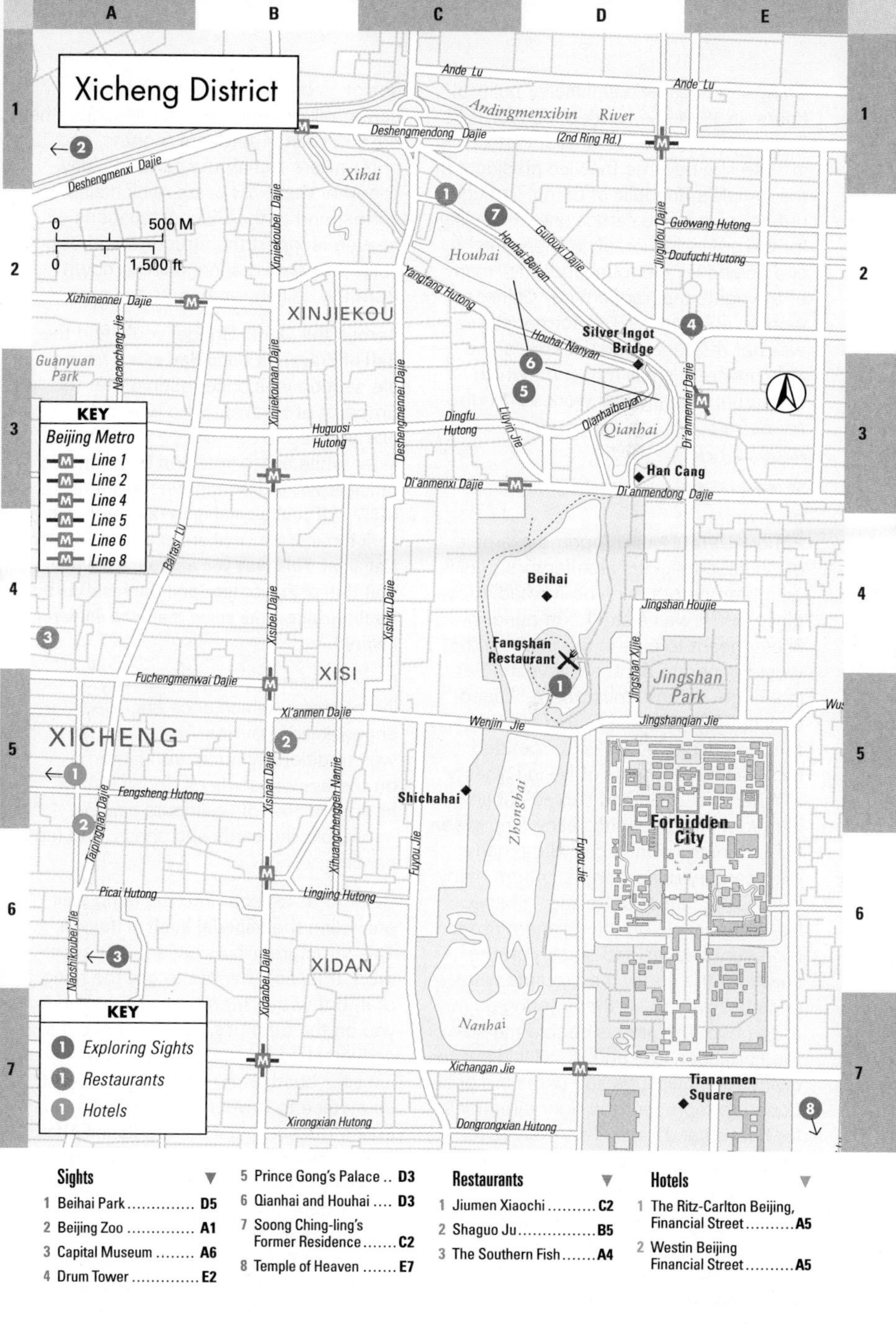

Sights

1 Beihai Park **D5**
2 Beijing Zoo **A1**
3 Capital Museum **A6**
4 Drum Tower **E2**
5 Prince Gong's Palace .. **D3**
6 Qianhai and Houhai **D3**
7 Soong Ching-ling's Former Residence **C2**
8 Temple of Heaven **E7**

Restaurants

1 Jiumen Xiaochi **C2**
2 Shaguo Ju **B5**
3 The Southern Fish **A4**

Hotels

1 The Ritz-Carlton Beijing, Financial Street **A5**
2 Westin Beijing Financial Street **A5**

Ching-ling became a significant political figure. In 1924 she headed the Women's Department of the Nationalist Party. Then in 1949 she became the vice president of the People's Republic of China. Throughout her career she campaigned tirelessly for the emancipation of women, and she helped lay the foundations for many of the rights that modern-day Chinese women enjoy today. This former palace was her residence and workplace and now houses a small museum, which documents her life and work. ✉ *46 Houhai Beiyan, Xicheng District* ☎ *010/6404–4205* 🎫 *Y20.*

★ **Temple of Heaven** (天坛 *Tiāntán gōngyuán*)

NATIONAL/STATE PARK | A prime example of Chinese religious architecture, this is where emperors once performed important rites. It was a site for imperial sacrifices, meant to please the gods so they would generate bumper harvests. Set in a huge, serene, mushroom-shaped park southeast of the Forbidden City, the Temple of Heaven is surrounded by splendid examples of Ming Dynasty architecture, including curved cobalt blue roofs layered with yellow and green tiles. Construction began in the early 15th century under Yongle, whom many call the "architect of Beijing." Shaped like a semicircle on the northern rim to represent heaven and square on the south for the earth, the grounds were once believed to be the meeting point of the two. The area is double the size of the Forbidden City and is still laid out to divine rule: buildings and paths are positioned to represent the right directions for heaven and earth. This means, for example, that the northern part is higher than the south.

The temple's hallmark structure is a magnificent **blue-roofed wooden tower** built in 1420. It burned to the ground in 1889 and was immediately rebuilt using Ming architectural methods (and timber imported from Oregon). The building's design is based on the calendar: 4 center pillars represent the seasons, the next 12 pillars represent months, and 12 outer pillars signify the parts of a day. Together these 28 poles, which also correspond to the 28 constellations of heaven, support the structure without nails. A carved dragon swirling down from the ceiling represents the emperor.

Across the Danbi Bridge, you'll find the **Hall of Prayer for Good Harvests.** The middle section was once reserved for the Emperor of Heaven, who was the only one allowed to set foot on the eastern side, while aristocrats and high-ranking officials walked on the western strip. ■ **TIP→ If you're coming by taxi, enter the park through the southern entrance (Tiantan Nanmen). This way you approach the beautiful Hall of Prayer for Good Harvests via the Danbi Bridge—the same route the emperor favored.**

Directly east of this hall is a long, twisting platform, which once enclosed the animal-killing pavilion. The Long Corridor was traditionally hung with lanterns on the eve of sacrifices. Today it plays host to scores of Beijingers singing opera, playing cards and chess, and fan dancing.

Be sure to whisper into the echo wall encircling the **Imperial Vault of Heaven.** This structure allows anyone to eavesdrop. It takes a minute to get the hang of it, but with a friend on one side and you on the other it's possible to hold a conversation by speaking into the wall. Tilt your head in the direction you want your voice to travel for best results. Just inside the south gate is the **Round Altar,** a three-tiered, white-marble structure where the emperor worshipped the winter solstice; it's based around the divine number nine. Nine was regarded as a symbol of the power of the emperor, as it's the biggest single-digit odd number, and odd numbers are considered masculine and therefore more powerful.

An afternoon stroll around the lake in Beihai Park is lovely, especially in the summer when paddle boats tool across the water.

The Hall of Abstinence, on the western edge of the grounds, is where the emperor would retreat three days before the ritual sacrifice. To understand the significance of the harvest sacrifice at the Temple of Heaven, it's important to keep in mind that the legitimacy of a Chinese emperor's rule depended on what is known as the *tian ming,* or the mandate of heaven, essentially the emperor's relationship with the gods.

A succession of bad harvests, for example, could be interpreted as the emperor losing the favor of heaven and could be used to justify a change in emperor or even in dynasty. When the emperor came to the Temple of Heaven to pray for good harvests and to pay homage to his ancestors, there may have been a good measure of self-interest to his fervor.

The sacrifices consisted mainly of animals and fruit placed on altars surrounded by candles. Many Chinese still offer sacrifices of fruit and incense on special occasions, such as births, deaths, and weddings.

■ TIP→ **We recommend buying an all-inclusive ticket. If you only buy a ticket into the park, you'll need to pay an additional Y20 to get into each building.**

Beijing's subway Line 5 (purple line) makes getting to the Temple of Heaven particularly simple. Get off at the Tiantandongmen (Temple of Heaven East Gate) stop. This line also runs direct to the Lama Temple (Yonghegong), so combining the two sites in a day makes a lot of sense.

Automatic audio guides (Y40) are available at stalls inside all four entrances.
⊠ *Yongdingmen Dajie (South Gate), Xuanwu District* ☎ *010/6702–8866*
🌐 *en.tiantanpark.com* 🎫 *From Y15*
Ⓜ *Tiantandongmen.*

Did You Know?

The Temple of Heaven's overall layout symbolizes the relationship between Heaven and Earth. Earth is represented by a square and Heaven by a circle. The temple complex is surrounded by two cordons of walls; the taller outer wall is semicircular at the northern end (Heaven) and shorter and rectangular at the southern end (Earth). Both the Hall of Prayer for Good Harvests and the Circular Mound Altar are round structures on a square yard.

Restaurants

Jiumen Xiaochi (九门小吃 *Jiǔ Mén Xiǎochī*)
$ | **ECLECTIC** | You can readily sample your way through culinary history at some of Beijing's oldest and most famous eateries, all grouped under the one roof of a house with a traditional courtyard. Soft bean curd topped, perhaps, with braised lamb and mushrooms, pot stickers shaped like traditional little satchels, or tripe served with a dipping sauce that's an old family secret are just some of what might be on offer. **Known for:** sticky red-bean sweets and other traditional snacks (sweet or savory); a setting as authentic as the food; popular with visitors. *Average main: Y90 1 Xiaoyou Hutong, Gulou Xidajie, just off Houhai lake, Xicheng District.*

Shaguo Ju (砂锅居 *Shāguō jū*)
$$ | **CHINESE** | A specialty of this historic restaurant is *shaoguo,* a traditional fatty-pork casserole. The dish was originated by the Manchus during the Qing Dynasty, when sacrificial offerings of whole pigs were common. **Known for:** Imperial cuisine; sweet tofu desserts; traditional Chinese furnishings. *Average main: Y100 60 Xisi Nan Dajie, Xicheng District 010/6602–1126 No credit cards Xidan.*

The Southern Fish (渔芙南 *Yúfúnán*)
$$$$ | **HUNAN** | At this achingly hip Hunan restaurant on the quieter side of town, the specialty is *fengminiurou,* a honey-cured beef that's stir-fried with generous amounts of chili. **Known for:** chic, monochromatic interior; lapidan (a kind of Chinese guacamole made by mashing preserved eggs and green peppers); busy at peak times (reservations essential). *Average main: Y250 49 Gongmenkou Toutiao, Xicheng District 010/6618–4915 No credit cards Fuchengmen.*

Hotels

Ritz-Carlton Beijing, Financial Street (北京金融街丽思卡尔顿酒店 *Běijīng Lìsīkǎ'ěrdùn jiǔdiàn*)
$$$$ | **HOTEL** | With ample amounts of glass and chrome, the Ritz-Carlton could be mistaken for one of the many sleek office buildings that crowd this very business-oriented area; the interior is equally swish and contemporary, with smart East-meets-West decor that's up to the Ritz standard—its location, excellent amenities, and eager-to-please staff make it popular with tour groups as well as businesspeople. **Pros:** impeccable service; luxurious atmosphere; world-class brand. **Cons:** far from the city's attractions; expensive; lobby lacks pizzazz. *Rooms from: Y2000 18 Financial St., Xicheng District 010/6601–6666 www.ritzcarlton.com 305 rooms No meals Fuchengmen.*

Westin Beijing Financial Street (威斯汀酒店 *Wēisītīng jiǔdiàn*)
$$ | **HOTEL** | It's business as usual at this worthwhile spot: comfortable rooms with plush beds, neutral tones and marble bathrooms; a plethora of amenities, including dining spots both formal and fun; and not forgetting the perhaps-to-be-expected, well-staffed executive lounge. **Pros:** sumptuous beds; high-tech gadgets; business location. **Cons:** glass between bathroom and bedroom not for the timid; gym could be bigger; not in a good spot for tourists. *Rooms from: Y1400 9B Financial St., Xicheng District 010/6606–8866 www.westin.com/beijingfinancial 483 rooms No meals Fuchengmen.*

Nightlife

BARS

East Shore Live Jazz Café (东岸咖啡 *Dōng'àn kāfēi*)

MUSIC CLUBS | There's no competition: This place has the most fabulous views of Houhai Lake, hands-down, and authentic jazz on stage every night. ✉ *2nd fl., 2 Qianhai Nanyanlu, west of post office on Di'anmen Waidajie, Xicheng District* ☎ *010/8403–2131*.

Performing Arts

ACROBATICS AND KUNG FU

Tianqiao Acrobatic Theater (天桥乐茶馆)

DANCE | The Beijing Acrobatics Troupe of China is famous for weird, wonderful shows. Content includes a flashy show of offbeat contortions and tricks, with a lot of high-wire action. There are two shows per night, usually scheduled for 5:30 and 7:15 pm, but it's best to phone ahead and check. ✉ *5 Tianqiao Shichang Lu, east end of Beiwei Lu, Xicheng District* ☎ *010/6303–7449*.

BEIJING OPERA

Huguang Guild Hall (湖广会馆 *Húguǎng huìguǎn*)

OPERA | Built in 1807, the Huguang Guild Hall was at its height one of Beijing's "Four Great" theaters. In 1925, the Guild Hall hosted Dr. Sun Yat-sen at the founding of the Chinese Nationalist Party (KMT). Today, the Guild Hall has been restored to its former glory and hosts regular opera performances. The venue also has a small museum of Peking opera artifacts. ✉ *3 Hufang Lu, Xicheng District* ☎ *010/6351–8284* Ⓜ *Caishikou*.

Lao She Teahouse (老舍茶馆 *Lǎoshě cháguǎn*)

OPERA | Named for famed Beijing author Lao She, this teahouse in the Qianmen area plays host to a variety of traditional performances, including acrobatics, opera, and vaudeville shows. Dinner is served on the premises; reservations are required one day in advance for the nightly shows. ✉ *Bldg. 3, 3 Qianmenxi Dajie, Xicheng District* ☎ *010/6303–6830*.

★ **Liyuan Theater** (梨园剧场 *Líyuán jùchǎng*)

OPERA | The unabashedly touristy shows here are still a great time. You can first watch performers put on makeup before the show (come early) and then graze on snacks and sip tea while watching English-subtitled shows. Glossy brochures complement the crooning. ✉ *1/F, Qianmen Hotel, 175 Yong'an Lu, Xicheng District* ☎ *010/6301–6688* 🌐 *www.liyuantheatreopera.com*.

MUSIC

Beijing Concert Hall (北京音乐厅 *Běijīng yīnyuètīng*)

MUSIC | One of Beijing's main venues for Chinese and Western classical-music concerts also hosts folk dancing and singing, and many celebratory events throughout the year. The 1,000-seat venue is also the home of the China National Symphony Orchestra. ✉ *1 Bei Xinhua Jie, Xicheng District* ☎ *010/6605–7006* Ⓜ *Tiananmen West*.

★ **Forbidden City Concert Hall** (北京中山公园音乐堂 *Zhōngshān gōngyuán yīnyuètáng*)

MUSIC | One of the nicest venues in Beijing, the 1,400-seat Forbidden City Concert Hall plays host to a variety of classical, chamber, and traditional music performances in plush surroundings and with world-class acoustics. Though the facilities are completely modern, concertgoers are treated to a moonlit walk through Zhongshan Park, a former imperial garden dotted with historical landmarks. ✉ *In Zhongshan Park, Xichang'an Jie, Xicheng District* ☎ *010/6559–8285* 🌐 *www.fcchbj.com* Ⓜ *Tiananmen West*.

THEATER

★ **National Centre for the Performing Arts** (国家大剧院. *Guójiā dàjùyuàn*)

CONCERTS | Architecturally, the giant silver dome of this performing arts complex is stunning, and its interior holds a state-of-the-art opera house, a music hall, and a theater. "The Egg," as it's been called, offers a world-class stage for national and international performers. If you don't wish to see a show, you can tour the inside of the building by paying for an entrance ticket. ✉ *2 Xi Chang'an Jie, Xicheng District* ☎ *010/6655–0000* 🌐 *www.chncpa.org* Ⓜ *Tiananmen West.*

Shopping

Xicheng is best known as the home of the Forbidden City, but it also has a few choice shopping areas. Located to the south of Tiananmen Square, **Qianmen** might not rank high on the authenticity scale, thanks to a pre-Olympics renovation, but it still offers plenty of color (as well as brand names)—a ride on the tram down what is one of the city's oldest shopping streets is a must. To the east lies the similarly spruced-up **Dashilar** area, a series of shiny hutongs (alleyways) that are a bit too clean to be real but house old-school Chinese medicine stores, silk shops, and "ancient" souvenirs aplenty.

Head northwest of the Forbidden City and you'll find Beijing's lake district of Shichahai, comprising Qianhai, Xihai, and Houhai. The latter is surrounded by a morass of hutongs that include Yandai Xiejie, a side street packed with stores and hawkers pushing jewelry, clothes, Mao-shape oddities, and plenty of stuff you don't need but simply can't resist. Meanwhile, farther west of here lies **Xidan**, a giant consumer playground swarming with high-rise malls and bustling underground markets stuffed with cheap clothing and accessories—it's the go-to place for Beijing's young and fashionable. At 13 stories, **Joy City** is the largest mall, while **Mingzhu** and **77th Street** are best for market browsing. And for those who are especially flush with cash, **Galeries Lafayette** is luxury-brand heaven, with the likes of Alexander McQueen, Jimmy Choo, and Gucci.

CHINESE MEDICINE

Tongrentang (同仁堂 *Tóngréntáng*)
LOCAL SPECIALTIES | A first-time consultation with a Chinese doctor can feel a bit like a reading with a fortune-teller. With one test of the pulse, many traditional Chinese doctors can describe the patient's medical history and diagnose current maladies. Serving as official medicine dispenser to the Imperial Court until its collapse, Tongrentang now has branches all over the city. At its 300-year-old store in Dashilan you can browse the glass displays of deer antlers and pickled snakes, dried seahorses and frogs, and delicate tangles of roots with precious price tags of Y48,000. If you don't speak Chinese and wish to have a consultation with a doctor, consider bringing along a translator. ✉ *24 Dashilan, Qianmen, Exit C, Xicheng District* ☎ *010/6303–1155* Ⓜ *Qianmen.*

■ TIP→ Chinese medicine can be effective, but that's unlikely to be the case when it's practiced by lab-coated "doctors" sitting behind a card table on the street corner. If you're seeking Chinese medical treatment, visit a local hospital, Tongrentang medicine shop, or ask your hotel concierge for a legitimate recommendation.

MARKET

Baoguo Temple Antiques Market (报国寺收藏品市场 *Bàoguósì shōucángpǐn shìchǎng*)
OUTDOOR/FLEA/GREEN MARKETS | This little-known market, atmospherically set in the grounds of Baoguosi Temple, is a smaller, more manageable version of Panjiayuan. It sees very few foreigners, and no one will speak English, but armed with a calculator, stallholders will get their point across. As well as memorabilia from the Cultural Revolution, look out for stalls that sell original photos, ranging from early-20th-century snaps to people posing with their first TVs in the 1970s. ✉ *Guanganmennei Dajie, Xicheng District* ☎ *8223–4583* Ⓜ *Caishikou.*

Did You Know?

There are more than 1,000 different kinds of makeup patterns used in the Beijing opera. Colors symbolize character traits. Red conveys bravery or loyalty, white signifies treachery, yellow suggests brutality, black stands for integrity or fierceness, and purple expresses wisdom. Bandits often have blue faces; gods and spirits are marked with gold and silver.

SILK AND FABRICS

Beijing Silk Shop (北京谦祥益丝绸商店 *Běijīng qiānxiángyì sīchóu shāngdiàn*)
TEXTILES/SEWING | Since 1830, the Beijing Silk Shop has been supplying the city with bolts of quality silks and other fabrics. There are tailors on-site to whip up something special, as well as ready-to-wear clothing on sale. ✉ *5 Zhubaoshi Jie, Xicheng District* ☎ *010/6301–4732* Ⓜ *Qianmen.*

SPECIALTY SHOPS

Tea Street (马连道茶叶批发市场 *Mǎliándaǒ cháyè chéng*)
FOOD/CANDY | Literally a thousand tea shops perfume the air of this prime tea-shopping district, west of the city center. Midway down this near-mile-long strip looms the **Teajoy Market,** the Silk Alley of teas. Unless you're an absolute fanatic, it's best to visit a handful of individual shops, crashing tea parties wherever you go. Vendors will invite you to sit down in heavy wooden chairs to nibble on pumpkin seeds and sample their large selections of black, white, oolong, jasmine, and chrysanthemum teas. Prices range from a few kuai for a decorative container of loose green tea to thousands of yuan for an elaborate gift set. Tea Street is also the place to stock up on clay and porcelain teapots and service sets. Green and flower teas are sold loose; black teas are sold pressed into disks and wrapped in natural-colored paper. Despite the huge selection of drinking vessels available, you'll find that most locals drink their tea from a recycled glass jar. ✉ *11 Maliandao Lu, Xicheng District* ✣ *South end of Maliandao Lu near Guang'anmen Waidajie* Ⓜ *Xuanwumen.*

TOYS

Three Stones Kite Store (三石斋风筝店 *Sānshízhāi fēngzhēng*)
TOYS | For something more traditional, go fly a kite. Here, for three generations, the same family has hand-painted butterflies and birds onto bamboo frames to delight adults and children alike. They're a far cry from the run-of-the-mill types you can find elsewhere. ✉ *25 Di'anmen Xidajie, Xicheng District* ☎ *010/8404–4505* 🌐 *www.cnkites.com* Ⓜ *Shichahai.*

Chaoyang District

There's precious little of Beijng's ancient history found in Chaoyang District, where much of the old has been razed to make way for the blingy new. Impeccably dressed Chinese women shop the afternoons away at gleaming new malls, young tycoons and princelings park their Ferraris on the sidewalks, and everyone who's anyone congregates at the booming nightclubs filled with hip-hop music and VIP bottle service.

GETTING HERE AND AROUND

The heart of Chaoyang District is accessible via Lines 1, 2, and 10 on the subway, but the district is huge and the sites are broadly distributed. Taking taxis between sites is usually the easiest way to get around. The 798 Art District is especially far away from central Beijing, so a taxi is also the best bet (about Y30–Y50 from the center of town). Buses go everywhere, but they're slow.

MAKING THE MOST OF YOUR TIME

You can spend years lost in Chaoyang District and never get bored. There's plenty to do, but there are very few historic sights. Spend a morning shopping at **Silk Alley Market** or **Panjiayuan Antiques Market** (best on weekend mornings) and the afternoon cooling off at **Ritan Park** or **Chaoyang Park,** the latter a large and pleasant park with a lot of activities for kids. Next, head to one of the numerous bar streets for refreshments. If you like contemporary art, browse the galleries at **798 Art District.** There are a number of nice cafés here as well.

Sights

Ancient Observatory (北京古观象台 *Běijīng gǔguānxiàng tái*)
BUILDING | This squat tower of primitive stargazing equipment peeks out next to the elevated highways of the Second Ring Road. It dates to the time of Genghis Khan, who believed that his fortunes could be read in the stars. To China's imperial rulers, interpreting the heavens was key to holding onto power; a ruler knew when, say, an eclipse would occur, or he could predict the best time to plant crops. Celestial phenomena like eclipses and comets were believed to portend change; if left unheeded they might cost an emperor his legitimacy—his mandate of heaven. Records of celestial observations at or near this site go back more than 500 years, making this the longest documented astronomical viewing site in the world.

The main astronomical devices are arranged on the roof. Writhing bronze dragon sculptures adorn some of the astronomy pieces at Jianguo Tower, the main building that houses the observatory. Among the sculptures are an armillary sphere to pinpoint the position of heavenly bodies and a sextant to measure angular distances between stars, along with a celestial globe. Inside, the dusty exhibition rooms shelter ancient star maps with information dating back to the Tang Dynasty. Most of the ancient instruments were looted by the Allied Forces in 1900, during the Boxer Rebellion, only to be returned to China at the end of World War I. ✉ *2 Dongbiaobei Hutong, Jianguomenwai Dajie, Chaoyang* ☎ *010/6524–2202* 🎫 *Y20* Ⓜ *Jianguomen.*

Ritan Park (日坛公园 *Rìtán gōngyuán*)
CITY PARK | A cool oasis of water, paths and trees just west of the Central Business District, Ritan Park (also known as "Temple of the Sun Park") is a popular place to go for some peace and quiet, and is where many locals head to stretch their legs. Stop in at the Stone Boat café if you're in need of refreshment. ✉ *Ritan Lu, northeast of Jianguomen, Chaoyang* ☎ *010/8563–5038* 🎫 *Free.*

Sanlitun (三里屯 *Sānlǐtún*)
NEIGHBORHOOD | Sanlitun is the nightlife hub of Beijing. Vics and Mix at the north gate of the Workers' Stadium are two clubs always packed with people looking for a big night out, while the bars at The Opposite House hotel are a swank respite. Taikoo Li, Beijing's hottest shopping complex, can be credited with changing the face of what was once a fairly seedy area. The Japanese-designed open-air center includes a number of international shops as well as a movie theater and some of Beijing's best restaurants and cafés, and has become the city's major hangout for the in-crowd, both local and foreign. ✉ *Chaoyang.*

★ **798 Art District** (798艺术区 *Qījiǔbā yìshù qū*)
ARTS VENUE | Chinese contemporary art has exploded in the past decade, and to see some of the finest examples of the scene look no further than 798 Art District, located in the northeast corner of the city. This was once the site of several state-owned factories, including Factory 798, that produced electronics. Beginning in 2002, artists and cultural organizations began to move into the area, gradually developing the old buildings into galleries, art centers, artists' studios, design companies, restaurants, and bars. Note that most if not all of the galleries here are closed on Mondays.

Experimenting with classical mediums such as paint and printmaking as well as forays into new and digital media, installation, and performance art, young Chinese artists are caught between old and new, Communism and capitalism, urban and rural, rich and poor, and East and West. These conflicts set the stage and color their artistic output, with varying results. Although more and more

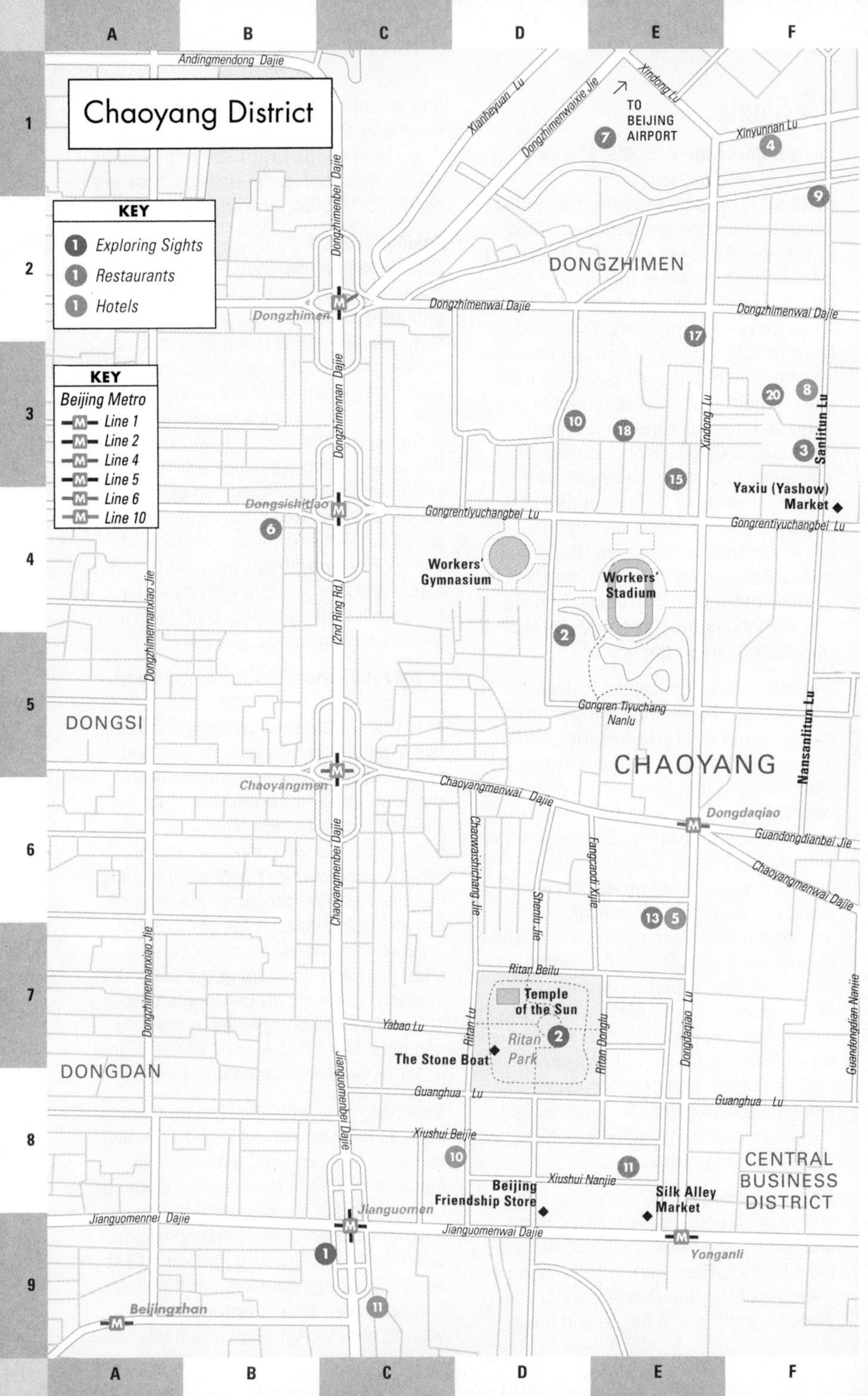

Chaoyang District
KEY
Exploring Sights
Restaurants
Hotels
KEY
Beijing Metro
Line 1
Line 2
Line 4
Line 5
Line 6
Line 10
A B C D E F
1 2 3 4 5 6 7 8 9
Andingmendong Dajie
Xianheyuan Lu
Dongzhimenwaixie Jie
Xindong Lu
TO BEIJING AIRPORT
Xinyunnan Lu
DONGZHIMEN
Dongzhimenbei Dajie
Dongzhimen
Dongzhimenwai Dajie
Dongzhimennan Dajie
Xindong Lu
Sanlitun Lu
Yaxiu (Yashow) Market
Dongsishitiao
Gongrentiyuchangbei Lu
Workers' Gymnasium
Workers' Stadium
(2nd Ring Rd)
Dongzhimennanxiao Jie
Gongren Tiyuchang Nanlu
DONGSI
Nansanlitun Lu
CHAOYANG
Chaoyangmen
Chaoyangmenwai Dajie
Dongdaqiao
Guandongdianbei Jie
Chaoyangmenbei Dajie
Chaowaishichang Jie
Fangcaodi Xijie
Shenlu Jie
Ritan Beilu
Temple of the Sun
Yabao Lu
Ritan Lu
Ritan Park
Ritan Donglu
Dongdaqiao Lu
Guandongdian Nanjie
The Stone Boat
DONGDAN
Jianguomenbei Dajie
Guanghua Lu
Xiushui Beijie
CENTRAL BUSINESS DISTRICT
Beijing Friendship Store
Xiushui Nanjie
Silk Alley Market
Jianguomen
Jianguomennei Dajie
Jianguomenwai Dajie
Yonganli
Beijingzhan

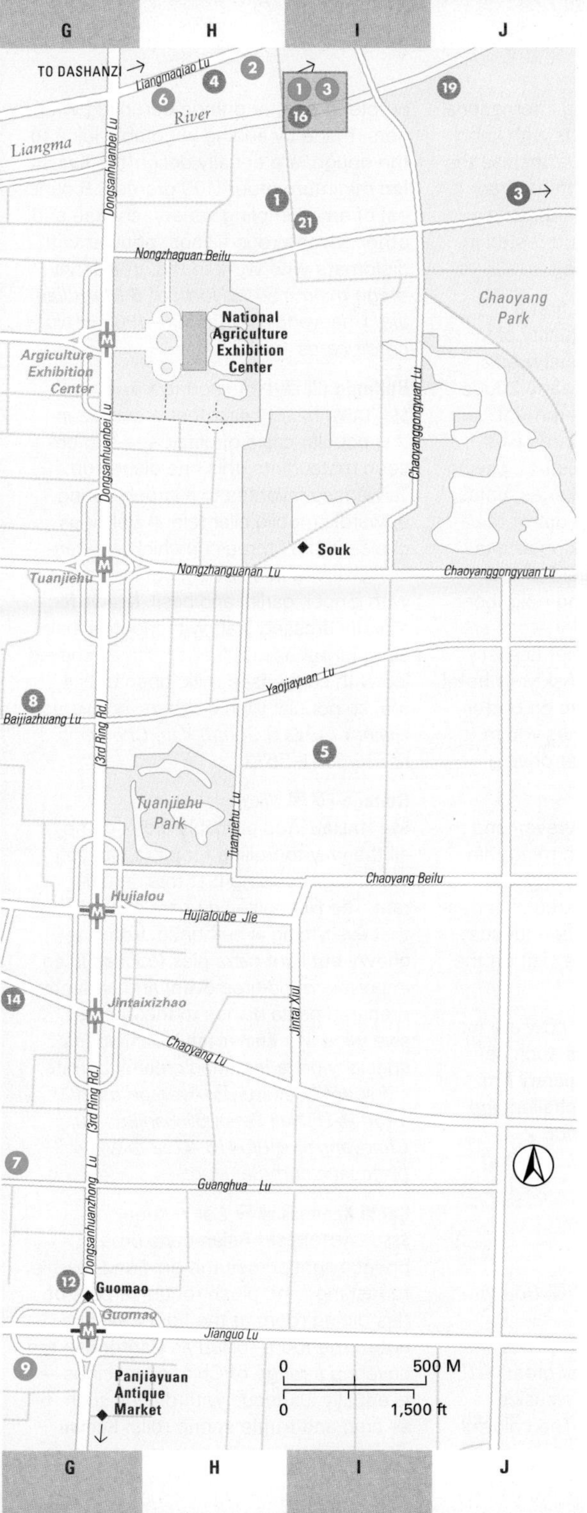

Sights

1 Ancient Observatory C9
2 Ritan Park.......................... D7
3 798 Art District J1

Restaurants

1 Baoyuan Dumpling H1
2 Bellagio D5
3 Bottega F3
4 Cai Yi Xuan H1
5 Comptoirs de France Bakery...... I5
6 Da Dong Roast Duck B4
7 Din Tai Fung E1
8 Haidilao G5
9 In and Out........................... F2
10 Jingzun Roast Duck Restaurant.................. D3
11 Makye Ame E8
12 Migas G8
13 Opera Bombana E6
14 Peking Duck, Private Kitchen G7
15 Rollbox E3
16 Sake Manzo I1
17 Sheng Yong Xing.................... E2
18 There Will Be Bread................ E3
19 Three Guizhou Men J1
20 Transit................................ F3
21 Yotsuba I2

Hotels

1 EAST Beijing I1
2 Four Seasons Hotel Beijing....... H1
3 Grace Beijing......................... I1
4 Hotel Bulgari F1
5 Hotel Ecla............................ E6
6 Kempinski Hotel Beijing Lufthansa Center H1
7 Kerry Centre Hotel.................. G8
8 The Opposite House................ F3
9 Park Hyatt Beijing G9
10 St. Regis D8
11 W Beijing Chang'an C9

Chinese artists are achieving international recognition, 798 still abounds with knock-offs of bad Western art. Nevertheless the area remains the hub of contemporary creative arts in Beijing and is definitely worth a visit if you're at all interested in the state of the arts in China.

Although the scene was at first a completely DIY affair, the quality of art produced and international media attention starting from the early 2000s meant that the district government took notice. Eventually the area was declared a protected arts district, paving the way for commercial galleries, cafés, and souvenir shops. Priced out of their original studios, many working artists have decamped further afield to the Caochangdi and Songzhuang neighborhoods. Both of these smaller areas are worth visiting, though neither is easily accessible except via taxi. Ask your hotel concierge for a detailed map or, better yet, call ahead to the galleries you're interested in visiting and get driving instructions.

798 is more accessible, however, and eminently walkable. Keep in mind that cabs are prohibited from driving into the complex, and much of the area is pedestrianized. Though it's also open Tuesday through Friday, most people visit on the weekend.

Many of the galleries there now are hit or miss, but establishments such as the **Ullens Center for Contemporary Arts (UCCA)** put on informative, challenging exhibitions. ✉ *798 Art District, 2–4 Jiuxianqiao Rd., Dashanzi, Chaoyang* 🌐 *www.798district.com.*

Restaurants

Baoyuan Dumpling (宝源饺子屋 *Bǎo yuán jiǎozi wū*)
$ | **NORTHERN CHINESE** | This cheerful, homey joint offers dozens of creative dumpling fillings alongside classics such as pork and cabbage. The colorful purple, green, or orange dumpling wrappers, made by adding vegetable juice to the dough, are equally delightful. **Known for:** minimum order (100 grams/3.5 ounces) of any dumpling variety; cheese and other adventurous fillings; popular with diplomats who work in the area. [$] *Average main: Y50* ✉ *North of 6 Maizidian Jie, Chaoyang* ☎ *010/6586–4967* 💳 *No credit cards.*

Bellagio (鹿港小镇 *Lùgǎng xiǎo zhèn*)
$$ | **TAIWANESE** | Like other branches in this popular chain of glitzy, see-and-be-seen restaurants, this one dishes up Taiwanese favorites to a largely young, upwardly mobile clientele. A delicious choice is the "three-cup chicken" (*sanbeiji*), served in a sizzling pot fragrant with ginger, garlic, and basil. **Known for:** smartly dressed staff with identical haircuts; Taiwanese desserts such as shaved ice with condensed milk; open until 4 am, so popular with clubbers. [$] *Average main: Y140* ✉ *6 Gongti Xilu, Chaoyang* ☎ *010/6551–3533.*

Bottega (意库 *Yìkù*)
$$ | **ITALIAN** | You probably didn't come all the way to Beijing for pizza, but you won't regret having it at this restaurant. The Neapolitan owners ensure that everything is authentic, from the chewy but light pizza pies (cooked in an imported wood-fired oven) and perfectly prepared pasta dishes to the impressive wine list. **Known for:** kitsch sodas; specialty pizza featuring creamy burrata; indulgent desserts. [$] *Average main: Y150* ✉ *2F Nali Patio, 81 Sanlitun Lu, Chaoyang* ☎ *010/6416–1752* 🌐 *www.bottegacn.com/Sanlitun.*

Cai Yi Xuan (采逸轩 *Cǎi Yì Xuān*)
$$$ | **CANTONESE** | Asian-style orbs bounce light across the gold and marble furnishings and plush rouge carpets of this dining room at the Four Seasons hotel. The food—billed as Cantonese but covering a range of Chinese cuisines—is equally luxurious with dishes such as crab and truffle spring rolls. **Known**

for: hong shao rou (braised pork with abalone) done to perfection; international celebrity spotting; intimate private dining rooms. *Average main: Y180* ✉ *Four Seasons Hotel Beijing, 48 Liangmaqiao Lu, Chaoyang* ☎ *010/5695–8520* 🌐 *www.fourseasons.com/beijing/dining* Ⓜ *Liangmaqiao.*

Comptoirs de France Bakery (法派 *Fǎpài*)
$ | **FRENCH** | Part of a small chain of contemporary French-managed patisseries, this is Beijing's go-to spot for Gallic confections. Goodies here include flaky croissants, sandwiches in crunchy house-made baguettes, and savory croquettes and quiches. **Known for:** unusual hot chocolate flavors; eye-catching birthday cakes; colorful macaroons. *Average main: Y80* ✉ *55–1 Xinfucun Zhong Lu, Chaoyang* ☎ *010/6530–5480* 🌐 *www.comptoirsdefrance.com* *No credit cards.*

★ **Da Dong Roast Duck** (北京大董烤鸭店 *Běijīng Dàdǒng kǎoyā diàn*)
$$$ | **NORTHERN CHINESE** | You won't go wrong with the namesake dish at this world-famous eatery. Dadong's version features crisp, caramel-hued skin (over meat that's less oily than tradition dictates) and is served with crisp sesame pockets in addition to the usual steamed pancakes. **Known for:** experimental takes on Chinese classics; guaranteed quality; skilled duck carvers. *Average main: Y180* ✉ *1–2 Nanxincang Guoji Dasha, 22 Dongsishitiao, Chaoyang* ☎ *010/5169–0328* 🌐 *dadongdadong.com* Ⓜ *Dongsishitiao.*

★ **Din Tai Fung** (鼎泰丰 *Dǐngtàifēng*)
$$ | **TAIWANESE** | This Taiwanese restaurant specializes in beautifully crafted *xiaolong bao*—steamed dumplings that are filled with piping hot, aromatic soup. Crab, chicken, and duck are lovely alternatives to the standard pork dumplings, or go wild with the black-truffle option. **Known for:** friendly, efficient service; the dandan mian (simple noodles with a chili sauce); several locations around town. *Average main: Y150* ✉ *24 Xinyuan Xili Zhongjie, Chaoyang* ☎ *010/6462–4502* 🌐 *www.dintaifung.com.cn* Ⓜ *Liangmaqiao.*

Haidilao (海底捞 *Hǎidǐlāo huǒguō*)
$ | **CHINESE** | Snacks and various forms of entertainment make the long waits to get into this hotpot restaurant almost enjoyable. Once inside, expect bubbling pots of broth and more sauces and things for dipping than you can count. **Known for:** manicures while you wait in line; dancing waiters; four different broths with a range of spice options. *Average main: Y90* ✉ *2A Baijiazhuang Lu, Chaoyang* ☎ *010/6595–2982* 🌐 *www.haidilao.com.*

In and Out (一坐一忘 *Yīzuò yīwàng*)
$ | **YUNNAN** | On a tree-lined street in the heart of Beijing's embassy district, this large, Yunnan restaurant, adorned with decorative crafts and paintings from China's southwest, serves as an excellent introduction to the light, fresh, and spicy flavors of the province. Staff in traditional dress dish up crispy potato pancakes, eggs stir-fried with fragrant jasmine flowers, or tilapia folded over lemongrass and lightly grilled. **Known for:** sticky pineapple rice; artisinal alcohols, such as fermented rice wine; pleasant outdoor terrace. *Average main: Y90* ✉ *1 Sanlitun Beixiaojie, Chaoyang* ☎ *010/8454–0086.*

Jingzun Roast Duck Restaurant
$ | **NORTHERN CHINESE** | Locals and foreigners alike pack this pleasant restaurant for affordable roast duck and tasty, varied Chinese fare with a Beijing slant. The roadside patio, garlanded by small, twinkling lights, is a lovely spot for warm weather dining. **Known for:** eye-wateringly spicy Chinese mustard greens; local draft beer; proximity to popular bars. *Average main: Y90* ✉ *4 Chunxiu Lu, opposite Holiday Inn Express, Chaoyang* ☎ *010/6417–4075.*

Did You Know?

Sanlitun became a favorite destination soon after the economic reforms of the late 1970s and early 1980s, when bars serving expatriates began to open. Today, the area is lined with bars, dance clubs, top-notch restaurants, and big-name shops, including the world's largest Adidas store.

Makye Ame (玛吉阿米 *Mǎjíāmǐ*)
$$ | **TIBETAN** | Fluttering prayer flags lead up to the second floor entrance of this Tibetan restaurant, where a pile of *mani* (prayer) stones and a large prayer wheel greet you. Elegant Tibetan Buddhist trumpets, lanterns, and handicrafts adorn the walls, and the kitchen serves a range of hearty dishes that run well beyond the region's staples of *tsampa* (roasted barley flour) and yak-butter tea. **Known for:** live cultural performances; good vegetarian options; Tibetan cheese. *Average main: Y110* ✉ *11 Xiushui Nanjie, 2nd fl., Chaoyang* ☎ *010/6506–9616* Ⓜ *Jianguomen.*

★ **Migas** (米家思 *Mǐ jiā sī*)
$$ | **SPANISH** | Migas is a whirlwind adventure in rustic Spanish gastronomy. The setting is glitzy, and the atmosphere is spirited, especially after 9 pm, when the bar and sprawling terrace really spring to life. **Known for:** stunning urban views; DJ music; free dance classes twice a week. *Average main: Y150* ✉ *NL7003 China World Mall, 1 Jianguomen Wai Dajie, Chaoyang* ☎ *010/6500–7579* 🌐 *migasbj.com* Ⓜ *Guomao.*

Opera Bombana
$$$$ | **ITALIAN** | Although this Italian restaurant is in a shopping mall, it has a gorgeous interior and serves decadent food. Langoustine carpaccio, Wagyu beef ravioli, and white truffle risotto are the types of dishes featured on the menu. **Known for:** critically acclaimed at home and abroad; the bombolini (sugary doughnuts with a rich lemony custard filling); blissful atmosphere. *Average main: Y260* ✉ *Parkview Green, 9 Dongdaqiao Lu, LG2-21, Chaoyang* ☎ *010/5690–7177* 🌐 *operabombana.com* Ⓜ *Dongdaqiao.*

Peking Duck, Private Kitchen (私房烤鸭 *Guǒguǒ sīfáng kǎoyā*)
$$ | **NORTHERN CHINESE** | Instead of the banquet-style scene found in Beijing's more traditional roast duckeries, the setting here is more laid-back, with diners lounging on comfortable sofas in a moderately sized, warmly lit dining room. The succulent signature dish is still made to exacting standards, and other popular dishes such as kung pao shrimp and green beans in sesame sauce are done well, too. **Known for:** intimate atmosphere; good value set menus; attentive service. *Average main: Y120* ✉ *Vantone Center, 6A Chaowai Dajie, FS2015, Chaoyang* ☎ *010/5907–1920* ⏲ *No lunch* Ⓜ *Dongdaqiao.*

Rollbox (越南三明治 *Yuènán Sānmíngzhì*)
$ | **VIETNAMESE** | This trendy, hole-in-the-wall Vietnamese eatery specializes in salads and banh mi sandwiches that are packed with punchy, fresh ingredients. **Known for:** delicious shrimp rolls; creative cocktails; Vietnamese coffee. *Average main: Y70* ✉ *39 Xingfu'ercun, Chaoyang* ☎ *177/1091–8725* 💳 *No credit cards.*

★ **Sake Manzo**
$$ | **JAPANESE** | Beijing's best all-round Japanese *izakaya*-style restaurant is the place to go for frothy mugs of Asahi draft, sublime soba noodles, and some of the best sushi and sashimi in the city for the price. The slow-cooked pork belly in miso broth with a poached egg gets rave reviews. **Known for:** minimalist decor; sake tasting flights; attentive service. *Average main: Y140* ✉ *Twenty-First Century Hotel, 40 Liangmaqiao Lu, Chaoyang* ☎ *010/6436–1608* Ⓜ *Liangmaqiao.*

Sheng Yong Xing (晟永興 *Shéng Yǒng Xìng*)
$$ | **NORTHERN CHINESE** | Of the branches in this classy, Beijing chain of Peking-duck restaurants, this one is the most popular thanks to a prime location in the Sanlitun nightlife district. The duck here is roasted in an open kitchen and served with an indulgent selection of traditional Beijing accompaniments. **Known for:** the foie gras–topped crispy duck skin; lengthy wine list; thoughtful side dishes. *Average main: Y150* ✉ *5 Xindong Lu, Chaoyang* ☎ *010/6567–3663* 💳 *No credit cards* Ⓜ *Agricultural Exhibition Center.*

There Will Be Bread (面包会有的 *Miànbāo huì yǒu de*)
$ | **FRENCH** | This patisserie takes its name from a Lenin speech and its aesthetic from Melbourne's contemporary coffee scene. Although the selection of pastries is limited, each freshly baked item is sure to hit the spot. **Known for:** flaky but moist almond croissants; dairy-free milk alternatives available; below a stylish Airbnb. *Average main: Y30 ✉ 5–155 Xingfucun Zhong Lu, Chaoyang ☎ 010/6460–7199 No credit cards.*

Three Guizhou Men (三个贵州人 *Sāngeguìzhōurén*)
$ | **CHINESE** | The popularity of Guizhou cuisine and its trademark spicy-sour flavors prompted three artist friends from the province to set up shop in Beijing. Noteworthy dishes include "beef on fire" (pieces of beef placed on a bed of chives over burning charcoal) accompanied by ground chilies; pork ribs; spicy lamb with mint leaves; and *mi doufu,* a rice-flour cake in spicy sauce. **Known for:** classy interior featuring the artist owners' sculptures and paintings; suantangyu (fish in a spicy-sour soup that's a regional specialty); blackened bamboo shoots. *Average main: Y90 ✉ Solana, 6 Chaoyang Park Lu, Chaoyang ☎ 010/5905–6855 No credit cards Ⓜ Zaoying.*

Transit (渡金湖 *Dùjīnhú*)
$$$ | **SICHUAN** | This is one of Beijing's hottest contemporary Chinese restaurants, and we're not just talking about the chilies. Located in the upscale Sanlitun Village North, this glam Sichuan establishment marries the region's famous spicy dishes with slick service and a designer interior entirely at home amid the surrounding luxury boutiques. **Known for:** floral gin and tonics; prettiest dandan noodles in town; inky black interiors. *Average main: Y160 ✉ Sanlitun Village North, N4–36, Chaoyang ☎ 010/6417–9090 transitrestaurant.com No lunch.*

★ **Yotsuba** (四叶 *Sìyè*)
$$$ | **JAPANESE** | This tiny, unassuming restaurant serves arguably the best sushi in the city. The seafood is flown in from Tokyo's Tsukiji fish market; the daily chef's selection (about Y280) is a wooden board of sushi made from the best catches of the day. **Known for:** authentic Japanese atmosphere; good lunch deals; reservations essential. *Average main: Y200 ✉ 39 Maizidian Jie, Chaoyang ☎ 010/6586–7166.*

Hotels

★ **EAST, Beijing** (北京东隅 *Běijīng Dōngyú*)
$$ | **HOTEL** | From the folks behind the Opposite House, EAST is a business hotel with pizzazz, from the contemporary, light-filled guest rooms done out with oak floors and huge windows (the corner rooms have the best views), to Xian, a hip bar, lounge and music venue with delicious wood-fired pizza and a connoisseur's selection of single malts. **Pros:** a business hotel with style; impeccable service; great in-house dining and drinking. **Cons:** far from the main sights (other than 798); no traditional Chinese features; brunch can be overrun with children. *Rooms from: Y1250 ✉ 22 Jiuxianqiao Lu, Jiangtai, Chaoyang ☎ 010/8426–0888 www.east-beijing.com 369 rooms No meals Ⓜ Jiangtai.*

★ **Four Seasons Hotel Beijing** (北京四季酒店 *Běijīng Sìjì jiǔdiàn*)
$$$ | **HOTEL** | Even the most modest "deluxe" rooms at the Four Seasons Beijing come with state-of-the-art tech, bathtubs with city views, and clever architecture that seems to amplify the already generous 46 square meters (500 square feet) of living space. **Pros:** some of the best service in the city; elegant rooms; impeccable attention to detail. **Cons:** very expensive; not particularly close to key tourist hubs; lobby feels a little cramped. *Rooms from: Y1800*

Chinese Cuisine

We use the following regions in our restaurant reviews.

Beijing: As the seat of government for several dynasties, Beijing has evolved a cuisine that melds the culinary traditions of many regions. Specialties include Peking duck, *zhajiang* noodles, flash-boiled tripe with sesame sauce, and a wide variety of sweet snacks.

Cantonese: A diverse cuisine that roasts, fries, braises, and steams. Spices are used in moderation, and flavors are light and delicate. Dishes include wonton soup, steamed fish or scallops, barbecued pork, roasted goose and duck, and dim sum.

Chinese: Catchall term used for restaurants that serve cuisine from multiple regions of China.

Guizhou: The two key condiments in Guizhou's spicy-sour cuisine are *zao lajiao* (pounded, dried, brined peppers) and fermented tomatoes (the latter used to make the region's hallmark sour fish soup, called *suantangyu*).

Hunan: Chili peppers, ginger, garlic, dried salted black beans, and preserved vegetables are the mainstays of this "dry spicy" cuisine. Signature dishes include "red-braised" pork, steamed fish head with diced salted chilies, and cured pork with smoked bean curd.

Northern Chinese: A catchall category encompassing the hearty stews and stuffed buns of Dongbei, the refined banquet fare of Shandong, Inner Mongolian hotpot, lamb and flat breads of Xinjiang, and the wheat noodles of Shaanxi Province.

Shanghainese and Jiangzhe: Cuisine characterized by rich, sweet flavors produced by braising and stewing, and the extensive use of rice wine. Signatures include steamed hairy crabs and "drunken chicken."

Sichuan (central province): Famed for bold flavors and "*mala*" spiciness created by combining chilies and mouth-numbing Sichuan peppercorns. Dishes include kung pao chicken, mapo doufu (tofu), *dandan* noodles, twice-cooked pork, and tea-smoked duck.

Taiwanese: This diverse cuisine centers on seafood. Specialties include oyster omelets, cuttlefish soup, and "three cups chicken," with a sauce made of soy sauce, rice wine, and sugar.

Tibetan: Cuisine reliant on foodstuffs that can grow or be produced at high altitudes, including barley flour, yak meat, milk, butter, and cheese.

Yunnan (southern province): This region is noted for its use of vegetables, fresh herbs, and mushrooms in its spicy preparations. Dishes include "crossing the bridge" rice noodle soup with chicken, pork, and fish; cured Yunnan ham with Bai-style goat cheese; and steamed or grilled fish with lemongrass.

✉ *48 Liangmaqiao Rd., Chaoyang* ☎ *010/5695–8888* 🌐 *www.fourseasons.com/beijing* 🛏 *313 rooms* 🍽 *No meals* Ⓜ *Liangmaqiao.*

Grace Beijing (一驿 *Géruìsī Běijīng*)
$$ | HOTEL | Housed in a redbrick Bauhaus factory building in Beijing's 798 art district, this stylish boutique hotel mixes French-colonial and art deco touches, with contemporary artworks dotted throughout the stylish guest rooms, which range from boxy singles to spacious suites with freestandng tubs. **Pros:** unique art-theme hotel; on-site restaurant is excellent; perfect for visiting 798. **Cons:** far from everything else; no subway; no pool. $ *Rooms from: Y1100* ✉ *D-Park, Jiuxianqiao Lu 2 Hao Yuan, 798 Art District, Chaoyang* ☎ *010/6436–1818* 🌐 *www.graciearthotel.com/en-us* 🛏 *30 rooms* 🍽 *Breakfast.*

Hotel Bulgari
$$$$ | HOTEL | Italian lifestyle brand Bulgari is known for modern luxury, and its Beijing property, where a cacophony of clicking heels and cards being swiped fills the sprawling lobby, doesn't disappoint. **Pros:** wonderful riverside views; unstuffy luxury; indulgent spa. **Cons:** overpriced and underwhelming restaurant; not a great location for sightseeing; very expensive. $ *Rooms from: 3200* ✉ *Bldg. 2, Courtyard 8,, 8 Xinyuan Nan Lu, Chaoyang* ☎ *010/8555–8555* 🌐 *www.bulgarihotels.com/en_US/beijing* 🛏 *119 rooms* Ⓜ *Liangmaqiao.*

Hotel Eclat (北京怡亨酒店 *Běijīng yí hēng jiǔdiàn*)
$$$$ | HOTEL | Attached to Parkview Green, Beijing's most artsy and upscale shopping mall, this playfully ultraluxe option has "lagoon" suites with their own private swimming pools, and a fabulous art collection that includes original works by Salvador Dalí and Andy Warhol. **Pros:** excellent service; free minibar and other welcome treats; attached to shopping mall. **Cons:** expensive; not that close to sights; immediate area lacks local color. $ *Rooms from: Y2300* ✉ *9 Dongdaqiao Lu, Chaoyang* ☎ *010/8561–2888* 🌐 *www.eclathotels.com/beijing/default-en.html* 🛏 *74 rooms* 🍽 *No meals* Ⓜ *Dongdaqiao, Line 6.*

Kempinski Hotel Beijing Lufthansa Center (凯宾斯基饭店 *Kǎibīnsījī fàndiàn*)
$$ | HOTEL | One of the capital's older luxury hotels, the Kempinski could stand to give its guest rooms a refresh, but the facilities remain first-rate thanks to a well-equipped gym, easy access to shopping in the attached Lufthansa Center, and plenty of dining opportunities. **Pros:** excellent service; a good bar; easy access to the airport. **Cons:** some areas are in need of renovation; far from the big tourist spots; the glamour is a bit faded. $ *Rooms from: Y1100* ✉ *50 Liangmaqiao Lu, Chaoyang* ☎ *010/6465–3388* 🌐 *www.kempinski.com* 🛏 *526 rooms* 🍽 *No meals* Ⓜ *Liangmaqiao.*

Kerry Centre Hotel (北京嘉里中心饭店 *Běijīng Jiālǐ zhōngxīn fàndiàn*)
$$ | HOTEL | FAMILY | This Shangri-La owned stalwart entices with its stylish Centro Bar, excellent all-day Kerry's Kitchen, and top-of-the-range health club that has a play area for kids. **Pros:** reasonably priced luxury; great for kids; nearby shopping. **Cons:** smallish rooms; congested area; expensive bar. $ *Rooms from: Y1250* ✉ *1 Guang Hua Lu, Chaoyang* ☎ *010/6561–8833* 🌐 *www.shangri-la.com/beijing/kerry* 🛏 *487 rooms* 🍽 *No meals* Ⓜ *Jintaixizhao.*

★ **The Opposite House** (瑜舍 *Yúshě*)
$$$ | HOTEL | In the heart of the Sanlitun nightlife district and designed by the famed architect Kengo Kuma, this exemplar of 21st-century China has a huge atrium and contemporary art in the stunning lobby, plus spacious and warm guest rooms kitted out with natural wood and Scandi-Asian minimalist chic. **Pros:** a design addict's dream; fantastic food and drink options (both within and around); unique experience. **Cons:** too trendy for some; not close to the tourist trail;

awful traffic. $ *Rooms from: Y1725* ✉ *11 Sanlitun Lu, Chaoyang* ☎ *010/6417–6688* 🌐 *www.theoppositehouse.com* ⇆ *98 rooms* 🍽 *No meals.*

★ **Park Hyatt Beijing** (北京柏悦酒店 *Běijīng Bòyuè jiǔdiàn*)

$$$$ | **HOTEL** | An easy-to-like (if costly) slice of luxury, this 63-story tower hotel offers plenty of pampering (just imagine your own spa-inspired bathroom with oversized rain shower, deep-soak tub, and heated floors), with large guest rooms that are a tad businesslike but packed with the obligatory modern amenities. **Pros:** spectacular views of the city; the hotel's buzzing Xue bar has a fab rooftop terrace; good location for business. **Cons:** pricey; lacks intimacy; hard area for walking around. $ *Rooms from: Y2000* ✉ *2 Jianguomenwai Dajie., Chaoyang* ☎ *010/8567–1234* 🌐 *beijing.park.hyatt.com* ⇆ *246 rooms* 🍽 *No meals* Ⓜ *Guomao.*

★ **St. Regis** (北京国际俱乐部饭店 *Běijīng guójì jùlèbù fàndiàn*)

$$ | **HOTEL** | At this favorite of business travelers and dignitaries, the luxurious interiors combine classic Chinese elegance with modern furnishings, but it's the facilities that really stand out: the health club is equipped with a Jacuzzi that gets its water directly from a natural hot spring, the glass-atrium swimming pool offers a sun-drenched backstroke, and the smart, wood-paneled Press Club Bar has the air of a private club. **Pros:** grand lobby and plush rooms; fantastic facilities and service; good Asian and European restaurants. **Cons:** the little extras really add up; local area a bit tired; not many good places to eat nearby. $ *Rooms from: Y1399* ✉ *21 Jianguomenwai Dajie, Chaoyang* ☎ *010/6460–6688* 🌐 *www.stregis.com/beijing* ⇆ *156 rooms* Ⓜ *Jianguomen.*

W Beijing Chang'an (北京長安街W 酒店 *Běijīng cháng'ān jiē W jiǔdiàn*)

$$ | **HOTEL** | True to form, the sassy Starwood brand W has tech-laden guestrooms (and corner rooms here have great city views), comfy beds, pillow menus, and free snacks. **Pros:** hip design; rooms loaded with creature comforts; excellent dining. **Cons:** a little farther out than the Wangfujing hotels; feels a bit corporate; area is full of traffic. $ *Rooms from: Y1288* ✉ *2 Jianguuomen Nan Dajie, Chaoyang* ☎ *010/6515–8855* 🌐 *w-hotels.marriott.com* ⇆ *349 rooms.*

Nightlife

BARS

The Black Moth

BARS/PUBS | Set on the fourth floor of the Mediterranean-style Nali Patio, this cocktail bar is an oasis of quirky sophistication overlooking the drunken revelry of the Sanlintun nightlife district below. Unconventional art adorns its walls, and creative concoctions—hot goji-berry tea spiked with rum, for example—are offered alongside classics on its drink menu. ✉ *4th fl., Nali Patio, 81 Sanlitun Lu, Chaoyang* ☎ *010/6816–8105.*

China Bar (北京亮酒吧 *Běijīng liàng jiǔbā*)

BARS/PUBS | Perched atop the 65-story Park Hyatt, this upmarket cocktail bar offers bird's-eye views of the city, smog and all. Dark and sultry, the modern Asian decor is minimalist and doesn't distract from the views, or the drinks. Cocktails are expertly mixed; Scotch purists can choose from a 20-plus strong list of single malts. ✉ *Park Hyatt, 2 Jianguomenwai Dajie, 65th fl., Chaoyang* ☎ *010/8567–1838* Ⓜ *Guomao.*

Ichikura (一藏 *Yī cāng*)

BARS/PUBS | This tiny bar is the place to go if you're a discerning whiskey drinker—there are hundreds of varieties on offer. The dimly lit interior, minimalist decor, and hushed conversation give it an air of exclusivity—it's worthy of James Bond. Drinks are taken very seriously here, and it shows in both the quality of the alcohol and the professionalism with which it's mixed by the Japanese-led bar staff. The entrance is via stairs at the south wall of the Chaoyang Theatre. ✉ *Chaoyang Theatre, 36 Dongsanhuan Beilu, 2nd fl., Chaoyang* ☎ *010/6507–1107* Ⓜ *Hujialou.*

Mokihi

BARS/PUBS | Behind an Italian-fusion restaurant amid several establishments along an unassuming strip mall near Chaoyang Park, Mokihi is a haven from the hustle and bustle of everyday Beijing. Have the Japanese-trained bartenders mix up one of their signature cocktails, and nibble on delightful hors d'oeuvres while engaging in quiet conversation. ✉ *C12, Haoyun Jie (Lucky St.), 3rd fl., Chaoyang* ☎ *010/5867–0244.*

★ **Scandal**

BARS/PUBS | Though hard to find, this treasure of a cocktail bar is worth the effort. *Miami Vice* meets Riviera chic in the slick interior, featuring double-height ceilings and lacquered, monochromatic floor tiles. Cocktails are simply named but artfully made thanks to okra, mustard seed, and other imaginative ingredients. Very cool. ✉ *Courtyard 4, 4 Gongti Bei Lu, Chaoyang* ☎ *010/6508–5150* Ⓜ *Tuanjiehu.*

Twilight (暮光 *Mùguāng*)

BARS/PUBS | Twilight is an oasis of cool in the otherwise somewhat-dry Central Business District (CBD). Have the bartender make you a perfect old-fashioned, which you can pair with one of the bar's tasty pizzas. ✉ *Bldg. 5, Jianwai SOHO, 39 Dongsanhuan Zhonglu, 3rd fl., Chaoyang* ☎ *010/5900–5376.*

Performing Arts

ACROBATICS AND KUNG FU

Chaoyang Theater (朝阳剧场 *Cháoyáng jùchǎng*)

DANCE | This space is the queen bee of acrobatics venues, especially designed to unleash oohs and ahhs. Spectacular individual and team acrobatic displays involving bicycles, seesaws, catapults, swings, and barrels are performed here nightly. It's touristy but fun. ✉ *36 Dongsanhuan Beilu, Chaoyang* ☎ *010/6507–2421* 🌐 *www.chaoyangjuchang.com* Ⓜ *Hujialou.*

THEATER

China National Puppet Theater (中国木偶剧院 *Zhōngguó guójiā mùǒujùyuà*)

THEATER | **FAMILY** | The shadow and hand-puppet shows at this theater convey traditional stories—it's lively entertainment for children and adults alike. This venue also attracts foreign performers, including the Moscow Puppet Theater. ✉ *1 Anhuaxili, Chaoyang* ☎ *010/6425–4847* 🌐 *www.puppetchina.com* Ⓜ *Anhuaqiao.*

Shopping

The vast Chaoyang District is *the* area to shop in Beijing, although given that it's the size of many cities, that is somewhat understating things. It stretches all the way from downtown to the airport, encompassing 798 Art District, Sanlitun, and the Central Business District areas. Its consumerist joys lie mainly in its collection of labyrinthine markets and ever more futuristic malls, with a smattering of boutiques in between. Parkview Green and Indigo are just some of the more impressive examples of shopping malls to dot this part of new-look China. Elsewhere, shopping highlights include Panjiayuan Antique Market, Silk Road Market, the indie stores of 798, and the local capitalist's mecca that is Sanlitun Village.

BOOKS

The Bookworm (书虫 *Shūchóng*)

BOOKS/STATIONERY | Thousands of English-language books fill the shelves at this pleasant café in the heart of Sanlitun. Read for free over a coffee or a simple bistro meal, or join the lending library for a fee. The Bookworm is also a good spot to buy new international magazines and

Did You Know?

Chinese acrobatics has existed for more than 2,000 years. Like vaudeville in the West, acrobatic performances in old China were considered low-class; they were even banned from theaters. Many of the acts used props such as chairs, tables, and plates. Today you'll see amazing feats like traditional group gymnastics, springboard stunts, and gymnastics on double-fixed poles.

best sellers. This is a popular venue for guest speakers, poetry readings, film screenings, and live-music performances. The kitchen offers a three-course set lunch and dinner. For a quick bite, sandwiches, salads, and a cheese platter are also available. ✉ *4 Sanlitun Nan lu, set back slightly in alley 50 meters south of Gongti Beilu junction, Chaoyang* ☎ *010/6586–9507* 🌐 *www.beijingbookworm.com* Ⓜ *Tuanjiehu.*

CLOTHING

UCCA Store (东八时区 *UCCA Shāngdiàn*)
HOUSEHOLD ITEMS/FURNITURE | The 798 Art District is home to a burgeoning collection of housewares, fashion, and design shops. The most innovative of these is an offshoot of the Ullens Center for Contemporary Art (UCCA), located just one door down from the gallery. Clothes, posters, ingenious knickknacks, and artist Sui Jianguo's iconic (and pricey) "Made in China" plastic dinosaurs make it a must-visit for anyone in the area. ✉ *798 Art District, 4 Jiuxianqiao Lu, Chaoyang* ☎ *010/5780–0224* 🌐 *ucca.org.cn/en/uccastore.*

HOUSEWARES

Spin (旋 *Xuán*)
HOUSEHOLD ITEMS/FURNITURE | This trendy ceramics shop near the 798 Art District features the work of several talented Shanghainese designers who take traditional plates, vases, and vessels and give them a unique and delightful twist. Prices are surprisingly inexpensive. ✉ *6 Fangyuan Xilu, Lido, Chaoyang* ☎ *010/6437–8649.*

MALLS AND DEPARTMENT STORES

China World Mall (国贸商城 *Guǒmào Shāngchéng*)
SHOPPING CENTERS/MALLS | Nothing embodies Beijing's lusty embrace of luxury goods quite like China World Mall, which is home to a giant branch of the Hong Kong designer emporium Joyce. The average spend here must run into millions of yuan. However, for smaller budgets, there are plenty of cafés and affordable restaurants; the cinema is decent, and there's also a good ice rink for kids. The mall is open every day, from 10 am to 9:30 pm. ✉ *1 Jianguomenwai Dajie, Chaoyang* ☎ *010/8535–1698* Ⓜ *Guomao.*

Indigo (颐堤港 *Yítígǎng*)
SHOPPING CENTERS/MALLS | Located just on the edge of Dashanzi (798 Art District), this complex is one of the city's many impressive "super malls." Light, airy, and with a few new stores still not open, the malls houses brands that include the GAP, H&M, and Sephora as well as the Parisian Bread and Butter and homebred earthy fashion house JNBY; there is also a branch of the excellent Page One bookstore. The indoor garden isn't much to write home about, but a gigantic outdoor park area often hosts family-friendly events. ✉ *18 Jiuxianqiao Lu, Chaoyang* ☎ *010/8426–0898* 🌐 *www.indigobeijing.com.*

Parkview Green, Fangcaodi (芳草地 *Fāngcǎodí*)
SHOPPING CENTERS/MALLS | Scattered in and around this giant, green pyramid-shaped "biodome" is a boutique hotel, a mall that doubles as a walk-through gallery, and one of the largest private collection of Salvador Dalí works on display outside Spain. For shoppers, stores by designers Stella McCartney and Mulberry rub shoulders with the likes of the GAP; meanwhile a branch of the world-famous Taiwanese dumpling-slingers Din Tai Fung is always worth a visit. Even if designer knickknacks aren't your thing, stopping by just to gawk at the sheer grandiosity of it all comes highly recommended. ✉ *9 Dongdaqiao Lu, Chaoyang* ☎ *010/5690–7000* 🌐 *www.parkviewgreen.com/eng* Ⓜ *Dongdaqiao.*

The Place (世贸天阶 *Shìmào tiān jiē*)
DEPARTMENT STORES | Shopping-wise you'll find all the usual suspects here—Zara, JNBY, et al.—even if a lack of good dining spots ensures that you won't linger too

long. However, visitors largely flock to The Place to witness its eye-wateringly gigantic LED screen, which bursts into life every hour in the evenings and shows some pretty stunning minimovies (the meteorites are the best!) before lapsing back into screensavers and commercials. ✉ *9 Guanghua Lu, Chaoyang* ☎ *010/6587–1188* 🌐 *www.theplace.cn* Ⓜ *Jintaixizhao.*

Taikoo Li (三里屯 太古里 *Sānlǐtún Taikoo Li*)
DEPARTMENT STORES | The default destination for all expats, this fashionable complex, split into two zones, gets the nod for its great range of stores at all price points, cool architecture, and fun people-watching. Taikoo Li South houses the biggest Adidas store in the world, as well as branches of Uniqlo, Steve Madden, I.T, and the busiest Apple store you'll ever see. The newer and more upscale Taikoo Li North has designer stores such as Alexander Wang and Emporio Armani. There's also a boutique cinema and some great restaurants and bars. ✉ *19 Sanlitun Jie, Chaoyang* ☎ *010/6417–6110* Ⓜ *Tuanjiehu.*

MARKETS

Panjiayuan Antiques Market (潘家园市场 *Pānjiāyuán shìchǎng*)
OUTDOOR/FLEA/GREEN MARKETS | Every day the sun rises over thousands of pilgrims rummaging in search of antiques and curios, though you'll find the biggest numbers of buyers and sellers (all told, there are about 1,000 of them) turn up on weekends. It's a sure bet that not every jade bracelet, oracle bone, porcelain vase, and ancient screen sold here is authentic, but most shoppers come for the reproductions anyway. Behold the bounty: watercolors, scrolls, calligraphy, Buddhist statues, opera costumes, old Russian SLR cameras, curio cabinets, Tibetan jewelry, tiny satin lotus-flower shoes, rotary telephones, jade dragons, antique mirrors, and infinite displays of "Maomorabilia." If you're buying jade, first observe the Chinese customers, how they hold a flashlight to the milky-green stone to test its authenticity. As with all Chinese markets, bargain with a vengeance, as many vendors inflate their prices astronomically for *waiguoren* ("outside-country people").

A strip of enclosed stores forms a perimeter around the surprisingly orderly rows of open-air stalls. Check out photographer Xuesong Kang and his **Da Kang** store (No. 63–B) for some fascinating black-and-white snaps of Beijing city life, dating from the start of the 20th century up to the present day. Also be sure to stop by the **Bei Zhong Bao Pearl Shop** (甲-007) for medium-quality freshwater pearls cultivated by the Hu family. Also here are a sculpture zoo, a book bazaar, reproduction-furniture shops, and an area stashing propaganda posters and Communist literature. Stalls start packing up around 4:30 pm, so make sure to get there on the early side. ✉ *18 Huaweili, Panjiayuan Lu, Chaoyang* ☎ *010/6774–1869* Ⓜ *Panjiayuan.*

★ **Silk Street Market** (秀水市场 *Xiùshuǐ shìchǎng*)
OUTDOOR/FLEA/GREEN MARKETS | Once a delightfully chaotic sprawl of hundreds of outdoor stalls, the Silk Alley Market is now corralled inside a huge shopping center. The government has been cracking down on an increasing number of certain copycat items, so if you're after a knockoff Louis Vuitton purse or Chanel jacket, just ask; it might magically appear from a stack of plastic storage bins. You'll face no dearth, however, of fake Pumas and Nikes or Paul Smith polos. Chinese handicrafts and children's clothes are on the top floors. Bargain relentlessly, carefully check the quality of each intended purchase, and guard your wallet against pickpockets. ✉ *8 Xiushui Dong Jie, Chaoyang* ☎ *010/5169–9003* 🌐 *www.silkstreet.cc* Ⓜ *Yong'anli.*

Haidian District

In the last decade or so Haidian has become Beijing's educational and technological center, although there's still a lot of Old Beijing left here, including the wonderful Summer Palace, with its lakes and ancient pavilions. The major IT players, including Microsoft, Siemens, NEC, and Sun, all have offices in this area, and in the Wudaokou and Zhongguancun neighborhoods you'll find kids geeking out over the latest gadgets at electronics superstores, studying in one of the many cafés, or blowing off steam at some of the area's dance clubs.

GETTING HERE AND AROUND

Subway Line 13 stops at Wudaokou, the heart of Haidian. Line 4 runs far into the northwest of the city with stops at the Summer Palace and the Old Summer Palace, though Fragrant Hills Park and the Beijing Botanical Garden are farther out still and best reached by taxi or tram (Xijiao Line). Take Line 10 to Baguo station and catch a cab or the tram from there.

MAKING THE MOST OF YOUR TIME

Because the **Summer Palace** is so large, with its lovely lakes and ancient pavilions, it makes for an entire morning of great exploring. The **Old Summer Palace** is close by, so visiting the two sites together is ideal (if you've got the energy).

Fragrant Hills Park makes for a charming outing, but keep in mind that it takes at least an hour and a half to get there from the city center. The **Botanical Garden,** with some 2,000 types of orchids, bonsai, and peach and pear blossoms, along with the **Temple of the Reclining Buddha,** is also fun, especially for green thumbs. Plan to spend most of a day if you go to either of these sites.

Sights

Beijing Botanical Garden (北京植物园 *Běijīng zhíwù yuán*)

GARDEN | Sitting at the feet of the Western Hills in Beijing's northwestern suburbs, the Beijing Botanical Garden, opened in 1955, hosts China's largest plant collection: 6,000 different plant species from all over northern China, including 2,000 types of trees and bushes, more than 1,600 species of tropical and subtropical plants, 1,900 kinds of fruit trees, and 500 flower species. With its state-of-the-art greenhouse and a variety of different gardens, this is a pleasant place to explore, especially in spring, when the peach trees burst with pretty blooms. An added feature is the wonderful Temple of the Reclining Buddha, which has an enormous statue that, it's said, took 7,000 slaves to build. ✉ *Xiangshan Wofosi, Haidian District* ☎ *010/8259–8771* 🎫 *From Y10* Ⓜ *Botanical Gardens.*

Big Bell Temple (大钟寺 *Dàzhōngsì*)

RELIGIOUS SITE | This 18th-century temple shields China's biggest bell and more than 400 smaller bells and gongs from the Ming, Song, and Yuan dynasties. The Buddhist temple—originally used for rain prayers—was restored after major damage inflicted during the Cultural Revolution. The bells here range from a giant 7 meters (23 feet) high to hand-sized chimes, many of them corroded to a pale green by time.

The giant, two-story bell, inscribed with the texts of more than 100 Buddhist scriptures (230,000 Chinese characters), is also said to be China's loudest. Believed to have been cast during Emperor Yongle's reign, the sound of this 46-ton relic can carry more than 15 km (10 miles) when struck forcibly. The bell rings 108 times on special occasions like Spring Festival, one strike for each of the 108 personal worries defined in Buddhism. People used to throw coins into

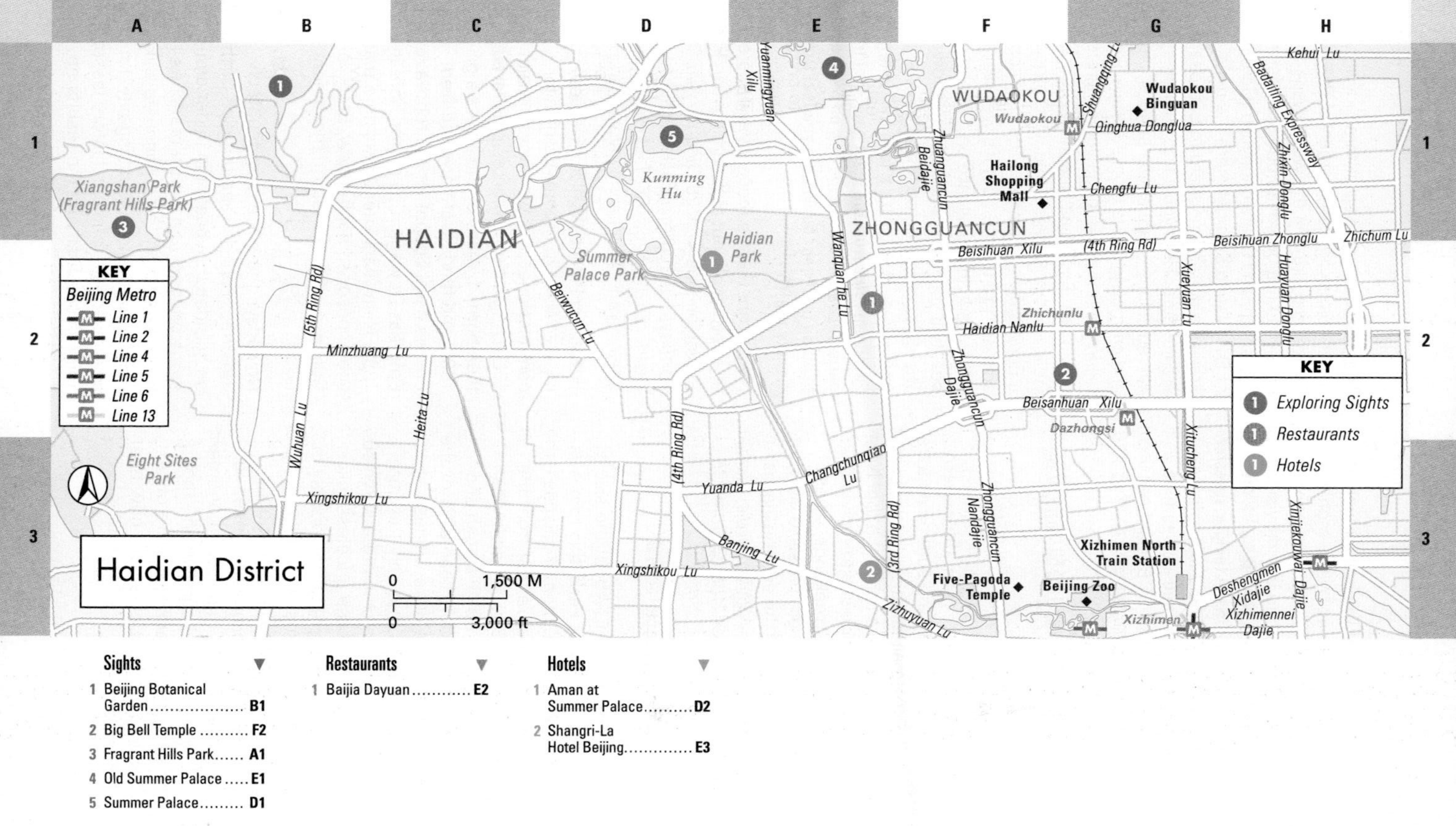

Sights

1 Beijing Botanical Garden **B1**
2 Big Bell Temple **F2**
3 Fragrant Hills Park...... **A1**
4 Old Summer Palace **E1**
5 Summer Palace......... **D1**

Restaurants

1 Baijia Dayuan **E2**

Hotels

1 Aman at Summer Palace.......... **D2**
2 Shangri-La Hotel Beijing.............. **E3**

a hole in the top of the bell for luck. The money was swept up by the monks and used to buy food. Enough money was collected in a month to buy provisions that would last for a year. ■ **TIP→ You can ride the subway to the temple: transfer from Dongzhimen on Line 2 to the aboveground Line 13 and go one stop north to Dazhong Si station.** ✉ *1A Beisanhuanxi Lu, Haidian District* ☎ *010/8213–2630* 🎫 *Y20* Ⓜ *Dazhong Si.*

Fragrant Hills Park (香山公园 *Xiāngshān gōngyuán*)
CITY PARK | Once an imperial retreat, Xiangshan Park is better known as "Fragrant Hills Park." From the eastern gate you can hike to the summit on a trail dotted with small temples. If you're short on time, ride a cable car to the top. Note that the park becomes extremely crowded on pleasant fall weekends, when Beijingers turn out en masse to view the changing colors of the autumn leaves. ✉ *Xiangshan Park, 40 Maimai Jie, Haidian District* ☎ *010/6259–1155* 🎫 *From Y10* Ⓜ *Fragrant Hill.*

★ **Old Summer Palace** (圆明园 *Yuánmíngyuán*)
ARCHAEOLOGICAL SITE | About the size of New York's Central Park, this ruin was once a grand collection of palaces—the emperor's summer retreat from the 15th century to 1860, when it was looted and blown up by British and French soldiers. More than 90% of the original structures were Chinese-style wooden buildings, but only the European-style stone architecture survived the fires. Many of the priceless relics that were looted are still on display in European museums, and China's efforts to recover them have been mostly unsuccessful. Beijing has chosen to preserve the vast ruin as a "monument to China's national humiliation," though the patriotic slogans that were once scrawled on the rubble have now been cleaned off.

The palace is made up of three idyllic parks: Yuanmingyuan (Garden of Perfection and Light) in the west, Wanchunyuan (Garden of 10,000 Springs) in the south, and Changchunyuan (Garden of Everlasting Spring) where the ruins are like a surreal graveyard to European architecture. Here you'll find ornately carved columns, squat lion statues, and crumbling stone blocks that lie like fallen dominoes. An engraved concrete wall maze, known as Huanghuazhen (Yellow Flower), twists and turns around a European-style pavilion. The park costs an extra Y15 to enter, but it's well worth it. The park and ruins take on a ghostly beauty if you come after a fresh snowfall. There's also skating on the lake when it's frozen over. ■ **TIP→ It's a long trek to the European ruins from the main gate. Electric carts buzz around the park; hop on one heading to Changchunyuan if you feel tired. Tickets are Y5.**

If you want to save money, travel there by subway; get out at Yuanmingyuan Park Station on Line 4. ✉ *28 Qinghua Xilu, northeast of Summer Palace, Haidian District* ☎ *010/6262–8501* 🎫 *Park and sites from Y10* Ⓜ *Yuanmingyuan Park.*

★ **Summer Palace** (颐和园 *Yíhéyuán*)
CASTLE/PALACE | Emperor Qianlong commissioned this giant royal retreat in 1750. Anglo–French forces plundered, then burned, many of the palaces in 1860, and funds were diverted from China's naval budget for the renovations. Empress Dowager Cixi retired here in 1889. Nine years later it was here that she imprisoned her nephew, Emperor Guangxu, after his reform movement failed.

Nowadays the place is undoubtedly romantic. Pagodas and temples perch on hillsides; rowboats dip under arched stone bridges; and willow branches brush the water. The greenery is a relief from the loud, bustling city. It also teaches a fabulous history lesson. You can see firsthand the results of

The marble ruins of the Old Summer Palace can be found in Changchunyuan (Garden of Everlasting Spring).

corruption: the opulence here was bought with siphoned money as China crumbled, while suffering repeated humiliations at the hands of colonialist powers. UNESCO placed the Summer Palace on its World Heritage list in 1998.

The **Hall of Benevolent Longevity** is where Cixi held court and received foreign dignitaries. It's said that the first electric lights in China shone here. Just behind the hall and next to the lake is the **Hall of Jade Ripples,** where Cixi kept the hapless Guangxu under guard while she ran China in his name. Strung with pagodas and temples, **Longevity Hill** is the place where you can escape the hordes of visitors.

Most of this 700-acre park is underwater. **Kunming Lake** makes up around three-fourths of the complex, and is largely man-made. The less-traveled southern shore near Humpbacked Bridge is an ideal picnic spot.

At the west end of the lake you'll find the **Marble Boat,** which doesn't actually float and was built by Dowager Empress Cixi with money meant for the navy. The **Long Corridor** is a wooden walkway that skirts the northern shoreline of Kunming Lake for about half a mile until it reaches the marble boat.

Subway Line 4 stops at the Summer Palace. Get off at Beigongmen and take Exit C for the easiest access to the north gate of the park. Otherwise, you'll have to take a taxi. It's best to come early in the morning to get a head start before the busloads of visitors arrive. You'll need the better part of a day to explore the grounds. Automatic audio guides can be rented for Y40 at stalls near the ticket booth. ✉ *Yiheyuan Lu and Kunminghu Lu, 12 km (7½ miles) northwest of downtown Beijing, Haidian District* ☎ *010/6288–1144,* 🌐 *www.summerpalace-china.com* 🎫 *Y60 summer (all-inclusive); Y50 winter (all-inclusive)* Ⓜ *Beigongmen.*

Restaurants

Baijia Dayuan (白家大宅门 *Báijiā dà zháimén*)

$$$$ | **CHINESE** | Staff dressed in richly hued, Qing-dynasty attire welcome you at this grand courtyard house, the Bai family mansion. Featured delicacies (ordered via an iPad) include bird's-nest soup, braised sea cucumber, abalone, and authentic imperial snacks. **Known for:** live Peking opera performances; historic setting; beautiful garden. *Average main: Y250* *15 Suzhou St., Haidian District* *010/6265–4186* *Suzhoujie.*

Hotels

★ **Aman at Summer Palace** (北京颐和安缦 *Běijīng yíhé ānmàn*)

$$$$ | **HOTEL** | The epitome of blissful indulgence, this luxury hotel (part of the famed Aman chain) is spread out across a series of carefully renovated ancient Qing Dynasty courtyards—it even has its own private entrance to the Summer Palace—with guest rooms decorated in restful earth tones (lovely traditional wooden screens and bamboo blinds) and grounds that are positively stunning. **Pros:** right next to the Summer Palace; fine-dining restaurants; beautiful setting. **Cons:** very pricey; extremely far from downtown; too isolated for some. *Rooms from: Y3300* *1 Gongmen Qian St., Haidian District* *010/5987–9999* *www.aman.com/resorts/aman-summer-palace* *51 rooms* *Breakfast* *Yiheyuan.*

Shangri-La Hotel, Beijing (北京香格里拉饭店 *Běijīng Xiānggélǐlā fàndiàn*)

$$ | **HOTEL** | With its landscaped gardens, luxury mall, and the addition of a more modern wing, the Shangri-La is a slice of charm for business travelers and those who don't mind being far from the city center; the service is spot-on throughout, from the pristine rooms to the efficient check-in, while the dining options are excellent. **Pros:** nice gardens; excellent amenities; great restaurants. **Cons:** far from the city center; no subway; older wing not as good as the newer one. *Rooms from: Y1230* *29 Zizhuyuan Lu, Haidian District* *010/6841–2211* *www.shangri-la.com* *670 rooms* *Breakfast.*

Nightlife

BARS

Lush

BARS/PUBS | The go-to hangout in the university district of Wudaokou, Lush is a home-away-from-home for many a homesick exchange student. With weekly pub quizzes, open-mike nights, and large, strong drinks, Lush is an excellent place to start the night for those in this part of town. *2nd fl., Bldg. 1, Huaqing Jiayuan, Chengfu Lu, Haidian District* *010/8286–3566* *www.lushbeijing.com* *Wudaokou.*

Shopping

If you're in Haidian, the chances are that you're a student, Korean, or both. An abundance of universities and a large Korean population around **Wudaokou** make this a rather bustling, fun area, although it's not worth the journey for that alone—unless you have a penchant for kimchi, cheap shots, and overcrowded dance floors. But, if you're on your way to the Summer Palace or Beijing Zoo, it's worth stopping by, if only to wind down with a massage at one of the many cheap Korean joints. Inexpensive and cheerful boutiques and restaurants are in abundance, while the usual mainstream chain stores can be found farther east at the shopping malls in **Zhongguancun**, which is also home to Beijing's largest IT and electronics market.

Inspecting the goods at the Panjiayuan Antiques Market

ELECTRONICS

Zhongguancun Electronics City (中关村电子城 *Zhōngguāncūn diànzǐ chéng*)

CAMERAS/ELECTRONICS | There's little in the world of IT and electronics that can't be found in Hailong, Dinghao, and the other multistory malls around the Zhongguancun subway station. Before you buy, make sure you compare prices among a few of the stalls (literally hundreds may be offering the same product or services). Never accept the initial quote without driving a hard bargain, and don't hesitate to pit sellers' prices against each other—it's the thing to do when the competition is this intense. ✉ *Zhongguancun Dajie, Haidian District* ☎ *010/8266–3883* 🎫 *Daily 9–7* Ⓜ *Renmin Daxue.*

Side Trips from Beijing

The wonders of Beijing aren't confined to the city center. Venturing into the outskirts and beyond, you'll discover a wealth of sights that provide a further look at imperial might, offer natural delights and some refreshing relief from city crowds, and even deliver a whiff of adventure.

Of course, the Great Wall is a good starting point for any exploration. Although it isn't (as the old propagandist myth goes) visible to the naked eye from space, and it might have failed to prevent the Manchus from invading, it's nonetheless an awesome sight. Few more soaring testimonies to human endeavor are more visually rewarding. You needn't stop there, though. Imperial tombs and Buddhist temples also surround the capital, with remarkable mausoleum complexes to the east near Changping and the west at Zunhua and a satisfying swath of temples in the western suburbs. A bit farther afield, a half-day's travel by train brings you to Chengde, where emperors left behind lavish summer pavilions, pagodas, and gardens. Beijing might be one of the most intriguing cities on Earth, and you'll soon discover the fascination extends well beyond the city limits.

Did You Know?

In a country increasingly filled with cars, shopping malls and pedestrian-only streets are becoming all the rage—and for good reason. Not only are the air and noise pollution less oppressive when there are no cars around, but dodging taxis tends to detract from one's shopping enjoyment.

The Great Wall

60–120 km (37–74 miles) north and west of Beijing.

Any visitor to Beijing should aside at least a day to visit one of the incredible sections of the Great Wall, just outside the city. Badaling is the closest to Beijing, just about an hour from the city center. The farther you get from Beijing, the more rugged the terrain, so you'll add the excitement of seeing the wall tumbling across the countryside.

See the highlighted feature in this chapter for more about the Great Wall.

GETTING HERE AND AROUND

The easiest and most comfortable way to visit the wall is by private car. Though taxis are occasionally willing to make the trip to more accessible sections like Badaling and Mutianyu, most hotels can arrange a four-passenger car and an English-speaking driver for eight hours at around Y500–Y700. Settle details in advance, and remember that it's polite to invite your driver to eat meals with you. To ensure your driver doesn't return to Beijing without you, pay after the trip is over.

TOURS

In addition to the tour buses that gather around Tiananmen Square, most hotels and tour companies offer trips (in comfortable, air-conditioned buses or vans) to Badaling, Mutianyu, Juyongguan, and Jinshanling. Smaller, private tours are generally more rewarding than large bus trips. Trips will run between Y400 and Y1,500 per person, but costs vary depending on the group size, and can sometimes be negotiated. Wherever you're headed, book in advance.

For further help in planning your trip to the wall, while adding a bit of adventure to the mix, consider the following:

Albatros Adventure Great Wall Marathon
SPECIAL-INTEREST | Not for the faint of heart, the Great Wall Marathon (and half marathon) takes place each May and covers approximately 6.5 km (4 miles) of the Great Wall, with the rest of the course running through lovely valleys in rural Tianjin. Visitors must book through Albatros, a Danish tour company that arranges weeklong packages, or a local operator. ✉ *Albatros, Tøndergade 16, Copenhagen* ☎ *45/3698–9838* 🌐 *great-wall-marathon.com.*

Beijing Hikers
SPECIAL-INTEREST | Arrange weekly day-treks to the wilder parts of the Great Wall throughout the year, as well as personalized tours. ☎ *010/6432–2786* 🌐 *www.beijinghikers.com.*

Beijing Service
GUIDED TOURS | Private guided tours by car include stops at Badaling, Mutianyu, Jinshanling, and Juyongguan for small groups of up to four people. ✉ *9–6 West Block of Chang An Block, Miyun* ☎ *010/5166–7026* 🌐 *www.beijingservice.com.*

Bespoke Beijing
GUIDED TOURS | This firm designs private tours with English-speaking guides to suit your interests. ✉ *107 Dongsi Bei, Dongcheng District* ☎ *010/6400–0133* 🌐 *www.bespoke-beijing.com.*

CITS (China International Tour Service)
BUS TOURS | The company runs bus tours to Badaling and private tours to Badaling, Mutianyu, and Jinshanling. ✉ *1 Dongdan Bei, Dongcheng District* ☎ *010/6522–2991* 🌐 *www.cits.net.*

Cycle China
GUIDED TOURS | This company runs good guided hiking tours of the unrestored wall at Jiankou. ✉ *12 Jingshan East St., opposite of east gate of Jingshan Park, Dongcheng District* ☎ *10/6402–5653* 🌐 *www.cyclechina.com.*

Continued on page 134

Did You Know?

The Great Wall is the longest man-made structure on earth. It was designated a UNESCO World Heritage Site in 1987. Sections were built from the 5th century BC to the 17th century AD.

THE GREAT WALL

For some people, the Great Wall is the main reason for a trip to China; for any visitor to Beijing, it's a must-see. Originally intended to keep foreigners out, the world's most famous wall has become the icon of an increasingly open nation. One of the country's most accessible attractions, the Great Wall promises both breathtaking scenery and cultural illumination.

Built by successive dynasties over two millennia, the Great Wall isn't one structure built at one time, but a series of defensive installations that shrank and grew. Especially vulnerable spots were more heavily fortified, while some mountainous regions were left un-walled altogether. The actual length of the wall remains a topic of considerable debate: at its longest, some estimates say the protective cordon spans 6,437 km (4,000 miles)—a distance wider than the United States. Although attacks, age, and pillaging (not to mention today's tourist invasion) have caused the crumbling of up to two-thirds of its length, new sections are being uncovered even today.

As kingdoms scrambled to protect themselves from marauding nomads, portions of wall cropped up, leading to a motley collection of northern borders. It was the first emperor of a unified China, Qin Shi-huang (circa 259–210 BC), founder of the Qin Dynasty, who linked these fortifications into a single network. By some accounts, Qin mustered nearly a million people, or one-fifth of China's workforce, to build this massive barricade, a mobilization that claimed countless lives and gave rise to many tragic folktales.

The Ming Dynasty fortified the wall like never before: for an estimated 5,000 km (3,107 miles), it stood 26 feet tall and 30 feet wide at its base. However, the wall failed to prevent the Manchu invasion that toppled the Ming in 1644. That historical failure hasn't tarnished the Great Wall's image, however. Although China once viewed it as a model of feudal oppression, the Great Wall is now touted as the national symbol. "Love China, Restore the Great Wall," declared Deng Xiaoping in 1984. Since then large sections have been repaired and opened to visitors, turning it also into a symbol of the tension between preservation and restoration in China.

AN ETERNAL WAIT

One legend concerns Lady Meng, whose husband was kidnapped on their wedding night and forced to work on the Great Wall. She traveled to the work site to await his return, believing her determination would bring him back. She waited so long that, in the end, she turned into a rock, which to this day stands at the head of the Great Wall in the beautiful seaside town of Qinhuangdao.

MATERIALS & TECHNIQUES

- During the 2nd century BC, the wall was largely composed of packed earth and piled stone.
- Some sections, like those in the Taklimakan Desert, were fortified with twigs, sand, and even rice (the jury's still out on whether workers' remains were used as well).
- The more substantial brick-and-mortar ruins that wind across the mountains north of Beijing date from the Ming Dynasty (14th–17th centuries). Some Ming mortar kilns still exist in valleys around Beijing.

VISITING THE GREAT WALL

As a visitor to Beijing, you simply must set aside a day to visit one of the glorious Great Wall sites just outside the capital.

At Mutianyu in the mountains on a clear summer day

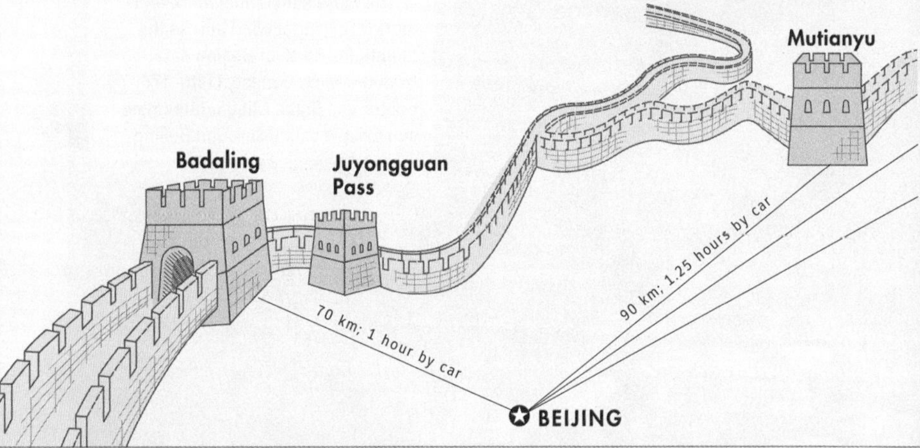

GREAT WALL SITES NEAR BEIJING

There are five Great Wall sites within relatively close proximity to the city of Beijing: depending on what you're looking for and how much time you have, there is one to fit your itinerary. Generally speaking, the farther you go from Beijing, the more rugged the terrain and the fewer tourists and hawkers you'll see. Badaling and Juyongguan are the most accessible sections of the Great Wall from Beijing, and these are where most of the tours go but there are tour options for all different kinds of Great Wall experiences. See the Great Wall Tours listings for some of our suggestions.

Part of the Great Wall of China at Badaling

Badaling is about an hour-long drive from Beijing and is great for photo ops, with amazing postcard views. Because it's easy to get to, though, there are often swarms of tourists, as well as lots of hawkers. The upside is that there are tourist-friendly facilities and there is better disability access here than elsewhere.

Juyongguan is also about an hour's drive from Beijing, and near Badaling. It has similarly impressive views and less crowds, but that's partly because the site has been heavily restored and feels a bit commercial.

If you're looking for a less-traveled section of the wall that is still accessible from Beijing, head to fantastic

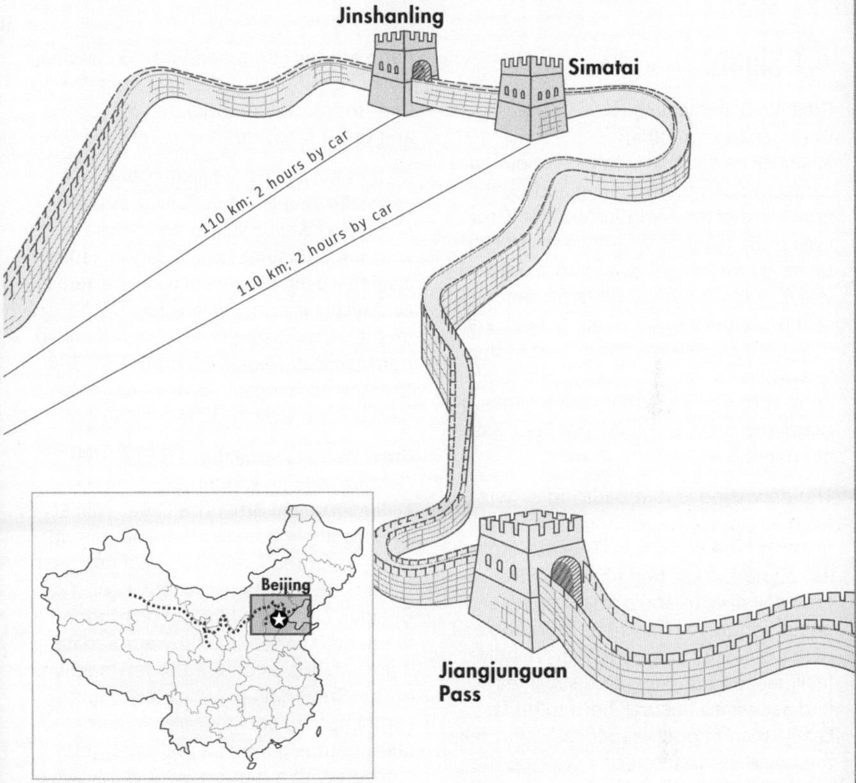

Mutianyu. It's only slightly farther from Beijing than Badaling but significantly more spectacular. Although you'll see the occasional souvenir stand, it's much less crowded than Badaling, and you'll be able to enjoy more solitude, along with amazing views from the towers and wall. Mutianyu is definitely more about hiking than Badaling or Juyongguan. It's a strenuous hour's hike out of the parking lot, although there is a cable car that can take you up to the wall, from where there are additional trails.

The Great Wall between Jinshanlin and Simatai

Jinshanling is the most rustic and the least touristed section of the Wall that's within easy proximity to Beijing. It's about a 2-hour drive from Beijing and most people come here on an overnight camping trip. This is an unforgettable experience if you have the time and like to camp.

Simatai is for adventure-seekers. It's remote and often precarious. It's also about a 2-hour drive from Beijing.

Great Wall at Badaling (**长城八达岭** *Chángchéng bādálǐng*)
ARCHAEOLOGICAL SITE | Only one hour by car from downtown Beijing and located not far from the Ming Tombs, the Great Wall at Badaling is where visiting dignitaries go for a quick photo op. Postcard views abound here, with large sections of the restored Ming Dynasty brick wall rising majestically to either side of the fort while, in the distance, portions of early-16th-century Great Wall disintegrate into more romantic but inaccessible ruins.

The downside is that Badaling suffers from its popularity, with tour groups flocking here en masse. This has led to its reputation as "one to be avoided" by those allergic to shoulder-bumping and being gouged by hawkers. Nevertheless, with popularity comes tourist-friendly facilities, and those with disabilities find access to the wall here to be far better than at other sections. Either take the cable car to the top or walk up the gently sloping steps, relying on handrails if necessary. On a clear day, you can see for miles across leafy, undulating terrain from atop the battlements. The admission price also includes access to the China Great Wall Museum and the Great Wall Circle Vision Theater.

A car for four people from central Beijing to Badaling should run no more than Y600 for five hours, and you can sometimes make arrangements to include a stop at the Thirteen Ming Tombs. By public transportation, trains leave Beijing North Station for Badaling Station (Y6) almost every hour from 6:12 am and take 1 hour 20 minutes. From there, it's just a 20-minute walk to the entrance to Badaling Great Wall. Or, take Line 2 on the subway to Jishuitan and walk to Deshengmen bus terminus. From there, take Bus 880 to Badaling (Y12). Be warned: private taxis hang around the station and drivers will try to convince you that it's easier to go with them. It isn't. Stick to your guns and get on that bus.

■TIP→ Most tours to Badaling will take you to the Thirteen Ming Tombs, as well. If you don't want a stop at the tombs—or at a tourist-trapping jade factory or herbal medicine center along the way—be sure to confirm the itinerary before booking. ✉ *Yanqing County, Beijing* ✣ *70 km (43 miles) northwest of Beijing* ☎ *010/6912–1383* 🌐 *www.badaling.cn* 🎫 *Wall Y45; cable car Y80 one-way, Y100 round-trip.*

Great Wall at Jinshanling (**长城金山岭** *Chángchéng jīn shānlǐng*)
ARCHAEOLOGICAL SITE | The Great Wall at Jinshanling is perhaps the least tamed of the restored Great Wall sections near Beijing, as well as the least visited. Besides being the starting point for a fantastic four-hour hike toward Simatai, it also stands as one of the few sections of the Great Wall on which overnight camping trips are available. A starry night here is gorgeous and unforgettable—go with a tour group such as Cycle China or Beijing Hikers. However, some have argued that unregulated tourism such as this goes against the efforts of others to preserve the wall, so tread carefully and leave nothing behind in order to reduce your impact. If you must take a souvenir, pack a piece of charcoal and paper to make rubbings of the bricks that still bare the stamp of the date they were made.

The trip by car to Jinhshanling from central Beijing should cost around Y700 and take about two hours. By public transportation, take a train from Beijing North Train Station to Luanping and a local bus or taxi from there. Trains leave almost every hour until 8 pm. ✉ *Jinshanling, Beijing* ✣ *110 km (68 miles) northeast of Beijing* ☎ *031/4883–0222* 🎫 *Apr.–Oct. Y65; Nov.–Mar. Y55; overnight stays at campsite Y150.*

Great Wall at Juyongguan (长城居庸关 *Chángchéng jūyōngguān)*
ARCHAEOLOGICAL SITE | Juyongguan is a quick, easygoing alternative for those not willing to blow a whole day traveling to Mutianyu or Jinshanling, or brave the more testing, unrestored sites such as Jiankou. It's the part of the wall that runs closest to Beijing and once guarded a crucial pass to the city, repelling hordes of Mongol and, latterly, Japanese invaders. The section also lies not far from Badaling, essentially acting as an overflow for its oversubscribed neighbor. It certainly loses nothing in the comparison, boasting similarly impressive views but with far less abrasive crowds. However, Juyongguan has been heavily restored and does feel a little sterile and commercial as a result.

The main attraction here is the Cloud Platform (or "Crossing Street Tower"), which was built in 1342 during the Yuan Dynasty. In appearance, it now resembles a rather squat Arc de Triomphe. The three white Tibetan stupas that originally sat atop it were destroyed during the early Ming period, only to be replaced with a Buddhist Tai'an temple, which was later toppled by fire in 1702. Today, carvings on the inner portal depicting the Four Heavenly Kings (Buddhist gods who defend the four compass points) and some elegant script work make for fascinating viewing on the way up the pass.

The trip by car from central Beijing to Juyongguan should cost around Y450 for the round trip and takes about an hour. By public transportation, take Line 13 on the subway to Longze. Exit the station and walk to the bus stop across the street to take Bus 58 (Y12) to Shahe; take bus 68 at the same stop to Juyongguan Gongjiaochang and walk to the wall from there. The trip takes about 2½ hours. ✉ *Juyongguan, Beijing* ⊕ *59 km (37 miles) northwest of Beijing* ☎ *010/6977–1665* 🎫 *Apr.–Oct. Y45; Nov.–Mar. Y28.*

Great Wall at Mutianyu (长城慕田峪 *Chángchéng mù tián yù)*
ARCHAEOLOGICAL SITE | Only slightly farther from downtown Beijing than Badaling, the Great Wall at Mutianyu is more spectacular and, despite the occasional annoyances of souvenir stands, significantly less crowded. This long section of wall, first built during the Northern Qi Dynasty (6th century) and restored and rebuilt throughout history, can offer a less busy Great Wall experience, with unforgettable views of towers winding across mountains and woodlands. On a clear day, you'll swear you can see the deserts of Mongolia in the distance.

The lowest point on the wall is a strenuous one-hour climb above the parking lot. As an alternative, you can take a cable car on a breathtaking ride to the highest restored section, from which several hiking trails descend. Take a gorgeous 1½-hour walk east to reach another cable car that returns to the same parking lot. Mutianyu is also known for its toboggan run—the perfect way to end a long hike.

The trip by car from central Beijing to Mutianyu should cost around Y600 and it takes about an hour. By public transportation, take bus 936 from Dongzhimen to Huairou bus stop. From there take a minibus to Mutianyu (Y25–Y30) or hire a taxi to take you there and back (about Y100–Y150 round-trip).

TIP→ For those taking a car, the road from Huairou, a suburb of Beijing, to Mutianyu follows a river upstream and is lined with restaurants selling fresh trout. In addition, Hongluo Temple is a short drive from the bottom of the mountain. ✉ *Huairou County, Beijing* ⊕ *90 km (56 miles) northeast of Beijing* ☎ *010/6162–6022* 🎫 *Apr.–Oct. Y25; cable car from Y80.*

Great Wall at Simatai (司马台长城 *sīmătái chángchéng)*
ARCHAEOLOGICAL SITE | This remote section of the Great Wall is ideal if you're seeking

adventure. It's been partially restored, but it's nowhere near as commercial as sections like Badaling and Mutianyu. Near the frontier garrison at Gubeikou, the wall traverses towering peaks and hangs precariously above cliffs. Be prepared for no-handrails hiking, tough climbs, and unparalleled vistas.

The first 10 of the watchtowers is currently accessible to visitors, and the hike to the top and back is just under two hours. Alternatively, a cable car takes you two-thirds of the way up; from there it's a steep 30-minute climb to the summit.

The trip by car from central Beijng to Simitai costs about Y800 and takes about two hours. By public transportation, take the 980 or 980快 (fast bus) from Dongzhimen bus stop to Miyun, getting off at Gulou. Cross the road to the opposite bus station and transfer to Bus 51 or 38 toward Simatai and get off at Gubeikou Water town (or Gubeikou Shuizhen). Follow directions to the ticket hall where you can pick up your prebooked online tickets for the wall.

■ TIP→ It's necessary to reserve a ticket online using a Chinese mobile number, to which a ticket code will be sent (your hotel or a travel agency can help with these arrangements). ✉ *Near Miyun, Miyun County, Beijing* ✣ *120 km (75 miles) northeast of Beijing* ☏ *010/8100–9999* 🌐 *www.wtown.com* 🎫 *From Y40.*

Thirteen Ming Tombs

48 km (30 miles) north of Beijing.

A narrow valley just north of Changping is the final resting place for 13 of the Ming Dynasty's 16 emperors (the first Ming emperor was buried in Nanjing; the burial site of the second one is unknown; and the seventh Ming emperor was dethroned and buried in an ordinary tomb in northwestern Beijing). Ming monarchs once journeyed here each year to kowtow before their clan forefathers and make offerings to their memory. These days, few visitors can claim royal descent, but the area's vast scale and imperial grandeur do convey the importance attached to ancestor worship in ancient China. A leisurely stroll down the Sacred Way, inspecting the series of charming larger-than-life statues of imperial officials and animals, is a wonderful experience. Many visitors combine a stop here with an excursion to the Badaling section of the Great Wall, which is found off the same expressway.

Zhaoling (昭陵墓 *Zhāolíngmù*)

ARCHAEOLOGICAL SITE | Allow ample time for a hike or drive northwest from Changling to the six fenced-off **unrestored tombs,** a short distance farther up the valley. Here, crumbling walls conceal vast courtyards shaded by pine trees. At each tomb, a stone altar rests beneath a stelae tower and burial mound. In some cases the wall that circles the burial chamber is accessible on steep stone stairways that ascend from either side of the altar. At the valley's terminus (about 5 km [3 miles] northwest of Changling), the Zhaoling Tomb rests beside a traditional walled village that's well worth exploring.

Picnics amid the ruins have been a favorite weekend activity among Beijingers for nearly a century; if you picnic here, be sure to carry out all trash. ✉ *Changping District, Beijing* 🎫 *Apr.–Oct. Y35; Nov.–Mar. Y25.*

The Western Temples

20–70 km (12–43 miles) west of Beijing.

Some of China's most spectacular temples and other monuments are on wooded hillsides west of Beijing. Here you'll discover magnificent murals at Fahai Temple, about an hour's drive from the center, and Jietai, an ancient

Buddhist site nearby. Tian Yi Mu is not a temple but the elaborate tomb of one of the high-ranking eunuchs who once played a vital role in affairs of state. Yunju Temple is best known for its mind-boggling collection of 14,278 minutely carved Buddhist tablets. While all these sights are in the western suburbs of Beijing, you will probably want to approach them as three separate excursions: Fahai Temple and Tian Yi Mu on one; Jietai Temple and nearby Tanzhe Temple on another; and Yunju Temple on a third. If traveling by taxi or private car, you could work visits to Fahai Temple, Tian Yi Mu, and Jietai and Tanzhe temples into one full day.

Sights

Fahai Temple (法海寺 *Fǎhǎi sì*)
RELIGIOUS SITE | The stunning works of Buddhist mural art at Fahai Temple, 20 km (12 miles) west of the central city, are among the most underappreciated sights in Beijing. Li Tong, a favored eunuch in the court of Emperor Zhengtong (1436–49), donated funds to construct Fahai Temple in 1443. The project was highly ambitious: Li Tong invited only celebrated imperial and court painters to decorate the temple. As a result, the murals in the only surviving chamber of that period, Daxiongbaodian (the Mahavira Hall), are considered the finest examples of Buddhist mural art from the Ming Dynasty. Sadly, statues of various Buddhas and one of Li Tong himself were destroyed during China's Cultural Revolution.

The most famous of the nine murals in Mahavira Hall is a large-scale triptych featuring Guanyin (the Bodhisattva of Compassion) and Wenshu (the Bodhisattva of Marvelous Virtue and Gentle Majesty) in the center, and Poxian (the Buddha of Universal Virtue) on either side. The depiction of Guanyin follows the theme of "moon in water," which compares the Buddhist belief in the illusoriness of the material world to the reflection of the moon in the water. Typically painted with Guanyin are her legendary mount Jin Sun and her assistant Shancai Tongzi. Wenshu is often presented with a lion, symbolic of the bodhisattva's wisdom and strength of will, while Poxian is shown near a six-tusked elephant, each tusk representing one of the qualities that leads to enlightenment. On the opposite wall is the *Sovereign Sakra and Brahma* mural, with a panoply of characters from the Buddhist canon.

The murals were painted during the time of the European Renaissance, and though the subject matter is traditional, there are comparable experiments in perspective taking place in the depiction of the figures, as compared with examples from earlier dynasties. Also of note is a highly unusual decorative technique; many contours in the hall's murals, particularly on jewelry, armor, and weapons, have been set in bold relief by the application of fine gold threads.

The temple grounds are also beautiful, but of overriding interest are the murals themselves. Visitors stumble through the dark temple with rented flashlights (free with your ticket). Viewing the murals in this way, it's easy to imagine oneself as a sort of modern-day Indiana Jones unraveling a story of the Buddha as depicted in ancient murals of unrivaled beauty. Fahai Temple is only a short taxi ride from Beijing's Pingguoyuan subway station. ✉ *Moshikou Lu, Shijingshan District* ✣ *Take an approximate Y19 taxi ride from Pinguoyuan subway station directly to temple* ☎ *010/8871–3975* 🎫 *From Y20.*

Jietai Temple (戒台寺 *Jiètái sì*)
RELIGIOUS SITE | The four main halls of one of China's most famous ancient Buddhist sites occupy terraces on a gentle slope up to Ma'an Shan (Saddle Hill), 35 km (22 miles) west of Beijing. Built in AD 622, the temple has been used for the ordination of Buddhist novices since the Liao Dynasty. The temple complex expanded over the centuries and grew to its current scale

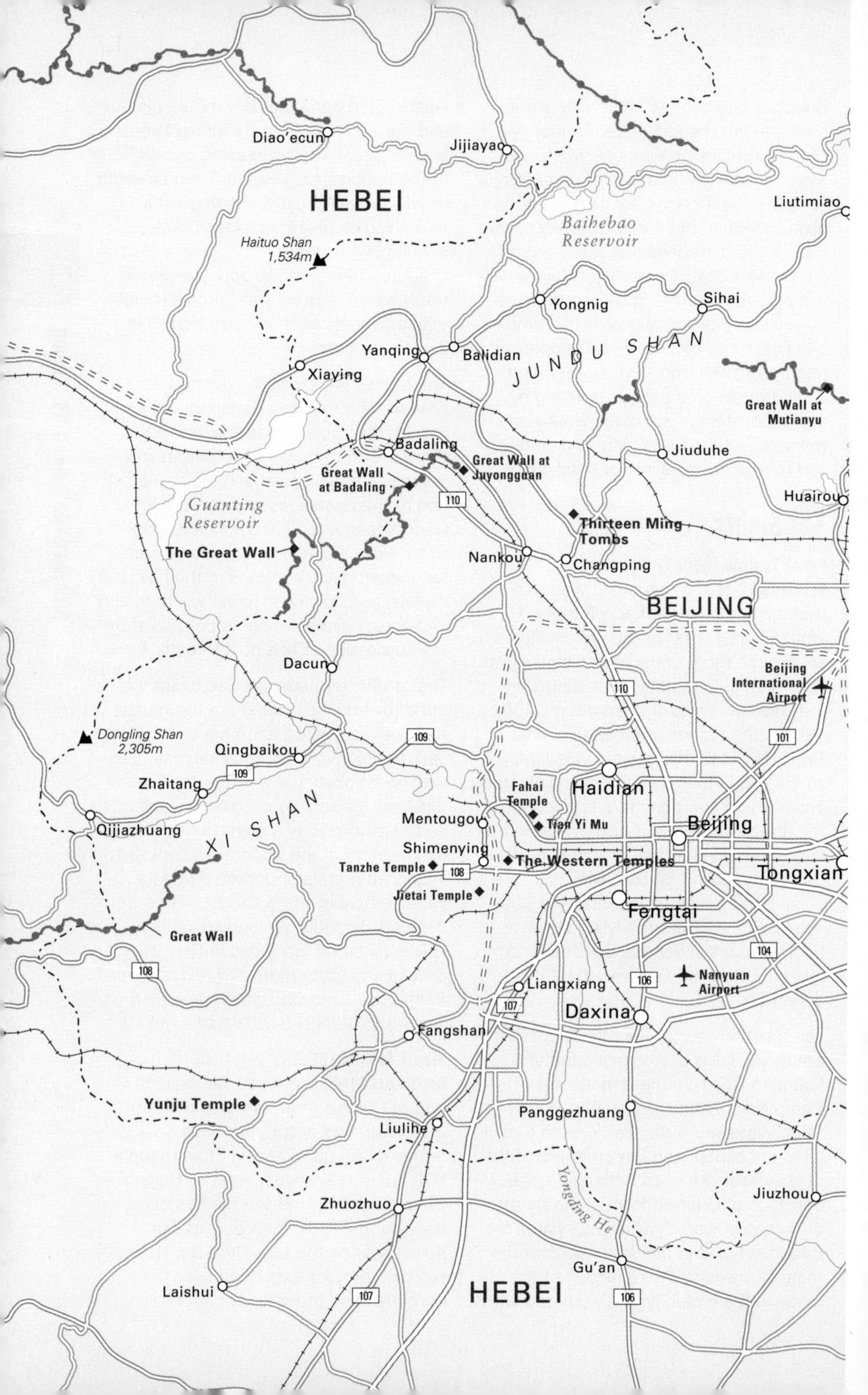

Diao'ecun
Jijiayao
HEBEI
Liutimiao
Baihebao Reservoir
Haituo Shan 1,534m
Yongnig
Sihai
Yanqing
Balidian
JUNDU SHAN
Xiaying
Great Wall at Mutianyu
Badaling
Jiuduhe
Great Wall at Juyongguan
Great Wall at Badaling
110
Huairou
Guanting Reservoir
Thirteen Ming Tombs
The Great Wall
Nankou
Changping
BEIJING
Dacun
Beijing International Airport
110
101
Dongling Shan 2,305m
109
Qingbaikou
109
Zhaitang
Haidian
Fahai Temple
Qijiazhuang
XI SHAN
Mentougou
Tian Yi Mu
Beijing
Shimenying
The Western Temples
Tanzhe Temple
108
Tongxian
Jietai Temple
Fengtai
Great Wall
104
108
Nanyuan Airport
106
Liangxiang
107
Daxina
Fangshan
Yunju Temple
Panggezhuang
Liulihe
Yongding He
Jiuzhou
Zhuozhuo
Gu'an
Laishui
HEBEI
107
106

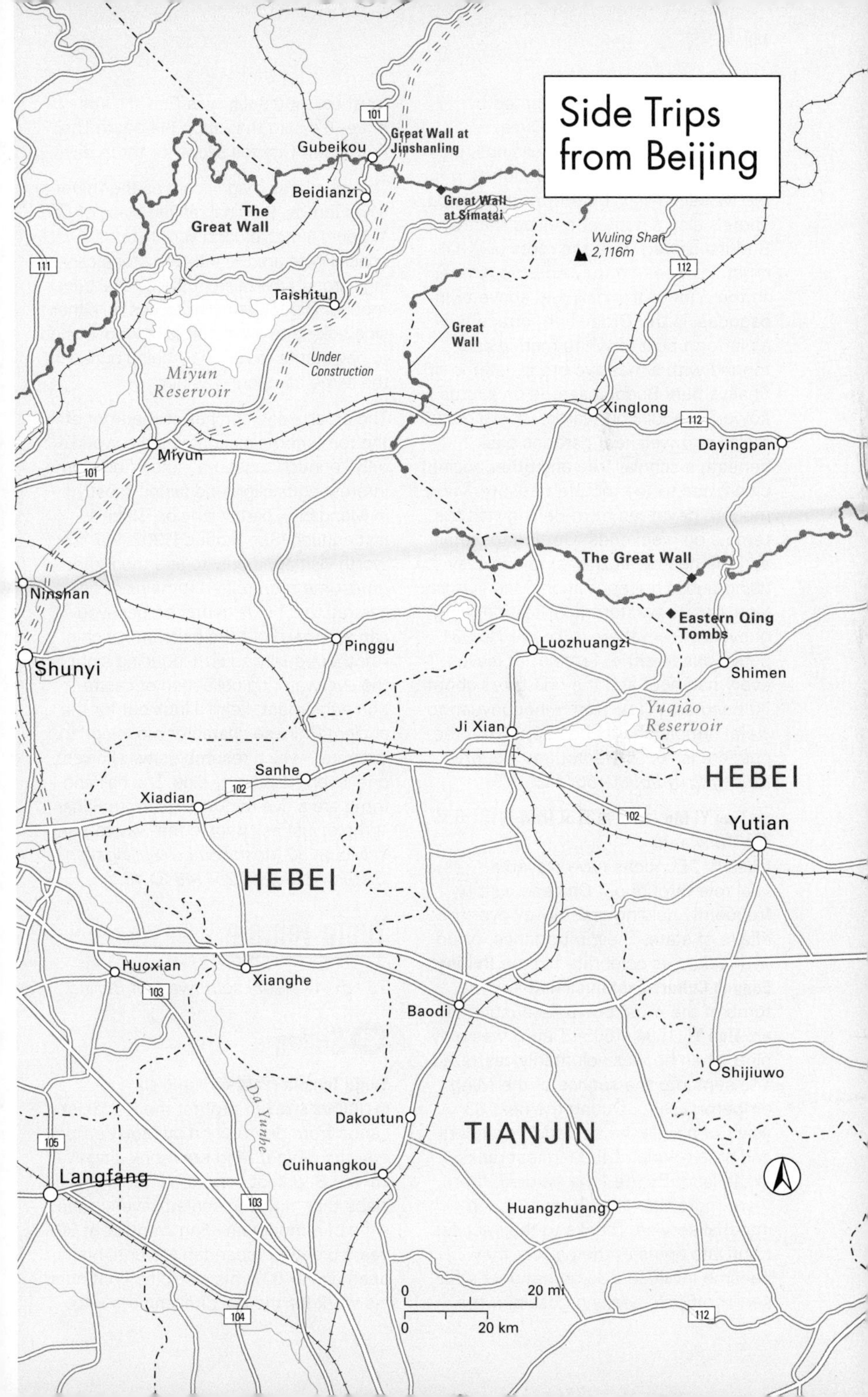

Side Trips from Beijing
Great Wall at Jinshanling
Gubeikou
Beidianzi
The Great Wall
Great Wall at Simatai
Wuling Shan 2,116m
Taishitun
Great Wall
Under Construction
Miyun Reservoir
Miyun
Xinglong
Dayingpan
The Great Wall
Eastern Qing Tombs
Ninshan
Shunyi
Pinggu
Luozhuangzi
Shimen
Ji Xian
Yuqiao Reservoir
HEBEI
Sanhe
Xiadian
Yutian
HEBEI
Huoxian
Xianghe
Baodi
Shijiuwo
Da Yunhe
Dakoutun
TIANJIN
Cuihuangkou
Langfang
Huangzhuang
0
20 mi
0
20 km
101
111
112
102
103
105
104

in a major renovation conducted by devotees during the Qing Dynasty (1644–1912). The temple buildings, plus three magnificent bronze Buddhas in the Mahavira Hall, date from this period. There's also a huge potbellied Maitreya Buddha carved from the roots of what must have been a truly enormous tree. To the right of this hall, just above twin pagodas, is the Ordination Terrace, a platform built of white marble and topped with a massive bronze statue of Shakyamuni Buddha seated on a lotus flower. Tranquil courtyards, where ornate stelae and well-kept gardens bask beneath a scholar tree and other ancient pines, add to the temple's beauty. Many modern devotees from Beijing visit the temple on weekends. Getting to Jietai and the nearby Tanzhe Temple is easy using public transportation. Take subway Line 1 to its westernmost station, Pingguoyuan. From there, take the No.931 public bus to either temple—it leaves every half hour and the ride takes about 70 minutes. A taxi from Pingguoyuan to Jietai Temple should be Y50 to Y60; the bus fare is Y6. ✉ *Mentougou County, Beijing* ☏ *010/6980–6611* 🎫 *Y45.*

★ **Tian Yi Mu** (**北京宦官文化陈列馆(田义幕)** *Tiányì mù*)
MUSEUM | Eunuchs have played a vital role throughout Chinese history, frequently holding great sway over the affairs of state. Their importance, often overlooked, is celebrated in the **Beijing Eunuch Culture Exhibition Hall** and the tomb of the most powerful eunuch of all, **Tian Yi** (1534–1605). Tian Yi was only nine when he was voluntarily castrated and sent into the service of the Ming emperor Jiajing. During the next 63 years of his life, he served three rulers and rose to one of the highest ranks in the land. By the time he died, there were more than 20,000 eunuchs in imperial service. Thanks to their access to private areas of the palace, they became invaluable as go-betweens for senior officials seeking gossip or the royal ear, and such was Tian Yi's influence. It's said that upon his death The Forbidden City fell silent for three days.

Though not as magnificent as the Thirteen Ming Tombs, the final resting place of Tian Yi befits a man of high social status. Of special note are the intricate stone carvings around the base of the central burial mound. The four smaller tombs on either side belong to other eunuchs who wished to pay tribute to Tian Yi by being buried in the same compound as him.

The small exhibition hall at the front of the tomb complex contains the world's only "eunuch museum" and offers some interesting background (albeit mostly in Mandarin), particularly on China's last eunuch, Sun Yaoting (1902–96). It's worth visiting, if only to see the rather gruesome mummified remains of one castrati that holds center stage—you can still make out the hairs on his chin. Another equally squirm-inducing sight is the eye-watering collection of castration equipment; keep a look out for the ancient Chinese character meaning "to castrate," which resembles two knives, one inverted, side by side. The hall and tomb are a five-minute walk from Fahai Temple; just ask people the way to Tian Yi Mu. ✉ *80 Moshikou Lu, Shijingshan District* ☏ *010/8872–4148* 🎫 *Y8.*

Yunju Temple

75 km (47 miles) southwest of Beijing.

Sights

Yunju Temple (**云居寺** *Yúnjū sì*)
RELIGIOUS SITE | To protect the Buddhist canon from destruction by Taoist emperors, the devout Tang-era monk Jing Wan carved Buddhist scriptures into stone slabs that he hid in sealed caves in the cliffs of a mountain. Jing Wan spent 30 years creating these tablets until his death in AD 637; his disciples continued his work for the next millennium into

The Eastern Qing Tombs are the most expansive burial grounds in China.

the 17th century, thereby compiling one of the most extensive Buddhist libraries in the world, a mind-boggling collection of 14,278 minutely carved Buddhist tablets. A small pagoda at the center of the temple complex commemorates the remarkable monk. Although the tablets were originally stored inside Shijing Mountain behind the temple, they're now housed in rooms built along the temple's southern perimeter.

Four central prayer halls, arranged along the hillside above the main gate, contain impressive Ming-era bronze Buddhas. The last in this row, the Dabei Hall, displays the spectacular *Thousand-Armed Avalokiteshvara.* This 13-foot-tall bronze sculpture—which actually has 24 arms and five heads and stands in a giant lotus flower—is believed to embody boundless compassion. A group of pagodas, led by the 98-foot-tall Northern Pagoda, is all that remains of the original Tang complex. These pagodas are remarkable for their Buddhist reliefs and ornamental patterns. Heavily damaged during the Japanese occupation and again by Maoist radicals in the 1960s, the temple complex remains under renovation.

Yunju Temple is 70 km (43 miles) southwest of central Beijing. By bus, take No. 917 from Tianqiao Long-distance Bus Station to Liangxiang Ximen, then change to Fangshan Bus Nos.12, 19, 31 to Yun Ju Si. ✉ *Off Fangshan Lu, Nanshangle Xiang, Fangshan County, Beijing* ☎ *010/6138–9612* 🎫 *Y40.*

Eastern Qing Tombs

125 km (78 miles) east of Beijing.

Modeled on the Thirteen Ming Tombs, the mausoleum complex at Zunhua, known as the Eastern Qing Tombs, replicate the Ming walkways, walled tomb complexes, and subterranean burial chambers. But they're even more extravagant in their scale and grandeur, and far less touristy.

These imposing ruins contain the remains of five emperors, 14 empresses, and 136 imperial concubines, all laid to rest in a broad valley chosen by Emperor Shunzhi (1638–61) while on a hunting expedition. By the Qing's collapse in 1911, the tomb complex covered some 18 square miles (46 square km) of farmland and forested hillside, making it the most expansive burial ground in all China.

The Eastern Qing Tombs are in much better repair than their older Ming counterparts—and considerably less crowded. Although several of the tomb complexes have undergone extensive renovation, none is overdone. Peeling paint, grassy courtyards, and numerous stone bridges and pathways convey a sense of the area's original grandeur. Often visitors are so few that you may feel as if you've stumbled upon an ancient ruin unknown beyond the valley's farming villages.

The tombs are a two- to three-hour drive from the capital and are surrounded by dramatic rural scenery, making this trip one of the best full-day excursions outside Beijing. Consider bringing a bedsheet, a bottle of wine, and boxed lunches, as the grounds are ideal for a picnic.

Sights

★ **Qingdongling** (清东陵 *Qīngdōnglíng*)
ARCHAEOLOGICAL SITE | The most elaborate of the Qing tombs was built for the infamous Empress Dowager Cixi (1835–1908). Known for her failure to halt Western-imperialist encroachment, Cixi once spent funds allotted to strengthen China's navy on a traditional stone boat for the lake at the Summer Palace. Her burial compound, reputed to have cost 72 tons of silver, is the most elaborate (if not the largest) at the Eastern Qing Tombs. Many of its stone carvings are considered significant because the phoenix, which symbolizes the female, is level with, or even above, the imperial (male) dragon—a feature ordered, no doubt, by the empress herself. A peripheral hall paneled in gold leaf displays some of the luxuries amassed by Cixi and her entourage, including embroidered gowns, jewelry, imported cigarettes, and even a coat for one of her dogs. In a bow to tourist kitsch, the compound's main hall contains a wax statue of Cixi sitting Buddha-like on a lotus petal flanked by a chambermaid and an eunuch. ✉ *Hebei province, Zunhua County, Malanguan* ☎ *0315/694–0888* 🎫 *Y152 (with rest of tombs).*

★ **Yuling** (清东陵 *Qīngdōnglíng*)
CEMETERY | Of the nine tombs open to the public, Yuling is not to be missed. This is the resting place of the Qing Dynasty's most powerful sovereign, Emperor Qianlong (1711–99), who ruled China for 59 years. Beyond the outer courtyards, Qianlong's burial chamber is accessible from inside Stela Hall, where an entry tunnel descends some 65 feet (20 meters) into the ground and ends at the first of three elaborately carved marble gates. Beyond, exquisite carvings of Buddhist images and sutras rendered in Tibetan adorn the tomb's walls and ceiling. Qianlong was laid to rest, along with his empress and two concubines, in the third and final marble vault, amid priceless offerings looted by warlords early in the 20th century. ✉ *Hebei province, Zunhua County, Malanguan* ☎ *0315/694–0888* 🎫 *Y152 (with rest of tombs).*

Chapter 4

BEIJING TO SHANGHAI

Updated by
Crystal Wilde

Sights ★★★★★ | Restaurants ★★★★☆ | Hotels ★★★★☆ | Shopping ★★★☆☆ | Nightlife ★★★☆☆

WELCOME TO BEIJING TO SHANGHAI

TOP REASONS TO GO

★ **Qingdao:** Hit the beach or explore the historic corners of the Bavarian-styled "Old City," with its mansions, churches, and burgeoning café culture.

★ **Huangshan:** Framed in spectral mist, Yellow Mountain's towering granite peaks have inspired artists and poets for centuries.

★ **Chengde:** Originally an imperial summer retreat, this town's magnificent temples, palaces, and deer-filled parks now attract weekenders hunting for culture.

★ **Suzhou:** Discover flower-filled classical gardens in a town still threaded with ancient waterways.

★ **Qufu:** Visit the birthplace of China's foremost philosopher and spiritual thinker, the "Great Sage" Confucius.

1 **Chengde.** The town's glory days were during the 18th century, after the Qing Emperor Kangxi had made it his summer retreat and hunting ground, establishing the country's largest royal garden and a bevy of opulent Buddhist temples on the surrounding hillsides.

2 **Beidaihe.** What used to be a quaint fishing village is now a popular, kitschy seaside retreat that gets wildly crowded during the summer months

3 **Shanhaiguan.** This is where the Great Wall meets the sea, and foreign visitors can experience a singularly Chinese take on the seaside vacation.

4 **Ji'nan.** The provincial capital is a great base for exploring Mount Tai, the most revered of all China's sacred mountains, and the walled town of Qufu, home of the philosopher Confucius.

5 **Qingdao.** China's most attractive coastal city and best known for its beaches, beer (sold as "Tsingtao" in the West), and Bavarian architecture.

6 **Nanjing.** Nanjing was the country's capital for six dynastic periods and was witness to turbulent historic events. The city abounds with mausoleums and memorials, ancient temples and palaces, and the region's finest cuisine.

7 **Yangzhou.** Renowned for its splendid gardens, Yangzhou's historic center is charming, laid-back, and small enough to see in a day, though you may want to linger.

8 **Suzhou.** Just an hour outside of Shanghai, Suzhou is known for its classical gardens and crisscrossing waterways. It's also a great jumping-off point for the famous water villages of Zhouzhuang, Tongli, and Luzhi.

9 **Huangshan.** Translated to Yellow Mountain, Huangshan is a sublime mountain range, where tens of thousands of steps lead to mist-covered vistas and soaring granite peaks.

10 **Tunxi.** This is the gateway to the Yellow mountain area.

11 **Shexian Country.** A nice day trip from Tunxi, this area is known for its historic buildings and natural beauty.

12 **Yixian Country.** Home to the UNESCO World Heritage site of Xidi Village.

INNER MONGOLIA
LIAONING
Chengde
1
BEIJING
GREAT WALL
3
Changping
Panshan
2
Shanhaiguan
BEIJING
Beidaihe
Tangshan
Tianjin
Baoding
TIANJIN
SHAANXI
Bohai Bay
Korea Bay
HEBEI
Hejian
Cangzhou
Shijiazhuang
Laizhou Bay
Yantai
Weihai
Dezhou
River
Laiyang
4
Ji'nan
Weifang
Handan
Zibo
Mt. Tai
Laoshan
Ti'an
SHANDONG
5
Qingdao
Yellow
Qufu
Yellow Sea
Jining
Linyi
Heze
Haizhou Bay
Lianyungang
Xuzhou
HENAN
Qingjiang
JIANGSU
0
100 mi
0
100 km
Bengbu
7
Yangzhou
Nanjing
Nantong
Zhenjiang
6
Hefei
8
Wuxi
Suzhou
Shanghai
Dabie Mountain
ANHUI
Tongli
Zhouzhuang
HUBEI
River
Wangpan Bay
Yangtzi
ZHEJIANG
Huangshan
12
11
9
10
JIANGXI

Tombs, temples, elegant gardens, and historic water towns are just the beginning of what this extraordinary region has to offer. This is where Confucius was born, where China's two great rivers and the Great Wall meet the sea, and where some of the country's most celebrated mountain landscapes have inspired pilgrimages for millennia.

Despite phenomenal development across Eastern China over the past decade, it's still possible to lose yourself in the canal-side walkways and idyllic gardens of Suzhou, the "Venice of the East," or pick a path through the cobbled streets of old Yangzhou. Several of China's 53 UNESCO World Heritage Sites dot this region, with Anhui's villages of Xidi and Hongcun and Shandong's Qufu, Confucius's ancestral birthplace, managing to retain most of their historic and artistic character. Buy Suzhou's famous silk from the owners of the silk-spinning worms, taste Tsingtao beer straight from the source in Qingdao, and sample the dim-sum delights of Huaiyang cuisine at its most authentic in Yangzhou.

Everyone from Emperor Qin to Chairman Mao has tackled the trail to the summit of Tai Shan, China's most sacred Taoist mountain. And they didn't have a cable car to help them. To the south, Huangshan's mysterious peaks, fringed with spindly pines and swathed in clouds, have inspired whole schools of Chinese painting.

Travel here has never been easier. Increasingly comfortable and internationally minded lodgings are springing up everywhere. Bullet trains have slashed journey times, whisking you from one destination to the next. Remember that the pedestrian in no way has the right of way in China, and take a business card with your hotel's address in Chinese to show a taxi when returning home after a long day's sightseeing.

MAJOR REGIONS

Stretching from Hebei, which is culturally and geographically Northern China, to the more refined province of Jiangsu, this region is accessible thanks to a well-developed tourism infrastructure. Hebei, Shanhaiguan, Jiangsu, and Anhui all have convenient air and rail links to the major transport hubs of Beijing and Shanghai. Wrapped around the nation's capital, Hebei's attractions are definitely worth a side trip. The Manchu summer retreat of **Chengde** puts on an almighty show of pomp and splendor, and **Beidaihe** and **Shanhaiguan** are Chinese-style beach resorts, with the Great Wall finally coming to an end at the ocean in Shanhaiguan. With its seventy active springes, **Ji'nan** is a good base for a pilgrimage to Mount Tai, the most revered of all China's sacred mountains. For the more earthly pleasures of sun, seafood, and suds, don't miss the seaside city of **Qingdao**, China's water sports (and drinking) capital. A witness to turbulent historic events, **Nanjing** abounds with mausoleums and memorials, ancient temples and palaces, and the region's finest cuisine. Nanjing was the country's capital for six dynastic periods. Nearby **Suzhou** and **Yangzhou** are renowned for their splendid gardens. It might be one of China's poorest provinces, but Anhui's wealth lies in its immaculately preserved villages, like the ones found in **Shexian Country**, and **Yixian Country**. **Tunxi** is a great base for visiting the sublime mountain scenery at **Huangshan**.

Planning

When to Go

Spring and summer is the best time to head to the coast at Qingdao and, farther north, Beidaihe and Shanhaiguan. Save the arduous ascents of Huangshan and Taishan for autumn, when the crowds have subsided and temperatures have dropped.

The eastern region of China is heavily populated, and sometimes it seems like everyone has taken to the road (or train or plane) at once. Avoid traveling during the Chinese New Year, which is based on the lunar calendar and falls between January and March. It's also good to avoid visits here during the busy, week-long National Day holiday at the start of October.

Getting Here and Around

With the exception of Chengde, every destination in this chapter is now connected by the China Highspeed Rail network, by far the most convenient and comfortable way to get around, though buses are very efficient, and you can usually buy same-day tickets. Airline tickets can be purchased close to the departure date and prices are fairly consistent, assuming you avoid traveling during a Chinese holiday, when prices can skyrocket.

Air Travel

In addition to the international airports in Beijing and Shanghai, domestic air hubs include Nanjing, Qingdao, and Shijiazhuang (the capital of Hebei Province). Unlike other areas of the country, distances between sights in this region aren't great. The main operators are Air China and China Eastern Airlines, though there are several regional carriers like Shandong Airlines and Hebei Airlines.

Bus Travel

With many thousands of destinations and departures, buses can be handy for short trips, especially to destinations outside the high-speed rail network (Nanjing to Yangzhou is a good example). Buses are usually in reasonable condition and have air-conditioning, assigned seating, and reliably punctual service. Remember to bring a pair of headphones, as you can usually expect a noisy kung-fu movie playing on the video monitor. Never patronize the army of touts who work at the main bus stations; always buy your tickets from the official counters or better yet, through your hotel.

Car Travel

Hiring a car and driver gives you the freedom to explore the region at your own leisure, but it can be costly. Expect prices of at least $150 a day if you book through an international hotel, and substantially more if you want an English-speaking guide.

Train Travel

China's excellent high-speed rail system has made Shandong and Jiangsu more accessible than ever before, with many trains whizzing along at over 300 kph (186 mph). Tickets can usually be purchased through your hotel (strongly recommended), online at 🌐 *www.ctrip.com* (after which they're couriered to your accommodation), or inside the station itself, although the lines are often long and vendors can be curt with non-Chinese speakers. Buy tickets at least 24 hours ahead (even more in advance during peak periods) of when you intend to travel. Passports are mandatory for buying tickets and boarding the train. If you miss your train, go to a ticket counter—they will usually put you on the next available service for a nominal fee. Note: only holders of Chinese ID cards can use the electronic ticket machines in stations.

Health and Safety

Take all prescription medicine with you. For minor ailments, such as headaches and stomachaches, Chinese pharmacies are widely available and stocked with both Chinese and Western medicine. Antibiotics can be purchased easily and cheaply over the counter. Carry waterless hand sanitizer and toilet paper. Safe bottled water is widely available.

Dining

Every locality has its own specialties—wild game in Hebei, braised chicken in Shandong, duck cooked myriad ways in Jiangsu. Try Qingdao's famous chili-fried clams, or Suzhou's sweet-and-sour river fish. Jiangsu cuisine, called Huaiyang, is considered one of China's four great cooking styles, and is light, fresh, and sweet (though not as sweet as in Shanghai). As you travel inland to Anhui, the food is famously salty, relying heavily on preserved ham and soy sauce to enhance flavors. Anhui chefs make good use of mountain-grown mushrooms and bamboo shoots. Vegetarian options, often available in or near Buddhist temples, showcase chefs who manipulate tofu, wheat gluten, and vegetables to create "mock" meat that even carnivores will appreciate.

What It Costs in Yuan

	$	$$	$$$	$$$$
RESTAURANTS	under Y50	Y50–Y99	Y100–Y165	over Y165

Lodging

Hotels in this region are improving every year, and most major cities now have a range of international brands. Don't expect to find luxury in smaller cities, where mid-range yet still comfortable lodgings are more the norm. English-speaking staff can be thin on the ground at cheaper Chinese-run hotels. Most places these days accept credit cards, and you'll get better rates if you book in advance. Chinese hotels are easy to book, often without prepaying, through the English-language Chinese website 🌐 *www.ctrip.com*. Although other international hotel booking websites list China properties, bookings

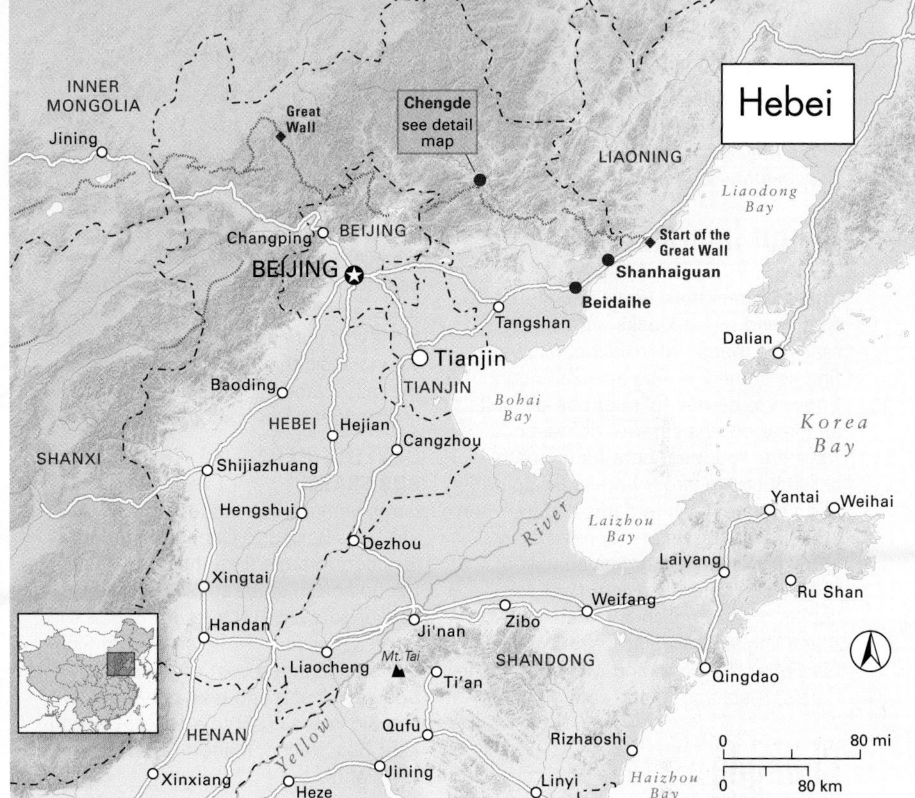

often disappear when made through anything other than Ctrip. *Hotel reviews have been shortened. For full information, visit Fodors.com.*

What It Costs in Yuan

$	$$	$$$	$$$$
HOTELS			
under Y1,100	Y1,100–Y1,399	Y1,400–Y1,800	over Y1,800

Tours

Group tours are always an option, but often feature unwelcome shopping stops, leaving less time to enjoy the sights. Do your research, ask questions, and if the package price seems too high or low, be skeptical. The best source of information is on Fodor's forums (🌐 *www.fodors.com*), where many travelers share the good, the bad, and the ugly, like pressured tipping, frequent shopping stops, and low-quality food.

Beijing Discovery Tours
PERSONAL GUIDES | This American-Chinese company can arrange private tours of Beijing, the surrounding sights, and beyond. The company is extremely reliable and thorough. ☎ *800/306–1264 in U.S., 130/1112–0229 in China* 🌐 *www.beijingdiscoverytours.com.*

★ **Bespoke Travel Company**
SPECIAL-INTEREST | Run by a friendly English woman who has spent most of her adult life in China, this energetic and knowledgeable tour company can arrange customized excursions to anywhere in China but specializes in trips to the east coast. It also offers interesting

"signature experiences" in Beijing and Shanghai. ✉ *07A110, 7th fl., 10 Jintong Xi Lu, Beijing* ☎ *151/0167–9082* 🌐 *www.bespoketravelcompany.com.*

Visitor Information

In the bigger cities, you'll find storefronts and street kiosks with signs reading "Tourist Information." However, finding someone who speaks enough English to be helpful might be difficult, as these booths cater to domestic travelers. Your best bets for in-depth assistance are larger hotels. Be polite and persistent. Write dates clearly when inquiring about tickets, speak slowly, and inspect any tickets given to you thoroughly before leaving. Look for copies of the English-language *Redstar* (Qingdao), *Map Magazine* or *The Nanjinger* (Nanjing), and *More Suzhou* in hotels, restaurants, and coffee shops.

Chengde

5 hrs (230 km [140 miles]) by train northeast of Beijing; 3 hrs by bus.

Recent development has not been particularly kind to Chengde, but the sights here are well tended, and in fine weather you can still glimpse the natural beauty of the river valley that so captivated Emperor Kangxi on a hunting trip in the late 1600s. With the Wulie River gurgling through and the Yanshan Mountains providing an impressive backdrop, Chengde was deemed an ideal spot for a retreat where the emperor could escape the summertime heat of the capital and indulge in hunting and fishing. Later Chengde would serve a crucial diplomatic function, its grand temples erected in honorific tribute to host visiting religious and political leaders of China's border ethnicities.

Today it is a UNESCO World Heritage Site, awarded collectively to the magnificent Mountain Resort and the Eight Outer Monasteries. Although children enjoy romping through the imperial gardens, there's little else to entertain younger visitors. It's generally considered best to visit in summer or early autumn to escape the heat of cities like Beijing, but a visit during the off-season is a good way to avoid the tourist hordes, and the rather steep admission prices are reduced after the first of November.

GETTING HERE AND AROUND

BUS TRAVEL

Long-distance bus is the fastest way to get from Beijing to Chengde, but rather less comfortable than the train, since the bus often stops to pick up extra passengers along the route. Two or three services an hour leave from Sihui bus station in the east of the city (on Subway Line 1) and take between 2½ and 3½ hours (Y85) to arrive at Chengde East Bus Station, a short taxi ride from the sights.

TRAIN TRAVEL

Most travelers arrive on the direct train from Beijing, of which there are several a day. No trains run between Chengde and Beidaihe or Shanhaiguan.

TRAIN CONTACT Chengde Train Station ✉ *Chezhan Lu.*

TAXI TRAVEL

Chengde is a small city, so you shouldn't have to pay more than Y20 to get from its center out to the temples.

TIMING

Most of the main attractions are bunched to the north and east of the Mountain Resort, so one or two full days should be enough time to see the sights. That said, the Mountain Resort is huge, and could easily take up a full day by itself. If you want to do any hiking in the surrounding countryside, plan on three full days.

Did You Know?

The 72 scenic spots that you'll see at Chengde's Mountain Resort are copies of famous Chinese gardens, grassy Mongolian plains, and forested mountains and valleys. Famous structures have also been replicated: the main building on Green Lotus Island, the Tower of Mist and Rain, is a copy of a tower in Nanhu Lake at Jiaxing in Zhejiang Province.

Sights

Don't waste your energy wandering around the city itself. The massive scale of the Mountain Resort, twice as large as Beijing's Summer Palace, means you will be doing plenty of walking. Bus route 6 links the Mountain Resort with the outer temples.

★ **Mountain Resort** (避暑山庄 *Bìshǔ shānzhuāng*)
MOUNTAIN—SIGHT | Charmed by Chengde's dramatic setting, pleasant climate, and plentiful game, Emperor Kangxi ordered construction of the first palaces of the Mountain Resort in 1703. Within a decade, this once sleepy settlement boasted dozens of ornate temples, pagodas, and walled grasslands spread out across 1,500 acres. By the end of the 18th century nearly 100 imperial structures had been built, with Chengde becoming the epicenter of Chinese political and cultural life whenever the emperor and his entourage decamped here from Beijing.

The Mountain Resort and its surrounding temples were more than just an Imperial retreat, however. Besides luxurious quarters for the emperor and his court, great palaces and temples were constructed to house visiting dignitaries—particularly China's border groups like the Mongols and Tibetans—and to woo them with the might and wealth of the Qing empire. Not forgetting, of course, that the Qing also came from beyond the Great Wall as the pastoral Manchu. The location was useful, as Chengde lay far enough away from Beijing to host talks with border groups who wouldn't otherwise set foot in the capital. From the interconnected palaces, each built in different architectural styles, to the replicas of famous temples representing different Chinese religions and ethnic groups, everything about the resort was designed to reflect China's diversity. In retrospect, it was as much a Qing statement of intent as it was a holiday home.

Today, the palace and its walled-off landscape of lakes, grasslands, hills, and forests dominates the center of Chengde. The steep hills in the northern half of the park, crowned by stone walls that resemble the Great Wall, afford beautiful panoramas, as does a slog up the nine-tiered pagoda in the center. Even during peak season (April to October) it rarely feels crowded. ✉ *Center of town* ☎ *0314/202–9771* 🎫 *Apr.–Oct., Y120; Nov.–Mar., Y90.*

Pule Temple (普乐寺 *Pǔ lè sì*)
RELIGIOUS SITE | The conical-roofed centerpiece of this serene hillside temple, the Pavilion of the Brilliance of the Rising Sun (*Xuguangge*), will be instantly recognizable if you've visited Beijing's Temple of Heaven. Built to host visiting Kazak, Uygher, and Kyrger dignitaries, as well as to commemorate certain Mongol tribes, Pule Temple was laid out to resemble a mandala of Tibetan Buddhism. From the south wall of the temple, it's a peaceful 40-minute walk up the hillside to Sledgehammer Rock. The Y50 ticket includes admission to Sledgehammer Rock and the lovely Anyuan Temple down the hill. ✉ *East of Mountain Resort* 🎫 *Y50.*

Puning Temple (普宁寺 *Pǔníng Sì*)
RELIGIOUS SITE | Located on the western banks of the Wulie River, this temple was built in 1755 to commemorate Emperor Qianlong's triumphant conquest of the warring Dzungar people from Xinjiang. Intended to mark a new period of peace, it was modeled after the Samye Monastery, a sacred Lamaist site in Tibet. Also known as "Big Buddha Temple," its main attraction is an awe-inspiring 72-foot-tall statue of Guanyin, a Buddhist deity of compassion. The statue is made from five types of wood, including pine, cypress, elm, and fir. ✉ *1 Puning Si Lu* ☎ *0314/205–8209* 🎫 *Apr.–Oct., Y80; Nov.–Mar., Y60.*

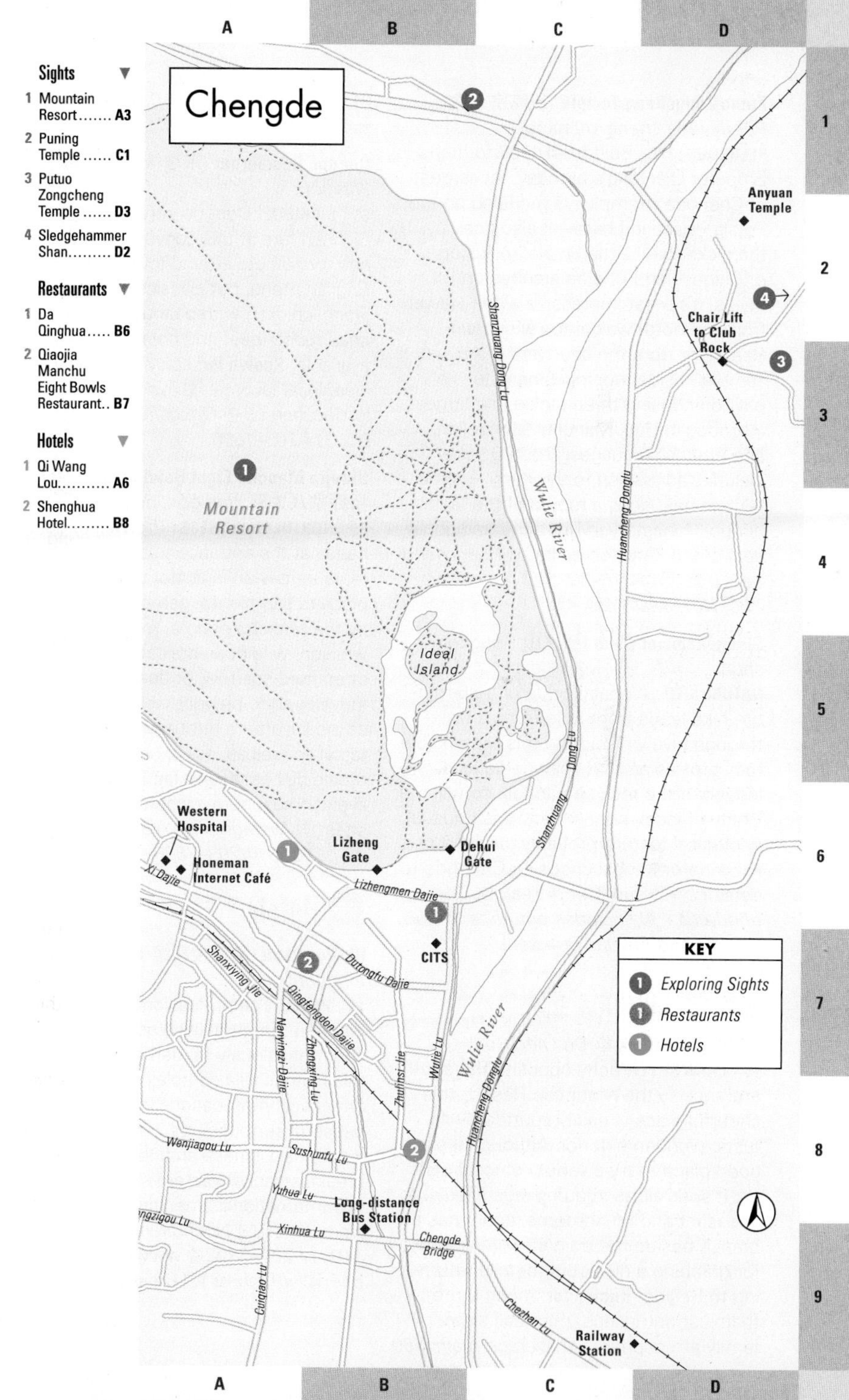

Chengde
Sights
1 Mountain Resort....... A3
2 Puning Temple...... C1
3 Putuo Zongcheng Temple...... D3
4 Sledgehammer Shan......... D2
Restaurants
1 Da Qinghua..... B6
2 Qiaojia Manchu Eight Bowls Restaurant.. B7
Hotels
1 Qi Wang Lou........... A6
2 Shenghua Hotel......... B8
A
B
C
D
1
2
3
4
5
6
7
8
9
Anyuan Temple
Chair Lift to Club Rock
Shanzhuang Dong Lu
Huancheng Donglu
Wulie River
Mountain Resort
Ideal Island
Western Hospital
Honeman Internet Café
Xi Dajie
Lizheng Gate
Dehui Gate
Lizhengmen Dajie
CITS
Shanxiying Jie
Dutongfu Dajie
Qingfengdon Dajie
Nanyingzi Dajie
Zhongxing Lu
Zhuhinsi Jie
Wulie Lu
Wenjiagou Lu
Sushunfu Lu
Yuhua Lu
Long-distance Bus Station
Xinhua Lu
Chengde Bridge
Cuiqiao Lu
Chezhan Lu
Railway Station
KEY
Exploring Sights
Restaurants
Hotels

Putuo Zongcheng Temple (普陀宗乘之庙 *Pǔtuó zōng chéng zhī miào*)
RELIGIOUS SITE | Built from 1767 to mark Emperor Qianlong's birthday, the largest of Chengde's temples is modeled on the Potala Palace in Lhasa—it also goes by the nickname "Little Potala." A fusion of Chinese and Tibetan architectural styles, it's most impressive when viewed from the north wall of the Mountain Resort, or from the courtyard of Anyuan Temple. Inside the imposing gate is a pavilion housing three stelae, the largest inscribed in Han, Manchu, Mongolian, and Tibetan languages. The Y80 ticket includes admission to the Xumi Fushou Temple next door, a replica of the Tashilhunpo Monastery in Tibet, the traditional seat of the Panchen Lama. ✉ *Huanchengbei Lu* ☎ *0314/216–3072* 🎫 *Apr.–Oct., Y80; Nov.–Mar., Y60.*

Sledgehammer Shan (棒槌山 *Bàngchuí shān*)
NATURE SITE | A chairlift ride or a 35-minute hike leads from Pule Temple up through lovely hillside to this remarkable rock protrusion that spawned a local legend: if the rock should fall, so will the virility of local men. In fact, this unusual geological feature probably played a part in Emperor Kangxi choosing Chengde to establish his summer retreat. ✉ *Chengde* 🎫 *Y50, includes entrance to Pule Temple and Anyuan Temple.*

Restaurants

Da Qinghua (大清华 *Dà Qīng Huā*)
$$ | **CHINESE** | Directly opposite the south entrance to the Mountain Resort, this cheerful place is easily spotted by its rustic wooden exterior. Although it's a good place to try a variety of local dishes, it specializes in dumplings filled with pheasant and mushrooms, and it has a branch beside the train station—perfect for grabbing a quick bite before returning to Beijing. **Known for:** much more than just dumplings; meatball soup; family atmosphere. 💲 *Average main: Y80* ✉ *Lizhengmen Dajie* ☎ *0314/2036–222* 💳 *No credit cards.*

Dongpo Restaurant (东坡饭店 *Dōngpō Fàndiàn*)
$$ | **SICHUAN** | Dongpo serves hearty Sichuan fare at this convenient branch and two others around town. There's no English menu, but classics like *gongbao jiding* (chicken with peanuts) and *niurou chao tudou* (beef and potatoes) are available. **Known for:** spicy food; brisk service; local favorite. 💲 *Average main: Y80* ✉ *Chezhan Lu* ✣ *Opposite train station* ☎ *0314/208–1886.*

Qiaojia Manchu Eight Bowls Restaurant (金桥乔家八大碗 *Jīnqiáo qiáo jiā bādà wǎn*)
$$ | **NORTHERN CHINESE** | The wall of deer heads at the entrance to this popular restaurant is an indicator that it's a good place to sample the game dishes beloved by the Manchu people. You can try venison, wild boar, braised camel hump, deep-fried sparrow, or deer-blood curd (developed to prevent wasting the blood of the kill after a hunt and surprisingly tasty) as well as less exotic meat or vegetable dishes. **Known for:** freaky feasts; lively atmosphere; close to mountain sites. 💲 *Average main: Y80* ✉ *1 Liushuigou Lu* ☎ *0314/203–7888.*

Hotels

Qi Wang Lou (绮望楼宾馆 *Qǐ wànglóu bīnguǎn*)
$$ | **HOTEL** | The professional service, wooden furniture–filled guest rooms, and meticulously tended gardens make this historic villa complex one of the finest accommodations in town. **Pros:** peaceful surroundings; central location; traditional Chinese architecture. **Cons:** breakfast lacks Western staples; no bar; few international amenities. 💲 *Rooms from: Y1100* ✉ *1 Bei Bifengmen Dong Lu* ☎ *0314/202–7898* 🌐 *www.qiwanglou.com* 🛏 *49 rooms* 🍽 *Breakfast.*

Shenghua Hotel (盛华大酒店 *shènghuá dàjiǔdiàn*)

$ | **HOTEL** | The carpets at the Shenghua could do with a scrub, but a few touches like having an on-site bilingual tour operator and guest rooms where teddy bears decorate the beds and bathrooms are equipped with tubs distinguish this average but well-run hotel from its peers. **Pros:** tasty restaurant; reliable service; near train station. **Cons:** needs a refurb; a bit far from the main sights; most staffers don't speak English. *Rooms from: Y800 ✉ 22 Wulie Lu ☎ 0314/227–1020 🌐 www.shenghuahotel.com 111 rooms 🍽 Breakfast.*

Beidaihe

2 hrs (260 km [160 miles]) by express train east of Beijing; 3 hrs (395 km [245 miles]) by train southwest of Shenyang; 1 hr (35 km [22 miles]) by minibus southwest of Shanhaiguan.

English railway engineers came across this small fishing village in the 1890s. Not long after, wealthy Chinese and foreign diplomats were visiting in droves. After Mao Zedong came to power, the new rulers developed a taste for sea air. Today the seaside retreat has an interesting mix of beach kitsch and political posturing, with Communist party members past and present owning villas here. Beidaihe is terrifyingly crowded during the summer and practically empty the rest of the year.

GETTING HERE AND AROUND

Most visitors come directly from Beijing, and the train is the most convenient option. The train station in Beidaihe is about a 15-minute taxi ride to the beachfront.

AIR TRAVEL

Qinhuangdao Beidaihe Airport is in Longjiadian, 34 km (23 milies) from Beidaihe. Flights run regularly from major Chinese cities, including Beijing and Shanghai.

AIR CONTACT Qinhuangdao Beidaihe Airport (秦皇岛北戴河机场 *Qínhuángdǎo běidàihé jīchǎng*) *✉ 62 Ji Chang Gao Su, Qinhuangdao.*

BUS TRAVEL

An excellent minibus service links Beidaihe, Qinhuangdao, and Shanhaiguan. Buses leave every 30 minutes. The station in Beidaihe is at the intersection of Heishi Lu and Haining Lu. Buy tickets on the bus.

BUS CONTACT Beidaihe Bus Station *✉ Beining Lu and Haining Lu.*

TRAIN TRAVEL

Trains traveling up the coast from Beijing all pass through Beidaihe, Shanhaiguan, and Qinhuangdao. Be sure to book the faster D or G class trains.

TRAIN CONTACT Beidaihe Train Station *✉ Zhannan Da Jie.*

TIMING

A half day is sufficient to see what the village has to offer, but if the weather allows, it can be a great place to bicycle ride and linger for a bit longer. Many visitors like to combine a trip here with a visit to the Great Wall at Shanhaiguan.

Sights

Lianfeng Shan Park (联峰山公园 *Liáfēngshān gōngyuán*)

CITY PARK | North of Middle Beach you'll find this lovely park, where quiet paths through a pine forest lead to the **Guanyin Temple** (Guānyīn sì). Look for the aviary, known as the Birds Singing Forest. There are also good views of the sea from the top of Lianfeng Hill. *✉ Lianfeng Lu and Jianqui Lu ☎ 0335/404–1591 Y30.*

Restaurants

★ **Bai Wei Jiaozi Cheng** (百味饺子城 *Bǎiwèi jiǎozǐ chéng*)

$$ | **CHINESE** | Set in the Qinhuangdao Sea View Hotel, this immensely popular restaurant is adorned with red lanterns

The rugged landscape around Shanhaiguan

and gold dragons. Although known for its huge array of truly juicy dumplings, it serves other Chinese specialties as well. **Known for:** fish dumplings; brisk service; huge menu. $ *Average main: Y80* ✉ *222 Gangcheng Main St., Qinhuangdao* ☎ *No phone.*

Qishilin Restaurant (起士林餐厅 *Qǐshìlín cāntīng*)
$$$ | **SEAFOOD** | On the grounds of the Kiessling Beidaihe Hotel, this popular restaurant, originally opened by Austrians, mixes a few Western dishes in with the menu's predominately Chinese fare. Its European-style café-bakery, on the main street, does a brisk business in freshly baked walnut cakes. **Known for:** sea-cucumber specialties; tasty beef stew; open year-round (unusual in Beidaihe). $ *Average main: Y130* ✉ *Kiessling Beidaihe Hotel, 95 Dongjing Lu* ☎ *0335/468–0000* 🌐 *www.qishilin.com.*

Hotels

Jinshan Hotel (金山大酒店 *Jīnshān dàjiǔdiàn*)
$ | **HOTEL** | On a quiet stretch of sand, this clean, comfortable hotel is made up of five two-story buildings linked by tree-lined paths. **Pros:** on the beach; clean rooms; friendly staff. **Cons:** some rooms are worn; lack of English; old-fashioned decor. $ *Rooms from: Y400* ✉ *4 Dongsan Lu* ☎ *0335/426–0666* 🌐 *jinshanhotelbeidaihe.ximantu.com* ⏱ *Closed Nov.–Mar.* *267 rooms* *No meals.*

Qinhuangdao Sea View Hotel (秦皇岛海景酒店 *Qínhuángdǎo hǎijǐng jiǔdiàn*)
$$$ | **HOTEL** | **FAMILY** | Nicer than many hotels in Beidaihe or Shanhaiguan (but a good 15 minutes from either by cab), this property has pleasant rooms overlooking a sandy beach and the Bohai Sea; other bonuses include a nice indoor pool and, more unusually, a staff that speaks a decent level of English. **Pros:** high standard of service; great beach access; lively Chinese vibe. **Cons:**

a cab ride from Beidaihe; uninspiring surrounding area; relatively expensive. $ *Rooms from: Y1560* ✉ *25 Donggang Lu, Qinhuangdao* ☎ *0335/343–0888* *274 rooms* *No meals.*

Sheraton Qinhuangdao Beidaihe Hotel (**秦皇岛北戴河华贸喜来登酒店** *Qínhuángdǎo běidàihé huá mào xǐláidēng jiǔdiàn*) **$$** | **HOTEL** | Although arguably not yet up to international standards in terms of service, the Sheraton Qinhuangdao Beidaihe is the first trusted luxury hotel brand in town. **Pros:** good breakfast; fast Wi-Fi; nice gym and pool. **Cons:** service needs work; lack of local flavor; relatively expensive. $ *Rooms from: Y1290* ✉ *16 Binhai Ave.* ☎ *335/428–1111* 🌐 *sheraton.marriott.com* *No meals.*

Shanhaiguan

2½ hrs (280 km [174 miles]) by train east of Beijing; 1 hr (35 km [22 miles]) by minibus northeast of Beidaihe; 2½ hrs (360 km [223 miles]) southwest of Shenyang.

On the northern tip of the Bohai Coast, Shanhaiguan is the end of the road for the Great Wall. After 8,850 km (5,500 miles), the massive structure plunges into the sea. During the Ming Dynasty, Shanhaiguan was fortified to prevent hordes of mounted Manchurian warriors from pushing to the south. Now local tourists swarm the town during the summer. An impressive wall still surrounds what was the Old Town, sadly razed in 2007 and rebuilt as a spiritless faux-historic area.

GETTING HERE AND AROUND

Shanhaiguan-bound express trains depart from Beijing several times daily, but it's also possible to take a train to Qinhuangdao and catch a taxi for the 20-minute drive to Shanhaiguan.

AIR TRAVEL

Regular flights run to Qinhuangdao Beidaihe Airport.

BUS TRAVEL

A minibus service runs from Beidaihe to Shanhaiguan, with departures every 30 minutes.

BUS CONTACT Shanhaiguan Bus Station ✉ *Nanguan Dajie, west side of railway station.*

TAXI TRAVEL

The half-hour taxi ride between Beidaihe and Shanhaiguan costs about Y80.

TRAIN TRAVEL

Shanhaiguan has limited train service; it might be necessary to take a train to Qinhuangdao and transfer to a bus or taxi to Shanhaiguan.

TRAIN CONTACT Shanhaiguan Train Station ✉ *Junction of Zhanqian Lu and Dongshuiguan St.*

TIMING

Shanhaiguan has enough to keep you occupied for one day, perhaps two if you plan on doing some serious Great Wall hiking. The town comes alive in the summer, but by late October many restaurants and other visitor facilities shut down for the season. The First Gate Under Heaven and Great Wall sections are open year-round, however.

Sights

First Gate Under Heaven (**天下第一关** *Tīanxià dìyīguān*)
BUILDING | The first heavy fortification along the Great Wall as it runs inland from the ocean, this mighty four-sided citadel guards the strategic Shanhai pass ("Shanhaiguan" in Chinese), around which the original town grew. Patrolling the battlements you can glimpse the Great Wall snaking up the sides of nearby mountains and grasp just how intimidating a barrier this must have presented to potential invaders. Not that it worked—the Manchus overran it in 1644, ultimately bringing down the Ming Dynasty. ✉ *Diyiguan Lu* ☎ *0335/505–1106* *Y50, includes admission to Great Wall Museum.*

Great Wall Museum (长城博物馆 *Cháng-chéng bówùguǎn*)
MUSEUM | Housed in a Qing Dynasty–style building past the First Gate Under Heaven, the Great Wall Museum has a diverting collection of historic photographs and cases full of military artifacts, including the fierce-looking weaponry used by attackers and defenders. There are some English captions. ✉ *South of First Gate Under Heaven, Diyiguan Lu* ☎ *0335/515–1314* 🎫 *Y50, includes admission to First Gate Under Heaven.*

Jiaoshan Great Wall (角山长城 *Jiāoshān chángchéng*)
BUILDING | One way to leave behind the crowds at the First Gate Under Heaven is to scale the wall as it climbs Jiao Mountain, about 3 km (2 miles) from the city. The first section has been restored and fitted with handrails and ladders up the sides of the watchtowers, but you can keep climbing until you reach a more wild, authentic stretch. After that you can take a path through trees that leads to the Qixian Monastery, or continue to the top for stunning if precarious views of the mountains and lakes beyond. A chairlift operates in high season. Jiaoshan is a 10-minute taxi ride from Shanhaiguan. ✉ *Jiaoshan Lu* ☎ *No phone* 🎫 *Y30.*

Jiumenkou Great Wall (九门口长城 *Jiǔménkǒu chángchéng*)
ARCHAEOLOGICAL SITE | Further from town than the Jiaoshan Great Wall, Jiumenkou is notable as the only section of the Great Wall to ford a river. Clamber up the battlements for dramatic views over the countryside. Jiumenkou is about 15 km (9 miles) north of Shanhaiguan; ask your taxi driver to wait for you for the return trip (a total of about Y120). ✉ *Zhijiu Xian* 🎫 *Y30.*

Mengjiangnu Miao (孟姜女庙 *Mèngjiāng-nǚ miào*)
MEMORIAL | About 8 km (5 miles) or 10 minutes in a taxi up the coast from Old Dragon Head is this shrine commemorating a local legend. As the story goes, a woman's husband died while building the Great Wall. She wept as she searched for his body, and in sympathy the wall split open before her, revealing the bones of her husband and others buried within. Overcome with grief, she threw herself into the sea. ✉ *Mengjiangnu Lu* ☎ *No phone* 🎫 *Y30.*

Old Dragon Head (老龙头 *Lǎolóngtóu*)
BUILDING | Legend has it that the Great Wall once extended into the Bohai Sea, ending with a giant carved dragon's head. Although the structure you see today was rebuilt in the 1980s, witnessing the waves smash against the massive base is a stirring sight. The admission price gets you into several rebuilt Ming Dynasty naval barracks, but you can just skip it altogether and head directly to the beach for the best photo ops. ✉ *1 Laolongtou Lu* ☎ *0335/515–2996* 🎫 *Y50.*

Restaurants

Wang Yang Lou (望洋楼饭店 *Wàngyánglóu fàndiàn*)
$$ | SEAFOOD | One of the town's most upmarket options, Wang Yang Lou serves tasty local seafood and an array of family-style Chinese dishes in a large though somewhat characterless dining room. There's no menu—order at the open kitchen to the left of the entrance by pointing at things swimming in the tanks, or at the displayed photos of dishes themselves. **Known for:** hosting big noisy families; large portions; point-and-pick fish tanks. $ *Average main: Y70* ✉ *51 Nanhai Xi Lu* ☎ *0335/513–4666* 💳 *No credit cards.*

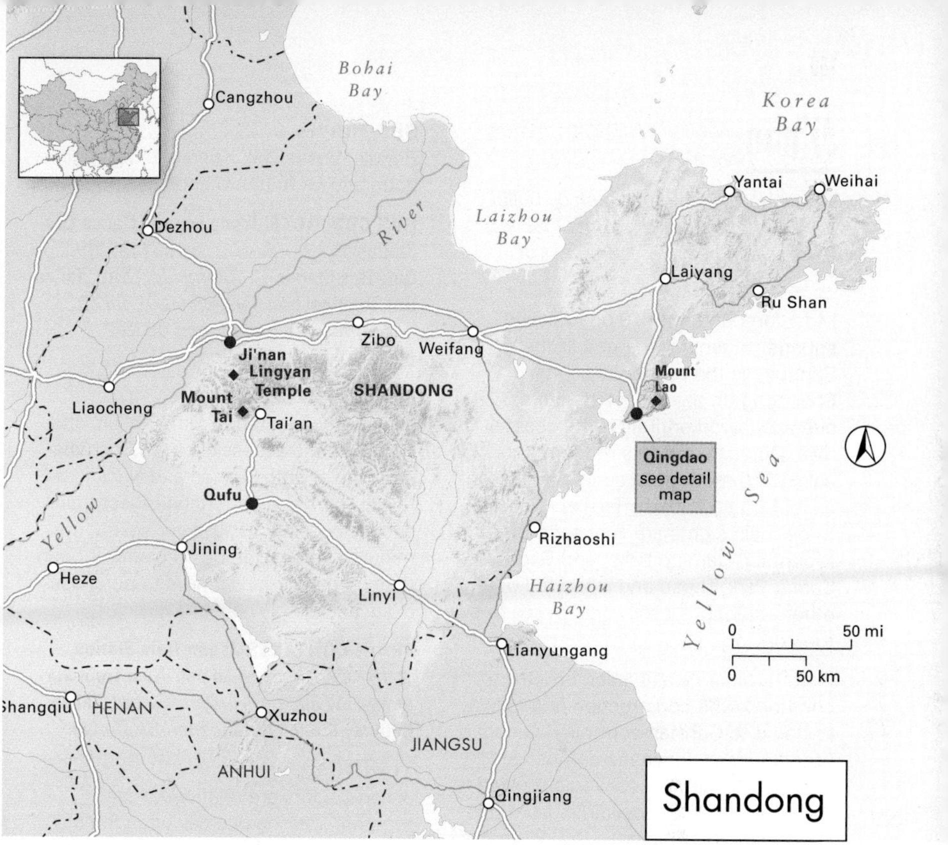

Hotels

Shanhai Holiday Hotel (山海假日酒店 *shānhǎi jiàrì jiǔdiàn*)
$ | HOTEL | One of the few lodgings inside the walls of the recently rebuilt "ancient city," this Qing Dynasty–style complex offers simply furnished rooms set around a series of courtyards. **Pros:** close to the First Gate Under Heaven; lots of local color; pretty complex. **Cons:** the "ancient city" is dead in the evenings; rooms are quite small; amenities are a little dated. *Rooms from: Y560* *6 Beimadao, beside the west gate* *0335/535–2800* *277 rooms* *Breakfast.*

Wanghai Vacational Village (望海度假 村 *wànghǎi dùjiàcūn*)
$ | HOTEL | Choose between simply furnished rooms or grandly restored villas at this resort hotel, a short march from Old Dragon Head and centered on a seafood restaurant in a greenhouse filled with tropical flora. **Pros:** lovely restaurant; on the beach; near the Great Wall. **Cons:** outside of town; furnishings a little dated; limited English. *Rooms from: Y680* *1 Wanghai Lu* *0335/535–0777* *44 rooms* *No meals.*

Ji'nan

1½ hrs (500 km [220 miles]) by bullet train south of Beijing; 2½ hrs (395 km [245 miles]) by bullet train west of Qingdao.

Most famous for its 70 or so active springs, Ji'nan, nicknamed "City of Springs," is the provincial capital of Shandong. In the tourist stakes it is overshadowed entirely by its coastal rival, Qingdao, but this modern and easygoing metropolis can be a pleasant base if visiting nearby Taishan. Ji'nan's three main sights are Thousand Buddha Mountain, Daming Lake, and Baotu Spring Park. These and a handful of other attractions easily occupy visitors for a day or so.

In 1901, Ji'nan was hauled into the 20th century by the construction of a railway linking it to German-controlled Qingdao. European and Japanese companies found Ji'nan to be a convenient place to do business. A few buildings from this concession era remain in the downtown area, although they are increasingly overshadowed by new shopping centers and hotels.

GETTING HERE AND AROUND

Far and away the best way to get here from Beijing is to catch one of the many daily bullet trains, which stop at Ji'nan Station or the newer Ji'nan West Station. The trip takes between 1½ and 2 hours.

AIR TRAVEL

Regular flights link Ji'nan Yaoqiang Airport with Beijing, Shanghai, Hong Kong, and other major Chinese cities. The airport is 40 km (25 miles) northeast of downtown Ji'nan. The journey takes 45 minutes in a taxi and costs around Y120.

AIR CONTACT Ji'nan Yaoqiang International Airport ✉ *1 Jichang Lu, Yaoqiang* ☎ *0531/96888* 🌐 *jnairport.com.*

BUS TRAVEL

Regular buses link Ji'nan with Tai'an (one hour) and Qufu (three hours).

BUS CONTACTS Ji'nan Long-Distance Bus Station ✉ *131 Jiluo Lu* ☎ *0531/96369.* **Qufu Bus Station** ✉ *Yulong Lu, Qufu.* **Tai'an Bus Terminal** ✉ *1 Taishan Dajie, Tai'an* ✣ *South of train station* ☎ *0538/218–8777* 🌐 *www.taqczz.com.*

TRAIN TRAVEL

Ji'nan is connected to Qufu, Tai'an, and Qingdao, and accessible from Shanghai, stopping at both Suzhou and Nanjing on route. There is no shortage of fast trains, and it's possible to buy your tickets mere minutes before getting on board, though during busy periods it pays to purchase in advance.

TRAIN CONTACTS Ji'nan Train Station ✉ *167 Chezhan Jie.* **Ji'nan West Train Station** ✉ *Weihai Lu, Huayin District.* **Tai'an Railway Station** ✉ *Lingshan St., Tai'an.*

TIMING

Ji'nan's sights are relatively close together, making one day enough time to comfortably visit them as well as walk around the city.

Sights

Baotu Spring Park (趵突泉 *Bàotūquán*)
HOT SPRINGS | Qing Dynasty Emperor Qianlong proclaimed this the finest of Ji'nan's many natural springs gurgling north from the foothills of Mount Tai. The spring is most active after the summer rains, when crowds gather under pavilions to watch it frothing and gushing. The pure water is said to be ideal for making tea; try it out at the Wangheting Teahouse, just east of the spring. A small museum in the park recounts the life of Jinan's most prized poetess Li Qingzhao, who lived near here in the 11th century. ✉ *91 Luoyuan* 🎫 *Y40.*

Burning incense at the Thousand Buddha Mountain

Daming Lake (大明湖 *Dàmíng hú*)
BODY OF WATER | **FAMILY** | Fed by artesian springs and garlanded by vivid banks of willows, Daming Lake has been inspiring Chinese poets and writers for 1,500 years. Surrounded by temples, pavilions, and leafy walkways, it's a pleasant spot for a stroll. There's a teahouse on top of the 50-meter tall pagoda on the island in the east of the lake. Climb up for pleasant views of Thousand Buddha Hill on clear days. ✉ *Daming Hu Lu* 🎫 *Free.*

Sacred Heart Cathedral (洪家楼耶稣圣心主教座堂 *Jīngsìlù jiàotáng*)
RELIGIOUS SITE | An interesting legacy of the German influence in Shandong is a handful of concession-era churches, this Gothic cathedral being the most impressive. Constructed around 1901 and resembling the Notre Dame in Paris, it can hold 800 worshippers. ✉ *1 Hongluo Lu* ✣ *Opposite entrance to old school of Shandong University.*

Thousand Buddha Mountain (千佛山 *Qiānfóshān*)
MOUNTAIN—SIGHT | **FAMILY** | On the southern edge of the city is Thousand Buddha Mountain, which gets its name from the multitude of Buddha images chiseled into the lofty cliffs since the early Sui Dynasty. It is still the focus of religious festivals, although many of the original statues have been lost to history, replaced by modern reconstructions. Getting to the top of the hill requires a 30-minute walk or a cable car ride (Y25 round-trip). Either way you'll be rewarded with a good view of Ji'nan—air quality permitting. For kids, there's an excellent slide to whiz back down to the bottom. ✉ *18 Jingshiyi Lu* ☎ *No phone* 🎫 *Y30.*

Restaurants

Foshan Yuan (佛山院素食店 *Fóshānyuàn sùshídiàn*)
$$ | **VEGETARIAN** | This comfy vegetarian restaurant specializes in dishes that look and taste remarkably like meat or fish. If sea cucumbers made from textured soy protein sounds like a gastronomic step too far, fear not: the delicious vegetable dumplings, braised mushrooms, and hearty tofu dishes are sure to satisfy. **Known for:** huge menu and a cheap buffet lunch; friendly regulars; tricky to find (locals can point you in the right direction, though). Ⓢ *Average main: Y60* ✉ *17 Foshan Yuan Xiao Qu* ✥ *Opposite entrance to Thousand Buddha Mountain* ☎ *0531/8868–0888* ▭ *No credit cards.*

Jufengde Restaurant (聚丰德饭店 *Jù fēng dé fàndiàn*)
$$ | **NORTHERN CHINESE** | This long-standing eatery is a well-liked spot to sample *Jinan lu cai,* a variation of one of the eight famous cuisines of China. The signature dish is *jiu zhuan da chang* (literally "nine turns intestine"), chewy braised spirals of pork chitterlings, but if that sounds extreme, try the sweet-and-sour fried carp, or their decent local take on roast duck with pancakes. **Known for:** huge portions; youxuan (Ji'nan's famously crispy fried bread snacks); local favorite. Ⓢ *Average main: Y70* ✉ *11 Jingwu Lu* ☎ *0531/8616–2888.*

★ **Malena Belgian Beer Bar** (玛莲娜啤酒吧 *Mǎliánnà Píjiǔ Bā*)
$$ | **BELGIAN** | With a huge beer list, decent cocktails, and great Western food, Malena is popular with travelers and expats. The people-watching here is good, too, thanks to a lively outdoor terrace and a Quancheng Square location. **Known for:** wood-fired pizza; good salads; English-speaking staff. Ⓢ *Average main: Y90* ✉ *Quancheng Sq.* ✥ *Tucked away down by moat at top of Quancheng Sq.* ☎ *0531/8601–6627* ▭ *No credit cards.*

Shunhe Seafood (舜和海鲜 *Shùn hé hǎixiān*)
$$$ | **SEAFOOD** | A must-try for seafood lovers, Shunhe is a bright and clean nautically themed restaurant with tank-upon-tank of live seafood. There are also plenty of Chinese classics to choose from on a foreigner-friendly point-and-pick photo wall. **Known for:** multiple shellfish varieties; free pickles station; good service. Ⓢ *Average main: Y100* ✉ *10 Wenhua Xi Lu* ✥ *Entrance around back* ☎ *0531/8608–1666* ▭ *No credit cards.*

Hotels

InterContinental Ji'nan City Center (洲际酒店 济南 *Zhōujì jiǔdiàn jǐnán*)
$ | **HOTEL** | This impressive luxury hotel with modern, well-appointed rooms is slap-bang in the middle of Ji'nan's commercial and tourism quarter—location doesn't get much better than this. **Pros:** exceptionally trained staff; international-standard buffet breakfast; fast Internet. **Cons:** relatively expensive; small pool; unromantic setting. Ⓢ *Rooms from: Y755* ✉ *3 Tiandi Tan Lu* ☎ *0531/8602–9999* ⊕ *www.intercontinental.com* 🍽 *No meals.*

Sheraton Ji'nan (济南喜来登 *Jǐ nán xǐ lái déng jiǔdiàn*)
$ | **HOTEL** | Overlooking the enormous, lotus-shape sports venue built to host the 11th Chinese National Games, this hotel has indoor and outdoor pools, an excellent spa, and spacious guest rooms with fabulous amenities, including Egyptian cotton sheets and rain-forest showers. **Pros:** excellent facilities; great Japanese restaurant; big, clean rooms. **Cons:** isolated location; fairly pricey; breakfast not up to par. Ⓢ *Rooms from: Y850* ✉ *8 Long Ao Bei Lu* ☎ *0531/8162–9999* ⊕ *sheraton.marriott.com* ⇨ *410 rooms* 🍽 *No meals.*

The Confucius Temple on top of the beautiful Mt. Tai

★ **Sofitel Ji'nan Silver Plaza** (苏菲特银座大酒店 *Sūfēité yínzuò dǎjiǔdiàn*)
$ | HOTEL | Looking somewhat like a tube of lipstick from the outside, this 49-story cylinder sits right in the center of town, boasting sleek and spacious guest rooms and a grand lobby with impressive chandeliers and marble columns. **Pros:** excellent location; eye-catching design; very good Italian restaurant. **Cons:** small bathrooms; road out front is hard to cross; some furnishings are tired. *Rooms from: Y750 ✉ 66 Luoyuan Dajie ☎ 0531/8606–8888 🌐 www.sofitel.com 426 rooms Free Breakfast.*

Nightlife

Banjo (班卓音乐酒吧 *Ban zhuo yin le jiu ba*)
BARS/PUBS | This funky, eclectic bar has live music most evenings, attracting a mix of young locals and expats. It's conveniently located among a row of Chinese, Japanese, and Korean restaurants that are very lively at night. *✉ 51 Foshan Jie ☎ 0531/8685–8585.*

Shopping

Shandong Curios City (山东古玩城 *Shāndōng Gǔwàn chéng*)
ANTIQUES/COLLECTIBLES | This cluster of small antiques shops is huddled around an attractive courtyard. Jade, jewelry, and regional antiques are beautifully displayed; expect to bargain for prices. *✉ 283 Quancheng Lu.*

Side Trip to Lingyan Temple

Shandong played a vital role in the spread of Buddhism in China. In the 4th century AD the Chinese Buddhist monk Faxian landed on the coast near present-day Qingdao to decode scriptures he'd gathered on travels to India, Sri Lanka, and Nepal. Ji'nan became the center of Buddhist culture for the whole province. During the Tang and Song dynasties, the Lingyan Temple was one of the most important Buddhist temples in China.

GETTING HERE AND AROUND

Lingyan Temple is about 76 km (46 miles) south of the city. The best way to get here is to arrange a car and driver through your hotel or a travel agency.

Lingyan Temple (灵岩寺 *Língyánsì*)
RELIGIOUS SITE | In a dramatic mountain setting, the 1,600-year-old Lingyan Temple is most famous for the Thousand Buddha Hall, with its cast of 40 hand-carved and painted wooden figures seated around the chamber. Unerringly lifelike, each one is distinct, from facial features to the folds of their robes. Dating back to the Song Dynasty, these are some of the finest religious sculptures in China. Several years ago, researchers cracked one of the life-sized statues open and found a full set of internal organs inside, made out of stuffed silk.

In the temple grounds, the Pagoda Forest (Da Lin) is a totemic graveyard of sculpted towers erected over centuries, each marking the passing of a prominent monk. The size and artistry of each tower points not to the status of the deceased, but the prosperity of the temple at the time. The cycle of boom and bust, it would seem, is eternal. ✉ *Pingshe Lu, Changqing District, Wande* ☎ *0531/8746–8099* 🎫 *Y40.*

Side Trip to Mount Tai

A destination for pilgrims for 3,000 years, the mountain was named a UNESCO World Heritage Site in 1987. Confucius is said to have climbed its slopes, scanned the horizon and observed: "The world is very small." Many centuries later, Mao Zedong reached the top and even more famously proclaimed: "The East is red."

GETTING HERE AND AROUND

Mount Tai is near the town of Tai'an, a major stop on the Shanghai–Beijing railway. Dozens of trains travel through Tai'an daily. By road, Tai'an is about 50 km (30 miles) south of Ji'nan. Buses to Tai'an leave Ji'nan's main bus station every 25 minutes between 5 am and 6 pm. From any spot in Tai'an, a taxi to Mount Tai (Taishan) takes less than 15 minutes and costs about Y20.

Confucius Souveniers

Many locals claim to be direct descendants of Confucius, and they take great pride in their heritage. Although the philosopher would have raised an eyebrow, the townspeople do a good line in Confucius-brand cookies, wine, and many other items.

Mount Tai (泰山 *Tàishān*)
MOUNTAIN—SIGHT | Reaching 5,067 feet above sea level, Mount Tai is the most venerated of the five sacred mountains of China. It is also reputedly the most climbed peak on earth, tamed by 7,000 steps over 7½ km (4½ miles) from base to summit, making it accessible to anyone with a sturdy pair of shoes and a head for heights. Over the ages, calligraphy has been etched into boulders and cliffs like graffiti, and temples of various faiths line the route, making a climb here a fascinating jaunt through Chinese history.

It's possible to follow the steps to the summit and back down in a day (a cinch if you use the cable car), but spending the night on the peak is also an option. The classic photo—sunrise over the cloud-hugged peaks—is actually a rare sight because of the mist. ✉ *Tai'an* 🎫 *Dec. 1–Jan. 31, Y100; Feb. 1–Nov. 30, Y125.*

Hotels

Ramada Plaza Tai'an (东尊华美达大酒店 *Dōngzūn huáměidá dàjiǔdiàn*)
$ | **HOTEL** | Request a mountain-view room at this resort-style hotel situated in the quiet foothills of Mount Tai and offering compact but comfortable rooms, soft beds, international TV channels, and thunderous showers. **Pros:** lovely setting; great facilities; large rooms. **Cons:** not on the summit; buffet breakfast just average; overpriced in-house restaurant. *Rooms from: Y500 ✉ 16 Yingsheng Dong Lu, Tai'an ☎ 0538/836–8888 ⇆ 328 rooms 🍴 Breakfast.*

Shenqi Hotel (泰山神憩宾馆 *Tàishān shénqì bīnguǎn*)
$$ | **HOTEL** | This is the only real hotel on the summit, so although it has unusual perks (a bell rings to wake you in time to catch the sunrise), it's overpriced considering the barely adequate rooms. **Pros:** perfect place to watch the sunrise; good Chinese breakfast; only mountain-top lodging. **Cons:** expensive for what you get; very basic rooms; hot water can be patchy. *Rooms from: Y1300 ✉ 18 Tai'an Tian Jie, Tai'an ☎ 0538/822–3866 ⇆ 62 rooms 🍴 Free Breakfast.*

Side Trip to Qufu

This sleepy provincial town is the birthplace of the country's foremost spiritual teacher and philosopher, Kong Fuzi, known to the West as Confucius. His impact was immense in China, and his code of conduct was a part of daily life here until it fell out of favor two millennia later during the Cultural Revolution. His teachings—that son must respect father, wife must respect husband, citizens must respect officials—were swept away by Mao Zedong because of their associations with the past. Qufu suffered greatly during the Cultural Revolution, with the Red Guards smashing statues and burning buildings. But the pendulum has swung back, and Confucius's teachings are again in vogue. Encircled by a Ming Dynasty wall, Qufu certainly has character, though there's little to do once the major sights close for the day.

Wiseman Pass

If you want to soak up as much Confucianism as possible during your visit to Qufu, get a ticket that grants access to all three sites. That's Y185 for a ticket that covers the Confucius Temple, Confucius Family Mansion, and the Confucian Forest.

GETTING HERE AND AROUND

A handful of Qufu-bound bullet trains leave Beijing each day, passing through Ji'nan and Tai'an on route. The trip takes about 2½ hours. Regular buses also run trips from Ji'nan to Qufu. The main bus station is south of the town center at the intersection of Shen Dao and Jingxuan Lu.

Sights

Confucian Forest (孔林 *Kǒnglín*)
CEMETERY | Confucius and his descendants have been buried in this tree-shaded cemetery for the past 2,000 years. Surrounded by a 10-km (6-mile) wall, Confucian Forest has more than 100,000 pine and cypress trees, jostling for space with burial mounds, grave stones, and statues commemorating generations of the Kong family. *✉ Lindao Lu 🎫 Y40.*

Confucius Family Mansion (孔府 *Kǒngfǔ*)
HOUSE | Beside the east wall of the Confucius Temple is the Confucius Family Mansion. A fascinating collection of stately abodes and gardens, it dates from the 16th century and illustrates the wealth and glory once enjoyed by Confucius's descendants. When the Kong

family were in residence, the mansion would have been heavily guarded; trespassing was punishable by death. The tallest structure here is the four-story "refuge tower," which the family could flee to in times of trouble. ✉ *Banbi Jie* 🎫 *Y60.*

Confucius Temple (孔庙 *Kŏngmiào*)
RELIGIOUS SITE | Within Qufu's restored city walls, the sprawling Confucius Temple comprises 66 buildings spread across more than 50 acres, making this one of the largest palace complexes from Imperial China. Like the Forbidden City, built 80 years earlier, its colonnaded halls and courtyards flow symmetrically along a central axis. The Hall of Great Achievements features mighty pillars entwined with dragons. Seek out the Apricot Platform in front, where it's said Confucius once preached beneath the shade of an apricot tree. September 28, the date of the Great Sage's birthday, is quite the party here. ✉ *Banbi Jie* 🎫 *Y90.*

Hotels

★ **Fuzi Binshe Family Education Culture Boutique Hotel** (夫子宾舍家教文化别墅酒店 *Fūzĭ bīn shě jiājiào wénhuà biéshù jiŭdiàn*)
$$ | **HOTEL** | This charming complex close to all of Qufu's main sights offers the best of two worlds: traditional design and modern amenities. **Pros:** large rooms; quiet location; traditional charm. **Cons:** staff speak no English; wooden chairs instead of comfy sofas; limited availability in busy season. *$ Rooms from: Y1300* ✉ *Sankong Scenic Area* ✣ *North of Bowen St.* ☎ *0537/709–1888* 🍽 *Free Breakfast* 💳 *No credit cards.*

★ **Shangri-La Qufu**
$ | **HOTEL** | Two kilometers (1 mile) south of the old walls, this elegant hotel set around a purpose-built lake was Qufu's first world-class accommodation, at last making the UNESCO-listed town a compelling destination for a luxury break or side trip that's complete with creature comforts. **Pros:** good food; nice escape from touristy center; top of the range facilities. **Cons:** at least a 20-minute walk to the sights; no local charm; some areas of service still need work. *$ Rooms from: Y650* ✉ *3 Chunqiu Middle Lu* ☎ *0537/505–8888* 🌐 *www.shangri-la.com/qufu/shangrila* 🛏 *322 rooms* 🍽 *Breakfast.*

Qingdao

4½ hrs (540 km [335 miles]) by bullet train southeast of Beijing; 2½ hrs by train (390 km [242 miles]) east of Ji'nan.

Qingdao has had a turbulent century, but it has emerged as one of China's most charming cities. It was a sleepy fishing village until the end of the 19th century, when Germany, using the killing of two German missionaries as a pretext, set up another European concession to take advantage of Qingdao's coastal position. The German presence lasted only until 1914, but locals continued to build Bavarian-style houses, and today a walk around the Old Town can feel like you've stumbled into a Black Forest village. Unlike many cities that had foreign concessions, Qingdao has recognized the historical value of these buildings and is enthusiastic about preserving them. With its seafront promenades, winding colonial streets, and pretty parks, Qingdao is probably China's best city for strolling.

Home to the country's best-known beer, Tsingtao, Qingdao is also very accommodating when it comes to alcohol consumption. (Look for beer being sold on the streets in plastic bags.) But wine drinkers should take heart: the region is also developing a much-talked-about wine industry.

The city is a destination for golfers, its courses especially popular with traveling Koreans and Japanese.

GETTING HERE AND AROUND

A comfortable way to get to Qingdao is aboard one of the several daily bullet trains that link it with Beijing (4½ hours). Buy tickets from travel agents or through your hotel, as lines are long and there are few English speakers at the station.

The long-distance bus terminal is opposite the train station. Taxis are a cheap way to get around. Getting anywhere in town will generally cost less than Y40.

Some parts of the Qingdao Metro underground network are up and running, with other lines under construction.

AIR TRAVEL

Qingdao Liuting Airport is 30 km (19 miles) north of the city. In a taxi, the journey takes 40 minutes and costs around Y90. Direct flights link Qingdao with Osaka and Seoul, as well as Hong Kong and other major Chinese cities.

AIR CONTACT Qingdao Liuting Airport (青岛机场 *Qīngdǎo jīchǎng*) ✉ *99 Minhang Lu* ☎ *0532/96567* 🌐 *www.qdairport.com.*

BOAT AND FERRY TRAVEL

Qingdao Ferry Termnal is located 2 km (1 mile) north of the train station. Ferries run domestically to Dalian and Weihai and internationally to North Korea and Japan.

BUS TRAVEL

Buses travel between Ji'nan and Qingdao every 20 minutes; the trip is 4–5 hours.

BUS CONTACT Qingdao Long-Distance Bus Station ✉ *2 Wenzhou Lu* ☎ *0532/8371–8060.*

TRAIN TRAVEL

Direct trains link Qingdao with Ji'nan (three hours), Beijing (4½ hours), and Shanghai (6½ hours).

TRAIN CONTACT Qingdao Train Station ✉ *2 Tai'an Lu.*

TIMING

Qingdao is a very pleasant seaside city. Two full days is just about enough to cram in all the sights, but the city has enough attractions to keep you happily occupied for longer.

ESSENTIALS

BOAT AND FERRY CONTACT Qingdao Ferry Terminal ✉ *6 Xinjiang Lu, 2 km (1 mile) north of train station.*

VISITOR AND TOUR INFORMATION Qingdao Tourism Administration ✉ *14th fl., 7 Minjiang Lu* ☎ *0532/8591–2029.*

Eight Passes (八大关 *Bādàguān*)
SCENIC DRIVE | Named after the Great Wall's eight strategic passes, this scenic area lies in-between Taiping and the Huiquan Cape. Sometimes referred to as "Little Switzerland," the grounds of more than 200 European-style villas are landscaped with pine, ginkgo, and peach trees. The serene No. 2 bathing beach and Granite Mansion are also here. ✉ *Juyongguan Lu.*

German Governor's Residence (青岛迎宾馆 *Qīngdǎo yíngbīnguǎn*)
MUSEUM | The cookie dough–colored German Governor's Residence, transformed into a museum in 1996, was where the mustachioed governor and his aristocratic entourage wined, dined, and held sway over Qingdao for their short but influential tenure. Built in 1906 on a commanding perch over the Old City, the interior resembles a Bavarian hunting lodge, with wood paneling, glazed-tile fireplaces, colored-glass chandeliers, and quirky grandfather clocks. Notable Chinese guests since include Mao Zedong, Zhou Enlai, and Deng Xiaoping. English audio guides are available. ✉ *26 Longshan Lu, below Xinhao Hill Park* 🎫 *Y20.*

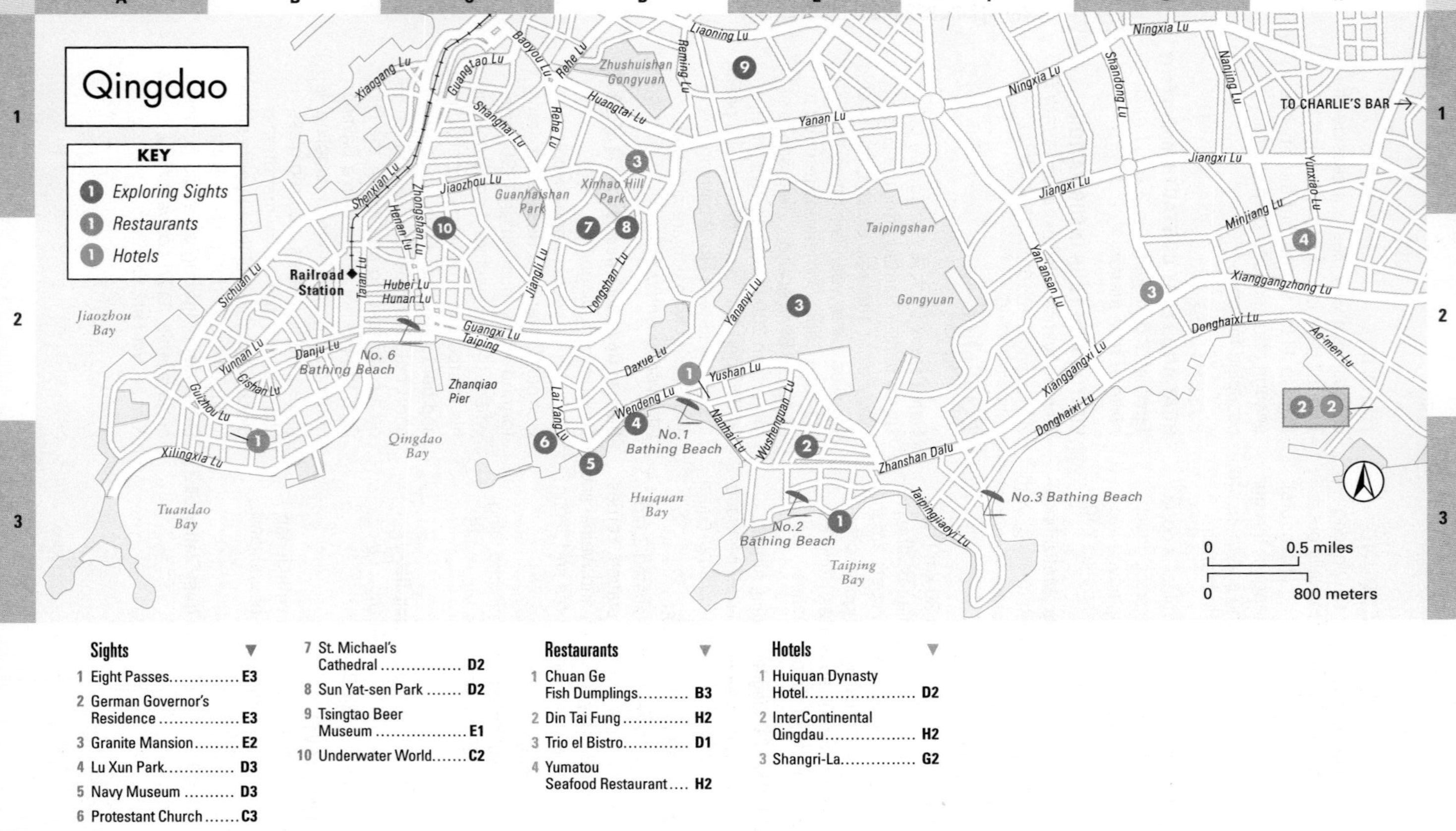

Sights	
1 Eight Passes	E3
2 German Governor's Residence	E3
3 Granite Mansion	E2
4 Lu Xun Park	D3
5 Navy Museum	D3
6 Protestant Church	C3
7 St. Michael's Cathedral	D2
8 Sun Yat-sen Park	D2
9 Tsingtao Beer Museum	E1
10 Underwater World	C2

Restaurants	
1 Chuan Ge Fish Dumplings	B3
2 Din Tai Fung	H2
3 Trio el Bistro	D1
4 Yumatou Seafood Restaurant	H2

Hotels	
1 Huiquan Dynasty Hotel	D2
2 InterContinental Qingdau	H2
3 Shangri-La	G2

Granite Mansion (花石楼 *Huāshí lóu*)
HOUSE | After the German Governor's Residence, the 1903 Granite Mansion is Qingdao's most famous example of concession-era German architecture. This miniature castle was built as a villa for a Russian aristocrat but soon became a fishing retreat for the governor. ✉ *18 Huanghai Lu* 🎫 *Y9.*

Lu Xun Park (鲁迅公园 *Lüxùngōngyuán*)
CITY PARK | Built in 1929, this park named for the distinguished Chinese writer and revolutionary sits on the rocky coastline of Huiquan Bay. It's a lovely park, with tree-shaded paths, elegant pavilions, and rugged reefs, making for attractive sea vistas. ✉ *26 Qinyu Lu* 🎫 *Free.*

Navy Museum (海军博物馆 *Hǎijūnbówùguǎn*)
MUSEUM | A short walk from the west entrance of Lu Xun Park is the Navy Museum, with an arsenal of archaic weaponry, Russian-made fighter planes, and several rusting naval vessels moored in the harbor. You can see much of it—and skip the entrance fee—by walking along the seawall to the Little Qingdao Isle with its charming lighthouse and excellent café. ✉ *8 Lai Yang Lu* ☎ *0532/8286–6784* 🎫 *Y50.*

Protestant Church (基督教堂 *Jīdū jiàotáng*)
RELIGIOUS SITE | Qingdao's charming Protestant Church is easy to spot: look for the ostentatious green spire resembling a medieval castle. It was built in 1910 at the southwest entrance of Xinhao Hill Park. Puff up the steps to the bell tower for sea views and to marvel at the German-engineered clock mechanism. ✉ *15 Jiangsu Lu* 🎫 *From 3Y.*

St. Michael's Cathedral (青岛天主教堂 *Qīngdǎo tiānzhǔ jiàotáng*)
RELIGIOUS SITE | With its towering 200-foot twin steeples and red-tile roof, St Michael's is probably Qingdao's most recognizable landmark. The classic Gothic Revival structure was built by the Germans in 1934 but was badly damaged during the Cultural Revolution. The surrounding area is worth a stroll, the streets a mix of sturdy concession buildings and contrastingly shabby modern architecture. The square in front of the cathedral is the most popular spot in town for wedding photos; an enormous "wedding banquet restaurant" is conveniently located opposite. ✉ *15 Zhejiang Lu* 🎫 *Y8.*

Ganbei!

Qingdao International Beer Festival
The Qingdao International Beer Festival, China's biggest, has been held since 1991. The state-sponsored fun is held early to mid-August, lasts for two weeks, and causes hotel prices to skyrocket. The focus is mostly on big-name brews from around the world, and you won't see any lederhosen, but it's still great fun. ✉ *Qingdao.*

Sun Yat-sen Park (中山公园 *Zhōngshān gōngyuán*)
CITY PARK | **FAMILY** | The largest of the city's parks is inland from Huiquan Bay and has a number of attractions, including a small zoo, a botanical garden, and the Zhanshan Buddhist Temple. Qingdao's TV tower, a city landmark, offers striking views from its observation deck. Originally planted by the Japanese in 1915, the park contains some 20,000 cherry trees. The annual Cherry Blossom Festival is held at the end of May. ✉ *28 Wendeng Lu* ☎ *0532/8287–0564* 🎫 *Free (attractions inside cost extra).*

Tsingtao Beer Museum (青啤博物馆 *Qīngpí bówùguǎn*)
WINERY/DISTILLERY | Beer fans should make a pilgrimage to the Tsingtao Beer Museum on Dengzhou Lu, also known as *Pijiu Jie* (Beer Street). The Germans established China's most famous brewery more than a century ago, and

Qingdao's seafront promenades, winding colonial streets, and pretty parks make it a great city for strolling.

a few of the original brick buildings still remain, alongside a modern bottling plant. The old photographs, beer labels, and dioramas are of middling interest; best of all are the beer samples you can enjoy along the way. The surrounding area is lined with bars, eateries, and bottle-shape benches where weary revelers can rest. ✉ *56 Dengzhou Lu* ☎ *0532/8383–3437* 🌐 *www.tsingtaomuseum.com* 🎫 *Y60.*

Underwater World (青岛海底世界 *Qīngdǎo hǎidǐshìjiè*)
ZOO | **FAMILY** | Located near No. 1 Beach, this family-friendly attraction features a moving platform with 360-degree views of the surrounding marine life. Four underground levels, interactive video displays, and tacky marine shows entertain the kids for hours. ✉ *2 Laiyang Lu* ☎ *0532/8289–2187* 🎫 *Y130.*

Restaurants

Chuan Ge Fish Dumplings (船歌鱼水饺 *Chuángē yúshuǐjiǎo*)
$$$ | **CHINESE** | A market-fresh spread of seafood, meats, and vegetables greets you at the entrance of this excellent eatery, a hit with well-heeled locals. Browse the live seafood (a small lobster, freshly steamed, will set you back about Y240), point at the dishes you want to try, and take your seat. **Known for:** signature moyu jiaozi (dumplings wrapped in dough blackened by cuttlefish ink); fast turnover; transparent pricing. $ *Average main: Y120* ✉ *39 Qutangxia Lu* ☎ *0532/8267–0026.*

Din Tai Fung (鼎泰丰 *Dǐngtàifēng*)
$$$ | **SHANGHAINESE** | Inside the posh Marina City Mall beside the Olympic Sailing Center, Din Tai Fung serves up its brand of precisely pleated dumplings to CBD execs and tourists staying at the InterCon nearby. The *xiaolongbao* dumplings from this renowned Taiwanese brand contain delicate fillings and

scalding soup—the perfectly steamed crab dumplings pair well with the ocean view. **Known for:** soup dumplings; kitchen viewing window; shoreside location. *$ Average main: Y100 ✉ Marina City Mall, 86 Ao'men Lu 🌐 www.dintaifungusa.com.*

★ Trio el Bistro
$$ | MEXICAN | Run by a young local guy who studied in Texas, this hole-in-the-wall taco bar serves up arguably the best Mexican food in town. All three of the hefty signature tacos are worth a try, and there's a decent selection of sides and craft beers, too. **Known for:** strong cocktails; expat following; hip setting. *$ Average main: Y60 ✉ 13 Laiwuer Lu ☎ 186/5321–9327 ⏲ Closed Tues.*

Yumatou Seafood Restaurant (渔码头海鲜舫 *Yúmǎtóu hǎixiānfǎng*)
$$ | SEAFOOD | At this quintessential seafood place, one of many on or around Minjiang Lu, rows of tanks swarm with live sea creatures, with prices marked per *jin* (about 500 grams, enough for two to share). Order the Qingdao signature: clams fried with chilis and garlic (*gala* in the local dialect), which pairs perfectly with Tsingtao beer, or try the scallops served *suanrong fensi* (steamed with garlic and vermicelli noodles). **Known for:** huge dining space; welcoming staff; good prices. *$ Average main: Y90 ✉ 24 Yunxiao Lu ☎ 0532/8577–9999.*

Hotels

Huiquan Dynasty Hotel (汇泉王朝大店 *huìquán wángcháo dàjiǔdiàn*)
$ | HOTEL | FAMILY | Looming over the city's most popular sandy stretch, this long-established hotel makes up for average rooms with terrific ocean views, easy beach access for kids, and friendly service. **Pros:** on-site shops; family-friendly; English-speaking staff. **Cons:** in high season rooms don't justify price; furniture a little dated; packed with kids. *$ Rooms from: Y920 ✉ 6 Nanhai Lu ☎ 0532/8299–9888 🌐 www.hqdynasty.com 405 rooms 🍽 No meals.*

InterContinental Qingdao (青岛海尔洲际酒店 *Hǎiěr zhōujì jiǔdiàn*)
$$$ | HOTEL | Adjacent to the Olympic Sailing Center and a short walk from the Marina City shopping complex, this ultramodern hotel has contemporary rooms, many with expansive marina or coastal views and all with dark wood paneling, built-in mood lighting, massive LCD TVs, and stand-alone bath tubs. **Pros:** one of Qingdao's most luxurious lodgings; marina location; gorgeous rooms. **Cons:** among the city's priciest hotels; a little far from city's main attractions; no-smoking floors and rooms don't always smell as such. *$ Rooms from: Y1800 ✉ 98 Ao Men Lu ☎ 0532/6656–6666 422 rooms 🍽 Free Breakfast.*

Shangri-La (香格里拉大酒店 *Xiānggélǐlā dàjiǔdiàn*)
$$$ | HOTEL | Insist on a room in the newer Valley Wing at the ever-reliable Shangri-La, which is a few hundred yards from the coast, near some of the best shopping and dining in town, and just a 15-minute cab ride from historic sights. **Pros:** convenient to beach; comfortable rooms; cozy bar. **Cons:** immediate area difficult to navigate on foot; some areas showing their age; relatively expensive. *$ Rooms from: Y1520 ✉ 9 Xiang Gang Zhong Lu ☎ 0532/8388–3838 🌐 www.shangri-la.com/qingdao 696 rooms 🍽 No meals.*

Nightlife

Laofei Bar (2nd Bar) (老菲酒吧 (第二店) *Lǎo fēi jiǔbā (dì èr diàn)*)
BARS/PUBS | This lively sports bar has numerous screens, games tables, an English-speaking staff, and a full bar with a decent menu of classic pub grub. A small crowd of friendly expats tends to gather here at night, so it's a great spot

if you're missing the camaraderie of your hometown pub. ✉ *162 Jiangxi Lu* ☎ *0532/8593–6566.*

★ **Strong Ale Works** (强麦啤酒 *Qiáng mài píjiǔ*)
BREWPUBS/BEER GARDENS | It's well worth seeking out this hidden gem, the only outlet of a long-standing local brewery run by an American and his Chinese partners. The pint-size, shabby-chic bar has great music and at least 10 incredibly tasty and inventive beers to sample at all times. ✉ *33 Huangxian Lu* ☎ *0532/8286–0252.*

Tsingtao Brewery Bar (青岛啤酒厂 *Qīngdǎo píjiǔchǎng jiǔbā*)
BREWPUBS/BEER GARDENS | At the Tsingtao Brewery Bar you can drink from the source. In front of the Tsingtao Brewery Museum, it's cavernous, brightly lit, and packed in high season with convivial gangs of beer-swilling Chinese tourists. ✉ *56 Dengzhou Lu* ☎ *0532/8383–3437.*

Shopping

Hong Ren Tang Pharmacy (宏仁堂 *Hóngrén táng*)
SPECIALTY STORES | This traditional family-run drug store has been operating here for more than 70 years. Inside, arcane displays and cabinets are stocked with thousands of herbs and other, more exotic items like antler and dried seahorses—all used to concoct Chinese medicines. Look for the English-speaking counter for foreign customers. This northern stretch of Zhongshan Lu is good for antiques, jade-carving, and other traditional businesses. ✉ *196 Zhongshan Lu, Shinan* ☎ *0532/8282–5279.*

Qingdao Arts and Crafts Store
CRAFTS | The city's largest antiques shop is the Qingdao Arts and Crafts Store, with four floors of porcelain, scroll paintings, silk, gold, jade, and other stones. ✉ *212 Zhongshan Lu* ☎ *0532/8281–7948.*

In the News

Qingdao has a lively foreign-restaurant and bar scene, with new venues opening up all the time. Get a copy of the local expat magazine *Redstar* from your hotel for the latest information, or check out their website (🌐 *www.myredstar.com*) for reviews, recommendations, and happenings around town.

Taidong Night Market (台东夜市 *Tái dōng yèshì*)
LOCAL SPECIALTIES | A lively mix of clothing, footwear, household goods, and souvenir tea sets can be found at this bustling street market walking distance from the Tsingtao Beer Museum. ✉ *Taidon Yi Lu.*

Activities

BEACHES

No. 1 Beach is the busiest, and in summer it can be difficult to find a place for your towel. If your goal is peace and quiet, head to **No. 2 Beach,** as fewer Chinese tourists venture out that way. In the summer, look out for the armies of brides and bridegrooms using the beaches for their wedding photos, and look out for another more recent phenomena: the facekini. This startlingly strange mask is worn by ladies to avoid getting a tanned face.

GOLF

Qingdao International Golf Club (青岛国际高尔夫俱乐部 *Qīngdǎo guójì gāo'ěrfū jùlèbù*)
GOLF | The 18-hole Qingdao International Golf Club is 20 minutes from downtown. It has driving ranges and a fine-dining restaurant. Booking ahead, especially on weekends, is recommended—it's particularly popular with South Korean golfers who appreciate the value

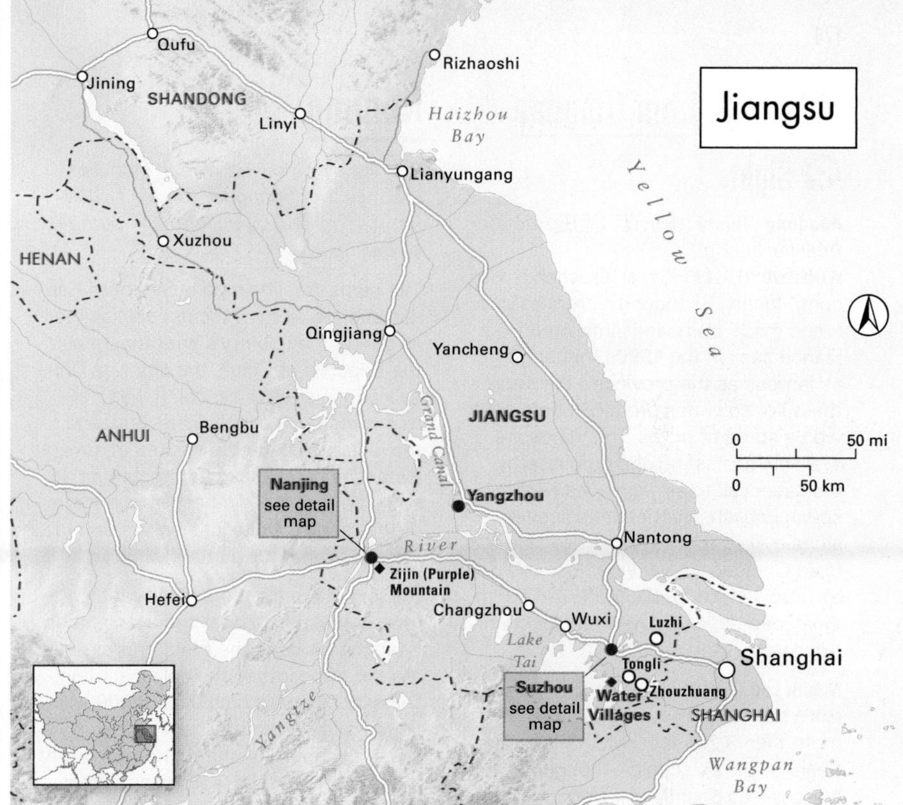

compared to their home country. ✉ *118 Songling Lu* ☎ *0532/8896–0001*.

WATER SPORTS

The waterfront at Fushan Bay has been completely transformed with the construction of the Olympic Sailing Center. Several other places will also help you get on or in the water.

Qingdao Qinhai Scuba Diving Club (青岛琴海潜水俱乐部 *Qīngdǎo qínhǎi qiánshuǐ jùlèbù*)

WATER SPORTS | Near No. 1 Bathing Beach, the Qingdao Qinhai Scuba Diving Club is one of the few government-approved diving clubs in northern China. Diving conditions here are variable, with visibility at about 4–5 meters on a good day. All equipment is provided for PADI certification courses or guided recreational dives. ✉ *1–6 Wendeng Lu* ☎ *0532/8388–1170*.

Yinhai International Yacht Club (银海国际游艇俱乐部 *Yínhǎi guójì yóutǐng jùlèbù*)

WATER SPORTS | One of the country's largest yacht clubs has vessels of all sizes for rent, and offers lessons to beginners and more experienced sailors. The club is in the east of town, past the Olympic Sailing Center. ✉ *30 Donghai Zhong Lu* ☎ *0532/8588–6666* 🌐 *www.yinhai.com.cn*.

Side Trips from Qingdao

Huadong Winery (华东百利酒庄 *Huádōng Bǎilì jiǔzhuāng*)
WINERY/DISTILLERY | Near Laoshan is Huadong Winery, Shandong's premier vinous brand made from vines imported from France back in the 1980s. Although not as famous as the province's brewery, the 30 or so wines produced here have won a string of prizes. The wines are available for tasting and purchase by the case; call to arrange a visit—they speak English. The beautiful scenery alone makes this a worthwhile side trip from Qingdao. ✉ *Nanlong Kou, Lao Shan* ☎ *189/5321–6136, 0532/8387–4778 to Quingdao Office* 🌐 *www.huadongwinery.com.*

Mount Lao (崂山 *Láoshān*)
MOUNTAIN—SIGHT | Rising to a height of more than 3,280 feet, Mount Lao (Lao Shan) is just as scenic—though not as famous—as Shandong neighbor Mount Tai. A place of pilgrimage for centuries, the craggy slopes of Laoshan once boasted nine palaces, eight temples, and 72 convents. Most have been lost over the years, but those remaining are worth seeking out for their elegant architecture and stirring sea views. With sheer cliffs and cascading waterfalls, Laoshan is the source of the country's best-known mineral water (a vital ingredient in the local brew, Tsingtao). It's possible to see the mountain's sights as a day trip. Tourist buses to Laoshan leave from the main pier in Qingdao, or hop on to public Bus 304. Mount Lao is 40 km (25 miles) east of Qingdao. 🎫 *Y90*

Nanjing

1½ hrs (309 km [192 miles]) by bullet train west of Shanghai; 3½ hrs (1,039 km [646 miles]) by bullet train southeast of Beijing.

The name *Nanjing* means Southern Capital, and for six dynastic periods, as well as during the country's brief tenure as the Republic of China, the city was China's administrative capital. It was never as successful a capital as Beijing, and the locals chalk up the failures of several dynasties here to bad timing, but it could be that the laid-back atmosphere of the Yangtze Delta just isn't as suited to political intrigue as the north.

Nanjing offers travelers significantly more sites of historical importance than Shanghai. Among the most impressive are the remnants of the colossal Ming Dynasty city wall, built by 200,000 laborers to protect the new capital in the 14th century. A number of important monuments, tombs, and gates reflect the glory and instability of Nanjing's incumbency.

The city lies on the Yangtze, and the Yangtze River Bridge or the more subdued park at Swallow Rock are great places for viewing the river. The sheer amount of activity on the water is testimony to its continued importance as a corridor for shipping and trade. Downtown, the streets are choked with traffic, but the chaotic scene is easily avoided with a visit to any of the large parks. You can also take a short taxi ride to Zijin (Purple) Mountain, where quiet trails lead between Ming Tomb and the grand mausoleum of Sun Yat-sen.

GETTING HERE AND AROUND

Regular daily flights connect Nanjing with all other major Chinese cities. The airport is located just 36 km (22 miles) from the city center.

Nanjing's position on the Beijing–Shanghai high-speed railway line makes train travel a great option. Bus travel in this area of China is considerably more comfortable than elsewhere, thanks to a network of highways linking the cities and a fleet of air-conditioned coaches with comfortable seats.

Getting around a city the size of Nanjing can be a daunting task, but the easy-to-use subway system has made navigating safer and easier. Useful stops for travelers on its 10 lines include Sanshan Jie (Confucius Temple area), Xuanwu Gate (Xuanwu Lake and Hunan Road area), and Yunjinlu (Nanjing Massacre Memorial). Fares are inexpensive, only Y2 to Y10, depending on how many stations you travel to.

Getting around Nanjing by taxi is both fast and inexpensive, though taxi drivers generally cannot speak any English, so be prepared with the address of your destination written in Chinese. If you're feeling more adventurous, note that the city is very bike-friendly, with mostly flat roads and many dedicated bike lanes. You can rent bicycles from some small hotels and tourist agencies, or you can download apps to use the multiple on-street share-bike options, such as Ofo and Mobike.

The best way to explore some of Nanjing's tourist destinations, once you're on Purple Mountain, is aboard the tourist buses (Y1, Y2, Y3) that run from the train station to Ming Tomb, Sun Yat-sen Botanical Gardens, Sun Yat-sen Mausoleum, and Spirit Valley Pagoda. The fare is Y3.

AIR TRAVEL

Most flights from Europe or North America go through Shanghai or Beijing before continuing on to Nanjing's Lukou Airport, but there are direct flights from Asian hubs like Seoul, Singapore, Nagoya, and Bangkok. From Nanjing several flights leave daily for Shanghai, Beijing, Guangzhou, Xiamen, Wuhan, and Hong Kong; flights leave daily for Xi'an, Chengdu, and Zhengzhou.

Taxis from Nanjing Lukou Airport, 36 km (22 miles) southwest of the city, should take between 20 and 30 minutes. The fare should be between Y100 and Y140.

AIR CONTACTS Air China ☎ *010/109–5583* 🌐 *www.airchina.com.cn/en.* **Nanjing Lukou Airport** ✉ *Lukou Jie, Jiangning District* ☎ *025/968–890* 🌐 *www.njiairport.com.*

BUS TRAVEL

Buses are the best way to reach Yangzhou, and they leave frequently from the main Zhongyangmen Long Distance Bus Station and take about an hour. The trip to Shanghai takes between three and four hours, and the trip to Suzhou can take as little as two hours; buses to both cities depart from the Zhongshan Nan Lu Bus Station.

BUS CONTACT Zhongyangmen Long Distance Bus Station ✉ *1 Jianning Lu.* **Zhongshan Nan Lu Long-Distance Bus Station** (**中山南路客运站** *Zhōngshān nánlù kèyùn zhàn*) ✉ *Junction of Shenzhou Lu and Zongshan Nan Lu.*

TRAIN TRAVEL

There are many bullet trains daily, arriving at either Nanjing Train Station or the newer Nanjing South Train station. Trains to Suzhou take about 90 minutes. The train to Yangzhou also takes 90 minutes, but it's a pleasant trip with the bonus of crossing the Yangtze via the Yangtze River Bridge.

TRAIN CONTACT Nanjing South Train Station ✉ *98 Yulan Lu, Yuhuatai District.* **Nanjing Train Station** ✉ *Zhongyang Gat, Long Pan Lu* ☎ *025/8582–2222.*

TIMING

Considering the massive size of the city and the sheer number of attractions, try to devote at least two to three full days exploring.

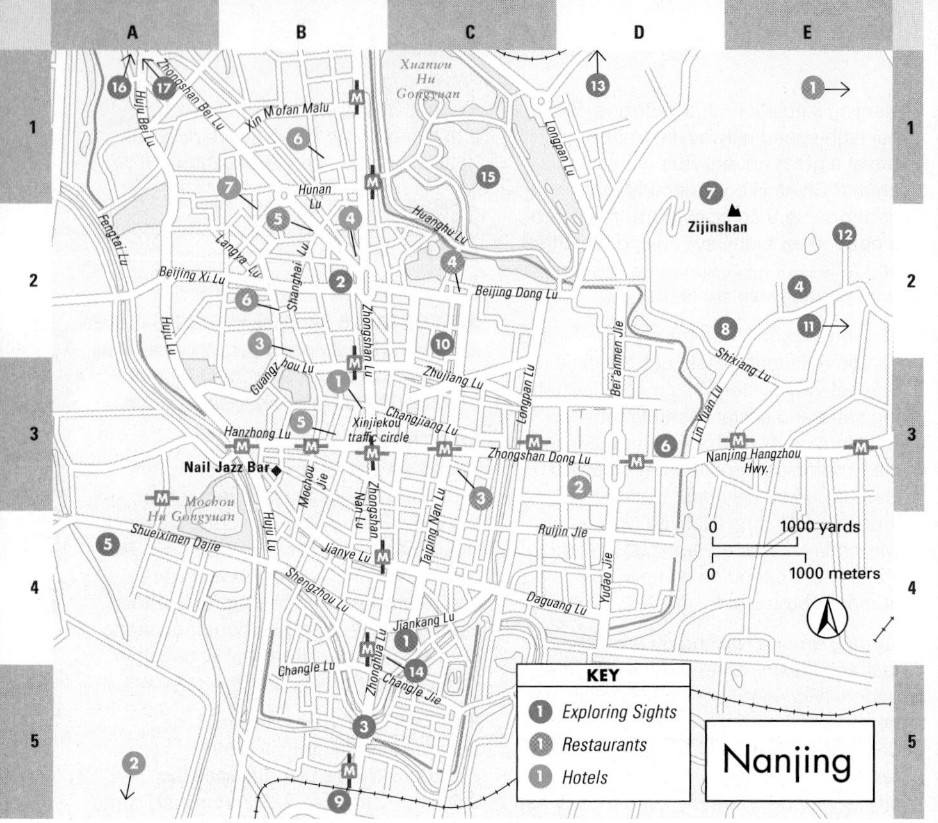

Sights

1 Confucian Temple **C4**
2 Drum Tower **B2**
3 Lingu Temple and Pagoda.............. **B5**
4 Ming Tomb................ **E2**
5 Nanjing Massacre Memorial **A4**
6 Nanjing Museum **D3**
7 National Dr. Sun Yat-sen Memorial Hall **D1**
8 Plum Blossom Hill and Sun Yat-sen Botanical Gardens....... **E2**
9 Rain Flower Terrace and Martyrs Memorial . **B5**
10 Shou Jia Massage....... **C2**
11 South Gate of City Wall **E2**
12 Sun Yat-sen Mausoleum............... **E2**
13 Swallow Rock........... **D1**
14 Taiping Heavenly Kingdom Museum **B4**
15 Xuanwu Lake Park....... **C1**
16 Yangtze River Bridge ... **A1**
17 Yuejiang Lo **A1**

Restaurants

1 Bellini **E1**
2 Da Pai Dang.............. **D3**
3 Hui Wei **C3**
4 Jimingsi Vegetarian Restaurant................ **C2**
5 Shizi Lou **B2**
6 Skyways Deli............. **B2**

Hotels

1 Central Hotel............. **B3**
2 Fairmont Nanjing **A5**
3 Grand Hotel **B2**
4 InterContinental Nanjing.................... **B2**
5 Jinling Hotel.............. **B3**
6 Lakeview Xuanwu Hotel....................... **B1**
7 Sofitel Galaxy Hotel **B2**

Sights

Confucian Temple (夫子庙 *Fūzǐmiào*)
RELIGIOUS SITE | Overlooking the Qinhuai River, a tributary of the Yangtze, a Confucian Temple has stood on this spot for 1,000 years, give or take. The present incarnation dates from the 1980s, rebuilt a few decades after it was destroyed by the Japanese in 1937. The surrounding area is the city's busiest shopping and entertainment district, festooned with neon at night and packed with tourists. The alleys behind the temple, once home to China's most famous district of courtesans, now house a market and curio shops. Boat rides along the Qinhuai River leave from in front of the temple every evening. ✉ *Zhongshan Lu and Jiankang Lu, on the Qinhuai River* 🎫 *Y25.*

Drum Tower (鼓楼 *Gǔlóu*)
BUILDING | First built in 1382, the Drum Tower (Gulou in Chinese) gives the central city district its name. In ancient times, drums housed inside were used to signal important events, from the changing of the night's watch to an enemy attack or the even greater threat of fire. Today just one drum remains. ✉ *1 Dafang Xiang, beside Gulou People's Sq.* ☎ *025/8663–1059* 🎫 *Y20.*

Lingu Temple and Pagoda (灵谷寺， 灵谷塔 *Línggǔsì and línggǔtǎ*)
RELIGIOUS SITE | Close to the Sun Yat-sen Memorial, this temple commemorates Xuan Zang, the roving monk who brought Buddhist scriptures back to China from India. Seek out the Beamless Hall, a magnificent 14th-century structure built entirely from bricks without wood or nails to help bear its roof. Today it has been given over to propagandistic Republic-era displays. Farther up the hill is an impressive nine-story granite pagoda built in 1929 as a memorial to fallen revolutionaries. Vendors sell balloons to toss from the upper balcony. ✉ *Lingusi Lu, southeast of Sun Yat-sen Memorial* 🎫 *Y80 (includes Sun Yat-sen Mausoleum).*

★ **Ming Tomb** (明孝陵 *Míngxiàolíng*)
MEMORIAL | One of the largest and most important burial mounds in China, this is the final resting place of Emperor Hong Wu, the founder of the Ming Dynasty. Born a peasant and orphaned at a young age, he became a monk and eventually led the army that overthrew the Yuan Dynasty, making Nanjing his capital in 1368 and building its mighty walls. You approach the tomb along the Spirit Way, flanked by auspicious stone lions, elephants, camels, and mythical beasts. Winding paths make the area around the tomb perfect for strolling. ✉ *Mingling Lu, on Purple Mountain* 🎫 *Y70 (includes Plum Blossom Hill and Sun Yat-sen Botanical Park).*

Nanjing Massacre Memorial (大屠杀纪念馆 *Dàtúshā jìniànguǎn*)
MEMORIAL | In the winter of 1937, Japanese forces occupied Nanjing. In the space of a few days, thousands of Chinese were killed in the chaos, which became known as the "Rape of Nanjing." This monument commemorates the victims, many of whom were buried in mass graves. Be advised, this is not for the squeamish. Skeletons have been exhumed from the "Grave of Ten Thousand" and are displayed with gruesomely frank explanations as to how each lost his or her life. The memorial also displays artifacts from the Sino-Japanese reconciliation after World War II, which ended the conflict between the two countries on a less strident, more hopeful note. To get here, take the subway to Yunjinlu (Line 2). ✉ *418 Shui Ximen Da Jie, west of Mouchou Lake Park* ☎ *025/8661–2230* 🌐 *www.nj1937.org* 🎫 *Free.*

Nanjing Museum (南京博物馆 *Nánjīng bówùguǎn*)
MUSEUM | This huge museum has a vast collection of artifacts, a whole host of dinosaur fossils, and a colorful exhibition on the Republic period after 1911. Note, too, that the Ming and Qing Imperial porcelain collection is one of the world's

The Spirit Way, lined with stone camels and other auspicious animals, leads to Ming Tomb.

largest. Also, keep an eye out for what might be the museum's singular treasure—a full-size suit of ceremonial armor made from jade tiles threaded with silver; it dates from the Eastern Han Dynasty. *⊠ 321 Zhongshan Dong Lu, inside Zhongshan Gate ☎ 025/8480–2119 🌐 www.njmm.cn 🎫 Free (bring passport).*

National Dr. Sun Yat-sen Memorial Hall (國立國父紀念館 *Guólì Guófù Jìniàn Guǎn*)
MEMORIAL | This enormous memorial to Dr. Sun Yat-sen, the founding father of the Republic of China, contains displays on the revered leader's life and revolution. The grounds are also home to a multipurpose social, cultural, and education center as well as a 300,000-title library. *⊠ At foot of second peak of Purple Mountain, Xuan Wu 🎫 Y100 for combo ticket to Open-air Music Hall, Xiaoling Mausoleum of Ming Dynasty, Linggu Temple, and Meiling Palace 🕒 Closed Mon. except holidays and Nov. 12 and Mar. 12 (anniversary of Dr. Sun Yat-sen's birth and death).*

Plum Blossom Hill and Sun Yat-sen Botanical Gardens (梅花山， 中山植物园 *Méihuāshān and Zhōngshān zhíwùyuán*)
GARDEN | March and April are the best months to visit Plum Blossom Hill, when peach, pear, plum, and cherry trees explode with color and fragrance. The rest of the year it's probably not worth a special trip, though exhibits at the botanical gardens, established in 1929, are a rewarding experience year-round for those interested in the country's flora. *⊠ 1 Shixiang Lu, northeast of Nanjing Museum 🎫 Y70 (includes Ming Tomb).*

Rain Flower Terrace and Martyrs Memorial (雨花台, 烈士陵园 *Yǔhuātái, lièshì língyuán*)
MEMORIAL | This scenic area gets its name from the legend of Yunzhang, a 15th-century Buddhist monk who supposedly pleased the gods so much with his recitation of a sutra that they showered flowers on this spot. It was put to a grim purpose in the 1930s, when the Nationalists executed thousands of their left-wing political enemies here. In

1950, after the founding of the People's Republic of China, it was transformed into a memorial park furnished with statues of heroic martyrs, soaring obelisks, and a museum. ✉ *215 Yuhua Lu, outside Zhonghua Gate* 🎫 *Free.*

Shou Jia Massage (手佳盲人按摩保健中心 *Shǒujiāmángrén ànmó bǎojiàn zhōngxīn*)
SPA—SIGHT | This health center is serious about traditional Chinese medicine. The center trains and employs the visually impaired for therapeutic massage treatments, and the friendly staff brings you endless cups of medicinal tea. ✉ *136 Chang Jiang Lu* ☎ *025/5871–7600.*

South Gate of City Wall (中华门 *Zhōnghuámén*)
ARCHAEOLOGICAL SITE | **FAMILY** | Built as the linchpin of the city's defenses, this is less a gate than a complete fortress, with multiple courtyards and tunnels where several thousand soldiers could withstand a siege. It was rarely attacked; armies wisely avoided it in favor of the less heavily fortified areas to the north. Today, bonsai enthusiasts maintain displays in several of the courtyards. ✉ *Southern end of Zhonghua Lu, south side of city wall* 🎫 *Y25.*

Sun Yat-sen Mausoleum (中山陵 *Zhōngshānlíng*)
MEMORIAL | Acknowledged by both the Nationalist and Communist governments as the father of modern China, Sun Yat-sen (also known as Zhong Shan) lies buried in a delicately carved marble sarcophagus, reached by a broad set of concrete steps rising up the hillside. His final resting place is the center of a solemn and imposing monument to the ideas that overthrew the imperial system. Steep trails wind around the pine-covered scenic area, which feels a world away from Nanjing's hyperkinetic buzz. **■ TIP→ The mausoleum gets crowded on weekends, so try to come during the week.** ✉ *Lingyuan Lu, east of Ming Tomb* 🎫 *Y80 (includes Linggu Temple and Pagoda).*

Pedestrian Streets

Confucius Temple Area Fuzimiao In the Confucius Temple Area are souvenir and shopping streets around the Qinhuai River. ✉ *Zhongshan Lu and Jiankang Lu.*

Hunan Road These streets are filled with snacks, shops, and restaurants. ✉ *Hunan Lu, west of Zhongshan North Rd. and east of Zhongyang Lu.*

Xinjiekou City Center Around the big malls and shopping centers are several bustling pedestrian streets. ✉ *Xinjiekou, between Huaihai Lu and Zhongshan Lu.*

Swallow Rock (燕子矶 *Yànzijī*)
CITY PARK | North of the city, this small park overlooking the Yangtze River is worth the trip for stirring views of Asia's longest waterway. The "rock" refers to a huge boulder jutting out into the water, a spot where Tang Dynasty poet Li Bai found inspiration. To get here, take Bus 8 to the last stop. ✉ *3 Linjiang Jie, Northeast of Mount Mufu, on Yangtze River* 🎫 *Y10.*

Taiping Heavenly Kingdom Museum (太平天国历史博物馆 *Tàipíngtiānguó lìshǐ bówùguǎn*)
MUSEUM | Commemorating a fascinating period of Chinese history, this museum follows the life of Hong Xiuquan, a Christian who led a peasant revolt in 1859. He ultimately captured Nanjing and ruled for 11 years. Hong, who set himself up as emperor, claimed to be the younger brother of Jesus. On display are artifacts from the period. After browsing through the museum, stroll through the grounds of the surrounding Ming Dynasty garden compound, once the home of high-ranking Taiping officials. In the evening there are performances of opera and

storytelling. ✉ *128 Zhanyuan Lu, beside the Confucian Temple* ☎ *025/5220–1849* 🎫 *Y30.*

Xuanwu Lake Park (玄武湖公园 *Xuánwǔhú gōngyuán*)
CITY PARK | More lake than park, this pleasant garden is bounded by one of the longer sections of the monumental city wall, which you can climb for a good view of the water. Purple Mountain rises in the east, and the glittering skyscrapers of modern Nanjing are reflected on the calm water. Causeways lined with trees and benches connect several large islands in the lake. Pedal-powered and battery-powered boats can be hired by the hour at a number of jetties. ✉ *1 Xuan Wu Xiang, outside the city wall* 🎫 *Y30.*

Yangtze River Bridge (长江大桥 *Chángjiāng dàqiáo*)
BRIDGE/TUNNEL | Completed in 1968 at the height of the Cultural Revolution, this bridge was the first truly great engineering project completed solely by the Communists, touted as a defining symbol of the spirit and ingenuity of the Chinese people. Decorated in a stirring Socialist-Realist manner, huge stylized flags sculpted from red glass rise from the bridge's piers, and groups of giant-size peasants, workers, and soldiers stride forward triumphantly. The Great Bridge Park lies on the southern side; from here you can take an elevator up to the top or browse a gallery of old photographs. Bus No. 1 from the Confucian Temple takes you to the bridge. ✉ *End of Daqiao Nan* 🎫 *Y15.*

Yuejiang Lou (阅江楼 *Yuèjiānglóu*)
BUILDING | Ming Dynasty founding emperor Hongwu wrote a poem describing his plans to have a tower built atop Lion Mountain, from where he could gaze out at the Yangtze River. Other imperial business got in the way, and, for several centuries, the building remained on paper. In 2001, his dreams were realized; a gargantuan, historically accurate, and slightly sterile tower arose. The views, though, are terrific. ✉ *202 Jianning Lu* ☎ *025/5880–3977* 🎫 *Y40.*

Restaurants

Bellini (贝丽妮意式餐厅 *Bèi lì nī yì shì cāntīng*)
$$ | ITALIAN | FAMILY | The crisp Neapolitan-style pizzas at this contemporary Italian eatery come recommended, but don't overlook the seafood specialities and wide range of pasta dishes. Ingredients and cooking techniques are authentic, and regular half-price deals (particularly on Tuesday) attract a local expat and student crowd. **Known for:** friendly Italian host; intimate vibe; great salmon Caesar salad. $ *Average main: Y85* ✉ *9 Wenfan Lu* ☎ *025/8579–1577* 🌐 *www.bellinirestaurants.com.*

★ **Da Pai Dang** (南京大牌档 *Nánjīng dàpáidǎng*)
$$ | MANDARIN | Lined with street-food-style stalls, this wildly popular, well-established dining hall—the original and best of five locations around town—dishes up Yangtze wetlands specialities, including appetizers and soups that emphasize local vegetables rather than the usual starchy offerings; Nanjing's famous salted duck, served sliced on the bone; and steamers full of duck dumplings. Order from the picture menu (with tiny English translations) or get up and browse, pointing to what you want and giving your table number to a costumed attendant. **Known for:** pretty interior; hearty portions; fresh produce. $ *Average main: Y60* ✉ *25 Ruijin Lu* ☎ *025/8448–8333.*

Hui Wei (回味 *Huí wèi*)
$ | FAST FOOD | Beloved by locals, Nanjing's very own fast-food chain is a great place to try two regional specialties: *xiaolongbao* (soup-filled pork dumplings) and *maoxue fensi tang* (rice noodle soup with duck blood cubes). Branches are

everywhere (the original is on Hunan Lu), but the nicest location is on the causeway crossing Xuanwu Lake, where you'll find tables at the water's edge. **Known for:** pretty location; Chinese comfort food; swift service. *Average main: Y30 Along causeway crossing Xuanwu Lake, Hunan Lu.*

Jimingsi Vegetarian Restaurant (鸡鸣寺百味斋茶社 *Jīmíngsì bǎiwèi zhāicháshè*)
$$ | **VEGETARIAN** | Inside the Jiming Temple, this establishment makes a good lunch stop. The chefs use wheat gluten and other ingredients to create mock pork, fish, chicken, and goose dishes; the tofu threads and the Sichuan-style "fish" are recommended. **Known for:** nice views of the temple grounds; visitor favorite; helpful staff. *Average main: Y60 1 Jimingsi Lu, south of Xuanwu Lake Park 025/5771–3690 No credit cards No dinner.*

Shizi Lou (狮子楼大酒店 *Shīzilóu dàjiǔdiàn*)
$$ | **CHINESE** | Near the Shanzi Road Market, this bustling restaurant is a popular purveyor of Huaiyang cuisine, one of the "four great traditions" of Chinese cooking. Try the signature "lion's head" meatballs (*shizitou*), large and succulent orbs of pork stewed with vegetables in a clear soup; the oversize potstickers (*guotie*); or, if you're feeling brave, the stinky tofu, malodorous but surprisingly tasty. **Known for:** popular among locals; simple but tasty food; saltwater duck. *Average main: Y90 29 Hunan Lu, near Shizi Bridge 025/8360–7888 No credit cards.*

Skyways Deli (云中食品店 *Yúnzhōng shípǐndiàn*)
$$ | **CAFÉ** | Popular with overseas students studying at Nanjing University, Skyways offers the perfect antidote to oily Chinese food. This clean, user-friendly deli offers a list of sandwiches and salads that lets you choose, check, and chow in a matter of minutes. **Known for:** grocery area with meat and cheese imports; great bakery known for its chocolate-dipped coconut macaroons; expat favorite. *Average main: Y70 160 Shanghai Lu 025/8331–7103 No credit cards.*

Hotels

Central Hotel (中心大酒店 *Zhōngxīn dàjiǔdiàn*)
$ | **HOTEL** | Steps from the heart of the city, this well-run hotel has an offbeat charm, with a bright, brash, and soaring lobby and stylish, reasonably priced guest rooms. **Pros:** good value; convenient location; nice decor. **Cons:** some rooms better than others (ask for a corner room); few English-speaking staff; needs a refurb. *Rooms from: Y520 75 Zhongshan Lu 025/8473–3888 339 rooms No meals.*

Fairmont Nanjing (南京费尔蒙 *Nánjīng fèi ěr méng*)
$$ | **HOTEL** | Occupying the uppermost floors of the Jimao Tower, designed so that its 62 concertina-like stories resemble a Chinese lantern, this international luxury hotel has state-of-the-art rooms, a fabulous spa (try the indoor mineral pool), and fawning service. **Pros:** international standard; convenient to airport; several on-site restaurants. **Cons:** slightly outside the center; smaller rooms than other international brands; lack of attention to detail in some areas. *Rooms from: Y1100 333 Jiangdong Zhong Lu, Jianye District 025/8672–8888 www.fairmont.com/nanjing 359 rooms Breakfast.*

Grand Hotel (南京古南都饭店 *Nánjīng gǔnándōu fàndiàn*)
$ | **HOTEL** | **FAMILY** | Overlooking the busy shopping centers in Nanjing's commercial center, the Grand Hotel is an affordable and reliable base for seeing the sights, with a decent Western restaurant, babysitting service, and other family-friendly extras. **Pros:** apartments with kitchens available; on-site shops and restaurants; helpful staff. **Cons:** some

rooms need renovations; limited equipment in gym; relatively small rooms. $ *Rooms from: Y550* ✉ *208 Guangzhou Lu* ☎ *025/8331–1999* 🌐 *nanjinggrandhotel.com* 🛏 *316 rooms* 🍽 *No meals.*

InterContinental Nanjing (**南京绿地洲际酒店** *nánjīng lǜdìzhōujì jiǔdiàn*)
$$ | **HOTEL** | This lofty hotel towers above its rivals in height, price, and, standards, although its amenities and decor—all blacks, creams, and chromes—are geared more to Chinese businessmen than foreign leisure travelers. **Pros:** stunning skyline views from some rooms; personalized touches; multiple on-site dining options. **Cons:** relatively expensive; very businesslike; spa is lacking. $ *Rooms from: Y1300* ✉ *1 Zhongyang Lu, Gulou District* ☎ *025/8353–8888* 🌐 *www.intercontinental.com/Nanjing* 🛏 *470 rooms* 🍽 *Breakfast.*

Jinling Hotel (**金陵饭店** *Jīnlíng Fàndiàn*)
$ | **HOTEL** | Something of an institution, Nanjing's original modern five-star hotel is worth a look for its great location in the center of town, solicitous service, and—in its newer tower—sparklingly modern rooms. **Pros:** luxurious accommodations; attentive service; large rooms. **Cons:** expensive rates; obligatory service charge in bar (unusual for China); slow Internet. $ *Rooms from: Y1000* ✉ *Xinjiekou Sq., 2 Hanzhong Lu* ☎ *025/8471–1888, 025/8472–2888* 🌐 *www.jinlinghotel.com/English/index.aspx* 🛏 *625 rooms* 🍽 *No meals.*

★ **Lakeview Xuanwu Hotel** (**南京玄武饭店** *Nánjīng xuánwǔ fàndiàn*)
$ | **HOTEL** | With rich textiles, sleek furnishings, and floor-to-ceiling windows, the guest rooms at this welcoming hotel are fine for the price; ask for an east-facing room, and you'll be treated to rousing vistas of Xuanwu Lake and the wall surrounding Nanjing's old city. **Pros:** fun revolving restaurant; good and varied breakfast; nice bedding. **Cons:** some outdated facilities; slow check-in/check-out; evidence of smoking in some no-smoking rooms. $ *Rooms from: Y600* ✉ *193 Zhongyang Lu* ☎ *025/8335–8888* 🛏 *305 rooms* 🍽 *No meals.*

★ **Sofitel Galaxy Hotel** (**苏菲特银河** *Sūfēitèyínhé dàjiǔdiàn*)
$ | **HOTEL** | If you're looking for luxury, this 48-story tower remains a fine choice despite all the recent competition; rooms and suites are chic and understated, with subtle Asian flourishes and all the trimmings you'd expect from the brand, including plasma TVs and rainfall showers. **Pros:** tasteful blend of Chinese and French design; great entertainment options nearby; lovely views. **Cons:** cigarette smoke in public areas; limited English among staff; some rooms are worn. $ *Rooms from: Y1050* ✉ *9 Shanxi Lu* ☎ *025/8371–8888* 🌐 *www.sofitel.com/Nanjing* 🛏 *278 rooms* 🍽 *No meals.*

Nightlife

Blue Marlin (**蓝枪鱼** *lánqiāngyú*)
DANCE CLUBS | Sandwiched between glitzy nightclubs, Blue Marlin is the place to kick off a night out. Big, brash, and commercial, it caters to all tastes with imported beers, decent cocktails, and finger food. Evenings bring televised sports and live music from a house band. ✉ *8 Changjiang Hou Jie* ☎ *025/8453–7376* 🌐 *www.bluemarlin.cn.*

Finnegan's Wake (**芬尼根酒吧** *Fēnnígēn jiǔbā*)
BARS/PUBS | Depending on which of the two owners pours your pint of Guinness or dram of Glenfiddich, expect a proper Irish or Scottish welcome at this beautifully designed pub. Get chatting, and you may well move on to one (or another) of the 70-odd whiskeys, best enjoyed by the fireplace in the upstairs lounge. An extensive menu includes Irish stew and the "ultimate" Dublin fried breakfast. There's live Celtic music most nights. ✉ *400 Zhongshan Nan Lu* ☎ *025/5220–7362* 🌐 *www.finneganswake.com.cn.*

Did You Know?

The Sun Yat-sen Memorial honors the father of modern China. He inspired the overthrow of the Qing Dynasty and was the first provisional president of the newly founded Republic of China in 1912. However, his real fame lies in his political philosophy, the Three Principles of the People: nationalism, democracy, and the people's livelihood.

Nail Jazz Bar (钉子酒吧 *Dīngzi jiǔbā*)
MUSIC CLUBS | This dark and cozy bar has the look and feel of a neighborhood jazz joint—sadly, it lacks a jazz band most of the time, opting for a bored-looking singer who warbles along to a backing track. It does, however, have a friendly atmosphere and the city's most eclectic selection of bottled beers. ✉ *8 Luolang Xiang, south of the Sheraton Nanjing* ☎ *139/5185–9244.*

★ **Prime** (南京绿地洲际酒店 *Nánjīng lǜdì zhōujì dàjiǔdiàn*)
BARS/PUBS | Jiangsu's high-flyers toast their bottom line over classy cocktails on the 78th floor of the Zifeng Tower, China's third-tallest building. Nestled atop the InterContinental Nanjing, the bar boasts the city's best wine selection, with a good number available by the glass. Smog permitting, there are stunning city views across Xuanwu Lake to the leafy mound of Zhongshan Park. ✉ *InterContinental Nanjing, 1 Zhongyang Lu, 78th fl.* ☎ *025/8353–8888.*

Shopping

Brocade Research Institute (南京云锦研究所有限公司 *Nánjīngyún jǐnyán jiūsuǒ yǒuxiàn gōngsī*)
TEXTILES/SEWING | On the UNESCO Intangible Cultural Heritage list, brocades are lavishly embroidered textiles unique to Nanjing and once used to make robes worn by emperors. The Brocade Research Institute is part-retail-outlet-part-workshop, where traditional brocades are still being made using huge, old-fashioned looms operated by two people at a time. The gift shop sells beautiful examples of the fabric. A fantastic museum has fashion shows and high-tech exhibits, including holographic displays and 360-degree film screenings. ✉ *240 Chating Dong Jie, behind Nanjing Massacre Memorial* ☎ *025/8651–8580.*

Chaotian Gong Antique Market (朝天宫古玩市场 *Cháo tiāngōng gǔwàn shìchǎng*)
ANTIQUES/COLLECTIBLES | In the courtyard of the Confucian Temple, the Chaotian Gong Antique Market has an array of curios, from genuine antiques to fakes of varying quality. A vendor's opening price can border on the ludicrous, especially with foreign customers, but some good-natured bargaining can yield success. The market is liveliest on weekend mornings. ✉ *77 Anpin Jie.*

Fabric Market (面料市场 *Miànliào shìchǎng*)
TEXTILES/SEWING | Northwest of the Drum Tower, the Fabric Market sells silks, linens, and traditional cottons. Bargaining is necessary, but the prices are reasonable. Expect to pay Y50 to Y60 per meter of silk. Many vendors can also arrange tailoring. ✉ *209 Zhongshan Bei Lu.*

Fashion Lady Mall (时尚莱迪商城 *Shíshàng lái dí shāngchéng*)
SHOPPING CENTERS/MALLS | **FAMILY** | This subterranean retail center contains literally hundreds of tiny shops all lit with colorful neon and hawking everything from bargain women's clothing and accessories to gems, jewelry, and beauty treatments like manicures and massages. A unique shopping experience (for the girls), it's great people-watching, too. Accessible directly from Xinjiekou subway station. ✉ *30 Xinjiekou Pedestrian St., Baixia District.*

Yangzhou

1 hr (106 km [66 miles]) by bus northeast of Nanjing; 3½ hrs (300 km [185 miles]) by bus from Shanghai; 2 hrs by train from Nanjing.

Despite rapid outward expansion, the historic center of Yangzhou has retained a laid-back feel not often found in Eastern China. Small enough to be seen in a day, its charm may encourage you to linger.

Due to its fortuitous position on the Grand Canal, Yangzhou has flourished since the Tang Dynasty. Drawing on thousands of years as a trade center for salt and silk, Yangzhou maintains a cosmopolitan feel. Indeed, some of the most interesting sites demonstrate a blending of cultures: Japanese relations are evidenced in the monument to Jian Zhen, a monk who helped spread Buddhist teachings to Japan. European influence is seen in the Sino-Victorian gardens of He Yuan, and Persian contact is preserved in the tomb of Puddahidin, a 13th-century trader and descendant of Mohammed.

GETTING HERE AND AROUND

The best way to get to Yangzhou is by bus. It lies on the Beijing–Shanghai and Nanjing–Nantong highways. Yangzhou's West Bus Station is the fastest way to get to Nanjing, while Yangzhou East Bus Station serves Suzhou and Shanghai.

AIR TRAVEL

Yangzhou Taizhou Airport is 30 km (21 miles) northeast of the city. It has daily flights from Beijing, Chengdu, and Guangzhou.

BUS TRAVEL

Frequent bus service runs between Yangzhou and Nanjing and Suzhou, and on to Shanghai. Most routes have air-conditioned buses. Yangzhou West Bus Station is about 6 km (4 miles) west of the city on Jiangyang Xi Lu. Yangzhou East Bus Station is east of the city along Yunhe Xi Lu.

BUS CONTACTS Yangzhou East Bus Station (扬州汽车东站 *Yángzhōu qìchē dōng zhàn*) ✉ *Junction of Yunhe Dong Lu and Shawan Lu.* **Yangzhou West Bus Station** ✉ *Jiangyang Xi Lu* ☎ *0514/8097–5108.*

TRAIN TRAVEL

Yangzhou has a recently built train station in the western outskirts beside the Shangri-La Hotel that's only practical if you are coming from nearby Nanjing.

TRAIN CONTACT Yangzhou Train Station ✉ *Wenchang Xi Lu* ☎ *0514/8554–6222.*

TIMING

Many travelers explore Yangzhou as a day trip from Nanjing, which is perfectly possible, but to get the most out of the city consider staying at least one night.

Sights

Da Ming Temple (大明寺 *Dàmíngsì*)

RELIGIOUS SITE | Built 1,600 years ago, the Da Ming Temple is one of the more interesting Buddhist shrines in Eastern China. The main attraction is a memorial to Tang Dynasty monk Jian Zhen, who traveled to Japan to spread the teachings of Buddha. It took the determined missionary six attempts to cross the East China Sea, and it cost him his eyesight. For refreshment, seek out the still-flowing Fifth Spring Under Heaven in the temple grounds. The water's high mineral content means it's great for tea, which you can sip in a small teahouse. ✉ *8 Pingshan Tang Lu, next to Slender West Lake* ☎ *0514/8734–0720* 🎫 *Y45.*

Garden Tomb of Puhaddin (普哈丁墓 *Pŭhādīngmù*)

MEMORIAL | Although largely ignored by domestic tourists, the tomb of Puhaddin is a reminder of the city's Islamic influences. It faces the Grand Canal, from where you climb a stairway to a graveyard of marble-slab headstones. Toward the back, a garden with a charming pavilion reveals both Persian and Chinese design elements. ✉ *167 Wenchang Zhong Lu, near Jiefang Bridge* 🎫 *Y15.*

Ge Garden (个园 *Gè yuán*)

GARDEN | This lovely garden is named for the bamboo plant's characteristic trio of leaves, which look like the Chinese character *ge* (个). There are more than 60 varieties of bamboo here, including yellow stalks, striped stalks, huge treelike stands, and the delicate-leaved dwarf. The garden was developed by a wealthy salt merchant named Huang Zhiyun, who believed bamboo represented the loyalty of a good man. As you wander, note the loose bricks in the path; they're arranged to clack under your footsteps. The garden is also accessible from an entrance on Dongguan Jie. ✉ *10 Yangfu Dong Lu, east of Yangzhou Hotel* ☎ *0514/8793–5233* 🌐 *www.ge-garden.net* 🎫 *Y40.*

He Garden (何园 *Héyuán*)
HOUSE | In the southeast part of the old town, the Victorian-influenced He Garden is notable for its melding of European and Chinese architecture and landscape design. Dating from the 1880s, it differs from a traditional Chinese garden partly because of the wooden pathway linking the buildings. Other East-meets-West aspects include Victorian-style fireplaces inside the residence. ✉ *66 Xuning Men Dalu, southeast corner of city* ☎ *0514/8790–0345* 🎫 *Y40.*

Slender West Lake (瘦西湖 *Shòuxīhú*)
NATIONAL/STATE PARK | Originally part of a river, Slender West Lake was created during the Qing Dynasty by wealthy salt merchants hoping to impress Emperor Qianlong on his many visits to Yangzhou. The park, laced with willows and dotted with pavilions, bridges, and tearooms, can be seen in an hour or savored for a half-day. The **Fishing Terrace** is where the emperor decided he'd try his hand at angling; the merchants reportedly had their servants wade into the lake and hook a fish on each line he cast. Another mark left by the emperor is the **White Pagoda,** a dome-shape Buddhist stupa. The emperor casually remarked that Slender West Lake only lacked a stupa to resemble Beijing's Beihai Park. By the time the sun shone through the morning mist, there was the emperor's stupa, hastily carved out of salt and convincing from a distance. A permanent structure was completed much later. It seems all the flattery had the desired effect; Yangzhou prospered as a trading center right up until the 20th century. ✉ *28 Da Hongqiao Lu, in northern part of city* ☎ *0514/8733–0189* 🎫 *Y100.*

Replanting Gardens

Many of the country's historic gardens have been recently pieced back together. Most were ravaged during the Cultural Revolution, when, for years, Red Guard troops were encouraged to smash China's heritage to pieces. To this day, China is still replanting gardens, repairing temples, and restoring historic architecture.

★ **Wang's Residence** (汪氏小苑 *Wāngshì xiǎoyuàn*)
HOUSE | This was once one among dozens of private mansions belonging to Yangzhou's prosperous merchant class, but it alone made it through the ravages of the Cultural Revolution largely intact, thanks to its conversion into a factory. Keep an eye out for the exquisite wood carving, especially the crisscrossing bamboo design carved in layers out of *nanmu,* a glimmering wood now extinct in this area of China. There's even a bomb shelter in the small inner garden—a reminder of the Japanese invasion. ✉ *14 Di Gong Di, between Taizhou Lu and Guoqing Lu* ☎ *0514/8732–8869* 🎫 *Y25.*

Yangzhou Museum (扬州博物馆 *Yángzhōu bówùguǎn*)
MUSEUM | Housed in an impressive building beside Mingyue Lake in the town's western suburbs, the Yangzhou Museum has seven exhibition halls packed with Chinese jade, earthenware, bronze vessels, porcelain, and paper-cutting. ✉ *468 Wenchang Xi Lu, Bowuguan Lu* ☎ *0514/8522–8018* 🎫 *Free.*

Adopting in China

For some, the gardens, the architecture, the history, and the scenery are all secondary reasons to visit Yangzhou. Theirs is a more personal and momentous trip. On the outskirts of town there is a white-tiled compound called the Yangzhou Social Welfare Institute. This is where American parents and Chinese children come together to form families. Since Chinese law began promoting foreign adoption in 1991, there has been a huge surge in the number of families adopting from China. More than 60,000 children have been brought to the United States from China over the past 20 years, although numbers have declined in recent years due to a tightening of restrictions and an increase in domestic adoption.

Around 95% of children in orphanages are female. There persists a strong preference for boys, especially in rural areas. This is largely due to a combination of bias and traditional social structures whereby girls marry out and males help provide for the family. An unintended consequence of the One Child Policy exacerbates prejudices against women. Some Chinese parents, desperate to have a male child, take drastic measures like abandoning girls at orphanages or even undergoing gender-selective abortion.

As these American-adopted children have matured, they have grappled with racial and cultural identity issues. Support groups, social organizations, and even specialized heritage tour groups have been established to help them learn more about their places of birth.

Restaurants

Fu Chun Teahouse (富春茶社 *Fùchūncháshè*)

$$ | **CHINESE** | Busiest at breakfast, this venerable institution steams all sorts of delicious buns and dumplings that are hungrily wolfed down by both locals and tourists who also sip cups of the light, fragrant, green, kui dragon (aka Monkey King) tea. Be sure to try the *xièfěn tāngbāo* (oversized crabmeat dumplings filled with rich soup that you slurp out through a straw) as well as the dish that Yangzhou gave to the world: fried rice. **Known for:** tasty dumplings; unusual teas; value-for-money combo deals. *$ Average main: Y60 ✉ 35 Desheng Qiao Lu ☎ 0514/8723–3326 No credit cards ⏲ No dinner.*

Hotels

★ **Changle Inn** (长乐客栈 *Chánglè kèzhàn*)

$ | **HOTEL** | It's worth dragging your suitcase along cobbled Donguang Street in the heart of old Yangzhou to reach this restored Qing Dynasty courtyard hotel, where quiet gardens and pavilions are connected by lantern-lit pathways and oval "moon gates," and modern guest rooms have well-equipped bathrooms. **Pros:** directly opposite Ge Garden; gorgeous setting; smart rooms. **Cons:** difficult to get taxis here; breakfast needs work; showing its age in places. *$ Rooms from: Y700 ✉ 357 Dongguan Jie, opposite Ge Garden ☎ 0514/8799–3333 🌐 www.yangzhoucentre-residence.com 80 rooms Breakfast.*

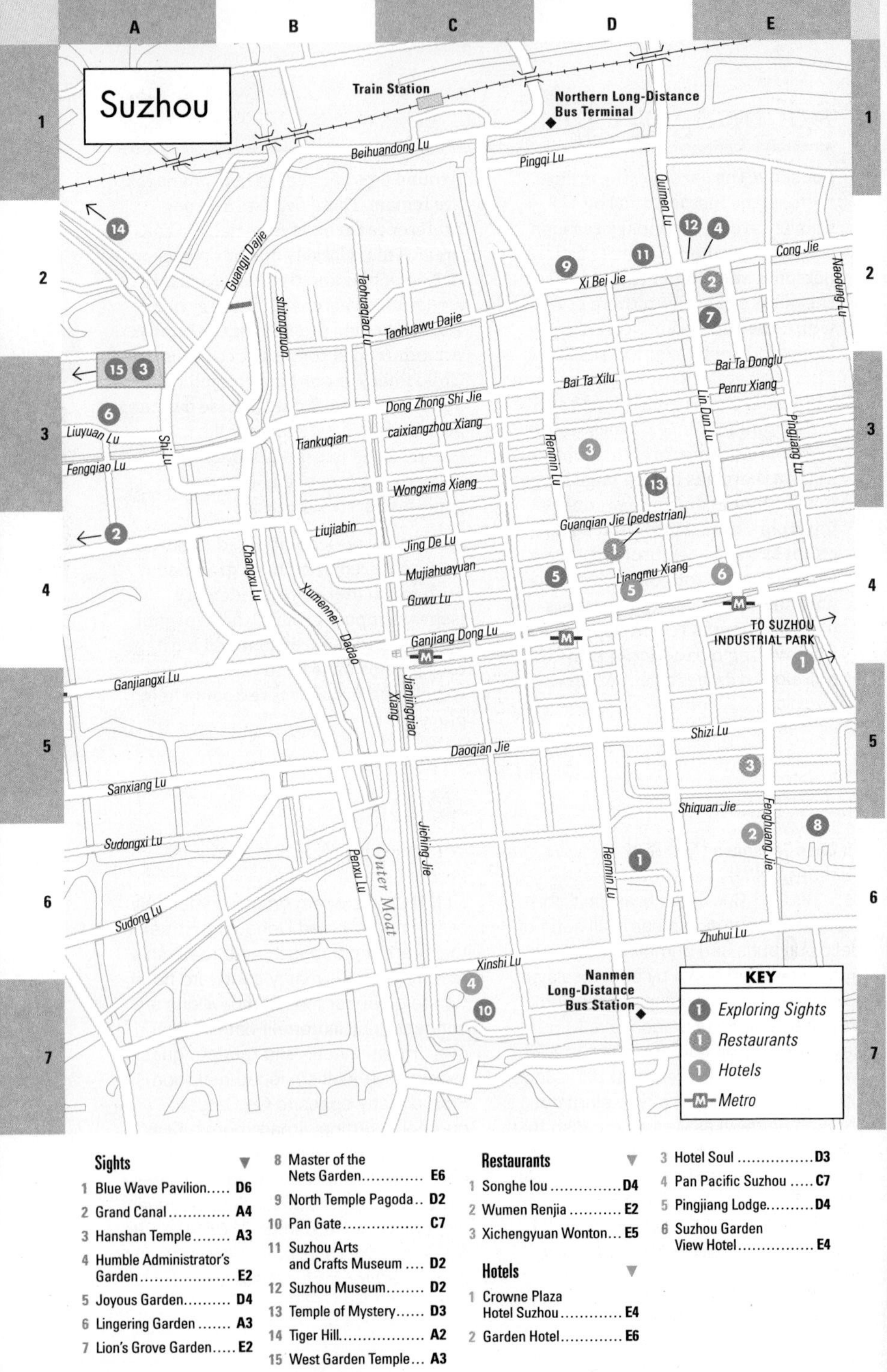

A
B
C
D
E
1
2
3
4
5
6
7
Suzhou
Train Station
Northern Long-Distance
Bus Terminal
Beihuandong Lu
Pingqi Lu
Quimen Lu
Cong Jie
Naodung Lu
Guangji Dajie
shitongnuon
Taohuaqiao Lu
Taohuawu Dajie
Xi Bei Jie
Bai Ta Donglu
Penru Xiang
Bai Ta Xilu
Lin Dun Lu
Pingjiang Lu
Dong Zhong Shi Jie
caixiangzhou Xiang
Tiankuqian
Liuyuan Lu
Shi Lu
Fengqiao Lu
Renmin Lu
Wongxima Xiang
Guanqian Jie (pedestrian)
Liujiabin
Jing De Lu
Changxu Lu
Mujiahuayuan
Liangmu Xiang
Xumennei
Dadao
Guwu Lu
Ganjiang Dong Lu
TO SUZHOU
INDUSTRIAL PARK
Ganjiangxi Lu
Jianjingqiao
Xiang
Shizi Lu
Daoqian Jie
Sanxiang Lu
Shiquan Jie
Fenghuang Jie
Sudongxi Lu
Jichiing Jie
Penxu Lu
Outer Moat
Sudong Lu
Zhuhui Lu
Xinshi Lu
Nanmen
Long-Distance
Bus Station
KEY
Exploring Sights
Restaurants
Hotels
Metro
Sights
1 Blue Wave Pavilion..... D6
2 Grand Canal............ A4
3 Hanshan Temple........ A3
4 Humble Administrator's Garden.................... E2
5 Joyous Garden.......... D4
6 Lingering Garden A3
7 Lion's Grove Garden..... E2
8 Master of the Nets Garden............ E6
9 North Temple Pagoda.. D2
10 Pan Gate................. C7
11 Suzhou Arts and Crafts Museum D2
12 Suzhou Museum........ D2
13 Temple of Mystery...... D3
14 Tiger Hill................. A2
15 West Garden Temple... A3
Restaurants
1 Songhe lou D4
2 Wumen Renjia E2
3 Xichengyuan Wonton... E5
Hotels
1 Crowne Plaza Hotel Suzhou............. E4
2 Garden Hotel............ E6
3 Hotel Soul D3
4 Pan Pacific Suzhou C7
5 Pingjiang Lodge..........D4
6 Suzhou Garden View Hotel................ E4

Ramada Plaza Yangzhou Casa Hotel (华美达凯莎酒店 *Huáměidá kǎishā jiǔdiàn*)
$ | **HOTEL** | Overlooking the Grand Canal and within striking distance of Slender West Lake and Ge Garden, the popular Ramada Plaza Yangzhou Casa is accented with bright shades of red and has up-to-date amenities and a great pool. **Pros:** great city center location; modern rooms; efficient facilities. **Cons:** lengthy check-in times; thin walls between rooms; limited English among staff. *$ Rooms from: Y600 ✉ 318 Wen Chang Zhong Lu ☎ 0514/8780–0000 🌐 www.ramada.com 204 rooms No meals.*

Shangri-La Yangzhou (扬州香格里拉酒店 *Yángzhōu Xiānggélǐlā jiǔdiàn*)
$$ | **HOTEL** | The Shangri-La makes up for its out-of-center location with sumptuous rooms and suites: the interior design nods to the city's cultural heritage—desks mimic traditional mah-jongg tables—while remaining completely contemporary. **Pros:** excellent service; high "chic" factor; indoor pool and other amenities. **Cons:** hidden among office buildings; a 15-minute taxi ride from the center; patchy Internet. *$ Rooms from: Y1100 ✉ 472 Wenchang Xi Lu ☎ 0514/8512–8888 🌐 www.shangri-la.com/yangzhou/shangrila 369 rooms No meals.*

Suzhou

Approximately 60 minutes (84 km [52 miles]) by bullet train west of Shanghai; 90 minutes (217 km [135 miles]) by bullet train southeast of Nanjing; 5 hrs (1,146 km [712 miles]) by bullet train south of Beijing.

Suzhou has long been known as a center of culture, beauty, and sophistication. The "Venice of the East" produced scores of artists, writers, and politicians over the centuries, developing a local culture based on refinement and taste. Famous around the world for its meticulously landscaped classical gardens and crisscrossing waterways, Suzhou's elegance extends even to its local dialect—a Chinese saying purports that two people arguing in the Suzhou dialect sound more pleasant than lovers talking in standard Chinese.

Unlike in other cities in Eastern China, glass-and-steel office parks have been barred from the Old City, and this preservation makes Suzhou a pleasant place to explore. There is also excellent English signage on the roads.

Only an hour outside of Shanghai, the tourist trail here is well worn, and during the high season you will find yourself sharing Suzhou's gardens with packs of foreign and domestic tour groups. It's worth getting up early to hit the most popular places before the crowds descend.

GETTING HERE AND AROUND

Buses and trains to Shanghai take about an hour. Buses bound for Nanjing (two hours) and Yangzhou (three hours) depart from the North Bus Station. Frequent trains to Nanjing take 90 minutes. It's a popular route, so be sure to buy tickets in advance.

AIR TRAVEL

Suzhou is served, rather inconveniently, by Shanghai's international airports, Hongqiao and Pudong. Hongqiao Airport is about 86 km (53 miles) from Suzhou, and shuttle buses run throughout the day. The trip takes less than two hours. If you are coming into Pudong, buses that make the long 120-km (74-mile) trip from the airport leave about once an hour.

AIR CONTACTS China Eastern Airlines *✉ 115 Ganjiang Xi Lu ☎ 0512/6522–2788 🌐 www.ce-air.com.*

BUS TRAVEL

Bus service between Suzhou and Nanjing is frequent. Suzhou has two long-distance bus stations. The North Bus Station is beside Suzhou Railway Station; the South Gate Bus Station is on the South Ring Road where it meets Yingchun Lu.

BUS CONTACT Suzhou North Bus Station ✉ *29 Xihui Lu* ☎ *0512/6753–0686*. **Suzhou South Gate Long Distance Bus Station** (苏州南门汽车客运站 *Sūzhōu nán mén qìchē kèyùn zhàn*) ✉ *601 Nanhuandong Lu*.

TRAIN TRAVEL

Trains arriving from Shanghai, Nanjing, and Beijing stop at Suzhou Train Station or the newer Suzhou North Train Station, a 25-minute taxi ride from the Old City. Tickets can usually be purchased through your hotel (advisable) or at the station.

TRAIN CONTACT Suzhou North Train Station ✉ *Chengtong Lu, Xiangcheng*. **Suzhou Train Station** ✉ *27 Suzhan Lu*.

TIMING

Suzhou has more than enough attractions to merit at least two full days. Gardens and other sights are spread throughout the city so traveling to and fro takes a bit of time.

Sights

Blue Wave Pavilion (沧浪亭 *Cānglàng tíng*)

GARDEN | The oldest existing garden in Suzhou, the Blue Wave Pavilion dates back more than 900 years to the Song Dynasty. With a rambling, maze-like design, the grounds feel a little wilder than other Suzhou gardens. The central pond is surrounded by a wooden walkway; gaze into the water at the reflection of the upturned eaves of the surrounding buildings. More than 100 different latticework motifs in the windows provide visual variety as you saunter through the covered corridor that winds through the grounds. The **Pure Fragrance Pavilion** showcases Qing Dynasty furniture at its most extreme; the entire suite is created from gnarled banyan root. ✉ *3 Canlanting Jie, between Shiquan Jie and Xinshi Lu* ☎ *0512/6519–4375* 🎫 *Mid-Apr.–Oct., Y20; Nov.–mid-Apr., Y15*.

Grand Canal (京杭大运河 *Jīngháng dàyùnhé*)

LOCAL INTEREST | Suzhou is threaded by a network of narrow waterways, with an outer moat surrounding its ancient center. The canals that now seem quaint were once choked with countless small boats ferrying goods between the city's merchants. All of these channels connect eventually to imperial China's main conduit of trade and travel, the **Grand Canal,** which passes through the town's southern outskirts. ✉ *Suzhou*.

Hanshan Temple (寒山寺 *Hánshānsì*)

RELIGIOUS SITE | Best known as a subject of one of the Tang Dynasty's most famous poems, which described the sound of its massive bell at midnight, this large, pristinely painted temple may leave those unfamiliar with the ancient poetry feeling a little underwhelmed. The place has the frenetic feel of a tourist attraction rather than the serenity of a temple. Literary pilgrims can line up to ring the temple bell themselves for an extra charge. ✉ *24 Hanshan Si Nong* ☎ *0512/6533–6634* 🎫 *Y20*.

★ **Humble Administrator's Garden** (拙政园 *Zhuōzhèng yuán*)

GARDEN | More than half of Suzhou's largest garden is occupied by ponds and lakes. The garden was built in 1509 by Wang Xianjun, an official dismissed from the imperial court. He chose the garden's name from a Tang Dynasty line of poetry reading "humble people govern," perhaps a bit of irony considering the magnificent scale of his private residence. In the warmer months the pond overflows with fragrant lotuses and the garden fills with tourists. Seek out the tiny museum near the exit for an informative display on the aesthetic differences between Chinese and Western garden design. ✉ *178 Dongbei Jie, 1 block east of Lindun Lu* 🌐 *www.szzzy.cn* 🎫 *Mid-Apr.–Oct., Y90; Nov.–mid-Apr., Y70*.

The Humble Administrator's Garden is the largest garden in Suzhou.

Joyous Garden (怡园 *Yíyuán*)
GARDEN | The youngest garden in Suzhou, Joyous Garden was built in 1874. It borrows elements from Suzhou's other famous gardens: rooms from the Humble Administrator's, a pond from the Master of the Nets. The most unusual feature is an oversize mirror, inspired by the founder of Zen Buddhism, who stared at a wall for years to find enlightenment. The garden's designer hung the mirror opposite a pavilion, to let the building contemplate its own reflection. From April to October the garden doubles as a popular teahouse in the evening. ✉ *343 Renmin Lu* ☎ *0512/6524–9317* 🎫 *Y15.*

Lingering Garden (留园 *Liú Yuán*)
GARDEN | Windows frame yet more windows, undulating rooflines recall waves, and a closed corridor opens out into a tranquil pool in this intriguing garden. The compound provides an endless array of architectural surprises: in a corner, an unexpected skylight illuminates a planted nook; windows are placed to frame bamboos as perfectly as if they were painted. The **Mandarin Duck Hall** is particularly impressive, with a picturesque moon gate engraved with vines and flowers. In the back of the garden stands a 70-foot-tall rock moved here from Lake Taihu. Occasional solo musical performances on erhu and zither enliven the halls. ✉ *338 Liuyuan Lu, west of moat* ☎ *0512/6557–9466* 🌐 *www.gardenly.com* 🎫 *Mid-Apr.–Oct., Y55; Nov.–mid-Apr., Y45.*

Lion's Grove Garden (狮子林 *Shīzilín*)
GARDEN | **FAMILY** | This garden employs countless craggy rock formations from nearby Lake Taihu to create a surreal moonscape. A labyrinth of caves surrounds a small lake; they're great fun for kids to explore, but watch for sharp edges. There's a popular local saying that if you talk to rocks, you won't need a psychologist, making this garden a good place to spend a 50-minute hour. A tearoom on the second floor of the main pavilion has nice views over the lake. ✉ *23 Yuanlin Lu, 3 blocks south*

of Humble Administrator's Garden ☎ *0512/6727–8316* 🌐 *www.szszl.com* 🎫 *Apr., May, and July–Oct., Y 40; Jan.–Mar., June, and Nov.–Dec., Y 30.*

★ **Master of the Nets Garden** (网师园 *Wǎngshī yuán*)
GARDEN | All elements of Suzhou style are here in precise balance: rocky hillscapes, layered planting, undulating walkways, and charming pavilions overlooking a central pond. Representing mountains, rivers, and the four seasons, it's a theme park of sorts, centuries before Walt Disney came along. It's also a fine example of how Chinese garden design creates the illusion of space, since this garden really isn't that big. To avoid the crowds, visit in the evening, when you can saunter from room to room enjoying traditional opera, flute, and dulcimer performances—as the master himself might have done. Evening performances are held from mid-March to mid-November. ✉ *11 Kuo Jia Tou Gang, south of Shiquan Lu, east of Daichengqiao Lu* ☎ *0512/6529–3190* 🌐 *www.szwsy.com* 🎫 *Mid-Apr.–Oct., Y30; Nov.–mid-Apr., Y20.*

North Temple Pagoda (北寺塔 *Běisìtǎ*)
BUILDING | One of the symbols of ancient Suzhou, this temple towers over the Old City. The complex has a 1,700-year history, dating to the Three Kingdoms Period. The wooden pagoda has nine levels; you can climb as high as the eighth level for what might be the best view of Suzhou. Within the grounds are the Copper Buddha Hall and Plum Garden, which, built in 1985, lack the history and complexity of Suzhou's other gardens. ✉ *1918 Renmin Lu, 2 blocks west of Humble Administrator's Garden* 🎫 *Y25.*

Pan Gate (盘门 *Pánmén*)
BUILDING | Traffic into Old Suzhou came both by road and canals, so the city's gates were designed to control access by both land and water. This gate—more of a small fortress—is the only one that remains. In addition to the imposing wooden gates on land, a double sluice gate can be used to seal off the canal and prevent boats from entering. A park is filled with colorful flowers, in contrast to the subdued hues in the city's traditional gardens. You can also climb the **Ruiguang Pagoda,** a tall, slender spire originally built more than 1,000 years ago. ✉ *1 Dong Dajie, southwest corner of Old City* ☎ *0512/6526–0004* 🎫 *Panmen Gate, Y40; Ruigang Pagoda, Y6.*

Precious Belt Bridge (宝带桥 *Bǎodàiqiáo*)
BRIDGE/TUNNEL | Spanning a small lake, this ancient bridge of 53 stone arches has a neglected air, overgrown with grass and surrounded by nondescript modern buildings. Seeing practically no tourists, it's a strangely forlorn and moving sight. By taxi it's about 25 minutes from the center of town. ✉ *Yingchun Nan Lu.*

Suzhou Arts and Crafts Museum (工艺美术博物馆 *Gōngyìměishùbówùguǎn*)
MUSEUM | This impressive collection of contemporary art is proof that Suzhou craftsmanship remains very healthy. It's just a shame that, all too often, ivory seems to be the material of choice. A highlight here is watching artists in action during high season, carving jade, cutting latticework fans from thin sheets of sandalwood, and fashioning traditional calligraphy brushes. Perhaps most amazing is the careful attention to detail of the women embroidering silk. The museum is amid attractive gardens and traditional buildings. ✉ *88 Xibei Jie, between Humble Administrator's Garden and North Pagoda* 🎫 *Y15.*

Suzhou Museum (苏州博物馆 *Sūzhōu bówùguǎn*)
MUSEUM | This is the most modern building to emerge amid a neighborhood of traditional architecture. The museum is the valedictory work for 90-year-old modernist master I.M. Pei. A controversy erupted over whether to allow Pei to construct the glass-and-steel structure in historical Suzhou. Like his crystal pyramid

in the courtyard of the Louvre, this building thrives on juxtapositions of old and new. The museum houses historical objects from Suzhou's ancient past and an impressive collection of Ming and Qing Dynasty paintings and calligraphy. English-language docent tours cost Y100. ✉ *202 Dongbei Jie, next to Humble Administrator's Garden* ☎ *0512/6757–5666* 🌐 *www.szmuseum.com* 🎫 *Free* 🕙 *Closed Mon.*

Temple of Mystery (玄妙观 *Xuánmiàoguān*)
RELIGIOUS SITE | One of the best-preserved Taoist complexes in Suzhou, the Temple of Mystery is a rare example of a wooden structure that has stood the test of time, with parts dating from the 12th century (it was founded in the 3rd century). Fortunately it suffered little damage in the Cultural Revolution and retains a splendid ceiling of carefully arranged beams and braces painted in their original colors. The temple grounds back on to a large square that is now a touristy market. ✉ *94 Guanqian Jie* ☎ *0512/6777–5479* 🎫 *Y10.*

Tiger Hill (虎丘 *Hǔqiū*)
MEMORIAL | This hill is the burial place of the king of the State of Wu, who founded the city in 514 BC. At the top of the approach is a huge sheet of stone called **Thousand Man Rock,** where legend has it that the workers who built the tomb were thanked for their labors with an elaborate banquet. The wine, alas, was drugged, so they perished to keep the tomb's entrance a secret. Modern archaeologists think they have discovered it hidden under the artificial lake. The secret may be out, but the king's wish to rest in peace is ensured by the fact that excavating the tomb would bring down the fragile Song Dynasty pagoda that stands above. The **Leaning Pagoda** is one of the most impressive monuments in Suzhou, with Persian influence evident in the arches and other architectural elements. A helpful audio guide explains many of the park's legends. ✉ *656 Huqiu Lu, northwest of city* ☎ *0512/6532–3488* 🎫 *Apr., May, and July–Oct., Y 80; Jan.–Mar., June, and Nov.–Dec., Y 60.*

West Garden Temple (西园寺 *Xīyuánsì*)
RELIGIOUS SITE | This temple is most notable for the **Hall of 500 Arhats** (*wubai luohan tang*), which houses 500 gold-painted statues of these Buddhist guides. Many of the carvings exhibit a playful humor: one struggling with dragons, another cradling a cat. ✉ *18 Xiyuan Nong, across from Lingering Garden* 🎫 *Y30.*

Restaurants

Songhelou (松鹤楼菜馆 *Sònghèlóu Càiguǎn*)
$$$$ | CHINESE | Ever since Emperor Qianlong, the Qing Dynasty's most famous tourist, declared the fish here a triumph, Songhelou has ridden on his yellow coattails. The town's most famous eatery, "Pine and Crane," as its name translates to in English, is pricey and overhyped—yet tourists still pack in to chow on braised tofu with crabmeat, pork belly with cherry sauce, and other local specialties. **Known for:** long lines; in-house specialties; creative presentation. $ *Average main: Y210* ✉ *72 Taijian Nong, south of Temple of Mystery* ☎ *0512/6727–2285.*

★ **Wumen Renjia** (吴门人家 *Wúmén rénjiā*)
$$$ | CHINESE | Shelled river shrimp (*wumen xiaren*) are a light and delicate signature dish at this lovely restaurant, accessed via a narrow alley north of Lion's Grove Garden. The busy kitchen also pulls off a crisp rendition of the region's famous *songshu guiyu* (squirrel fish), scored and fried so that the white meat fans outward in chopstick-friendly mouthfuls; sweet-and-sour sauce completes the experience. **Known for:** lively atmosphere; family friendly; good tea menu. $ *Average main: Y130* ✉ *31 Panru Xiang, north of Lion's Grove Garden* ☎ *0512/6728–8041.*

Stroll Into the Past

Pingjiang Lu is an ancient, well-preserved cobbled street in the center of the Old City, following the course of a narrow canal. Dating back 800 years, this north-to-south lane and its side streets feature bygone scenes of daily life. Quaint whitewashed canal-side houses with overhanging balconies and black-tiled roofs cluster under weeping willows and jasmine trees. Arched bridges reflected in the canals are picture-perfect. The area has become trendy in recent years, drawing new bars, restaurants, and art galleries, but for now the old and new coexist in relative harmony. Moreover, it's possible to duck into one of the alleyways and discover locals clinging to a way of life relatively unchanged for hundreds of years. It's here where you'll find the living echoes of old Suzhou.

★ **Xichengyuan Wonton** (熙盛源馄饨 *Xīchéngyuán húntún*)
$ | **SHANGHAINESE** | Locals squeeze around tables at this simple eatery, a quick hop from the Master of the Nets Garden, to lunch on mouthwateringly zingy wonton soup and *xiaolongbao* (freshly steamed, soup-filled pork dumplings). There is no menu—order at the entrance, take a number, and find a seat. **Known for:** authentic local fare; low prices; unfussy, practical atmosphere. *$ Average main: Y30 ✉ 43 Fenghuang Jie ☎ 0512/6512–8707.*

Hotels

Crowne Plaza Hotel Suzhou (中茵皇冠假日酒店 *Zhōngyín xīngguān jiàrì jiǔdiàn*)
$$ | **HOTEL** | Eight decks of spacious rooms wrap around a nautical-theme lobby bar at this shipshape luxury hotel on Jinji Lake; splurge on one of the Captain's Suites if you want to enjoy a soak in a private hot tub while you gaze out at the water. **Pros:** whimsical design; light-filled rooms; lovely pool. **Cons:** pricey in-room Internet access; outside the city center; small standard rooms. *$ Rooms from: Y1100 ✉ 168 Xinggang Lu ☎ 0512/6761–6688 🌐 www.crowneplaza.com ⮐ 344 rooms 🍽 No meals.*

Garden Hotel (南园宾馆 *Nányuán bīnguǎn*)
$ | **HOTEL** | After a day exploring Suzhou's many gardens, return to one of your own—10 acres, to be precise, complete with flowering trees, tranquil ponds, and colorful pagodas, with rooms spread across six low-slung buildings. **Pros:** pleasant, peaceful grounds; convenient location; great service. **Cons:** interior a little sterile; some rooms overdue for renovations; small standard rooms. *$ Rooms from: Y1000 ✉ 99 Daichengqiao Lu ☎ 0512/6778–6778 ⮐ 104 rooms 🍽 No meals.*

Hotel Soul (苏哥利酒店 *sūgēlì jiǔdiàn*)
$ | **HOTEL** | This centrally located design hotel is by no means the quintessential Suzhou experience, but the comfortable beds, international cable channels, and a bistro-style restaurant could be just the ticket after a long day exploring classical gardens; rooms are spacious, but beware of the inexpensive, windowless "atrium" rooms. **Pros:** great value; playful design (don't miss the "spaceship" elevator capsule); friendly service.

The canals of Tongli, one of the water villages near Suzhou.

Cons: no historic value; gym very basic; limited English among staff. $ *Rooms from: Y550* ✉ *27–33 Qiaosikong Xiang, east of Pingan Fang* ☎ *0512/6777–0777* 🌐 *www.hotelsoul.com.cn* *225 rooms* *No meals.*

★ **Pan Pacific Suzhou** (吴宫泛太平洋酒店 *Sūzhōu wúgōng tàipǐngyángdàjiǔdiàn*)
$ | **HOTEL** | **FAMILY** | The two-story stone entrance to this luxury hotel is topped by a pagoda that's modeled after the nearby Pan Gate; try to snag a courtyard-facing room (with garden views) or a newer Pacific Club room (pricier but with more perks). **Pros:** unique architecture; peaceful gardens; pretty pool. **Cons:** in an older part of town; uninspiring lounge food; confusing to navigate. $ *Rooms from: Y900* ✉ *259 Xinshi Lu* ☎ *0512/6510–3388* 🌐 *www.panpacific.com/suzhou* *481 rooms* *No meals.*

★ **Pingjiang Lodge** (平江客栈 *Píngjiāng kèzhàn*)
$ | **B&B/INN** | This grand old mansion next to historic Pingjiang Jie balances period atmosphere and contemporary comfort; just ask to see a few rooms before check-in—antique furniture and modern bathrooms are a given, but a cramped, awkward layout and lack of natural light can be issues. **Pros:** quaint historic style; great location; affordable rates. **Cons:** service can be a little frosty; some rooms a bit dark; ready for a refurb. $ *Rooms from: Y600* ✉ *33 Niu Jia Xiang, southern end of Pingjiang Jie* ☎ *0512/6523–3888* 🌐 *www.pingjiang-lodge.com/* *50 rooms* *No meals.*

Suzhou Garden View Hotel (苏州人家大酒店 *Sūzhōu rěnjià dàjiǔdiàn*)
$ | **HOTEL** | Beside a canal and a short stroll to historic Pingjiang Lane, this comfortable and well-run hotel wraps around a peaceful courtyard and Suzhou-style garden. **Pros:** great value; distinctive touches; tranquil surroundings. **Cons:** difficult to find taxi; small bathrooms; poor amenities. $ *Rooms from: Y500* ✉ *66 Luo Guaqia, Lindun Lu* ☎ *0512/6777–8888* *188 rooms* *No meals.*

Nightlife

The Bookworm (老书虫 *Lǎoshūchóng*)
BARS/PUBS | Visit this canal-side town house to peruse a wide selection of English-language books and magazines while sipping imported wines and beers. At night, there's often live music. ✉ *77 Gunxi Fang, off Shiquan Jie* ☎ *0512/6526–4720* 🌐 *www.suzhoubookworm.com.*

Le Ble D'or (金色三麥 *Jīnsè sānmài*)
BARS/PUBS | This enormous brewpub has servers garbed in Bavarian dirndls, a jarringly French name, and a self-described "American style." Occupying the entire fourth floor of a high-rise building, it's the local outpost of a popular Taiwanese chain. Three types of craft beer are brewed on the premises, and the menu includes sticky barbecue pork ribs, fried chicken, and truffle fries in portions meant for sharing. The Munich-inspired *bierkeller* interior can seat a staggering 900 people at its long tables. ✉ *Jinhe Guoji Dasha Building, 34 Shishan Lu, 4th fl., East New Town* ☎ *0512/6665–5909* 🌐 *www.lebledor.com.*

Shopping

Su Embroidery Studio (苏绣工作室 *Sūxiù gōngzuò shì*)
TEXTILES/SEWING | Pick up fine examples of hand-embroidered silk as well as Suzhou double-sided embroidery at this showroom and workshop. Custom pieces can be ordered and shipped internationally. ✉ *1902 Senso International Plaza, 98 Bei Dongwu Lu* ☎ *0512/5887–1762* 🌐 *www.suembroidery.com.*

Suzhou Cultural Relics Store (苏州文物商店 *Sūzhōu wénwù shāngdiàn*)
ANTIQUES/COLLECTIBLES | Since 1956, the Suzhou Cultural Relics Store has been selling antiques, calligraphy, jades, and other items. Prepare to bargain on price. ✉ *1208 Renmin Lu* ☎ *0512/6523–3851.*

Suzhou Silk Museum Shop (苏州丝绸博物馆 *Sūzhōu sīchóu bówùguǎn*)
TEXTILES/SEWING | Near the North Pagoda, the well-stocked Suzhou Silk Museum Shop is the main reason folks come to the Silk Musuem. ✉ *2001 Renmin Lu* ☎ *No phone.*

Side Trips from Suzhou: Water Villages

Centuries-old villages, preserved almost in their original state, surround Suzhou. Bowed bridges span narrow canals along which traditional oared boats are paddled, creating an almost picture-perfect scene of life long past. A trip to one of these villages could well be the photographic highlight of your trip to Eastern China.

Be warned, though: the tourism revenue that has saved some of these villages from the wrecking ball has also changed their character to differing degrees. Those closest to the larger cities are swamped by tour groups. Trekking to an out-of-the-way destination can pay off by letting you find a village that, outside of high season, you might have mostly to yourself.

Zhouzhuang

30 km (19 miles) southeast of Suzhou.

Sights

Zhouzhuang (周庄 *Zhōuzhuāng*)
TOWN | The most renowned of the water villages is undoubtedly Zhouzhuang. Its fame is partly due to its proximity from Suzhou and Shanghai, just 45 minutes and an hour away, respectively. As a result, more than 2½ million annual visitors elbow their way through its streets, diminishing the town's charm in an en-masse attempt to experience Old

China. Next to the "ancient memorial archway," which isn't ancient at all, is a ticket window. The entrance fee of Y100 gets you into the water-village-turned-gift shop.

Crowds aside, Zhouzhuang is fun for families. Several residences, some 500 years old, let you peek in to see what life was like in the Ming and Qing dynasties. There are several storefronts where you can see brick making, bamboo carving, and basket weaving—traditional crafts that, up until recently, were widely practiced in the countryside. In terms of souvenirs, skip the usual snuff bottles and teapots, and opt for items you're less likely to find elsewhere: homemade rice wine, rough-hewn ox-horn combs, and bamboo rice baskets, say. The food here is typical country fare, making it a nice break from the fancier cuisines of Suzhou and Shanghai. Braised pork belly, crunchy stir-fried water chestnuts, pickled vegetables, and wild greens abound.

Buses bound for Zhouzhuang depart from Suzhou's North Bus Station every 20 minutes between 7 and 5. The 90-minute trip costs Y25. ⊠ *Suzhou.*

Tongli

18 km (11 miles) southeast of Suzhou.

Sights

Tongli (同里 *Tónglǐ*)
TOWN | Supremely photogenic and a pleasure to explore, the largest of the water villages is 30 minutes from Zhouzhuang and 90 minutes from Suzhou. Although Tongli can become crowded, it has a more-authentic atmosphere, thanks to cobbled streets devoid of cars and a populace that still lives as well as works here. To get a better feel for an earlier era, avoid the often-busy main thoroughfares, and seek out the quaint side streets and narrow alleyways that open onto canals and bridges. Near the entrance gate are several private homes offering beds, and throughout the village are tea shops and local restaurants with small tables set out in front of the canals. Hiring a boat (Y100 for up to six people) to be punted along the waterways gives a different perspective on the town. The admission fee is Y100.

The fastest buses to Tongli leave from Suzhou South Bus Station every 20 minutes between 7 and 5. The journey costs Y12. Most taxis in town will also take you; when you negotiate a fee, aim for about Y150. This is by far the fastest way to get there, and you can take the bus back. ⊠ *Suzhou.*

Luzhi

25 km (15 miles) east of Suzhou.

Sights

Luzhi (甪直 *Lùzhí*)
HISTORIC SITE | Even farther off the beaten path than Zhouzhuang or Tongli is the water village Luzhi, roughly half an hour from Suzhou. Though it's a popular tourist destination, it remains one of the more peaceful communities in the area. Described as a "museum of bridges," the village has more than 40 in all shapes and styles. Many of the older women in the village preserve traditional customs, wearing folk headdresses and skirts.

Luzhi-bound buses leave from Suzhou's North Bus Station every 30 minutes between 6:30 am and 6:30 pm. The 40-minute ride costs Y10. ⊠ *Suzhou* *Y100.*

Baosheng Temple (保圣寺 *Bǎoshèngsì*)
RELIGIOUS SITE | Luzhi is notable for the spectacular Baosheng Temple, a yellow-walled compound built in the year 503 that is famous for its breathtaking collection of Buddhist arhats. Arranged on a wall of stone, these clay

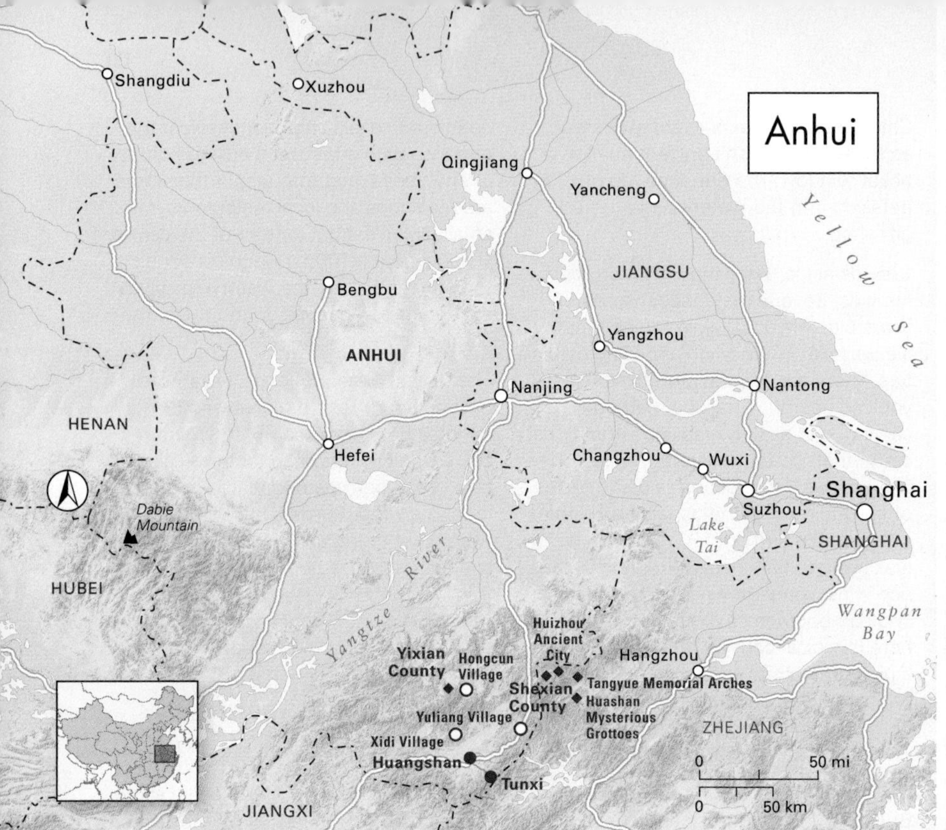

sculptures are the work of Yang Huizhi, a famous Tang Dynasty sculptor. Made more than 1,000 years ago, they depict Buddhist disciples who have gained enlightenment. The temple also features a well-preserved bell from the end of the Ming Dynasty. ✉ *Wenhua Wu* ☎ *0512/6501–0011* 🎟 *Free.*

Huangshan

5½ hrs (250 km [155 miles]) by train west of Nanjing; 3½ hrs by long-distance bus.

Huangshan (Yellow Mountain) is Eastern China's most dreamlike mountain landscape, where delicate songshu pines cling to the vertiginous sides of soaring granite peaks. Its mist-swathed vistas are a recurring motif in Chinese art and literature, and, tamed by tens of thousands of stone steps (and a few cable cars), are accessible to anyone with a head for heights.

GETTING HERE AND AROUND

Most long-distance transportation, including trains and airplanes, arrives in Tunxi, the largest city near Huangshan. Be aware, however, that Tunxi is still about an hour from the entrance to the scenic mountain area. Minibuses to Tangkou and other destinations around the base of the mountain leave from the plaza in front of Tunxi's Huangshan Railway Station, costing around Y15 to Y30. There are also plenty of taxi drivers who are happy to offer their services, usually for around Y70–Y100 per carload.

Some buses from Nanjing, Hangzhou, and Shanghai go directly to Tangkou, the entrance at the base of the mountain.

The airport is close to Tunxi, about a Y15 to Y20 cab ride from the center of town.

AIR TRAVEL

If you plan to fly to Huangshan, you'll land at the Huangshan City Airport near Tunxi, about 60 to 90 minutes by car from the mountain. There are direct flights from Beijing, Guangzhou, Shanghai, and Ji'nan.

TAXI AND MINIBUS TRAVEL

In Tunxi, minibuses and taxis that congregate around the train station will take you to Huangshan. For about Y20 they will drop you at the main gate at the bottom of the mountain or at the beginning of the climbing section.

TRAIN TRAVEL

There is one overnight train from Shanghai to Huangshan Railway Station, arriving at about 9 am. From the station you can catch a minivan or taxi to Huangshan.

TIMING

Allow at least two days for a visit to Huangshan, and another day or so to see the villages around Tunxi. Thanks to the cable cars on the mountain (each trip costing Y80 per person), it is possible to take in a lot of scenery in one full day. On weekends or holidays you can expect lengthy queues at the cable cars.

Sights

There are two primary hiking routes up the mountain. The Eastern Steps, a straightforward path through forests, is both the shortest and the easiest. The Southern Steps (some guidebooks call these the Western Steps, which causes confusion with another set of steps used primarily by porters) require more effort, but they pay off with remarkable scenery. The steep, winding path reveals sheer peaks and precipitous lookouts over mist-enshrouded valleys.

Climbing up is physically taxing, but climbing down is mentally exhausting, requiring far more concentration. If you have the time and the leg muscles, it's nice to ascend the Southern Steps, where the scenery stretches before you. The views are a good excuse to stop and catch your breath.

★ **Huangshan** (黄山 *Huángshān*)
MOUNTAIN—SIGHT | Eastern China's most impressive natural landscape, Yellow Mountain's peaks thrust upward through rolling seas of clouds, spindly pines clinging precipitously to their sides. It was a favorite retreat of emperors and poets past, and its vistas have inspired some of China's most outstanding artworks and literary endeavors. So beguiling were they that centuries of labor went into constructing the paths and stone stairways, some ascending gently through virgin forest, others sharp and steep. Since 1990, the area has been designated a UNESCO World Heritage Site.

The common English translation—Yellow Mountain—is misleading. Huangshan is not a single mountain but a range of peaks stretching across four counties. To complicate matters, the name is not a reference to color. The region was originally called the "Black Mountains," but a Tang Dynasty emperor renamed it to honor Huangdi, the Yellow Emperor. And according to legend, it was from these slopes that he rode off to heaven on the back of a dragon.

The mountain is renowned for its gnarled stone formations, many sporting fanciful names to describe their shape. Some will require a stretch of the imagination, while others will leap out at you on first glance. Generations of Chinese poets and travelers have humanized these peaks and forests in this way, and left their mark on the area.

■ **TIP→ Be forewarned: Huangshan has its own weather.** More than 200 days a year, precipitation obscures the famous views. It can be sunny below, but in the mountains it's damp and chilly. That said, even on the foggiest of days

Did You Know?

Climbing the rough-hewn steps of Huangshan is not something you'll quickly forget. More than 60,000 steps have been carved into the side of the mountains, some as far back as 1,500 years ago.

the wind is likely to part the mist long enough to offer a satisfactory glimpse of the famous peaks. *Mar.–Nov., Y300; Dec.–Feb., Y150.*

EASTERN STEPS

The Eastern Steps are quicker than the Southern Steps, but the scenery isn't as rewarding, and there are fewer scenic side routes. Along the way is a building called **Fascinating Pavilion,** most notable as a rest stop along the way. There's a short half-hour side hike to **Pipeng,** with a good view out over a number of the smaller eastern peaks. By the time you reach **Cloud Valley,** the landscape that makes Huangshan famous begins to come into view. **Beginning to Believe Peak** is the start of the awe-inspiring landscape, and the first true majestic vista on this path.

Cloud Valley Temple Cable Car Station (云谷寺索道 *Yúngŭsì suŏdào*)

TRANSPORTATION SITE (AIRPORT/BUS/FERRY/TRAIN) | The Eastern Steps begin at the Cloud Valley Temple Cable Car Station. The cable car takes eight minutes to traverse what takes hikers three or more hours. Large windows provide an aerial view of the mountain and bamboo forests below. This area was once home to several monasteries, nunneries, and temples. By the beginning of the 20th century, they had been largely abandoned, but the name Cloud Valley Temple Area remains. ✉ *Close to Cloud Valley Temple* *Mar.–Nov., Y80; Dec.–Feb., Y65.*

SOUTHERN STEPS

The steep Southern Steps are by far the tougher path. However, the climb pays off with great views and some beautiful side trails. Although the Eastern Steps feel like a walk through the woods, the Southern Steps truly feel like an ascent into the clouds. The steps begin around the Hot Springs, at the **Mercy Light Temple** area. **Midway Mountain Temple** has facilities to rest, eat, and even stay overnight, but no temple. It's here that the splendor of Huangshan comes into full view. At

Be Prepared

Most paths are well maintained with good steps and sturdy handrails, but Huangshan still has sheer drop-offs and steep, uneven, rain-slicked steps. A walking stick (sturdy wooden dragon-head staffs are on sale around the mountain) will help steady your ascent. It can get very cold on the peaks, and rain can come unexpectedly. Dress in layers, and consider bringing a hooded sweatshirt to stay warm.

the **Three Islands at Penglai,** a trio of peaks emerge from a sea of mist. If you're feeling energetic, a side tour of **Heavenly Capital Peak** affords spectacular views out over the rest of the range. The effort is worth a try even if it looks cloudy, because the mist can sometimes clear by the time you get to the top. This may not be the highest peak in the range, but it is one of the steepest.

Jade Screen Cable Car (玉屏索道 *Yùpíng suŏdào*)

TRANSPORTATION SITE (AIRPORT/BUS/FERRY/TRAIN) | The Jade Screen Cable Car runs parallel to the Southern Steps, leaving riders close to the Welcoming Guests Pine. It can close unexpectedly in inclement weather. ✉ *Huangshan* *Mar.–Nov., Y90; Dec.–Feb., Y75.*

THE SUMMIT

The entrance to the summit area, also known as Tianhai, is announced by the **Welcoming Guest Pine,** a lone pine clinging to the edge of a cliff, one branch outstretched. Behind it a sheer stone slope rises out of the clouds. Continuing onward, you can climb **Lotus Peak,** the tallest in the province. A walk through **Turtle Cave,** an arched pathway straight through the hillside, brings the weary traveler to **Bright Top Peak,** slightly lower than Lotus, and an easier climb.

The **Xihai Grand Canyon** loop starts at the Cloud Dispelling Pavilion and ends at the Haixin Ting Pavilion. Rock formations called "Upside Down Boot" and "Lady Playing Piano" may be clumsily translated, but they are stunning. The farther along you walk, the fewer travelers you'll come across. At the southern end of the loop, near Haixin, the trail reaches the **Immortal's Walk Bridge,** a dizzying arch over the misty abyss that leads to a terrace on one of the mountain's spires. A huge landscape spreads out beneath, without a single tour group in sight.

A highlight of any trip is sunrise, visible from several places on the mountain. Most hikers arrive well after dawn, but you'll be rewarded with the spectacle of Huangshan materializing from the shadows if you arrive just before first light, weather permitting of course. A popular viewing spot near the Beihai Hotel is the **Dawn Pavilion.** There are several less crowded peaks with equally good views a little farther from the hotels. **Refreshing Terrace, Lion Peak,** and **Red Cloud Peak** all provide unobstructed views of the rising sun.

Compared to the ascent, the summit area is relatively level, but there is still a good amount of stair climbing. It takes about three to four hours to walk the full summit circle, and considerably more if you take side trails.

Restaurants

Celebrity's Banquet (喜来大酒店 *Xǐlái dàjiǔdiàn*)
$$ | CHINESE | The best restaurant on the summit, Celebrity's Banquet inside the Xihai Hotel celebrates local culture with a range of traditional Hui dishes. Soups of dried vegetables, jellied tofu, braised pork, and a delicately flavored pumpkin soup shouldn't be missed. **Known for:** stewed chicken wings; fried "rocky" frogs; tofu soup. *Average main: Y80 ✉ Xihai Hotel, Grand Canyon Loop, Summit Area ☎ 0559/558–8888.*

Tangzhen Hotel Restaurant (汤镇大酒店 *Tāngzhèn dàjiǔdiàn*)
$$ | CHINESE | This hotel is nothing to write home about, but the Hui cuisine here is especially good, attracting locals from around the area. Specialties include cured mandarin fish, home-cured pork with bamboo, and stewed dishes served in clay pots. **Known for:** traditional dishes; picturesque setting; tasty pork. *Average main: Y80 ✉ Tangzhen Hotel, Tangchuan Rd., Tangkou ✣ At main entrance to Huangshan ☎ 0559/556–2665 No credit cards.*

Hotels

Several small, basic huts can be found along the Southern Steps, but it would be better to push on to the hotels in the Summit Area. They are your only option if you want to catch the sunrise. As a bonus, you'll have the dew-drenched forests to yourself for a few hours before the latecomers arrive. Reservations are strongly recommended, especially for weekends; this is a popular destination for Chinese travelers, as well as tourists from Japan and Korea.

Baiyun Hotel (白云宾馆 *Báiyún bìnguǎn*)
$ | HOTEL | From the Yungu Cable Car station (or top of the Eastern Steps for hikers), this is the first of the four main hotels at the summit area that you'll reach; middling rooms are made up for somewhat by a good restaurant downstairs. **Pros:** good location; great restaurant; short hike to viewpoint. **Cons:** few amenities; nothing special about the rooms; no Wi-Fi. *Rooms from: Y700 ✉ Summit Area ☎ 0559/558–2708 81 rooms No meals.*

Beihai Hotel (北海宾馆 *Běihǎi bìnguǎn*)
$ | HOTEL | With rooms set among flowering rhododendrons and azaleas, the Beihai Hotel is a decent choice for a night on the mountain; ask for a front-facing room which has better views. **Pros:** ideal location; soothing sauna; amazing

The shops and restaurants on Old Street in Tunxi

views. **Cons:** uninspiring decor in rooms; overpriced restaurant; service needs work. *Rooms from: Y900 Huangshan Scenic Area 0559/556–2555 139 rooms No meals.*

★ **Xihai Hotel** (黄山西海饭店 *Huángshān xīhǎi fàndiàn*)

$$ | HOTEL | At this classy summit hotel, you can count on comfortable, spacious double rooms (ask for one in the newer building) that come with down jackets, a welcome touch if you plan to brave the predawn chill to catch the sunrise. **Pros:** high-standard accommodations in south building; good on-site restaurant; great views. **Cons:** relatively expensive; some bathroom amenities cost extra; north building not air-conditioned. *Rooms from: Y1200 Xihai Scenic Area 0559/558–8186 www.hsxihaihotel.cn/en/index.html 180 rooms.*

Tunxi

5½ hrs (250 km [155 miles]) by train west of Nanjing; 3½ hrs by long-distance bus.

This is the gateway to the Yellow Mountain area. Apart from being a transportation hub, Tunxi also has a charming strip of shops and restaurants and is a convenient place from which to take trips to Shexian and Yixian counties, famous for their historical architecture.

GETTING HERE AND AROUND

Unless you arrive on a long-distance bus bound for Tangkou, your bus or train is probably bound for Tunxi, around 65 km (40 miles) from the mountain.

AIR TRAVEL

Huangshan Tunxi International Airport, located near Tunxi, welcomes flights from Beijing, Guangzhou, Chengdu, Xi'an, and Shanghai. There are also roughly two flights a week from Hong Kong. Taxis to Tunxi cost Y15 to Y30.

AIR CONTACTS Huangshan Tunxi International Airport (黄山机场 *Huángshān jīchǎng*) ✉ *Jichang Dadao, west of city, Huangshan* ☎ *0559/293–4111* 🌐 *www.hsairport.com.*

BUS TRAVEL

Buses are a convenient way of getting to Tunxi from Zhejiang, Jiangsu, and even Shanghai. Buses that run hourly from Hangzhou take 3½ hours and cost Y65. The route takes you through some gorgeous scenery. Buses from Nanjing take around five hours and cost Y80. From Shanghai, buses take eight to nine hours and cost Y120.

BUS CONTACT Tunxi Bus Station ✉ *95 Huangshan Dong Lu, Huangshan.*

TRAIN TRAVEL

Several trains depart daily for Nanjing (6 hours), and there are two trains each day for Shanghai (11½ hours).

TRAIN CONTACT Huangshan Train Station ✉ *Northern end of Qianyuan Beilu, Huangshan* ☎ *0559/211–6222.*

TIMING

Tunxi is mostly a place to spend a night before your Huangshan trek. It can also be a good place to arrange tours of the area.

Sights

Tunxi Old Street (屯溪老街 *Túnxī lǎojiē*)

NEIGHBORHOOD | In Tunxi, the best place to stroll is along Old Street. The avenue is quiet during the day, but comes alive in the early evening. Shops along the way stay open until about 10 or 11. Wade through the tourist offerings and you may find some treasures. ✉ *Huangshan.*

Restaurants

Diyilou (老街第一楼 *Lǎojiēdìyīlóu*)

$$ | **CHINESE** | You order by pointing to plated dishes at this lively restaurant in a traditional house, where local specialties include tender bamboo shoots, four-mushroom soup, braised tofu, and a must-try mushroom-wrapped meatball. **Known for:** huge menu; good prices; friendly staff. ⓢ *Average main: Y70* ✉ *247 Tunxi Lao Jie, at Lao Jie, Huangshan* ☎ *0559/253–9797.*

Hotels

Crowne Plaza Huangshan Yucheng (昱城皇冠假日酒店 *Yùchéng huángguān jiàrì jiǔdiàn*)

$ | **HOTEL** | Huangshan's first world-class hotel is a really good bet for a night of creature comforts after you've hiked the trails and returned to Tunxi. **Pros:** Reliable international brand; nice pool; just 3 km (2 miles) from Tunxi's Old Street. **Cons:** lacks personality; restaurant food nothing special; relatively expensive. ⓢ *Rooms from: Y850* ✉ *1 Huizhou Lu, Huangshan* ☎ *0871/423–4917* *485 rooms* *Breakfast.*

Huashan Holiday Hotel (華山賓館 *Huàshān bīnguǎn*)

$ | **HOTEL** | At this well-appointed hotel just a block from the city's main shopping district, the enormous guest rooms come as a pleasant surprise, even if service can be confused at times. **Pros:** great access to shops and restaurants; plenty of room to spread out; decent value for the money. **Cons:** so-so in-house restaurant; some rooms a little musty; limited English among staff. ⓢ *Rooms from: Y300* ✉ *3 Yanan Lu, Huangshan* ☎ *0559/232–2888* *200 rooms* *No meals.*

★ **Pig's Inn** (猪栏酒吧 *Zhūlánjiǔbā*)

$ | **B&B/INN** | Wake to crowing roosters at this curio-filled boutique hotel opened by a Shanghai artist; it's in a 400-year-old stone house outside Xidi, an hour's drive from Tunxi, so a stay here lets you experience ancient village life—without forsaking air-conditioning or Internet access. **Pros:** traditional lodging; beautiful surroundings; drivers at the ready. **Cons:** a bit far from Huangshan; staff knows very little English; basic furnishings. $ *Rooms from: Y800* ✉ *Renrang Li, Xidi* ☎ *0559/515–4555* *5 rooms* 🍽 *No meals.*

Shopping

Sanbai Yanzhai (三百砚斋 *Sānbǎi yànzhāi*)
LOCAL SPECIALTIES | When shopping along Lao Jie, the best offerings are traditional calligraphy ink and paper. The best ink stones are sold at Sanbai Yanzhai. ✉ *173 Lao Jie, Huangshan* ☎ *0559/253–5538.*

Side Trip to Shexian County

25 km (15 miles) east of Tunxi.

Shexian County has been called a living architectural art museum because of its natural beauty and array of historic buildings. Over the centuries, it has inspired philosophers, poets, and painters. Today, there is no lack of tourists, as it's a pleasant day trip from Tunxi.

GETTING HERE AND AROUND

Buses run throughout the day from the Tunxi long-distance bus station. The trip should take about 45 minutes and cost approximately Y15. Once you get to Shexian Bus Station in Huizhou Old City, you can board a minibus or take a taxi to outlying scenic spots. However, if you are traveling with several people, it's best to hire a car and driver for the day, as many of these places are quite remote and spread out.

Sights

Huashan Mysterious Grottoes (华山谜窟 *Huàshān míkū*)
CAVE | The Huashan Mysterious Grottoes are a combination of impressive natural caves and rooms carved into rock illuminated with colored lights. No one seems quite certain when or why they were built, but it makes for a distracting excursion. ✉ *Wu Village, Between Xiongcun and Tunxi, Huangshan* ☎ *0559/235–9888* 🌐 *www.huashanmiku.cn* 🎫 *Y70.*

Huizhou Ancient City (惠州城 *Huìzhōu lǎochéng*)
TOWN | This site boasts several examples of Huizhou architecture that demonstrates the wealth of the merchants who lived here. Highlights include the centuries-old city wall and a magnificent four-sided memorial gate guarded by sculptures of frolicking lions. ✉ *Huangshan* ☎ *0559/527–8899* 🎫 *Free to visit; Y180 for a combo ticket to enter various buildings and gardens.*

Tangyue Memorial Arches (堂樾牌楼群 *Tángyuè páióuqún*)
BUILDING | Almost 100 memorial archways, a recurring feature of Huizhou architecture, dot Shexian County, but this well-preserved row of seven is the most famous. It commemorates the wealthy Bao family and has elements that reflect morality, piety, female chastity, and other traditional values. ✉ *Tangyue Village, 5 km (3 miles) west of Huizhou Old Town, Tangyue* 🎫 *Y100.*

Yuliang Village (渔梁古镇 *Yúliáng gǔzhèn*)
TOWN | Near Huizhou Old Town, Yuliang Village overlooks an ancient Tang Dynasty dam with water still gurgling over its sloped sides. Fishermen in wooden skiffs still make their living here. A narrow street parallel to the river is a pleasant spot for a stroll. Most families leave their doors open, allowing a peak into simple homes where pages from magazines are often used as wallpaper. Inexpensive pedicabs travel here from the Shexian Bus Station in Huizhou Old City, or you can catch Bus 1 from the train station. ✉ *Changxi Xian, Yuliang* 🎫 *Y30.*

Side Trip to Yixian County

A pleasant day trip from Tunxi, Yixian County is the site of some beautiful and ancient rural architecture set in bucolic surroundings. Yixian County receives nearly 2½ million visits per year, but don't let that deter you, as the UNESCO World Heritage Sites in the area are eminently photogenic.

GETTING HERE AND AROUND

To reach Yixian County, take the buses that leave from in front of Tunxi's train station. They cost about Y15 and depart every 20 minutes.

Sights

Hongcun Village (宏村 *Hóng cūn*)
TOWN | A delicately arched bridge leads into Hongcun, a delightfully preserved settlement laid out to resemble a water buffalo. Two 600-year-old trees mark its horns, a lake its belly, and streams diverted for irrigation are its intestines! A number of films have used Hongcun as a location, including *Crouching Tiger, Hidden Dragon*. Several large halls and old houses are open to visit. The Salt Merchant's House is especially well preserved, with intricate decorations and carvings that fortunately survived the Cultural Revolution. ✉ *Northwest corner, Yi Xian, Hongcun* ☎ *0559/251–7464* 🎫 *Y104 (ticket valid for 3 days with unlimited entries).*

Xidi Village (西递村 *Xīdīcūn*)
TOWN | A UNESCO World Heritage Site, Xidi Village is known for its exquisite memorial gate. There were once a dozen gates, but they were destroyed during the Cultural Revolution. The existing gate was left standing as a "bad example" to be criticized. There are several houses in the village with excellent examples of brick carving and an impressive Clan Temple with massive ginkgo columns and beams. ✉ *Off Taohuayuan Lu, Xidi* ☎ *0559/515–4030* 🎫 *Y104.*

Chapter 5

SHANGHAI

Updated by
Cat Nelson

Sights ★★★☆☆

Restaurants ★★★★★

Hotels ★★★★☆

Shopping ★★★☆☆

Nightlife ★★★★☆

WELCOME TO SHANGHAI

TOP REASONS TO GO

★ **Skyline Views:** Head to the top of the Shanghai World Financial Center, known to locals as the "bottle opener," the pagoda-inspired Jin Mao, or the gargantuan Shanghai Tower, and look straight into the clouds.

★ **Modern Art:** The far-flung Power Station of Art is a contemporary hub worth the trek down to the former World Expo site.

★ **People-Watching:** A strong sense of community and small living spaces push life out onto the street, where locals chit chat, play cards, exercise, ballroom dance, and stroll about.

★ **Yu Garden:** When not too crowded, the garden offers a few minutes of peace and beauty amid the clamor of the city, with rocks, trees, and walls curved to resemble dragons, bridges, and pavilions.

★ **The Bund:** This waterfront promenade is lined with regal colonial buildings in 52 architectural styles, and it looks much as it did during Shanghai's Golden Age nearly a century ago.

1 Old City. This is where Chinese locals lived when foreigners filled the concessions.

2 Xintiandi and City Center. City Center encompasses Xintiandi and People's Square. Eat, drink, and shop in restored *shikumen* (stone gatehouses).

3 The Bund and Nanjing Dong Lu. Pedestrian-only Nanjing Dong Lu ends at Shanghai's iconic waterfront boulevard.

4 Former French Concession. Wander these wonderful streets, or hop in a cab and explore the emerging West Bund district.

5 Jing'an and Changning. Nanjing Dong (east) Lu turns into Nanjing Xi (west) Lu, and the shops go from mass market to ultraluxury.

6 Pudong. Home to the central business district in Lujiazui and three supertall skyscrapers.

7 Hongkou and Putuo. Quiet Hongkou is steeped in history. Putuo has the gallery strip M50.

8 Xujiahui, Hongqiao, and Gubei. These neighborhoods have malls and are popular with business travelers.

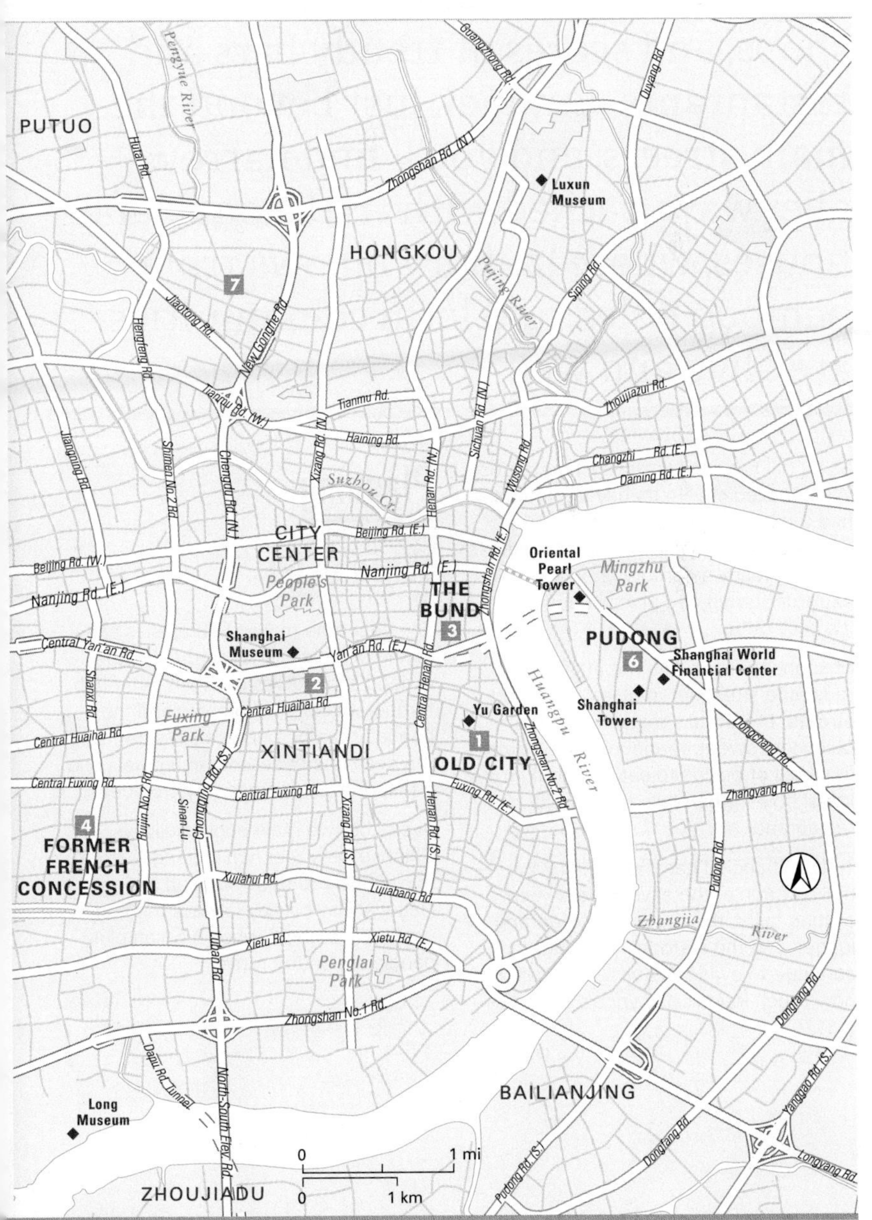
PUTUO
HONGKOU
Luxun Museum
7
Pengyue River
Guangzhong Rd.
Duyang Rd.
Zhongshan Rd. (N.)
Hutai Rd.
Jiaotong Rd.
Hengfeng Rd.
New Gonghe Rd.
Pujing River
Siping Rd.
Tianmu Rd.
Tianmu Rd. (W.)
Zhoujiazui Rd.
Haining Rd.
Sichuan Rd. (N.)
Wusong Rd.
Jiangning Rd.
Shimen No.2 Rd.
Chengdu Rd. (N.)
Xizang Rd. (N.)
Henan Rd. (N.)
Changzhi Rd. (E.)
Daming Rd. (E.)
Suzhou Cr.
CITY CENTER
Beijing Rd. (E.)
Beijing Rd. (W.)
Nanjing Rd. (E.)
People's Park
THE BUND
3
Zhongshan Rd. (E.)
Oriental Pearl Tower
Mingzhu Park
PUDONG
6
Shanghai World Financial Center
Shanghai Tower
Shanghai Museum
Central Yan'an Rd.
Yan'an Rd. (E.)
2
Central Henan Rd.
Huangpu River
Shanxi Rd.
Central Huaihai Rd.
Fuxing Park
Yu Garden
1
XINTIANDI
OLD CITY
Zhongshan No.2 Rd.
Dongchang Rd.
Central Fuxing Rd.
Fuxing Rd. (E.)
Zhangyang Rd.
4
Ruijin No.2 Rd.
Sinan Lu
Chongqing Rd. (S.)
Xizang Rd. (S.)
Henan Rd. (S.)
FORMER FRENCH CONCESSION
Xujiahui Rd.
Lujiabang Rd.
Pudong Rd.
Zhangjia River
Xietu Rd.
Xietu Rd. (E.)
Penglai Park
Luban Rd.
Zhongshan No.1 Rd.
Dongfang Rd.
Dapu Rd. Tunnel
North-South Elev. Rd.
BAILIANJING
Yanggao Rd. (S.)
Long Museum
Pudong Rd. (S.)
Longyang Rd.
0
1 mi
0
1 km
ZHOUJIADU

Shanghai is a city of two faces. It is home to some of the world's tallest skyscrapers, miles of luxury goods shops, and scores of trendy bars and restaurants. But look just beyond the main streets, and you'll find narrow alleyways packed with traditional lane houses, where laundry billows from bamboo poles, and local communities are alive and well.

Shanghai has always been China's most Westernized city. In its heyday, Shanghai had the best nightlife, the greatest architecture, and the strongest business in Asia. Nearly a century later, after extreme tumult and political upheaval, it's back on top.

Shanghai's charm lies not in a list of must-see sites, but in quiet, tree-lined streets, the Bund's majestic colonial buildings, sweet boutiques, and a dizzying array of places to eat and drink, from literal hole-in-the-walls to celebrity chef restaurants.

Today, Shanghai has more than 24 million people, the skyscrapers keep getting taller, the metro keeps getting longer, and the historical buildings continue to evade the wrecking ball. For how much longer is anyone's guess.

Planning

When to Go

The best time to visit Shanghai is early spring or early fall, when the weather is good and crowds diminish. Although temperatures are scorching and the humidity can be unbearable, summer is the peak tourist season, and hotels and transportation can get very crowded.

Avoid the two main public holidays, Chinese New Year (which ranges from mid-January to mid-February) and the National Day holiday (always the first week of October), when a billion-plus people are on the move.

Shanghai's Storied Past

Until 1842, the "City Above the Sea" was a small fishing village. After the first Opium War, the village was carved up into autonomous concessions administered concurrently by the British, French, and Americans.

With dance halls, glitzy restaurants, international clubs, brothels, opium dens, and a racetrack, Shanghai catered to the rich. The "Paris of the East" was known as a place of vice and indulgence. It was amid this glamour and degradation that the Communist Party held its first meeting in 1921.

In the '30s and '40s, the city suffered raids, invasions, and occupation by the Japanese. After the war's end, Nationalists and Communists fought a three-year civil war for control of China. The Communists declared victory in 1949 and established the People's Republic of China. Between 1950 and 1980, Shanghai's industries soldiered on through periods of extreme famine and drought, reform, and suppression. Politically, the city was central to the Cultural Revolution and the Gang of Four's base. The January Storm of 1967 purged many of Shanghai's leaders, and Red Guards set out to destroy the "Four Olds": old ways of ideas, living, traditions, and thought.

In 1972, with the Cultural Revolution still going, Shanghai hosted the historic meeting between Premier Zhou Enlai and U.S. President Richard Nixon. In 1990, China's leader, Deng Xiaoping, chose Shanghai as the center of the country's commercial renaissance, and it has again become a place of hedonism and capitalism, one of China's most ideologically, socially, culturally, and economically open cities.

Getting Here and Around

AIR TRAVEL

Shanghai's two major international airports—Pudong (PVG) and Hongqiao (SHA)—make it easy to get here from the rest of the world. Many major world cities have direct flights: United Airlines runs daily direct flights from Newark to Pudong; Delta flies direct from Pudong to Atlanta; Air France offers direct flights between Paris and Pudong. A few budget airlines, such as Air Asia, fly from Shanghai (to Kuala Lumpur for example), with most leaving from Pudong.

GROUND TRANSPORTATION

Most international flights go through Pudong International Airport (PVG), which is 45 km (30 miles) east of the city, whereas many domestic routes and some flights from Hong Kong, Taiwan, Japan, and Korea operate out of the older Hongqiao International Airport (SHA), 15 km (9 miles) west of the city center.

Taking a taxi is the most comfortable way into town from Pudong International Airport. Expect to pay around Y200 to Y260 for the 45-minute trip to downtown Puxi; for a cab to Hongqiao, a western suburb, tack on Y80. Puxi is the west side of the Huangpu River and Pudong is the east side. With the exception of Pudong, all areas listed here are in Puxi, which is home to Shanghai's historic center. From Pudong Airport, getting to places in Pudong takes 25–30 minutes and should cost no more than Y115. At rush hour, these times and rates can easily double; if you will be arriving between 8 and 9:30 am or 4 and 7 pm, it's best to book a car service that charges a flat rate.

For the quickest ride, catch the Maglev train, which tops out at 431 kph (268 mph). At the Longyang Lu metro station in Pudong it connects to Lines 2, 7, and 16 which can get you downtown in about 25 minutes. It costs Y50 for a single trip (Y40 if you present your ticket from a same-day flight) and Y80 per round-trip. For a mere Y7, you can hop on metro Line 2 at Pudong International Airport, cross the platform at Guanglan Road Station, and be downtown in just over an hour. Note that the Maglev train runs 7 am–9:40 pm and the metro 6 am–10 pm, so these are not early-morning or late-night options.

From Hongqiao Airport, a taxi downtown will cost you Y55–Y85 and takes 30 to 40 minutes; it takes about half an hour to an hour to reach Pudong depending on traffic. You can take metro Lines 2 and 10 from Hongqiao for Y5. A taxi from one airport to the other takes about an hour and 20 minutes and costs upward of Y270. Metro Line 2 also connects Hongqiao Airport and Pudong Airport, making trips between the two significantly cheaper.

Many hotels offer free airport transfers to their guests. Otherwise, shuttle buses link Pudong Airport with a number of hotels (routes starting with a letter) and transport hubs (routes starting with a number) in the city center. Most shuttle buses depart every 10 to 20 minutes between roughly 7 am and midnight. Trips to Puxi take about 90 minutes and cost between Y25 and Y40. From Hongqiao Airport, Bus 71 runs along the Yan'an Lu overpass with stops near Jing'an Temple and People's Square. It costs Y2.

The best bus for travelers going *to* Pudong Airport is the direct airport bus from Jing'an Temple. It's well known and easy to find. If you are standing in front of Jing'an Temple facing West Nanjing Road, it's a few minutes' walk to your left. The bus departs every 15 minutes from the ground-level parking lot; tickets cost Y22 and can only be paid for in cash.

BIKE TRAVEL

Few hotels rent bikes, but you can inquire at bike shops like Giant, where the rate starts from Y50 a day depending on the bike, plus a large refundable deposit. Giant does not rent helmets. Note that for about Y200 you can buy your own basic bike at Tesco or Carrefour. Shanghai's frenzied traffic is not for the faint of heart, though secondary streets in quieter neighborhoods like the Former French Concession are calmer. In recent years, bike-sharing companies like Mobike and Ofo have flooded the city with dockless bikes that can be unlocked via an app on your phone and used for as little as Y1 per hour. The apps require digital payment, like Apple Pay or domestic services like WeChat or Alipay, and can be found via Apple or Android app stores. ■ **TIP→ If you plan to do a lot of cycling during your trip, it's best to bring your own helmet.**

BUS TRAVEL

Taking buses is possible—the stops are called out in English—but as they are often crowded, slow, and the maps are only in Chinese, it is easier to stick to other forms of transportation.

FERRY TRAVEL

Ferries run around the clock every 10 minutes between the Bund and Pudong's terminal just south of the Riverside Promenade. The per-person fare is Y2 each way.

SUBWAY TRAVEL

Shanghai's quick and efficient subway system—called the Shanghai Metro—is an excellent way to get around town, and the network is growing exponentially every year. English maps and exit signs abound, and the single-ticket machines have an English option, too. In-car announcements for each station are given in both Chinese and English. Keep your ticket handy: you'll need to use it at a second turnstile as you exit at your destination.

■ **TIP→ Refillable transport cards costing Y20 are available from the info booths at metro stations. Add as much money as you like, and use them to pay for taxi, metro, ferry, and bus rides. They can also be added to Apple Pay on later model iPhones, which can then be used in lieu of the card itself.** The transport cards aren't discounted, but they'll save you time you would have spent joining queues and fumbling for cash. To purchase, say, *Wo yao yi zhang jiaotong ka* (我要一张交通卡) which means "I want a transportation card."). Shanghai is a sprawling city with large districts, but the downtown area is fairly compact, and the subway reaches nearly all places you'll want to visit.

TAXI TRAVEL

Taxis were once plentiful, cheap, and easy to spot. While they are still all of the above, since the introduction of ride-hailing app Didi (China's equivalent to Uber), it can be difficult to get a taxi to pick you up, especially as a foreigner. Your hotel concierge can call for one by phone, or you can try hailing one on the street. The available ones have a small lighted sign on the passenger side. If you're choosing a cab from a line, peek at the driver's license on the dashboard. The lower the license number, the more experienced the driver. Drivers with a number below 200,000 can usually get you where you're going, though pretty much all drivers rely (at times to their detriment) on GPS navigation. You can also download the Didi app, which has an English version and also supports payment from international bank cards. ■ **TIP→ Drivers don't speak English, so it's best to give them a piece of paper with your destination written in large Chinese characters or show them the characters on your phone.** (Keep a card with the name of your hotel on it handy for the return trip.) Between 5 am and 11 pm, taxis start at Y14 for the first 3 km, then Y2.40 for every additional km and, exceeding 10 km, Y3.60 per km; after 11 pm this jumps to Y18 for 3km, Y3.10 per additional km and, exceeding 10 km, Y4.10 per km.

TRAIN TRAVEL

Several train stations, the newest of which is Hongqiao Railway Station, right next to Hongqiao Airport, serve Shanghai well. You can hop a train to Guangzhou (7 hours), Beijing (5 hours), Nanjing and Shaoxing (1½ hours), Hangzhou (45 minutes), Suzhou (25 minutes), as well as a few other nearby places. The G- and D-trains are the fastest and the only type you'll want to board. You'll need your passport to buy tickets, which, outside of Chinese New Year and Golden Week (first week of October) can generally be purchased day-of at the station. Popular routes like Shanghai–Beijing can sell out in advance, so it's best to book these a few days prior to your trip.

Restaurants

You'll notice that most Chinese restaurants in Shanghai have large, round tables. The reason becomes clear the first time you eat a late dinner at a local restaurant and are surrounded by jovial, laughing groups of people toasting and topping off from communal bottles of beer, sharing cigarettes, and spinning the lazy Susan loaded with food. Whether feting guests or demonstrating their wealth, hosts will order massive, showy spreads.

Shanghai's standing as China's most international city is reflected in its dining scene. You can enjoy *xiaolongbao* (soup dumplings) for breakfast, foie gras for lunch, and Korean barbecue for dinner. In many restaurants, it's traditional to order several dishes to share among your party for family-style dining. Tipping is not expected, but more upmarket restaurants will tack on a 10%–15% service charge. Although you can eat at Chinese restaurants for less than Y50 per person, Western meals go for Western prices.

Some restaurants in Shanghai offer set lunches at a fraction of the dinner price. Check out the dining section of *Time Out Shanghai, That's Shanghai* or Smartshanghai.com, all of which list dining discounts and promotions around town.

What it Costs in Yuan

$	$$	$$$	$$$$
RESTAURANTS			
under Y100	Y100–Y150	Y151–Y200	over Y200

Hotels

Shanghai's stature as China's business capital hasn't stopped it from catering both to business and leisure travelers, especially with its handful of boutique hotels. Business hotels can be divided into two categories: modern Western-style properties, with all the latest amenities, and older hotels built during the city's glory days. The latter make up for a lack of service, modern fixtures, and convenient facilities with an abundance of charm, tradition, and history.

Judging by the number of international chain hotels in Shanghai, the city has proven just how much it has opened to the outside world. Many aren't merely hotels; they're landmarks on the Shanghai skyline. Even the historic properties feel the pressure to update their rooms and facilities.

Shanghai may have an excellent subway system and cheap, plentiful taxis, but if you want to take full advantage of the city's popular sights, restaurants, and nightlife, opt to stay in downtown Puxi, incorporating the quiet, leafy green Former French Concession, the historic Bund promenade, and the bustling shopping street of Nanjing Dong Lu. From these neighborhoods you'll have easy access to the rest of Shanghai.

What it Costs in Yuan

$	$$	$$$	$$$$
HOTELS			
under Y1,100	Y1,100–Y1,400	Y1,401–Y1,800	over Y1,800

Nightlife

Offerings range from world-class swank to dark and dingy dens or from places with young Shanghainese kids screaming experimental punk to Filipino cover bands singing "Hotel California" in a hotel basement. Prices range just as wildly.

The Former French Concession is full of small cocktail bars and speakeasies shrouded in varying degrees of secrecy. Farther east, The Bund is also a good place for upscale bars.

Nightlife streets are constantly changing, subject to government regulations, renovation plans, and the like. Just as there is a move to push restaurants into malls, there's also seemingly an initiative to concentrate bars and clubs where possible. Found 158 on Julu Lu on the edge of the Former French Concession is the major example of this, though areas like Xintiandi and Columbia Circle similarly boast clusters of places to go for a drink alongside their restaurants.

Shopping

Shanghai is chock-a-block with places to spend money. The markup on luxury goods is extremely high in China, and even clothes at American chains are pricier here than in the States. Malls usually don't open until 10 am; boutiques open at 11 am. The upside is that chain stores tend to stay open later, with many closing at 10 pm. Independent shops close by 7:30 pm. Markets generally start earlier, at around 7:30 or 8 am, and close around 6 pm. Most stores are open seven days a week.

Navigating Shanghai Streets

The Streets

The Huangpu River divides Shanghai into east and west sides. The metro area is huge, but the city center is a relatively small district in Puxi, west of the river. On the east side is Pudong, which has undergone massive urbanization in the past two decades. The city is loosely laid out on a grid, and most neighborhoods are easily explored on foot. Massive construction in many neighborhoods makes the pavement uneven and the air dusty, but if you can put up with this, walking is the best way to really get a feel for the city and its people. Taxis are readily available and good for traveling longer distances, and the subway network covers all of downtown and many far-flung areas.

Major east–west roads are named for Chinese cities and divide the city into *dong* (east), *zhong* (middle), and *xi* (west) sections. North–south roads divide the city into *bei* (north) and *nan* (south) segments. The heart of the city is found on its chief east–west streets—Nanjing Lu, Huaihai Lu, and Yan'an Lu overpass.

■ TIP→ Street signs in Shanghai are written in Chinese and English, not in pinyin, the transliteration of Chinese. When asking for directions, pinyin will guide your pronunciation; for this reason, our listings have street names written as Nanjing Xi Lu or Shiji Dadao, not West Nanjing Road or Century Avenue. Our maps, however, follow the city's street signs; they are written as West Nanjing Road, not Nanjing Xi Lu.

The Vocabulary

Below are some terms you'll see on maps and street signs and in the names of most places you'll go:

Dong (东) is east, **xi** (西) is west, **nan** (南) is south, **bei** (北) is north, and **zhong** (中) means middle. **Jie** (街) and **lu** (路) mean street and road, respectively, **da dao** (大道) means avenue, **da** (大) means big, and **xiao** (小) means small.

Qiao (桥) or bridge, is part of the place-name at just about every entrance and exit on the ring roads. **Men** (门), meaning door or gate, indicates a street that passed through an entrance in the fortification wall that surrounded the city hundreds of years ago. The entrances to parks and some other places are also referred to as *men*. For example, Xizhimen literally means Western Straight Gate.

Yu Garden, a major tourist haunt in the Old City area of Shanghai, can be overwhelming, but if you're looking for tchotchkes, hard bargaining brings rewards. Here is where you'll find imitation jade, tiny Buddha statues, costume jewelry, scarves, and the like. Also check out these streets that specialize in specific traditional products: **Fenyang Lu,** in the French Concession, and **Jinling Lu,** west of the Bund, for musical instruments; **Fuzhou Lu, between People's Square and the Bund,** in City Center, for books and art supplies, including calligraphy supplies; **Changle Lu** and **Maoming Lu** in the Former French Concession for *qipao* (Chinese-style dresses).

For a traditional massage, you'll find hundreds of blind massage parlors, inexpensive no-frills salons whose blind masseurs are closely attuned to the body's soft and sore spots. At the other end of the spectrum lie the hotel spas, luxurious retreats where pampering is at a premium.

Tours

Tours are a nice way to unwind post-flight, and can help you get your bearings on that stressful first afternoon.

BOAT TOURS

Huangpu River boat tours afford a great view of Pudong and the Bund, but after that it's mostly ports and cranes.

Cruises from Oriental Pearl Tower

BOAT TOURS | Forty-five-minute boat tours run day and night along the Bund from the Pearl Tower's cruise dock in Pudong. Tickets, excluding Pearl Tower admission, can be purchased at the gate to the tower. ✉ *Oriental Pearl Cruise Dock, 1 Shiji Dadao (Century Ave.), Pudong* ☎ *021/5879–1888* 🎫 *From Y140.*

Huangpu River Cruises

BOAT TOURS | Boats run nightly 6–9 pm, leaving every 30 minutes and traveling for 45–60 minutes up and down the Huangpu River to where it meets the Yangtze. You'll see barges, bridges, and factories, but not much scenery. ✉ *Shilipu Docks, 501 Zhongshan Dong Er Lu, The Bund* ☎ *130/6199–1834* 🎫 *From Y120.*

BUS TOURS

Gray Line Tours

BUS TOURS | On offer are half- and full-day group coach tours of Shanghai, as well as one-day trips to Suzhou, Hangzhou, and other nearby waterside towns. ✉ *5A, 5F, 1399 Beijing Xi Lu, Jing'an* ☎ *021/6289–5221, 800/820–0006 Shanghai area only hotline* 🌐 *www.grayline.com/travel-guide/shanghai* 🎫 *From $50.*

HERITAGE TOURS

Bespoke Shanghai

PERSONAL GUIDES | As the name suggests, this China-founded company specializes in custom-made tours tailored entirely around the guests. The company also arranges car hire and a selection of signature experiences, including a street photo workshop with a professional photographer and an architect-guided tour of the city's landmark buildings. Prices, which vary widely, are based on the type of tour and the number of participants. ✉ *Shanghai* ☎ *151/0167–9082* 🌐 *www.bespoketravelcompany.com.*

Context Travel

WALKING TOURS | U.S.-based Context runs small group and private walking tours in Shanghai and Beijing. Offerings, which focus on food, history, art, architecture, and urban planning, are led by academics and other experts. Group tours cost Y550–Y620 per person; private tours run Y2,500–Y2,960. ✉ *Shanghai* ☎ *215/392–0303 U.S. office* 🌐 *www.contexttravel.com/cities/shanghai/tours.*

Historic Shanghai

WALKING TOURS | A historic society formed by a few dedicated Shanghai history buffs in 1989, Historic Shanghai is on a long-term mission to help preserve and understand the city's rich, often overwritten, history. The group offers well-researched regular public and private walking tours away from the tourist traps. Public tours start from Y250 per person and private tours from Y3,000 for two people. ✉ *Shanghai* ☎ *No phone* 🌐 *www.historic-shanghai.com.*

Shanghai Jewish Tours

SPECIAL-INTEREST | Available in Hebrew or English and led by an Israeli photojournalist, this half-day tour takes you to the sites of Shanghai's Jewish history, such as the 1920 Ohel Rachel Synagogue. ✉ *Shanghai* ☎ *130/0214–6702* 🌐 *www.shanghai-jews.com* 🎫 *From Y100.*

★ UnTour Food Tours

SPECIAL-INTEREST | Cuisine is an integral part of Chinese culture, and UnTour offers unfamiliar visitors the opportunity to explore the essentials of it with a variety of walking tours covering everything from breakfast street food to night eats, dumplings, and more. ✉ *Shanghai* ☎ *No phone* 🌐 *www.untourfoodtours.com/Shanghai* 🎫 *From Y520.*

Did You Know?

Nanjing Road is the main shopping street in Shanghai and has been so for more than a century. At the start of the 20th century, the street was home to a number of franchised stores, eight big department stores, and at least one casino. Today, West Nanjing Road is lined with luxury goods shops and a long swath of East Nanjing Road is pedestrian only.

Visitor Information

The best thing to hit Shanghai since an extended metro system is the Shanghai Call Centre (*962288*), where a host of English-speaking operators answer any question you have, help you communicate with taxi drivers, and provide directions to restaurants, bars, shops, and museums. There are also a number of French-, German-, and Spanish-speaking operators. Though you'll see what appear to be information kiosks on the street, bypass these; they're staffed by well-meaning college students who rarely offer valuable information.

VISITOR INFORMATION Shanghai Tourist Information & Service Center (Yu Garden) **(上海旅游咨询服务中心（豫园）** *Shànghǎi lǚyóu zīxún fúwù zhōngxīn (yùyuán))* ✉ *Yu Garden, 149 Jiujiaochang Lu, Huangpu* ☎ *021/6355–5032.*

Old City

Tucked away in the east of Puxi are the remnants of Shanghai's Old City. Once encircled by a thick wall, a fragment of which still remains, the Old City has a sense of history among its fast disappearing old shikumen (stone gatehouses), temples, and markets; it wasn't until 1854 that Chinese were allowed to move out of the so-called Chinese City and into the foreign concessions. Delve into narrow alleyways where residents still hang their washing out on bamboo poles and chamber pots remain in use. Burn incense with the locals in small temples, sip tea in a teahouse, or get a taste of Chinese snacks and street food. This is the place to get a feeling for Shanghai's past, but come soon: the wrecker's ball knows no mercy.

GETTING AROUND

This area could take a very long afternoon or morning, as it's a good one to do on foot. Browsing the souvenir stalls around Yu Garden might add an hour. Metro Line 10 has a Yu Garden station, and it's a 30-minute walk from Nanjing Dong Lu station on Lines 2 and 10.

Sights

Chen Xiangge Temple (陈向阁寺 *Chénxiànggé sì)*
RELIGIOUS SITE | If you find yourself passing by this tiny temple on your exploration of the Old City, you can make an offering to Buddha with the free incense sticks that accompany your admission. Built in 1600 by the same man who built Yu Garden, it was destroyed during the Cultural Revolution and rebuilt in the 1990s. The temple is now a nunnery, and you can often hear the women's chants rising from the halls beyond the main courtyard. ✉ *29 Chenxiangge Lu, Old City* ☎ *021/6320–3431* 🎫 *Y5.*

City God Temple (城隍庙 *Chénghuángmiào)*
RELIGIOUS SITE | At the southeast end of the Yu Gardens bazaar stands this Taoist temple, built during the early part of the Ming Dynasty and destroyed by fire in 1924. The main hall was rebuilt in 1926, and has been renovated many times over the years. Inside are gleaming gold figures, and atop the roof you'll see statues of crusading warriors—flags raised, arrows drawn. This is a popular place for locals to light incense; expect it to be crowded around major holidays like Chinese New Year. ✉ *249 Fangbang Zhong Lu, Old City* ☎ *021/6328–4494* 🌐 *shchm.org* 🎫 *Y10.*

Old City Wall (上海古城墙大 *Shànghǎi gǔchéng qiángdà)*
ARCHAEOLOGICAL SITE | The Old City used to be completely surrounded by a wall, built in 1553 as a defense against Japanese pirates. Most of it was torn down in 1912, except for one 50-yard-long (40-meter-long) piece that still stands at Dajing Lu and Renmin Lu. You can walk through the remnants and check out the rather simple museum nearby, which is dedicated to the history of the Old City (signs are in Chinese). You can

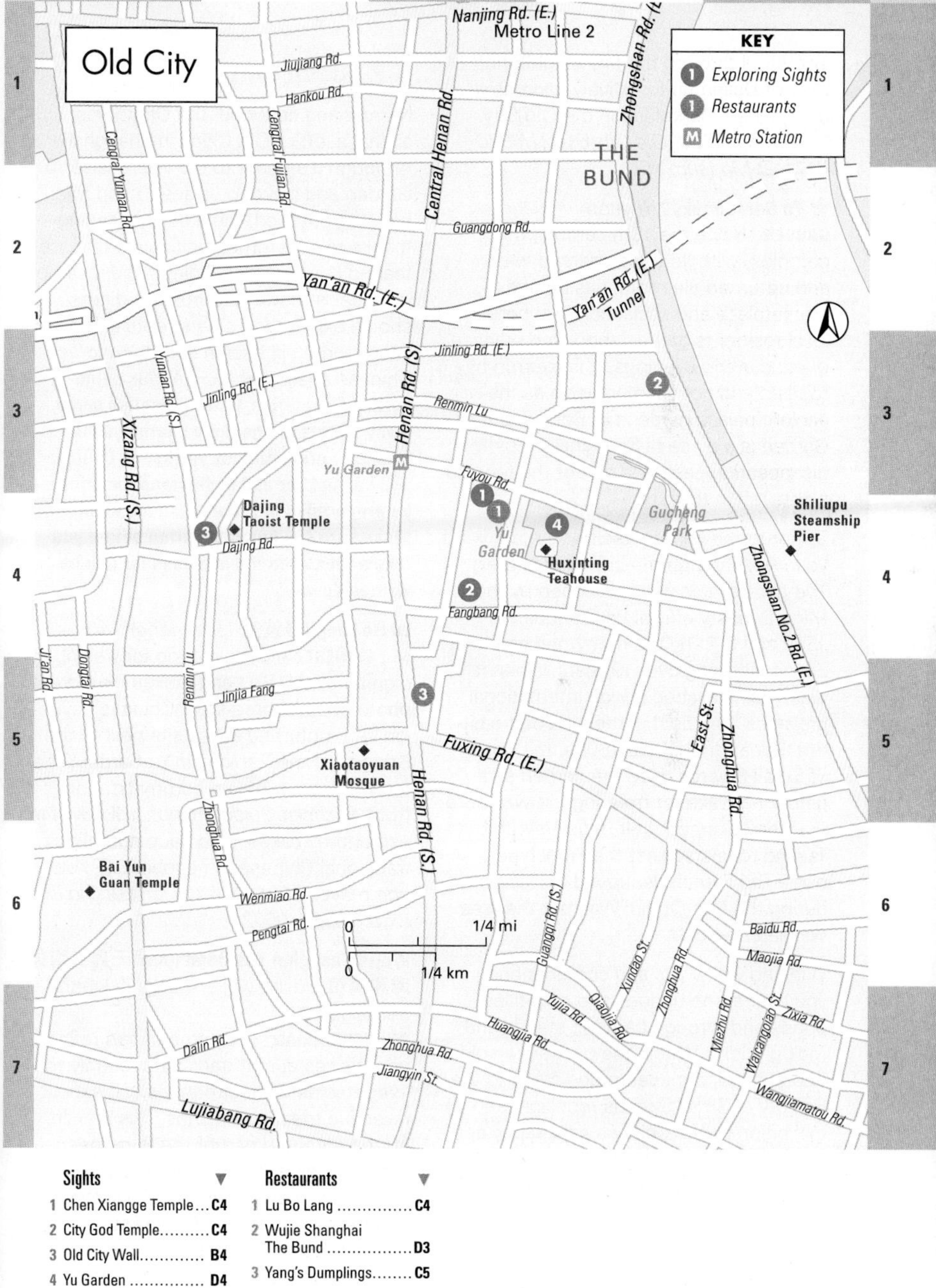

Sights

1 Chen Xiangge Temple ... **C4**
2 City God Temple **C4**
3 Old City Wall **B4**
4 Yu Garden **D4**

Restaurants

1 Lu Bo Lang **C4**
2 Wujie Shanghai The Bund **D3**
3 Yang's Dumplings........ **C5**

also stroll through the tiny neighboring alley of Dajing Lu for a lively panorama of crowded market life in the Old City. ✉ *269 Dajing Lu, Old City* ☎ *021/6326-6171* 🎫 *Museum Y5.*

★ **Yu Garden** (豫园 *Yùyuán*)
GARDEN | Since the 18th century, this complex, with its traditional red walls and upturned tile roofs, has been a marketplace and social center where local residents gather, shop, and practice *qi gong* in the evenings. It is overrun by tourists and not as impressive as the ancient palace gardens of Beijing, but Yu Garden is a piece of Shanghai's rapidly disappearing past, and one of the few old sights left in the city.

To get to the garden itself, you must wind your way through the crowded bazaar. The garden was commissioned by the Ming Dynasty official Pan Yunduan in 1559 and built by the renowned architect Zhang Nanyang over 19 years. When it was finally finished it won international praise as "the best garden in southeastern China." In the mid-1800s, the Society of Small Swords used the garden as a gathering place for meetings. It was here that they planned their uprising with the Taiping rebels against the French colonists. The French destroyed the garden during the first Opium War, but the area was later rebuilt.

Winding walkways and corridors bring you over stone bridges and carp-filled ponds and through bamboo stands and rock gardens. Within the park are an old opera stage, a museum dedicated to the Society of Small Swords rebellion, and an exhibition hall of Chinese calligraphy and paintings. ✉ *218 Anren Lu, bordered by Fuyou Lu, Jiujiaochang Lu, Fangbang Lu, and Anren Lu, Old City* ☎ *021/6328–2465* 🌐 *www.yugarden.com.cn* 🎫 *Y40 (Apr. 1–June 30; Sept. 1–Nov. 30); Y30 (July 1–Aug. 31; Dec. 1–Mar. 31).*

Restaurants

Narrow and crowded, the Old City is all that's left of Old China in Shanghai. Although it's home to the impressive Yu Garden and is a good place to find traditional street food, the area is changing thanks to government initiatives that are tearing down older buildings and revamping older streets. Adventurous diners should explore the side streets around Fangbang Lu in search of authentic Chinese snacks. **■ TIP→ At this neighborhood's eateries, with no English menu, many sellers are going to charge you the foreigner price. Unless you speak Chinese and can ask for and understand the price, be prepared to pay more than the locals. Make sure you know the price before you take a bite, even if that means for it to be written down.**

Lu Bo Lang (绿波廊 *Lǜ bō láng*)
$$ | **CHINESE** | A popular stop for visiting dignitaries, Lu Bo Lang makes for a great photo op: the three-story Chinese pavilion with upturned eaves sits next to the Bridge of Nine Turnings in Yu Garden. The food is good, with a recommendation from *Michelin Guide Shanghai.* **Known for:** osmanthus cakes; crab soup dumplings; traditional Chinese atmosphere. $ *Average main: Y150* ✉ *115 Yuyuan Lu, Old City* ☎ *021/6328–0602.*

Wujie Shanghai The Bund (大蔬无界上海外滩和美馆 *Dàshū wújiè shànghǎi wàitān héměiguǎn*)
$$ | **VEGETARIAN** | The name of this refined, upscale restaurant translates roughly to "vegetables without bounds," so expect inventive meat-free dishes. This branch, on the southern part of the Bund near the Old City, is the flagship location, so you can also expect a peaceful setting and excellent service. **Known for:** seasonal prix-fixe menus; great use of uncommon Chinese ingredients; fried-tofu "ribs." $ *Average main: Y120* ✉ *Bund 22, 22 Zhongshan Dong Er Lu, 4th fl., Old City* ☎ *021/6375–2818.*

Cheap snacks can be found on the streets around the Old City.

Yang's Dumplings (小杨生煎 *Xiǎoyáng shēngjiān*)

$ | **SHANGHAINESE** | **FAMILY** | Yang's, which has 150 branches around town, specializes in the highly addictive *shengjianbao* (meaty soup dumplings panfried on one side and sprinkled with sesame seeds), which come in sets of four or six. Like all the other shops, this one is a casual, in-and-out, fast-food-style place, where you order at the counter under harsh neon lights. **Known for:** extremely popular chain; classic shrimp- or pork-filled shengjianbao; no-fuss approach to service. *$ Average main: Y12 ✉ Hong Kong Metropolis, 489 Henan Nan Lu, Unit 132–133, Old City ☎ 021/6333–0212.*

Xintiandi and City Center

Xintiandi is Shanghai's showpiece restoration project. Reproduction shikumen (stone gatehouses) contain expensive bars, restaurants, and chic boutiques. On warm nights, the restaurants' outdoor tables are filled with diners watching the world go by.

Another good people-watching spot is the area around People's Square, which has some magnificent examples of historical architecture and a smattering of museums. The adjoining People's Park is a pleasant green space where it's possible to escape the clamor of the city for awhile.

GETTING AROUND

People's Square metro station is the point of convergence for metro Lines 1, 2, and 8. The often-packed underground passageways can be confusing, so it's best to take the first exit and then find your way aboveground. Xintiandi can be reached by taking Line 10 to the Xintiandi stop or Line 1 to the Huangpi Nan Lu station, which is a block or two north of Xintiandi.

The sights in this area are divided into two neat clusters—those around People's Square and those around Xintiandi. You can easily walk between the two in 20 minutes. Visiting all the museums in the People's Square area could take a good half day. Xintiandi's sights don't take very long at all, so you could go in the

A nighttime view of a teahouse in Yu Garden

afternoon, check out the museums, and then settle down for a predinner drink.

Sights

Grand Theater (**上海大剧院** *Shànghǎi dàjùyuàn*)
STORE/MALL | The spectacular front wall of glass shines as brightly as the star power in this magnificent theater. Its three stages present the best domestic and international performances. The dramatic curved roof atop a square base is meant to follow the ancient Chinese philosophy that "the earth is square and the sky is round." The best time to see it is at night. ✉ *People's Square, 300 Renmin Dadao, City Center* ☎ *021/6386–8686, 400/1068–686 info hotline* 🌐 *shgtheatre.com.*

Park Hotel (**国际饭店** *Guójì fàndiàn*)
HOTEL—SIGHT | This art deco structure overlooking People's Park was once the tallest hotel in Shanghai. Completed in 1934, it was known for its luxurious rooms, fabulous nightclub, and chic restaurants. Today the lobby is the most vivid reminder of its glorious past. It was an early inspiration for architect I.M. Pei (creator of the glass pyramids at the Louvre). ✉ *People's Sq., 170 Nanjing Xi Lu, City Center* ☎ *021/6327–5225* 🌐 *park.theshanghaihotels.com/en/.*

People's Park (**人民公园** *Rénmín gōngyuán*)
CITY PARK | In colonial days this park was the northern half of the city's racetrack. Today the 30 acres of flower beds, lotus ponds, and trees are crisscrossed by a large number of paved paths. It's also home to the **Museum of Contemporary Art** and the **Urban Planning Exhibition Hall.** **■ TIP→ The marriage market, held in the park weekends noon–5 pm, is not to be missed.** Desperately seeking spouses for their children, the parents and grandparents of unmarried adults post flyers advertising their child's height, job, income, Chinese Zodiac sign, and more. ✉ *231 Nanjing Xi Lu, City Center* ☎ *021/6327–1333* 🎟 *Free.*

★ **People's Square** (人民广场 *rénmín guǎngchǎng*)

CITY PARK | Home of the Shanghai Museum, the city's enormous main square is a social center for locals. During the day, residents stroll, practice tai chi, and fly kites. In the evening, kids roller-skate, and ballroom dancers hold group lessons. There is also a small amusement park. Weekends here are extremely busy—particularly on Xizang Road—and are not for the agoraphobic. ✉ *120 Renmin Dadao, City Center* ✣ *Enter at Xizang Lu.*

★ **Shanghai Museum** (上海博物館 *Shànghǎi bówùguǎn*)

MUSEUM | Look past the eyesore of an exterior—this museum holds the country's premier collection of relics and artifacts. Eleven galleries exhibit Chinese artistry in all its forms: paintings, bronzes, sculpture, ceramics, calligraphy, jade, furniture of the Ming and Qing dynasties, coins, seals, and art by indigenous populations. Its bronze collection is one of the best in the world, and its dress and costume gallery showcases intricate handiwork from several of China's 55 ethnic minority groups. There are signs and an audio guide available in English. You can relax in the museum's pleasant tearoom or head to the shop for postcards, crafts, and reproductions of the artwork. ✉ *201 Renmin Dadao, City Center* ☎ *021/6372–3500* 🌐 *www.shanghaimuseum.net/en* 🎫 *Free, Y40 for English-language audio guide (with Y400 deposit or passport)* 🕙 *Closed Mon.*

★ **Shanghai Urban Planning Center** (上海城市规划展示馆 *Shànghǎi chéngshì guīhuà zhǎnshìguǎn*)

MUSEUM | To understand the true scale of Shanghai and its ongoing building boom, visit the Master Plan Hall of this museum. Sprawled out on the third floor is a 6,400-square-foot planning model of Shanghai—the largest of its kind in the world—showing the metropolis as city planners expect it to look in 2020. You'll find familiar existing landmarks like the Pearl Tower and Shanghai Center as well as a detailed model of the Shanghai Expo, complete with miniature pavilions. ✉ *People's Sq., 100 Renmin Dadao, City Center* ☎ *021/6372–2077* 🎫 *Y30* 🕙 *Closed Mon.*

Shikumen Open House Museum (石库门博物馆 *Shíkùmén bówùguǎn*)

MUSEUM | Just off Xintiandi's main thoroughfare is this beautifully restored shikumen (stone gatehouse) filled with furniture and artifacts collected from the other nearby shikumen (now turned shops). Exhibits explain the European influence on shikumen design, the history of the neighborhood's renovation, and future plans for the entire 128-acre project. ✉ *No. 25, Xintiandi North Block, 118 Taicang Lu, Xintiandi* ☎ *021/3307–0337* 🌐 *www.xintiandi.com* 🎫 *Y20.*

Site of the First National Congress of the Communist Party (共产党第一次全国代表大会址纪念馆 *Gòngchǎndǎng dì yī cì quánguó dàibiǎo dàhuì huìzhǐ jìniànguǎn*)

HISTORIC SITE | The secret meeting on July 31, 1921 that marked the first National Congress was held at the Bo Wen Girls' School, where 13 delegates from Marxist, Communist, and Socialist groups gathered from around the country. The upstairs of this restored shikumen is a well-curated museum detailing the rise of communism in China. Downstairs lies the very room where the first delegates worked. It remains frozen in time, the table set with matches and teacups. Ironically, the site today is surrounded by Xintiandi, Shanghai's center of capitalist conspicuous consumption. ✉ *76 Xinye Lu, City Center* ☎ *021/5383–2171* 🎫 *Free, audio tour Y10* 🕙 *Closed Mon.*

★ **Xintiandi** (新天地 *Xīntiāndì*)

STORE/MALL | By World War II, more than two-thirds of Shanghai's residents lived in a shikumen (stone gatehouse). Most have been razed in the name of progress, but this 8-acre collection of them has been transformed into an upscale

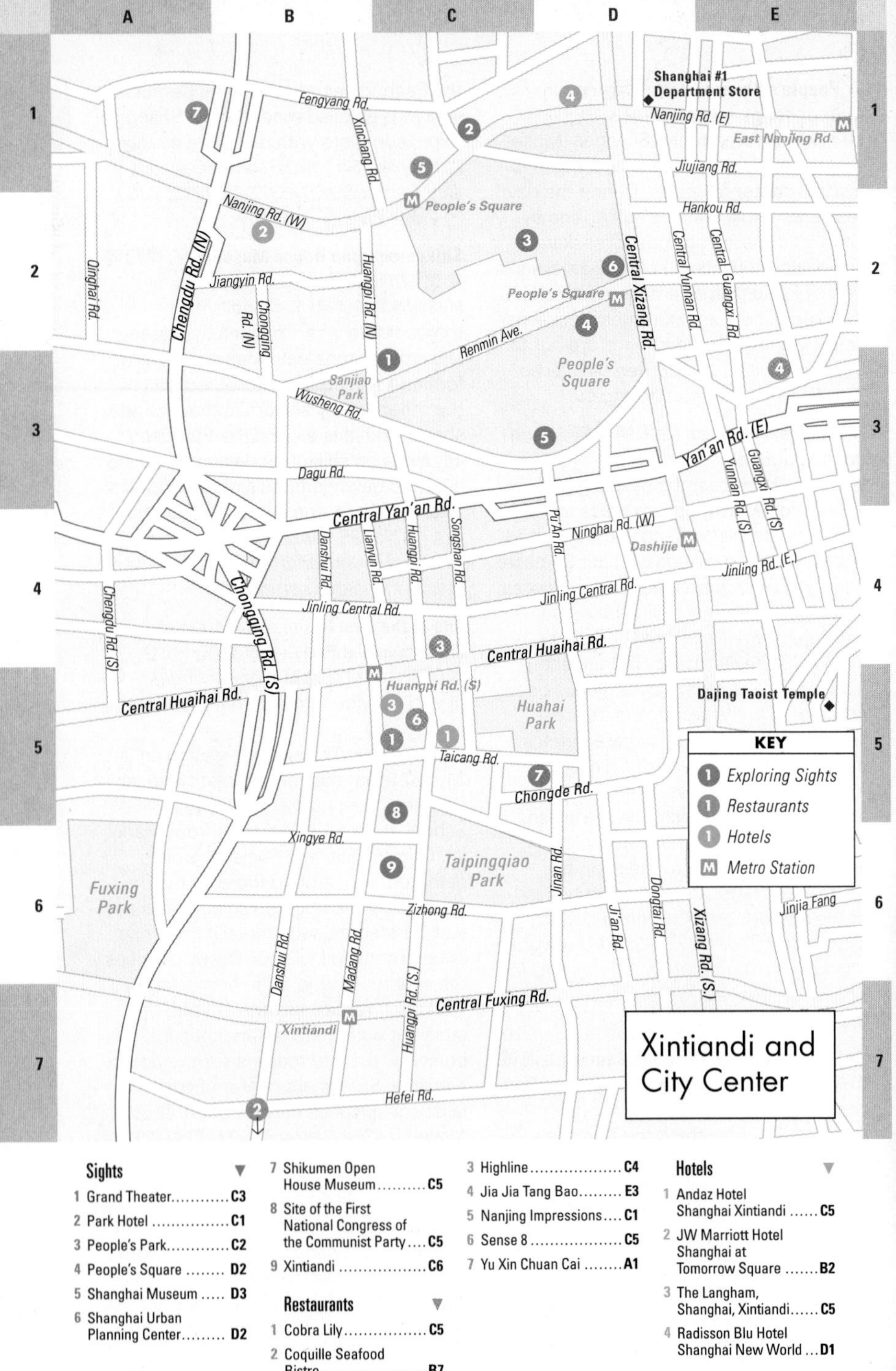

Sights

1 Grand Theater............ C3

2 Park Hotel C1

3 People's Park............. C2

4 People's Square D2

5 Shanghai Museum D3

6 Shanghai Urban Planning Center......... D2

7 Shikumen Open House Museum.......... C5

8 Site of the First National Congress of the Communist Party.... C5

9 Xintiandi C6

Restaurants

1 Cobra Lily................. C5

2 Coquille Seafood Bistro...................... B7

3 Highline.................... C4

4 Jia Jia Tang Bao......... E3

5 Nanjing Impressions.... C1

6 Sense 8 .... C5

7 Yu Xin Chuan Cai A1

Hotels

1 Andaz Hotel Shanghai Xintiandi C5

2 JW Marriott Hotel Shanghai at Tomorrow Square B2

3 The Langham, Shanghai, Xintiandi...... C5

4 Radisson Blu Hotel Shanghai New World ... D1

shopping-and-dining complex called Xintiandi, or "New Heaven on Earth." The restaurants are busy from lunch until past midnight, especially those with patios—perfect places from which to watch the passing parade of shoppers. ✉ *181 Taicang Lu, bordered by Madang Lu, Zizhong Lu, and Huangpi Nan Lu, Xintiandi* ☎ *021/5127–0808* 🌐 *www.shxintiandi.com.*

Restaurants

Cobra Lily (镜花水月 *Jìnghuāshuǐyuè*)
$$ | **ASIAN FUSION** | From the team behind local craft brewery Boxing Cat and American eatery Liquid Laundry comes this hip Southeast Asian fusion concept. Spread over two floors and tucked into a renovated shikumen on Xintiandi's main drag, the space is beautiful by day, when it's flooded with light, but you should come in the evening when you won't feel so bad sampling the excellent cocktails. **Known for:** butter chicken; lemongrass carnitas banh mi; scallion-oil noodles. $ *Average main: Y110* ✉ *No. 19, Lane 181, Taicang Lu, Xintiandi* ☎ *021/5351–0116* 💳 *No credit cards.*

Coquille Seafood Bistro
$$$$ | **FRENCH** | The scent of butter and brine waft from the kitchen of this lovely French restaurant, the brainchild of Californian banker-turned-restaurateur John Liu and set in a refurbished space that was previously his mother's Vietnamese restaurant. While seated in a brasserie chair at a marble- or wood-topped table, you can tuck into platters of seafood and slurp French onion soup; while seated at the bar, you can watch the frenetic concocting of cocktails. **Known for:** ultrafresh seafood; beef Wellington; foie-gras crème brûlée. $ *Average main: Y220* ✉ *29 Mengzi Lu, City Center* ☎ *021/3376–8127* 🌐 *www.coquille.com.cn* ⏲ *Closed Mon. No lunch.*

Dragon Boat Day

About 2,000 years ago, a poet named Qu Yuan threw himself into the river in protest against the emperor. To commemorate him, people now race dragon boats and eat *zongzi* (sticky rice dumplings). The date of the Dragon Boat Festival varies, but is often in late May or early June.

Highline
$$$ | **AMERICAN** | Perched on the sixth floor of the Ascott Residences, this modern American eatery has a lust-worthy terrace—complete with a sleek firepit—that looks onto a park and surrounding cityscape. Trendy young Chinese pack out the 1960s-inspired space; brunch is particularly popular. **Known for:** chicken and waffles; red velvet sundae; slow-roasted beef rib rack;. $ *Average main: Y200* ✉ *Ascott Residences, 282 Huaihai Zhong Lu, 6th fl., Xintiandi* ☎ *021/6333–0176* 💳 *No credit cards.*

Jia Jia Tang Bao (佳家汤包 *Jiājiā tāngbāo*)
$ | **CHINESE** | **FAMILY** | The soup dumplings here are arguably the best in town; once the kitchen runs out of them, the restaurant closes for the day. It's a proper local hole-in-the-wall, with orange plastic chairs and grimy tabletops and floors, but eating here is an authentic, delicious, not-to-be-missed experience. **Known for:** local feel; crab xiaolongbao; century egg and seawood soup. $ *Average main: Y20* ✉ *90 Huanghe Lu, City Center* ☎ *021/6327–6878* 💳 *No credit cards* ⏲ *No dinner.*

Nanjing Impressions (南京大牌档 *Nánjīng dàpái dàng*)
$ | **CHINESE** | It feels like old Nanjing at this restaurant—part of a Chinese chain—where glowing bamboo and paper

lanterns swing from the ceiling, and food stalls are set against the walls. The authentic dishes are great, and though the menu's English translations leave something to be desired, the pictures will help muddle your way through ordering. **Known for:** palace chicken with pickled peppers; Nanjing Impressions potstickers; celestial roast duck dumplings. $ *Average main: Y30* ✉ *Shimao Shopping Center, 258 Nanjing Xi Lu, 3rd fl., City Center* ☎ *400/187–7177* ▭ *No credit cards.*

Sense 8 (誉八仙 *Yùbāxiān*)
$$ | **CANTONESE** | The black-lacquer woods and hanging red lanterns at this Cantonese restaurant recall old Wong Kar Wai flicks. The setting and the decent dim sum and roast-meat classics make this a good place for a lunch or dinner experience you won't get outside of China. **Known for:** over-the-top interior; old-school teahouse atmosphere; upscale, polished Cantonese experience. $ *Average main: Y100* ✉ *Xintiandi, No. 8, Lane 181, Taicang Lu, Xintiandi* ☎ *021/6373–1888.*

Yu Xin Chuan Cai (渝信川菜 *Yúxìn chuāncài*)
$ | **SICHUAN** | Locals love the spicy Sichuan food at this restaurant inside an office building (take the escalators or elevator to the third floor). Book ahead, or be prepared to wait 30 to 60 minutes for a table. **Known for:** shuizhu yu ("water-boiled" fish); tea-smoked duck; koushui ji ("mouthwatering" chicken). $ *Average main: Y90* ✉ *Zhaoshangju Square, 333 Chengdu Bei Lu, 3rd fl., City Center* ☎ *021/5298–0438* ▭ *No credit cards.*

Hotels

Andaz Hotel Shanghai Xintiandi (上海新天地安达仕酒店 *Shànghǎi xīntiāndì āndá shì jiǔdiàn*)
$$ | **HOTEL** | **FAMILY** | Set in the heart of bustling and beautiful shopping, drinking, and dining area, Xintiandi, this stylish boutique hotel offers the usual Andaz freebies like tea and coffee in the reception and free soft drinks and snacks in the minibar. **Pros:** incredible location; free canapes and drinks at Xuan Bar 6–8 pm daily; family-friendly play areas. **Cons:** divisive LED-light feature carried through the interiors; long waits at reception during peak times; service standard slips. $ *Rooms from: Y1300* ✉ *88 Songshan Lu, Xintiandi* ☎ *021/2310–1234, 400/819–8070 for reservations only* 🌐 *shanghai.andaz.hyatt.com* *307 rooms* 🍽 *No meals.*

JW Marriott Hotel Shanghai at Tomorrow Square (上海明天广场JW万豪酒店 *Shànghǎi míngtiān guǎngchǎng JW wànháo jiǔdiàn*)
$$$ | **HOTEL** | Outside, this 60-story tower on the edge of People's Square turns heads with its futuristic design; inside, the decor follows more classic lines, with Chinese celadon vases, wedding boxes, and ornamental jades complementing soft green-and-yellow palettes and warm fiddleback woods in the spacious rooms. **Pros:** fantastic location; amazing city views from all rooms; wonderful rooftop pool. **Cons:** exterior far more contemporary than interiors; small service issues; rooms are fairly basic but comfortable. $ *Rooms from: Y1550* ✉ *399 Nanjing Dong Lu, City Center* ☎ 🌐 *www.jwmarriottshanghai.com* *347 rooms* 🍽 *No meals.*

The Langham Shanghai, Xintiandi (上海新天地朗廷酒店 *Shànghǎi xīntiāndì lǎngtíng jiǔdiàn*)
$$$$ | **HOTEL** | Since it opened, The Langham Shanghai, Xintiandi has been receiving nothing but praise for service that's impeccable without being intrusive and rooms that are big and plush. **Pros:** great service; well-kept pool; excellent location. **Cons:** light sleepers may find street-facing rooms a tad noisy; no views from the basement gym; three Michelin-starred restaurant Tang Court requires a reservation one month in advance. $ *Rooms from: Y2000* ✉ *99 Madang*

The iconic Bund has 52 buildings dating from the late 19th to early 20th centuries. Architectural styles include Baroque Revival, Romanesque Revival, Renaissance Revival, Gothic Revival, Neo-Classical, Beaux-Arts, and Art Deco.

Lu, Xintiandi ☎ *021/2330–2288* 🌐 *www.langhamhotels.com/en/the-langham/shanghai* 🛏 *357 rooms* 🍽 *No meals.*

Radisson Blu Hotel Shanghai New World (**上海新世界丽笙大酒店** *Shànghǎi xīnshìjiè lìshēngdà jiǔdiàn*)
$$ | **HOTEL** | **FAMILY** | A prominent skyline landmark—topped by a revolving, 45th-floor restaurant in what looks like a flying saucer—this hotel caters primarily to business travelers with lower Park Tower rooms that face People's Square and higher City Tower rooms. **Pros:** prime location; city views; distinctive architecture. **Cons:** somewhat dated decor; location makes it hard to get taxis; lacks the character of boutique options. $ *Rooms from: Y1100* ✉ *People's Sq., 88 Nanjing Xi Lu, City Center* ☎ *021/6359–9999* 🌐 *www.radissonblu.com/en/newworldhotel-shanghai* 🛏 *520 rooms* 🍽 *No meals.*

Nightlife

BARS

Barbarossa (**爸爸露沙** *Bābālùshā*)
BARS/PUBS | This is a popular evening destination especially with nearby office workers who come by for happy hour. The interior is straight out of *Arabian Nights,* with billowing draperies swathing the space. Usually quiet and classy, it switches to hot, hip, and hopping on weekend nights, especially in summer. It's the ambience, not the food or drink, that bring people in. ✉ *Inside People's Park, 231 Nanjing Xi Lu, next to Shanghai Art Museum, City Center* ☎ *021/6318–0220* 🌐 *www.barbarossa.com.cn.*

Constellation (**酒池星座** *Jiǔ chí xīngzuò*)
BARS/PUBS | The fourth sibling in the ever-growing Constellation bar family is just south of Xintiandi, a stone's throw from the metro station. It sticks to a tried-and-true formula of cigars, mid-volume jazz, and high-quality Japanese-style cocktails. ✉ *398 Zizhong Lu, Xintiandi* ☎ *021/6333–7009.*

Lots of eating and drinking options in Xintiandi.

CLUBS

M2

DANCE CLUBS | The original and most popular location of the Muse chain offers a Chinese-style megaclub experience, with theme parties and a musical line-up that includes hip-hop, house, and electro. Loud and crowded, M2 is where people end up after hitting a few other drinking establishments. All the branches are popular with young locals who order bottle service and stay until the sun comes up. ✉ *Hong Kong Plaza, 283 Huaihai Zhong Lu, 4th fl., City Center* ☎ *131/6606–1720.*

KARAOKE

Karaoke is ubiquitous in Shanghai; most nights, the private rooms at KTV (Karaoke TV) establishments are packed with Shanghainese crooning away with their friends. Many bars employ "KTV girls" who sing along with male patrons and serve cognac and expensive snacks. (Note, though, that at some establishments, KTV girls are also prostitutes.)

Haoledi (好乐迪KTV *Hāolèdī KTV*)

BARS/PUBS | Crowded at all hours with locals of all ages crooning pop favorites, the popular Haoledi chain has branches virtually everywhere. A few of the outlets in downtown are on the sixth floor of New World Mall at 479 Nanjing Dong Lu, near People's Square, and on the seventh floor of mall Metro City, at 1111 Zhaojiabang Lu in Xujiahui. ✉ *438 Huaihai Zhong Lu, 3rd, 5th and 6th fl., City Center* ☎ *021/6311–5858.*

LIVE MUSIC

MAO Livehouse (光芒 *Guāngmáng*)

MUSIC CLUBS | To the west and south of Xintiandi is one of Shanghai's best live-music venues, with foreign as well as up-and-coming local bands taking to the stage to play everything from heavy metal, indie, and punk rock to folk music. Past performers have included Thee Oh Sees, Grimes, and Gang of Four. ✉ *308 Chongqing Nan Lu, 3F, City Center* ☎ *021/6445–0086.*

Performing Arts

CHINESE OPERA

Yifu Theatre (逸夫舞台 *Yîfû wûtái*)
OPERA | Not only Beijing Opera but also China's other regional operas, such as Huju, Kunqu, and Yueju, are performed regularly at this theater in the heart of the city center. Considered the marquee theater for opera in Shanghai, it's just a block off People's Square. ✉ *701 Fuzhou Lu, City Center* ☎ *021/6322–5294*.

DANCE AND CLASSICAL MUSIC

Shanghai Concert Hall (上海音乐厅 *Shàng-hǎi yīnyuètīng*)
DANCE | More than a decade ago, city officials spent $6 million to move this venerable concert hall two blocks to avoid the rumble from the nearby high-way. Only then did they discover that it now sat over an even more rumbling subway line. Oops. It's known for hosting top-level classical musicians from around China and the world. ✉ *523 Yan'an Dong Lu, City Center* ☎ *400/891–8182* 🌐 *www.shanghaiconcerthall.org*.

Shopping

Exclusive and expensive stores are housed in reproduction traditional shiku-men—stone gatehouses. Your plastic will get plenty of work here, but step outside Xintiandi proper and you'll find charming streets upon which pajama-clad citizens still do their marketing.

CLOTHING

Alter
CLOTHING | Founded by fashionista Sonja Long Xiao in 2010, this multibrand shop was started as a reaction to the Chinese luxury market's focus on huge name megabrands. The store carries interesting, arty designer labels from around the world as well as Xiao's own in-house brand Roll-ing Acid. Even if you don't plan on buying, the layout and design of the store itself is provocative. ✉ *245 Madang Lu, Shop L116, Xintiandi* ☎ *021/6302–9889* 🌐 *www.alterstyle.com*.

Shanghai Tang (上海滩 *Shànghǎitān*)
CLOTHING | This is one of China's leading fashion brands, with distinctive acid-bright silks, soft-as-a-baby's-bottom cash-mere, and funky housewares. Sigh at the beautiful fabrics and designs, and gasp at the inflated prices. ✉ *181 Taicang Lu, City Center* ☎ *021/6384–1601* 🌐 *www.shanghaitang.com*.

Uma Wang
CLOTHING | When the Central St. Martins grad launched her eponymous line in 2005, little did she know her designs would soon be on the catwalks of Lon-don, Paris, New York, and Milan. Knitwear is Wang's signature design and, in her industrial chic shop, you'll find chunky vests, mohair dresses, and cardigans that can double as scarves. For the average shopper, the space is more gallery than viable shopping destination—as Wang's star has risen, so too have her prices; a dress now goes for more than Y3,500. ✉ *Xintiandi Style, L229, 245 Madang Lu, City Center* ☎ *021/3331–5109*.

GIFTS

Shanghai Museum Shop (上海博物馆商店 *Shanghǎi bówùguǎn shāngdiàn*)
GIFTS/SOUVENIRS | This selection of books on China and Chinese culture is impres-sive, and there are also some interesting children's books. Expensive reproduction ceramics are available, as are more affordable gifts like magnets, scarves, and notebooks. ✉ *Shanghai Museum, 201 Renmin Dadao, People's Sq., City Center* ☎ *021/6372–3500* ⏲ *Closed Mon.*

SPAS

Yu Massage (愉庭保健会所 *Yútíng bǎojiàn huìsuǒ*)
SPA—SIGHT | Expats flock to this tranquil spa, where the front desk staff speak English well and can help you choose one of their handful of massages. Body massages are done in private rooms; foot massages take place in a nook lined with

plush recliners. Prices are very reasonable. ✉ *199 Huangpi Bei Lu, City Center* ☎ *021/6315–2915.*

The Bund and Nanjing Dong Lu

On the bank of the Huangpu River is the Bund, Shanghai's most recognizable sightseeing spot, lined with massive foreign buildings that predate 1949. Some of these buildings have been developed into lifestyle complexes with spas, restaurants, bars, galleries, and designer boutiques. The Bund is also an ideal spot for that photo of Pudong's famous skyline. Running perpendicular to the Bund, pedestrian-only Nanjing Dong Lu is lined on both sides with shops and their glowing neon signboards. It's a popular shopping spot for locals who flock to massive outposts of American chains. Some of the adjacent streets still have a faded glamour, and some—lined with shops selling hardware or bicycle parts—are great for a peek at local life. The best time to visit Nanjing Dong Lu is at night.

GETTING AROUND

The simplest way to get here is to take metro Line 2 or 10 to Nanjing Dong Lu station, and then head east for the Bund or west for the main shopping area of Nanjing Dong Lu. Alternatively, you can take Line 1, 2, or 8 to People's Square station and walk east for about 30 minutes to the Bund or 15 minutes to Nanjing Dong Lu.

Sights

Bank of China (中国银行 *Zhōngguó yínháng*)
BUILDING | British art deco and Chinese elements combine in this 1937 building, which was designed to be the tallest in the city. However, opium magnate Victor Sassoon insisted that no building surpass his Cathay Hotel (now the Peace Hotel). Were it not for the Cathay Hotel's copper-faced pyramid roof, the bank would indeed be taller. ✉ *23 Zhongshan Dong Yi Lu, The Bund* ☎ *021/6329–1979.*

★ **The Bund** (外滩 *Wàitān*)
NEIGHBORHOOD | Shanghai's waterfront boulevard best shows both the city's pre-1949 past and its focus on the future. Both the northern and southern ends of Bund are constantly changing, with hotels and restaurants popping up amid scooter repair shops and hardware stores.

On the riverfront side of the Bund, Shanghai's street life is in full force. You'll find Chinese tourists as well as foreigners here, ogling the Pudong skyline. If you have blonde hair, prepare to be stopped for photos. In the morning, just after dawn, the Bund is full of people ballroom dancing, doing aerobics, and practicing kung fu, qi gong, and tai chi. The rest of the day, people walk the embankment, snapping photos of the Oriental Pearl Tower, the Huangpu River, and each other. In the evenings, lovers come out for romantic walks amid the floodlit buildings and tower. ■ **TIP→ Be prepared for the aggressive souvenir hawkers; while you can't completely avoid them, just ignore them—and watch your pockets and bags.** ✉ *Zhongshan Dong Yi Lu, between Jinling Lu and Suzhou Creek, The Bund* 🌐 *www.waitan.cn.*

Former HSBC Building (浦东发展银行 *Pǔdōng fāzhǎn yínháng*)
BANK | When this beautiful neoclassical structure was built by the British in 1923, it was the second-largest bank building in the world. It served as the headquarters of the Shanghai branch of The Hongkong and Shanghai Banking Corporation. After the building was turned into offices for the Communist Party in 1955, the beautiful 1920s Italian-tile mosaic in the building's dome was deemed too extravagant and was covered by white paint. Ironically enough, this protected it from being

destroyed by the Red Guards during the Cultural Revolution. The mural was then forgotten until 1997, when the Pudong Development Bank renovated the building. If you walk in and look up, you'll see the circular mosaic in the dome—an outer circle portraying the cities where the bank had branches at the time: London, Paris, New York, Bangkok, Tokyo, Calcutta, Hong Kong, and Shanghai; a middle circle made up of the 12 signs of the zodiac; and the center painted with a large sun and Ceres, the Roman goddess of abundance. ✉ *12 Zhongshan Dong Yi Lu, The Bund* ☎ *021/6161–8550* 🎟 *Free.*

Peace Hotel (**和平饭店** *Hépíng fàndiàn*)
HOTEL—SIGHT | This hotel at the corner of the Bund and Nanjing Dong Lu is among Shanghai's most treasured buildings. If any establishment will give you a sense of Shanghai's past, it's this one. Its high ceilings, ornate woodwork, and streamlined fixtures are still intact. Following a renovation in 2010, the hotel reopened as the Fairmont Peace Hotel, with the jazz bar, tea lounge, restaurant, shopping arcade, and ballroom all restored to their original glory, evoking old Shanghai cabarets and galas. On the mezzanine level is a small but fascinating gallery chronicling the hotel's past.

The south building, formerly the Palace Hotel (and now the Swatch Art Peace Hotel), was built in 1906. The north building, once the Cathay Hotel, built in 1929, is more famous. It was known as the private playroom of its owner, Victor Sassoon, a wealthy landowner who invested in the opium trade. Sassoon lived and entertained his guests in the copper penthouse. The hotel was rated on a par with the likes of Raffles in Singapore and the Peninsula in Hong Kong. It was *the* place to stay, see, and be seen in old Shanghai. Noël Coward wrote *Private Lives* here. ✉ *20 Nanjing Dong Lu, The Bund* ☎ *021/6138–6888* 🌐 *www.fairmont.com/peace-hotel-shanghai.*

★ **Rockbund Art Museum** (**上海外滩美术馆** *Shànghǎi wàitān měishùguǎn*)
MUSEUM | **FAMILY** | The detailing on this 1932 art deco building is as enticing as the artwork inside. Rockbund has no permanent collection, which keeps things exciting. When exhibitions are being installed, the museum is closed, so check the website before you go. Exhibits showcase works by both Chinese and international artists, and some include interactive elements. Lectures and film screenings are held often; many are in English, and some are family-friendly. On the top floor is a quiet, airy seating area and, the cherry on the sundae, the museum's roof deck. ✉ *20 Huqiu Lu, just off Beijing Dong Lu, The Bund* ☎ *021/3310–9985* 🌐 *www.rockbundartmuseum.org* 🎟 *Y50* 🕙 *Closed Mon.*

Restaurants

The Bund is the heart of modern Shanghai, with the colonial history of Puxi facing the towering steel and glass of Pudong. The stellar river and city views have attracted some of the finest (and often most expensive) restaurants in town.

Canton Table (**三号黄浦会** *Sānhào huángpǔ huì*)
$$$$ | **CANTONESE** | Though the decor here is thoroughly modern, it still evokes old Canton, with gorgeous tiled floors and painted murals of women in qipao dresses. The classic Cantonese dishes have been refined, elevated, and updated to perfectly match the stunning contemporary view of the Pudong skyline. **Known for:** whole abalone puffs; Cantonese barbecue platter; sauteed beef with matsutake mushroom. $ *Average main: Y250* ✉ *Three on the Bund, 3 Zhongshan Dong Yi Lu, 5th fl., The Bund* ☎ *021/6321–3737.*

Cejerdary (**蟹家大院** *Xièjiā dàyuàn*)
$$$$ | **CHINESE** | Outfitted in gorgeous pale wood with an aesthetic that feels almost Japanese in its minimalism, this light,

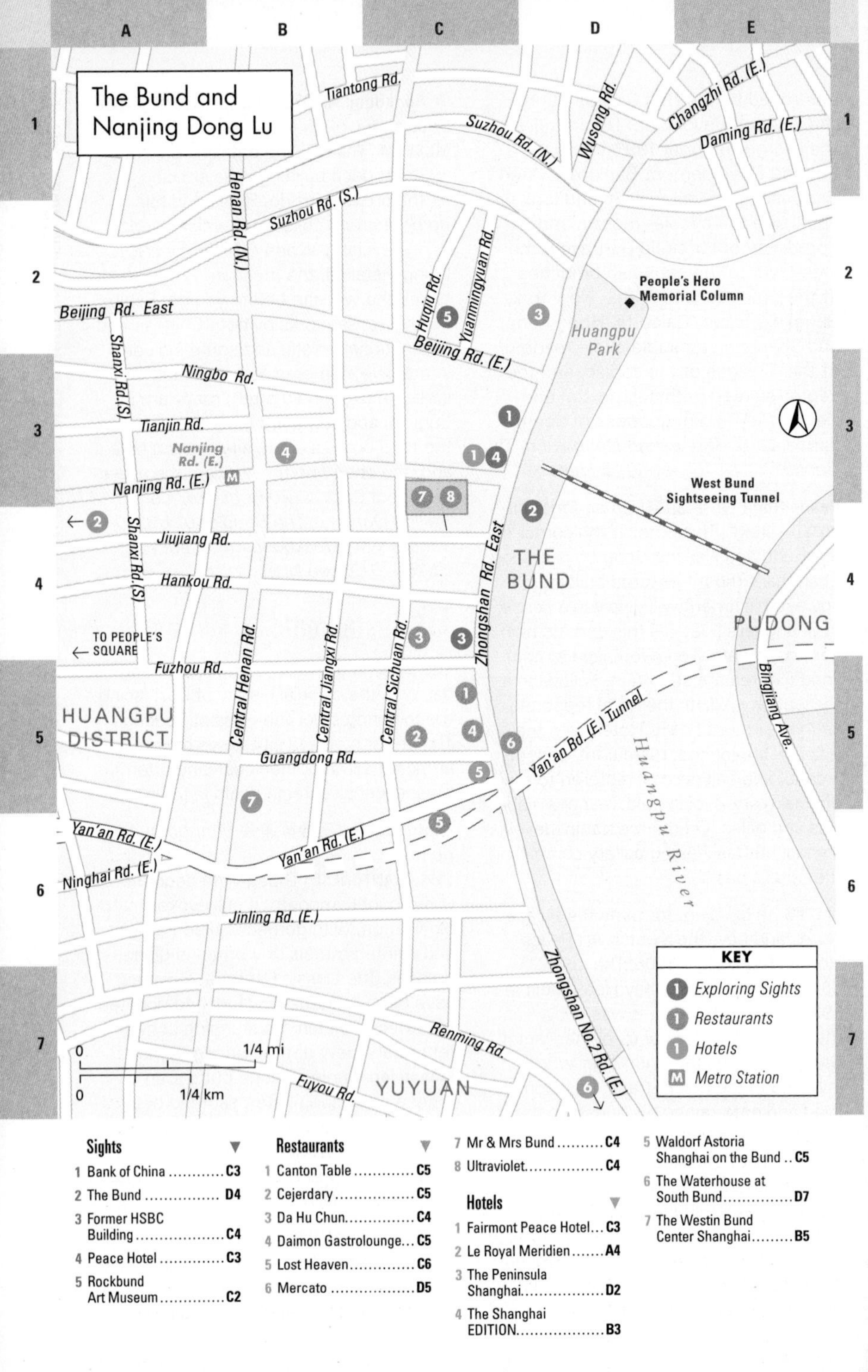

A
B
C
D
E
1
2
3
4
5
6
7
The Bund and Nanjing Dong Lu
Tiantong Rd.
Suzhou Rd. (N.)
Wusong Rd.
Changzhi Rd. (E.)
Daming Rd. (E.)
Henan Rd. (N.)
Suzhou Rd. (S.)
Yuanmingyuan Rd.
Huqiu Rd.
People's Hero Memorial Column
Huangpu Park
Beijing Rd. East
Shanxi Rd.(S)
Beijing Rd. (E.)
Ningbo Rd.
Tianjin Rd.
Nanjing Rd. (E.)
Nanjing Rd. (E.)
West Bund Sightseeing Tunnel
Jiujiang Rd.
Hankou Rd.
THE BUND
Zhongshan Rd. East
PUDONG
TO PEOPLE'S SQUARE
Fuzhou Rd.
Central Henan Rd.
Central Jiangxi Rd.
Central Sichuan Rd.
Bingjiang Ave.
HUANGPU DISTRICT
Yan'an Rd. (E.) Tunnel
Huangpu River
Guangdong Rd.
Yan'an Rd. (E.)
Yan'an Rd. (E.)
Ninghai Rd. (E.)
Jinling Rd. (E.)
Zhongshan No.2 Rd. (E.)
KEY
Exploring Sights
Restaurants
Hotels
Metro Station
Renming Rd.
0
1/4 mi
0
1/4 km
Fuyou Rd.
YUYUAN
Sights
1 Bank of China C3
2 The Bund D4
3 Former HSBC Building C4
4 Peace Hotel C3
5 Rockbund Art Museum C2
Restaurants
1 Canton Table C5
2 Cejerdary C5
3 Da Hu Chun............... C4
4 Daimon Gastrolounge... C5
5 Lost Heaven............. C6
6 Mercato D5
7 Mr & Mrs Bund C4
8 Ultraviolet................ C4
Hotels
1 Fairmont Peace Hotel... C3
2 Le Royal Meridien A4
3 The Peninsula Shanghai.................. D2
4 The Shanghai EDITION.................. B3
5 Waldorf Astoria Shanghai on the Bund .. C5
6 The Waterhouse at South Bund............. D7
7 The Westin Bund Center Shanghai......... B5

airy shop specializes in one thing: crab noodles. They don't come cheap, but you can taste the care and craftsmanship in each serving—plus, the premium bowls are topped with gold flakes. **Known for:** singular, specialized menu; high price tag; beautiful design. *$ Average main: Y360 ✉ 59 Guangdong Lu, The Bund ☎ 021/6969–7777 ▭ No credit cards.*

Daimon Gastrolounge (厨魔馆 *Chúmóguǎn*)
$$ | CHINESE FUSION | Hong Kong "Demon Chef" Alvin Leung does playful, inventive, excellent takes on Hong Kong street food at this casual-concept restaurant, where a dimly lit interior features neon signs and pumping music. If you're feeling flush with funds, book a seat at Leung's upscale Bo Shanghai speakeasy (it's hidden behind an unmarked wall), for a fine-dining tour of regional cuisines remixed with Western flair. **Known for:** over-the-top hipness; barbecue pork buns; chili crab xiaolongbao. *$ Average main: Y150 ✉ Five on the Bund, 5 Zhongshan Dong Yi Lu, 6th fl., The Bund ☎ 021/5383–2031.*

Da Hu Chun (大壶春 *Dàhúchūn*)
$ | SHANGHAINESE | This hole-in-the-wall shop makes traditional Shanghaiese shengjianbao (fried soup dumplings) with wrappings that are pillowy and soft rather than thin and chewy. Take care not to scald your mouth with the piping-hot soup inside the dumplings, and try to come off-hours to avoid the inevitable morning and lunchtime crowds. **Known for:** local favorite; pork or shrimp-and-pork shengjianbao; shrimp wonton soup. *$ Average main: Y10 ✉ 136 Sichuan Zhong Lu, The Bund ☎ 021/6313–0155 ▭ No credit cards.*

★ **Lost Heaven** (话马天堂 *Huāmǎtiāntáng*)
$$ | YUNNAN | Southern China's Yunnan cuisine—with Burmese, Vietnamese, and Thai influences—is highlighted at this restaurant, which has a second location in the Former French Concession. Though service at this branch lacks a bit, the dining room is romantic, with dim lighting and exotic, traditional decor; in warmer months, try for a table on the spacious roof deck. **Known for:** Yunnan wild vegetable cakes; Dalí-style chicken; ghost chicken salad. *$ Average main: Y120 ✉ 17 Yan'an Dong Lu, The Bund ☎ 021/6330–0967 🌐 www.lostheaven.com.cn.*

Mercato
$$$$ | ITALIAN | Prolific restaurateur Jean-Georges Vongerichten's namesake restaurant has delighted Shanghai for quite a few years now, but Mercato is a whole different animal—one where the kitchen really shines with its smaller plates and pizza. Also polished is the industrial chic interior featuring iron, steel, reclaimed wood, and black-leather and wooden chairs that celebrate form and function. **Known for:** black-truffle pizza; house-made ricotta with fruit compote; classy but unfussy atmosphere. *$ Average main: Y230 ✉ Three on the Bund, 17 Guangdong Lu, 6th fl., The Bund ☎ 021/6321–9922 🌐 www.jean-georges.com/restaurants/china/shanghai/mercato ⏲ No lunch.*

Mr & Mrs Bund (先生和小姐外滩的 *Xiānshēng hé xiǎojiě wàitāndé*)
$$$$ | FRENCH | Open into the wee hours, chef Paul Pairet's Bund-side eatery features not only satisfying modern French dishes but also a lengthy list of wines by the glass. If you're not a night owl, come for lunch or brunch, when the terrace views of Pudong's skyine are especially gorgeous. **Known for:** late-night bites; romantic setting; locally renowned chef. *$ Average main: Y250 ✉ Bund 18, 18 Zhongshan Dong Yi Lu, 6th fl., The Bund ☎ 021/6323–9898 🌐 www.mmbund.com.*

Ultraviolet
$$$$ | ECLECTIC | To reach this Paul Pairet (of Mr & Mrs Bund fame) restaurant, you board a minibus bound for a secret, 10-seat location, somewhere near Suzhou Creek, where you're served several courses, each one paired with

Did You Know?

On one short stretch of the famous Bund, there are 52 buildings in architectural styles, including Romanesque, Gothic, Renaissance, Baroque, Neoclassical, Beaux-Arts, and, of course, Art Deco. In fact, Shanghai features some of the finest Art Deco architecture in the world.

广 场

customized video projections, songs, and aromas. Several different dining experiences are offered, but all of them are as pricey (seats start at Y4,000) and exclusive (deposits and reservations accepted three months out) as they are unique. **Known for:** totally immersive experience; high price tag; critically acclaimed. *Average main: Y4000* *Mr & Mrs Bund, 18 Zhongshan Dong Yi Lu, 6th fl., The Bund* *021/6142–5198* *www.uvbypp.cc* *No lunch. Closed Mon.*

Hotels

Fairmont Peace Hotel (上海和平饭店 *Shànghǎi hépíng fàndiàn*)
$$$ | **HOTEL** | Originally The Cathay Hotel, built by the wealthy Sassoon family in 1929, the Fairmont Peace Hotel pairs modern-day skyline views with rich history in rooms that maintain the glamour of art deco–era Shanghai. **Pros:** stunning architecture; exudes luxury and extravagance; home to Shanghai's oldest jazz band. **Cons:** very busy location; outside can be loud at night; dining outlets aren't as impressive as the rest of the hotel. *Rooms from: Y1700* *20 Nanjing Dong Lu, The Bund* *021/6138–6888* *www.fairmont.com/peace-hotel-shanghai* *270 rooms* *No meals.*

Le Royal Meridien (上海世茂皇家艾美酒店 *Shìmào huángjia àiměi jiǔdiàn*)
$ | **HOTEL** | When it opened, Le Royal Meridien, which dominates the foot of pedestrian-only Nanjing Dong Lu, changed the face of Puxi hospitality with its attentive staff, excellent amenities, and stately rooms. **Pros:** central location; excellent facilities; great weekend brunch. **Cons:** service hiccups; annoying elevator system; small design flaws. *Rooms from: Y1009* *505 Nanjing Dong Lu, Nanjing Dong Lu* *021/3318–9999* *www.leroyalmeridienshanghai.com* *761 rooms* *No meals.*

★ **The Peninsula Shanghai** (上海半岛酒店 *Shànghǎi bàndǎo jiǔdiàn*)
$$$$ | **HOTEL** | No detail is too small at the luxurious Peninsula, where the rooms are plush and have a classic design that recalls early 20th–century Shanghai, and the dining options and other amenities are world-class. **Pros:** houses two Michelin-starred restaurants; stunning facilities, including an art deco–inspired pool and excellent spa; exceptional afternoon tea. **Cons:** service and decor can feel stuffy; no lounge offering free drinks or snacks; high price point. *Rooms from: Y2600* *32 Zhongshan Dong Yi Lu, The Bund* *021/2327–2888* *www.peninsula.com/en/shanghai/5-star-luxury-hotel-bund* *235 rooms* *Free Breakfast.*

The Shanghai EDITION (上海艾迪逊酒店 *Shànghǎi àidíxùn jiǔdiàn*)
$$$$ | **HOTEL** | Sleek, design-savvy rooms done in muted-beige tones and an array of wining and dining options draw cosmopolitan travelers to this Ian Schrager/Marriott International property just off the Bund. **Pros:** good location near the metro; excellent dining options; fabulous views. **Cons:** can feel more like a social hub than a retreat; not inexpensive; on a very busy street. *Rooms from: Y2300* *199 Nanjing Dong Lu, The Bund* *021/5368–9999* *www.editionhotels.com/shanghai* *145 rooms* *No meals.*

Waldorf Astoria Shanghai on the Bund (上海外滩华尔道夫酒店 *Shànghǎi wàitān huáěr dàofū jiǔdiàn*)
$$$$ | **HOTEL** | The fact that one part of this Bund-side hotel occupies what was once the Shanghai Club contributes to its history-steeped, picture-perfect elegance: from the moment you step inside, you'll be dazzled by the marble flooring and crystal chandeliers. **Pros:** incredible views of the iconic skyline; lavish decor; home to the city's longest bar (more than 110 feet). **Cons:** pricey room rates; location can be noisy; views from some rooms less impressive than from others. *Rooms from: Y2500* *2 Zhongshan*

Dong Yi Lu, The Bund ☎ 021/6322–9988 🌐 www.waldorfastoriashanghai.com/en 🛏 260 rooms 🍽 Free Breakfast.

The Waterhouse at South Bund (水舍上海南外滩 *Shuǐshě shànghǎi nánwàitān*)
$ | HOTEL | Aesthetics dominate at this hotel in a converted, 1930s warehouse—designed by local architecture champions Neri & Hu—and though rooms might feel too minimalist for some, there's no arguing that they aren't beautiful in their simplicity. **Pros:** intimate setting; rooftop bar overlooking the Pudong skyline; quiet location. **Cons:** small rooms; tucked away from main Bund sights; 15-minute walk to the nearest metro station. $ *Rooms from: Y1000 ✉ No. 1–3 Maojiayan Lu, The Bund ☎ 021/6080–2988 🌐 www.waterhouseshanghai.com 🛏 19 rooms.*

The Westin Bund Center Shanghai (上海威斯汀大饭店 *Shànghǎi wēisītīng dàfàndiàn*)
$$ | HOTEL | FAMILY | With its distinctive room layouts, glittering glass staircase, and 90-plus works of art on display, the Westin Shanghai is a jewel on the Bund. **Pros:** very attentive service; five-minute walk from The Bund; peaceful area. **Cons:** outmoded furnishings; some rooms feel small; no spa. $ *Rooms from: Y1100 ✉ Bund Center, 88 Henan Zhong Lu, The Bund ☎ 021/6335–1888, 888/6335–1888 🌐 www.westinshanghai.com 🛏 570 rooms 🍽 No meals.*

Nightlife

BARS

Char (上海外滩英迪格酒店 *Shànghǎi wàitān yīng dí gé jiǔdiàn*)
BARS/PUBS | Though somewhat dated, Hotel Indigo's rooftop bar and steak house is still a prime place to take in unimpeded views of the Pudong skyline and Huangpu River while sipping drinks and snacking from a charcuterie board for two. ✉ *Hotel Indigo, 585 Zhongshan Dong Er Lu, 29-31F, The Bund ☎ 021/3302–9995.*

Glam (魅蓝 *Mèi lán*)
NIGHTLIFE OVERVIEW | Glam attracts a well-heeled crowd of media types, intellectuals, and artists with its idiosyncratic design, its creative cocktails that include customizable gin and tonics, its casual, lounge-food menu (try the truffle cheese toasties), and its occasional film screenings or other cultural offerings. It's a welcome retreat from the busy Bund; it's also across from its sister restaurant, M. ✉ *Five on the Bund, 20 Guangdong Lu, 7th fl., The Bund ☎ 021/6329–3751 🌐 www.m-restaurantgroup.com/glam.*

CLUBS

Bar Rouge
BARS/PUBS | In the trendy Bund 18 complex, Bar Rouge has been the destination of choice among Shanghai's beautiful people for years. Pouting models, visiting celebrities, and, seemingly, all of the city's French expats are among the regular clientele. The Pudong views are knockout—as are the drink prices. ✉ *Bund 18, 18 Zhongshan Dong Yi Lu, 7th fl., The Bund ☎ 021/6339–1199 🌐 www.bar-rouge-shanghai.com.*

M1NT
DANCE CLUBS | Two-parts club, one part bar, M1NT is one of the few places in Shanghai with a strict door policy. The club is on the 24th floor of an office tower situated on a quiet side street just behind the Bund. There's no set dress code, but men should not wear shorts. Although bottle service is popular, plenty of revelers stick to buying drinks and shots from the bar, whose lines can be three deep. The shark tank is partiers' favorite photo backdrop. ✉ *318 Fuzhou Lu, 24th fl., The Bund ☎ 021/6391–2811 🌐 www.m1ntglobal.com/club-shanghai.*

LIVE MUSIC

House of Blues and Jazz (布鲁斯与爵士之屋 *Bùlǔsī yǔ juéshì zhīwu*)
MUSIC CLUBS | Several music sets nightly and loads of ambience—dark-wood paneling, low-lighting, memorabilia from 1930s Shanghai—make the House of

Local Brews

Northern Chinese swear by their *baijiu*, a strong, usually sweet, clear liquor, but Shanghainese opt for milder poison. Most beloved is *huangjiu*, a brown brew from Shaoxing with a mild taste that resembles whiskey, which may explain why the latter is the most popular foreign liquor among locals. Huangjiu's quality is determined by whether it was brewed 2, 5, or 10 years ago. It is usually served warm, sometimes with ginger or dried plum added for kick.

Beer is also widely consumed; although there is a Shanghai beer brand, it is cheap, very bitter, and mostly found in the suburbs. Stores stock brands like Suntory, Asahi, Harbin Snow, and any number of imported beers. Bars serve Tsingtao and imports like Tiger, Heineken, and Budweiser, which are more expensive. You'll find Sinkiang Black at Xinjiang restaurants. Craft beer can be had at Shanghai's small but strong homegrown breweries, and, increasingly, at fancier spots around town.

Blues and Jazz a must visit. ✉ *60 Fuzhou Lu, The Bund* ☎ *021/6323–2779.*

Jazz at Lincoln Center Shanghai (林肯爵士乐上海中心 *Línkěn juéshìyuè shànghǎi zhōngxīn*)
MUSIC CLUBS | Just off the Bund, the Shanghai outpost of New York City's famed Jazz at Lincoln Center venue doesn't drip with the local history that places like Peace Hotel do. Its musical programming is excellent, though, so it's worth checking the schedule if you like jazz. ✉ *139 Nanjing Dong Lu, 4th fl., The Bund* ☎ *021/6330–9218* ⊕ *jalcsh.com/en* ☞ *Closed Mon.*

Peace Hotel Jazz Bar (和平饭店爵士酒吧 *Hépíng fàndiàn juéshì jiǔbā*)
PIANO BARS/LOUNGES | The average age of the musicians in the Old Jazz Band is 80, but you wouldn't know it when listening to them jam. The food and drinks are inspired by what the bar served in the 1920s and '30s, when Shanghai was in its golden age, and the Peace Hotel was *the* place to see and be seen. Dark woods, heavy red curtains, and warming cocktails make this bar an especially good choice for winter. ✉ *20 Nanjing Dong Lu, The Bund* ☎ *021/6321–6888* ⊕ *www.fairmont.com/peace-hotel-shanghai/dining/thejazzbar.*

Shopping

BOOKS

Shanghai Foreign Language Bookstore
BOOKS/STATIONERY | You could while away an hour or two in this massive bookstore, which has a huge selection of English-language books for children and adults. The downside here is that there's so much, it's not always organized well, and few of the clerks speak English. Still, wander the floors, and you'll find new and back issues of magazines ranging from *Vogue* to *National Geographic*, and shelf upon shelf of novels and nonfiction books. Prices are higher than what you'd pay in the States but not terribly so. ✉ *390 Fuzhou Lu, The Bund* ☎ *021/2320–4888.*

CERAMICS

Blue Shanghai White (海上青花 *Hǎishàngqīnghuā*)
CERAMICS/GLASSWARE | The eponymous colored ceramics here are designed and hand-painted by the owner and are made in Jingdezhen, once home

to China's imperial kilns. Some larger pieces are made with wood salvaged from demolition sites around Shanghai. ✉ *17 Fuzhou Lu, Room 103, The Bund* ☎ *021/6323–0856.*

SHOES

Suzhou Cobblers (**苏州臭皮匠** *Sūzhōu chòu píjiang*)

CLOTHING | Sold here are beautifully embroidered handmade shoes and slippers for men and women, with quirky designs such as cabbages. You'll also find funky round handled bags, gorgeous children's shoes and more intricate accessories and trinkets. ✉ *17 Fuzhou Lu, Room 101, The Bund* ☎ *021/6321–7087* 🌐 *www.suzhou-cobblers.com.*

SPAS

Waldorf Astoria Spa (**华尔道夫水疗** *Huáěr dàofū shuǐliáo*)

SPA/BEAUTY | At the Waldorf Astoria's exquisite spa, every room is kitted out with its own steam room and rain shower. Have yourself a private spa party (up to four people), with three hours in the VIP Spa Suite, including a 90-minute Oriental Stress Massage, a 30-minute facial, and an afternoon tea service that concludes with a bottle of Champagne. ✉ *The Waldorf Astoria Shanghai, 2 Zhongshan Dong Yi Lu, The Bund* ☎ *021/6322–9988* 🌐 *www.waldorfastoriashanghai.com/en/SpaFitness.*

Former French Concession

With its tree-lined streets and crumbling old villas, the Former French Concession is Shanghai's most visitor-friendly area, with ample shade and sidewalks meant to be pounded. **■ TIP→ If you're looking at a larger city map, the Former French Concession is located in North Xuhui District, South Jing'an District and West Huangpu Districts.** The area is a wonderful place to go wandering and make serendipitous discoveries of stately architecture, groovy boutiques and galleries, or cozy cafés. Much of Shanghai's past beauty remains, although many of the old buildings are in a desperate state of disrepair. One of the major roads through this area, Huaihai Lu, is a popular shopping location, with all the big foreign chains and an assortment of local brands. Julu Lu, Fumin Lu, Donghu Lu, Xiangyang Lu, Fuxing Xi Lu, and Anfu Lu are where many of Shanghai's restaurants, bars, and clubs are located, so if you are looking for an evening out, head to this area.

GETTING AROUND

This is a lovely area to walk around, so it's best to leave cabs behind and go on foot. The only site that is at a distance is Soong Ching-ling's Former Residence, which is a bit farther down Huaihai Lu. Access it via metro Lines 10 and 11 at Jiaotong University. Any of the three Line 1 metro stops (Shaanxi Nan Lu, Changshu Lu, or Hengshan Lu) will land you somewhere in the Former French Concession area. Line 7 connects at Changshu Lu and Line 10 at Shaanxi Nan Lu.

Sights

Cathay Theatre (**国泰电影院** *Guótài diànyǐngyuàn*)

ARTS VENUE | The art deco–style Cathay Cinema was one of the first movie theaters in Shanghai and, indeed, still shows a mix of Chinese and Western films. The theater was a favorite of Shanghainese author Eileen Chang, of *Lust, Caution* fame. ✉ *870 Huaihai Zhong Lu, French Concession* ☎ *021/5404–2095* 🌐 *www.guotaifilm.com.*

Former Residence of Dr. Sun Yat-sen (**上海孙中山故居纪念馆** *Shànghǎi sūnzhōngshān gùjū jìniànguǎn*)

MUSEUM | Sun Yat-sen, the father of the Republic of China, lived in this two-story house from 1919 to 1924. His wife, Soong Qing-ling, of the illustrious Soong family, continued to live here until 1937.

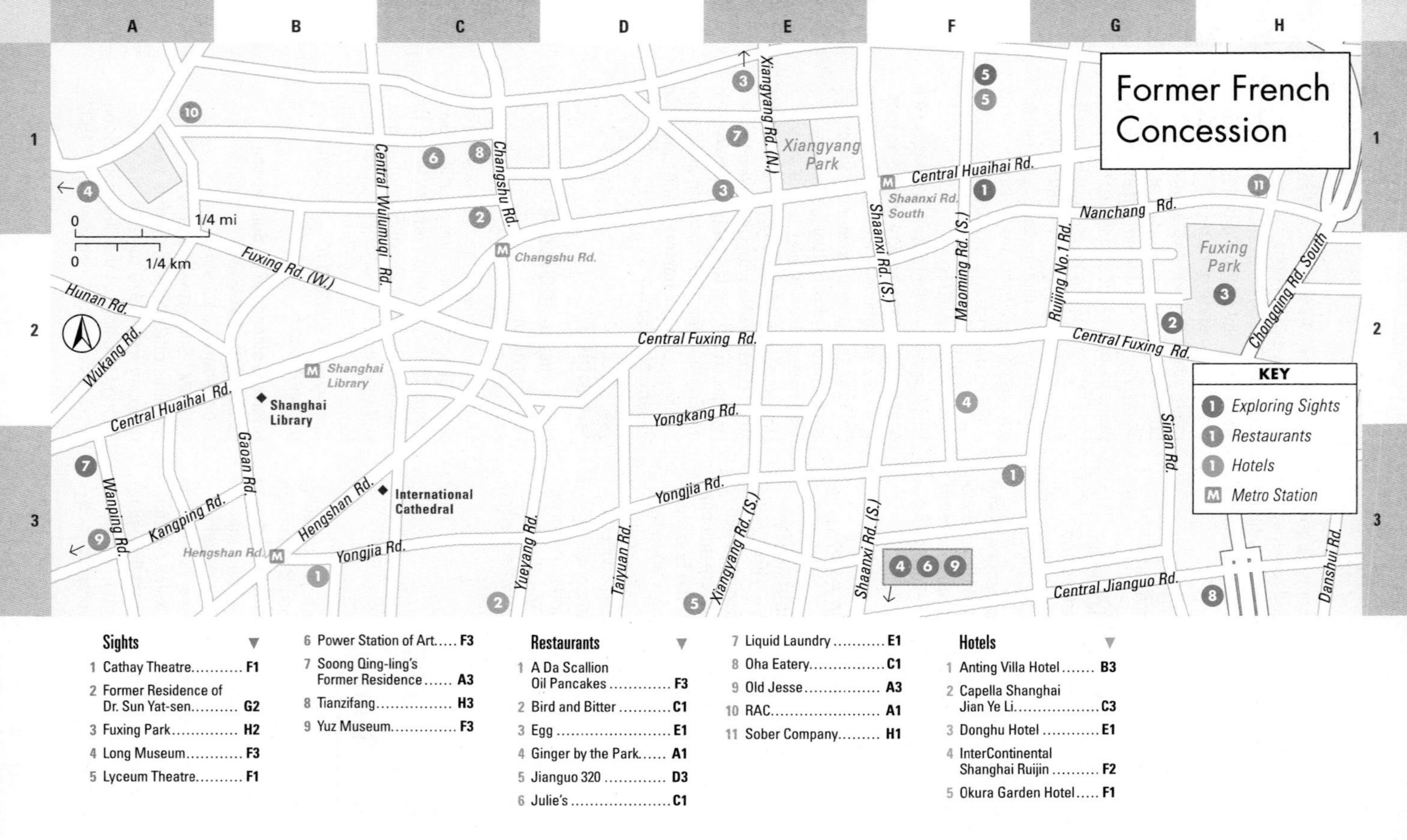

Sights

1 Cathay Theatre........... F1
2 Former Residence of Dr. Sun Yat-sen.......... G2
3 Fuxing Park.............. H2
4 Long Museum............ F3
5 Lyceum Theatre.......... F1
6 Power Station of Art..... F3
7 Soong Qing-ling's Former Residence...... A3
8 Tianzifang................ H3
9 Yuz Museum.............. F3

Restaurants

1 A Da Scallion Oil Pancakes F3
2 Bird and Bitter C1
3 Egg E1
4 Ginger by the Park...... A1
5 Jianguo 320 .... D3
6 Julie's C1
7 Liquid Laundry E1
8 Oha Eatery................ C1
9 Old Jesse................. A3
10 RAC...................... A1
11 Sober Company......... H1

Hotels

1 Anting Villa Hotel B3
2 Capella Shanghai Jian Ye Li.................. C3
3 Donghu Hotel E1
4 InterContinental Shanghai Ruijin F2
5 Okura Garden Hotel..... F1

Today it's a museum, where tours are conducted in Chinese and English. ✉ *7 Xiangshan Lu, French Concession* ☎ *021/5306–3361* 🎫 *Y20.*

Fuxing Park (**复兴公园** *Fùxīng gōngyuán*)
GARDEN | This European-style park, once open only to Shanghai's French residents, is one of downtown's most tranquil spots. Here you'll find people strolling hand in hand, practicing tai chi, and playing cards and mah-jongg. There is a tiny amusement park and, on weekends and holidays, art projects for kids. The open spaces double as dance floors, with elderly couples dancing away the day—visitors are welcome to join in. ✉ *516 Fuxing Zhong Lu, French Concession* ☎ *021/5386–1069* 🎫 *Free.*

Long Museum (**龙美术馆** *Lóng měishùguǎn*)
MUSEUM | Billionaire art collectors Liu Yiqian and Wang Wei don't do anything halfway; their Long Museum, designed by Shanghai-based firm Atelier Deshaus, is a testament to the money flowing into supporting contemporary Chinese art. The museum hosts rotating exhibitions, from Qing Dynasty paintings to a show on the past, present, and future of silver in Mexico. Long Museum is also walking distance from Yuz Museum. On the first Tuesday of every month, Long Museum offers free entry. Note that the museum is in the up-and-coming West Bund gallery and arts district to the south. Although you can easily reach the West Bund by taxi from anywhere in central Shanghai, the Former French Concession provides the best public-transit access via metro Lines 7 and 12. ✉ *3398 Longteng Dadao, Old City* ☎ *021/6422–7636* 🌐 *thelongmuseum.org* 🎫 *Y50* ⏲ *Closed Mon.* Ⓜ *Longhua Zhong Lu.*

Lyceum Theatre (**兰心大戏院** *Lánxīn dàxìyuàn*)
ARTS VENUE | In the days of Old Shanghai, the Lyceum Theatre was the home of the British Amateur Drama Club. The old stage is still in use as a concert hall. On the third floor is Candor, an intimate cocktail bar and stage outfitted in plush red velvet. The atmosphere draws on the 1920s era, with cabaret and burlesque-style shows. ✉ *57 Maoming Nan Lu, French Concession* ☎ *021/6217–8530.*

★ **Power Station of Art** (**上海当代艺术博物馆** *Shànghǎi dāngdài yìshù bówùguǎn*)
MUSEUM | **FAMILY** | The site of the Shanghai World Expo was a barren wasteland until this massive contemporary art museum, housed in a former power plant, opened in late 2012. It did so with a bang, opening the ninth Shanghai Biennale and simultaneously hosting an exhibition from the Centre Pompidou in Paris. Rather than a permanent collection, the museum hosts one large-scale exhibition after another. It pulls in top Chinese artists like Cai Guoqiang and is the city's home for major touring exhibitions. Every Tuesday is free entry for all visitors. The PSA is actually about 2½ miles south of the Old City, on the edge of the Huangpu River. You can get here from the Old City or Xintiandi/City Center by taxi or via metro Lines 4 and 8 (and a 15-minute walk from the metro station). ✉ *200 Huayuangang Lu, Old City* ☎ *021/3110–8550* 🌐 *www.powerstationofart.org/en* 🎫 *From Y50, depending on exhibition* ⏲ *Closed Mon.* Ⓜ *Xizangnan Lu.*

Soong Qing-ling's Former Residence (**上海宋庆龄故居纪念馆** *Shànghǎi sòngqìnglíng gùjū jìniànguǎn*)
HISTORIC SITE | A daughter of the prominent Soong family, Soong Qing-ling (also known as Madame Sun Yat-sen) was first a Nationalist and then a Communist. Her sister Mei-ling married Chiang Kai-shek, who was the head of the Nationalist government from 1927 to 1949. This three-story house, built in 1920 by a German ship owner, was Soong's primary residence from 1948 to 1963. It has been preserved as it was during her lifetime; in the study are her 4,000 books and, in the bedroom, the furniture that her parents

gave as her dowry. The small museum next door has some nice displays from Soong Qing-ling and Sun Yat-sen's life, including pictures from their 1915 wedding in Tokyo. ✉ *1843 Huaihai Zhong Lu, French Concession* ☎ *021/6474–7183* 🌐 *www.shsoong-chingling.com* 🎫 *Y20.*

Tianzifang (田子坊 *Tiánzi fāng*)
COMMERCIAL CENTER | **FAMILY** | If Xintiandi is the government's orderly, sanitized shikumen restoration project, Tianzifang is the opposite. The former residential district is a labyrinth of alleyways between redbrick lane houses. Restaurants, cafés, and a few galleries fill the spaces today, as do shops selling everything from kitschy souvenirs emblazoned with retro propaganda to leather journals and shoes, tea, and qipao dresses. **■ TIP→ You can also enter Tianzifang from the back side, at 155 Jianguo Zhong Lu.** ✉ *Enter at 210 or 248 Taikang Lu, between Ruijin Er and Sinan Lu, French Concession.*

★ **Yuz Museum** (余德耀美术馆 *Yúdéyào měishùguǎn*)
MUSEUM | **FAMILY** | In a former airport hangar and within walking distance of the Long Museum, the Yuz Museum is the brainchild of Chinese-Indonesian art collector Budi Tek. The massive, light-flooded space is perfect for showcasing installations like Maurizio Cattelan's *Untitled*, an olive tree planted in a cube of dirt, which was featured in his retrospective at New York's Guggenheim. Chinese artists get plenty of showtime, too; in the same exhibition, you will find Ren Jian's painting *Stamp Collection*, six acrylic-on-canvas versions of stamps from African nations. The museum has Wi-Fi throughout, a small gift shop, and a café where you can watch the sun set. Its cement courtyard, with several sets of stairs, ramps, and a few sculptures, is a good place for kids to roam. Note that, like the Long Museum, the Yuz is in the emerging West Bund arts area, readily reached from the Former French Concession by taxi or metro Line 11. ✉ *35 Fenggu Lu, Old City* ☎ *021/6426–1901* 🌐 *www.yuzmshanghai.org* 🎫 *Y150* 🕙 *Closed Mon.* Ⓜ *Yunjin Lu.*

Restaurants

A Da Scallion Oil Pancakes (阿大葱油饼 *Ā dà cōngyóubǐng*)
$ | **SHANGHAINESE** | The scallion-oil pancakes at this shop are incredibly popular, with long lines forming from the 6 am opening time until closing—around 3 pm, which is when the pancakes usually sell out. Indeed, demand for A Da's delicious take on this traditional Shanghai street food is so fierce that the owner has placed a limit on the number of pieces each customer can order. **Known for:** great craftsmanship; long waits; efficient service. $ *Average main: Y7* ✉ *120 Ruijin Er Lu, French Concession* ✥ *Entrance on Yongjia Lu* ☎ *No phone* 🕙 *Closed Wed.* ▬ *No credit cards.*

Bird and Bitter
$$ | **INTERNATIONAL** | A narrow driveway is all that separates this couplet of venues on a leafy lane. Bird, an intimate, relaxed wine bar and kitchen, has a changing menu of unfussy small-plate dishes with fusion twists and a list of wines with interesting stories. **Known for:** casual, welcoming environment; creative menu; great coffee. $ *Average main: Y100* ✉ *50 and 58 Wuyuan Lu, French Concession* ☎ *135/0172–6412.*

Egg
$ | **CAFÉ** | Laptop-equipped freelancers and other trendy locals frequent this petite, friendly, Australian-style café. The menu focuses on breakfast/brunch fare; small plates, often featuring local ingredients; and, of course, delicious hot- or cold-brew coffees. **Known for:** avocado toast; pumpkin spice latte; meeting place for local creatives. $ *Average main: Y58* ✉ *12 Xiangyang Bei Lu, French Concession* 🌐 *eggshanghai.com* ▬ *No credit cards.*

Ginger by the Park
$ | **CAFÉ** | Ginger is a Southeast Asian eatery with a strong European flavor. The food is excellent, and the intimate indoor space, the patio, and the relatively tranquil park-side setting make it a good place to enjoy quiet conversation over a meal or a cup of coffee. **Known for:** laksa; crispy honey-herbed chicken; black cod with lemongrass. *Average main: Y75 ✉ 91 Xingguo Lu, French Concession ☎ 021/3406–0599 🌐 www.gingerfoods.com.*

Jianguo 320 (建国328号 *Jiànguó 328 hào*)
$ | **SHANGHAINESE** | Locals and visitors alike are drawn to this restaurant for its relaxed, casual atmosphere; its home-style Shanghainese classics; and its no-MSG policy. It's often packed, so consider calling ahead, especially if you plan to order the signature "duck with eight delicacies" dish, which must be ordered in advance as it's limited to five per day. **Known for:** scallion-roasted yellow croaker; scallion oil noodles; hongshao rou (red-cooked pork). *Average main: Y50 ✉ 328 Jianguo Xi Lu, French Concession ☎ 021/6471–3819 No credit cards.*

Julie's (香 *Xiāng*)
$ | **YUNNAN** | A wall of picture windows looks out onto leafy Anfu Lu, so you can watch passersby from this simply furnished dining room. Wash down your pickled mashed potatoes, *ru bing* (rectangles of panfried goat cheese), or other home-style Yunnan dishes with a Belgian beer or one of the house juices. **Known for:** jasmine scrambled eggs; dry-fried potato threads; vanilla-scented ribs. *Average main: Y90 ✉ 45 Anfu Lu, French Concession ☎ 021/5403–5266 No credit cards.*

Liquid Laundry
$$ | **MODERN AMERICAN** | **FAMILY** | By day, this modern gastropub appeals to families with its crispy pizzas and other delicious lunch and brunch favorites. At night, house-brewed beer, good cocktails, and Friday and Saturday DJ events attract a trendy party crowd. **Known for:** buzzing brunches; rotisserie chicken; inventive pizzas. *Average main: Y100 ✉ Kwah Center, 1028 Huaihai Zhong Lu, 2nd fl., French Concession ✣ Entrance is on Donghu Lu, just off Huaihai; look for bank ICBC ☎ 021/6445–9589 🌐 www.theliquidlaundry.com.*

Oha Eatery
$$ | **CHINESE FUSION** | A meal at sleek, wood-adorned Oha is sure to introduce you to new flavors. Tucked behind a small coffee window, this intimate restaurant is easy to miss but well worth finding for its contemporary Chinese food—influenced heavily by Guizhou's regional cuisine, with some modern twists—craft cocktails, and natural wines. **Known for:** fermented tofu salad; lard rice; pinewood smoked beans and pork. *Average main: Y100 ✉ 23 Anfu Lu, French Concession ☎ 136/2164–7680 🌐 www.ohashanghai.com/project/oha-eatery/ No credit cards.*

Old Jesse (老吉士 *Lǎo jíshì*)
$$ | **SHANGHAINESE** | The well-established Old Jesse is a must-try. Its unforgettable renditions of classic Shanghai dishes are widely considered the best in town; its brusk service and ramshackle dining room are merely part of its authentic charm. **Known for:** scallion-oil noodles; whole fish head with scallions; hongshao rou (red-cooked pork). *Average main: Y150 ✉ 41 Tianping Lu, French Concession ☎ 021/6282–9260 No credit cards.*

RAC
$ | **FRENCH** | The tiny RAC empire occupies a courtyard at the juncture of Anfu Lu and Wukang Lu. Streetside, it has takeaway coffee and ice cream (summer only) windows; in the courtyard, it has a relaxed French eatery that serves delicious sweet or savory crepes, as well as other casual brunch and lunch fare. **Known for:** avocado toast; natural wine; Breton-style galettes. *Average main: Y80 ✉ 322 Anfu Lu, French Concession ☎ No phone No credit cards.*

Sober Company

$$ | **ASIAN FUSION** | This multilevel space offers several venues in one spot. The café has light, Asian-influenced fare, as well as good coffee and coffee or tea cocktails; the upstairs restaurant with New York–inspired decor touches serves modern dim sum and well-done fusion dishes; and the adjacent Sober Society bar features excellent cocktails as well as the Tipsy Room (a secret bar within the bar). **Known for:** uni ban mian (sea urchin noodles); foie gras "Snickers"; inventive cocktails. *Average main: Y150* *99 Yandang Lu, French Concession* *021/5309–8261* *No credit cards.*

Unique Spot

Magnolia B&B is one of Shanghai's most charming budget boutique hotels and a must if you're looking for a personalized experience that the larger hotels just can't offer.

Hotels

Anting Villa Hotel (安亭别墅花园酒店 *Antíng biéshù huayuán jiǔdiàn*)

$ | **HOTEL** | Although conveniently situated two blocks from the Hengshan Road nightlife district, the Anting Villa Hotel is a surprisingly quiet, side-street retreat with cedar-shaded grounds and basic rooms. **Pros:** central location; well-priced for the neighborhood; very local. **Cons:** faded; can be hard to communicate; feels budget. *Rooms from: Y400* *46 Anting Lu, French Concession* *021/6433–1188* *www.antingvillahotel.com* *143 rooms* *No meals.*

Capella Shanghai Jian Ye Li (上海建业里嘉佩乐酒店 *Shànghǎi jiànyèlǐ jiāpèilè jiǔdiàn*)

$$$$ | **HOTEL** | A collection of private villas in restored, traditional, 1930s shikumen (stone gate) houses, Capella Shanghai is a secluded and stunning sanctuary in the heart of the Former French Concession. **Pros:** unique to Shanghai; tailored service from individual personal assistants; beautiful pastries from in-house bakery. **Cons:** steep prices; some guests may encounter difficulties with the stairs; staying here can feel like you're in a bubble. *Rooms from: Y3980* *480 Jianguo Xi Lu, French Concession* *021/5466–6688* *www.capellahotels.com/en/capella-shanghai* *55 villas* *Free Breakfast.*

Donghu Hotel (東湖賓館 *Dōnghú bīnguǎn*)

$ | **HOTEL** | Just off the frenzied shopping street of Huaihai Lu is one of Shanghai's best-preserved hotels from the city's 1920s heyday, with grand rooms in the older guesthouse annex and newer but plainer (and more geared to business travelers) main-building rooms. **Pros:** traditional and elegant; indoor pool; a stone's throw from the metro. **Cons:** poor service; rooms in original building need refurbishment; rowdy location near lots of bars. *Rooms from: Y530* *70 Donghu Lu, French Concession* *021/6415–8158* *www.donghuhotelshanghai.cn* *280 rooms* *No meals.*

InterContinental Shanghai Ruijin

$ | **HOTEL** | **FAMILY** | Although this property has two newer buildings, the beautifully restored Morris Estate villas showcase how opulently Shanghai's *tai-pan* (expatriate millionaire businessmen) once lived; rooms here have plush beds, cozy reading areas, and art deco–inspired decor. **Pros:** sprawling grounds; historical grandeur; prime location. **Cons:** service is uneven; taxis can be hard to find; slightly more impressive from the outside than inside. *Rooms from: Y1098* *118 Ruijin Er Lu, French Concession* *021/6472–5222* *www.ihg.com/intercontinental* *238 rooms* *No meals.*

Okura Garden Hotel (花园饭店 *Huāyuán fàndiàn*)
$$ | HOTEL | A parklike setting in the heart of the Former French Concession makes this 33-story tower set on the grounds of the old French Club a favorite retreat, especially among Japanese travelers familiar with the Okura name. **Pros:** gorgeous surroundings; historic building; convenient to shops, restaurants, and the metro. **Cons:** you're paying more for beauty and location than service; furnishings a little dated; towering design detracts from the historical charm of the grounds. *Rooms from: Y1200 ✉ 58 Maoming Nan Lu, French Concession ☎ 021/6415–1111 🌐 www.gardenhotelshanghai.com/Pages/en 471 rooms No meals.*

Nightlife

BARS

Cotton's (棉花酒吧 *Miánhuā jiûbā*)
BARS/PUBS | This friendly, laid-back favorite moved many times before settling into the current old garden house. Busy without being loud, Cotton's is a rare place where you can have a conversation with friends—or make some new ones. The patio here is one of Shanghai's loveliest, but the food menu is not, so stick to drinks. ✉ *132 Anting Lu, French Concession* ☎ *021/6433–7995* 🌐 *www.cottons-shanghai.com.*

Epic
BARS/PUBS | Housed on several levels of an old lane house, this intimate cocktail bar feels perfectly Shanghai—a contrast of old and new, with forward-thinking drinks in a traditional setting. Cocktails are intricate without being pretentious, and you'll have trouble only stopping at one. ✉ *17 Gaoyou Lu, French Concession* ☎ *021/5411–1189.*

Senator Saloon
PIANO BARS/LOUNGES | In true speakeasy style, this swinging spot is easy to miss, situated as it is behind an unmarked door on a quiet street. Step inside to travel back in time, with big-band music playing in the background, velvet damask wallpaper, a pressed-tin ceiling, and classic as well as contemporary cocktails. ✉ *98 Wuyuan Lu, French Concession* ☎ *021/5423–1330.*

Speak Low (彼楼 *Bǐlóu*)
BARS/PUBS | This spot led Shanghai's speakeasy trend and continues to garner international acclaim with regular appearances on lists of the world's (and Asia's) 50 best bars. Each of its four floors has a different cocktail bar and menu. All four of them serve some of Shanghai's best drinks. All are also equally popular; be prepared to wait on weekends. ✉ *579 Fuxing Zhong Lu, French Concession* ☎ *021/6416–0133.*

Union Trading Company
BARS/PUBS | A local favorite, Union feels like a neighborhood pub but has the prices and service of a posh cocktail bar. The drink list includes 100-plus concoctions, some classic, others creative; the small-bites menu features elevated American comfort food. ✉ *64 Fenyang Lu, entrance is on Fuxing Lu, just west of Fenyang, French Concession.*

LIVE MUSIC

Heyday
MUSIC CLUBS | There's not a bad seat to be had at this intimate jazz-club gem, tucked on a quiet street. A vintage feel and great drinks complement nightly performances by local, expat, and international acts. ✉ *50 Taian Lu, French Concession* ☎ *021/6236–6075* 🌐 *www.heydayjazz.cn.*

JZ Club (爵士酒吧 *Juéshì jiǔbā*)
MUSIC CLUBS | At the king of Shanghai's jazz offerings, house bands and stellar guest performers mix it up nightly. Look for plush seating and drink prices to match. JZ Club is also the organizer of JZ Festival, which they claim is Asia's largest jazz fest. It takes place in the fall and outdoors along the Huangpu River. ✉ *Found 158, 158 Julu Lu, B1, French Concession* ☎ *021/6431–0269* 🌐 *www.jzclub.cn/en.*

★ **Shake**

MUSIC CLUBS | Funk and soul supper club Shake hits exactly the right notes for a great night out. A curated lineup of guest artists alongside the club's regular rotating resident singer and band put on quite the live show, belting out Motown classics and hits from the '60s and '70s. The cocktails are tasty, and the kitchen turns out excellent Asian-inspired contemporary dishes. ✉ *46 Maoming Nan Lu, 3rd fl., French Concession* ☎ *021/6230–7175* 🌐 *www.shakeclub.cn* ☞ *Closed Mon.*

Who Are the Miao?

Famous for their intricate embroidery work, the Miao are one of the oldest ethnic-minority groups in China and represent one of the largest ethnic groups in Southwest China. The Miao may have been in China as early as 200 BC, in the Han Dynasty.

Performing Arts

DANCE AND CLASSICAL MUSIC

Shanghai Symphony Orchestra Hall (上海交响乐团 *Shànghǎi jiāoxiǎngyuè tuán*)

CONCERTS | Home to the Shanghai Symphony Orchestra, this magnificent concert hall holds regular classical music performances between its two performance spaces: The 1,200-seat concert hall and the smaller 400-seat chamber music hall. Set in the heart of the Former French Concession, it's open daily and also houses a delightful café. ✉ *1380 Fuxing Zhong Lu, French Concession* ☎ *400/821–0522* 🌐 *www.shsymphony.com.*

THEATER

Lyceum Theatre (兰馨大戏院 *Lánxīn dàxìyuàn*)

THEATER | Although the renovation of Shanghai's oldest theater sadly replaced the richly stained wood with glaring marble and glass, the design of the space makes for an intimate theater experience. The Lyceum regularly hosts drama and music from around China as well as smaller local plays and Chinese opera performances. On the third floor is cocktail bar and stage Candor which puts on burlesque-style shows in plush, red velvet surrounds. ✉ *57 Maoming Nan Lu, French Concession* ☎ *021/6217–8530.*

★ **Shanghai Dramatic Arts Center** (上海话剧艺术中心 *Shànghǎi huàjù yìshù zhōngxīn*)

THEATER | The city's premier theater venue and troupe, the Shanghai Dramatic Arts Center presents an award-winning lineup of its own original pieces, plus those of other cutting-edge groups around China. It also stages Chinese-language adaptations, sometimes very inventive, of Western works, such as a festival of Samuel Beckett works reinterpreted through Chinese opera. ✉ *288 Anfu Lu, French Concession* ☎ *021/6473–4567* 🌐 *www.china-drama.com.*

Shopping

A playground for shopaholics, the Former French Concession's streets are lined with high-end, chic boutiques selling designer wares from local creatives. On the eastern edge of the Former French Concession, **Tianzifang,** often referred to as Taikang Lu, after the street on which it's on, is a former residential area whose redbrick lane houses are now a maze of quaint boutiques, cafés, restaurants, and bars.

CLOTHING AND SHOES

Chou Chou Chic

CLOTHING | This irresistible French–Chinese children's-wear shop is your go-to when you're looking to spoil your fashion-focused nieces and nephews. Think adorable qipaos and unique sweaters adorned with Chinese button knots. ✉ *Tianzifang, Lane 285, Taikang Lu, No. 47, French Concession* ☎ *021/6415–0520* 🌐 *www.chouchouchic.com.*

Culture Matters (飞跃回力国货专售 *Fēiyuè huílì guóhuò zhuān shòu*)
SHOES/LUGGAGE/LEATHER GOODS | Shanghai's iconic sneaker brand, Feiyues, can get comparatively pricey when bought internationally, but in Shanghai, where they're made, you can pick up a pair very cheaply. The classic designs are canvas with rubber soles, but there's a variety of styles on offer, including felt models, rubber sneakers that are good for wet weather, an intricate line decorated with traditional Chinese drawings, and a cute collection for kids. ✉ *206 Wulumuqi Zhong Lu, French Concession* ☎ *136/7188–2040.*

Dong Liang
CLOTHING | For one-of-a-kind designs from up-and-coming (and a few well known) Chinese designers, carefully curated multibrand store Dong Liang is a stunning—albeit pricey—one-stop-shop. ✉ *184 Fumin Lu, French Concession* ☎ *021/3469–6926* 🌐 *en.dongliang-china.com.*

Urban Tribe
CLOTHING | An eco-conscious clothing line, Urban Tribe's creations are made with natural fabrics adopting traditional methods used by Chinese tribes including hand weaving, vegetable dyes, and embroidery. ✉ *133 Fuxing Xi Lu, French Concession* ☎ *021/6433–5366* 🌐 *www.urbantribe.cn.*

GIFTS AND HOUSEWARES

★ **Brut Cake** (Brut Cake 創意製作社 *Brut Cake chuàngyì zhìzuò shè*)
HOUSEHOLD ITEMS/FURNITURE | Taiwanese designer Nicole Teng's showroom is welcoming, with comfy oversize chairs (for sale), reclaimed wood, and quirky ceramic pieces on every surface. In addition to dinnerware and ceramic lampshades, Brut Cake sells beautiful handwoven and dyed fabrics. ✉ *232 Anfu Lu, French Concession* ☎ *021/5448–8159* 🌐 *brutcake.com.*

★ **Madame Mao's Dowry** (毛太设计 *Máotài shèjì*)
ANTIQUES/COLLECTIBLES | This shop claims its covetable collection of mostly propaganda items from the '50s, '60s, and '70s is sourced from the countryside and areas in Sichuan Province and around Beijing and Tianjin. Whether they're authentic is up for debate. Shelves and racks are filled with women's clothing from local and international designers. Look for beautiful wrapping paper from Paper Tiger and dish towels, notecards, and T-shirts from Pinyin Press; both are indie, Shanghai-based design companies. Although this could be your one-stop shopping experience, remember this is communism at capitalist prices. ✉ *207 Fumin Lu, French Concession* ☎ *021/5403–3551.*

★ **Propaganda Poster Art Centre** (上海杨培明宣传画收藏艺术馆 *Shànghǎi yángpéimíng xuānchuánhuà shōucáng yìshùguǎn*)
GIFTS/SOUVENIRS | This small-but-mighty museum, housing a collection of Chinese propaganda posters from 1949 through the 1970s, has an equally impressive pint-size shop attached selling original and replica posters, postcards, and more excellent keepsakes for history buffs. Tip: the museum is a little hard to find, tucked away in the basement of a nondescript apartment compound, but on-site guards will point you in the right direction. ✉ *868 Huashan Lu, Room B-OC, French Concession* ☎ *021/6211–1845* 🌐 *www.shanghaipropagandaart.com.*

Zen Lifestore (钲艺廊 *Zhēng yì láng*)
CERAMICS/GLASSWARE | The porcelain goods here are truly lovely, available in an eye-popping array of colors. Designs range from delicate Chinese landscapes to modern geometric prints. You'll also find pretty candles, incense holders,

and pipe-and-water-spigot candelabras (which are very cool, but a bit large to carry home). ✉ *7 Dongping Lu, French Concession* ☎ *021/6437–7390.*

SPAS

Double Rainbow Massage House (双彩虹按摩 *Shuangcaihong ànmúo*)

SPA—SIGHT | With instructions clearly spelled out in English, Double Rainbow Massage House provides an inexpensive introduction to traditional Chinese massage. Choose a masseur; state your preference for soft, medium, or hard pressure; then keep your clothes on for a 45- to 90-minute massage. There's no ambience, just a clean room with nine massage tables. ✉ *45 Yongjia Lu, French Concession* ☎ *021/6473–4000.*

Dragonfly (悠亭保健会所 *Yōutíng bǎojiàn huìsuǒ*)

SPA—SIGHT | This local spa chain has claimed the middle ground between expensive hotel spas and workmanlike blind-man massage parlors. Don the suede-soft treatment robes for traditional Chinese massage, or take them off for an aromatic oil massage. Dragonfly also has waxing and nail services. ✉ *206 Xinle Lu, French Concession* ☎ *021/5403–9982.*

★ **Subconscious Day Spa** (桑格水疗会所 *Sānggéshuǐ liáohuìsuǒ*)

SPA/BEAUTY | Give your stressed-out body a bit of TLC at this great value spa. The bright, minimalist decor and soothing staff create a calming environment in the busy city. Get centered with a signature hot stone massage, or treat yourself to some extra pampering with a manicure or eyelash extensions. ✉ *183 Fumin Lu, French Concession* ☎ *021/6415–0636* 🌐 *www.subconsciousdayspa.com.*

TEA

Wanling Tea House

FOOD/CANDY | British expat James and his wife Wan Ling, who hails from the tea-producing province Fujian, have built a tidy tea business in Shanghai. In addition to their Shanghai teahouse, where you can purchase a slew of teas from China and India and teapots and cups, they sell in the U.K. and Australia. The selection of tea here is ample, and foreigners can feel safe in the knowledge they won't be ripped off. ✉ *No. 1, Lane 619, Jianguo Xi Lu, French Concession* ☎ *021/6054–0246* 🌐 *www.wanlingteahouse.com.*

Jing'an and Changning

Shanghai's glitziest malls are on or near the main street in this area, Nanjing Xi Lu. If you're into designer threads, luxury spas, or expensive brunches, you can satisfy your spending urges and max out your credit here. For those of a more spiritual bent, Jing'an Temple, which is as gilded as its surroundings, is one of Shanghai's largest temples and stands in sharp contrast to its materialistic neighbors. The small Jing'an Park across the street is popular with couples. North of the temple is an interesting network of back streets, filled with independent bars and restaurants. It's become the cheaper alternative to the Former French Concession, attracting creatives and young professionals. Sandwiched between Hongqiao, Gubei, and Jing'an is Changning District, which has a number of quiet, very local neighborhoods alongside commercial hubs. Similarly boasting cheaper rents alongside proximity and convenient transportation, East Changning District is quickly developing.

GETTING AROUND

Sights are thin in this area, but if you like international designer labels, this is where you can work the plastic, albeit at a huge markup from prices you'd find in the States. Metro Line 2 takes you to the Nanjing Xi Lu stations, and Lines 2 and 7 take you to Jing'an Temple. To wander the small streets behind Jing'an Temple, take Line 7 to Changshou Lu station and walk south. If you want to take a taxi afterward, joining the line at the Shanghai Centre/Portman Ritz-Carlton is a good idea, especially when it's raining.

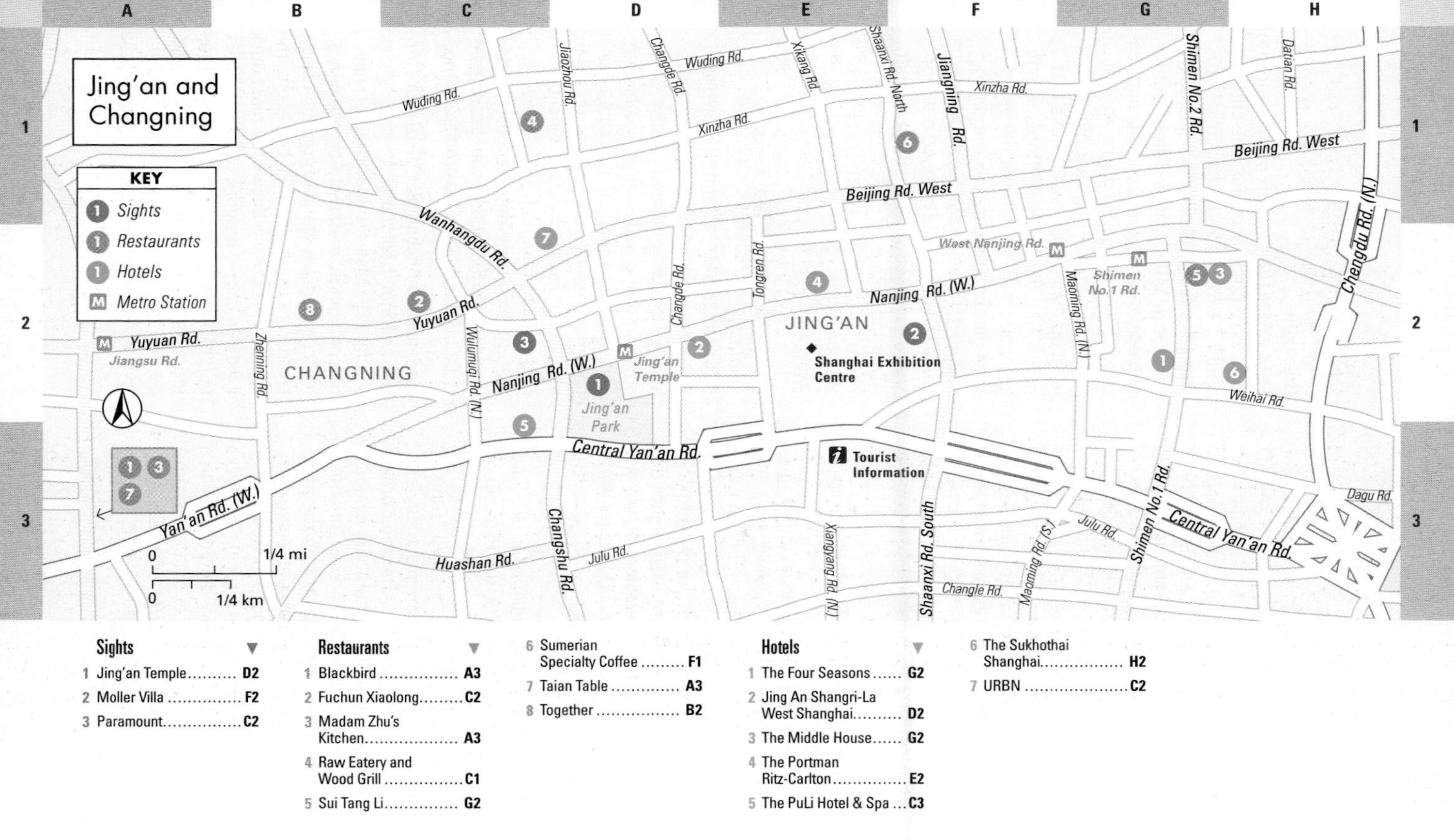

Sights

1 Jing'an Temple.......... D2
2 Moller Villa F2
3 Paramount................ C2

Restaurants

1 Blackbird A3
2 Fuchun Xiaolong......... C2
3 Madam Zhu's Kitchen.................. A3
4 Raw Eatery and Wood Grill C1
5 Sui Tang Li............... G2
6 Sumerian Specialty Coffee F1
7 Taian Table A3
8 Together B2

Hotels

1 The Four Seasons G2
2 Jing An Shangri-La West Shanghai.......... D2
3 The Middle House...... G2
4 The Portman Ritz-Carlton............... E2
5 The PuLi Hotel & Spa ... C3
6 The Sukhothai Shanghai................. H2
7 URBN C2

Sights

Jing'an Temple (静安寺 *Jìng'ān Sì*)
RELIGIOUS SITE | Originally built about AD 300, this temple has had a tumultuous history of destruction and rebuilding, with a brief stint as a plastics factory during the Cultural Revolution. What you see today dates from the 1980s. The temple's main draw is its copper Hongwu bell, cast in 1183 and weighing 3½ tons. The gilded temple, on one of Shanghai's busiest thoroughfares, is an interesting contrast to the surrounding skyscrapers, shopping malls, and luxury boutiques. ✉ *1686 Nanjing Xi Lu, next to the Jing'an Temple subway entrance, Jing'an* ☎ *021/6256–6366* 🌐 *www.shjas.org/* 🎫 *Y50.*

Moller Villa (马勒别墅饭店 *Mǎlēibiéshù fàndiàn*)
BUILDING | Built by Swedish shipping magnate Eric Moller in 1936, this massive villa resembles a fairy-tale castle. It's a surprising sight when you come down from the pedestrian bridge that leads from Jing'an into the Former French Concession. Inside is a rather gaudy hotel. ✉ *30 Shaanxi Nan Lu, Jing'an* ☎ *021/6247–8881* 🌐 *www.mollervilla.com.*

Paramount (百樂門 *Bǎilèmén*)
BUILDING | Built in 1933, the Paramount was considered the finest dance hall in Asia. Until 1949, the so-called "Gate of 100 Pleasures" was the place for very late, very wild nights. After the Communist Revolution, Paramount closed and reopened as Red Capitol Cinema, showing propaganda films. In the past two decades, it underwent a series of renovations, openings, and closings before re-opening yet again in 2017 as a glitzy, retro, multistory nightclub, with a fourth-floor ballroom and plenty of private karaoke rooms. ✉ *218 Yuyuan Lu, Jing'an* ☎ *021/6249–8866.*

Restaurants

Blackbird
$$ | **CHINESE FUSION** | Part of the renovated Columbia Circle complex, the carousing spot for American expats in the 1930s, Blackbird features different spaces on three levels. The chic first-floor lounge serves contemporary cocktails and Chinese-influenced small plates and casual mains; the fine-dining Table Black, one level up, has a regional-Chinese tasting menu; and the lovely rooftop space is complete with an outdoor bar and an herb garden that supplies the downstairs kitchens. **Known for:** interesting wine and cocktail lists; good outdoor space; polished yet casual atmosphere. $ *Average main: Y150* ✉ *Columbia Circle, 1262 Yan'an Xi Lu, Building 8, Changning* ☎ *187/0199–0479* 💳 *No credit cards.*

Fuchun Xiaolong (富春小笼 *Fùchūn xiǎolóng*)
$ | **SHANGHAINESE** | Outfitted to evoke 1920s Shanghai, Fuchan regularly appears on lists of the city's best soup-dumpling restaurants. This branch was renovated in 2018, making it a particularly pleasant place to soak up a retro atmosphere over breakfast, lunch, or dinner. **Known for:** pork soup dumplings; fried pork cutlet; wonton soup. $ *Average main: Y15* ✉ *650 Yuyuan Lu, Jing'an* ☎ *021/6252–5117* 💳 *No credit cards.*

Madam Zhu's Kitchen (汉舍中国菜馆 *Hànshě zhōngguó càiguǎn*)
$ | **CHINESE** | Mall shoppers appreciate this mid-range, sit-down Chinese chain for its expansive menu of excellent contemporary dishes inspired by flavors from across the country. **Known for:** roast duck; fried rice cake with pork and shepherd's purse; braised pork with cuttlefish. $ *Average main: Y90* ✉ *The Place, 100 Zunyi Lu, 5th fl., Hongqiao* ☎ *021/6237–0681* 💳 *No credit cards.*

Raw Eatery and Wood Grill
$$$ | **INTERNATIONAL** | If you've tired yourself out on the city's excellent Chinese food and just want a steak, head to this often-packed but laid-back Spanish eatery. It relies on incredibly high-quality ingredients and a Josper charcoal oven to make the magic happen. **Known for:** foie-gras terrine; Chilean Wagyu beef tartare; Josper-oven steaks. *Average main: Y175 98 Yanping Lu, 2nd fl., Jing'an 021/5175–9818 Closed Mon. No credit cards.*

Sumerian Specialty Coffee (Sumerian精品咖啡 *Sumerian Jīngpǐn kāfēi*)
$ | **CAFÉ** | **FAMILY** | As the bags of beans sitting out, the variety of offerings, and the high prices indicate, coffee is serious business here. But the expertly prepared hot or cold brews are served without a hint of pretension, as are the salad bowls, sandwiches (on house-made bagels), and baked goods. **Known for:** laid-back environment; bulletproof coffee; great selection of cakes. *Average main: Y50 415 Shaanxi Bei Lu, Jing'an 136/3651–8753 sameriancoffee.com No dinner.*

★ **Sui Tang Li** (随堂里 *Suí táng lǐ*)
$$$ | **CANTONESE** | On the second floor of The Middle House Residences, this polished restaurant delivers excellent contemporary renditions of regional Chinese fare, including modern takes on dim sum. Stellar service and tasty Chinese-inspired cocktails combine with the elevated cuisine to make this a must-try eatery. **Known for:** black-truffle soup dumplings; panfried foie gras and chicken dumplings; jasmine tea-smoked pomfret. *Average main: Y188 The Middle House Residences, 366 Shimen Yi Lu, Jing'an 021/3216–8068 www.themiddlehousehotel.com.*

Taian Table (泰安门 *Tài'ān mén*)
$$$$ | **INTERNATIONAL** | For a treat, head to Stefan Stiller's Michelin-starred Taian Table, where most seating is at a bar that wraps around a truly open and impressively orderly kitchen. The meticulously prepared dishes on the (mandatory) eight-course tasting menu change regularly and can be supplemented with equally well-made classic dishes and seasonal specials from an à la carte menu. **Known for:** sea urchin on sourdough; lobster royal; roasted cauliflower with beef cheek. *Average main: Y1128 No. 161, Lane 465, Zhenning Lu, Changning 173/0160–5350 www.taian-table.com.*

Together (愚舍 *Yú shě*)
$$$ | **FRENCH FUSION** | Helmed by Bina Yu, a young Korean chef who trained under Jean-Georges Vongerichten, Together typifies Shanghai's contemporary dining scene—a sleek but casual setting serving unfussy but interesting food. Developed and co-owned by the Neri & Hu design firm, the space is brilliant, as is Yu's thoughtful blend of French and Korean flavors. **Known for:** octopus with gochujang (red-chili paste); ume miso–glazed salmon; rustic, home-style cakes and ice cream. *Average main: Y178 546 Yuyuan Lu, Jing'an 021/5299–8928 No credit cards.*

Hotels

The Four Seasons (四季酒店 *Sìjì jiǔdiàn*)
$$ | **HOTEL** | **FAMILY** | Amid bustling downtown Puxi, this 37-story luxury hotel is an elegant oasis, with a lobby that has palm trees, fountains, and golden-hue marble as warm as sunshine, and with spacious rooms (just 12 or 15 to a floor) that have a chic gold palette. **Pros:** impeccable service; convenient location; family programs. **Cons:** restaurants lacking atmosphere; set on a busy road; mismatched design features. *Rooms from: Y1200 500 Weihai Lu, Jing'an 021/6256–8888, 800/819–5053 www.fourseasons.com/shanghai/ 422 rooms No meals.*

Jing An Shangri-La, West Shanghai (静安香格里拉大酒店 *Jìng'ān xiānggélǐlā dà jiǔdiàn*)
$$$ | **HOTEL** | Perfectly primed for business and pleasure, this plush, modern hotel is smack bang in the center of downtown Shanghai's action, with easy access to metro Lines 2 and 7. **Pros:** sweeping city views, especially from the lounge; excellent steak house; next to Jing An Kerry Centre mall. **Cons:** can get very crowded; standards at all-day buffet restaurant not always up to scratch; busy area. *Rooms from: Y1688* ✉ *1218 Yan'an Zhong Lu, Jing An Kerry Centre, Jing'an* ☎ *021/2203–8888* 🌐 *www.shangri-la.com/shanghai/jinganshangrila* *508 rooms* *No meals.*

★ **The Middle House** (上海镛舍 *Shànghǎi yōngshě*)
$$$$ | **HOTEL** | Tucked in the busy HKRI Taikoo Hui mall complex, The Middle House from Swire Hotels is centrally located and sleek, with sophisticated public spaces and rooms designed by Italian architect Piero Lissoni. **Pros:** sprawling, state-of-the art gym and spa; excellent restaurants; elegant Chinese-inspired design. **Cons:** not particularly child-friendly; busy location not suitable for guests seeking peace; premium room rates. *Rooms from: Y2600* ✉ *366 Shimen Yi Lu, Jing'an* ☎ *021/3216–8199* 🌐 *www.themiddlehousehotel.com* *111 rooms* *No meals.*

The Portman Ritz-Carlton (波特曼丽嘉酒店 *Bō tè màn lì jiā jiǔdiàn*)
$$ | **HOTEL** | **FAMILY** | It's hard to beat the Portman Ritz-Carlton's prime Shanghai Centre location or its family-friendly facilities, which include a large fitness center, basketball courts, a playground, and a trampoline. **Pros:** superb location; family programs; rooftop pool. **Cons:** breakfast buffet hit-or-miss; rooms need refurbishing; standards don't match those in newer area hotels. *Rooms from: Y1380* ✉ *1376 Nanjing Xi Lu, Jing'an* ☎ *021/6279–8888* 🌐 *www.ritzcarlton.com/en/hotels/china/shanghai* *593 rooms* *No meals.*

★ **The PuLi Hotel & Spa** (璞丽酒店 *Púlì jiǔdiàn*)
$$$ | **RESORT** | The cutting-edge, glass-and-steel PuLi lives up to its billing as an urban resort: with spalike guest rooms—as well as an actual spa, a stunning indoor pool, a garden terrace, and a library replete with fireplaces—it's truly an oasis of calm in Shanghai's bustling center, just off Nanjing Xi Lu. The mellow lobby has low-slung seating, modern porcelain pieces, and windows overlooking adjacent Jing'an Park. **Pros:** long list of complimentary amenities; great location; quiet. **Cons:** service can be stiff; doesn't cater to children or babies; some rooms feel dated. *Rooms from: Y1770* ✉ *1 Changde Lu, Jing'an* ☎ *021/3203–9999* 🌐 *www.thepuli.com/en* *229 rooms* *Breakfast.*

The Sukhothai Shanghai (上海素凯泰酒店 *Shànghǎi sùkǎitài jiǔdiàn*)
$$$$ | **HOTEL** | Designed by renowned architectural firm Neri & Hu, The Sukhothai Shanghai is a gorgeous, modern property, where brass accents contrast with natural materials like terrazzo, wood, and raw silk throughout both public spaces and rooms. **Pros:** design forward; sound environmentally friendly practices; excellent restaurant and bars. **Cons:** minimalist rooms may feel too stark; not child-friendly; busy location. *Rooms from: Y2100* ✉ *380 Weihai Lu, Jing'an* ☎ *021/5237–8888* 🌐 *www.sukhothai.com/shanghai/en* *201 rooms* *No meals.*

★ **URBN** (雅悦酒店 *Yǎyuè jiǔdiàn*)
$$ | **HOTEL** | Set in a former warehouse that was transformed using recycled materials, Shanghai's first carbon-netural hotel has a superb design and well-trained staffers who make you feel at home the moment you enter the tree-shaded courtyard. **Pros:** eco-friendly vibe; luxe setting; quiet location. **Cons:** not suitable for guests with mobility

impairments; some rooms are on the small side; basic gym with limited facilities. *Rooms from: Y1400* ✉ *183 Jiaozhou Lu, Jing'an* ☎ *021/5153–4600* ⊕ *www.urbnhotels.com* *26 rooms* *Free Breakfast.*

Nightlife

BARS

The Cannery

BARS/PUBS | Equal parts bar and restaurant, this hip gastrolounge appeals to a clientele that ranges from trendy young Chinese and foreigners to old-school business types. Choose from any number of house-created cocktails—perhaps paired with pickled clams or other bar snacks—to sip under the copper-tiled ceiling. ✉ *1107 Yuyuan Lu, Jing'an* ☎ *021/5276–0599.*

El Ocho

BARS/PUBS | Comfortable and welcoming, El Ocho is the kind of place where friends meet to catch up over unpretentious but exceptionally good (and smart) cocktails. It's spacious, with vaulted wooden ceilings, and has significant talent behind the bar. ✉ *Zhongyuan Plaza, 99 Taixing Lu, 3rd fl., Jing'an* ☎ *021/6256–3587.*

The Zuk Bar

BARS/PUBS | A hotel bar that doesn't feel like a "hotel bar," this petite spot has a pared back, minimalist, black-and-white tile interior with just a few tables as well as terrace with seating that spills out to the sidewalk on warm-weather days. The cocktail program is innovative, with a zero-waste agenda and drinks of a complexity that rivals anything you'd get in London or New York. ✉ *The Sukhothai Shanghai, 380 Weihai Lu, Shanghai* ☎ *021/5237–8888* ⊕ *www.sukhothai.com/shanghai/en/dining/the-zuk-bar.*

LIVE MUSIC

The Wooden Box

CAFES—NIGHTLIFE | On a quiet lane off busy Nanjing Xi Lu, this café and bar mimics the inside of a tree house, with high ceilings and wood paneling on the rounded walls. The performers here play a variety of jazz and acoustic music, which you can listen to while sipping wine, beer, and cocktails. The food is nothing to write home about and best skipped unless you're starving. ✉ *9 Qinghai Lu, Jing'an* ☎ *021/5213–2965.*

Yuyintang (育音堂 *Yùyīntáng*)

MUSIC CLUBS | No one has done as much to bring Shanghai rock out from the underground and into the open as has this collective. Headed by a sound engineer and former musician, the group started hosting regular concerts around town and eventually opened its own space. Shows, usually on Friday, Saturday, or Sunday night, spotlight the latest in young Chinese music, especially punk and rock, and the occasional Western act. ✉ *851 Kaixuan Lu, enter behind metro station, Changning* ☎ *021/5237–8662.*

Performing Arts

ACROBATICS

Shanghai Acrobatics Troupe (上海杂技团 *Shànghǎi zájìtuán*)

DANCE | This troupe performs remarkable gravity-defying stunts at the Shanghai Centre Theater, inside the Portman Ritz-Carlton. ✉ *Shanghai Centre Theater, 1376 Nanjing Xi Lu, Jing'an* ☎ *021/6279–8948* *From Y180* ☞ *Performances are not daily, but schedule can be found here: www.shanghaicentre.com/cn/theatre/theatre_schedule.php.*

Shopping

GIFTS AND HOUSEWARES

Brocade Country (锦绣纺 *Jǐnxiùfǎng*)

GIFTS/SOUVENIRS | The English-speaking owner, Liu Xiao Lan, has a Miao mother and a broad knowledge of her pieces. The Miao sew their history into the cloth, and she knows the meaning behind each piece, some of which are collector's items. Antique embroidery can cost an arm and a leg, but smaller embroidery pieces are affordable and easy to slip into a suitcase. Ms. Liu has also started designing more wearable items. ✉ *616 Julu Lu, Jing'an* ☎ *021/6279–2677.*

★ **Piling Palang** (噼呤啪啷 *Pīlīng pālāng*)
CERAMICS/GLASSWARE | Designers Judy Kim and Bingbing Deng, who hails from Tianjin, founded their line of cheerful ceramics in Paris in 2010. Their Jing'An boutique is packed with bowls, vases, plates, trays, and beautiful cloisonné tiffin carriers in a rainbow of bright colors. ✉ *Shanghai Centre, 1376 Nanjing Xi Lu, Shop 116, Jing'an* ☎ *021/6219–5020* 🌐 *pilingpalang.com/en.*

★ **Spin** (旋 *Xuán*)
CERAMICS/GLASSWARE | Halfway between a gallery and a shop, Spin sells reasonably priced contemporary Chinese pottery handmade in Jingdezhen, China's pottery capital. Treasures include chopstick rests shaped like bone fragments and too-cute dim sum paperweights in a little bamboo steamer. The ceramics sell for a fraction of the price of what they go for in New York City, where they're available at venues like Bergdorf Goodman. Note that this shop was once closer to the city center but moved to the northern Zhabei district in 2018. ✉ *5i Center II, 538 Hutai Zhi Lu, F1, Bldg. D2, Zhabei* ☎ *021/6279–2545.*

TEA

Tianshan Tea City (大不同天山茶城 *Dàbùtóng tiānshān chāchéng*)
FOOD/CANDY | This place stocks all the tea in China, and then some. More than 300 vendors occupy three floors, but most vendors sell the same tea, so find a seller with whom you have a rapport, and sit down for a taste test. You can buy such famous teas as West Lake dragon well (*longjing*) tea, from nearby Hangzhou, and Wuyi red-robe tea, as well as the tea sets to serve them in. Though the vendors encourage you to taste all their teas, as you should, they are not terribly pushy. ✉ *520 Zhongshan Xi Lu, Changning.*

Pudong

Shanghai residents used to say that it was better to have a bed in Puxi than an apartment in Pudong, but the neighborhood has come a long way in recent years. It's now a futuristic city of wide boulevards and towering skyscrapers topped by the Shanghai Tower. Apartments here are some of the most expensive in Shanghai. Although a little on the bland side, it is home to expat compounds designed in a bizarre medley of architectural styles, international schools, and malls. However, there are a few sites here worth visiting, particularly if you have children. **■ TIP→ To avoid crushing crowds, do not visit family favorites such as Disneyland, the aquarium, or the science and technology museum on weekends and during school holidays.**

GETTING AROUND

The Bund Tourist Tunnel is a strange and rather garish way of making the journey under the Huangpu River to Pudong. You might get a few laughs from the light displays. Otherwise, you can take the metro on Line 2 to Lujiazui, or catch the ferry from the Bund.

Outside of the Lujiazui metro stop and Century Park, Pudong is not a pedestrian-friendly area, as there are large, rather featureless distances between the sights. You can either take the metro to get around or jump in a cab. If you visit all the sights, you could easily spend a day out here.

Sights

Century Park (世纪公园 *Shìjì gōngyuán*)
CITY PARK | FAMILY | If you're staying in Pudong, this giant swath of green is a great place to take kids, as it has a variety of bicycles for hire, good flat paths for Rollerblading, and pleasure boats. On a nice day, pack a lunch and head to the designated picnic areas, fly a kite in the open areas, or take a walk among

the trees. ✉ *1001 Jinxiu Lu, bordered by Huamu Lu and Fangdian Lu, Pudong* ☎ *021/3876–0588* 🎫 *Y10.*

★ **China Art Museum** (中华艺术宫 *Zhōnghuá yìshù gōng*)

MUSEUM | Housed inside the China Pavilion at the 2010 Shanghai World Expo (which had sites on both sides of the river in Pudong and Puxi), this gleaming homage to contemporary art has a whopping 27 exhibition halls. Much of the work is underwhelming, but be sure to stop by the animation hall, where you can catch shorts and feature-length films from the '50s to the '90s. The touring exhibits are often a real treat; besides a huge Picasso retrospective, the museum has hosted works from New York's Whitney Museum, London's British Museum, and Paris's Maisons de Victor Hugo. Look for works from David Hockney, Jasper Johns, and Rodin. ✉ *205 Shangnan Lu, Pudong* ☎ *400/921–9021* 🌐 *www.artmuseumonline.org* 🎫 *Free, special exhibits Y20; audio guides Y20 (with Y200 deposit and ID)* ⏲ *Closed Mon.*

Jin Mao Tower (金茂大厦 *Jīn Mào Dàshà*)

BUILDING | Rising 88 floors—eight being the Chinese number imparting wealth and prosperity—this tower combines the classic 13-tier Buddhist pagoda design with postmodern steel and glass. It houses one of the highest hotels in the world—the Grand Hyatt Shanghai occupies the 53rd to 87th floors. The 88th-floor observation deck, reached in 45 seconds by two high-speed elevators, offers 360-degree views of the city. The brave can also try the tower's Skywalk experience, a glass pathway without rails outside the 88th floor. ■ **TIP→ Skip the line and instead spend what you would've shelled out for a ticket to the observation deck at the 87th-floor Cloud 9 bar.** ✉ *88 Shiji Dadao (Century Ave.), Pudong* ☎ *021/5047–6688* 🌐 *www.jinmao88.com/en* 🎫 *Observation deck: Y120; Skywalk Y388.*

Oriental Pearl Tower (东方明珠塔 *Dōngfāng Míngzhūtǎ*)

BUILDING | Looking like a stucture straight out of *The Jetsons*, the Oriental Pearl Tower was built when much of Pudong was still farmland. It's especially kitschy at night when it flashes with colored lights. A museum in the base recalls Shanghai's pre-1949 history. Each with its own observation deck, the three spheres are supposed to represent pearls (as in the city's nickname, the "Pearl of the Orient"). Go to the top sphere for a 360-degree bird's-eye view of the city, or grab a drink in the tower's revolving restaurant (skip the food). ✉ *1 Shiji Dadao (Century Ave.), Pudong* ☎ *021/5879–1888* 🌐 *www.orientalpearltower.com* 🎫 *From Y160.*

Riverside Promenade (滨江大道 *Bīnjiāng dàdào*)

PROMENADE | Although this park along the Huangpu River has a sterile atmosphere, it offers the most beautiful views of the Bund. As you stroll on the grass and concrete, you get a perspective of Puxi unavailable from the west side. ✉ *Binjiang Dadao, Pudong* ✥ *From Dongchang Lu to Pudong Nan Lu, near Oriental Pear Tower* 🎫 *Free.*

Shanghai Disneyland (上海迪士尼乐园 *Shànghǎi díshìní lèyuán*)

AMUSEMENT PARKS | **FAMILY** | The first Disney resort in Mainland China opened in 2016. It's high on the must-see list for most domestic and international visitors, so expect it to be busy, particularly on weekends and during holidays. The park is well laid out, with an Adventure Isle, Fantasyland, Gardens of Imagination, Toy Story Land, Tomorrowland, and Treasure Cove. Smaller children will love the whole experience; teenagers and parents will find the Tron ride particularly entertaining. ✉ *310 Shendi Xi Lu, Pudong* ☎ *021/2099–8002* 🌐 *www.shanghaidisneyresort.com/en* 🎫 *From Y399.*

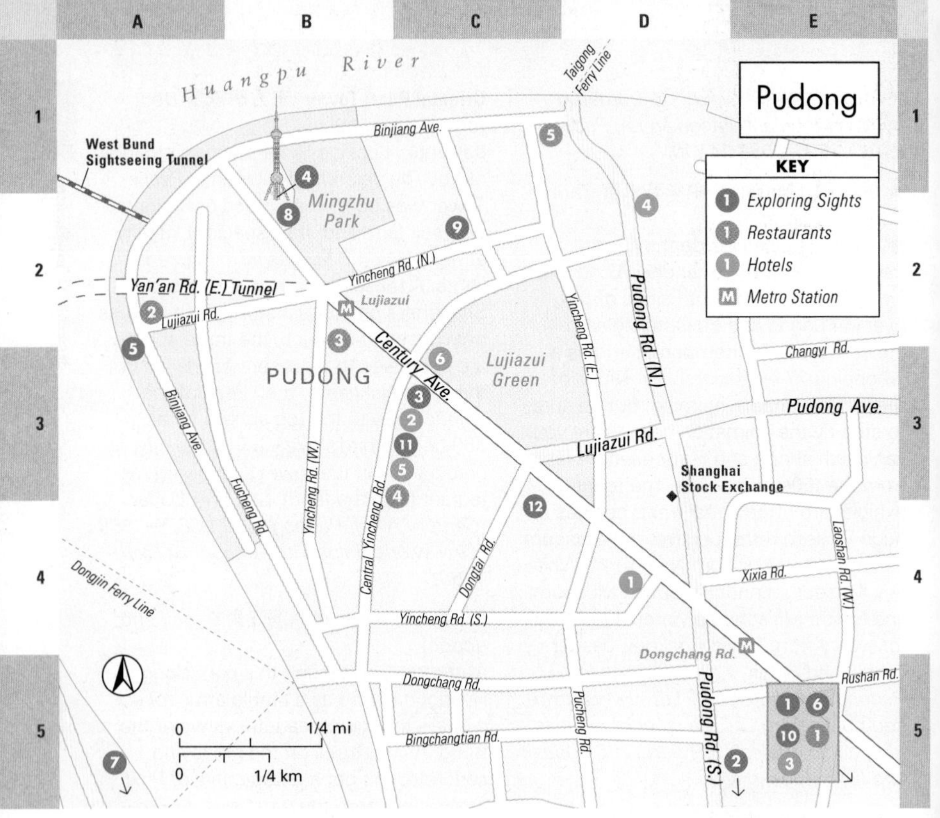

Sights

1 Century Park E5
2 China Art Museum....... E5
3 Jin Mao Tower........... C3
4 Oriental Pearl Tower ... B2
5 Riverside Promenade .. A2
6 Shanghai Disneyland.... E5
7 Shanghai Minsheng Art Museum............. A5
8 Shanghai Municipal History Museum B2
9 Shanghai Ocean Aquarium C2
10 Shanghai Science and Technology Museum.... E5
11 Shanghai Tower C3
12 Shanghai World Financial Center C4

Restaurants

1 Brut Eatery E5
2 Din Tai Fung A2
3 Golden Mauyra B2
4 Paradise Dynasty........ C3
5 Yong Yi Ting............... C1

Hotels

1 Four Seasons Pudong.................... D4
2 Grand Hyatt C3
3 Kerry Hotel, Pudong, Shanghai................. E5
4 Mandarin Oriental Pudong, Shanghai....... D2
5 Pudong Shangri-La, East Shanghai............ C3
6 Ritz-Carlton Shanghai Pudong........ C3

Shanghai Minsheng Art Museum (上海民生现代美术馆 *Shànghǎi mínshēng xiàndài měishùguǎn*)
MUSEUM | This sleek museum is on the site of Shanghai's 2010 World Expo, which was held in areas along both sides of the river. It takes its name from its sponsor, Minsheng Bank, which opened it to showcase contemporary art in all mediums, from photography to sound, by artists from China and beyond. The museum is housed in the former French expo pavilion and is within walking distance from China Art Palace. ✉ *1929 Shibo Dadao (Expo Ave.), just off Expo Park, Pudong* ☎ *021/6105–2121* 🌐 *www.minshengart.com/en* 🎫 *Free* 🕙 *Closed Mon.*

Shanghai Municipal History Museum (上海城市历史发展陈列馆 *Shànghǎi chéngshì lìshǐ fāzhǎn chénliè guǎn*)
MUSEUM | **FAMILY** | This impressive museum in the base of the Pearl Tower recalls Shanghai's pre-1949 history. Inside, you can stroll down a re-created Shanghai street circa 1900, or check out a streetcar that used to operate in the concessions. Dioramas depict battle scenes from the Opium Wars, shops found in a typical turn-of-the-20th-century Shanghai neighborhood, and grand Former French Concession buildings of yesteryear. ✉ *1 Shiji Dadao (Century Ave.), Pudong* ☎ *021/5879–1888* 🎫 *Y35.*

Shanghai Ocean Aquarium (上海海洋水族馆 *Shànghǎi hǎiyáng shuǐzúguǎn*)
ZOO | **FAMILY** | As you stroll through the aquarium's 120-meter (394-foot) glass viewing tunnel, you may feel like you're walking your way through the seven seas—or at least five of them. The aquarium's 10,000 fish represent 300 species, five oceans, and four continents. You'll also find penguins and species representing all 12 of the Chinese zodiac symbols, such as the tiger barb, sea dragon, and seahorse. ✉ *1388 Lujiazui Huan Lu, Pudong* ☎ *021/5877–9988* 🌐 *www.sh-soa.com* 🎫 *Y160.*

Shanghai Science and Technology Museum (上海科技馆 *Shànghǎi kējì guǎn*)
MUSEUM | **FAMILY** | This family favorite has more than 100 hands-on exhibits in its sprawling galleries. Earth Exploration takes you through fossil layers to the earth's core for a lesson in plate tectonics. Spectrum of Life introduces you to the animal and plant kingdoms in a simulated rain forest. Light of Wisdom explains basic principles of light and sound through interactive exhibits, and simulators in AV Paradise put you in a plane's cockpit and on television. Children's Technoland has a voice-activated fountain and a miniature construction site. Two IMAX theaters and a "4-D" IWERKS theater screen larger-than-life movies, though some are in Chinese. All signs are in English. ✉ *2000 Shiji Dadao (Century Ave.), Pudong* ☎ *021/6862–2000* 🌐 *www.sstm.org.cn* 🎫 *Y60* 🕙 *Closed Mon.*

Shanghai Tower (上海中心 *Shànghǎi Zhōngxīn*)
BUILDING | The newest skyscraper in Lujiazui was completed in early 2017. At the time of this writing, it's the country's tallest structure and the second tallest in the world (beat out by the Burj Khalifa in Dubai). The 127-story building, with five additional levels below ground, rises more than 2,000 feet and houses a hotel, offices, restaurants, and shops. Its sky-high observation deck on the 118th floor is the world's highest, a few floors above that in the Burj Khalifa, and is reached by the world's fastest elevator. There is an excellent exhibit about the world's super-tall buildings in the basement floor on your way to the observation deck. ✉ *479 Lujiazui Huan Lu, Pudong* ☎ *021/2064–6999* 🌐 *www.shanghaitower.com* 🎫 *Observation deck Y180.*

Shanghai World Financial Center (上海环球金融中心 *Shànghǎi huánqiú jīnróng zhōngxīn*)
BUILDING | The iconic "bottle opener" has three observation decks, the highest of which is on the 100th floor. The Park Hyatt is housed on floors 79 to 93, giving it a loftier perch than its older sibling, the neighboring Grand Hyatt. The view from up here is a knockout; on a clear day, you can see far and wide; on an overcast day, you'll feel as though you're floating in the clouds. **TIP→ Consider skipping the observation decks in favor of the hotel. Afternoon tea at the 87th-floor Living Room is a treat.** ✉ *100 Shiji Dadao (Century Ave.), Pudong* ☎ *400/1100–555* 🌐 *www.swfc-observatory.com* 🎫 *Observatory Y180.*

Restaurants

Brut Eatery (悦璞食堂 *Yuèpú shítáng*)
$ | ASIAN FUSION | FAMILY | This branch of Brut Eatery is a good choice if you're staying near Century Park and/or are traveling with children. The casual café offers a good selection of Western-inspired dishes, with the occasional Asian touch, and has a large play area where kids can run about while you relax and sip coffee. **Known for:** family-friendly; chicken and waffles; adorable ceramic mugs created by the founder. $ *Average main: Y60* ✉ *199 Fangdian Lu, Pudong* ☎ *021/5078–2797* 💳 *No credit cards.*

Din Tai Fung (鼎泰豐 *Dǐng tài fēng*)
$$ | TAIWANESE | FAMILY | The star attractions at this Taiwanese chain are the delicate, impeccably folded xiaolongbao (soup dumplings). Be sure to try the particularly delectable pork and black truffle version. **Known for:** good service; very family-friendly; about 10 locations around town. $ *Average main: Y110* ✉ *Super Brand Mall, 168 Lujiazui Xi Lu, 3rd fl., Lujiazui* ☎ *021/5047–8883.*

Golden Maurya (金孔雀 *Jīn kǒngquè*)
$$ | SICHUAN | With a gold- and marble-filled interior, this restaurant makes a statement that lives up to its "Golden Peacock" name. Its serves excellent and fiery Sichuan classics and is a higher-end version of the group's popular Maurya chain. **Known for:** Chongqing fragrant peas and mandarin fish; spicy tofu; crispy "hand grab" cake. $ *Average main: Y125* ✉ *International Finance Centre, 8 Shiji Dadao, Bldg. D, B1, Pudong* ☎ *021/5757–5578* 💳 *No credit cards.*

Paradise Dynasty (乐忻皇朝 *Lèxīn huángcháo*)
$ | CHINESE | FAMILY | While written off as gimmicky by some, this Singaporean chain's playful eight-color, eight-flavor take on xiaolongbao draws a steady stream of locals. Steamers of the soup dumplings come with small cards identifying each variety—from black truffle to garlic to foie gras. **Known for:** eight-color soup dumplings; fun, family-friendly spot; great lunch option near Shanghai Tower. $ *Average main: Y60* ✉ *Shanghai Tower, 501 Yincheng Zhong Lu, B2, Pudong* ☎ *021/5830–3068* 🌐 *www.paradisegp.com* 💳 *No credit cards.*

★ **Yong Yi Ting** (雍颐庭 *Yōngyítíng*)
$$$$ | CHINESE | You'd expect nothing less than an exquisite experience from a restaurant in the Mandarin Oriental, and Yong Yi Ting delivers. The nuanced dishes—which focus on China's famous Huaiyang cuisine from Yangzhou in Jiangsu Province near Shanghai—are light in flavor and skillfully prepared. **Known for:** crispy fried pomfret with sweet soy; braised beef ribs with walnuts; crispy mandarin fish with sweet sour sauce and pine nuts. $ *Average main: Y250* ✉ *Mandarin Oriental, 111 Pudong Nan Lu, LG, Pudong* ☎ *021/2082–9978* 🌐 *www.mandarinoriental.com/shanghai/pudong.*

Hotels

Four Seasons Pudong (浦东四季酒店 *Pǔdōng sìjì jiǔdiàn*)
$$$$ | **HOTEL** | The Pudong outpost of the Four Seasons is flashier and hipper than its older sister in Jing'an, but style doesn't diminish substance: the service is polished, and the beds are sublime. **Pros:** sleek design; prompt service; nice little terrace. **Cons:** it's a long walk to restaurants; no nearby nightlife; not ideal for exploration on foot beyond Lujiazui. *Rooms from: Y2050* *210 Shiji Dadao, Pudong* *021/2036–8888* *www.fourseasons.com/pudong* *187 rooms* *No meals.*

Grand Hyatt (上海金茂君悦大酒店 *Shànghǎi jīnmàojūn yuè dà jiǔdiàn*)
$$ | **HOTEL** | Views, views, views are what this hotel is all about—occupying floors 53 through 87 of the spectacular Jin Mao Tower, the Grand Hyatt's interior is defined by contemporary lines juxtaposed with Space Age grillwork. **Pros:** beautiful rooms; lovely decoration throughout the hotel; fantastic city views. **Cons:** somewhat outdated; no guarantee of clear views; soundproofing lacking. *Rooms from: Y1300* *Jin Mao Tower, 88 Shiji Dadao, Pudong* *021/5049–1234* *shanghai.grand.hyatt.com/en/hotel/home* *548 rooms* *No meals.*

Kerry Hotel, Pudong, Shanghai (上海浦东嘉里大酒店 *Shànghǎi pǔdōng jiā lǐ dà jiǔdiàn*)
$$$ | **HOTEL** | **FAMILY** | This hotel is great if you're traveling with kids: not only is it across from Century Park, where tandem bikes and pleasure boats are available, but it also has an indoor play area with slides, climbing equipment, and a giant ball pit. **Pros:** comfortable, spacious rooms; family-friendly, with easy access to greenery; on metro lines and connected to Kerry Parkside Mall. **Cons:** far from downtown; not near popular tourist sights; cookie-cutter design. *Rooms from: Y1488* *1388 Huamu Lu, Pudong* *021/6169–8800* *www.shangri-la.com/shanghai/kerryhotelpudong* *574 rooms* *No meals.*

★ **Mandarin Oriental Pudong, Shanghai** (上海浦东文华东方酒店 *Shànghǎi pǔdōng wénhuá dōngfāng jiǔdiàn*)
$$$ | **HOTEL** | Situated just outside of the Pudong CBD and offering world-class everything—from generously sized rooms to impeccable service to exceptional restaurants and other facilities—the Mandarin Oriental Pudong is almost flawless. **Pros:** walking distance to Pudong landmarks; free one-way shuttle service to destinations in Lujiazui; ultra-luxe fitness and wellness facilities. **Cons:** far from Puxi's sights; neighborhood lacks historic charm; area better suited to business travelers. *Rooms from: Y1800* *111 Pudong Nan Lu, Pudong* *021/2082–9888* *www.mandarin-oriental.com/shanghai/pudong* *362 rooms* *No meals.*

★ **Pudong Shangri-La, East Shanghai** (浦东香格里拉酒店 *Pǔdōng xiānggélǐlā jiǔdiàn*)
$$ | **HOTEL** | Although it's not the newest or most high-tech hotel, it still attracts both business and leisure travelers with its breathtaking views, white-glove service, spacious rooms, and prime location—overlooking the Huangpu River, opposite the Bund, and near the Pearl Tower. **Pros:** fantastic location; good restaurants; glorious views. **Cons:** somewhat dated; nearby restaurants are in shopping malls; immense property can be overwhelming. *Rooms from: Y1188* *33 Fucheng Lu, Pudong* *021/6882–8888* *www.shangri-la.com/shanghai/pudong-shangrila* *951 rooms* *No meals.*

Ritz-Carlton Shanghai Pudong (上海浦东丽思卡尔顿酒店 *Shànghǎi pǔdōng lìsīkǎ'ěrdùn jiǔdiàn*)
$$$$ | **HOTEL** | **FAMILY** | The Ritz-Carlton Pudong has a 55th-floor spa with staggering views of the Huangpu River and the entire downtown skyline, an impressive Italian restaurant, and a rooftop bar

that's such a good lookout point you may never want to leave. **Pros:** great extras and activities for kids; only a two-minute walk to Lujiazui metro station; great views. **Cons:** all nearby restaurants are in malls; high room rates; busy location. *$ Rooms from: Y2300 ✉ Shanghai IFC, 8 Shiji Dadao (Century Ave.), Pudong ☎ 021/2020–1888 🌐 www.ritzcarlton.com/en/hotels/china/shanghai-pudong 210 rooms No meals.*

Nightlife

BARS

The Brew (酿餐厅 *Niàng cāntīng*)
BREWPUBS/BEER GARDENS | **FAMILY** | The Kerry Hotel's microbrewery is tightly run and one of the best options for a drink in the Century Park neighborhood. The crisp cider is very good for those who don't love beer, while the Pilsner and IPA are the most popular among brew-heads. Shooting pool, tossing back peanuts from a tin pail, and sipping brewskies, you may well forget you're in China. On weekend afternoons, this is a family-friendly bar. ✉ *Kerry Hotel Pudong, 1388 Huamu Lu, Pudong ☎ 021/6169–8886 🌐 www.shangri-la.com/shanghai/kerryhotelpudong/dining/bars-lounges/the-brew/.*

Flair (顶层餐厅酒吧 *Dǐngcéng cāntīng jiǔbā*)
BARS/PUBS | The view here can only be described as jaw-dropping. The open-air bar on the 58th floor of the Ritz-Carlton Pudong sits you so close to the Oriental Pearl Tower that you could almost touch it. You'll pay for the sight of Shanghai laid out before you, with pricey cocktails and a minimum spend for tables on the terrace, but it's worth coming at least for one drink. ✉ *Ritz-Carlton Pudong, 8 Shiji Dadao, 58th fl., Pudong ☎ 021/2020–1717 🌐 www.ritzcarlton.com/en/hotels/china/shanghai-pudong/dining/flair.*

Jade on 36 (翡翠36酒吧 *Fěicuì 36 jiǔbā*)
BARS/PUBS | This swanky spot in the newer tower of the Pudong Shangri-La offers decent cocktails, but it's the excellent design and equally excellent views (when Shanghai's fog and pollution levels cooperate) that make it popular with locals. You may still feel like you're in a hotel bar, but you'll have a stiff drink and some amazing city vistas. ✉ *Pudong Shangri-La, 33 Fucheng, 36th fl., Pudong ☎ 021/6882–8888.*

Performing Arts

DANCE AND CLASSICAL MUSIC

Shanghai Oriental Art Center (上海东方艺术中心 *Shànghǎi dōngfāng yìshù zhōngxīn*)
DANCE | This cultural powerhouse presents traditional Chinese works as well as a superb selection of Western shows. The Royal New Zealand Ballet, Munich Philharmonic Orchestra, and Netherlands Symphony Orchestra are just three among a slew of groups that have performed here. ✉ *425 Dingxiang Lu, Pudong ☎ 021/4006–466–406 🌐 en.shoac.com.cn.*

Shopping

MALLS

ifc Mall
SHOPPING CENTERS/MALLS | Like its Hong Kong sister, this shiny mall is packed with luxury goods stores. The basement food court has everything from octopus balls to Japanese-style crepes, as well as very expensive imported groceries. The upper levels are dotted with restaurants serving various fare, high in quality and in price. **TIP→ The Lujiazui station of metro Line 2 is inside the mall.** ✉ *8 Shiji Dadao, Pudong ☎ 021/2020–7070.*

Super Brand Mall (正大广场 *Zhèngdà guǎngchǎng*)
SHOPPING CENTERS/MALLS | One of Asia's largest malls, this 10-story behemoth has a mind-boggling array of international

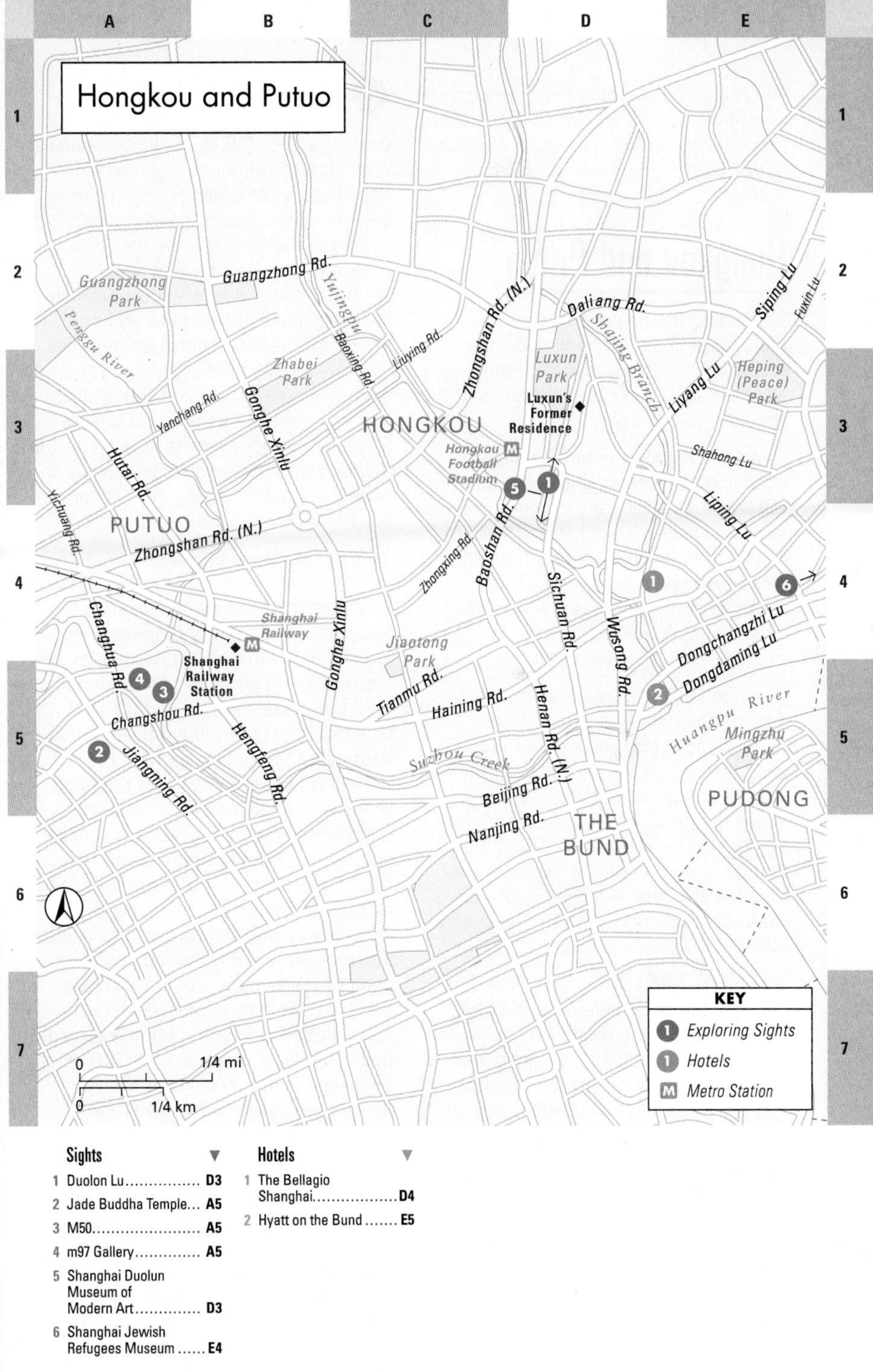

Sights

1 Duolon Lu **D3**

2 Jade Buddha Temple ... **A5**

3 M50 .... **A5**

4 m97 Gallery **A5**

5 Shanghai Duolun Museum of Modern Art **D3**

6 Shanghai Jewish Refugees Museum **E4**

Hotels

1 The Bellagio Shanghai **D4**

2 Hyatt on the Bund **E5**

shops and food stops, as well as a cineplex. It can be overwhelming if you don't love to shop. ✉ *168 Lujiazui Lu, Pudong* ☎ *021/6887–7888* 🌐 *www.superbrand-mall.com.*

Hongkou and Putuo

Although often neglected in favor of more glamorous neighborhoods, the northern Shanghai districts of Putuo and Hongkou offer interesting sites and shouldn't be ignored.

Hongkou District is relatively undeveloped and unchanged, and buildings from the past are visible behind cheap clothing stores. Shanghai's old Jewish Quarter is here, too. An area with an interesting history, Hongkou has the most sights worth seeing, as well as the lush green sweep of Lu Xun Park.

In Putuo, the old buildings and warehouses around Suzhou Creek, which feeds into the Huangpu, have been turned into hip-and-happening artsy venues. Of particular note is the M50 development, which—in typical Shanghai fashion—is slated for still more renovation and development in the near future. Also in Putuo District is another one of Shanghai's main temples, the Jade Buddha Temple, which is an easy walk from Jing'an, the district just to the south.

GETTING AROUND

For the Jade Buddha Temple and M50, you can hop off the metro Line 3 or 4 at Zhongtan Lu, and then it's a short walk to M50 and a longer one to Jade Buddha. You can take Line 3 to Dongbaoxing Lu and Hongkou Stadium for Lu Xun Park and Duolun Lu. The easiest way to get around is by taxi or on foot.

The galleries at M50 open later in the morning, so it may be best to head to some other sites first. All galleries are closed on Monday and some on Tuesday.

Sights

Duolun Lu (多伦文化街 *Duōlún wénhuà jiē*)
HISTORIC SITE | Although this road has been heavily restored, its architecture and general ambience takes you back in time to the 1930s, when the 1-km (½-mile) lane was a favorite haunt of writer Lu Xun and fellow social activists. Bronze statues of those literary luminaries dot the lawns between the villas and row houses whose ground floors are now home to cafés, antiques shops, and art galleries. As the street takes a 90-degree turn, its architecture shifts 180 degrees with the seven-story stark gray Shanghai Duolun Museum of Modern Art. ✉ *Off Sichuan Bei Lu, Hongkou.*

Jade Buddha Temple (玉佛禅寺 *Yùfó chán sì*)
RELIGIOUS SITE | Completed in 1918, this temple is fairly new by Chinese standards. During the Cultural Revolution, the monks pasted portraits of Mao Zedong on the outside walls so that the Red Guards couldn't tear them down without destroying Mao's face as well. The temple is built in the style of the Song Dynasty, with symmetrical halls and courtyards, upturned eaves, and bright yellow walls. The temple's great treasure is its 2-meter (6½-foot) seated Buddha made of white jade with a robe of precious gems, originally brought to Shanghai from Burma. Frightening guardian gods of the temple populate the halls, home to a collection of Buddhist scriptures and paintings. The temple is madness at festival times. **■ TIP→ There's a simple vegetarian restaurant serving inexpensive noodle dishes.** ✉ *170 Anyuan Lu, Putuo* ☎ *021/6266–3668* 🌐 *www.yufotemple.com* 🎫 *From Y20.*

M50 (M50创意园 *M50 chuàngyì yuán*)
MUSEUM | This cluster of art galleries and artist studios, inside a sprawling former textile mill and slated for even more renovation and development in the near future, sits beside Suzhou Creek. The

Did You Know?

Different Buddhist sects wear different colors, and there are many theories on the significance of color. This is one of our favorites: Buddhist monks and nuns wear yellow because when one looks at a tree, it's easy to tell which leaves will fall based on the yellow, orange, or brown color. Yellow is a constant reminder of the importance of letting go.

galleries are filled almost exclusively with work by Chinese artists, but a few showcase foreign work. There are also a few shops selling music and art supplies and a couple coffee shops. Don't be shy about nosing around—occasionally artists will be up for a chat. ■ **TIP→ Mind the weather, as some galleries lack heating and cooling systems.** ✉ *50 Moganshan Lu, Putuo* 🌐 *www.m50.com.cn/en* 🎫 *Free.*

★ **m97 Gallery** (m97画廊 *M97 huàláng*)
MUSEUM | Situated in the M50 arts district for about 10 years before moving to this location in 2016, this gallery and project space specializes in photography. Look for works by both Chinese and foreign artists, such as Holland's Robert Van Der Hilst and Germany's Michael Wolf. It's open every day but Monday, when viewings are by appointment only. ✉ *363 Changping Lu, 1st fl. and 2nd fl., Bldg. 4, Jing'an* ☎ *021/6266–1597* 🌐 *www.m97gallery.com.*

Shanghai Duolun Museum of Modern Art (上海多伦现代美术馆 *Shànghǎi duō lún xiàndài měishù guǎn*)
MUSEUM | Covering more than 14,400 square feet, Shanghai's first state-owned modern art gallery wraps around a metal spiral staircase that's a work of art in itself. The frequently changing exhibits are cutting-edge for Shanghai. They've showcased electronic art from American artists, examined gender issues among the Chinese people, and featured musical performances ranging from Chinese electronica to the *dombra,* a traditional Kazak stringed instrument. A tiny shop sells art books. ✉ *27 Duolun Lu, Hongkou* ☎ *021/6587–2530* 🎫 *Free* ⏲ *Closed Mon.*

★ **Shanghai Jewish Refugees Museum** (上海犹太难民纪念馆 *Shànghǎi yóutài nànmín jìniànguǎn*)
RELIGIOUS SITE | Built in 1927, the Ohel Moishe Synagogue was the spiritual center of Shanghai's Jewish ghetto in the '30s and '40s, and now houses the excellent Shanghai Jewish Refugees Museum. More than 20,000 Central European refugees fled to Shanghai during World War II, and the museum has a good selection of photos and newspaper clippings. Around the corner is Huoshan Park, where a memorial tablet has been erected in honor of Israeli prime minister Yitzhak Rabin's 1993 visit. ✉ *62 Changyang Lu, Hongkou* ☎ *021/6512–6669* 🎫 *Y20.*

Roof Top Drinking

Sip cockails at the elegant Vue bar on top of the Hyatt and enjoy the picture-perfect views over the Bund and across to Pudong.

Restaurants

The Bellagio Shanghai (上海苏宁宝丽嘉酒店 *Shànghǎi sūníng bǎolìjiā jiǔdiàn*)
$$$$ | **HOTEL** | With a black-and-gold color scheme and spacious, opulently outfitted rooms, the Bellagio pairs Las Vegas sparkle with classic Shanghai views of Suzhou Creek and the Pudong skyline. **Pros:** whirlpool tub overlooks historic Waibaidu Bridge and Pearl Tower; excellent Italian restaurant LAGO by Julian Serrano; quiet location. **Cons:** Bund prices just off the main stretch; dark design theme can feel a little gloomy; not all staff speak English. 💲 *Rooms from: Y2100* ✉ *188 Bei Suzhou Lu, Hongkou* ☎ *021/3680–6666* 🌐 *www.bellagioshanghai.com* 🛏 *162 rooms* 🍽 *No meals.*

Hyatt on the Bund (外滩茂悦大酒店 *Wàitān mào yuè dà jiǔdiàn*)
$$$ | **HOTEL** | Near the banks of Suzhou Creek, the Hyatt on the Bund offers beautifully appointed rooms in an airy and modern building. **Pros:** gorgeous facilities; views are hard to beat; short

walk from the Bund. **Cons:** rather bland neighborhood; the food underwhelms; can be difficult to get taxis. *Rooms from: Y1500 ✉ 199 Huangpu Lu, near Wuchang Lu, Hongkou ☎ 021/6393–1234 🌐 shanghaithebund.hyatt.com 620 rooms No meals.*

Nightlife

GAY–LESBIAN BARS AND CLUBS

Lai Lai Dancehall (来来舞厅 *Lái lái wǔtīng*)
DANCE CLUBS | This is one of Shanghai's gems, a sweet, simple dance hall where local men can come three nights a week and dance to tender Chinese pop songs from an earlier time. Songs are played by a band, which sometimes dresses in drag, as does one of the owners. There are a number of regulars, and strangers aren't shy about asking for a dance, but it's all quite chaste. Foreigners are most welcome and treated no differently than locals. In general, photos are not allowed. *✉ 235 Anguo Lu, 2nd fl., near Zhoujiazui Lu, Hongkou ☎ 150/2174–7399 Y10.*

LIVE MUSIC

Bandu Cabin (半度雨棚 *Bàndù yǔpéng*)
MUSIC CLUBS | Also known as Bandu Music, this unpretentious café and bar in the M50 art compound sells hard-to-find CDs and occasionally holds concerts of traditional Chinese folk music. When touring the M50 galleries, this is a nice place for a break. *✉ M50, 50 Moganshan Lu, Unit 11, 1st fl., Putuo ☎ 021/6276–8267.*

Shopping

Right by Suzhou Creek, **Moganshan Lu** in Putuo was once home to poor artists, but the area has been developed and repackaged as M50, a creative hub with an exciting collection of galleries set in old, refurbished factories. The space is known for exhibiting contemporary art works from an eclectic mixture of established and up-and-coming artists, making it a worthy (and photo-friendly) place to while away an afternoon.

ART

ShanghART (香格纳上海 *Xiānggénà shànghǎi*)
ART GALLERIES—ARTS | A long-established contemporary art gallery, ShanghART is an M50 mainstay—also with a newer outpost in the burgeoning West Bund Art District. The art space is dedicated to pushing forward China's contemporary art scene with exhibitions featuring a range of mediums, including multimedia, sculpture, and photography. *✉ M50, 50 Moganshan Lu, Bldg. 16, Shanghai ☎ 021/6359–3923 🌐 www.shanghartgallery.com ☞ Closed Mon.*

SPAS

Banyan Tree Spa On The Bund (上海外滩悦榕Spa *Shànghǎi wàitān yuèróng Spa*)
SPA/BEAUTY | The spa in the Banyan Tree Shanghai On The Bund hotel spans three ultraluxe floors and offers treatments reflecting *wu xing*, the five elemental energies in Chinese philosophy: earth, metal, water, wood, and fire. Relax and choose from a menu of massages, facials, and body scrubs, or indulge in a package that combines the three. *✉ The Banyan Tree on the Bund, 19 Gongping Lu, Hongkou ☎ 021/2509–1188 🌐 www.banyantreespa.com.*

Xujiahui, Hongqiao, and Gubei

Buyers throng the large malls in the shopping precinct at Xujiahui, which shines with neon and giant billboards. To the west are the districts of Hongqiao and Gubei, each of which has large resident populations of Western and other Asian expats. Although these neighborhoods don't have as much to offer visitors as other areas of the city, there are a couple intriguing sights that might make them worth a trip.

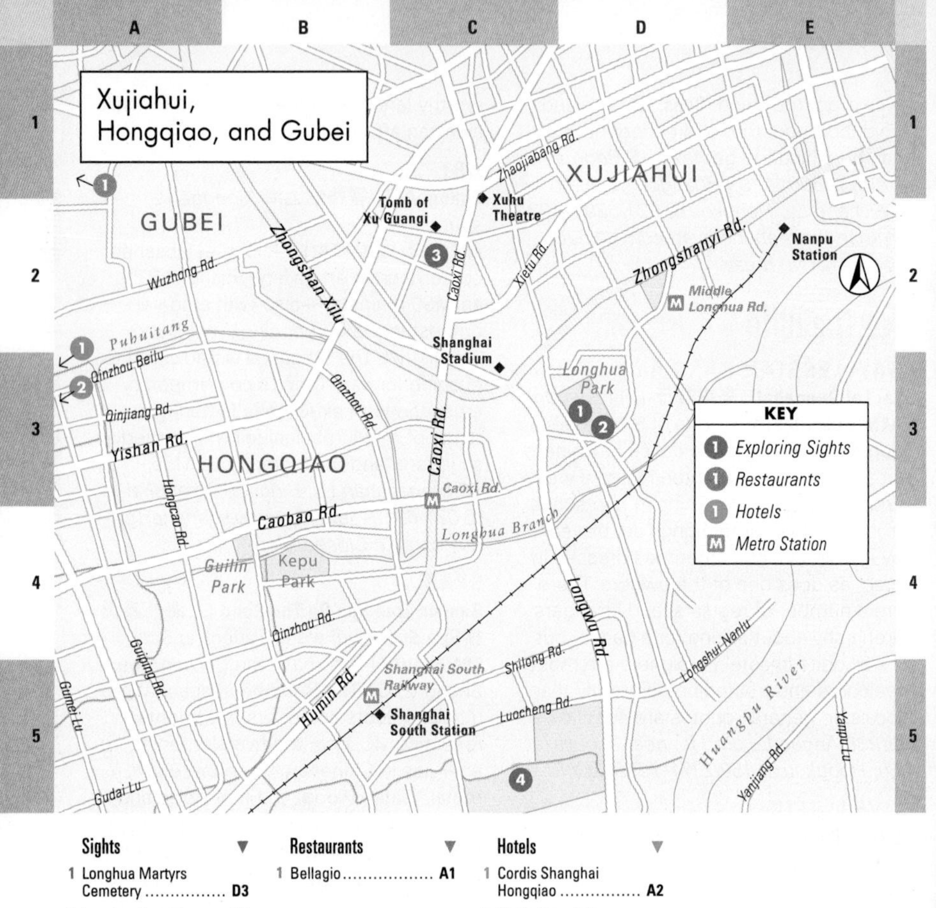

Sights

1 Longhua Martyrs Cemetery D3
2 Longhua Temple D3
3 St. Ignatius Cathedral C2
4 Shanghai Botanical Gardens........ C5

Restaurants

1 Bellagio........ A1

Hotels

1 Cordis Shanghai Hongqiao A2
2 Melia Shanghai Hongqiao A3

GETTING AROUND

Metro Line 1 takes you right into the depths of the Grand Gateway Mall at Xujiahui. The other sights are fairly far-flung, so a taxi is a good idea. If you are going to places like the Shanghai Botanical Gardens, be prepared for a hefty fare. Otherwise, you can get off at Shanghai South Railway Station.

Sights

Longhua Martyrs Cemetery (龙华烈士陵园 *Lónghuá lièshì língyuán*)
CEMETERY | It may seem tranquil now, but Longhua Martyrs Cemetery was the execution site of many Communists, particularly during the Guomingdang crackdown in 1927. The small, unkempt, grassy execution area—accessed by a tunnel—is chilling. In the 1950s, the remains of murdered Communists were found here still wearing leg irons. A glass, pyramid-shape museum in the center of the grounds contains paintings and other items. Elsewhere, Soviet-style sculptures dot immaculate lawns. ✉ *180 Longhua Xi Lu, Xujiahui* ☎ *021/6468–5995* 🌐 *www.slmmm.cn* 🎫 *Free* 🕑 *Museum closed Mon.*

Longhua Temple (龙华寺 *Lónghúa Sì*)
RELIGIOUS SITE | Shanghai's largest and most active temple has as its centerpiece a seven-story, eight-sided pagoda. While the temple, which made a cameo in Spielberg's *Empire of the Sun*, is thought to have been built in the 3rd century, the pagoda dates from the 10th century; it's not open to visitors. Near the front entrance stands a three-story bell tower, where a 3.3-ton bronze bell is rung at midnight every Lunar New Year's Eve. Along the side corridors you'll find a room filled seven rows deep with small golden statues. The third hall is the most impressive. Its three giant Buddhas sit beneath a swirled red and gold dome. ✉ *2853 Longhua Lu, Xujiahui* ☎ *021/6456–6085, 021/5410–3445* 🌐 *www.longhua.org* 🎫 *Y10.*

St. Ignatius Cathedral (圣依纳爵主教座堂 *Shèng yī nà jué zhǔjiào zuò táng*)
RELIGIOUS SITE | Just a hop from the traffic-clogged roads surrounding Xujiahui metro station and its periphery of malls is this Neo-Gothic Roman Catholic cathedral, which opened in 1910. In 1966, with the start of the Cultural Revolution, its beautiful stained glass windows, the ceiling, and spires were destroyed by the Red Guards. The church spent the next 10 years as a State-owned grain warehouse. Finally, in the 1980s, the cathedral was restored; today it remains the headquarters of the Roman Catholic Diocese of Shanghai. ✉ *158 Puxi Lu, Xujiahui* ☎ *021/6441–2211, 021/6438–2595.*

Shanghai Botanical Gardens (上海植物园 *Shànghǎi zhíwùyuán*)
GARDEN | This 200-acre urban garden is best visited during spring, when it's covered in roses, azaleas, bamboo, and orchids. Do visit the penjing garden; *penjing* translates as "pot scenery" and describes the Chinese art of creating a miniature landscape in a container. More than 2,000 bonsai trees line the penjing garden's courtyards and corridors. The Chinese cymbidium garden has more than 300 varieties. Within the Grand Conservatory are towering palms and more than 3,000 varieties of tropical plants. ✉ *1111 Longwu Lu, Xujiahui* ☎ *021/5436–3369* 🌐 *www.shbg.org* 🎫 *From Y15.*

Restaurants

Bellagio (鹿港小镇 *Lùgǎng xiǎozhèn*)
$ | **TAIWANESE** | **FAMILY** | Taiwanese expats pack the Bellagio (which also has branches in Hongqiao and downtown), so you know it offers an authentic taste of Taiwan. Carrying classic dishes such as three-cup chicken, waitresses with short, chic hairstyles move efficiently between the closely spaced black tables and red fabric–covered chairs. **Known for:** favorite with Asian and Western expats;

pineapple fried rice; Bellagio Breeze shaved ice. *Average main: Y90* *778 Huangjin Cheng Dao, Gubei* *021/6278–0722* *No credit cards.*

Hotels

Cordis Shanghai Hongqiao (**上海虹桥康得思酒店** *Shànghǎi hóngqiáo kāngdésī jiǔdiàn*)
$$ | **HOTEL** | Within walking distance of Hongqiao airport and train station, this hotel is an ideal base for on-the-go business travelers or tourists in transit. **Pros:** near Hongqiao airport and railway and metro stations; modern facilities; decent selection of restaurants and shops nearby. **Cons:** far from central tourist spots; lacking atmosphere; hotel restaurants are average. *Rooms from: Y1300* *333 Shenhong Lu, Minhang* *021/5263–9999* *www.cordishotels.com/en/shanghai-hongqiao* *396 rooms* *No meals.*

Melia Shanghai Hongqiao (**上海虹桥美利亚酒店** *Shànghǎi hóngqiáo měilìyǎ jiǔdiàn*)
$ | **HOTEL** | Popular with business travelers for its location near Hongqiao Airport and the National Exhibition and Convention Centre, this hotel offers sophisticated setting for your stay. **Pros:** great value; modern facilities; spacious rooms. **Cons:** a 30-minute-plus drive to the city center; almost easy to forget you're in Shanghai; Nespresso machines only in club level rooms. *Rooms from: Y420* *1118 Gaojing Lu, Minhang* *021/8028–9888* *www.melia.com/en/hotels/china/shanghai/melia-shanghai-hongqiao* *187 rooms* *No meals.*

Nightlife

BARS

Shanghai Brewery (**上海啤酒工坊** *Shànghǎi píjiǔ gōngfāng*)
BREWPUBS/BEER GARDENS | **FAMILY** | It's a family affair at Shanghai Brewery, where you're equally likely to find a group of footballers and a posse of parents with toddlers in tow. There are seven house-made brews here, including a Black-Eyed Bear Stout and the sweet, summery peach beer. The food menu is all over the place, with both Western dishes and a handful of Asian options, but it's all solid. *3338 Hongmei Lu, Hongqiao* *021/3463–5188* *shanghaibrewery.com.*

Shopping

Where major shopping malls and giant electronics complexes converge, **Xujiahui** looks like it's straight out of mid-'90s Tokyo. Shop 'til you drop, or play with the gadgets and compare prices at the electronics shops.

ANTIQUES

Hu & Hu Antiques (**古悦家俱** *Uyuè jiājù*)
ANTIQUES/COLLECTIBLES | Co-owner Marybelle Hu worked at Taipei's National Palace Museum as well as Sotheby's in Los Angeles before opening this shop with her sister-in-law Lin in 1998. The bright, airy showroom contains Tibetan chests and other rich furniture as well as a large selection of accessories, from lanterns to mooncake molds. The prices are higher than their competitors', but so is their standard of service. *601–38 Qingxi Lu, Hongqiao* *021/3431–1212* *www.hu-hu.com.*

Chapter 6

EASTERN CHINA

Updated by
Jamie Fullerton

Sights	Restaurants	Hotels	Shopping	Nightlife
★★★☆☆	★★★☆☆	★★★★☆	★★☆☆☆	★★★☆☆

WELCOME TO EASTERN CHINA

TOP REASONS TO GO

★ **Hangzhou Teatime:** Sip sublime longjing (Dragon Well) tea and stroll in the footsteps of Marco Polo at Hangzhou's romantic West Lake.

★ **Qiantang Tidal Bore—marvel at one of nature's most enthralling spectacles:** the mighty tidal bore at the mouth of Zhejiang's Qiantang River, best seen during the fall equinox.

★ **Gulangyu:** Wander through narrow alleyways filled with a fascinating blend of Chinese and European architecture, and recharge in seaside garden pavilions on this historic, car-free island, just a five-minute boat ride from Xiamen.

★ **Shaoxing Wine:** Dramatized by one of China's most famous writers, Lu Xun, Shaoxing wine is celebrated throughout the region. Potent to be sure, Shaoxing wine is de rigueur for local dining.

★ **Hakka Roundhouses:** The founder of the Republic of China, Dr. Sun Yat-sen, came from China's proud Hakka minority group, whose ancient tradition of rounded-home architecture is now treasured.

1 Hangzhou. Described by Marco Polo as the finest and noblest city in the world, Hangzhou is famous for the inspiringly beautiful West Lake. In recent years, Hangzhou has also emerged as one of China's most vibrant cities. A little way outside the city, visit the plantations that produce the area's famous Longjing tea, or stroll in forested hills to take in the views of the surrounding area.

2 Shaoxing. Shaoxing is famed for its historic homes and many traditional bridges. This small, well-preserved town is perhaps the best place to experience the historic atmosphere of a traditional Yangzi Delta town. Visit the stunning Figure 8 Bridge, which is shaped like a figure eight and erected over 800 years ago. Bearded moss hangs from its arches like the characters in local author Lu Xun's sagas. Don't miss the Catholic church with Italian–Chinese inspired decor.

3 Ningbo. A perfect blend of old and new, this bustling seaside metropolis is the ideal place to comfortably veer off the standard tourist trail. Climb the ancient Tianfeng Pagoda to survey the busy masses and, come nightfall, head over to *laowaitan* (old Bund), the city's entertainment district complete with a centuries-old Portuguese church and a handful of international bars and restaurants.

4 Xiamen. With a bird's-eye view of the Taiwan Straight, Xiamen is well poised to profit from the windfall of increased economic activity between Taiwan and the mainland. Famous for its party atmosphere and popular with young expats, its trendy clubs and upscale restaurants are now becoming as commonplace as Xiamen's famous beaches and botanical gardens. Although Xiamen is known for its fresh seafood, the city's Buddhist population means it has excellent vegetarian cuisine. Xiamen is probably the best place outside of Taiwan to experience Taiwanese cuisine, and many restaurants advertise their *Taiwan wei kou* (Taiwanese appetite) and *Taiwan xiao chi* (Taiwanese snacks).

JIANGSU
SHANGHAI
Huzhou
Jiaxing
Wangpan Bay
ANHUI
Hangzhou
1
Shaoxing
2
Ningbo
3
Fuyang
Qiantian
Shengzhou
Yiwu
Jinhua
ZHEJIANG
Linhai
Jiaojiang
Huangyan
Quzhou
Lishui
Wenzhou
Rui'an
JIANGXI
Wuyi Mountain Natural Reserve
Shaowu
Fu'an
Xiapu
Ningde
Taiwan Strait
Nanping
Fuzhou
Sanming
FUJIAN
Fuqing
HAITAN ISLAND
Changting
Putian
NANRI ISLAND
Nan'an
Quanzhou
Longyan
Hakka Settlements of Yongding
4
Xiamen
KINMEN ISLAND
Zhangzhou
Gulangyu Island
GUANGDONG
TAIWAN
0
75 mi
0
75 km

In Eastern China, the past's rich legacy and the challenges of, and aspirations for, China's future combine in a present that is dizzying in its variety and speed of transformation. Zhejiang and Fujian, often overlooked on the standard Beijing–Shanghai–Hong Kong tourist trail, offer some of the country's most verdant scenery and a plethora of diversions, like hiking through ancient villages, bicycling along lush tea fields, and lounging on lively beaches.

Zhejiang has always been a hub of culture, learning, and commerce. Its cities, with their elegant gardens, elaborate temples, and fine crafts, evoke the sophisticated and refined world of classical China's literati. Since the Southern Song Dynasty (1127–79), large numbers of Fujianese have immigrated to Southeast Asia. As a result, Fujian Province has strong ties to overseas Chinese. In 1979, Fujian was allowed to form in Xiamen the first Special Economic Zone (SEZ)—a testing ground for a capitalist market economy. Today, although Xiamen is a wealthy place with a vibrant economy, the city has managed to retain its old-world charm.

MAJOR REGIONS

A center of culture and trade, Zhejiang is also one of China's wealthiest provinces. The capital city of **Hangzhou** is famous for West Lake, which is visited by millions of tourists annually. **Shaoxing's** small-town flavor of a city-on-canals survives, despite a growing population. **Ningbo** is not set up for tourists, which makes it an interesting and authentic city to explore. The port city of **Xiamen** is beautiful, and remarkably green, with notable beaches. Once a paradise of undisturbed colonial architecture, car-free **Gulangyu** island has since become a not-so-hidden gem, drawing hordes of visitors to its shores on weekends.

Planning

When to Go

Fall and spring are the ideal times to visit the region. Spring, especially April and May, has very comfortable temperatures, and the trees and flowers are in full bloom. Hangzhou's spectacular cherry blossoms are out in spring, dotting the gardens surrounding the West

Lake. Summers are hot and muggy, and winters are short (the temperature rarely dips below zero) but miserably wet, windy, and chilly. Typhoons can strike any time from late summer through autumn. The region has a long and very pleasant fall season, with moderate weather and clear skies lasting into early December. Chinese tourists flood in during the long weekends in April, May, and June (which change according to the lunar calendar), "Golden Week" (always the first week of October), and during Chinese New Year (late January to mid-February), so avoid traveling during these times.

Getting Here and Around

Shanghai is generally the best place from which to begin exploring Eastern China. It has good amenities, and with two airports and four train stations, it offers myriad connections across the country. Most major travel agents in Shanghai speak English. If you want to make Hangzhou your base, many cheap flights there are available, and the list of connecting destinations is constantly growing.

AIR TRAVEL

Air travel in Eastern China is very straightforward but often delayed. Hangzhou's Xiaoshan International Airport is modern and well connected, and domestic flights are abundant. Hangzhou is increasingly adding more international routes, already including Amsterdam (KLM), Kuala Lumpur (AirAsia), Tokyo (Air Nippon), Seoul (Asiana Airlines), Bangkok (China Eastern Airlines), Malé (Mega Maldives), Hong Kong (Hong Kong Airlines), and Paris (Hainan Airlines). Ningbo offers direct flights to Taipei (China Eastern Airlines), Hong Kong (Dragonair), and Beijing (China Eastern Airlines). Xiamen is well connected to Jakarta (Air China), Singapore (Xiamen Airlines), Hong Kong (Dragonair), and Manila (China Southern).

BUS TRAVEL

Traveling by bus in Eastern China is a great way to get around, as even tiny cities and villages have a station. Large cities such as Hangzhou have several stations. Buses in Eastern China are usually relatively new, air-conditioned vehicles, and almost always leave on time. The biggest headache you'll likely encounter is trying to navigate through the masses at the stations to buy your tickets. Ask your hotel to purchase tickets in advance, as line etiquette in China can be frustrating, especially for non-Mandarin speakers. Buses between major cities such as Hangzhou and Ningbo leave frequently, so just show up and get on the next available departure.

CAR TRAVEL

Hiring a driver is possible and, for a large group, makes far more sense than hailing cabs. Plan on paying at least $165 for an eight-hour day. Hangzhou Car Service operates an impressive fleet of international vehicles and can arrange city tours, intercity transport, and airport pickup. Since taxis are cheap and plentiful, navigating within cities is fairly easy, but it's essential to have your destinations mapped out and written down in Chinese ahead of time.

TRAIN TRAVEL

Bullet trains are the easiest, quickest, and most comfortable option. For the shortest journeys, look for G- or D-coded trains, or the letters CHR (China High-Speed Rail). Shanghai to Hangzhou, for example, takes approximately an hour, and there are roughly 30 daily departures. D-coded trains take 1 hour and 15 minutes. Slower trains are uncomfortable for long distances and best avoided.

Restaurants

Zhejiang cuisine is often steamed or roasted, and has a subtle, salty flavor; specialties include yellow croaker with Chinese cabbage, sea eel, drunken chicken, and stewed chicken. In Shaoxing, locals traditionally start the day by downing a bowl or two of *huang jiu* (yellow rice wine), the true breakfast of champions. Shaoxing's most famous dish is its deep-fried *chou dofu,* or stinky tofu. Try it with a touch of the local chili sauce.

The cuisine of Fujian has its own characteristics. Spareribs are a specialty, as are soups and stews using a soy and rice-wine stock. The coastal cities of Fujian offer a wonderful range of seafood, including river eel with leeks, fried jumbo prawns, and steamed crab.

What it Costs in Yuan

$	$$	$$$	$$$$
RESTAURANTS			
under Y50	Y50–Y99	Y100–Y165	over Y165

Hotels

Hotels in this region cater to all budgets, all the way up to luxurious resorts and international chains offering every creature comfort. Besides a general lack of amenities, cheaper options may not be able to accept foreign credit cards. Family-run guesthouses are rare, as are boutique hotels. Consider a domestic chain called the Orange Hotel, with dozens of locations throughout China, including Hangzhou and Ningbo. Comfortable rooms are available from US$50 to US$85 a night.

Hotel reviews have been shortened. For full information, visit Fodors.com.

What it Costs in Yuan

$	$$	$$$	$$$$
HOTELS			
under Y1,100	Y1,100–Y1,399	Y1,400–Y1,800	over Y1,800

Tours

Discover Fujian

SPECIAL-INTEREST | Experience the Fujian *tulou* (round earthen structures) with Discover Fujian. The company leads reasonably priced day trips, as well as four- to five-day journeys to these ancient, circular houses. ✉ *1118 Xiahe Lu, 10th fl., Xiamen* ☎ *0592/398–9901* 🌐 *www.discoverfujian.com* 🎫 *From Y500 per person.*

Seven Cups

SPECIAL-INTEREST | Tea lovers should consider Seven Cups, which offers 12- to 15-day visits to tea gardens, as well as hands-on experience with the harvest and production methods of some of China's finest teas. ☎ *520/628–2952* 🌐 *www.sevencups.com* 🎫 *From US$4,550.*

Visitor Information

Tourist kiosks are ubiquitous in major cities and tourist destinations, but mostly cater to domestic travelers. The best sources for visitor information are the English-language city magazines like *More Hangzhou* (🌐 *www.more-hangzhou.com*) and *What's On Xiamen* (🌐 *www.whatsonxiamen.com*), both of which can be found at international hotels and restaurants.

Hangzhou

Approximately an hr (202 km [126 miles]) southwest of Shanghai by train.

Hangzhounese are immensely proud of their city, and will often point to a classical saying that identifies it as an "earthly paradise." Indeed, for locals, Hangzhou is one of the country's most livable cities, thanks to lots of green space and plenty of parks. The city retains much of its historic charm despite an overly robust tourism market. Visitors come from all over China to see West Lake, the temples, and the silk markets. Beyond the major tourist draws, there's a small but growing mix of local shops and low-key restaurants, as well as an increasing number of fine-dines and bars, making Hangzhou a pleasant day or overnight trip.

GETTING HERE AND AROUND

Travel between Shanghai and Hangzhou is very efficient. Fast trains take about an hour and usually leave from the Hangzhou East station, while local trains take two hours or more. Hangzhou East is enormous and buying tickets can take a long time, so have your hotel book and deliver tickets in advance. Buses will get you here from Shanghai in 3 hours or from Suzhou in 2½ hours. Trains also run to Suzhou (1½ hours), Nanjing (about 2 hours), and most cities in Fujian.

Hangzhou Xiaoshan International Airport, about 30 km (18 miles) southeast of the city, has frequent flights to Hong Kong, Guangzhou, and Beijing, which are all about two hours away. There are also flights from other major cities around the region.

Major hotels offer limousine service to the airport. Taxis to the airport cost around Y100. A bus (Y20 per person) leaves from the CAAC office on Tiyuchang Lu at least every 30 minutes between 7:30 am and 11 pm.

Hangzhou's taxi fleet ferries visitors from West Lake to far-flung sights like the Temple of the Soul's Retreat and the China Tea Museum. You'll need your destination written down in Chinese characters. Fares usually run Y30 to Y45. You can also book cabs by the hour (about Y100) or half day (Y400), and this is much easier than flagging one down. If you're hailing a cab on the street, make sure the meter is being used; many drivers will not turn on the meter or will insist that it's broken. ■ **TIP→ Avoid looking for a taxi between 4 and 5 pm, as virtually all drivers are finishing their shifts and refuse to pick anyone up.**

TIMING

Give yourself at least two full days to explore the city. West Lake and the pagodas and gardens that dot its periphery will occupy at least a full day. Hefang Pedestrian Street, Lingyin Temple, and a variety of museums will fill another day.

Rent a Bike

West Lake is one of East China's most pleasant places for bicycling. Its path, away from car traffic, is also a quick way to move between the area's major sights. Numerous public bike-rental agencies are scattered around the lake, especially near Orioles Singing in the Willows and on Hubin Lu, down the road from the Hyatt and adjacent to a Starbucks and Dairy Queen. Rentals are free for the first hour, maxing out at Y3 per hour after three hours, between 6 am and 10 pm. A Y200 deposit and some form of identification are required, and we do not recommend using your passport as ID.

Sights

China National Silk Museum (中国丝绸博物馆 *Zhōngguó sīchóu bówùguǎn*)

MUSEUM | From worm to weave, the huge China National Silk Museum explores traditional silk production, illustrating every step of the process. By the end, you'll comprehend the cost of this fine fiber made from cocoons of mulberry-munching larvae. On display are looms, brocades, and a rotating exhibit of historic robes from different Chinese dynasties. The first-floor shop has the city's largest selection of silk, and sells it by the meter. The museum is south of West Lake, on the road to Jade Emperor Hill. ✉ *73–1 Yuhuangshan Lu* ☎ *0571/8703–5150* 🌐 *www.chinasilkmuseum.com* 🎫 *Free.*

★ **China Tea Museum** (中国茶叶博物馆 *Zhōngguó cháyé bówùguǎn*)

MUSEUM | Surrounded by tranquil tea plant fields, this engaging museum explores all facets of China's tea culture. Galleries contain fascinating information about the varieties and quality of leaves, brewing techniques, and gathering methods, all with good English explanations. A shop offers a wide range of teas, without the bargaining you'll encounter at Dragon Well Tea Park. ✉ *88 Longjing Lu, north of Dragon Well Tea Park* ☎ *0571/8796–4221* 🌐 *www.teamuseum.cn* 🎫 *Free.*

Dragon Well Tea Park (龙井茶园 *Lóngjǐng cháyuán*)

CITY PARK | This park is named for an ancient well whose water is considered ideal for brewing the famous local longjing (Dragon Well) tea. Distinguishing between varieties and grades of tea can be confusing for novices, especially under high pressure from the eager hawkers. It's worth a preliminary trip to the nearby tea museum to bone up on

A picture-perfect sunset over West Lake

what's what. The highest quality varieties are very expensive, but once you take a sip you will taste the difference. Prices are intentionally high, so be sure to bargain. ✉ *Longjing Lu, next to Dragon Well Temple.*

Dreaming of the Tiger Spring (虎跑梦泉 *Hǔ pǎo mèng quán*)

FOUNTAIN | According to legend, a traveling monk decided this setting would be perfect for a temple, but was disappointed to discover that there was no source of water. That night he dreamed that two tigers had ripped up the earth around him. When he awoke he was lying next to a spring. On the grounds is an intriguing "dripping wall" cut out of the mountain. Locals line up with jugs to collect the water that pours from its surface, believing that the water has special qualities—and it does. Ask someone in the temple's souvenir shop to float a coin on the surface of the water to prove it. ✉ *Hupao Lu, near the Pagoda of Six Harmonies* 🎫 *Y15.*

★ **Evening Sunlight at Thunder Peak Pagoda** (雷锋夕照 *Léifēng xīzhào*)

BUILDING | On the southeastern shore of West Lake is the Evening Sunlight at Thunder Peak Pagoda. Local legend says that the original Thunder Peak Pagoda was constructed to imprison a snake-turned-human who lost her mortal love on West Lake. The pagoda collapsed in 1924, perhaps finally freeing the White Snake. A new tower, completed in 2002, sits beside the remains of its predecessor. There's a sculpture on each level, including one that depicts the tragic story of the White Snake. The foundation dates from AD 976 and is an active archaeological site, where scientists uncovered a miniature silver pagoda containing what is said to be a lock of the Buddha's hair; it's on display in a separate hall. The view of the lake is breathtaking, particularly at sunset. ✉ *15 Nanshan Lu* ☎ *0571/8798–2111* 🎫 *Y40.*

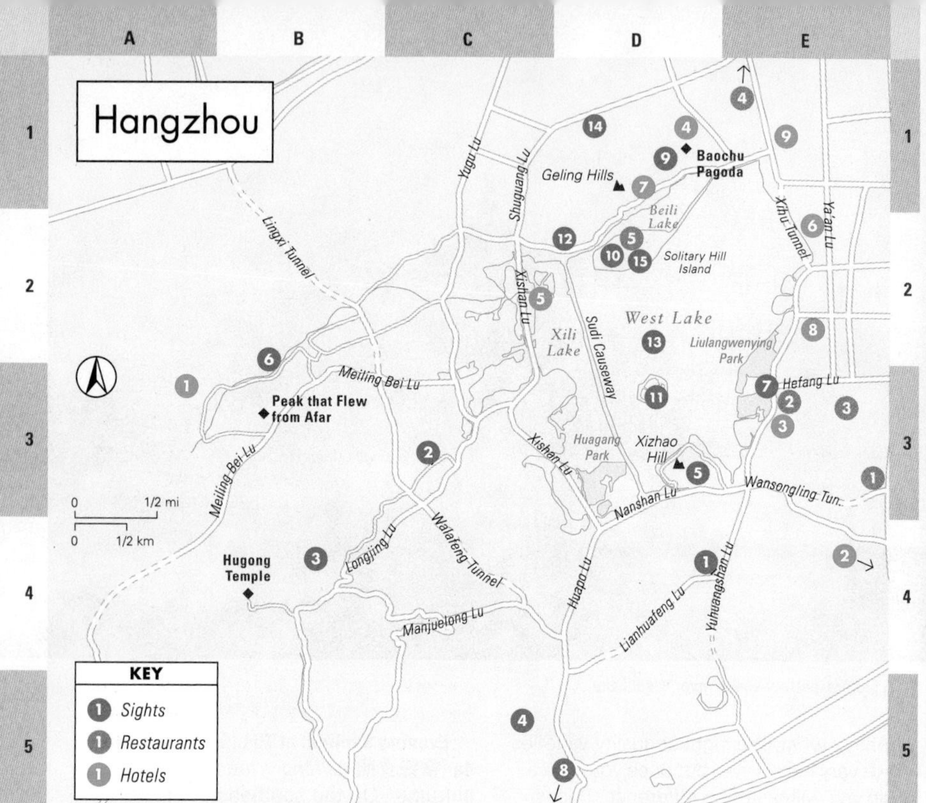

Sights	
1 China National Silk Museum	D4
2 China Tea Museum	C3
3 Dragon Well Tea Park	B4
4 Dreaming of the Tiger Spring	C5
5 Evening Sunlight at Thunder Peak Pagoda	D3
6 Lingyin Temple	B2
7 Orioles Singing in the Willows	E3
8 Pagoda of Six Harmonies	D5
9 Precious Stone Hill	D1
10 Solitary Hill Island	D2
11 Three Pools Mirroring the Moon	D3
12 Tomb of Yue Fei	D2
13 West Lake	D2
14 Yellow Dragon Cave	D1
15 Zhejiang Provincial Museum	D2

Restaurants	
1 Dong Yi Shun	E3
2 Hanyan Coffee House	E3
3 Honeymoon Dessert	E3
4 Lingyin Si Vegetarian Restaurant	E1
5 Louwailou	D2

Hotels	
1 Amanfayun Resort	A3
2 The Azure Qiantang	E4
3 Crystal Orange Hotel	E3
4 The Dragon	D1
5 Four Seasons Hotel Hangzhou at West Lake	C2
6 Hyatt Regency Hangzhou	E2
7 Shangri-La Hotel Hangzhou	D1
8 Sofitel Hangzhou Westlake	E2
9 Wyndham Grand Plaza Royale Hangzhou	E1

★ Lingyin Temple (灵隐寺 *Língyǐn sì*)
RELIGIOUS SITE | One of the major Zen Buddhist shrines in China, Lingyin Temple (Temple of the Soul's Retreat) was founded in AD 328 by Hui Li, a Buddhist monk from India. He looked at the surrounding mountains and exclaimed, "This is the place where the souls of immortals retreat," hence the name. This site is especially notable for religious carvings on the nearby **Peak Flown From Afar** (Feilai Feng). From the 10th to the 14th century, monks and artists carved more than 300 statues in and around these grottos. Uprisings, revolutions, and wars have changed the face of the shrine. The main temple was restored in 1974 following the end of the Cultural Revolution. About 5 km (3 miles) west of West Lake, the temple and carvings are among the most popular spots in Hangzhou and as such are positively teeming come weekends. **■ TIP→ To avoid crowds, visit on weekdays.** ✉ *End of Lingyin Lu* ☎ *0571/8796–8665* *Carvings Y45, temple Y30.*

Orioles Singing in the Willows (柳浪闻莺 *Liǔlàngwényíng*)
CITY PARK | Along the eastern bank of West Lake is Orioles Singing in the Willows, a nice park from which to watch boats traverse the water. The park comes alive during Lantern Festival, which falls on the 15th day of the first lunar month, usually in February or March. Paper lanterns are set to float on the river under the willow boughs. ✉ *11 Nanshan Lu, near intersection of Hefang Jie and Nanshan Lu.*

Pagoda of Six Harmonies (六和塔 *Liù hétǎ*)
BUILDING | Atop Moon Mountain stands the impressive Pagoda of Six Harmonies, also referred to as the Liuhe Pagoda. Those who climb to the top of the seven-story pagoda are rewarded with great views across the Qiantang River. Originally lanterns were lit in its windows and the pagoda served as a lighthouse for ships navigating the river. On the 18th day of the eighth lunar month, the pagoda is packed with people wanting the best seat to view the Qiantang Tidal Bore. On this day, the flow of the river reverses itself, creating large waves that for centuries have delighted observers. Behind the pagoda is a large park, one of our favorite family-friendly spaces in Hangzhou. The grounds house an exhibit of 100 or so miniature pagodas, representing every Chinese style. The pagoda is 4 km (2½ miles) south of West Lake. ✉ *16 Zhijiang Lu, on Qiantang River* ☎ *0571/8717–9617* *Y30.*

For the Kids

Pagoda of Six Harmonies Garden (六和塔 *Liùhétǎ*)
The garden behind the Pagoda of Six Harmonies in Hangzhou is a very child-friendly place. Climb the stairs of the seven-story pagoda, picnic among the flower beds, and play among the miniature versions of China's most famous pagodas and temples. The pagoda is 2½ km (1½ miles) south of West Lake. ✉ *Fuxing Jie, on the Qiantang River* *Y20.*

Precious Stone Hill (宝石山 *Bǎoshí shān*)
NATURE SITE | The slender spire of Baochu Pagoda rises atop the romantically named Precious Stone Hill Floating in Rosy Clouds. The brick and stone pagoda is visible from just about anywhere on the lake. From the hilltop you can see across the lake to the city. Numerous paths from the lake lead up the hill, which is dotted with Buddhist and Taoist shrines. Several caves provide shade from the hot summer sun. ✉ *North of West Lake.*

Solitary Hill Island (孤山 *Gū shān*)
ISLAND | A palace for the exclusive use of the emperor during his visits to Hangzhou once stood on Solitary Hill Island, the largest island in West Lake.

West Lake Is the Best

There's a well-known Chinese poem that says, "Of all the lakes, north, south, east and west, the one at West Lake is the best." Start exploring where Pinghai Lu meets Hubin Lu in the northeastern part of the lake. There's a popular boardwalk with weeping willows, restaurants, and a lakeside teahouse.

Wending north, you can cross the street to ascend a small hill capped with the Baochu Pagoda. Here the views of West Lake are some of the best in the city. Once you climb down, you can venture to the Baidi and Sudi causeways through the middle of the lake. Don't miss the classical Lingyin Temple, nestled in the nearby hills.

By night, take a guided boat from the southern shore to see one of Hangzhou's best views: the Three Pools Mirroring the Moon. When candles are set inside the trio of miniature pagodas, the glow creates a silhouette on the water resembling the moon.

On its southern side is a small, carefully composed park with several pavilions and a pond. A path leads up the hill to the Xiling Seal Engraver's Society, where professional carvers design and create seals. The society's garden has one of the best views of the lake. ✉ *Bai Causeway* 🎫 *Free.*

Three Pools Mirroring the Moon (三潭印月 *Sāntányínyué*)
ISLAND | Here you'll find walkways surrounding several large ponds, all connected by zigzagging bridges. Off the island's southern shore are three Ming Dynasty–era mini stone pagodas. During the Mid-Autumn Moon Festival, held in the middle of September, lanterns are lit in the pagodas, creating the reflections that give the island its name. Leisure boats from several spots around the lake, including a dock near Yue Fei's memorial, will shuttle you to the pagodas for around Y55. ✉ *Southern side of West Lake* 🎫 *Y55, includes boat ride.*

Tomb of Yue Fei (岳飞墓 *Yuèfēi mù*)
MEMORIAL | Near Solitary Hill Island stands this shrine to honor General Yue Fei (1103–42), who led Song Dynasty armies against foreign invaders. When he was a young man, his mother tattooed his back with the commandment "Repay the nation with loyalty." This made Yue Fei a hero both for his patriotic loyalty and filial piety. At the height of his success, a jealous rival convinced the emperor to have Yue Fei executed. A subsequent leader pardoned the warrior and enshrined him as a national hero. Statues of Yue Fei's accusers kneel in shame nearby. Traditionally, visitors would spit on statues of the traitors, but now a sign near the statue asks them to glare instead. ✉ *80 Beishan Lu, west of Solitary Hill Island* ☎ *0571/8798–6653* 🎫 *Y25* 🕙 *Closed Mon.*

Yellow Dragon Cave (黄龙洞 *Huánglóng dòng*)
CAVE | At the foot of Gem Hill is Yellow Dragon Cave, famous for a never-ending stream of water spurting from the head of a yellow dragon. Nearby are a lovely garden plus a stage for traditional Yue opera performances, and you can take a pleasant 25-minute hike through the woods to the Tomb of Yue Fei from the site. ✉ *69 Shuguang Lu* ☎ *0571/8797–2468* 🎫 *Y15.*

West Lake (西湖 *Xīhú*)
AMUSEMENT PARK/WATER PARK | With arched bridges stretching over the water, West Lake is the heart of Hangzhou. Originally a bay, the area has been built up gradually throughout the years by a combination of natural changes and human shaping of the land. The photogenic shores are enhanced by meandering paths, artificial islands, and countless pavilions with upturned roofs. Two pedestrian causeways cross the lake: **Bai** in the north and **Su** in the west. They are named for two poet–governors from different eras who invested in landscaping and developing the lake. Ideal for strolling or biking, both walkways are lined with willow and peach trees, crossed by bridges, and dotted with benches where you can pause to admire the views. **■ TIP→ The lake's pathways are jam-packed on weekends and during holidays, particularly Golden Week (first week of October).** ✉ *Along Nanshan Lu.*

Zhejiang Provincial Museum (浙江省博物馆 *Zhéjiāng shěng bówùguǎn*)
MUSEUM | Solitary Hill Island is home to the Zhejiang Provincial Museum, which has a good collection of archaeological finds, as well as bronzes, paintings, and exhibits focusing on the province's ethnic minority groups. English signage isn't great here, but the visuals themselves are enticing. ✉ *25 Gushan Lu* ☎ *0571/8798–0281* 🌐 *www.zhejiangmuseum.com* 🎫 *Free* ⏲ *Closed Mon.*

Restaurants

Dong Yi Shun (东伊顺 *Dōngyīshùn*)
$ | **MIDDLE EASTERN** | All day, lines form at the takeout window here, with people eager to order sesame-coated naan bread and plump, well-seasoned, skewered meats. Sit inside for a large picture menu of Western Chinese and Middle Eastern dishes. **Known for:** delicious lamb or chicken skewers; offers a break from oilier Chinese cuisine; neon-lit Gaoyin Street is a great place to walk off calories. Ⓢ *Average main: Y45* ✉ *99 Gaoyin Jie* ☎ *0571/8780–5163* 💳 *No credit cards.*

Hanyan Coffee House (寒烟梧桐 *Hányān kāfēiguǎn*)
$$ | **INTERNATIONAL** | This Himalayan café brews some of the city's best java. The eclectic space is outfitted with quilted tablecloths, comfy sofas, knit blankets, and walls stacked with books and knickknacks. **Known for:** loaded with character; steamy tea (as well as coffee) and tasty sandwiches; well-stocked bar. Ⓢ *Average main: Y50* ✉ *1142 Xueyuan Jie* ☎ *0571/8996–7075.*

Honeymoon Dessert (满記甜品 *Mǎnjì tiánpǐn*)
$ | **CAFÉ** | Trendy Hangzhou locals pack in at all hours for the inventive and exotic creations. The mango or durian pancakes filled with fresh whipped cream are especially yummy. **Known for:** bright, sleek, spotless interior; prime West Lake area locale; has English picture menus. Ⓢ *Average main: Y25* ✉ *98 Youdian Lu* ☎ *0571/8706–7050* 🌐 *www.honeymoon-dessert.com* 💳 *No credit cards.*

Lingyin Si Vegetarian Restaurant (灵隐寺面馆 *Língyǐn Sì miànguǎn*)
$ | **VEGETARIAN** | Inside the Temple of the Soul's Retreat (Lingyin Si), this restaurant has turned the Buddhist restriction against eating meat into an opportunity to invent a range of delicious vegetarian dishes. Soy replaces chicken and beef, meaning your meal is as benevolent to your health as to the animal world. **Known for:** busy on weekends and holidays; feel-good menu and vibe; overall serene setting. Ⓢ *Average main: Y45* ✉ *End of Lingyin Si Lu, western shore of West Lake* ☎ *0571/8796–8665* 🌐 *www.lingyinsi.org* 💳 *No credit cards* ⏲ *No dinner.*

Buddha sculptures on the face of the Peak Flown From Afar

★ **Louwailou** (楼外楼 *Lóuwàilóu*)
$$$ | **CHINESE FUSION** | Back in 1848, this place was a simple fish shack. Business boomed, and it became the most famous restaurant in the province, focusing on Zhejiang cuisine and specializing in steamed lake perch served with vinegar sauce. **Known for:** West Lake dining classic; renowned beggar's chicken (wrapped in lotus leaves and baked in a clay shell); truly tender dongpo rou (pork slow cooked in yellow rice wine). *Average main: Y150 30 Gushan Lu, southern tip of Solitary Hill Island 0571/8796–9682 www.louwailou.com.cn.*

Hotels

Amanfayun Resort (法云安缦酒店 *Ānmànfǎyún jiǔdiàn*)
$$$$ | **RESORT** | Surrounded by tea fields, forests, and romantic courtyards, Amanfuyan tastefully re-creates the feel of a traditional Chinese village, with buildings that incorporate lots of stone, clay, and brick, and rooms decked out in earth tones. **Pros:** local design touches; luxurious spa; on-site restaurants and nearby teahouse. **Cons:** far from city center; expensive. *Rooms from: Y5000 22 Fayun Nong 0571/8732–9999 www.amanresorts.com 82 rooms Free Breakfast.*

The Azure Qiantang (尊蓝钱江豪华精选酒店 *Zūnlán qiánjiāng háohuá jīng xuǎn jiǔdiàn*)
$$ | **HOTEL** | Named after *Memories of the South*, a famous Tang Dynasty poem by Bai Ju Yi, this luxury property incorporates shades of blue throughout, and its big windows give you front row seats for the tidal bore. **Pros:** excellent Qiantang River views; central location; good pool and fitness center. **Cons:** busy during tidal bore and holidays; some service hiccups. *Rooms from: Y1126 39 Wangjiang Dong Lu 0571/2823–7777 www.theluxurycollection.com/azureqiantang 205 rooms No meals.*

The Qiantang Tidal Bore

During the autumnal equinox, when the moon's gravitational pull is at its peak, huge waves crash up the Qiantang River. Every year at this time, crowds gather at a safe distance to watch what begins as a distant line of white waves approaching. As it nears, it becomes a towering, thundering wall of water.

The phenomenon, known as a tidal bore, occurs when strong tides surge against the current of the river. The Qiantang Tidal Bore is the largest in the world, with recorded speeds of up to 25 miles an hour and heights of 30 feet. The Qiantang has the best conditions in the world to produce these tidal waves. Incoming tides are funneled into the shallow riverbed from the Gulf of Hangzhou and the bell shape narrows and concentrates the wave. People have been swept away in the past, so police now enforce a strict viewing distance.

★ **Crystal Orange Hotel** (桔子水晶酒店 *Júzi shuǐjīng jiǔdiàn*)
$ | **HOTEL** | Branches of this quirky, beloved, boutique-hotel chain have popped up in other Chinese cities, but the Hangzhou location is a step up from the rest, with an airy, artful lobby decorated with Andy Warhol's pop art; a glass elevator that gives you a bird's-eye view; and clean, quiet rooms. **Pros:** excellent location near West Lake; bicycle rental; free Wi-Fi. **Cons:** disappointing breakfast; few amenities; limited English. *Rooms from: Y500* *122 Qingbo Jie* *0571/2887–8988* *www.orangehotel.com.cn* *205 rooms* *No meals.*

The Dragon (黄龙饭店 *Huánglóngfàndiàn*)
$ | **HOTEL** | Guest rooms have earthy interiors with lots of wood at this massive hotel, whose five towers are set amid peaceful courtyards dotted with ponds, a small waterfall, and a gazebo—all within walking distance of Diamond Hill and Yellow Dragon Cave. **Pros:** good location; reasonable rates; free Wi-Fi. **Cons:** indifferent service; hit-and-miss English. *Rooms from: Y900* *120 Shuguang Lu, at Hangda Lu* *0571/8799–8833* *www.dragon-hotel.com* *598 rooms* *Free Breakfast.*

Four Seasons Hotel Hangzhou at West Lake (杭州西子湖四季酒店 *Hángzhōu xīzǐ hú sìjì jiǔdiàn*)
$$$$ | **HOTEL** | Under a pagoda-style roof, contemporary Chinese decor and modern amenities combine with superlative service to create a luxurious retreat with plush, spacious rooms—some with private terraces that have excellent views, all with bathrooms that have soaking tubs and separate showers. **Pros:** great location; boat pickup from West Lake; beautiful landscaping. **Cons:** outdoor pool lacks privacy; heavy traffic to and from the hotel; an extra Y200 for breakfast. *Rooms from: Y3500* *5 Lingyin Lu* *0571/8829–8888* *www.fourseasons.com* *86 rooms* *No meals.*

★ **Hyatt Regency Hangzhou** (杭州凯悦酒店 *Hángzhōu kǎi yuè jiǔdiàn*)
$$$ | **HOTEL** | Hangzhou's most recognizable and centrally located hotel offers attentive service and comfortable, sleekly furnished rooms; be sure to ask for one on an upper floor for unobstructed views. **Pros:** ultrasoft beds; good spa and health club; excellent pool. **Cons:** long

Did You Know?

More than 4.3 million metric tons of tea are produced worldwide each year; after water, tea is the world's favorite drink. In China, tea is usually grown on large plantations and is always picked by hand.

check-in time; some areas are outdated; service can be a bit stiff. $ *Rooms from: Y1400* ✉ *28 Hubin Lu* ☎ *0571/8779–1234* 🌐 *www.hyatt.com* *390 rooms* *Free Breakfast.*

★ **Shangri-La Hotel Hangzhou** (杭州香格里拉饭店 *Hángzhōu xiānggélǐlā fàndiàn*)
$ | **HOTEL** | On the site of an ancient temple, amid 40 acres of camphor and bamboo trees that merge seamlessly into the gardens and walkways of surrounding West Lake, this historic landmark hotel has two wings of rooms with high ceilings and heavy damask fabrics. **Pros:** picturesque location; fun quirks such as talking birds in lobbies; free strong Wi-Fi. **Cons:** starting to show its age; English language skills of staff not always great; rooms have a formal feel. $ *Rooms from: Y890* ✉ *78 Beishan Lu* ☎ *0571/8797–7951* 🌐 *www.shangri-la.com* *380 rooms* *Free Breakfast.*

Sofitel Hangzhou Westlake (杭州索菲特西湖大酒店 *Hángzhōu suǒ fēi tè xīhú dà jiǔdiàn*)
$ | **HOTEL** | Thoughtfully designed rooms—with sleek desks, soothing beige palettes, and big bathrooms—and a distinctive lobby with grand columns and gauzy curtains distinguish this hotel, which is set amid a lively neighborhood just a block north of West Lake's Orioles Singing in the Willows. **Pros:** great location; helpful staff; free Wi-Fi. **Cons:** some mediocre views; breakfast costs another Y200; pool is in the basement. $ *Rooms from: Y950* ✉ *333 Xihu Dadao* ☎ *0571/8707–5858* 🌐 *www.sofitel.com* *233 rooms* *No meals.*

Wyndham Grand Plaza Royale Hangzhou (杭州温德姆至尊豪廷大酒店 *Wēn dé mǔ dà jiǔdiàn*)
$ | **HOTEL** | This spaceship-shaped hotel just steps from West Lake offers excellent customer service and spacious rooms with big balconies and ergonomic furniture. **Pros:** knowledgeable guest-service ambassadors; flawless mountain, lake, city, and garden views; excellent location. **Cons:** too-firm mattresses; inconsistent restaurant service. $ *Rooms from: Y900* ✉ *555 Fengqi Lu* ☎ *0571/8761–6888* 🌐 *www.wyndham.com* *295 rooms* *No meals.*

Nightlife

Eudora Station (亿多瑞站 *Yìduōruìzhàn*)
MUSIC CLUBS | An integral part of Nanshan Road's ever-expanding foreign bar and restaurant scene, Eudora Station fills up on the weekend thanks to live music and cheap drink specials. The pizzas and salads are decent and make up for the sometimes blunt service. ✉ *101–7 Nanshan Lu* ☎ *0571/8791–4760* 🌐 *www.eudorastation.com.*

★ **JZ Club** (黄楼酒吧 *Huánglóu jiǔbā*)
MUSIC CLUBS | For a refined night out, head to the southeastern edge of West Lake and visit this well-established jazz club with a cultured clientele. The large three-story spot is known for its steady stream of talented jazz and blues performers, plus it has one of the city's best wine and whiskey lists. ✉ *6 Liuying Lu, at intersection of Nanshan Lu* ☎ *0571/8702–8298.*

Schanke Beer Bar (喧客德国啤酒酒吧餐厅 *Xuān kè déguó píjiǔ jiǔbā cāntīng*)
BARS/PUBS | For locally brewed beers and German flavors, head here. The beer hall makes its own dark and wheat brews, serves tasty sausages, and has a bustle-fun atmosphere during big sports events. ✉ *Rooms 1–3 and 2–2, 32 Qingchunfang* ☎ *0571/5666–0999.*

Vesper Bar (炼金术 *Liàn Jīn Shù*)
BARS/PUBS | This intimate cocktail bar has great views from the second-story balcony, as well as an impressive range of whiskeys. The bartender can also whip up inventive cocktails inspired by Hangzhou, like the Foggy West Lake, in which Shaoxing yellow wine is mixed with tequila and a homemade syrup made with Chinese spices. ✉ *7 Paomachang Lu* ☎ *0571/8880–9701.*

The best souvenirs to buy in Hangzhou are green tea and silk, but all sorts of wooden crafts, silk fans and umbrellas, and antiques are sold in small shops sprinkled around town. For the best longjing tea, head to Dragon Well Tea Park or the China Tea Museum.

China Silk Town (中国丝绸城 *Zhōngguó sīchóuchéng*)
CLOTHING | On either side of a nearly 4,000-foot-long pedestrian street, the stalls and shops of China Silk Town sell silk ties, pajamas, and shirts, plus silk straight off the bolt. ✉ *227 Xinhua Lu, between Fengqi Lu and Jiankang Lu* ☎ *0571/8510–0192.*

★ **Hefang Jie** (河坊街 *Héfāng jiē*)
SHOPPING NEIGHBORHOODS | Also known as Qinghefang Historic Block, Hefang Street is a lively, crowded pedestrian street that's not to be missed on a visit to Hangzhou. Restored old buildings are beautifully illuminated at night and house tea shops, traditional apothecaries, and boutiques selling *qipaos* (traditional silk Chinese dresses), scrolls, calligraphy, and wooden fans. Artists draw caricatures, candy makers sculpt sugar into art, blind masseurs alleviate tension, and storytellers re-create ancient Chinese legends. Start at Wushan Square and walk west. At night the glowing Chenghuang Pavilion, perched on a mountaintop next to the square, is enchanting. ✉ *Hefang Jie, enter at Wushan Square.*

Wushan Night Market (吴山夜市 *Wúshān yèshì*)
OUTDOOR/FLEA/GREEN MARKETS | The Wushan Night Market has stalls selling late-night local snacks as well as those purveying accessories of every kind—ties, scarves, pillow covers—knockoff designer goods, and imitation antiques. It's open nightly from around 6. ✉ *Huixing Lu, near Renhe Lu.*

Xihu Longjing Tea Company (西湖龙井茶叶有限公司 *Xīhú lóngjǐng cháyè yǒuxiàn gōngsī*)
FOOD/CANDY | A few blocks north of the China Tea Museum, the Xihu Longjing Tea Company has a nice selection of the famed longjing (Dragon Well) tea. ✉ *38 Lingyin Lu* ☎ *0571/8796–2219.*

Shaoxing

64 km (40 miles) east of Hangzhou.

Shaoxing is alive in the Chinese imagination thanks to the famous writer Lu Xun, who set many of his classic works in this sleepy southern town. A literary revolutionary, Lu Xun broke tradition by writing in the vernacular of everyday Chinese, instead of the stiff, scholarly prose previously held as the only appropriate language for literature.

Today, much of the city's charm is in exploring its narrow cobbled streets. The older sections of the city are made up of low stone houses connected by canals crisscrossed by arched bridges. East Lake is no match for the grandeur of Hangzhou's West Lake, but its bizarre rock formations and caves make for interesting tours. Shaoxing is also famous for its celebrated yellow rice wine, used by cooks everywhere.

GETTING HERE AND AROUND

The most reliable and comfortable way to travel to Shaoxing is by train. Regular train and luxury bus services run to Shaoxing from Hangzhou and Shanghai a few times a day.

Trains between Hangzhou and Shaoxing take about 20 minutes, from Hangzhou's East station to Shaoxing's North station. It's a little farther out of the city than Shaoxing's Central train station, but the ultramodern trip is an impressive example of China's sophisticated railway system. Spring for business or

One of Shaoxing's famous waterways

first-class seats for just a few more yuan (Y15–Y63).

Although Shaoxing is small enough that walking is the best way to get between many sights, the city's small red taxis are relatively inexpensive. Most trips are Y15–Y30.

TIMING

Shaoxing's major attractions can be seen in a day trip from Hangzhou, but don't rush: the city's slow pace and historic charm can fill two full days if you move at a leisurely pace.

Sights

★ **Bazi Bridge** (八字桥 *Bāzíqiáo*)
BRIDGE/TUNNEL | In a city of bridges, the Bazi Bridge is the finest and best known. Its long, sloping sides rise to a flat crest that looks like the character for eight, an auspicious number. The bridge is more than 800 years old, built in the Southern Song Dynasty, and is draped with a thick beard of ivy and vines. It sits in a quiet area of old stone houses with canal-side terraces where people wash clothes and chat with neighbors. ✉ *Bazi Qiao Zhi Jie, off Renmin Zhong Lu.*

Catholic Church of St. Joseph (St. Joseph 天主教堂 *Tiānzhǔ jiàotáng*)
RELIGIOUS SITE | Near the Bazi Bridge is the bright pink Catholic Church of St. Joseph, dating from the turn of the 20th century. A hybrid of styles, the Italian-inspired interior is decorated with Bible passages written in Chinese calligraphy. ✉ *Bazi Qiao Zhi Jie, off Renmin Zhong Lu.*

East Lake (东湖 *Dōng hú*)
BODY OF WATER | The narrow East Lake runs along the base of a rocky bluff rising up from the rice paddies. The crazily shaped cliffs were used as a rock quarry over the centuries, and today their sheer gray faces jut out in sheets of rock. You can hire a local boatman to take you along the base of the cliffs in a traditional black awning boat for around Y50. ✉ *Yundong Lu, 5 km (4 miles) east of city center.*

What's Cooking

Shaoxing secured its place in the Chinese culinary pantheon with Shaoxing wine, the best yellow rice wine in the country. Although cooks around the world know the nutty-flavored wine as a marinade and seasoning, in Shaoxing the fermented brew of glutinous rice is put to a variety of uses, from drinking straight up (as early as breakfast) to sipping as a medicine (infused with traditional herbs and remedies). Like grape wines, Shaoxing mellows and improves with age, as its color deepens to a reddish brown. It is local custom to bury a cask when a daughter is born and serve it when she marries.

The wine is an excellent accompaniment to Shaoxing snacks such as pickled greens, baked rice cakes, and the city's most popular street food, *chou doufu* (stinky tofu). Usually paired with a bright red chili sauce, the golden-fried squares of tender tofu have a pleasant flavor and texture, if you can get past the pungent odor. Also, look for dishes made with another Shaoxing product, fermented bean curd, colloquially known as "moldy bean curd." With a flavor not unlike an aged cheese, it's rarely eaten by itself but complements fish and sharpens the flavor of meat dishes.

Former Residence of Cai Yuanpei (蔡元培故居 *Càiyuánpéi gùjū*)
HOUSE | The city's quiet northern neighborhoods are great places to wander, with several historic homes and temples that are now preserved as museums. The largest is Cai Yuanpei's house. Once the president of Peking University, Cai was a famous democratic revolutionary and educator during the republic, and his family's large compound is decorated with period furniture. ✉ *13 Bifei Nong, off Xiaoshan Lu* ☎ *0575/8511–0652* 🎫 *Y5.*

Lu Xun Native Place (鲁迅故居 *Lüxùn gùjū*)
HOUSE | As its name implies, Lu Xun Native Place is devoted to the literary giant and social critic Lu Xun. In this historic quarter, visit the Lu Xun Family Home (*241 Luxun Zhong Lu, 0575/8513–2084; free entry, passport required*), where the writer was born. His extended family lived around him in a series of courtyards, and today, you can tour this traditional Shaoxing home and see some beautiful antique furniture. ■ **TIP→ To avoid the crowds, visit in the morning or early evenings.** Down the street is the local school where Lu honed his writing skills, as well as a large square and a memorial that's dedicated to the famed writer. ✉ *235 Luxun Zhong Lu, 1 block east of Xianhen Hotel.*

Yanyu Tea House (雁雨茶艺馆 *Yànyǔ cháyì guǎn*)
STORE/MALL | This idyllic little teahouse sits right along one of Shaoxing's famous waterways. The historic building is a little musty, but the antique furniture, artwork, drapes and meticulous tea service is an experience in itself. Ask for snacks, and you'll be rewarded with assorted bowls of fresh cherry tomatoes, dates, seeds, and regional fruits. ✉ *Huanshan Rd., right across from park called City Plaza* ☎ *0575/8511–5102.*

Zhou Enlai Family Home (周恩来故居 *Zhōu ēnlái gùjū*)
HOUSE | The Zhou Enlai Family Home belonged to the first premier of Communist China, who came from a family of prosperous Shaoxing merchants. Zhou is credited with saving some of China's

most important historic monuments from destruction at the hands of the Red Guards during the Cultural Revolution. The compound, a showcase of traditional architecture, houses exhibits on Zhou's life, ranging from his high-school essays to vacation snapshots with his wife. ✉ *369 Laodong Lu* ☎ *0575/8513–3368* 🎫 *Y18.*

Restaurants

Xianheng Winehouse (咸亨酒店 *Xánhēng jiüdiàn*)
$$ | CHINESE | More than 100 years old, this popular, buzzing cafeteria is where the writer Lu Xun's most famous fictional character, small-town scholar Kong Yiji, would sit on a bench, sipping wine and eating boiled beans. The beans aren't for everyone, though they're worth a try, as are the fermented bean curd and the pork belly with dried veggies—local delicacies that pair well with a bowl of Shaoxing rice wine. **Known for:** historical and literary landmark; often crowded, especially on weekends; local food and flavor. $ *Average main: Y50* ✉ *179 Lu Xun Zhong Lu, 1 block east of the Sanwei Jiulou* ☎ *0575/8522–3317* 💳 *No credit cards.*

Xunbaoji Zhuangyuan Restaurant (寻宝记状元楼 *Xúnbǎo jì zhuàngyuán lóu*)
$$ | CHINESE | Get here early or risk waiting in line for the famous Shaoxing delicacies, including the ubiquitous stinky tofu, pork belly with dried vegetables, and chicken cooked in local wine. **Known for:** authentic but chaotic; picture-menus to help you order; picturesque historic district setting. $ *Average main: Y50* ✉ *114 Cangqiaozhi Jie* ☎ *0575/8522–3317.*

Hotels

New Century Grand Hotel Shaoxing (绍兴开元名都大酒店 *Shàoxīng kāiyuán míng dū dà jiǔdiàn*)
$ | HOTEL | The New Century's contemporary rooms are decorated in muted shades with pops of bright red and have bathrooms equipped with rain showers. **Pros:** comfy beds and sleek baths; free Wi-Fi; good value for the money. **Cons:** a little removed from major sites; indifferent service; limited English; rooms in need of a revamp. $ *Rooms from: Y458* ✉ *278 Remin Dong Lu* ☎ *0575/8809–8888* 🌐 *www.sxkymd.com* *355 rooms* 🍴 *Breakfast.*

★ **Xianheng Hotel** (绍兴咸亨大酒店 *Shàoxīng xiánhēng dà jiǔdiàn*)
$ | HOTEL | Though it's difficult to prove the Xianheng's claims that it's the province's first eco-friendly hotel, other things about it are undeniable: its traditionally accented rooms are plush and comfortable, its setting amid courtyards with canals is pretty, and its Chinese-style spa has extensive facilities and services. **Pros:** centrally located; reasonably priced; free Wi-Fi. **Cons:** spotty English; could do with a refresh; quality varies from room to room (ask to see yours before booking). $ *Rooms from: Y448* ✉ *179 Lu Xun Zhong Lu* ☎ *0575/8806–8688* 🌐 *www.xianhengchina.com* *217 rooms* 🍴 *Breakfast.*

Shopping

Lu Xun Zhong Lu (鲁迅中路 *Lǔxùn zhōng lù*)
LOCAL SPECIALTIES | In addition to calligraphy brushes, and fans, scrolls, and other items decorated with calligraphy, this street has several shops selling the local tin wine pots. In the traditional way of serving yellow rice wine, the pots are placed on the stove to heat up wine for a cold winter's night. Also popular are traditional boatmen's hats, made of thick waterproof black felt. ✉ *Shaoxing.*

Ningbo

150 km (95 miles) southeast of Hangzhou; 220 km (136 miles) south of Shanghai.

Ningbo is one of the country's biggest ports and most prosperous cities. It's an easy place to explore on foot. Rivers and canals flow through a city that is generously sprinkled with tranquil gardens and parks. Colonial architecture and centuries-old pagodas and temples are mixed (rather unfortunately) with featureless, Eastern Bloc apartment blocks and hideous glass and steel towers. Unlike Shanghai, Hangzhou, and Suzhou, Ningbo is not set up for tourism. This makes it a relaxing and authentic place to explore. Join the locals for bottomless cups of tea and mah-jongg in one of the many parks, or burn through some cash in the city's lively markets, ritzy shopping malls, and trendy nightclubs.

Ningbo, translated as "tranquil waves," sits at the confluence of three rivers (the Yuyao, the Fenghua, and the Yong) that snake their way to the nearby sea. Ningbo's history stretches back thousands of years. In the 7th century, the Tang Dynasty developed a complicated system of canals, and trade with Japan and Korea boomed. The Portuguese, with their keen eye for location, settled in as early as the 16th century, and left behind a fair number of churches that are still in use today. More recently, during the Second World War, the Japanese bombed the city with fleas carrying the bubonic plague.

GETTING HERE AND AROUND

It's best to travel by rail, as express trains connect Ningbo with both Hangzhou (1 hour) and Shanghai (1¾ hours). If you prefer to take a bus, there is a steady stream heading to Hangzhou, Shanghai, and beyond, departing from the South Bus Station (across the street from the Asia Garden Hotel) every 10–15 minutes from 6 am to 8 pm. Be aware that buses can get stuck in traffic and that drivers are prone to somewhat reckless driving.

A 25-minute drive from downtown is Ningbo's Lishe International Airport. There are connections to all major Chinese cities, as well as Hong Kong and Seoul. Major hotels offer free airport shuttle buses. An airport-bound bus (Y12) leaves from the CAAC office every hour from 7 am to 6 pm.

Taxis are cheap and plentiful. Areas of interest are not far apart and should cost no more than Y15, with about Y50 to the airport.

TIMING

Ningbo has enough to occupy you for two full days, but the major attractions can be seen in one day. The city center is compact and can be explored on foot.

Drum Tower (鼓楼 *Gŭlóu*)
BUILDING | This large yellow pavilion, complete with a medieval clock tower, was built in AD 821. Climb to the top for a bird's-eye view of the city. The tower marks the entrance to Gulou Pedestrian Street, lined with restored Ming Dynasty–style buildings. Here you'll find tiny shops, makeshift stalls, every kind of local snack imaginable, as well as, of course, McDonald's. It's an ideal spot for people-watching. ✉ *Gongyuan Lu and Zhongshan Xi Lu* 🎫 *Free.*

Jiangbei Catholic Church (江北基督教圣教堂 *Jiangbei sheng jiao tang*)
RELIGIOUS SITE | Home to China's highest percentage of Christians, Ningbo has several active churches. Marking the beginning of the Laowaitan district, this church was built by the Portuguese in 1872 and is considered to be the best preserved in Zhejiang Province. Sunday morning services are well attended and welcoming. ✉ *2 Zhong Ma Lu, Laowaitan* ☎ *0574/8735–5903* 🎫 *Free.*

Moon Lake (月湖 *Yuè hú*)
CITY PARK | The lovely park that surrounds this 1,400-year-old lake is dotted with quaint teahouses and pavilions with upturned eaves. Weeping willows line crooked paths that wrap around bamboo groves. In addition to being a peaceful place for a leisurely stroll, the park is centrally located in the city center and a useful point of reference. ✉ *Yanyue Lu, near Yaohang Jie* ☎ *0574/8386–8555.*

Tianfeng Pagoda (天封塔 *Tiān fēng tǎ*)
RELIGIOUS SITE | Seven stories high, this ancient hexagonal structure was first built in AD 695, then destroyed and rebuilt several times over. The current building was finished in the 14th century and is surrounded by a tiny garden complete with gigantic rocks and several inviting stone benches. For a great view of the pagoda, walk directly across the street from the main entrance, enter the market, and walk up to the second floor. Continue climbing to the top for only Y5 and you'll be rewarded with panoramic cityscapes. ✉ *Near intersection of Jiefang Nan Lu and Kaiming Jie* ☎ *0574/8729–4523* 🎟 *Y5.*

★ **Tianyi Pavilion** (天一阁 *Tiān yī gé*)
BUILDING | Down a peaceful alley off Changchun Lu, the Tianyi Pavilion is the oldest private library in China. Built in 1596 and founded by politician Fan Qin, this spiritual place features gold-plated, wood-paneled buildings, bamboo groves, pools, and a rockery. The scholarly setting, worth a visit for the architecture alone, preserves an atmosphere of seclusion and contemplation. ✉ *10 Tianyi Lu, west of Moon Lake* ☎ *0574/8729–3856* 🌐 *www.tianyige.com.cn* 🎟 *Y30.*

Zhongshan Park (中山公园 *Zhōngshān gōngyuán*)
CITY PARK | In one of Ningbo's most delightful parks, winding stone paths snake over arched bridges, and slender canals flow past pavilions and teahouses. During the humid summer months, the city's senior citizens fan themselves with oversized paper fans, crack sunflower seeds, gossip, and drink tea. Impromptu groups of musicians huddle together; old men play traditional Chinese instruments as women belt out ear-piercing renditions of Chinese opera. This is a wonderful place to relax and soak up the atmosphere. ✉ *Gongyuan Lu, end of Drum Tower pedestrian street* 🎟 *Free.*

Restaurants

★ **Gang Ya Gou** (缸鸭狗 *Gāng yā gǒu*)
$$ | **CHINESE** | There's no better place to sample the city's famous *tangyuan* (multicolor sugar dumplings served in a bowl of syrup and eaten like soup) than Gang Ya Gou. To get here, look for the hard-to-miss logo depicting a dog and a duck fighting over a pot of rice—or simply follow the crowds. **Known for:** tofu pancakes; crabmeat dumplings; local favorite. $ *Average main: Y55* ✉ *68 Shuijing Jie, Tianyi Sq.* ☎ *0574/8908–1926* 💳 *No credit cards.*

★ **Lebanese Restaurant** (黎巴嫩餐厅 *Líbānèn cāntīng*)
$$ | **LEBANESE** | On the eastern edge of Moon Lake, this Middle Eastern restaurant has consistently excellent food. One bite of the olive-oil-and-pine-nut-drizzled hummus, and you'll be hooked. **Known for:** favorite of the city's Islamic community; delicious lamb kebabs and fresh mint yogurt; English-language picture menu. $ *Average main: Y55* ✉ *320 Zhenming Lu* ☎ *0574/8731–5861.*

Vegetarian Lifestyle (枣子树净素餐厅 *Zǎozǐ shù jìng sù cāntīng*)
$ | **VEGETARIAN** | The spinach dumplings and mock-meat dishes served at this vegetarian restaurant are as nourishing as they are delicious. Ordering is a breeze, thanks to an English-language picture menu. **Known for:** outpost of a renowned Shanghai restaurant; refreshing house-made juices; no-smoking policy enforced (unusual in China). $ *Average main: Y45* ✉ *16 Liuting Jie, 2nd fl.*

⊕ *Inside Yifu Theater building; entrance just east of big China Construction Bank branch* ☎ *0574/8730–1333* ▭ *No credit cards.*

Zhuang Yuan Lou Restaurant (状元楼酒店 *Zhuàngyuánlóu jiǔdiàn*)

$$$$ | **CHINESE** | At this restaurant on the Yu Yao River, near the He Yi shopping complex's western end, you step through gigantic red-and-gold doors into an antiques-filled dining room, where hostesses in elaborate silk dresses welcome you. The Ningbo cuisine is as traditional as the setting: steamed turtle, fried yellow-fish with fresh blueberries, pork ribs. **Known for:** quality and freshness; opulent decor; convenient location. Ⓢ *Average main: Y200* ✉ *He Yi Shopping Center, He Yi Lu* ☎ *0574/2796–6666* ▭ *No credit cards.*

Hotels

★ **Shangri-La Ningbo** (香格里拉酒店 *Xiānggélǐlā jiǔdiàn*)

$ | **HOTEL** | Overlooking the confluence of three rivers, Ningbo's most opulent international hotel offers personalized service, first-rate facilities, and elegantly appointed rooms with floor-to-ceiling windows that frame urban panoramas. **Pros:** sleek indoor lap pool; outdoor tennis courts; free Wi-Fi. **Cons:** mandatory bathing cap in the pool; loud lobby area; tour groups can flood the facilities. Ⓢ *Rooms from: Y850* ✉ *88 Yuyuan Jie* ☎ *0574/8799–8808* ⊕ *www.shangri-la.com/ningbo* *562 rooms* *No meals.*

Sheraton Ningbo (喜来登酒店 *Xǐláidēng jiǔdiàn*)

$ | **HOTEL** | A massive marble lobby features an unusual spiky chandelier, and spiral staircases lead to guest rooms at this hotel, whose excellent service and convenient location make it an ideal base from which to explore the city. **Pros:** impressive breakfast buffet; free Wi-Fi; free shuttle to Shanghai. **Cons:** busy lobby; aging facilities. Ⓢ *Rooms from: Y950* ✉ *50 Caihong Bei Lu* ☎ *0574/8768–8688* ⊕ *www.starwoodhotels.com* *378 rooms* *Free Breakfast.*

Sofitel Wanda

$ | **HOTEL** | Next to popular shopping complex Wanda Plaza, the Sofitel Wanda combines French flair and touches of Chinese culture for a sophisticated result. **Pros:** friendly staff; impressive breakfast buffet; nice spa. **Cons:** inconsistent service; outside city center. Ⓢ *Rooms from: Y600* ✉ *899 Siming Zhong Lu* ☎ *0574/2889–9888* ⊕ *www.sofitel.com* *291 rooms* *No meals.*

Nightlife

If you're looking for a fun night out, head over to Laowaitan, the city's entertainment strip and Ningbo's pint-size answer to Shanghai's Bund. It's designed to look like a mini European city, complete with cobblestone streets. The charming setting is popular with local couples who come here to take wedding photos.

Bar Constellation

BARS/PUBS | One of the better bars on Laowaitan has earned a following thanks to its romantic ambience and professional pourers. The whisky list is more like a tome, with more than 150 brands, including familiar faces like Maker's Mark alongside more exotic options such as Nikka from Japan. You can even enjoy a Cuban cigar while you're at it. ✉ *72 Renmin Lu, Laowaitan* ☎ *0574/8765–8280.*

O'Reilly's Pub (奥赖利爱尔兰酒吧 *Ào lài lì ài'ěrlán jiǔbā*)

BARS/PUBS | For a low-key evening, head to the warm and welcoming O'Reilly's Pub, which has Guinness and Strongbow Cider on tap, a hodgepodge of Irish paraphernalia on the walls, and tasty Western bar grub. There's often live Celtic, folk, and pop music. ✉ *46–9 Caihong Bei Lu* ☎ *0574/8770–4282.*

Off the Path

Putuo Mountain. On this tiny island, only 12½ square km (8 square miles), is Putuoshan, one of China's four sacred Buddhist mountains. Legend has it that a 9th-century Japanese monk got caught in a storm, and Guanyin, the Buddhist goddess of mercy, miraculously appeared and guided him safely to the mountain. In thanks, he erected Puji Si, the area's most famous temple, of which there are more than 30. The island can easily be explored on foot and completely circumnavigated in a day. Take time to lounge on Thousand Step Beach, photograph the enormous 108-foot-high bronze Guanyin statue, eat fresh seafood, and climb Putuoshan (or take the cable car) for fabulous island vistas. The population is only between 3,000 and 4,000, about 1,000 of whom are monks and nuns. Getting to the island is fairly easy, with frequent boats leaving from Ningbo's wharf. The island can get crowded, so avoid weekends and holidays.

Shopping

Antiques Market Curio Bazaar (宁波市范宅古玩集市 *Níngbō shì fàn zhái gǔwàn jí shì*)
ANTIQUES/COLLECTIBLES | Small clusters of galleries and stalls here sell a variety of jade pieces and antique bric-a-brac of varying levels of authenticity. Chinese scrolls with traditional watercolor paintings and kitschy Mao-era memorabilia make good souvenirs. Bargain hard; prices are inflated for tourists. ✉ *85–97 Zhongshan Xi Lu.*

Gulou Pedestrian Street (鼓楼步行街 *Gǔlóu bùxíngjiē*)
ANTIQUES/COLLECTIBLES | If you head east down Zhongshan Xi Lu to Gulou (drum tower) Pedestrian Street, you'll come to a row of restored buildings packed with everything from inexpensive DVDs to tea to ceramics. In between the busy shops, there's the odd restaurant and night club. The area can get pretty crowded on weekends, but it is a great place to soak up modern Chinese culture while shopping for souvenirs. ✉ *Gulou Pedestrian St., between Zhongshan Xi Lu and Zhongshan Park.*

Heyi Avenue (和義大道購物中心 *Héyì dàdào gòuwù zhòngxīn*)
SHOPPING NEIGHBORHOODS | Ningbo's crème de la crème shop for luxury items at posh Heyi Avenue stores such as Gucci, Dior, Armani, Montblanc, and Swarovski. There's plenty of riverfront dining and nightlife, too. ✉ *66 Heyi Lu.*

Tianyi Square (天一广场 *Tiānyī guǎngchǎng*)
SHOPPING NEIGHBORHOODS | Just east of the Tianfeng Pagoda is the Tianyi Square shopping-and-entertainment complex, a popular local meeting point, thanks to plentiful outdoor seating around a central fountain. There's also a slew of electronics and fashion outlets and a wide selection of fast-food and low-key local restaurants (don't miss the Ningbo dumplings at Gang Ya Gou). If you need a break from the crowds, look for the enormous Yaohang Street Catholic Church just outside the square. ✉ *88 Zhongshan Dong Lu.*

Xiamen

262 km (163 miles) southwest of Fuzhou by car; 469 km (291 miles) northeast of Hong Kong by air.

Dating from the late 12th century, Xiamen is a new city by Chinese standards. It was a stronghold for Ming loyalist Zheng Chenggong (better known as Koxinga), who later fled to Taiwan after China was overrun by the Qing. Xiamen's place as a dynasty-straddling city continues to this day due to its proximity to Taiwan. Some see Xiamen as a natural meeting point between the two sides in the decades-long separation. Only a few miles out to sea are islands that still technically belong to the Republic of China, as Taiwan is officially known in Mainland China.

Today, Xiamen is one of the most prosperous cities in China, with beautiful parks, impressive temples, and waterfront promenades that neatly complement historic architecture. Since around 2014, it has also cultivated a reputation as an increasingly "cool" city, with young fashion designers and artists choosing to live here, away from the bustle of bigger cities.

Just off Xiamen's west coast, the small island of Gulangyu makes a fun day trip. Its pleasant parks, gardens, statues, museums, and colonial-style buildings draw huge numbers of visitors, though, so it's best to come early on a weekday. The attractions are well signposted; the main ones, such as the Piano Museum inside the charming Shuzhuang Garden, can be accessed with a Y100 combo ticket available from booths outside site entrances. To reach the island take a 25-minute ferry ride from the second floor of the Xiamen Ferry port (Y50 round-trip, passport required).

GETTING HERE AND AROUND

The best way to reach Xiamen is by plane. The city is accessible by long-distance trains and buses, but these entail much longer travel times.

Xiamen Gaoqi International Airport, one of the largest and busiest in China, lies about 10 km (6.2 miles) northeast of the city. A taxi from downtown should cost no more than Y50, and takes between 20 and 30 minutes, depending on traffic. Most carriers service Xiamen, which has connections to many cities in China and international destinations like Bangkok, Kuala Lumpur, Jakarta, Manila, Penang, Singapore, and Amsterdam. A popular regional carrier is Xiamen Airlines.

Xiamen has luxury bus service to all the main cities along the coast as far as Guangzhou and Shanghai. There are two long-distance bus stations.

Xiamen North Train Station, about a half-hour taxi ride from the main Xiamen island, handles high-speed trains in and out of the city. It takes about 11 ½ hours to get to or from Beijing, four hours for Shenzhen, eight hours for Wuhan, and between five and eight hours for Shanghai. Although the more central Xiamen Station was renovated in 2016, it doesn't handle high-speed trains to or from major cities.

In Xiamen, taxis can be found around hotels or on the streets; they're a convenient way to visit the sights on the edge of town. Taxi drivers rarely speak any English, so make sure your addresses are written in Chinese. For farther-flung destinations, it is common to hire a taxi for an hour or two (about Y120 per hour) so you don't get stranded.

TIMING

Xiamen is a very pleasant city, well worth a few days of exploring and hiking. Much cleaner and more environmentally conscious than other Chinese cities, it's a great place to recharge and take in some fresh air.

Bright Moon Garden (皓月园 *Hàoyuè yuán*)
GARDEN | This sculpture garden on the southeastern tip of Gulangyu Island is a fitting seaside memorial to Zhen Chenggong, also known as Koxinga, a famous Ming general who fought to protect China from the invading Manchus. A massive stone statue of him stares eastward from a perch hanging over the sea. ✉ *3 Zhangzhou Lu, Gulangyu* 🎫 *Y15.*

Ding'aozai Cat Street
NEIGHBORHOOD | In 2014, Xiamen-based artist Guo Mingming decided that the Ding'aozai area, a short walk from the university district attractions, was boring and launched a project to liven it up with a plethora of paintings and statues of cats. Now the stretch is a fun, feline-filled, selfie mecca–filled, with little coffee shops and restaurants. Also, don't miss the Xiamen Cat Museum (400 Siming Nan Lu), which is more of a shop, really, but which has a gang of cats living in a weird train carriage–like house. ✉ *Xiamen* ✣ *Ding'aozai* ☎ *0592/2084–065 to Xiamen Cat Museum.*

Hakka Roundhouses (客家土楼 *Kéjiā tǔlóu*)
ARCHAEOLOGICAL SITE | Legend has it that, when these huge doughnut-shape residential structures were first spotted by the American military, fear spread that they were silos for some massive unknown missile site. Many were created centuries ago by the Hakka, an offshoot of the Han Chinese who settled all over southeastern China. Peppering the countryside of Yong Ding, 225 km (140 miles) northwest of Xiamen, these beautiful examples

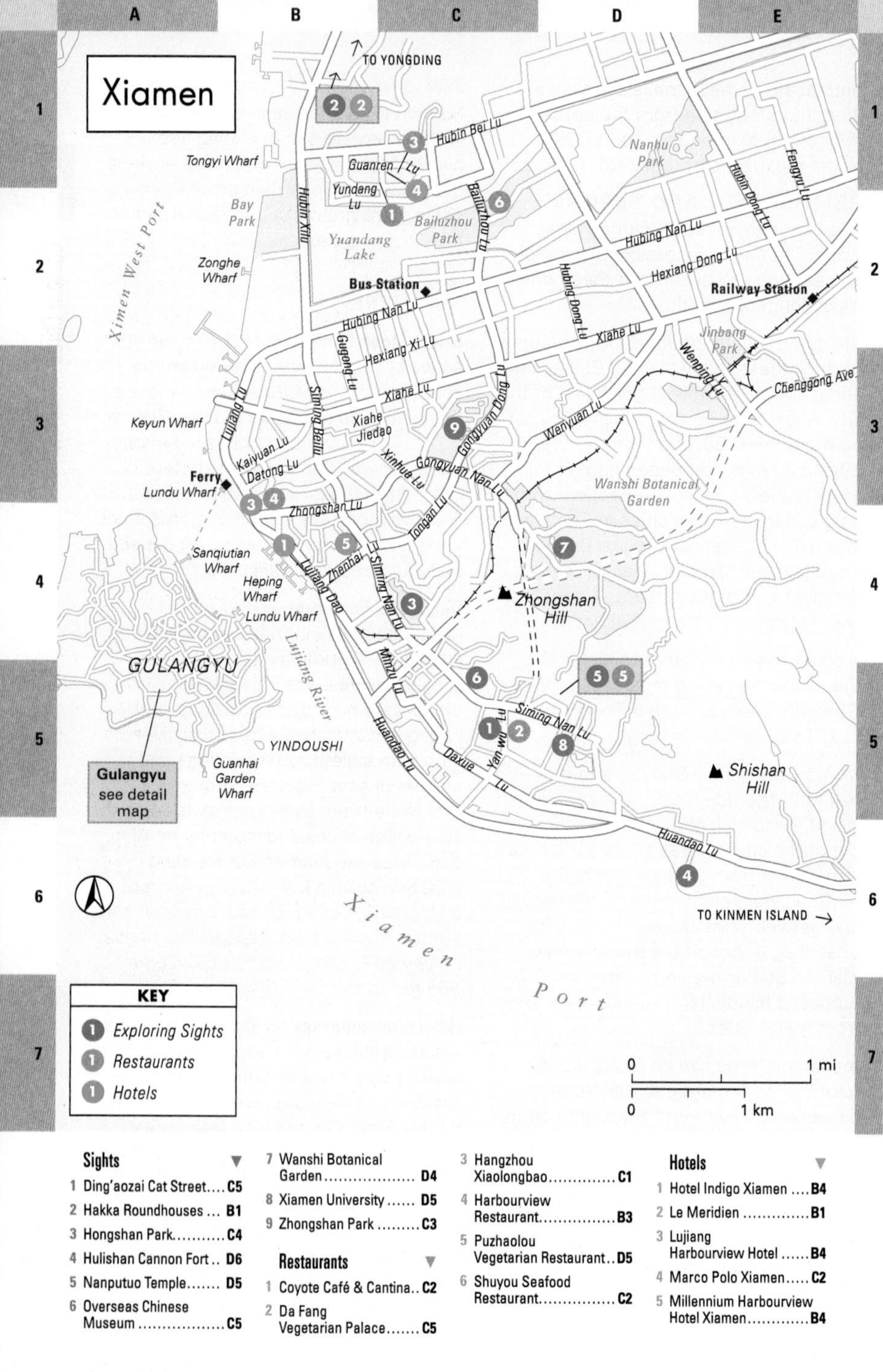

Sights

1 Ding'aozai Cat Street.... **C5**
2 Hakka Roundhouses ... **B1**
3 Hongshan Park........... **C4**
4 Hulishan Cannon Fort .. **D6**
5 Nanputuo Temple....... **D5**
6 Overseas Chinese Museum **C5**
7 Wanshi Botanical Garden **D4**
8 Xiamen University **D5**
9 Zhongshan Park **C3**

Restaurants

1 Coyote Café & Cantina.. **C2**
2 Da Fang Vegetarian Palace....... **C5**
3 Hangzhou Xiaolongbao.............. **C1**
4 Harbourview Restaurant................ **B3**
5 Puzhaolou Vegetarian Restaurant.. **D5**
6 Shuyou Seafood Restaurant................ **C2**

Hotels

1 Hotel Indigo Xiamen **B4**
2 Le Meridien **B1**
3 Lujiang Harbourview Hotel **B4**
4 Marco Polo Xiamen..... **C2**
5 Millennium Harbourview Hotel Xiamen............. **B4**

of Hakka architecture are made of raw earth, sand, brown sugar and glutinous rice, reinforced with bamboo and wood. Joining a tour group or hiring a private car is your best option for getting to one. ✉ *Yong Ding.*

Hongshan Park (**鸿山公园** *Hóngshān gōngyuán*)
CITY PARK | Built into a hillside, Hongshan Park has a small Buddhist temple, a lovely waterfall, and beautiful views of the city and the harbor. The steep park shoots straight up from a busy street, so wear comfortable shoes if you're eager to explore. ✉ *Siming Nan Lu, one block east of Zhenhai Lu* 🎫 *Free.*

Huaijiu Gulangyu Museum (**珍奇世界** *Zhēn qí shí jié*)
MUSEUM | Throughout its various exhibition spaces, the truly unique Gulangyu Nostalgia Museum highlights the history of Fujian and Taiwan and showcases furnishings, decorative arts, curios, and curiosities. ✉ *38 Huangyan Lu, Gulangyu* ☎ *0592/206–9933* 🎫 *Y60.*

Hulishan Cannon Fort (**胡里山砲台** *Húlǐshān pàotái*)
HISTORIC SITE | A symbol of China's westernization in the 19th and 20th centuries, Hulishan Cannon Fort was built with help from Germany. When constructed in 1894, the fort was considered one of China's most technologically advanced fortresses and served as the central command of the coast. It also played a major part in the defense against the Japanese in 1900 and 1937, thanks, in part, to two massive, 19th-century, German Krupp cannons. Today, the fortress retains its east-meets-west architectural style, with beautiful views of the coast, a castle, and one of the famed cannons. Regular performances by horseback riders dressed in old-fashioned military attire help bring history to life here. ✉ *2 Huandao Lu* ☎ *0592/208–8313* 🎫 *Y25.*

Nanputuo Temple (**南普陀寺** *Nán pǔtuó sì*)
RELIGIOUS SITE | Dating from the Tang Dynasty, Nanputuo Temple has roofs decorated with brightly painted clusters of flowers and statues of sinewy serpents and mythical beasts. It has been restored many times, most recently in the 1980s, with more touch-ups in recent years. Pavilions on either side of the main hall contain tablets commemorating the suppression of secret societies by Qing Dynasty emperors. As the most important of Xiamen's temples, it is nearly always buzzing as monks and worshippers mix with tour groups. The latter often miss the intriguing small statues embedded in stone crannies behind the back of the main complex. ✉ *Siming Nan Lu, next to Xiamen University* 🌐 *www.nanputuo.com/npten* 🎫 *Free.*

Overseas Chinese Museum (**华侨博物馆** *Huáqiáo bówùguǎn*)
MUSEUM | Housed in an imposing cream-color building, this museum was founded by wealthy industrialist Tan Kah Kee. With pictures and documents, personal items, and associated relics, three large halls tell the story of the great waves of emigration from southeastern China during the 19th century. ✉ *493 Siming Nan Lu* ☎ *0592/208–4028* 🎫 *Free* 🕑 *Closed Mon.*

Piano Museum (**钢琴博物馆** *Gāngqín bówùguǎn*)
MUSEUM | Gulangyu holds a special place in the country's musical history, thanks to the large number of Christian missionaries who called the island home in the late 19th and early 20th centuries. Gulangyu has more pianos per capita than anyplace else in China, and the Piano Museum houses more than 70 beautifully preserved instruments that were once owned by famous pianists. Tucked away up a steep hill in the Shuzhuang Garden, this charming collection is a must for any music lover. ✉ *45 Huangyan Lu, Gulangyu* ☎ *0592/206–0238* 🎫 *Y30, included in Shuzhuang Garden ticket.*

Continued on page 304

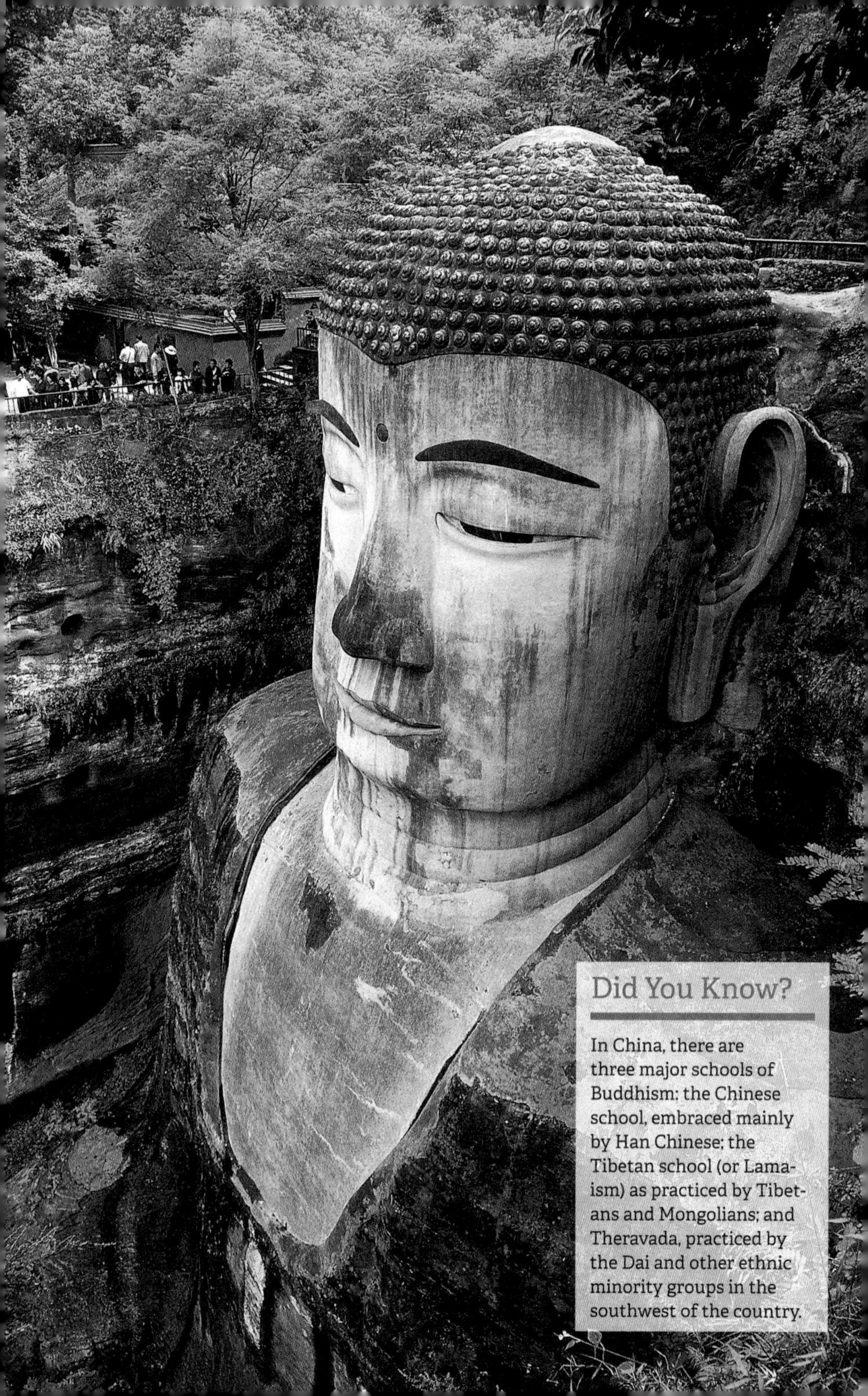

Did You Know?

In China, there are three major schools of Buddhism: the Chinese school, embraced mainly by Han Chinese; the Tibetan school (or Lamaism) as practiced by Tibetans and Mongolians; and Theravada, practiced by the Dai and other ethnic minority groups in the southwest of the country.

SPIRITUALITY IN CHINA

Even though it's officially an atheist nation, China has a vibrant religious life. What are the differences between China's big three faiths of Buddhism, Taoism, and Confucianism? Like much else in the Middle Kingdom, the lines are often blurred.

Walking around the streets of any city in China, it's hard to believe that only four decades ago the bulk of the Middle Kingdom's centuries-old religious culture was destroyed by revolutionary zealots, and that the few temples, mosques, monasteries, and churches that escaped outright destruction were desecrated and turned into warehouses and factories, or put to other ignoble uses. Those days are long over, and religion in China has sprung back to life. Even though the official line of the Chinese Communist Party is that the nation is atheist, China is rife with religious diversity.

Perhaps the faith most commonly associated with China is Confucianism, an ethical and philosophical system developed from the teachings of the sage Confucius. Confucianism stresses the importance of relationships in society and of maintaining proper etiquette. These aspects of Confucian thought are associated not merely with China (where its modern-day influence is dubious at best, especially in a crowded subway car), but also with East Asian culture as a whole. Confucianism also places great emphasis on filial piety, the respect that a child should show an elder (or subjects to their ruler). This may account for Confucianism's status as the most officially tolerated of modern China's faiths.

Taoism is based on the teachings of the *Tao Te Ching,* a treatise written in the 4th century BC, and blends an emphasis on spiritual harmony with that of the individual's duty to society. Taoism and Confucianism are complementary, though to the outsider, the former might seem more steeped in ritual and mysticism. Think of it this way: Taoism is to Confucianism as Catholicism is to Protestantism. Taoism's mystic quality may be why so many westerners come to China to study "the way," as Taoism is sometimes called.

Buddhism came to China from India in the second century AD and quickly became a major force in the Middle Kingdom. The faith is so ingrained here that many Chinese openly scoff at the idea that the Buddha wasn't Chinese.

Buddhism teaches that the best way to alleviate suffering is to purify one's mind.

TIPS FOR TEMPLE VISITS

■ Chinese worshippers are easygoing. Even at the smallest temple or shrine, they understand that some people will be visitors and not devotees. Temples in China have relaxed dress codes, but you should follow certain rules of decorum:

■ You're welcome to burn incense, but it's not required. If you do decide to burn a few joss sticks, take them from the communal pile and be sure to make a small donation. This usually goes to temple upkeep or local charities.

■ Be careful when shaking lit incense.

■ Respect signs reading no photo in front of altars and statues. Taoist temples seem particularly sensitive about photo taking. When in doubt, ask.

■ Avoid stepping in front of a worshipper at an altar or censer (where incense is burned).

■ Speak quietly and silence mobile phones inside of temple grounds.

■ Don't touch Buddhist monks of the opposite sex.

■ Avoid entering a temple during a ceremony.

TEMPLE OBJECTS

For many, temple visits are among the most culturally edifying parts of a China trip. Large or small, Chinese temples incorporate a variety of objects significant to religious practice.

INCENSE

Incense is the most common item in any Chinese temple. In antiquity, Chinese people burned sacrifices both as an offering and as a way of communicating with spirits through the smoke. This later evolved into a way of showing respect for one's ancestors by burning fragrances that the dearly departed might find particularly pleasing.

BAGUA

Taoist temples will have a bagua: an octagonal diagram pointing toward the eight cardinal directions, each representing different points on the compass, elements in nature, family members, and more esoteric meanings. The bagua is often used in conjunction with a compass to make placement decisions in architectural design and in fortune telling.

"GHOST MONEY"

Sometimes the spirits need more than sweet- smelling smoke, and this is why many Taoists burn "ghost money" (also known as "hell money" or "joss"), a scented paper resembling cash. Though once more popular in Taiwan and Hong Kong (and looked upon as a particularly capitalist superstition on the mainland), the burning of ghost money is now gaining ground throughout the country.

CENSER

Every Chinese temple will have a censer in which to place joss sticks, either inside the hall or out front. Larger temples often have a number of them. These large stone or bronze bowls are filled with incense ash from hundreds of joss sticks placed by worshippers. Some censers are ornate, with sculpted bronze rising above the bowls.

STATUES

Visitors will find a variety of statues of deities and mythical figures. Confucius is usually rendered as a wizened man with a long beard, and Taoist temples have an array of demon deities.

PRAYER WHEEL

Used primarily by Tibetan Buddhists, the prayer wheel is a beautifully embossed hollow metal cylinder mounted on a wooden handle. Inside the cylinder is a tightly wound scroll printed with a mantra. Devotees believe that the spinning of a prayer wheel is a form of prayer that's just as effective as reciting the sacred texts aloud.

CHINESE ASTROLOGY

According to legend, the Jade Emperor wanted to designate an animal to each calendar year. As the animals rushed to be the first to arrive, the rat snuck a ride on the ox's back. Just as the ox was about to cross the threshold, the rat jumped past him and arrived first. This is why the rat was given first place in the astrological chart. Find the year you were born to determine what your astrological animal is.

RAT

1936 · 1948 · 1960 · 1972 · 1984 · 1996 · 2008 · 2020

Charming and hardworking, Rats are goal setters and perfectionists. Rats are quick to anger, ambitious, and lovers of gossip.

OX

1937 · 1949 · 1961 · 1973 · 1985 · 1997 · 2009 · 2021

Patient and soft-spoken, Oxen inspire confidence in others. Generally easygoing, they can be remarkably stubborn, and they hate to fail or be opposed.

TIGER

1938 · 1950 · 1962 · 1974 · 1986 · 1998 · 2010 · 2022

Sensitive, and thoughtful, Tigers are capable of great sympathy. Tigers can be short-tempered, and are prone to conflict and indecisiveness.

RABBIT

1939 · 1951 · 1963 · 1975 · 1987 · 1999 · 2011 · 2023

Talented and articulate, Rabbits are virtuous, reserved, and have excellent taste. Though fond of gossip, Rabbits tend to be generally kind and even-tempered.

DRAGON

1940 · 1952 · 1964 · 1976 · 1988 · 2000 · 2012 · 2024

Energetic and excitable, short-tempered and stubborn, Dragons are known for their honesty, bravery, and ability to inspire confidence and trust.

SNAKE

1941 · 1953 · 1965 · 1977 · 1989 · 2001 · 2013 · 2025

Snakes are deep, possessing great wisdom and saying little. Snakes are considered the most beautiful and philosophical of all the signs.

HORSE

1942 · 1954 · 1966 · 1978 · 1990 · 2002 · 2014 · 2026

Horses are thought to be cheerful and perceptive, impatient and hot-blooded. Horses are independent and rarely listen to advice.

GOAT

1943 · 1955 · 1967 · 1979 · 1991 · 2003 · 2015 · 2027

Wise, gentle, and compassionate, Goats are elegant and highly accomplished in the arts. Goats can also be shy and pessimistic, and often tend toward timidity.

MONKEY

1944 · 1956 · 1968 · 1980 · 1992 · 2004 · 2016 · 2028

Clever, skillful, and flexible, Monkeys are thought to be erratic geniuses, able to solve problems with ease. Monkeys are also thought of as impatient and easily discouraged.

ROOSTER

1945 · 1957 · 1969 · 1981 · 1993 · 2005 · 2017 · 2029

Roosters are capable and talented, and tend to like to keep busy. Roosters are known as overachievers, and are frequently loners.

DOG

1946 · 1958 · 1970 · 1982 · 1994 · 2006 · 2018 · 2030

Dogs are loyal and honest and know how to keep secrets. They can also be selfish and stubborn.

PIG

1947 · 1959 · 1971 · 1983 · 1995 · 2007 · 2019 · 2031

Gallant and energetic, Pigs have a tendency to be single-minded and determined. Pigs have great fortitude and honesty, and tend to make friends for life.

The Hakka Roundhouses were added to the UNESCO World Heritage List in 2008.

Shuzhuang Garden (菽庄花园 *Shūzhuāng huāyuán*)
GARDEN | This lovely, peaceful garden on Gulangyu is immaculately kept and dotted with pavilions and bridges, some extending out to rocks just offshore. Built in 1913 by a wealthy Taiwanese merchant, the garden is home to several key sights, including the Piano Museum and the Twelve Cave Paradise, which comprises 12 caves formed from multicolor sandstone. ✉ *Tianwei Lu, Gulangyu* 🎫 *Y30, includes entry to Piano Museum.*

Wanshi Botanical Garden (万石植物园 *Wàn shí zhíwùyuán*)
GARDEN | Surrounding a pretty lake at the base of Wanshi Mountain, this garden has a fine collection of more than 6,500 species of tropical and subtropical flora, ranging from eucalyptus and bamboo trees to orchids and ferns. Pathways wind past interesting rock formations, a rose garden, and several temples, including the notable Heaven's Border Temple. Don't miss the atmospheric "rain forest" section, and be sure to wear comfy shoes: this huge park is worth hours of exploration. ■ **TIP→ Soar over the park in a cable car (Y70 round-trip), embarking next to where the east end of Huxiyan Lu crosses Huyuan Lu, at the base of the mountain.** ✉ *Huyuan Lu, off Wenyuan Lu* 🎫 *Y40.*

Xiamen University (厦门大学 *Xiàmén dàxué*)
COLLEGE | Right by Nanputuo Temple, housed in an interesting mix of modern and traditional colonial buildings, is Xiamen University. It was founded in the 1920s with the help of Chinese living abroad. ■ **TIP→ For some peace and quiet, take a stroll here in the early morning.** ✉ *End of Siming Nan Lu, near Danan Lu* 🌐 *www.xmu.edu.cn* 🎫 *Free; bring ID.*

Zhongshan Park (中山公园 *Zhōngshān gōngyuán*)
CITY PARK | Commemorating Dr. Sun Yat-sen—who is known in Chinese as Sun Zhongshan—Zhongshan Park was built in 1927 and is centered on a bronze statue of the great man. It has a small zoo,

pretty lakes, and canals you can explore by paddleboat. The annual Lantern Festival is held here. ✉ *Zhongshan Lu and Zhenhai Lu* 🎫 *Free.*

Restaurants

Coyote Café and Cantina (凯奥特咖啡馆酒馆 *Kǎiàotè kāfēiguǎn jiǔguǎn*)
$$ | **MEXICAN** | The theme is heavy-handed, but Xiamen's most beloved Mexican restaurant serves steak fajitas and genuinely good burritos. Don't expect generous sides of sour cream or guacamole, but it won't matter after a few well-poured margaritas. **Known for:** attractive daily drink deals; friendly staff; local favorite. 💲 *Average main: Y75* ✉ *Yang Ming Bldg., 20–22 Jianye Lu* ☎ *0592/508–0737* 🌐 *www.coyotecafe.asia* 💳 *No credit cards.*

Da Fang Vegetarian Palace (大方素食馆 *Dà fāng sùshí guǎn*)
$ | **VEGETARIAN** | Don't opt for this restaurant just for its location down the street from the Nanputo Temple. Come for its house-special rice noodles, mock duck, or sizzling beef with pepper buns. **Known for:** reasonably priced dishes with English descriptions; friendly service; convenient location. 💲 *Average main: Y40* ✉ *3 Nanhua Lu, along Siming Nan Lu* ☎ *0592/209–3236* 💳 *No credit cards.*

★ **Hangzhou Xiaolongbao** (杭州小笼包 *Hángzhōu xiǎolóngbāo*)
$ | **CHINESE** | Thanks to its bright-red sign and big tower of steamers out front, this little hole-in-the-wall is easy to spot. Although the family who runs it doesn't speak English, they will happily play charades in an effort to take your order for dishes such as steamed Hangzhou-style *xiaolongbao* (soup dumplings). **Known for:** standout among foodstalls on Guanren Lu; well-seasoned pork; friendly owners. 💲 *Average main: Y20* ✉ *26 Guanren Lu* 💳 *No credit cards.*

★ **Harbourview Restaurant** (观海餐厅 *Guānhǎi cāntīng*)
$$$ | **SEAFOOD** | The Chinese chef at the rooftop restaurant in the waterfront Lujiang Harbourview Hotel prepares particularly good dim sum specialties like sweet pork buns and shrimp dumplings. The à la carte menu includes English descriptions and some pictures. **Known for:** stellar bay views from terrace area (book ahead to dine here); delicious seafood dishes; buffet-dining option. 💲 *Average main: Y150* ✉ *Lujiang Harbourview Hotel, 54 Lujiang Lu, 7th fl.* ☎ *0592/266–1398* 🌐 *www.lujiang-hotel.com.*

Puzhaolou Vegetarian Restaurant (普照楼素菜馆 *Pǔzhào lóu sù càiguǎn*)
$$ | **VEGETARIAN** | The comings and goings of monks add to the atmosphere at this restaurant next to Nanputuo Temple, where the menu isn't translated into English. Point to its few pictures or to items being served at other tables to order popular dishes such as black-mushroom soup with tofu and stewed yams with seaweed. **Known for:** nutritious and delicious food; authentic local atmosphere; long waits at peak hours. 💲 *Average main: Y75* ✉ *Nanputuo Temple, 515 Siming Nan Lu* ☎ *0592/208–5908* 🌐 *www.nptveg.com* 💳 *No credit cards.*

Shuyou Seafood Restaurant (舒友海鲜大酒楼 *Shū yǒu hǎi xiān dà jiū lóu*)
$$ | **SEAFOOD** | Downstairs at this loud, boisterous restaurant, tanks are filled with lobster, prawns, and crabs. Upstairs, diners feast on other types of dishes cooked in Cantonese and Fujian styles. **Known for:** extremely fresh seafood; popular with locals; also serves an excellent Peking duck. 💲 *Average main: Y100* ✉ *1 Bailuzhou Lu, near Swan Hotel Xiamen* ☎ *0592/533–0888.*

Hotels

Hotel Indigo Xiamen (**厦門海港英迪格酒店** *Xiàmén hǎigǎng yīngdígé jiǔdiàn*)
$ | **HOTEL** | Trendy travelers appreciate this boutique hotel's smart design, friendly service, space-efficient but comfortable (and colorful) rooms, and harborside location. **Pros:** friendly service; free Wi-Fi; some rooms have private terraces. **Cons:** lobby can get noisy; some city views; spotty check-in service. *$ Rooms from: Y900 ✉ 16 Lujiang Lu ☎ 0592/226–1666 🌐 www.ihg.com/hotelindigo 161 rooms 🍽 Free Breakfast.*

Le Meridien (**艾美酒店** *Ài měi jiǔdiàn*)
$ | **HOTEL** | **FAMILY** | With sweeping views of Xiamen Bay, this stunning, family-friendly property feels less like an urban Chinese hotel and more like a Southeast Asian resort—albeit one with sleek guest rooms decorated with mid-century-inspired pieces (think Barcelona chairs) and equipped with iPod docking stations and DVD players. **Pros:** lots of amenities for kids; good for sporty types; great natural setting. **Cons:** outside the city center; slow service; breakfast costs Y172. *$ Rooms from: Y720 ✉ 7 Guanjun Lu ☎ 0592/770–9999 🌐 www.lemeridien.com 342 rooms 🍽 No meals.*

★ **Lujiang Harbourview Hotel** (**鹭江宾馆** *Lùjiāng bīnguǎn*)
$ | **HOTEL** | In a nicely renovated colonial building, this hotel has an ideal location opposite the ferry pier and the waterfront boulevard; indeed, many of its stylishly furnished rooms have ocean views. **Pros:** phenomenal location; complimentary Wi-Fi; bike rental services. **Cons:** busy pedestrian intersection; hard to hail cab; rooms on the small side. *$ Rooms from: Y525 ✉ 54 Lujiang Lu ☎ 0592/202–2922 🌐 www.lujiang-hotel.com 153 rooms 🍽 No meals.*

Coffee Street

Coffee Street (**咖啡一条街** Kāfēi yītiáo jiē) If you need to take a break, the best place for coffee in Xiamen is on the waterfront outside the Marco Polo hotel. Along Yundang Lu, aka Coffee Street, you will find nearly five blocks of cafés—some more modern looking than others. *✉ Yundang Lu 💳 No credit cards.*

★ **Marco Polo Xiamen** (**马可波罗大酒店** *Mǎkěbōluó dà jiǔdiàn*)
$ | **HOTEL** | Sitting pretty between the historic sights and the commercial district, the Marco Polo is one of the best options for both business and leisure travelers. **Pros:** excellent location; helpful staff; right by a restaurant and bar hub. **Cons:** aging facilities; breakfast costs another Y138; area's expat scene might not appeal to some. *$ Rooms from: Y720 ✉ 8 Jianye Lu ☎ 0592/509–1888 🌐 www.marcopolo-hotels.com 153 rooms 🍽 No meals.*

Millenium Harbourview Hotel Xiamen (**厦门海景千禧大酒店** *Xiàmén hǎijǐng qiān xǐ dà jiǔdiàn*)
$ | **HOTEL** | Spacious and comfortable rooms, a friendly and attentive staff, and an excellent location overlooking the harbor make this hotel a practical base. **Pros:** excellent service; free Wi-Fi; some rooms recently refurbished. **Cons:** can be noisy; some rooms very dark. *$ Rooms from: Y730 ✉ 12–8 Zhenhai Lu ☎ 0592/202–3333 🌐 www.millenniumhotels.com/en/xiamen/millennium-harbourview-hotel-xiamen 353 rooms 🍽 Breakfast.*

Nightlife

Although the Zhongshan Lu pedestrian street near the ferry pier can be crazy-busy with tourists, it still has its nighttime charms: colonial-style buildings aglow with gentle neon and a waterfront

Sights

1 Bright Moon Garden...... D4

2 Huaijiu Gulangyu Museum C3

3 Piano Museum C4

4 Shuzhuang Garden...... C5

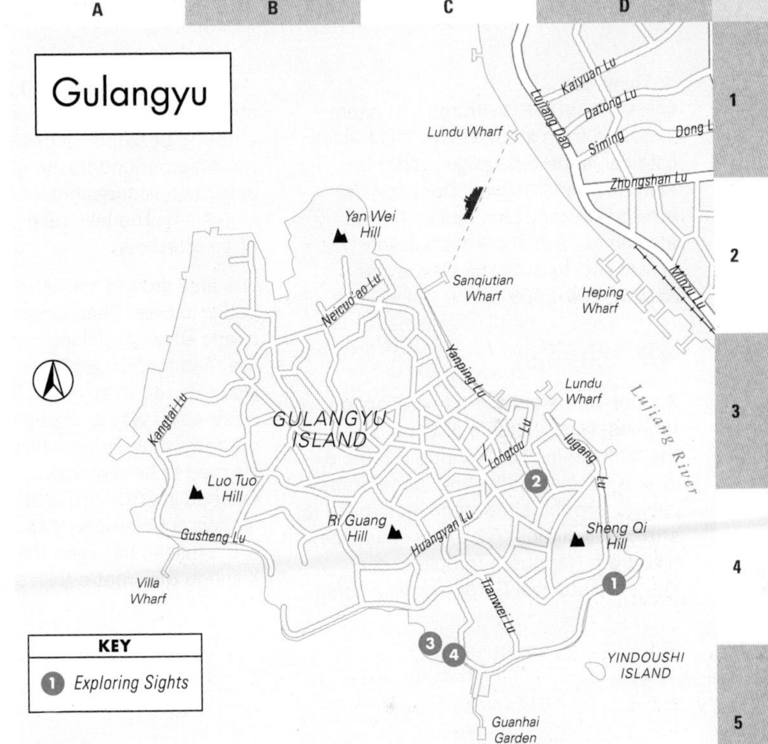

promenade where young couples walk arm in arm. Since its opening in 2014, however, the Shapowei Art Zone complex has become the city's "cool" spot.

Bay Park (海湾公园 *Hǎiwān gōngyuán*)
GATHERING PLACES | FAMILY | For a pleasant evening stroll, head north along the waterfront promenade and then take one of the tree-lined walkways into the center of this park. The nightly carnival here is great for kids, and there's a small street-food market next to a beautiful footbridge that connects with the Marco Polo Hotel. ✉ *Haiwan Park, off Hubin Xi Lu.*

Pub Street (槟榔酒吧街 *Bīnláng jiǔbā jiē*)
GATHERING PLACES | Make like the expats and head to Pub Street, on Guanren Lu behind the Marco Polo Hotel, where there are lively pubs and clubs to keep your thirst quenched. The favorite in town is the Londoner (5–8 Guanren Lu), voted the best bar for several years running, but there's something for all tastes. Most of the bars along this leafy strip have nice outdoor tables—particularly lovely in the spring and autumn when the humidity has died down. ✉ *Guanren Lu* ☎ *0592/508–9783 Londoner.*

Shapowei Art Zone
BARS/PUBS | Every night this trendy complex teems with drinkers, skateboarders and shoppers checking out its arty independent stalls. Inside, Fat Fat Beer Horse, a large craft beer hall in a converted fish processing plant, is one of China's coolest bars, architecturally speaking. There are also nightclubs and roof terrace bars inside the main building to the east of FFBH. ✉ *60 Daxue Jie* ☎ *187/5023–0350 to Fat Fat Beer Horse.*

★ Thank You

CAFES—NIGHTLIFE | With retro furniture imported from around Asia, this friendly café/bar is the top hangout spot for Xiamen's hip creatives. Decent Western-style brunch plus noodle dishes are served. Ask about the seasonal fruit cocktails. ✉ *162 Daxue Jie* ☎ *0592/208–2609.*

Xiamen offers excellent hiking opportunities. Most notable of these are the hills behind the Nanputuo Temple, where winding paths and stone steps carved into the sheer rock face make for strenuous climbs. For a real challenge, hike from Nanputuo Temple to the Wanshi Botanical Garden or vice versa. If you're still in the mood for a climb after spending a few hours enjoying the garden's beautiful landscape, another more serpentine trail (a relic of the Japanese occupation) leads to Xiamen University. The hike takes the better part of an afternoon.

The area around Xiamen has decent public shores. Beachgoers abound nearly anywhere along Huandao Lu, the road that circles the island, which is also referred to as Island Ring Road. A more novel way to experience the city's outdoors is to ride the bicycle skyway, claimed to be the world's longest. Opened in 2017, it runs above Xiamen's highways for around 9 kilometers (roughly 5½ miles), between the Hongwen and Xianhou BRT metro train stations.

Chapter 7

HONG KONG

Updated by
Kate Springer

Sights	Restaurants	Hotels	Shopping	Nightlife
★★★★☆	★★★★★	★★★★★	★★★★☆	★★★★☆

WELCOME TO HONG KONG

TOP REASONS TO GO

★ **Harbor views:** The skyline that launched a thousand postcards ... See it on a stroll along the Tsim Sha Tsui waterfront, from a Star Ferry crossing the harbor, or from atop Victoria Peak.

★ **Dim sum:** As you bite into a moist siu mai it dawns on you why everyone says you haven't done dim sum until you've done it in Hong Kong.

★ **Cultural immersion:** The Hong Kong Heritage Museum chronicles the city's history. On a Lantau Island hill, the 242-ton Tian Tan Buddha statue sits in the lotus position beside the Po Lin Buddhist Monastery.

★ **Shopping as religion:** In Kowloon's street markets, clothes, electronics, and souvenirs compete for space with food carts. Antiques fill windows along Hollywood Road.

★ **Horsing around:** Every year, Hong Kongers gamble billions of dollars, and the Happy Valley Racetrack is one of their favorite places to do it.

1 **Hong Kong Island.** It's only 78 square km (30 square miles), but it's where the action is, from high finance to nightlife to luxury shopping.

2 **Kowloon.** This peninsula on the Chinese mainland is just across from Central and bounded in the north by the string of mountains that give it its poetic name: *gau lung*, "nine dragons."

3 **Lantau Island.** Off the west coast of Hong Kong Island lies Lantau Island. Home to the Tian Tau Buddha, Lantau is connected by ferries to Hong Kong Island and by a suspension bridge to west Kowloon.

4 **New Territories.** The expanse between Kowloon and the Chinese border feels far removed from urban congestion and rigor. Nature reserves (many with great trails), temples, and traditional Hakka villages fill its 200 square miles.

5 **Macau.** Most people visit Macau to gamble in the Cotai area and to shop. But don't overlook its timeless charms and unique culture, born from centuries of both Portuguese and Chinese influence.

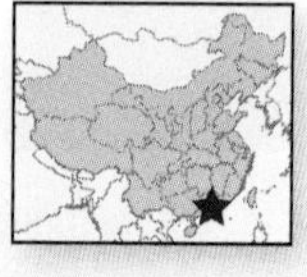

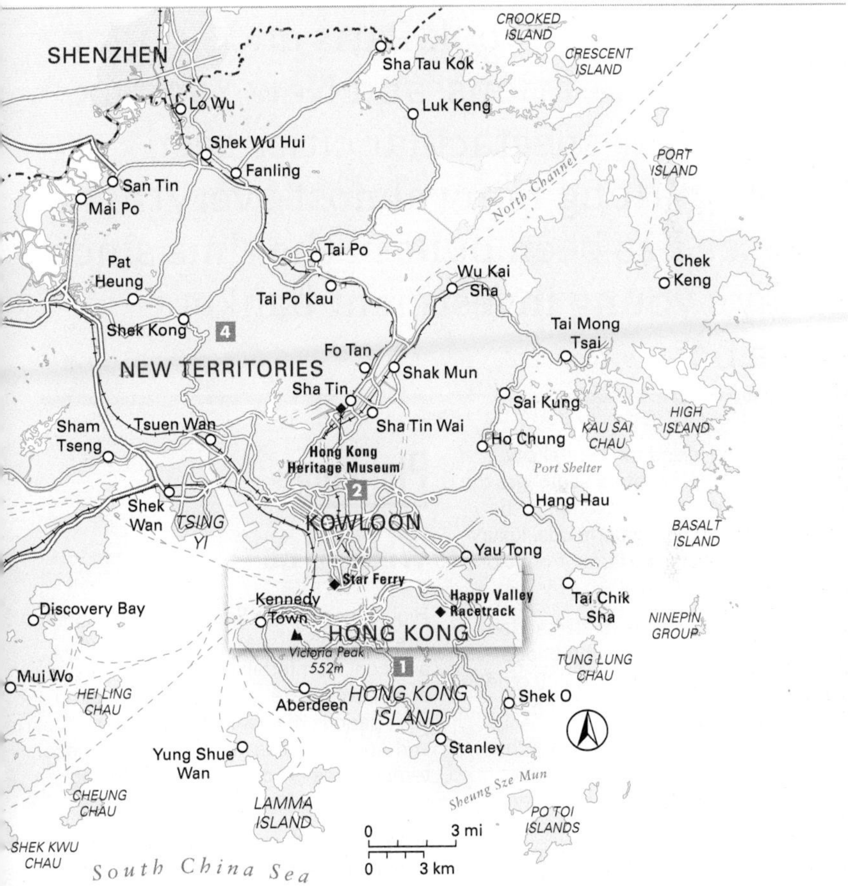

SHENZHEN
CROOKED ISLAND
CRESCENT ISLAND
Sha Tau Kok
Lo Wu
Luk Keng
Shek Wu Hui
Fanling
San Tin
Mai Po
PORT ISLAND
North Channel
Tai Po
Pat Heung
Tai Po Kau
Wu Kai Sha
Chek Keng
Shek Kong
4
Tai Mong Tsai
Fo Tan
NEW TERRITORIES
Shak Mun
Sha Tin
Sai Kung
Sham Tseng
Tsuen Wan
Sha Tin Wai
HIGH ISLAND
Ho Chung
KAU SAI CHAU
Hong Kong Heritage Museum
Port Shelter
2
Hang Hau
Shek Wan
TSING YI
KOWLOON
BASALT ISLAND
Yau Tong
Star Ferry
Kennedy Town
Happy Valley Racetrack
Tai Chik Sha
Discovery Bay
HONG KONG
NINEPIN GROUP
Victoria Peak 552m
1
TUNG LUNG CHAU
Mui Wo
HEI LING CHAU
Aberdeen
HONG KONG ISLAND
Shek O
Yung Shue Wan
Stanley
Sheung Sze Mun
CHEUNG CHAU
LAMMA ISLAND
PO TOI ISLANDS
0 3 mi
0 3 km
SHEK KWU CHAU
South China Sea

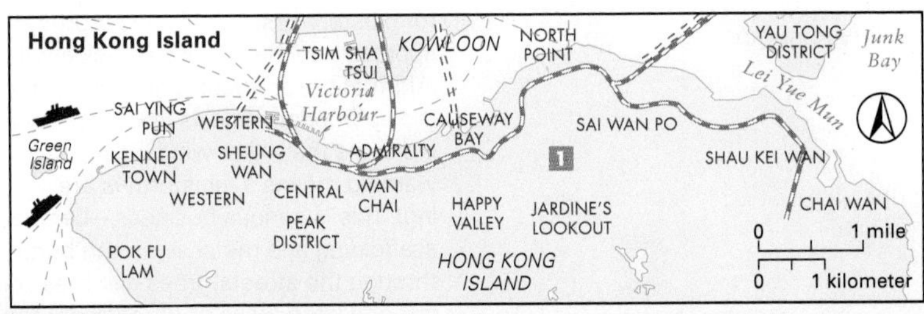
Hong Kong Island
TSIM SHA TSUI
KOWLOON
NORTH POINT
YAU TONG DISTRICT
Junk Bay
Victoria Harbour
Lei Yue Mun
SAI YING PUN
WESTERN
CAUSEWAY BAY
SAI WAN PO
Green Island
KENNEDY TOWN
SHEUNG WAN
ADMIRALTY
1
SHAU KEI WAN
WESTERN
CENTRAL
WAN CHAI
HAPPY VALLEY
JARDINE'S LOOKOUT
CHAI WAN
PEAK DISTRICT
0 1 mile
POK FU LAM
HONG KONG ISLAND
0 1 kilometer

The Hong Kong Island skyline, with its ever-growing number of skyscrapers, speaks to the triumph of ambition over fate. Whereas it took Paris and London 10 to 20 generations, and New York six, to build the spectacular cities seen today, in Hong Kong almost everything you see has been built in the time since today's young investment bankers were born.

On Hong Kong Island the central city goes only a few kilometers south into the island before mountains rise up. In the main districts and neighborhoods, luxury boutiques are a stone's throw from old hawker stalls.

West of Hong Kong Island, Lantau Island is connected by a suspension bridge to west Kowloon. More than 200 other islands also belong to Hong Kong.

Hong Kong's older areas—the southern side of Central, for example—show erratic street planning, but the newer developments and reclamations follow something closer to a grid system. Streets are usually numbered odd on one side, even on the other. There's no baseline for street numbers and no block-based numbering system.

Planning

When to Go

High season, from September through late December, sees sunny, dry days and cool, comfortable nights. January and February are mostly cool and damp, with periods of overcast skies. March and April are pleasant, and by May the temperature is consistently warm and comfortable.

June through August are the cheapest months for one reason: they coincide with the hot, sticky, and very rainy typhoon season. Hong Kong is prepared for blustery assaults; if a big storm approaches, the airwaves crackle with information, and your hotel will post the appropriate signals (a No. 10 signal indicates the worst winds; a black warning means a rainstorm is brewing). This is serious business—bamboo scaffolding and metal signs can hurtle through the streets, trees can break or fall, and large areas of the territory can flood. Museums, shops, restaurants, and transport shut down at signal No. 8, but supermarkets, convenience stores, and cinemas typically stay open.

Getting Here and Around

AIR TRAVEL

Modern, easy to navigate, and full of amenities, Hong Kong International Airport (HKG) is a traveler's dream. Terminal 1, the third-largest terminal in the world, services the departures for most major airlines, as well as all arriving flights. The newer but smaller Terminal 2 handles all other airlines, including budget carriers.

The Airport Express train service is the quickest and most convenient way to and from the airport. High-speed trains whisk you to Kowloon in 21 minutes and Central in 24 minutes. Citybus runs five buses ("A" precedes the bus number) from the airport to popular destinations. They make fewer stops than regular buses (which have an "E" before their numbers). Two useful routes are the A11, serving Central, Admiralty, Wan Chai, and Causeway Bay and ending in North Point; and the A21, going to Tsim Sha Tsui, Jordan, and Mong Kok.

Taxis from the airport are reliable and plentiful. Trips to Hong Kong Island destinations cost around HK$280–HK$320, while those to Kowloon are around HK$240. There is also an HK$5 charge per piece of luggage stored in the trunk.

BOAT AND FERRY TRAVEL

With fabulous views of both sides of Victoria Harbour, the Star Ferry is so much more than just a boat. It's a Hong Kong landmark in its own right, and has been running across the harbor since 1888. Double-bowed, green-and-white vessels connect Central and Wan Chai with Kowloon in less than 10 minutes, daily from 6:30 am to 11:30 pm.

BUS TRAVEL

An efficient network of double-decker buses covers most of Hong Kong. More intrepid visitors can take a chance on a minibus. These cream-colored vehicles seat 16–19 people and rattle through the city at breakneck speeds. Routes and prices are prominently displayed in front. While faster than buses, minibuses are risky if you aren't sure of your destination.

SUBWAY TRAVEL

By far the best way to get around Hong Kong is on the MTR, which now provides all subway and train services in Hong Kong. The network's trains are among the cleanest in the world, with hardly any litter to be found. Eating or drinking on the trains or in the paid areas is prohibited, with fines of HK$2,000.

The five major lines are color-coded for convenience. The Island line (blue) runs along the north coast of Hong Kong Island; the Tsuen Wan line (red) goes from Central under the harbor to Tsim Sha Tsui, then up to the western New Territories. Mong Kok links Tsim Sha Tsui to eastern New Kowloon via the Kwun Tong line (green). Also serving this area is the Tseung Kwan O line (purple), which crosses back over the harbor to Quarry Bay and North Point. Finally, the Tung Chung line (yellow) connects Central and West Kowloon to Tung Chung on Lantau, near the airport.

You can buy tickets from ticket machines (using coins or notes) or from English-speaking staff behind glass-windowed customer-service counters near the turnstile entrances. Fares range from HK$3 to HK$42.50, depending how far you travel. An alternative is the Tourist Day Pass. For HK$65, this pass allows you unlimited travel on the MTR, excluding the Airport Express, for one day. However, you cannot use the pass on other public transport or to purchase items.

TAXI TRAVEL

Taxis are easy to find in Hong Kong, although heavy rush hour traffic in Central, Causeway Bay, and Tsim Sha Tsui means they aren't always the best option for getting around the city quickly. They're most useful at other times of the day, especially after the MTR closes. Drivers usually know the terrain well, but many don't speak English; having your destination written in Chinese is a good idea.

TRAIN TRAVEL

The ultra-efficient MTR train network connects Kowloon to the eastern and western New Territories. Trains run every five to eight minutes, and connections to the subway are relatively quick. This is a commuter service and, like the subway, has sparkling-clean trains and stations—smoking, eating, and drinking are strictly forbidden.

TRAM TRAVEL

Old-fashioned double-decker trams have been running along the northern shore of Hong Kong Island since 1904. Most routes start in Kennedy Town or Western Market, and go eastward all the way through Central, Wan Chai, Causeway Bay, North Point, and Quarry Bay to Shau Kei Wan. A branch line turns off in Wan Chai toward Happy Valley, where horse races are held in season.

Destinations are marked on the front of each tram, and route maps are displayed at the stops; you board at the back and get off at the front, paying a flat rate of HK$2.60 as you leave.

Restaurants

Many restaurants in Hong Kong serve main dishes that are meant to be shared, so take this into account with respect to prices. When you get your check, don't be shocked that you've been charged for everything, including tea, rice, and those side dishes placed automatically on your table. At upmarket and Western-style restaurants tips are appreciated (10% is standard); the service charge on your bill doesn't always go to the staff.

Book ahead during Chinese holidays and the eves of public holidays, or at high-end hotel restaurants like Amber or Caprice. Certain classic Chinese dishes (especially beggar's chicken, whose preparation in a clay pot takes hours) or Peking duck require reserving not just a table but the dish itself. Do so at least 24 hours in advance. You'll also need reservations for a meal at one of the so-called private kitchens—unlicensed culinary speakeasies, which are often the city's hottest tickets. Book several days ahead, and be prepared to pay a deposit. Reservations are virtually unheard of at small, local restaurants.

A typical Hong Kong breakfast is often congee (a rice porridge), noodles, or plain or filled buns. Most hotels serve Western-style breakfasts, however, and coffee, pastries, and sandwiches are readily available at local coffee shops and Western cafés. Lunchtime is between noon and 2 pm; normal dinner hours are from 7 until 11 pm, but Hong Kong is a 24-hour city, and you'll be able to find a meal here at any hour. Dim sum can begin as early as 7:30 am and, though it's traditionally a daytime food, you'll find plenty of specialist restaurants that serve dim sum late into the evening.

What It Costs in Hong Kong Dollars

	$	$$	$$$	$$$$
RESTAURANTS	under HK$100	HK$100–HK$200	HK$201–HK$300	over HK$300

Hotels

Whether you're a business traveler or a casual tourist, you'll inevitably be caught up with the manic pace of life in Hong Kong. Luckily, hotels are constantly increasing their efforts to provide guests with a restful haven, often bundling spectacular views of the famous skyline and harbor with chic luxury, snazzy amenities, and soothing ambience.

From budget guesthouses to gleaming towers, you're sure to find a style and site to fit your needs. Prices tend to reflect quality of service and amenities as well as location, so it's worth the effort to examine neighborhoods closely when making your choice—you may end up paying the same to stay exactly where you want to be as you would to be off the beaten path.

The rock stars of Hong Kong's hotel industry are perfectly situated around Victoria Harbour, offering unobstructed harbor views, sumptuous spas, and reputable service to compete for the patronage of business-suited jet-setters, and any visitor willing to splurge for uncompromised luxury. Farther up the hills on both Kowloon and Hong Kong Island, cozy hotels seduce travelers who simply want a safe and practical place to crash in a trendy locale.

Travelers familiar with European cities might be surprised by the lack of provenance among Hong Kong hotels—the Peninsula passes as the venerable old-timer in this brashly new city where most hotels are perched in modern towers. And the scene keeps changing: Hong Kong's continued growth as a top tourist destination and business capital means that when it comes to choice of lodging, the next big thing is always around the corner.

Prices vary depending on season and occupancy. Most hotels offer their best rates and special offers on their websites—look for long-stay or advanced-purchase discounts, or for that matter, last-minute booking deals. Hong Kong's high seasons are generally May through June and October through November, though rates also go up during certain holiday periods and for events such as the Hong Kong Sevens rugby tournament or Art Basel in March. While many hotels put on lavish breakfast buffets, breakfast is usually extra and not included in basic room rates.

What It Costs in Hong Kong Dollars

	$	$$	$$$	$$$$
HOTELS	under HK$1,500	HK$1,500–HK$2,499	HK$2,500–HK$4,000	over HK$4,000

Nightlife

The neighborhoods of Wan Chai, Lan Kwai Fong, Sheung Wan, and SoHo are packed with bars, pubs, and nightclubs that cater to everyone from the hippest trendsetters to bankers ready to spend their bonuses and more laid-back crowds out for a pint. Partying in Hong Kong is a way of life; it starts at the beginning of the week with a drink or two after work, progressing to serious barhopping and clubbing on the weekends. Wednesday is a big night out here, too. Work hard, play harder is the motto in Hong Kong, and people follow it seriously.

Shopping

It's true that the days when everything in Hong Kong was mind-bogglingly cheap are over. It *is* still a tax-free port, so you can get some good deals. But it isn't just about the savings. Sharp contrasts and the sheer variety of experiences available make shopping here very different from back home.

You might find a bargain or two elbowing your way through a chaotic open-air market filled with haggling vendors selling designer knockoffs, the air smell of curried fish balls simmering at a nearby food stand. But then you could find lines outside luxury shops in a hushed marble-floor mall, the air scented by the designer fragrances of your fellow shoppers. What's more, in Hong Kong the two extremes are often within spitting distance of each other.

Visitor Information

For a guide to what's happening in Hong Kong, check out the Hong Kong Tourist Board's excellent website (🌐 *www.discoverhongkong.com/eng*).

Hong Kong Island

When you're on Hong Kong Island and feeling disoriented, remember that the water is always north. Central, Admiralty, and Wan Chai, the island's main business districts, are opposite Tsim Sha Tsui on the Kowloon Peninsula. West of Central are Sheung Wan and the other (mainly residential) neighborhoods that make up Western. Central backs onto the slopes of Victoria Peak, so the districts south of it—the Mid-Levels and the Peak—look down on it. Causeway Bay, North Point, Quarry Bay, Shau Kei Wan, and Chai Wan East run east along the shore after Wan Chai. Developments on the south side of Hong Kong Island are scattered: the beach towns of Shek O and Stanley sit on two peninsulas in the southeast, and industrial Aberdeen sits to the west.

Western

Despite its name, the Western District is the part of Hong Kong that has been least affected by Western influence. Many of the narrow, jammed streets that climb the slopes of Victoria Peak seem to be light-years from the dazzle of Central, just a 15-minute walk down the road. Though developers are making short work of the traditional architecture, Western's colonial buildings, rattling trams, old-world medicine shops, and lively markets still recall bygone times. Western is also a foodie's idea of heaven, as you'll soon discover when you step into Sheung Wan Market and Cooked Food Center on Queen's Road Central or browse the dried delicacies—abalone, bird's nests, sea cucumbers, mushrooms—in shops around Wing Lok Street and Des Voeux Road.

The Mid-Levels Escalator forms a rough boundary between Western and Central. Several main thoroughfares run parallel to the shore, each farther up the slope: Des Voeux Road (where the trams run), Queen's Road, Hollywood Road (where SoHo starts), and Caine Road (where Mid-Levels begin).

As to how far west Western goes, it technically reaches all the way to Kennedy Town, where the tram lines end, but there isn't much worth noting beyond Sheung Wan.

GETTING HERE AND AROUND

The most scenic way to Sheung Wan, Sai Ying Pun, and Kennedy Town is on a tram along Des Voeux Road. From Central or Admiralty it's probably the quickest, too: no traffic, no subway lines, no endless underground walks. There are stops every two or three blocks. The Island Line terminates in Kennedy Town, with Sheung Wan station bringing you within spitting distance of Western Market.

Sights

Hong Kong Museum of Medical Sciences

MUSEUM | You can find out all about medical breakthroughs at this private museum, which is housed in an Edwardian-style building at the top of Ladder Street. The 11 exhibition galleries cover

Shopping at the Western Market

10,000 square feet, and present information on both western and Chinese medical practices. ✉ *2 Caine La., Mid-Levels* ☎ *2549–5123* 🌐 *www.hkmms.org.hk* 🎟 *HK$10* Ⓜ *Central.*

★ University Museum and Art Gallery

MUSEUM | Set inside a heritage building, the peaceful rooms of this museum and gallery are filled with a small but excellent collection of Chinese antiquities. On view are ceramics and bronzes, some dating from 3,000 BC, as well as paintings, lacquerware, and carvings in jade, stone, and wood. Some superb ancient pieces include ritual vessels, decorative mirrors, and painted pottery. The museum has the world's largest collection of Nestorian crosses, dating from the Mongol Period (1280–1368). There are usually two or three well-curated temporary exhibitions on view; contemporary artists who work in traditional mediums are often featured. The collection is spread between the T.T. Tsui Building, where there is a Tea Gallery, and the Fung Ping Shan Building, which you access via a first-floor footbridge. The museum is a bit out of the way—20 minutes from Central via Buses 3B, 23, 40, 40M, or 103, or a five-minute uphill walk from Sheung Wan MTR—but it's a must for the true Chinese art lover. ✉ *University of Hong Kong, 90 Bonham Rd., Western* ☎ *2241–5500* 🌐 *www.umag.hku.hk* 🎟 *Free* Ⓜ *Sheung Wan.*

Western Market

BUILDING | The Sheung Wan district's iconic market, a hulking Edwardian-era brick structure, is a good place to get your bearings. Built in 1906, it functioned as a produce market for 83 years. Today it's a shopping center selling trinkets and fabrics—the architecture is what's worth the visit. Nearby you'll find herbal medicine on Ko Shing Street and Queen's Road West, dried seafood on Wing Lok Street and Des Voeux Road West, and ginseng and bird's nest on Bonham Strand West. ✉ *323 Des Voeux Rd. Central, Sheung Wan, Western* ☎ *6029–2675* 🌐 *www.westernmarket.com.hk* Ⓜ *Sheung Wan, Exit B or C.*

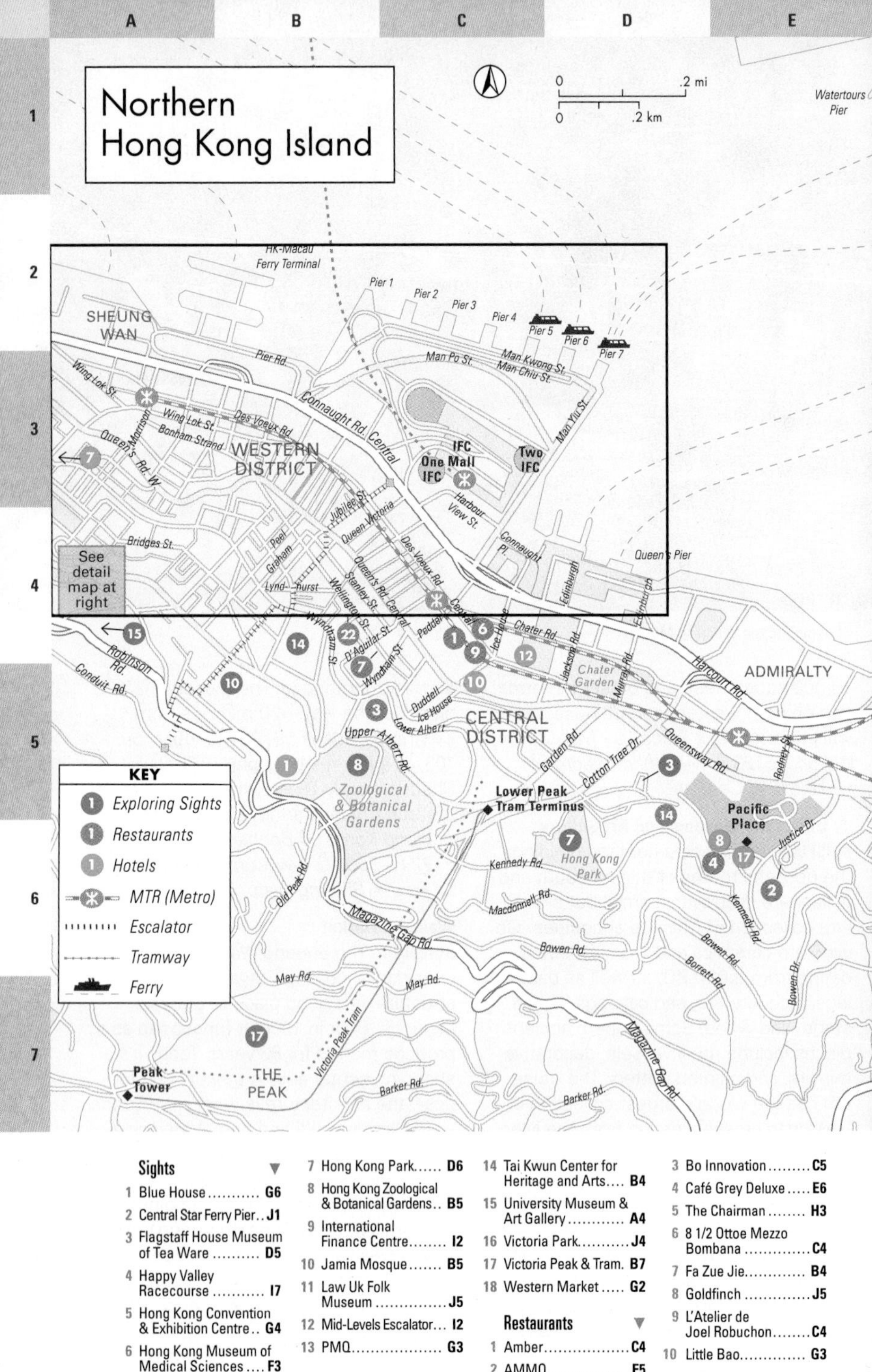

Sights

1 Blue House........... **G6**
2 Central Star Ferry Pier.. **J1**
3 Flagstaff House Museum of Tea Ware **D5**
4 Happy Valley Racecourse **I7**
5 Hong Kong Convention & Exhibition Centre.. **G4**
6 Hong Kong Museum of Medical Sciences **F3**
7 Hong Kong Park...... **D6**
8 Hong Kong Zoological & Botanical Gardens.. **B5**
9 International Finance Centre........ **I2**
10 Jamia Mosque....... **B5**
11 Law Uk Folk Museum **J5**
12 Mid-Levels Escalator... **I2**
13 PMQ.................. **G3**
14 Tai Kwun Center for Heritage and Arts.... **B4**
15 University Museum & Art Gallery............ **A4**
16 Victoria Park........... **J4**
17 Victoria Peak & Tram. **B7**
18 Western Market..... **G2**

Restaurants

1 Amber................. **C4**
2 AMMO................. **E5**
3 Bo Innovation......... **C5**
4 Café Grey Deluxe..... **E6**
5 The Chairman........ **H3**
6 8 1/2 Ottoe Mezzo Bombana **C4**
7 Fa Zue Jie............. **B4**
8 Goldfinch **J5**
9 L'Atelier de Joel Robuchon........ **C4**
10 Little Bao............. **G3**

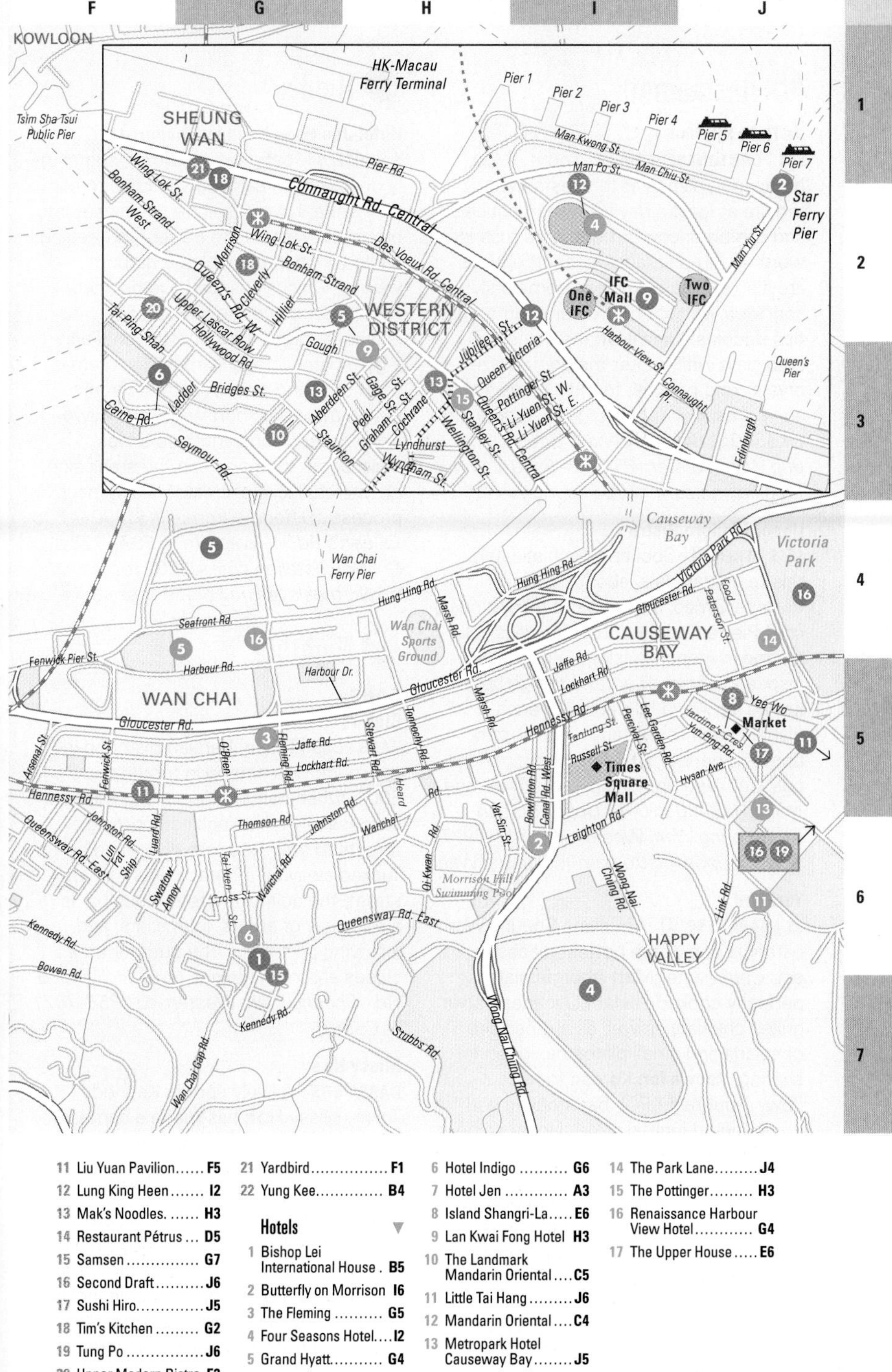

11 Liu Yuan Pavilion...... **F5**
12 Lung King Heen....... **I2**
13 Mak's Noodles. **H3**
14 Restaurant Pétrus ... **D5**
15 Samsen **G7**
16 Second Draft.......... **J6**
17 Sushi Hiro............. **J5**
18 Tim's Kitchen **G2**
19 Tung Po **J6**
20 Upper Modern Bistro. **F2**
21 Yardbird................ **F1**
22 Yung Kee............. **B4**

Hotels

1 Bishop Lei International House . **B5**
2 Butterfly on Morrison **I6**
3 The Fleming **G5**
4 Four Seasons Hotel.... **I2**
5 Grand Hyatt........... **G4**
6 Hotel Indigo **G6**
7 Hotel Jen **A3**
8 Island Shangri-La..... **E6**
9 Lan Kwai Fong Hotel **H3**
10 The Landmark Mandarin Oriental.... **C5**
11 Little Tai Hang **J6**
12 Mandarin Oriental **C4**
13 Metropark Hotel Causeway Bay........ **J5**
14 The Park Lane......... **J4**
15 The Pottinger......... **H3**
16 Renaissance Harbour View Hotel............ **G4**
17 The Upper House **E6**

Restaurants

★ Tim's Kitchen

$$$ | CANTONESE | FAMILY | Some of the homespun dishes at this restaurant require at least a day's advance notice and can be pricey, but the extra fuss is worth it. Simpler (and cheaper) options are also available, such as pomelo skin sprinkled with shrimp roe or panfried flat rice noodles. **Known for:** the signature crab claw with winter melon; fist-size crystal king prawns; friendly service and an impressive wine list. $ *Average main: HK$300* ✉ *84–90 Bonham Strand, Sheung Wan, Western* ☎ *2543–5919* 🌐 *www.timskitchen.com.hk* Ⓜ *Sheung Wan.*

Upper Modern Bistro

$$$$ | FRENCH | Cool and sophisticated, this restaurant is a labor of love for Philippe Orrico, a protégé of revolutionary chef Pierre Gagniare. Though classically trained in French cuisine, Orrico takes inspiration from all around the globe. **Known for:** Asian-influenced French dishes, such as Brittany oysters with ponzu; a perfect 63-degree egg; generous weekend brunch spread. $ *Average main: HK$400* ✉ *6–14 Upper Station St., Sheung Wan, Western* ☎ *2517–0977* 🌐 *www.upper-bistro.com* Ⓜ *Sheung Wan.*

Yardbird

$$ | JAPANESE | This bustling Sheung Wan eatery is one of the hottest places to eat. Chef-owner Matt Abergel plates perfectly cooked *yakitori* (Japanese-style grilled chicken) as well as a repertoire of salads and small plates designed for sharing. **Known for:** Korean fried cauliflower (dubbed KFC); bar stocked with house-brand junmai sake, Japanese beer, and whiskey; long waits and a no-reservations policy. $ *Average main: HK$150* ✉ *154–158 Wing Lok St., Sheung Wan, Western* ☎ *2547–9273* 🌐 *www.yardbirdrestaurant.com* ⏲ *No lunch. Closed Sun.* Ⓜ *Sheung Wan.*

Hotels

Hotel Jen Hong Kong by Shangri-La

$ | HOTEL | Most guest quarters, soothingly decorated in calming shades of cream and white, have cushioned seats set into bay windows that are perfect for reading while taking in the city and harbor views—which you may have plenty of time to do, since the surrounding area is quiet at night. **Pros:** rooftop pool and a gym with Victoria Harbour panoramas; MTR stop and numerous restaurants within minutes; short walk to Hollywood Road galleries and antiques shops. **Cons:** some rooms are on the small side; on-site bar lacks character; slow check-in process. $ *Rooms from: HK$1200* ✉ *508 Queen's Rd. W, Western* ☎ *2974–1234* 🌐 *www.hoteljen.com* *283 rooms* 🍴 *No meals* Ⓜ *HKU Station.*

Nightlife

BARS

Club 71

BARS/PUBS | This bohemian diamond-in-the-rough was named in tribute to July 1, 2003, when half a million Hong Kongers successfully rallied against looming threats to their freedom of speech. Tucked away on a terrace down a side street, the quirky, unpretentious bar is a mainstay of artists, journalists, and left-wing politicians. The outdoor area closes around midnight. ✉ *67 Hollywood Rd., Sheung Wan, Western* ☎ *2858–7071* Ⓜ *Central.*

Missy Ho's

BARS/PUBS | A lively spot in Kennedy Town, Missy Ho's has made a name for itself as much for the swing hanging from the ceiling and dress-up closet as for its Asian-inspired cocktails. Dark but inviting, it's the kind of place where the bartender will urge you to enjoy tequila shots on a Tuesday night. The crowd tends to be mostly young people looking to party, but all will feel welcome. A sign that Hong Kong's nightlife epicenter is moving ever westward, the bar comes into its own on weekends when it is often full to the brim with revelers. ✉ *Sincere Western House, 48 Forbes St., Kennedy Town, Western* ☎ *2817–3808* 🌐 *www.casteloconcepts.com.*

★ Ping Pong 129 Gintonería

BARS/PUBS | Hidden behind an unmarked red door is one of the coolest bars in up-and-coming Sai Ying Pun. Converted from an old table-tennis parlor, the basement space serves gin and tonics in authentic Spanish G&T balloon glasses and features works by local artists on the walls. It also offers an array of Spanish-inspired snacks. ✉ *Nam Cheong House, Basement, 129 2nd St., Western* ☎ *9835–5061* 🌐 *www.pingpong129.com* Ⓜ *Sai Ying Pun.*

GAY AND LESBIAN SPOTS

FLM

BARS/PUBS | A friendly, mixed crowd of gays, lesbians, and their friends enjoys this club's free admission and open-door policy. Thursday "game nights" are a staple of the scene, luring visitors and locals alike with alternating themes such as drag bingo, trivia, or karaoke. Weekends are reliably hyper, with dance anthems filling the floor until the wee hours. ✉ *62 Jervois St., Sheung Wan, Western* ☎ *2799–2883* 🌐 *www.flmhk.net* Ⓜ *Sheung Wan.*

Petticoat Lane

DANCE CLUBS | Championing inclusivity and eschewing labels, Petticoat Lane is a lively bar that's known to draw a diverse crowd. It's also a great place for a midweek pick-me-up: "Gay Night" every Wednesday promises topless bartenders and free vodka mixers from 11 pm to midnight. ✉ *Basement, 57–59 Wyndham St., Central* ☎ *2808–2738* 🌐 *www.petticoatlane.club* ☞ *Closed Sun. and Mon.* Ⓜ *Central.*

Shopping

ANTIQUES AND COLLECTIBLES

Yue Po Chai Antique Co

ANTIQUES/COLLECTIBLES | One of Hollywood Road's oldest shops is at the Cat Street end, next to Man Mo Temple. Its vast and varied stock includes porcelain, stone carvings, and ceramics. ✉ *Ground fl., 132 Hollywood Rd., Sheung Wan, Western* ☎ *2540–4374* ⏲ *Closed Sun.* Ⓜ *Sheung Wan, Exit A2.*

ART GALLERIES

★ Above Second

ART GALLERIES—ARTS | Known for its dynamic collections of graffiti-style art and illustrations, this contemporary urban art gallery in Sai Ying Pun is the only one of its kind in Hong Kong. Since opening in 2010, the gallery's rotating exhibits have included a mix of up-and-coming regional and international artists such as Daisuke Tajima, The London Police, and Pure Evil. You can take home original works or commission something new. ✉ *9 1st St., Western* ☎ *6330–7759* 🌐 *www.abovesecondgallery.com* Ⓜ *Sai Ying Pun.*

Asia Art Archive

ART GALLERIES | The AAA saw it before the rest of us: contemporary Asian art is big. In 2000, the Asian Art Archive set out to address the lack of information on the emerging field and to record its growth. It provides comprehensive research resources through its website, library, and reading facilities, which are open to the public. ✉ *11th fl., Hollywood Centre, 233 Hollywood Rd., Sheung Wan, Western* ☎ *2815–1112* 🌐 *www.aaa.org.hk* ⏲ *Closed Sun.* Ⓜ *Sheung Wan.*

CLOTHING

Grana

CLOTHING | Founded by Pieter Paul Wittgen and Luke Grana, this online-offline fashion company is known for must-have basics made with quality fabrics, such as Peruvian pima cotton, Japanese denim, French linen, and Mongolian cashmere.

Head over to The Fitting Room in Central to try on products first-hand, before placing an order online. Grana delivers internationally—a perfect solution for travelers who are fretting over suitcase space. That said, if you want to take home pieces instantly, make your way down to the warehouse in Wong Chuk Hang. ✉ *108 Hollywood Rd., Sheung Wan* ☎ *6013–2118* 🌐 *www.grana.com* Ⓜ *Sheung Wan.*

Lee Kung Man Knitting Factory

CLOTHING | This hole-in-the-wall shop has a surprisingly long history: it dates back to the early 1920s in Guangzhou, where the brand got its start before moving to Hong Kong. Lee Kung Man uses 1950's-era machines to make simple cotton tees and tanks, but the underwear is what brings shoppers flocking in. Despite a loyal hipster following, the store has kept prices relatively affordable, running between about HK$90 and HK$350 per top. Look for the signature cicada logo or the prancing deer at one of the four shops around town. ✉ *111 Wing Lok St., Sheung Wan, Western* ☎ *2543–8579* 🌐 *leekungman.com* Ⓜ *Sheung Wan, Exit A2.*

Vivienne Tam

CLOTHING | You know it when you walk into a Vivienne Tam boutique—the strong Asian-motif prints and modern updates of traditional women's clothing are truly distinct. But don't let the bold, ready-to-wear collections distract you from the very pretty accessories, which include leather handbags and other items with artistic embellishments. Tam, who has seven shops here, is one of the best-known designers in Hong Kong—and, even though she's now based in New York, the city still claims her as its own. ✉ *Shop SG03, PMQ, 35 Aberdeen St., Sheung Wan, Western* ☎ *2721–1818* 🌐 *www.viviennetam.com* Ⓜ *Central.*

MARKET

Western Market

OUTDOOR/FLEA/GREEN MARKETS | This red-brick Edwardian-style building in the Sheung Wan district is a declared monument and the oldest existing market building in Hong Kong; when built in 1906 it was used as a produce market. These days, kitschy commerce dominates its ground floor, where a few unmemorable shops sell crafts, toys, jewelry, and collectibles. Skip these, and head up the escalator, where you'll find a remarkable selection of fabric: satins, silks, and sequins are all here and worth a look. A more authentic experience is lunch, dinner, or high tea in the Grand Stage Ballroom Restaurant on the top floor. After a great Chinese meal, you can while away the afternoon with the old-timers trotting around the room to a live band belting out the cha-cha and tango. The restaurant is also a popular spot for weddings and receptions. Visit in the evening, and you're likely to snap up cashmere and chiffon while a violin sings overhead. ✉ *323 Des Voeux Rd., Sheung Wan, Western* ☎ *6029–2675* 🌐 *www.westernmarket.com.hk* Ⓜ *Sheung Wan.*

SHOES, HANDBAGS, AND LEATHER GOODS

Chateau Zoobeetle

JEWELRY/ACCESSORIES | As the only international outpost from French leather goods maison Zoobeetle Paris, this stylish Sheung Wan address combines a few of the best things in life: wine, cheese, charcuterie ... and accessories. Stop in for a glass of Burgundy, then shop for gleaming leather weekenders, ready-to-wear clothes, jewelery, books, wallets, and colorful clutches. ✉ *38 Sai St., Sheung Wan* ☎ *5331–5126* 🌐 *www.zoobeetle.com* Ⓜ *Sheung Wan.*

★ Select 18 and Mido Eyeglasses

JEWELRY/ACCESSORIES | Across from the sprawling Oolaa restaurant, two of Hong Kong's best vintage hangouts are in one convenient store. Select 18 has everything from typewriters to 1970s

Hermès blouses. If you can tear yourself from the heaps of jewelry and handbags, a treasure trove awaits. Tucked in back, you'll find literally thousands of retro-styled specs from Mido Eyeglasses, priced from a couple of hundred to several thousand Hong Kong dollars. The big question: tortoise-shell cat eyes or classic wayfarers? ✉ *18 Bridges St., Sheung Wan, Western* ☎ *2858–8803* Ⓜ *Sheung Wan, Exit A2.*

★ **Squarestreet**

SHOES/LUGGAGE/LEATHER GOODS | You might stumble upon this local gem while wandering around Sheung Wan's evolving Po Hing Fong neighborhood. Founded and designed by Stockholm native Alexis Holm and watch collector William Cheung, the low-key boutique features slick Scandinavian watches, eyewear, and accessories. ✉ *15 Square St., Sheung Wan, Western* ☎ *2362–1086* 🌐 *www.squarestreet.se* Ⓜ *Sheung Wan.*

Central

Shopping, eating, drinking—Central lives up to its name when it comes to all of these. But it's also Hong Kong's historical heart, packed with architectural reminders of the early colonial days. They stand in stark contrast to the soaring masterpieces of modern architecture for which the city is famous. Somehow the mishmash works. With the harbor on one side and Victoria Peak on the other, Central's views—once you get high enough to see them—are unrivaled. It's a hot spot for both locals and expatriates, packed with people, sights, and life.

The streets between Queen's Road Central and the harbor are laid out more or less geometrically. The south side of Queen's Road, however, is a confusion of steep lanes. Overhead walkways connect Central's major buildings, an all-weather alternative to the chaotic streets below.

GETTING HERE AND AROUND

Central MTR station is a mammoth underground warren with a host of far-flung exits. A series of "travelators" (escalators and inclined moving walkways) join it with Hong Kong Station, under the IFC Mall, where Tung Chung Line and Airport Express trains arrive and depart. Rattling old trams along Des Voeux Road reliably get you into Western, or as far east as Shau Kei Wan, with views along the way. Star Ferry vessels to Kowloon leave Pier 7 every 6 to 12 minutes.

Sights

Central Star Ferry Pier

MARINA | Take in the view of the Kowloon skyline on this pier, from which sturdy green-and-white Star Ferry vessels cross the harbor. Naturally, the views are even better from the open water. ✉ *Pier 7, Central Ferry Pier, Man Kwong St., Central* ☎ *2367–7065* 🌐 *www.starferry.com.hk* Ⓜ *Hong Kong Station.*

★ **Flagstaff House Museum of Tea Ware**

MUSEUM | All that's good about British colonial architecture is exemplified in this museum's simple white facade, wooden monsoon shutters, and colonnaded verandas. Hundreds of delicate tea sets from the Tang (618–907) through the Qing (1644–1911) dynasties fill rooms that once housed the commander of the British forces. **■ TIP→ Skip the lengthy, confusing tea-ceremony descriptions and concentrate on the porcelain pieces themselves.** Be on the lookout for the unadorned brownish-purple clay of the Yixing pots, whose beauty hinges on perfect form. ✉ *Hong Kong Park, 10 Cotton Tree Dr., Central* ☎ *2869–0690* 🌐 *www.lcsd.gov.hk* 🎫 *Free* 🕒 *Closed Tues.* Ⓜ *Admiralty.*

★ **Hong Kong Park**

CITY PARK | **FAMILY** | One of the prettiest parks in the city proper is a sprawling mix of rock gardens and leafy pathways. It's

Hop on the Peak Tram, the world's steepest funicular railway, and enjoy the views from Victoria Peak, arguably the city's most famous attraction.

common to stumble on locals practicing tai chi or reading in a secluded spot. This welcome respite from the surrounding skyscrapers occupies the site of a garrison called the Victoria Barracks, and some buildings from 1842 and 1910 are still standing. The park is home to the Flagstaff House Museum of Tea Ware and the Edward Youde Aviary. ✉ *19 Cotton Tree Dr., Central* ☎ *2521–5041* 🌐 *www.lcsd.gov.hk* 🎫 *Free* ⏲ *Closed mornings the 1st and 3rd Mon. of each month* Ⓜ *Admiralty, Exit C1.*

Hong Kong Zoological and Botanical Gardens

ZOO | FAMILY | This welcoming green space includes a children's playground and gorgeous gardens with more than 1,000 plant species, but the real attractions are the dozens of mammals housed in the zoo. If you're a fan of primates, look for rare sightings like the golden lion tamarin and the black-and-white ruffed lemur. Buses 3B, 12, and 13 run from various other stops in Central; the walk from the Central MTR stop is long and uphill. ✉ *Albany Rd., between Robinson and Upper Albert Rds., Central* ☎ *2530–0154* 🎫 *Free* Ⓜ *Central.*

International Finance Centre

BUILDING | One building towers above the Central skyline: Two IFC. The slender second tower of the International Finance Centre has been compared to at least one—unprintable—thing and is topped with a clawlike structure. Designed by Argentine architect Cesar Pelli, its 88 floors top a whopping 1,352 feet. Opposite stands its dinky little brother, the 38-floor One IFC. The massive IFC Mall stretches between the two, and Hong Kong Station is underneath. If you wish to see the breathtaking views from Two IFC, visit the 55th-floor Hong Kong Monetary Authority. While there, take a quick look at exhibits tracing the history of banking in Hong Kong. Upon arrival, you might need to register your passport with the concierge. ✉ *8 Finance St., Central* 🌐 *www.ifc.com.hk* 🎫 *Free* Ⓜ *Hong Kong Station, Exit A2.*

Jamia Mosque

RELIGIOUS SITE | The Mid-Levels Escalator zooms by the first mosque in Hong Kong. Commonly known as the Lascar Temple, the original 1840s structure was rebuilt in 1915 and shows its Indian heritage in the perforated arches and decorative facade work. The mosque isn't open to non-Muslims, but it occupies a small, verdant enclosure that's a welcome retreat. ✉ *30 Shelley St., above Caine Rd., Central* ☎ *2523–7743* 🌐 *www.amo.gov.hk* Ⓜ *Central, Exit D1.*

Mid-Levels Escalator

TRANSPORTATION SITE (AIRPORT/BUS/FERRY/TRAIN) | The unimaginatively named Mid-Levels district is halfway up the hill between the Western and Central districts and Victoria Peak. Running through it is the world's longest covered outdoor escalator, which connects to several main residential streets and walkways. Free of charge and protected from the elements, this series of moving walkways makes the uphill journey a cinch. Before 10 am the escalators only move downward, carrying an endless stream of workers and their cups of coffee. ✉ *Next to 100 Queen's Rd. Central, Central* Ⓜ *Central, Exit D1.*

PMQ

ARTS VENUE | This hip and happening area has a long history: back in the 1880s, this was the campus of the Central School, where Dr. Sun Yat-sen studied. After suffering severe damage in World War II, the area became the city's first Police Married Quarters. After standing empty for more than a decade, it reopened in 2014 as a design hub where locals could showcase their art, host workshops, arrange pop-up shops—there's even an atmospheric night market and a handful of excellent restaurants and cozy cafés. **■ TIP→ Take advantage of one of the free guided tours of the underground foundations and historic architecture.** ✉ *35 Aberdeen St., SoHo, Central* ☎ *2870–2335* 🌐 *www.pmq.org.hk.*

★ Tai Kwun Centre for Heritage and Arts

ARTS VENUE | After more than a decade of construction, this complex opened in 2018 in the location of the 19th-century Central Police Station; indeed, its name means "big station" in colloquial Cantonese. It's the largest restoration project ever to be completed in Hong Kong, stretching across 16 heritage buildings and 156,077 square feet. In addition to a wide range of restaurants—from dazzling design and Cantonese cuisine at Madame Fu to French fair in charming Cafe Claudel—the complex has local-designer boutiques, performing arts events, film screenings, art exhibitions, and a lovely open-air courtyard. With its red bricks and beautiful verandas, the old-world architecture contrasts delightfully with the adjacent, avant-garde JC Contemporary building—a center for contemporary arts with a metal facade so futuristic that it looks as if the entire building could take off for space at any moment. **■ TIP→ Tai Kwun is free to visit, however, the number of visitors might be restricted during peak hours. It's advised to apply online for a Tai Kwun Pass to ensure access.** ✉ *10 Hollywood Rd., Central* ☎ *3559–2600* 🌐 *www.taikwun.hk* 🎫 *Free* Ⓜ *Central, Exit D2.*

★ Victoria Peak and the Victoria Peak Tram

NEIGHBORHOOD | As you step off the Victoria Peak Tram, you might be surprised to encounter two shopping arcades crowning Hong Kong's most prized mountaintop. But venture up the escalators to the free viewing platforms—yep, through the Peak Galleria mall—and the view will astound you. Whatever the time, whatever the weather, be it your first visit or your 50th, this is Hong Kong's one unmissable sight. Spread below you is a glittering forest of skyscrapers; beyond them the harbor and—on a clear day—Kowloon's eight mountains. On rainy days wisps of clouds catch on the buildings' pointy tops, and at night both sides of the harbor burst into color. Consider having dinner at one of the restaurants near the Upper Terminus. ■ **TIP→ Skip the Peak Tower's observation deck, which is pricey. The free sights from atop the Galleria are just as good.**

Soaring just over 1,805 feet above sea level, Victoria Peak looks over Central and beyond. The steep funicular tracks up to the peak start at the **Peak Tram Terminus,** near St. John's Cathedral on Garden Road. Hong Kong is proud that its funicular railway is the world's steepest. Before it opened in 1888, the only way to get up to Victoria Peak was to walk or take a bumpy ride in a sedan chair on steep steps. At the Lower Terminus, the Peak Tram Historical Gallery displays a replica of the first-generation Peak Tram carriage. On the way up, grab a seat on the right-hand side for the best views of the harbor and mountains. The trams, which look like old-fashioned trolley cars, are hauled the whole way in seven minutes by cables attached to electric motors. En route to the Upper Terminus, 1,300 feet above sea level, the cars pass four intermediate stations, with track gradients varying from 4 to 27 degrees.

The well-signed nature walks around Victoria Peak offer wonderful respites from the commercialism. Before buying a return ticket on the tram or on a bus, consider taking one of the beautiful low-impact trails back to Central. You'll be treated to spectacular views in all directions on the **Hong Kong Trail,** an easygoing 40- to 60-minute paved path that begins and ends at the Peak Tram Upper Terminus. Start by heading north along fern-encroached Lugard Road. There's another stunning view of Central from the lookout, 20 minutes along, after which the road snakes west to an intersection with Hatton and Harlech roads. From here Lantau, Lamma, and—on incredibly clear days—Macau come into view. The longer option from here is to wind your way down Hatton to the University of Hong Kong campus in Western District.

Buses 15 and 15B shuttle you between the Peak Tram Lower Terminal and Central Bus Terminal near the Star Ferry Pier, every 15 to 20 minutes, for HK$9.80 ✉ *Between Garden Rd. and Cotton Tree Dr., Central* ☎ *2522–0922* 🌐 *www.thepeak.com.hk* 🎫 *HK$37 one-way, HK$52 round-trip.*

Restaurants

Amber

$$$$ | **FRENCH** | As you would expect from a restaurant in the Landmark Mandarin Oriental, Hong Kong Amber will linger in your memories for its modern style, impeccable service, and creative cuisine. Chef Richard Ekkebus's menu of creative European dishes still doesn't fail to impress. **Known for:** playful amuse bouche, including famous foie gras lollipops; well-heeled diners; fantastic wine-paired lunch on weekends. $ *Average main: HK$1000* ✉ *7th fl., Landmark Mandarin Oriental, 15 Queen's Rd., Central* ☎ *2132–0066* 🌐 *www.amberhongkong.com* Ⓜ *Central.*

AMMO

$$$$ | **ITALIAN** | Few places in Hong Kong have the kind of stunning garden views that you'll find at AMMO. Housed in a former ammunition compound (hence the name) that was converted into the Asia Society Hong Kong Center, the restaurant's interiors and menus blend the old with the new resulting in an impressive and dynamic dining experience. **Known for:** Italian culinary techniques with Asian flourishes; insanely satisfying panfried brioche; beautiful interior design in a heritage building. $ *Average main: HK$350* ✉ *9 Justice Dr., Asia Society Hong Kong Center, Admiralty, Central* ☎ *2537–9888* 🌐 *www.ammo.com.hk* Ⓜ *Admiralty.*

★ **Café Gray Deluxe**

$$$$ | **CONTEMPORARY** | Celebrated chef Gray Kunz's restaurant offers expertly prepared modern European fare in a casual and relaxed 49th-floor locale with

stunning urban vistas. A fan of fresh, seasonal ingredients, Kunz incorporates local produce into the ever-evolving menu whenever possible, often adding Asian flavors to excellent effect. **Known for:** steak tartare and signature pasta fiore; a fine selection of creative cocktails and wines; amazing views from every seat. *Average main: HK$450 The Upper House, Pacific Place, 88 Queensway, 49th fl., Central 3968–1106 www.cafegrayhk.com Admiralty.*

★ The Chairman

$$$ | **CANTONESE** | Premium ingredients, traditional recipes, elegant interiors ... there's a reason The Chairman is often booked out weeks in advance. The forward-thinking Cantonese restaurant is dedicated to sourcing many of its ingredients—from crabs and fish to chicken, pork, and veggies—from local fishmongers and farmers. **Known for:** signature steamed flower crab in rice wine; a slow-cooking philosophy and house-made sauces; eschewing dishes such as shark's fin and bird's nest. *Average main: HK$220 18 Kau U Fong, Central www.thechairmangroup.com Sheung Wan.*

★ 8½ Otto e Mezzo Bombana

$$$$ | **ITALIAN** | Spearheaded by Umberto Bombana (the former executive chef of the Ritz-Carlton Hong Kong and often lauded as the best Italian chef in Asia), this glitzy space delivers everything it promises. The service is crisp, the wine list is extensive, and the interior is nothing less than glamorous. **Known for:** authentic Italian food, including the famed handmade pastas; magnificent mains such as the Tajima short rib; a degustation menu that offers a neat sampling of Bombana's best. *Average main: HK$600 Shop 202, 2nd fl., Landmark Alexandra, 18 Chater Rd., Central 2537–8859 www.ottoemezzobombana.com Closed Sun. Central.*

★ Fa Zu Jie

$$$$ | **SHANGHAINESE** | This place is good—really, *really* good. Tucked away in a nondescript building in a hidden alley off Lan Kwai Fong, this reservations-only private kitchen plates up inventive, French-inspired Shanghainese dishes that are prepped in a polished open kitchen. **Known for:** the drunken quail (cooked in Chinese Hua Diao wine); prix-fixe menu that's tweaked regularly; cozy dining room with just a handful of tables. *Average main: HK$600 1st fl., 20A D'Aguilar St., Central 3487–1715 No credit cards No lunch. Closed Sun. Central.*

L'Atelier de Joël Robuchon

$$$$ | **FRENCH** | Joël Robuchon, one of the world's most iconic chefs, claims that his atelier (or "artist's workshop") is for contemporary casual dining. Diners sit on barstools around a counter designed like a modern Japanese sushi bar so that everyone can watch the chefs at work in the open kitchen. **Known for:** immaculate presentations; superb croissants and cakes at the tea salon one floor below; the quail with foie gras, with deservedly famous mashed potatoes. *Average main: HK$680 Shop 401, The Landmark, 15 Queen's Rd. Central, Central 2166–9000 www.robuchon.hk Central.*

★ Little Bao

$ | **ECLECTIC** | Slide into one of the dozen-some seats and tuck into the delicious *baos*—fluffy steamed buns sandwiched with all types of delicious ingredients. The rest of the menu is globally inspired and includes to-share plates such as drunken clams, short-rib dumplings, and truffle fries. **Known for:** perpetual lines out the door; signature braised pork belly baos; creative cocktails and refreshing high balls. *Average main: HK$90 66 Staunton St., Central 2194–0202 little-bao.myshopify.com Sheung Wan.*

★ Lung King Heen

$$$$ | **CHINESE** | This place has made a serious case for being the best Cantonese restaurant in Hong Kong, especially after winning and retaining three Michelin stars every year since 2009. Where other contenders tend to get too caught up in prestige dishes and name-brand chefs, Lung King Heen focuses completely on taste. **Known for:** divine barbecued suckling pig and crispy shrimp dumplings; extensive premium tea and wine list; harbor views and handsome interiors. *Average main: HK$350* *4th fl., Four Seasons Hotel, 8 Finance St., Central* *3196–8880* *www.fourseasons.com* *Hong Kong.*

Mak's Noodles

$ | **CHINESE** | Mak's may look like any other Hong Kong noodle shop, but this tiny storefront is one of the best known in town, with a reputation that belies its humble decor. The real test of a good Cantonese noodle shop, however, is its wontons, and here they're fresh, delicate, and filled with whole shrimp. **Known for:** truly famous wonton noodles; sauce-tossed noodles with pork; sui kau dumplings, filled with diced mushrooms and shrimp. *Average main: HK$40* *77 Wellington St., Central* *2854–3810* *www.maksnoodle.com* *No credit cards* *Central.*

Restaurant Petrus

$$$$ | **FRENCH** | From atop the Island Shangri-La Hong Kong, Restaurant Petrus scales the upper Hong Kong heights of prestige, formality, and price. This is one of the city's few flagship hotel restaurants that has not attempted to reinvent itself as fusion—sometimes traditional French haute cuisine is the way to go. **Known for:** grand design and breathtaking harbor views; memorable wine list, with more than 1,800 vintages; exceptional foie gras. *Average main: HK$600* *56th fl., Island Shangri-La, Hong Kong, Pacific Place, Supreme Court Rd., Admiralty, Central* *2820–8590* *www.shangri-la.com* *Admiralty.*

Yung Kee

$$ | **CHINESE** | **FAMILY** | Close to Hong Kong's famous nightlife and dining district of Lan Kwai Fong, Yung Kee has been a local institution since it first opened as a food stall in 1942. The food is authentic Cantonese, served amid riotous decor and writhing gold dragons. **Known for:** signature roast goose with beautifully crisp skin and tender meat; excellent dim sum in an upscale environment; thousand-year-old preserved eggs for more adventurous palates. *Average main: HK$150* *32–40 Wellington St, Central* *2522–1624* *www.yungkee.com.hk* *Central.*

 Hotels

★ Bishop Lei International House

$ | **HOTEL** | If you've ever dreamed of living a life of privilege in the Mid-Levels without having to pay through the nose for it, this is your chance—all the better if you go for a slightly pricier harbor-view room. **Pros:** unique perch near escalators, saving you countless steps up and down to SoHo and Central; good value for the location; beautiful views from some rooms. **Cons:** escalator runs upward-only after 10 am, so lots of steps down in the morning; decor could use a revamp; relatively small rooms. *Rooms from: HK$800* *4 Robinson Rd., Mid-Levels, Central* *2868–0828* *www.bishopleihtl.com.hk* *227 rooms* *No meals* *Central.*

★ Four Seasons Hotel Hong Kong

$$$$ | **HOTEL** | Few comforts are neglected, with amenities ranging from sumptuous Chinese-accented furnishings to all sorts of high-tech gadgetry, but the main features are the knockout views of the harbor and Victoria Peak through walls of glass. **Pros:** elite service and attention to detail; outstanding business center and executive lounge; direct

access to the International Finance Centre. **Cons:** breakfast not included in high rates; some views are better than others; lobby can be busy and crowded. *Rooms from: HK$4600* *International Finance Centre, 8 Finance St., Central* *3196–8888* *www.fourseasons.com/hongkong* *399 rooms* *No meals* *Central.*

Island Shangri-La, Hong Kong

$$$ | **HOTEL** | A city icon towering above Pacific Place drips with old-world charm and offers spacious and luxurious accommodations with an Asian twist, along with fine dining and impeccable service. **Pros:** grand lobby; beautiful pool deck with a great up-close skyline view; elevator access to Pacific Place Mall. **Cons:** no full-service spa; rooms due for a refurbishment; restaurants often very busy. *Rooms from: HK$3300* *Pacific Place, Supreme Court Rd., Admiralty, Central* *2877–3838* *www.shangri-la.com* *565 rooms* *No meals* *Admiralty.*

Lan Kwai Fong Hotel

$ | **HOTEL** | **FAMILY** | The scent of lemongrass and cozy feel of an old Hong Kong apartment building extend to the small but beautiful rooms enlarged by bay windows and plunging views of the surrounding cityscape. **Pros:** free happy hour at Breeze lounge; some rooms have balconies; complimentary data-enabled smartphone. **Cons:** surrounding narrow roads are often congested; can be hard to get a taxi; breakfast can be crowded. *Rooms from: HK$1300* *3 Kau U Fong, Central* *3650–0000* *www.lankwaifonghotel.com.hk* *162 rooms* *No meals* *Sheung Wan.*

★ The Landmark Mandarin Oriental

$$$$ | **HOTEL** | Some of the city's most spacious, beautifully designed rooms also have huge spa-style bathrooms with massive circular tubs. **Pros:** you can't get more central in Central; elegant rooms by Hong Kong designer Joyce Wang; complimentary daily treats from Amber. **Cons:** relatively small lobby; city views only; can be hard to get a cab. *Rooms from: HK$4900* *The Landmark, 15 Queen's Rd. Central, Central* *2132–0188* *www.mandarinoriental.com/landmark* *111 rooms* *No meals* *Central.*

★ Mandarin Oriental Hong Kong

$$$$ | **HOTEL** | Over the past 50 years, Hong Kong's most famous hotel has lost none of its opulence, colonial charm, or shine: it still features impeccable service as well as spacious rooms with daybeds tucked beneath huge windows; TV screens set next to bathroom sinks; and closet cubbyhole "valet boxes," where your daily paper, newly shined shoes, and room-service meal magically appear. **Pros:** spacious, open, beautifully designed rooms with harbor views; old-world ambience at its finest; exquisite spa, salon, and barber. **Cons:** in-room Wi-Fi isn't free; small indoor pool; Clipper Lounge decor feels dated. *Rooms from: HK$4500* *5 Connaught Rd., Central* *2522–0111* *www.mandarin-oriental.com/hongkong* *501 rooms* *No meals* *Central.*

The Pottinger Hong Kong

$$$ | **HOTEL** | Overlooking the stony, historic staircase from which it takes its name, The Pottinger weaves romantic elements of local heritage into its chic chinoiserie-inspired bedrooms, where pretty silkscreen headboards and latticed dividers sit beside history books, and where treats give you a taste of old Hong Kong. **Pros:** centrally located just steps from shops and restaurants; local touches in the snacks, art, and decor; big bathrooms. **Cons:** no pool; limited amenities; underwhelming views in some rooms. *Rooms from: HK$2600* *21 Stanley St., Central* *2308–3188* *www.thepottinger.com* *68 rooms* *No meals.*

★ The Upper House

$$$$ | **HOTEL** | Even standard rooms in this haven of stylish luxury are suites—tranquil havens of design and indulgence that feature huge window-side bathtubs, walk-in rain showers, and free mini-bars (or Maxi-Bars as they call them). **Pros:** minimalist design with works by contemporary Asian artists; world-class mountain, city, and harbor views; incredibly personalized service. **Cons:** no spa or pool; can be difficult to get a taxi; no reception so check-in can be confusing. *Rooms from: HK$4500 ✉ Pacific Place, 88 Queensway, Admiralty, Central ☎ 2918–1838 🌐 www.upperhouse.com 117 suites No meals Ⓜ Admiralty.*

Nightlife

On weekends the streets of Lan Kwai Fong are liberated from traffic, and the swilling hordes from both sides of the street merge into one heaving organism. Hong Kong is proud of this très chic area, a warren of streets stuffed with commensurately priced restaurants, bars, and late-night boutiques. Midway between Lan Kwai Fong's madness and SoHo's bohemian glamour is Wyndham Street, home to an array of sophisticated bars, nightclubs, and restaurants and strict domain of the over 25s.

BARS

Bar De Luxe

BARS/PUBS | Japanophiles will want to make a beeline for this sleek bar and lounge, which shares a space with Attire House—a high-end menswear store that also houses a tailor and barber shop. As the first international outpost from legendary bartender Hidetsugu Ueno—the brains behind Ginza's famous Bar High Five—Bar De Luxe offers a luxurious drinking experience, complete with hand-crafted cocktails, premium Japanese whiskies, delicious bar snacks, and views of Hong Kong's famous skyline. Sundowners here will set you back a few hundred Hong Kong dollars, so skip this lofty spot if you're strapped for cash. *✉ 30th fl., Asia Pacific Centre, 8 Wyndham St., Central ☎ 3706–5716 🌐 attire-house.com ☞ Closed Sun. Ⓜ Central.*

★ The Globe

BARS/PUBS | In a trendy SoHo space, this British-expat hangout evokes the feel of southwest London. The owner is a beer fanatic, and the place has one of Hong Kong's best selections of local and international craft brews. It's a fun and convivial spot, with a mix of ages and a pretty even split between expats and locals. You can book the sectioned-off "Lounge" to watch broadcasts of the World Series, Super Bowl, Rubgy Sevens, World Cup soccer, or other sporting events with a group of friends. *✉ 45–53 Graham St., SoHo, Central ☎ 2543–1941 🌐 www.theglobe.com.hk Ⓜ Central.*

★ IFC Rooftop

BREWPUBS/BEER GARDENS | On the roof of IFC Mall, the outdoor terrace is an ideal place to watch the sun set. The entire rooftop seating area is public space—a rarity in Hong Kong—so do what the locals do: buy your drinks from the CitySuper downstairs, and enjoy one of the city's best views on the cheap. *✉ 4th fl., 2 IFC, 8 Finance St., Central, Central ☎ 2295–3308 🌐 ifc.com.hk Ⓜ Central.*

Le Jardin

BARS/PUBS | The leafy setting belies the down-and-dirty vibe at this casual bar with a terrace overlooking the colorful dining strip known locally as "Rat Alley." This refreshingly low-key bar is a little tricky to find: walk through the dining area and up a flight of steps. The place is packed on weekends. *✉ 10 Wing Wah La., Lan Kwai Fong, Central ☎ 2526–2717 Ⓜ Central.*

MO Bar

BARS/PUBS | A destination for the corporate lunch crowd and stylish tipplers, this plush bar and restaurant in the Landmark Mandarin Oriental appeals to a civilized crowd. You'll pay top dollar for the signature drinks (up to HK$200), but the super-modern interior and live DJ beats make it worthwhile. The ground floor location means the best views will be of the other well-heeled patrons, but that's OK: this is a place to be seen as much as to see. Upstairs, at the back of the room, make a reservation at PDT (Please Don't Tell)—a speakeasy by way of New York City that's accessed through a faux phone booth. Just dial 1 and emerge into a wood-paneled world of craft cocktails and premium hot dogs. ✉ *Landmark Mandarin Oriental, 15 Queen's Rd. Central, Central* ☎ *2132-0077* 🌐 *www.mandarinoriental.com/landmark* Ⓜ *Central.*

★ The Pontiac

BARS/PUBS | Styled as a retro rock 'n' roll Americana dive bar, The Pontiac is constantly abuzz. Award-winning bartender Beckaly Franks designs the excellent cocktail menu and sets the tone for the predominantly female staff. Stick around 'til midnight when bartenders hop atop the bar and pour shots of Becherovka herbal liqueur into customers' mouths. ✉ *13 Old Bailey St., Central* Ⓜ *Central.*

Solas Gastro Lounge

BARS/PUBS | Positioned a floor below dance club dragon-i, this bar is Wyndham Street's party central. Expect a mostly expat crowd of twenty- and thirtysomethings who come straight from work in their business suits. With good music—everything from electronic dance music to Cardi B—and a well-lubricated crowd, Solas is a great place to cut loose. The interior is dark and extremely basic, but the party routinely spills into the street out front. ✉ *Shop 1, 60 Wyndham St., SoHo, Central* ☎ *3162-3710* 🌐 *www.solas.com.hk* Ⓜ *Central.*

Staunton's Wine Bar & Cafe

BARS/PUBS | Adjacent to Hong Kong's famous outdoor escalator is this stalwart bistro-style café and bar. As the weekend approaches the place gets crowded, but the upstairs balcony is still the perfect perch from which to people-watch. You can come for a drink at night or coffee during the day. It's also a Sunday-morning favorite for nursing hangovers over brunch. ✉ *10–12 Staunton St., SoHo, Central* ☎ *2973-6611* 🌐 *www.stauntonsgroup.com* Ⓜ *Central.*

DISCOS AND NIGHTCLUBS

★ dragon-i

DANCE CLUBS | Around for more than a decade, dragon-i has lost none of its popularity, which is rare for a nightclub in Hong Kong. Have a drink on the deck, or step inside the vivid red playroom, which doubles as a Chinese restaurant earlier in the day. It's the domain of the city's young, rich, and beautiful (if not necessarily classy) crowd, and attracts a busy roster of international acts and DJs. ✉ *The Centrium, 60 Wyndham St., Central* ☎ *3110-1222* 🌐 *www.dragon-i.com.hk* Ⓜ *Central.*

Drop

DANCE CLUBS | This pint-size gem is *the* after-hours party spot in Central. Hidden down an alley beside a late-night food stand, its obscure location only adds to the speakeasy feel. Drop gets crowded on weekends, and it can be hard to get inside, so arrive early and wait for the party to pop off. ✉ *Basement level, On Lok Mansion, 39–43 Hollywood Rd., Central* ☎ *2543-8856* 🌐 *www.drophk.com* ☞ *Closed Mon.* Ⓜ *Central.*

Oma

DANCE CLUBS | The space is a bit of a dank hole, but thanks to the top-of-the-line sound system and strong drinks, nobody seems to notice or care. Expect great tech house music, international DJs alongside local talent, and parties that go all night. ✉ *Lower basement level, Harilela House, 79 Wyndham St., Central* ☎ *2521-8815* ☞ *Closed Sun.–Tues.* Ⓜ *Central.*

ANTIQUES AND COLLECTIBLES

Altfield Gallery

ANTIQUES/COLLECTIBLES | If only your entire home could be outfitted by Altfield. Established in 1980, the elegant gallery carries exquisite antique Chinese furniture, Asia-related maps and topographical prints, Southeast Asian sculpture, and decorative arts from around Asia, including silver and rugs. Altfield Interiors, on nearby Queen's Road, features a selection of larger furniture pieces, framed art, and contemporary home accessories. ✉ *2nd fl., Shop 249, Prince's Bldg., 10 Chater Rd., Central* ☎ *2537–6370* 🌐 *www.altfield.com.hk* Ⓜ *Central.*

Teresa Coleman Fine Arts Ltd.

ANTIQUES/COLLECTIBLES | Teresa Coleman specializes in finely woven and embroidered costumes and textiles from the imperial courts of the Qing and Ming dynasties (circa 1368–1912). The centrally located gallery also displays a wide collection of Tibetan rugs, Himalayan Buddhist art, antique painted and carved fans, lacquered boxes, prints, and paintings. There's a small ground-floor gallery that's open for walk-ins, as well as a spacious gallery on the upper floor that's by appointment only. ✉ *Ground fl., 55 Wyndham St., Central* ☎ *2526–2450* 🌐 *www.teresacoleman.com* Ⓜ *Central.*

ART GALLERIES

Grotto Fine Art

ART GALLERIES | Director and chief curator Henry Au-yeung writes about, curates, and gives lectures on 20th-century Chinese art. His tucked-away gallery focuses exclusively on local Chinese artists, with an interest in the newest and most avant-garde works. Look for paintings, sculptures, prints, mixed-media pieces, and conceptual installations. ✉ *2nd fl., 31C–D Wyndham St., Central* ☎ *2121–2270* 🌐 *www.grottofineart.com* Ⓜ *Central, Exit G.*

Hanart TZ Gallery

ART GALLERIES | This is a rare opportunity to compare and contrast cutting-edge and experimental Chinese art selected by one of the field's most respected authorities. Unassuming curatorial director Johnson Chang Tsong-zung also cofounded the Asia Art Archive and has curated exhibitions at the São Paolo and Venice biennials. ✉ *4th fl., Room 401, Pedder Bldg., 12 Pedder St., Central* ☎ *2526–9019* 🌐 *www.hanart.com* Ⓜ *Central.*

CLOTHING

A-Man Hing Cheong Co., Ltd.

CLOTHING | People often gasp at the very mention of A-Man Hing Cheong, in the Mandarin Oriental Hotel. For some it symbolizes the ultimate in fine tailoring, with a reputation that extends back to its founding in 1898. For others it's the lofty prices that elicit a reaction. Regardless, this is a trustworthy source of European-cut suits, custom shirts, and excellent service. ✉ *Mezzanine, Mandarin Oriental, 5 Connaught Rd., Central* ☎ *2522–3336* Ⓜ *Central, Exit H.*

Ascot Chang

CLOTHING | This self-titled "gentleman's shirtmaker" makes it easy to find the perfect shirt, even if you could get a better deal in a less prominent shop. Ascot Chang has upheld exacting Shanghainese tailoring traditions in Hong Kong since 1953, and now has stores in New York, Beverly Hills, Manila, and Shanghai. The focus here is on the fit and details, from 22 stitches per inch to collar linings crafted to maintain their shape. Among the countless fabrics, Italian 330s three-ply Egyptian cotton by David & John Anderson is one of the most coveted and expensive. Like many shirtmakers, Ascot Chang does pajamas, robes, boxer shorts, and women's blouses, too. It also has ready-made lines of shirts, T-shirts, neckties, and other accessories available for online ordering. Other branches are located in the IFC Mall, Elements Mall, and the Peninsula Hotel. ✉ *Shop 131, Prince's Bldg., 10 Chater Rd., Central* ☎ *2523–3663* 🌐 *www.ascotchang.com* Ⓜ *Central.*

Barney Cheng Couture

CLOTHING | One of Hong Kong's best-known local designers, Barney Cheng made a name for himself with his expert tailoring and entrance-making gowns. He's crafted many a bride's dream dress, and his masterfully tailored evening gowns range from HK$40,000–HK$100,000, depending on style, detailing, and fabric. Though he still designs extravagant special-occasion ware, Cheng's services have expanded to include sophisticated menswear, exotic skins, and bespoke jewels. Consultations are available by appointment only. ✉ *12th fl., World Wide Commercial Bldg., 34 Wyndham St., Central* ☎ *2530–2829* 🌐 *www.barneycheng.com* ⏲ *Closed Sun.* Ⓜ *Central, Exit D2.*

Blanc de Chine

CLOTHING | Relying on word of mouth, Blanc de Chine has catered to high society and celebrities, such as actor Jackie Chan, for years. The small, refined tailoring shop neatly displays exquisite fabrics from Switzerland, France, and Italy used for tailor-made as well as ready-made women's wear, menswear, and home accessories. Items here are extravagances, but they're worth every penny. ✉ *Shop 123, LANDMARK Prince's Bldg., 10 Chater Rd., Central* ☎ *2104–7934* 🌐 *www.blancdechine.com* Ⓜ *Central.*

Episode

CLOTHING | Locally owned and designed Episode collections focus on accessories and elegant clothing for working women and Hong Kong "tai tais" (aka ladies who lunch). The looks tend to be simple yet elegant, with an emphasis on high-quality cashmere and knits, stylish business attire, and flowy weekend dresses—beautiful tailoring is a hallmark of the brand. Episode has a second store in Harbour City. ✉ *Shop 109, Man Yee Arcade, 68 Des Voeux Rd. Central, Central* ☎ *2259–5117* 🌐 *www.episode-intl.com* Ⓜ *Central.*

Fang Fong Projects

CLOTHING | Fang Fong fell in love with the vintage feel of the SoHo district as a design graduate and vowed to move in. She chose a light-filled studio space to display her floaty, 1970s-inspired clothing line, with its bold prints and sexy wisps of lace and silk. She also brought her friends with her, or at least those who suited her vibe. ✉ *Shop 1, 69–71 Peel St., SoHo, Central* ☎ *3105–5557* Ⓜ *Sheung Wan, Exit E2.*

Joyce

CLOTHING | Local socialites and couture addicts still thank Joyce Ma, the fairy godmother of luxury retail in Hong Kong, for bringing must-have labels to the city. Others may be catching up, but her Joyce boutiques are still ultrachic havens outfitted with a Vogue-worthy wish list of designers and beauty brands. Not so much a shop as a fashion institution, hushed Joyce houses the worship-worthy creations of fashion's greatest gods and goddesses. McCartney, McQueen, Oscar de la Renta: the stock list is practically a mantra. Joyce sells unique household items, too, so your home can live up to your wardrobe. The flagship store is in New World Tower. ✉ *New World Tower, 16 Queen's Rd. Central, Central* ☎ *2810–1120* 🌐 *www.joyce.com* Ⓜ *Central.*

★ Loom Loop

CERAMICS/GLASSWARE | Homegrown brand Loom Loop is known for its bold style and sustainable ethos. Made from a mixture of heritage Canton fabrics, sourced in Guangzhou, the collections tend to revolve around bright colors, cooling silks, and decidedly urban cuts. In addition to apparel, the brand also works with leftover textiles, such as denim and knitwear, to create upcycled accessories. ✉ *Studio S205, PMQ, 35 Aberdeen St., Central* ☎ *2548–7837* 🌐 *www.loom-loop.com* Ⓜ *Central.*

Lu Lu Cheung

CLOTHING | A fixture on the Hong Kong fashion scene for decades, Lu Lu Cheung creates designs that ooze comfort and warmth. In both daytime and evening wear, natural fabrics and forms are represented in practical yet imaginative ways. ✉ *62 Wellington St., Central* ☎ *2539–4133* 🌐 *www.lulucheung.com.hk* Ⓜ *Central.*

★ Shanghai Tang

CLOTHING | Make your way past the perfumes, scarves, and silk-embroidered Chinese souvenirs to the second floor, where you'll find a rainbow of fabrics at your fingertips. In addition to the brilliantly hued—and expensive—silk and cashmere clothing, you'll see custom-made suits starting at around HK$30,000, including fabric. You can also have a cheongsam (a sexy slit-skirt silk dress with a Mandarin collar) made for around HK$10,000, including fabric. Ready-to-wear Mandarin suits are in the HK$15,000–HK$20,000 range. There are stores scattered across Hong Kong, including the airport's Terminal One. ✉ *Ground–3rd fl., 1 Duddell St., Central* ☎ *2525–7333* 🌐 *www.shanghaitang.com* Ⓜ *Central, Exit D2.*

★ Tai Kwun

CLOTHING | On the grounds of the 19th-century Central Police Station complex, Hong Kong's largest revitalization project to date, Tai Kwun debuted in 2018. It stretches across 38,750 square feet and hosts several restaurants, bars, art exhibitions, and local boutiques. Shopping here runs the gamut from traditional tailors like Yuen's Tailor to avant garde apparel by Harrison Wong. **■ TIP→ While you're here, check out the Heritage Storytelling Spaces. From the Central Magistry to the old prison, eight distinct areas transport you back in time.** ✉ *10 Hollywood Rd., Central* ☎ *3559–2600* 🌐 *www.taikwun.hk* Ⓜ *Central.*

W. W. Chan & Sons Tailors Ltd.

CLOTHING | Chan is known for excellent-quality suits and shirts in classic cuts and has an array of fine European fabrics. It's comforting to know that you'll be measured and fitted by the same master tailor from start to finish. The store features a mirrored, hexagonal changing room so you can check every angle. Tailors from here travel to the United States several times a year to fill orders for their customers; if you have a suit made and leave your address, they'll let you know when they plan to visit. ✉ *Unit B, 8th fl., Entertainment Bldg., 30 Queen's Rd. Central, Central* ☎ *2366–9738* 🌐 *www.wwchan.com* Ⓜ *Central.*

GIFTS AND SOUVENIRS

Mountain Folkcraft

CRAFTS | A little old-fashioned bell chimes as you open the door to this fantastic shop filled with handicrafts and antiques from around China. Amid the old treasures, carved woodwork, rugs, and curios, are stunning folk-print fabrics. **■ TIP→ To reach the store from Queen's Road Central, walk up D'Aguilar Street toward Lan Kwai Fong, then turn right onto Wo On Lane.** ✉ *Ground fl., 12 Wo On La., Central* ☎ *2523–2817* 🌐 *www.mountain-folkcraft.com* Ⓜ *Central.*

Tittot

CRAFTS | This Taiwanese brand has taken modern Chinese glass art global. Glassworks here are made using the laborious lost-wax casting technique, employed by artists for centuries to create a bronze replica of an original wax or clay sculpture. The collection—which includes tableware, paperweights, glass Buddhas, and jewelry—can be purchased in Lane Crawford department stores. ✉ *Lane Crawford, IFC Mall, 8 Finance St., Central* ☎ *2118–3638* 🌐 *www.tittot.com* Ⓜ *Hong Kong.*

JEWELRY AND ACCESSORIES

Edward Chiu

JEWELRY/ACCESSORIES | Everything about Edward Chiu is *fabulous,* from the flamboyant way he dresses to his high-end jade jewelry. The minimalist, geometric pieces use the entire jade spectrum, from deep greens to surprising lavenders. Inspired in part by art deco, Chiu is also famous for contrasting black-and-white jade, setting it in precious metals, and adding diamond or pearl touches. ✉ *Shop 108, Prince's Bldg., 10 Chater Rd., Central* ☎ *2525–2325* 🌐 *www.edwardchiu.com* Ⓜ *Hong Kong.*

Qeelin

JEWELRY/ACCESSORIES | With ancient Chinese culture for inspiration and *In the Mood for Love* actress Maggie Cheung as the muse, something extraordinary was bound to come from Qeelin, whose name is cleverly derived from the Chinese mythical animal and icon of love. Classic gold, platinum, and diamonds are mixed with colored jades, black diamonds, and unusual materials for truly unique effects. The meaningful creations of designer Dennis Chan are exemplified in the signature collection: Wulu, a minimalist form representing the mythical gourd as well as the lucky number eight. The IFC Mall store is one of five in Hong Kong. ✉ *Shop 2059, IFC Mall, 8 Finance St., Central* ☎ *2389–8863* 🌐 *hk.qeelin.com* Ⓜ *Hong Kong.*

Ronald Abram

JEWELRY/ACCESSORIES | Looking at the rocks in these windows can feel like a visit to a natural history museum. Large white- and rare-color diamonds sourced from all over the world are a specialty here, but the shop also deals in emeralds, sapphires, and rubies. With years of expertise, Abrams dispenses advice on both the aesthetic merits and the investment potential of each stone or piece of jewelry. ✉ *Mezzanine, Mandarin Oriental, 5 Connaught Rd., Central* ☎ *2525–1234* 🌐 *www.ronaldabram.com* Ⓜ *Central.*

TAYMA Fine Jewellery

JEWELRY/ACCESSORIES | Unusual colored "connoisseur" gemstones are set by hand in custom designs by Hong Kong–based jeweler Tayma Page Allies. The collection is designed to bring out the personality of the individual wearer, and includes oversize cocktail rings, distinctive bracelets, pretty earrings, and more. ✉ *Shop 225, 2nd fl., LANDMARK Prince's Bldg., 10 Chater Rd., Central* ☎ *2525–5280* 🌐 *www.taymajewellery.com* Ⓜ *Central, Exit K.*

MALLS AND SHOPPING CENTERS

★ IFC Mall

SHOPPING CENTERS/MALLS | A quick glance at the directory—Tiffany & Co., Kate Spade, Bvlgari, Chaumet—lets you know that the International Finance Centre isn't for the faint of pocket. Designer department store Lane Crawford chose to open its flagship store here, and J.Crew followed suit in 2014. Even the mall's cinema multiplex is special: the deluxe theaters have super-comfy seats with extra legroom and a wine bar for classy refreshments. If you finish your spending spree at sunset, go for a cocktail at Dear Lilly or LA RAMBLA by Catalunya, two posh spots with fabulous harbor views. The Hong Kong Airport Express station (with in-town check-in service) is under the mall, and the Four Seasons Hotel connects to it. **■ TIP→ Avoid the mall between 12:30 and 2, when it's flooded with lunching office workers from the two IFC towers.** ✉ *8 Finance St., Central* ☎ *2295–3308, 2295–3308 hotline* 🌐 *www.ifc.com.hk* Ⓜ *Hong Kong, Exit F.*

SHOES, HANDBAGS, AND LEATHER GOODS

Kow Hoo Shoe Company

SHOES/LUGGAGE/LEATHER GOODS | If you like shoes made the old-fashioned way, then Kow Hoo—one of Hong Kong's oldest, circa 1946—is for you. It also does great cowboy boots (there's nothing like knee-high calfskin!). Just be sure to make an appointment before you go. ✉ *2nd fl., Shop 243, LANDMARK Prince's Bldg., 10 Chater Rd., Central* ☎ *2523–0489* 🌐 *kowhoo.com.hk* ⏲ *Closed Sun.* Ⓜ *Central.*

Kwanpen

SHOES/LUGGAGE/LEATHER GOODS | Renowned for its crocodile bags and shoes, Kwanpen got its start in 1938, when master craftsman Kwan Pen Song became the go-to handbag designer among British aristocrats in Hong Kong. Over the years, Kwan's sons grew the business into a global force, running two stand-alone shops in Pacific Place and Elements malls, as well as several international boutiques in countries like Japan, Qatar, and the UK. ✉ *Shop 310, Pacific Place, 88 Queensway, Admirality, Central* ☎ *2918–9199* 🌐 *www.kwanpen.com* Ⓜ *Admiralty.*

Lianca

SHOES/LUGGAGE/LEATHER GOODS | This is one of those unique places that make you want to buy something even if there's nothing you need. Lianca, first and foremost a manufacturer, sells well-made leather bags, wallets, frames, key chains, and home accessories in timeless, simple designs. It's an unbranded way to be stylish. ✉ *Basement fl., 27 Staunton St., entrance on Graham St., SoHo, Central* ☎ *2139–2989* 🌐 *www.liancacentral.com* Ⓜ *Central, Exit D2.*

LIII LIII COUTURE

SHOES/LUGGAGE/LEATHER GOODS | The Chan Brothers have an illustrious history in Hong Kong and have certainly left a trail of satisfied customers in their wake; however, reviews these days speak of hit-and-miss experiences at this bespoke shoe boutique. Prices have also shot up over the last few years (from around HK$1,500 for sandals and HK$2,300 for high heels). Still, when they are good, they are very, very good. ✉ *1st fl., Tower 2, Shop 75, Admiralty Centre, 18 Harcourt Rd., Central* ☎ *2865–3989* Ⓜ *Admiralty, Exit A.*

Mayer Shoes

SHOES/LUGGAGE/LEATHER GOODS | Since the 1960s, Mayer has been making excellent custom-order shoes and accessories in leather, lizard, crocodile, and ostrich. Go to them for the classic pieces for which they became famous rather than this season's "it" bag. Prices for ladies shoes start at several hundred U.S. dollars and peak at roughly US$2,000. ✉ *Mandarin Oriental, 5 Connaught Rd., Central* ☎ *2524–3317* ⏲ *Closed Sun.* Ⓜ *Central.*

Wan Chai, Causeway Bay, and Beyond

The Happy Valley horse races are a vital part of Hong Kong life, so it's only fitting that they're in one of the city's most vital areas. A few blocks back from Wan Chai's new office blocks are crowded alleys where you might stumble across a wet market, a tiny furniture-maker's shop, or an age-old temple. Farther east, Causeway Bay pulses with Hong Kong's best shopping streets and hundreds of restaurants. At night the whole area comes alive with bars, restaurants, and discos, as well as establishments offering some of Wan Chai's more traditional services (think red lights and photos of seminaked women outside).

GETTING HERE AND AROUND

Both Wan Chai and Causeway Bay have their own MTR stops, but a pleasant way to arrive from Central is on the tram along Hennessy Road. If you're going beyond Wan Chai, check the sign at the front: some continue to North Point and Shau Kei Wan, via Causeway Bay, while others go south to Happy Valley.

The underground MTR stations are small labyrinths, so read the signs carefully to find the best exit. Traffic begins to take its toll on journey times to places beyond Causeway Bay, and the MTR is often the quickest way to travel.

Sights

Blue House

BUILDING | An excellent example of a traditional *tong lau* (20th-century tenement building), the Blue House in Wan Chai sits in the center of a color-coded complex that also includes the aptly named Yellow and Orange houses. As the story goes, the original owners only had blue paint on hand, thus the high-voltage shade of cyan. Thanks to a preservation campaign by city conservationists, the cluster of distinctive buildings has been gracefully restored, winning an Award of Excellence in the UNESCO Asia-Pacific Awards for Cultural Heritage Conservation in 2017. Inside the 1920s buildings, you can get a good sense of the neighborhood's roots. There's a community center, restaurants, cultural tours, movie screenings, craft workshops, and architectural exhibits. ✉ *72–74A Stone Nullah Lane, Wan Chai* ☎ *2117–5843* 🌐 *www.vivabluehouse.hk* 🎫 *Free* Ⓜ *Wan Chai, Exit A3.*

★ Happy Valley Racecourse

SPORTS VENUE | The biggest attraction east of Causeway Bay for locals and visitors alike is this local legend, where millions of Hong Kong dollars make their way each year. The exhilarating blur of galloping hooves under jockeys dressed in bright silk jerseys is a must-see. The races make great Wednesday nights out on the town. Aside from the excitement of the races, there are restaurants, bars, and even a racing museum to keep you amused. The public entrance to the track is a 20-minute walk from Causeway Bay MTR Exit A (Times Square), or simply hop on the Happy Valley tram, which terminates right in front. **■ TIP→ Every Wednesday night during race season (September through June), the first of about eight races kicks off at 7:15.** ✉ *Sports Rd. at Wong Nai Chung Rd., Happy Valley, Causeway Bay* 🎫 *HK$10* Ⓜ *Causeway Bay, Exit A.*

Hong Kong Convention and Exhibition Centre

CONVENTION CENTER | Land is so scarce in Hong Kong that developers usually only build skyward, but the HKCEC juts into the harbor instead. Curved-glass walls and a swooping roof make it look like a tortoise lumbering into the sea or a gull taking flight, depending on who you ask. Of all the international trade fairs, regional conferences, and other events held here, by far the most famous was the 1997 Handover Ceremony. An obelisk commemorates it on the waterfront promenade, which also affords great views of Kowloon.

Outside the center stands the *Golden Bauhinia*. This gleaming sculpture of the bauhinia flower, Hong Kong's symbol, was a gift from China. The police hoist the flag daily at 7:50 am; on the first of every month, there is an enhanced flag-raising ceremony with musical accompaniment at 7:45 am. ✉ *1 Expo Dr., Wan Chai* ☎ *2582–8888* 🌐 *www.hkcec.com* Ⓜ *Wan Chai, Exit A.*

Law Uk Folk Museum

MUSEUM | This restored Hakka house was once the home of the Law family, who arrived here from Guangdong in the mid-18th century. It's the perfect example of a triple- *jian,* double- *lang* residence. Jian are enclosed rooms—here, the bedroom, living room, and workroom at the back. The front storeroom and kitchen are the *lang,* where the walls don't reach up to the roof, and thus allow air in. Although the museum is small, informative texts outside and displays of rural furniture and farm implements inside give a powerful idea of what rural Hong Kong was like. It's definitely worth a trip to bustling industrial Chai Wan, at the eastern end of the MTR, to see it. Photos show what the area looked like in the 1930s—these days a leafy square is the only reminder of the woodlands and fields that once surrounded this buttermilk-color dwelling. ✉ *14 Kut Shing*

St., Chai Wan, Eastern ☎ *2896–7006* 🌐 *www.lcsd.gov.hk* 🎫 *Free* ⏲ *Closed Thurs.* Ⓜ *Chai Wan, Exit B.*

Victoria Park

NATIONAL/STATE PARK | Hong Kong Island's largest park is a welcome breathing space on the edge of Causeway Bay. It's beautifully landscaped and has recreational facilities for soccer, basketball, swimming, lawn bowling, and tennis. At dawn every morning hundreds practice tai chi chuan here. During the Mid-Autumn Festival it's home to the Lantern Carnival, when the trees are a mass of colorful lights. Just before Chinese New Year (late January to early February), the park hosts a huge flower market. On the eve of Chinese New Year, after a traditional family dinner at home, much of Hong Kong happily gathers here to shop and wander into the early hours of the first day of the new year. ✉ *1 Hing Fat St., Causeway Bay* ☎ *2890–5824* 🌐 *www.lcsd.gov.hk* 🎫 *Free* Ⓜ *Tin Hau, Exit A2.*

Restaurants

WAN CHAI

Bo Innovation: The Hong Kong Story

$$$$ | **CHINESE** | The mastermind behind this three-Michelin-starred restaurant is Alvin Leung, who dubs himself the "demon chef" and has the moniker tattooed on his arm. Bo Innovation serves what he calls "X-treme Chinese" cuisine, applying contemporary twists to traditional Cantonese dishes. **Known for:** signature xiao long bao (soup dumpling); two different (Red or Blue) multicourse tasting menus; thoughtful design with Hong Kong motifs and artwork. Ⓢ *Average main: HK$2600* ✉ *Shop 8, Podium, 1st fl., J Senses, 60 Johnston Rd., Wan Chai* ☎ *2850–8371* 🌐 *www.boinnovation.com* ⏲ *No lunch Sat. Closed Sun.* Ⓜ *Wan Chai.*

★ **Liu Yuan Pavilion**

$$ | **CHINESE** | **FAMILY** | Often regarded as one of the best Shanghainese restaurants in town, Liu Yuan's cooking style stays loyal to tradition with a no-fuss mentality that has worked in their favor for years. Easy favorites include sweet strips of crunchy eel, panfried meat buns, and steamed *xiao long bao* dumplings plumped up with minced pork and broth. **Known for:** favored by Hong Kong's Shanghainese community; elegant interiors; comfortable booths. Ⓢ *Average main: HK$120* ✉ *The Broadway, 54–62 Lockhart Rd., 3rd fl., Wan Chai* ☎ *2804–2000* Ⓜ *Wan Chai.*

★ **Samsen**

$$ | **THAI** | Chef Adam Cliff made his name at Chachawan in Sheung Wan before opening this, his very own, Thai noodle shop on a historic Wan Chai street. You can spot the open-air restaurant from a mile away, due to the nonstop line out the door—the wait is worth it for Cliff's fresh and flavorful Thai boat noodles, pad Thai, pomelo salads, crab omelettes, and lots of street-style classics. **Known for:** super-slurpable Wagyu beef boat noodles; refreshing Thai watermelon juice—spiked with vodka; colorful, retro-inspired Thai shophouse decor. Ⓢ *Average main: HK$120* ✉ *68 Stone Nullah La., Wan Chai* ☎ *2234–0001* Ⓜ *Wan Chai.*

CAUSEWAY BAY

Goldfinch Restaurant

$$ | **STEAKHOUSE** | **FAMILY** | Travel back to the romantic 1960s at this retro restaurant. Both the decor and the food have remained largely unchanged since the restaurant's heyday, and you'll find local interpretations of borscht, gravy-covered steaks, and other western dishes. **Known for:** the backdrop of director Wong Kar-wai's film, In the Mood for Love; nostalgic charm; big portions. Ⓢ *Average main: HK$200* ✉ *13 Lan Fong Rd., Causeway Bay* ☎ *3427–916.*

Street food in Hong Kong is cheap and delicious.

★ **Second Draft**

$$ | **ASIAN FUSION** | A mecca for craft beer and creative Chinese cuisine, Second Draft anchors Little Tai Hang hotel in its namesake neighborhood. Decked out in retro Hong Kong–inspired decor and wooden booths, the gastropub is always buzzing thanks to the welcoming atmosphere and easy-to-share plates. **Known for:** extensive craft beer list, including varieties from co-owners Young Master Brewery; the mapo burrata and the squid ink croquettes; horseshoe-shape bar, which makes chatting easier. Ⓢ *Average main: HK$150 ✉ 98 Tung Lo Wan Rd., Causeway Bay ☎ 2656–0232 ⊕ www.facebook.com/SecondDraftHK Ⓜ Causeway Bay.*

Sushi Hiro

$$$$ | **JAPANESE** | *Uni* (sea urchin), *ikura* (salmon roe), *o-toro* (the fattiest of fatty tuna) ... if these dishes make you drool, then make a beeline for Sushi Hiro, hidden in an office building but quite possibly the best place in town for raw fish. Dinner can be pricey, but lunch sees some fantastic deals. **Known for:** fresh fish filleted in front of you; truly Japanese minimalist interior; intimate seating perfect for couples and small groups. Ⓢ *Average main: HK$350 ✉ Henry House, 42 Yun Ping Rd., 10th fl., Causeway Bay ☎ 2882–8752 ⊕ www.sushihiro.com.hk Ⓜ Causeway Bay.*

EASTERN

★ **Tung Po**

$$ | **CANTONESE** | **FAMILY** | Arguably Hong Kong's most famous—if not most perpetually packed—indoor dai pai dong has communal tables large enough to fit 18 guests and walls scribbled with an ever-growing list of specials. The food is Hong Kong cuisine with fusion innovations, and you should wash everything down with a cold beer (served here in Chinese soup bowls). **Known for:** spaghetti with cuttlefish and fresh squid ink; seafood dishes and stir-fries; owner Robby Cheung, who's known to blast pop songs and moonwalk;. Ⓢ *Average main: HK$110 ✉ 2nd fl., Java Road Municipal Services Bldg., 99 Java Rd., Eastern*

☎ 2880–5224, 2880–9399 ▭ No credit cards ⏲ No lunch Ⓜ North Point.

Hotels

WAN CHAI

The Fleming

$$$ | HOTEL | An homage to the famous Star Ferry, this boutique hotel in the heart of Wan Chai delivers beautiful rooms done in shades of bottle green and eggshell white and kitted out with retro brass fixtures—all of which recall the vessels that have been plying Hong Kong's harbor for more than a century. **Pros:** comfy beds with goose-down duvets; beautiful design details in every corner; great happy hours at ground-floor restaurant. **Cons:** rooms relatively snug; no harbor views; little natural light in some rooms. *$ Rooms from: HK$3000 ✉ 41 Fleming Rd., Wan Chai 🌐 thefleming.com 66 rooms No meals Ⓜ Wan Chai.*

Grand Hyatt Hong Kong

$$$ | HOTEL | FAMILY | A direct connection to the Hong Kong Convention and Exhibition Centre makes this a business-first hotel, but leisure travelers also enjoy the elegant rooms, with sweeping harbor views and luxurious touches such as an oversize square bathtub and mirror TV. **Pros:** excellent service; extensive sports facilities; Plateau spa is a beautiful sanctuary. **Cons:** quiet outside the hotel at night; difficult to get reservations in popular restaurants; hotel pool is packed on summer days. *$ Rooms from: HK$3600 ✉ 1 Harbour Rd., Wan Chai ☎ 2588–1234 🌐 www.hongkong.grand.hyatt.com 542 rooms No meals Ⓜ Wan Chai, Exit A1.*

Hotel Indigo

$$ | HOTEL | This standout boutique hotel has serious architectural chops—the exterior resembles a circling dragon—as well as photogenic interiors, where exquisitely designed guest rooms have dramatic floor-to-ceiling windows, colorful contemporary decor, and funky tiled-wall murals. **Pros:** complimentary smartphone, with unlimited local calls and 3G data; eclectic neighborhood near nightlife and restaurants; panoramas from the higher floors. **Cons:** pricey drinking and dining options; over-air-conditioned public spaces; tiny fitness center. *$ Rooms from: HK$2000 ✉ 242–246 Queen's Rd. E, Wan Chai ☎ 3926–3888 🌐 www.ihg.com/hotelindigo 138 rooms No meals Ⓜ Wan Chai.*

Renaissance Harbour View Hotel Hong Kong

$$ | HOTEL | FAMILY | The modest guest rooms in this Hong Kong Convention and Exhibition Centre hotel are simply outfitted with attractive modern decor; although many have harbor views, some overlook a sprawling outdoor pool, a driving range, a jogging trail, and a playground that should help keep the kids busy. **Pros:** great harbor views; harborside recreational garden; spacious lobby for working or relaxing. **Cons:** a walk from the subway but near the Star Ferry; lobby can be packed with corporate cats at lunchtime; perpetual construction outside. *$ Rooms from: HK$2000 ✉ 1 Harbour Rd., Wan Chai ☎ 2802–8888 🌐 www.renaissanceharbourviewhk.com 861 rooms No meals Ⓜ Wan Chai.*

CAUSEWAY BAY

Butterfly on Morrison

$$ | HOTEL | FAMILY | Standard rooms are small and don't have views, so consider upgrading to a larger, upper-floor room, where the surrounding skyline and Happy Valley Racecourse form a dramatic backdrop. **Pros:** chic contemporary-style rooms; some rooms specially designed for families; excellent tech amenities, including free 4G pocket Wi-Fi device. **Cons:** few in-hotel facilities; mixed bag when it comes to views; lobby can feel overrun with groups. *$ Rooms from: HK$2400 ✉ 39 Morrison Hill Rd., Causeway Bay ☎ 3962–8333 🌐 www.butterflyhk.com 98 rooms No meals Ⓜ Causeway Bay.*

★ Little Tai Hang

$$ | **HOTEL** | A design-forward hotel in the charming Tai Hang neighborhood combines a unique location with apartment-style rooms, harbor views, a 24/7 gym, a lounge with complimentary drinks and snacks, and free DIY laundry facilities. **Pros:** excellent harbor and city views; spacious rooms, some with kitchenettes; charming neighborhood with cafés, restaurants, and boutiques. **Cons:** check-in process can be slow; some rooms have better views than others; limited amenities and services. *Rooms from: HK$1700* ✉ *98 Tung Lo Wan Rd., Causeway Bay* 🌐 *www.little-taihang.com* *91 rooms* *No meals* Ⓜ *Causeway Bay.*

Metropark Hotel Causeway Bay

$$ | **HOTEL** | The views of the skyline and adjacent Victoria Park are beautiful, whether enjoyed from the simple but effectively designed modern rooms with all the basics or the pleasant rooftop pool. **Pros:** spectacular views for less; across from Victoria Park; easy access to shopping and affordable street food in Causeway Bay. **Cons:** limited facilities; small lobby; few in-room amenities. *Rooms from: HK$1500* ✉ *148 Tung Lo Wan Rd., Causeway Bay* ☎ *2600–1000* 🌐 *www.metroparkhotel.com* *266 rooms* *No meals* Ⓜ *Tin Hau.*

The Park Lane Hong Kong, a Pullman Hotel

$$ | **HOTEL** | Guest rooms are as airy as the views at this elegant landmark, where glass-top furnishings and glass walls accent the open outlooks over Victoria Park greenery, the harbor, and the skyline. **Pros:** excellent views; close to Causeway Bay shopping; free Wi-Fi and complimentary data-enabled phone. **Cons:** often crowded; no pool; mediocre breakfast buffet. *Rooms from: HK$1788* ✉ *310 Gloucester Rd., Causeway Bay* ☎ *2293–8888* 🌐 *www.parklane.com.hk* *832 rooms* *Breakfast* Ⓜ *Causeway Bay.*

Nightlife

Wan Chai is the pungent night flower of the nocturnal scene, where the way of life served as inspiration for the novel *The World of Suzie Wong*. It now shares the streets with hip wine bars, salsa nights, old men's pubs, and after-parties that continue past sunrise. The seedy "hostess bars" in this neighborhood are easy to spot and avoid, with curtained entrances guarded by old ladies on stools and suggestive names in neon. But some things never change: the busiest nights are still when there's a navy ship in the harbor on an R&R stopover. Wednesday's ladies' night, with free or half-price drinks, is also a big draw.

BARS

Djiboutii

BARS/PUBS | Confusingly, the Middle Eastern and Mediterranean menu doesn't have much to do with the African country of Djibouti, but no matter. This gem hidden along a quiet alleyway is a favorite among young professionals looking for a relaxed night out and well-priced drinks. Like an open-air living room, the bar comes dressed up with beautiful artwork, botanical wallpaper, stylish lounge furniture, and a glowing purple-hued bar. The tea-focused cocktails are refreshing, too, particularly during Hong Kong's steamy summer nights. ✉ *Alleyway off 2 Landale St., Wan Chai* ☞ *Closed Sun.* Ⓜ *Wan Chai.*

Ophelia

MUSIC CLUBS | Extravagant and theatrical, Ophelia pays homage to Hong Kong's 19th-century opium dens. From lounging cheongsam-clad "muses" to dancers dressed as peacocks, everything is unapologetically decadent. The menu's colorful, quirky cocktails perfectly complement the larger-than-life atmosphere. ✉ *1st fl., Shop 39A, The Avenue, 200 Queen's Rd. East, Wan Chai* ✣ *Entrance on Lee Tung Ave.* ☎ *2520–1117* 🌐 *www.ophelia.com.hk* Ⓜ *Wan Chai.*

Hong Kong is the perfect destination if you're looking to drop some cash on the three Rs—retail, restaurants, and recreation

The Pawn

BARS/PUBS | FAMILY | As its name suggests, this Wan Chai mainstay occupies a 19th-century heritage building that was once the famous Woo Cheong Pawn Shop. The stylish interior features light woods and an uplifting color palette, while a long balcony overlooks the iconic Hong Kong tramway. Upstairs is the Kitchen restaurant, serving light and refined British cuisine. ✉ *62 Johnston Rd., Wan Chai* ☎ *2866–3444* 🌐 *www.thepawn.com.hk* Ⓜ *Wan Chai.*

Rio

DANCE CLUBS | A nice alternative to the dives of Wan Chai, sophisticated Rio has a plush bar with low-key live music and a dance club complete with a light-up floor. On weekends the party runs until very late. ✉ *Basement, Dannies House, 68–82 Luard Rd., Wan Chai* ☎ *2527–3777* 🌐 *www.rioclub.hk* Ⓜ *Wan Chai.*

NIGHTCLUB

Joe Bananas

MUSIC CLUBS | Considered a Hong Kong landmark—at least, on the nightlife circuit—Joe Bananas is known for its live bands and handsome interiors. It tends to draw an after-hours crowd, since the doors stay open until 5:30 am almost every day of the week. During the day, this is also a popular spot to watch sports games and enjoy comfort foods with a cold beer. ✉ *23 Luard Rd., Wan Chai* ☎ *2537–4618* 🌐 *www.joebananas.hk* Ⓜ *Wan Chai.*

Shopping

CAMERAS AND ELECTRONICS

Broadway

CAMERAS/ELECTRONICS | Like its more famous competitor, Fortress, Broadway is a large electronic-goods chain. It caters primarily to the local market, so some staff members speak better English than others. Look for familiar name-brand cameras, computers, sound systems, home appliances, and mobile phones. ✉ *8th fl., Shop 814, Times Square, 1 Matheson St., Causeway Bay* ☎ *2506–0228* 🌐 *www.broadwaylifestyle.com* Ⓜ *Causeway Bay.*

DG Lifestyle Store

CAMERAS/ELECTRONICS | As Apple Authorized Resellers, DG Lifestyle stores carry the latest iPhone, iPad, Mac, and Apple Watch products. In addition to Apple products, find high-design gadgets, accessories, and software by other brands; these add-ons meld with the sleek design philosophy. ✉ *Shop 917, 9th fl., Times Square, 1 Matheson St., Causeway Bay* ☎ *2506–1338* 🌐 *www.dg-lifestyle.com* Ⓜ *Causeway Bay.*

★ Fortress

CAMERAS/ELECTRONICS | Part of billionaire Li Ka-shing's empire, this extensive chain of shops sells electronics with warranties—a safety precaution that draws the crowds. It also has good deals on printers and accessories, although selection varies by shop. You can spot a Fortress by looking for the big orange sign. For the full list of outlets, visit the website. ✉ *Times Square, Shop 818–821, Shop 914, 8th and 9th fl., 1 Matheson St., Causeway Bay* ☎ *2506–1082* 🌐 *www.fortress.com.hk* Ⓜ *Causeway Bay.*

Wanchai Computer Centre

CAMERAS/ELECTRONICS | You can find decent deals on computer goods and accessories in the labyrinth of shops spanning several floors. It's not as easy to negotiate prices here as it once was, but there are technicians who can help you put together a computer in less than a day if you're rushed; otherwise, two days is normal. The starting price is around HK$3,250 depending on the hardware, processor, and peripherals you choose. This is a great resource, whether you're a techno-buff who's interested in assembling your own computer (a popular pastime in Hong Kong) or a technophobe looking for quality headphones. ✉ *130 Hennessy Rd., Wan Chai* ☎ *2834–7685* Ⓜ *Wan Chai, Exit A5.*

CLOTHING

45R

CLOTHING | Around since 1978, Japanese brand 45R has garnered a reputation for ultracomfortable, exquisitely crafted jeans. Following the successes of outposts in Paris and New York, a flagship store opened on Star Street in 2008. Amid the minimalist surroundings, find heaps of its famous hand-dyed denim as well as breezy button-downs, wooly sweaters, and understated frocks. ✉ *Ground fl., Vincent Mansion, 7 Star St., Wan Chai* ☎ *2861–1145* 🌐 *www.45rpm.jp* Ⓜ *Wan Chai.*

Initial

CLOTHING | This team of local designers creates simple but whimsical clothing with a trendy urban edge. The bags and accessories strike a soft vintage tone, fitting the store's fashionably worn interiors, casually strewn secondhand furniture, and sultry jazz soundtrack. In Causeway Bay, you'll find distinct men's and women's stores. To shop both together under one roof, you'll have to trek up to Sha Tin. ✉ *19 Yun Ping Rd., Causeway Bay* ☎ *2526–8862* 🌐 *www.initialfashion.com* Ⓜ *Causeway Bay.*

kapok

CLOTHING | Hip utilitarian bags, soft fabrics, minimalist watches, comfy kicks, music, stationery—kapok is a one-stop shop for lifestyle products and accessories from independent brands. Meanwhile, the boutique's café serves up steamy French coffee that you're welcome to sip while browsing. If you're lucky, you'll catch one of the store's many exhibitions and pop-up collaborations. ✉ *3 Sun St., Wan Chai* ☎ *2520–0114* 🌐 *www.ka-pok.com* Ⓜ *Admiralty.*

Microwave

CLOTHING | Vintage Japanese boutique Microwave fills its racks with preloved and upcycled looks—all of which are made to turn heads. The youthful range runs the gamut from statement shirts to tasseled jewelry to frilly dresses adorned with dramatic layers of tulle, lace, and ruffles. Pieces range from HK$300 to HK$1,200, depending on the style and designer. ✉ *7 School St., Causeway Bay* ☎ *2566–8823* 🌐 *www.microwavehk.tictail.com* Ⓜ *Causeway Bay.*

Olivia Couture

CLOTHING | The surroundings are functional, but the gowns, wedding dresses, and cheongsams by local designer Olivia Yip are lavish. With a growing clientele—including socialites looking to stand out—Yip is quietly making a name for herself and her Parisian-influenced pieces. ✉ *Ground fl., Shop 3, Redana Centre, 25 Yiu Wah St., Causeway Bay* ☎ *2838–6636* 🌐 *www.oliviacouture.com* Ⓜ *Causeway Bay.*

Spy Henry Lau

CLOTHING | Local bad boy Henry Lau brings an edgy attitude to his fashion for men and women. Bold and often dark, with a touch of bling, his clothing and accessories lines are not for the fainthearted. In Central, you can visit the store at 125 Wellington Street. ✉ *1st fl., Shop B, Cleveland Mansion, 5 Cleveland St., Causeway Bay* ☎ *3580–1197* 🌐 *www.spyhenrylau.com* Ⓜ *Causeway Bay.*

VEIN on the Yard

CLOTHING | Modern and minimalist, VEIN on the Yard's decor is in perfect harmony with its Nordic apparel. The combination boutique and gallery on St. Francis Yard is a spinoff of Vein, and offers up a mix of Scandinavian luxury labels and home accessories. The lineup changes every four to six weeks, but you can usually find at least a dozen stalwart, simple-yet-elegant brands, including Filippa K and Won Hundred. Expect straight lines, a gray-scale palette, and unexpected splashes of color. ✉ *Shop 2, St. Francis Yard, Wan Chai* ☎ *2804–1038* 🌐 *www.bvein.com* Ⓜ *Wan Chai, Exit B2.*

JEWELRY AND ACCESSORIES

Wing On Jewelry Ltd.

JEWELRY/ACCESSORIES | There's a nostalgic charm to the butterflies, birds, and natural forms fashioned from jade, pearls, precious stones, and gold here. Everything looks like an heirloom inherited from your grandmother. With on-site gemologists and artisans, and a commitment to postsale service, this store has a long list of repeat customers. If, however, you lean toward Scandinavian aesthetics and clean lines, this probably isn't the place for you. Wing On Jewelery also has a Causeway Bay branch at 459 Hennessy Road. ✉ *146 Johnston Rd., Wan Chai* ☎ *2572–2332* 🌐 *www.wingonjewelry.com.hk* Ⓜ *Wan Chai.*

MALL

★ **Times Square**

SHOPPING CENTERS/MALLS | This gleaming mall packs most of Hong Kong's best-known stores into 16 frenzied floors, organized thematically. Lane Crawford and Marks & Spencer both have big branches here, as does favored local gourmet grocer City'super. Many beauty brands are located in the basement, giving way to names like Gucci and De Beers on the second floor, and midrange options like Zara higher up. The electronics, sports, and outdoors selection is particularly good. An indoor atrium hosts everything from rock bands to fashion shows to local movie stars. ■ **TIP→ Among the dozen or so eateries, classic Lei Garden is a good pick, thanks to its excellent dim sum menu and Zen interior.** ✉ *1 Matheson St., Causeway Bay* ☎ *2118–8900* 🌐 *www.timessquare.com.hk* Ⓜ *Causeway Bay.*

Kowloon

There's much more to Kowloon than rock-bottom prices and goods of dubious provenance. Just across the harbor from Central, this piece of Chinese mainland takes its name from the string of mountains that bound it in the north: *gau lung,* "nine dragons" (there are actually eight mountains, the ninth represented the emperor who named them). Although less sophisticated and wilder than its island-side counterpart, Kowloon's dense, gritty urban fabric is the backdrop for Hong Kong's best museums and most interesting spiritual sights. And there's street upon street of hard-core consumerism in every imaginable guise.

Kowloon's southernmost district is Tsim Sha Tsui (TST), home to the Star Ferry Pier. The waterfront extends a few miles to TST East. Shops and hotels line Nathan Road, which runs north from the waterfront through the market districts of Jordan, Yau Ma Tei, and Mong Kok.

New Kowloon is the unofficial name for the sprawl beyond Boundary Street. The district just north is Kowloon Tong. Two spiritual sights—Wong Tai Sin and Lok Fu—are a little farther east. The tongue sticking out into the sea to the south was the runway of the old Kai Tak Airport. Kowloon City is a stone's throw west.

GETTING HERE AND AROUND

The most romantic passage from Hong Kong Island to Tsim Sha Tsui (TST) is by Star Ferry. There are crossings from Central every 6 to 12 minutes and a little less often from Wan Chai.

TST is also accessible by MTR. Underground walkways connect the station with the Tsim Sha Tsui East station on the East Rail Line, where trains depart every 10 to 15 minutes for the eastern New Territories. Connecting with Austin station on the West Rail, the Kowloon Airport Express station sits amid the West Kowloon Cultural District (home to concerts, festivals, and the M+ visual arts museum. Hotel shuttles link the area to the rest of Kowloon.

The MTR is your best bet for Jordan, Yau Ma Tei, Mong Kok, and other sights in far-flung Kowloon, including Wong Tai Sin Temple, and Chi Lin Nunnery. In West Kowloon, you will also find the terminus of the Beijing–Guangzhou–Shenzhen–Hong Kong high-speed railway, which connects Hong Kong and Shenzhen in 14 minutes and Guangzhou in 48 minutes. In the future, this rail will also connect Hong Kong with more than a dozen major cities in China, including Beijing and Shanghai.

Tsim Sha Tsui

You'll probably come to this district hugging the waterfront at the southern tip of Kowloon (in Chinese the name means "pointed sandy mouth") to see one or more of Hong Kong's top museums. These collections are within easy reach of one another amid high-rises, hotels, shops, and Kowloon Park, a coveted parcel of green space.

★ Hong Kong Museum of Art

MUSEUM | An extensive collection of Chinese art is packed inside this landmark art museum, which emerged from a years-long face-lift with new exhibitions and experiences. The collections include a heady mix of Qing ceramics, ancient calligraphic scrolls, bronze, jade, lacquerware, textiles, and contemporary canvases. It's all well organized into thematic galleries. The museum sits on the Tsim Sha Tsui waterfront in Kowloon, a few minutes from the Star Ferry and Tsim Sha Tsui MTR stop. ✉ *10 Salisbury Rd., Tsim Sha Tsui* ☎ *2721–0116* 🌐 *hk.art.museum* 🎫 *HK$10* Ⓜ *Tsim Sha Tsui MTR, Exit F.*

Hong Kong Museum of History

MUSEUM | For a comprehensive hit of history, this museum's popular Hong Kong Story should do the trick. The exhibit starts 400 million years ago in the Devonian period and makes its way all the way through to the 1997 Handover, with spectacular life-size dioramas that include village houses and a colonial-era shopping street. The ground-floor Folk Culture section offers an introduction to the history and customs of Hong Kong's main ethnic groups. Upstairs, gracious stone-walled galleries whirl you through the Opium Wars and the beginnings of colonial Hong Kong. Don't miss the chilling account of conditions during the Japanese occupation or the colorful look at Hong Kong life in the '60s. **TIP→ Unless you're with kids who dig models of cavemen and bears, skip the prehistory and dynastic galleries.**

Allow at least two hours to stroll through—more if you linger in every gallery and make use of the interactive elements. Pick your way through the gift shop's clutter to find local designer Alan Chan's T-shirts, shot glasses, and notebooks. His retro-kitsch aesthetic is based on 1940s cigarette-girl images. To get here from the Tsim Sha Tsui MTR walk along Cameron Road, then left for a block along Chatham Road South. A signposted overpass takes you to the museum. ✉ *100 Chatham Rd. S, Tsim Sha Tsui* ☎ *2724–9042* 🌐 *hk.history.museum* 🎫 *HK$10; free Wed.* Ⓜ *Tsim Sha Tsui, Exit B2.*

Kowloon Park

NATIONAL/STATE PARK | **FAMILY** | These 33 acres, crisscrossed by paths and meticulously landscaped, are a refreshing retreat after a bout of shopping. In addition to children's playgrounds, a fitness trail, soccer field, aviary, Chinese garden, and sculpture garden, on Sunday and public holidays there are stalls with arts and crafts, as well as a kung fu corner. ✉ *22 Austin Rd., Tsim Sha Tsui* ☎ *2724–3344* 🌐 *www.lcsd.gov.hk* 🎫 *Free* Ⓜ *Tsim Sha Tsui MTR, Exit A1; Jordan, Exit C1.*

Nathan Road

STORE/MALL | Running for several miles, this street is filled with hotels, restaurants, malls, and boutiques—retail space is so costly that the southern end is dubbed the Golden Mile. The mile's most famous tower block is ramshackle Chungking Mansions, packed with cheap hotels and Indian restaurants. The building was a setting for local director Wong Kar-Wai's film *Chungking Express.* To the left and right are mazes of narrow streets with even more shops selling jewelry, electronics, clothes, souvenirs, and cosmetics. ✉ *Nathan Rd. between Salisbury Rd. and Boundary St., Tsim Sha Tsui* Ⓜ *Tsim Sha Tsui.*

West Kowloon Cultural District

ARTS VENUE | After years of construction, portions of this massive development project—slated to convert 40 hectares (99 acres) of harborfront into green space and to transform Hong Kong into "Asia's arts and cultural capital"—were finally completed in 2018. The first openings included the M+ Museum, one of the world's largest visual arts museums with 17,000 square meters (183,000 square feet) of performance and theater space, and the Xiqu Centre, a beautiful Cantonese opera center, with the 1,000-seat Grand Theatre and more-intimate, 200-seat Tea House Theatre. Come 2022, the cultural district will welcome the waterfront Lyric Theatre Complex for music, theater, and dance; the Hong Kong Palace Museum, devoted to imperial Chinese art; and an Art Park, complete with an outdoor cinema, bar, café, and live-music stage. **TIP→ SmartBikes, which you can rent with cash or an Octopus card, make it easy to explore the vast peninsula.** ✉ *West Kowloon, Tsim Sha Tsui* ☎ *2200–0217* 🌐 *www.westkowloon.hk* 🎫 *Free* Ⓜ *Kowloon Station, Exit E4.*

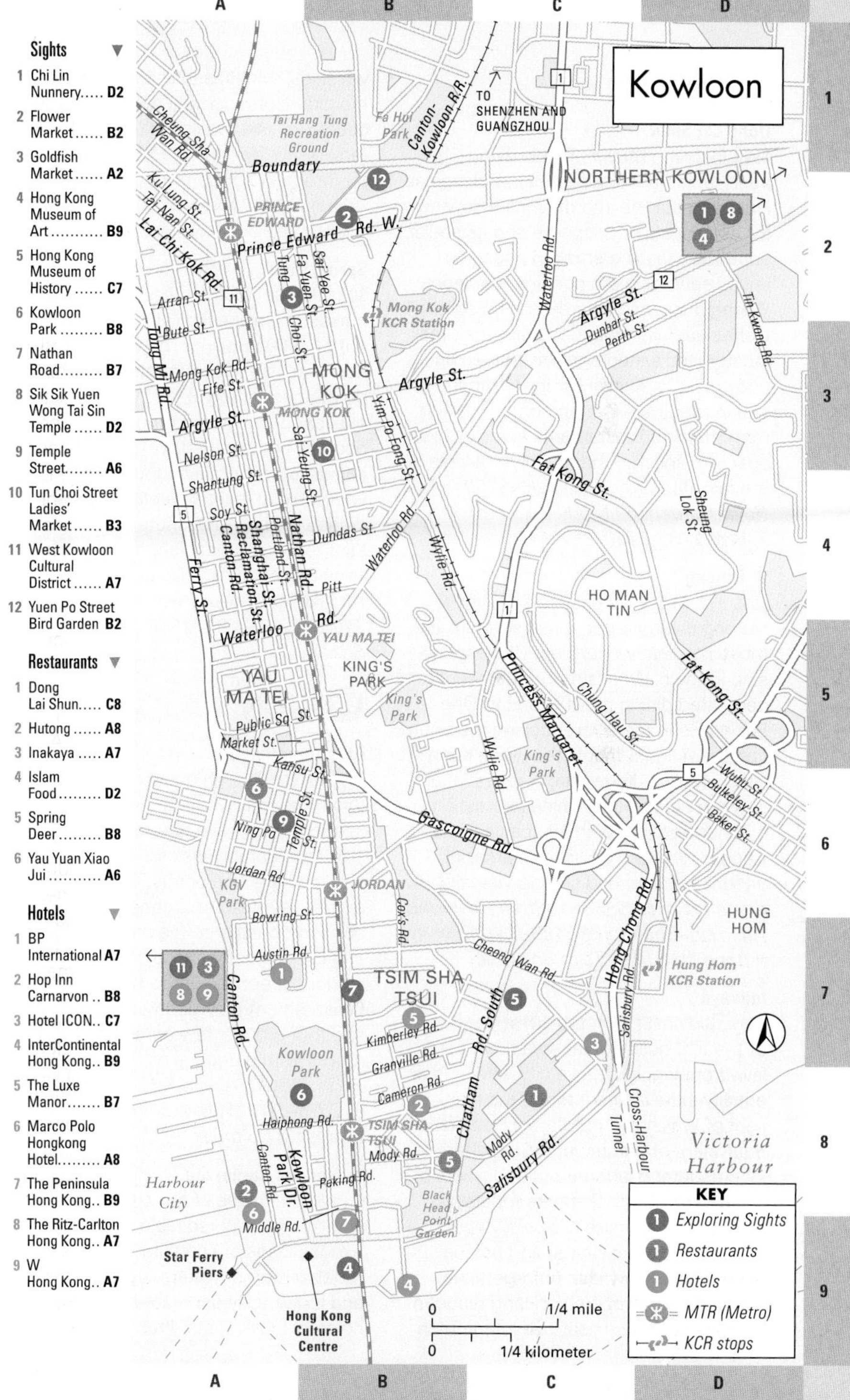

Kowloon
Sights
1 Chi Lin Nunnery..... D2
2 Flower Market...... B2
3 Goldfish Market...... A2
4 Hong Kong Museum of Art........... B9
5 Hong Kong Museum of History...... C7
6 Kowloon Park......... B8
7 Nathan Road......... B7
8 Sik Sik Yuen Wong Tai Sin Temple...... D2
9 Temple Street........ A6
10 Tun Choi Street Ladies' Market...... B3
11 West Kowloon Cultural District...... A7
12 Yuen Po Street Bird Garden B2
Restaurants
1 Dong Lai Shun..... C8
2 Hutong...... A8
3 Inakaya..... A7
4 Islam Food......... D2
5 Spring Deer......... B8
6 Yau Yuan Xiao Jui........... A6
Hotels
1 BP International A7
2 Hop Inn Carnarvon .. B8
3 Hotel ICON.. C7
4 InterContinental Hong Kong.. B9
5 The Luxe Manor....... B7
6 Marco Polo Hongkong Hotel......... A8
7 The Peninsula Hong Kong.. B9
8 The Ritz-Carlton Hong Kong.. A7
9 W Hong Kong.. A7
TO SHENZHEN AND GUANGZHOU
NORTHERN KOWLOON
MONG KOK
YAU MA TEI
KING'S PARK
HO MAN TIN
TSIM SHA TSUI
HUNG HOM
Victoria Harbour
Harbour City
Star Ferry Piers
Hong Kong Cultural Centre
Tai Hang Tung Recreation Ground
Fa Hui Park
King's Park
KGV Park
Kowloon Park
Black Head Point Garden
PRINCE EDWARD
MONG KOK
YAU MA TEI
JORDAN
TSIM SHA TSUI
Mong Kok KCR Station
Hung Hom KCR Station
Canton-Kowloon R.R.
Boundary
Prince Edward Rd. W.
Cheung Sha Wan Rd.
Ku Lung St.
Tai Nan St.
Lai Chi Kok Rd.
Arran St.
Bute St.
Tong Mi Rd.
Mong Kok Rd.
Fife St.
Argyle St.
Nelson St.
Shantung St.
Soy St.
Ferry St.
Canton Rd.
Reclamation St.
Shanghai St.
Portland St.
Nathan Rd.
Tung Choi St.
Fa Yuen St.
Sai Yee St.
Sai Yeung St.
Yim Po Fong St.
Dundas St.
Pitt
Waterloo Rd.
Wylie Rd.
Dunbar St.
Perth St.
Tin Kwong Rd.
Fat Kong St.
Sheung Lok St.
Princess Margaret
Chung Hau St.
Public Sq. St.
Market St.
Kansu St.
Ning Po
Temple St.
Jordan Rd.
Gascoigne Rd.
Wuhu St.
Bulkeley St.
Baker St.
Bowring St.
Austin Rd.
Cox's Rd.
Cheong Wan Rd.
Hong Chong Rd.
Salisbury Rd.
Chatham Rd. South
Kimberley Rd.
Granville Rd.
Cameron Rd.
Haiphong Rd.
Mody Rd.
Peking Rd.
Middle Rd.
Kowloon Park Dr.
Cross-Harbour Tunnel
A
B
C
D
1
2
3
4
5
6
7
8
9
0
1/4 mile
1/4 kilometer
KEY
Exploring Sights
Restaurants
Hotels
MTR (Metro)
KCR stops

Restaurants

Dong Lai Shun

$$$ | **CHINESE** | **FAMILY** | This buzzing Chinese restaurant specializes in Beijing and Huaiyang cuisine and draws a following for its upscale atmosphere and its stellar appetizers (try the smoked eggs and crispy eel), hand-cut noodles, traditional Peking duck, and award-winning combo dishes such as wok-fried crabmeat, rock lobster, and salted egg yolk served on rice crackers. **Known for:** Inner Mongolian shuan yang rou (mutton hotpot); having more than 100 restaurants across China; special hairy crab menu (only available in the fall). [$] *Average main: HK$250* ✉ *The Royal Garden, 69 Mody Rd., Tsim Sha Tsui* ☎ *2733–2020* 🌐 *www.rghk.com.hk.*

★ Hutong

$$$$ | **CHINESE** | It's easy to see why Hutong is a hot spot: it has some of the most imaginative northern Chinese cuisine in town. What's more, the beautifully decorated dining room sits atop One Peking Road Tower overlooking the entire festival of lights that is the Hong Kong island skyline. **Known for:** a sensational selection of regional Chinese creations; a Sunday brunch with 18 specialties and free-flowing Veuve Clicquot; amazing Victoria Harbour and skyline views. [$] *Average main: HK$368* ✉ *28th fl., 1 Peking Rd., Tsim Sha Tsui* ☎ *3428–8342* 🌐 *www.hutong.com.hk* [M] *Tsim Sha Tsui.*

Inakaya

$$$$ | **JAPANESE** | On the 101st floor of the ICC building, Inakaya flaunts a jaw-dropping, bird's-eye city view and an equally extravagant interior, the highlight of which is a *robatayaki* (Japanese equivalent of barbecue) room, where a long counter is adorned with baskets of fresh ingredients. Because robatayaki is served in bite-size morsels, prices can add up, but it's a fun and unique experience. **Known for:** unforgettable grilled dishes prepared on long wooden paddles in front of your eyes; top-notch whiskies, wines, and sakes to sip among the clouds; teppanyaki A5 Wagyu, multicourse kaiseki meals, deluxe sushi platters. [$] *Average main: HK$600* ✉ *101st fl., International Commerce Centre, 1 Austin Rd. W, Kowloon* ☎ *2972–2666* 🌐 *www.jcgroup.hk* [M] *Austin.*

Spring Deer

$$ | **CHINESE** | **FAMILY** | The floral interior makes this place look like something out of 1950s Beijing. The Peking duck, however, is a showstopper (it might be the best in town), and you'll see an old-school crowd enjoying it as well as noodles and stir-fried wok meat dishes. **Known for:** extremely popular—book your table at least a week in advance; delectable boiled peanuts for snacking; stir-fried wok meat dishes and not-to-miss Peking duck. [$] *Average main: HK$180* ✉ *42 Mody Rd., 1st fl., Tsim Sha Tsui* ☎ *2366–4012, 2366–5839* [M] *Tsim Sha Tsui.*

Hotels

BP International

$$ | **HOTEL** | Though guest rooms in this modern town on the north side of Kowloon Park have few frills and vary in size considerably (ask for a larger one), they do have one bonus: views over an extensive swath of greenery or the harbor. **Pros:** on-site coffee shop, restaurant, and lounge; self-service coin laundry; glorious green views from most rooms. **Cons:** can get crowded with business and tour groups; few amenities; small rooms with dated decor. [$] *Rooms from: HK$1900* ✉ *8 Austin Rd., Tsim Sha Tsui* ☎ *2376–1111* 🌐 *www.bpih.com.hk* *529 rooms* *No meals* [M] *Tsim Sha Tsui.*

★ Hop Inn Carnarvon

$ | **B&B/INN** | One of the city's most charming and personable budget hotels exudes loads of character in tidy, comfortable rooms that are well organized and individually decorated with lots of color by local artists. **Pros:** fun, beautifully original decor for budget lodgings; friendly staff; private bathrooms. **Cons:** not too many amenities, but the price is right; decor in need of refurbishment; rooms near elevators or reception can be noisy. *Rooms from: HK$650 9th fl., James S. Lee Mansion, 33–35 Carnarvon Rd., Tsim Sha Tsui 2881–7139 www.hopinn.hk 27 rooms No meals Tsim Sha Tsui.*

★ Hotel ICON

$$$ | **HOTEL** | The interiors throughout this hotel are designed to make a statement, from the vertical garden hanging above the lobby café to the stylish, panoramic, top-floor lounge—and, in between, are gorgeous, view-filled guest rooms outfitted with cozy woods, natural fabrics, and high-tech amenities. **Pros:** a designer's dream; dedication to guest experience; complimentary smartphones with free mobile data. **Cons:** surrounding area is thick with crowds at times; long walk from the MTR; lobby can feel busy when small tour groups arrive. *Rooms from: HK$2600 17 Science Museum Rd., Tsim Sha Tsui 3400–1000 www.hotel-icon.com 262 rooms No meals Tsim Sha Tsui East.*

★ InterContinental Hong Kong

$$ | **HOTEL** | Its location at the tip of the Kowloon peninsula ensures panoramic, front-row harbor views from most of the restaurants and contemporary guest rooms, which feature sunken tubs in marble bathrooms, 24-hour butler service, and complimentary Handy smartphones with data. **Pros:** exceptional views; service, as expected, is impeccable; extravagant spa and excellent restaurant lineup. **Cons:** the Avenue of Stars, just outside the hotel, is under redevelopment; can be hard to get reservations at the popular restaurants; long walk from the MTR. *Rooms from: HK$1900 18 Salisbury Rd., Tsim Sha Tsui 2721–1211 www.hongkong-ic.intercontinental.com 503 rooms No meals Tsim Sha Tsui.*

The Luxe Manor

$$ | **HOTEL** | In the absence of views, rooms are a show in themselves, with audacious design, artsy decor, and plenty of luxury and comfort. **Pros:** a trippy experience for art and design lovers; close to nightlife and shopping; live music at the hotel's bar and lounge. **Cons:** no views; lobby feels deserted at times; the over-the-top design is not for everyone. *Rooms from: HK$1600 39 Kimberley Rd., Tsim Sha Tsui 3763–8888 www.theluxemanor.com 159 rooms No meals Tsim Sha Tsui.*

Marco Polo Hongkong Hotel

$$ | **HOTEL** | **FAMILY** | Spacious rooms with sweeping views of Hong Kong Island are near the shopping hub along Canton Road and linked to Harbour City's immense shopping complex. **Pros:** westward views; convenient to Star Ferry and other transport; easy access to Harbour City shopping. **Cons:** full in late March during the Hong Kong Rugby Sevens tournament; boisterous crowds during German Bierfest; busy atmosphere. *Rooms from: HK$2000 Harbour City, Canton Rd., Tsim Sha Tsui 2113–0088 www.marcopolohotels.com 665 rooms No meals Tsim Sha Tsui.*

★ The Peninsula Hong Kong

$$$$ | **HOTEL** | Even in a city with so many world-class hotels, The Peninsula—opened in 1928 and the luxury brand's flagship—stands apart from the rest, an oasis of old-world glamour, with Kowloon and harbor views that'll make you feel like you own Hong Kong and high-ceilinged, apartment-like rooms furnished with chic, residential-style elegance and updated with guest-oriented technology. **Pros:** legendary dining and service; state-of-the-art room facilities; extensive on-site facilities. **Cons:** rooms are pricey; the lobby feels like a tourist trap in the afternoon; no outdoor pool. *Rooms from: HK$5080 Salisbury Rd., Tsim Sha Tsui 2920–2888*

hongkong.peninsula.com *300 rooms* *No meals* *Tsim Sha Tsui, Exit L3.*

★ The Ritz-Carlton, Hong Kong

$$$$ | **HOTEL** | **FAMILY** | At the world's highest hotel, occupying the 102nd through the 118th floors of West Kowloon's ICC skyscraper, every large, luxurious guest room enjoys a stupendous vantage point. **Pros:** earth-shattering views; top-class service and amenities; sanctuary of a spa. **Cons:** pricey rates and food; surrounding Kowloon area lacks nightlife; famous Ozone bar feels overpriced and touristy. *Rooms from: HK$4700* *International Commerce Center, 1 Austin Rd. W, Kowloon* *2263–2263* *www.ritzcarlton.com* *312 rooms* *No meals* *West Kowloon.*

★ W Hong Kong

$$$$ | **HOTEL** | A hip, young vibe prevails, though guest rooms are veritable urban oases—soundproof and spacious; alternately colorful or sleek on even and odd floors; and equipped with mood lighting, surround audiovisual systems, big mirrors, and even bigger harbor views. **Pros:** spacious and colorful rooms; panoramic views; exciting bars and restaurants. **Cons:** noisy atmosphere outside rooms; construction nearby; long walk from the MTR through the mall. *Rooms from: HK$6000* *1 Austin Rd. W, Kowloon Station, Kowloon* *3717–2222* *www.w-hongkong.com* *393 rooms* *No meals* *West Kowloon.*

Nightlife

★ Aqua Spirit

BARS/PUBS | Inside an impressive curvaceous skyscraper, this very cool bar sits on the mezzanine level of the top floor. The high ceilings and glass walls offer up unrivaled views of Hong Kong and the surrounding harbor filled with ferries and ships. Tables are placed in front of the windows so you never have to crane your neck to see the skyline. *30th fl., One Peking, 1 Peking Rd., Tsim Sha Tsui* *3427–2288* *www.aqua.com.hk* *Tsim Sha Tsui.*

Delaney's

BARS/PUBS | This Irish pub has interiors that were shipped here from the Emerald Isle, and the mood is as authentic as the furnishings. Guinness and Delaney's ale (a specialty microbrew) are on tap, and there's a traditional Irish menu. The crowd includes some Irish regulars, so get ready for spontaneous outbursts of fiddling and other Celtic traditions. *Basement fl., Mary Bldg., 71–77 Peking Rd., Tsim Sha Tsui* *2301–3980* *www.delaneys.com.hk* *Tsim Sha Tsui.*

★ Felix

BARS/PUBS | High up in the Peninsula Hong Kong, this bar is immensely popular with visitors. It not only has a brilliant view of the island, but the dramatic interiors are by the visionary designer Philippe Starck. Another memorable feature: tthe women's bathroom overlooks the harbor, while the men's has great city views. *28th fl., Peninsula Hong Kong, Salisbury Rd., Tsim Sha Tsui* *2696–6778* *hongkong.peninsula.com* *Tsim Sha Tsui.*

Shopping

CLOTHING

Dorfit

CLOTHING | A longtime cashmere manufacturer and retailer, Dorfit caters to a variety of men's, women's, and children's tastes. Knitwear here comes in pure cashmere as well as blends, so be sure to ask which is which. *6th fl., Room 601, Mary Bldg., 71–77 Peking Rd., Tsim Sha Tsui* *2312–1013* *www.dorfit.com.hk* *Tsim Sha Tsui.*

Giordano

CLOTHING | Hong Kong's version of the Gap is the most established and ubiquitous local source for basic T-shirts, jeans, and casual wear. Like its U.S. counterpart, the brand now has a bit more fashion sense, but prices are still reasonable. Although the flagship store is in Manson House on Nathan Road, you'll have no problem finding one on almost every major street. ✉ *Ground fl., Manson House, 74–78 Nathan Rd., Tsim Sha Tsui* ☎ *2926–1028* 🌐 *www.giordano.com.hk* Ⓜ *Tsim Sha Tsui, Exit B1.*

giordano ladies

CLOTHING | If Giordano is the Gap, giordano ladies is the Banana Republic, albeit with a more Zen aesthetic. Find clean-line modern classics in neutral black, gray, white, and beige; each collection is brightened by a soft highlight color, such as leafy green, indigo, or rusty orange. Everything is elegant enough for the office and comfortable enough for the plane. ✉ *1st fl., Manson House, 74–78 Nathan Rd., Tsim Sha Tsui* ☎ *2926–1331* 🌐 *www.giordanoladies.com* Ⓜ *Tsim Sha Tsui.*

Maxwell's Clothiers Ltd.

CLOTHING | After you've found a handful of reputable, high-quality tailors, one way to choose between them is price. Maxwell's is known for its competitive rates. It's also a wonderful place to have favorite men's and women's shirts and suits copied. It was founded by third-generation tailor Ken Maxwell in 1961 and follows Shanghai tailoring traditions, while also providing the fabled 24-hour suit upon request. The showroom and workshop are in Kowloon, but son Andy and his team take appointments in the United States, Canada, Australia, and Europe twice annually. ✉ *13th fl., Maxwell Centre, 39–41 Hankow Rd., Tsim Sha Tsui* ☎ *2366–6705* 🌐 *www.maxwells-clothiers.com* Ⓜ *Tsim Sha Tsui, Exit A1.*

Mode Elegante

CLOTHING | Don't be deterred by the somewhat dated mannequins in the windows. Mode Elegante is a favorite source for custom-made suits among women and men in the know. Tailors here specialize in European cuts. You'll have your choice of fabrics from the United Kingdom, Italy, and elsewhere. Your records are put on file so you can place orders from abroad. It'll even ship the completed garment to you almost anywhere on the planet. Alternatively, you can make an appointment with director Gary Zee, one of Hong Kong's traveling tailors, who makes regular visits to North America, Australia, Europe, and Japan. ✉ *11th fl., Room 1127A, Star House, 3 Salisbury Rd., Tsim Sha Tsui* ☎ *2366–8153* 🌐 *www.modeelegante.com* Ⓜ *Tsim Sha Tsui.*

★ Pearls & Cashmere

CLOTHING | Warehouse prices in chic shopping arcades? It's true. This old Hong Kong favorite is elegantly housed on both sides of the harbor. In addition to quality men's and women's cashmere sweaters in classic designs and in every color under the sun, they also sell reasonably priced pashminas, gloves, and socks, which make great gifts for men and women. In recent years the brand has developed the more fashion-focused line, BYPAC. ✉ *Mezzanine, Peninsula Hotel Shopping Arcade, Salisbury Rd., Tsim Sha Tsui* ☎ *2723–8698* 🌐 *bypac.com* Ⓜ *Tsim Sha Tsui, Exit L4.*

Raja Fashions

CLOTHING | A three-generation haberdasher that's been dressing Hong Kong *tai pans* since 1957, Raja Fashions has a presence in 13 countries around the world. At the Hong Kong flagship on Cameron Road, gents will be spoiled for choice when it comes to suit fabrics—there are more than 20,000 on offer, including big names such as Ermenegildo Zegna, Loro Piana, and Guabello. ✉ *34–C Cameron Rd., Tsim Sha Tsui* ☎ *2366–7624* 🌐 *www.raja-fashions.com* Ⓜ *Tsim Sha Tsui.*

★ Sam's Tailor

CLOTHING | Unlike many famous Hong Kong tailors, you won't find the legendary Sam's in a chic hotel or sleek mall. But don't be fooled. These digs in humble Burlington House, a tailoring hub, have hosted everyone from U.S. presidents (back as far as Richard Nixon) to performers such as the Black Eyed Peas, Kylie Minogue, and Blondie. This former uniform tailor to the British troops once even made a suit for Prince Charles in a record hour and 52 minutes. The men's and women's tailor does accept 24-hour suit or shirt orders, but will take about two days if you're not in a hurry. Founded by Naraindas Melwani in 1957, "Sam" is now his son, Manu Melwani, who runs the show with the help of his own son, Roshan, and about 57 tailors behind the scenes. In 2004 Sam's introduced a computerized bodysuit that takes measurements without a tape measure (it uses both methods, however). These tailors also make biannual trips to Europe and North America: schedule updates are listed on the website. ✉ *Burlington House, 94 Nathan Rd., Tsim Sha Tsui* ☎ *2367–9423* 🌐 *www.samstailor.com* Ⓜ *Tsim Sha Tsui.*

JEWELRY AND ACCESSORIES

Artland Watch Co Ltd.

JEWELRY/ACCESSORIES | Elegant but uncomplicated, the interior of this established watch retailer is like its service. The informed staff will guide you through the countless luxury brands on show and in the catalogs from which you can also order. Prices here aren't the best in Hong Kong, but they're still lower than at home. ✉ *Ground fl., Mirador Mansion, 62A Nathan Rd., Tsim Sha Tsui* ☎ *2366–4508* Ⓜ *Tsim Sha Tsui.*

TSL Jewellery

JEWELRY/ACCESSORIES | One of the big Hong Kong chains, TSL (Tse Sui Luen) specializes in diamond jewelry, and manufactures, retails, and exports its designs. Its range of 100-facet stones includes the Estrella cut, which reflects nine symmetrical hearts and comes with international certification. Although its contemporary designs use platinum settings, TSL also sells pure, bright, yellow-gold items targeted at Chinese customers. ✉ *G5–G7, Park Lane Shopper' Blvd., Nathan Rd., Tsim Sha Tsui* ☎ *2375–2661* 🌐 *www.tsljewellery.com* Ⓜ *Tsim Sha Tsui.*

MALLS AND SHOPPING CENTERS

★ Festival Walk

SHOPPING CENTERS/MALLS | Located in residential Kowloon Tong, about 20 minutes from Central on the MTR, Festival Walk stretches across six floors, with Marks & Spencer, an Apple store, MUJI, and H&M serving as anchors. Vivienne Tam and PS by Paul Smith draw the elite crowds; I.T. and agnès b. keep the trend spotters happy. If you want a respite from the sometimes scorching-hot weather, Festival Walk also has one of the city's largest ice rinks, a multiplex cinema, and more than 30 restaurants and cafés. ■ **TIP→ There's free Wi-Fi throughout the mall, as well as excellent brews at Coffee Academics.** ✉ *80 Tat Chee Ave., Kowloon* ☎ *2844–2200* 🌐 *www.festivalwalk.com.hk* Ⓜ *Kowloon Tong.*

★ Harbour City

SHOPPING CENTERS/MALLS | The four interconnected complexes that make up Harbour City contain almost 500 shops between them—if you can't find it here, it probably doesn't exist. Pick up a map on your way in, as it's easy to get lost. **Ocean Terminal,** the largest section, runs along the harbor and is divided thematically, with kids' wear and toys on the ground floor, and sports and cosmetics on the first. The top floor is home to white-hot department store LCX. Near the Star Ferry pier, the **Marco Polo Hong Kong Hotel Arcade** has branches of the department store Lane Crawford. Louis Vuitton, Chanel, and Burberry are some of the posher boutiques that fill the **Ocean Centre** and **Gateway Arcade,** parallel to Canton Road. Most of the complex's restaurants are here, too. A cinema and three hotels round out Harbour City's offerings. ■ **TIP→ Free Wi-Fi is available.** ✉ *3–27 Canton Rd., Tsim Sha Tsui* 🌐 *www.harbourcity.com.hk* Ⓜ *Tsim Sha Tsui.*

Yau Ma Tei, Mong Kok, and Northern Kowloon

North of Tsim Sha Tsui, the vibrant area of Yau Ma Tei teems with people and is home to several street markets. Around Jordan Road, follow the little offshoots to find boutique shops, quiet temples, and low-key *cha chaan tengs* (1950s-style diners). The Jordan MTR stop is another good place to start your exploring.

Mong Kok lives up to its Chinese name, which translates roughly as "busy corner." The neighborhood is the epicenter of Hong Kong street fashion—the trends that originate from these bustling streets are known as "MK style."

Sights

★ Chi Lin Nunnery

RELIGIOUS SITE | Not a single nail was used to build this nunnery, which dates from 1934. Instead, traditional Tang Dynasty architectural techniques involving wooden dowels and bracket work hold everything together. Most of the 15 cedar halls house altars to bodhisattvas (those who have reached enlightenment)—bronze plaques explain each one. The Main Hall is the most imposing—and inspiring—part of the monastery. Overlooking the smaller second courtyard, it honors the first Buddha, known as Sakyamuni. The soaring ceilings are held up by cedar columns that support the roof. The principles of feng shui governed all construction: buildings face south toward the sea, to bring abundance; they're backed by the mountain, a provider of strength and good energy. The temple's clean lines are a vast departure from most of Hong Kong's colorful religious buildings ✉ *5 Chi Lin Dr., Kowloon* ☎ *2354–1888* 🎫 *Free* Ⓜ *Diamond Hill, Exit C2.*

Flower Market

MARKET | Stalls containing local and imported fresh flowers, potted plants, and even artificial blossoms cover Flower Market Road, as well as parts of Yuen Po Street, Yuen Ngai Street, Prince Edward Road West, and Playing Field Road. ✉ *Flower Market Rd. between Yuen Ngai St. and Yuen Po St., Mong Kok* 🎫 *Free* Ⓜ *Mong Kok East, Exit C; Prince Edward, Exit B1.*

Goldfish Market

STORE/MALL | FAMILY | A few dozen shops at the northern end of Tung Choi Street, starting at the intersection with Nullah Road, sell the ubiquitous fish, which locals believe to be lucky. There are other types of animals as well. ✉ *Tung Choi St. and Nullah Rd., Mong Kok* 🎫 *Free* Ⓜ *Mong Kok East, Exit C; Prince Edward, Exit B2.*

★ Sik Sik Yuen Wong Tai Sin Temple

RELIGIOUS SITE | There's a practical approach to prayer at one of Hong Kong's most exuberant places of worship. Here the territory's three major religions—Taoism, Confucianism, and Buddhism—are all celebrated under the same roof. You'd think that ornamental religious buildings would look strange with highly visible vending machines and LCD displays in front of them, but Wong Tai Sin pulls it off in cacophonous style. The temple was established in the early 20th century, on a different site on Hong Kong Island, when two Taoist masters arrived from Guangzhou with the portrait of Wong Tai Sin—a famous monk who was born around AD 328—that still graces the main altar. In the '20s the shrine was moved here and expanded over the years.

Start at the incense-wreathed main courtyard, where the noise of many people shaking out *chim* (sticks with fortunes written on them) forms a constant rhythm. After wandering the halls, take time out in the Good Wish Garden—a peaceful riot of rockery—at the back of the complex. At the base of the complex is a small arcade where soothsayers and palm readers are happy to interpret Wong Tai Sin's predictions for a small fee. At the base of the ramp to the Confucian Hall, look up behind the temple for a view of Lion Rock, a mountain in the shape of a sleeping lion. ■ **TIP→ If you feel like acquiring a household altar of your own, head for Shanghai Street in Yau Ma Tei, the Kowloon district north of Tsim Sha Tsui, where religious shops abound.** ✉ *Wong Tai Sin Rd., Kowloon* ☎ *2327–8141* 🌐 *www.siksikyuen.org.hk* 🎫 *Donations expected. Good Wish Garden HK$2* Ⓜ *Wong Tai Sin, Exit B2 or B3.*

Temple Street

NEIGHBORHOOD | In the heart of Yau Ma Tei, Temple Street is home to Hong Kong's biggest night market. Stalls selling kitsch of all kinds set up in the late afternoon in the blocks north of Public Square Street. Fortune-tellers, open-air cafés, and street doctors also offer their services here. ✉ *Temple St. between Jordan Rd. and Kansu St., Yau Ma Tei* Ⓜ *Yau Ma Tei, Exit C; Jordan, Exit A.*

Tung Choi Street Ladies' Market

MARKET | Despite the name, the stalls here are filled with no-brand clothing and accessories for both sexes. The shopping is best between Dundas and Argyle. ✉ *Tung Choi St. between Dundas St. and Argyle St., Mong Kok* 🎫 *Free* Ⓜ *Mong Kok.*

Yuen Po Street Bird Garden

STORE/MALL | **FAMILY** | Adjacent to the Flower Market, this street has more than 70 stalls selling different types of twittering, fluttering birds. Pretty wooden birdcages, starting from about HK$500, are also on offer. ✉ *Yuen Po St. between Boundary St. and Prince Edward Rd. W, Mong Kok* Ⓜ *Mong Kok East, Exit C; Prince Edward, Exit B1.*

Shopping

DEPARTMENT STORE

★ Yue Hwa Chinese Products Emporium

DEPARTMENT STORES | This popular purveyor of Chinese goods has 14 stores across Hong Kong, and the flagship one features seven floors laden with everything from clothing and housewares to traditional medicine. The logic behind its layout is hard to fathom, so go with time to rifle around. As well as the predictable tablecloths, silk pajamas, and chopsticks, there are cheap and colorful porcelain sets and offbeat local favorites like mini-massage chairs. The fifth floor has a selection of tea—you can pick up a HK$50 packet of leaves or an antique Yixing teapot stretching into the thousands. ✉ *301–309 Nathan Rd., Jordan, Yau Ma Tei* ☎ *3511–2222* 🌐 *www.yuehwa.com* Ⓜ *Jordan.*

Restaurants

Islam Food

$ | **CHINESE** | This might not be the prettiest restaurant you've ever seen, but its panfried beef patties (translated as "veal goulash" on the menu) are incredibly delicious. The browned pastry packets arrive at the table piping hot and bursting with tender minced beef—good luck stopping after just one. **Known for:** tasty halal food; tender lamb brisket curry, panfried mutton dumplings, hot-and-sour soup; lines out the door at peak hours. Ⓢ *Average main: HK$65* ✉ *1 Lung Kong Rd., Kowloon* ☎ *2382–1882, 2382–8928* 🌐 *www.islamfood.com.hk* 💳 *No credit cards.*

★ Yau Yuan Xiao Jui

$ | **CHINESE** | It might look like any other tiny, storefront noodle joint, but its humble appearance belies its culinary prowess. The restaurant serves authentic Shaanxi snacks, which can be best described as some of the heartiest and delicious chow that China has to offer. **Known for:** handmade dumplings fattened up with lamb and scallion oil; signature biang biang mien (long, wide, al dente noodles with chili oil and marinated spareribs); brusque yet efficient service;. $ *Average main: HK$40* ✉ *36 Man Yuen St., Jordon, Jordan* ☎ *5300–2682* ▭ *No credit cards* Ⓜ *Austin.*

JEWELRY AND ACCESSORIES

Sandra Pearls

JEWELRY/ACCESSORIES | You might be wary of the lustrous pearls hanging at this little Jade Market stall. But the charming owner does, in fact, sell genuine cultured and freshwater pearl necklaces and earrings at reasonable prices. Some pieces are made from shell, which Sandra is always quick to point out, and could pass muster among the snobbiest collectors. ✉ *Stall 437 and 447, Jade Market, Kansu St., Yau Ma Tei* ☎ *9485–2895* Ⓜ *Jordan, Exit A.*

MARKET

★ Temple Street Night Market

OUTDOOR/FLEA/GREEN MARKETS | Each evening, as darkness falls, the lamps strung between the stalls of this Yau Ma Tei street market slowly light up, and the air fills with aromas wafting from myriad food carts. Hawkers try to catch your eye by flinging up clothes; Cantonese opera competes with swelling pop music and the sounds of spirited haggling; fortune-tellers and street performers add another element to the sensory overload. Granted, neither the garments nor the cheap gadgets sold here are much to get excited about, but it's the atmosphere people come for—any purchases are a bonus. The market stretches for almost a mile and is one of Hong Kong's liveliest nighttime shopping experiences. ✉ *Temple St., Yau Ma Tei* Ⓜ *Jordan, Exit A.*

Southside

For all the unrelenting urbanity of Hong Kong Island's north coast, its south side consists largely of green hills and a few residential areas around picturesque bays. With beautiful sea views, real estate is at a premium; some of Hong Kong's wealthiest residents live in beautiful houses and luxurious apartments here. Southside is a breath of fresh air—literally and figuratively. The people are more relaxed, the pace is slower, and there are lots of sea breezes.

GETTING HERE AND AROUND

You can get here by bus from the center of the city, and the trip will take anywhere from 20 to 50 minutes. Note that express buses skip Aberdeen and Deep Water Bay, heading directly to Repulse Bay and Stanley. Buses run less frequently in the evening, so it's more convenient to grab a taxi (they're everywhere). A faster option is the MTR, which connects Admiralty Station with Ocean Park, Wong Chuk Hang. Kei Tung, and South Horizons (in Aberdeen) in about 4–11 minutes.

Sights

Aberdeen

TOWN | Aberdeen's harbor contains about 3,000 junks and sampans, and each might be home to multiple generations of one family. During the Tin Hau Festival in April and May, hundreds more boats converge along the shore. On Aberdeen's side streets you'll find outdoor barbers hard at work and any number of dim sum restaurants serving up dishes you won't find at home. You'll also see traditional sights like the Aberdeen Cemetery, with its enormous terraced gravestones, and yet another shrine to the goddess of the sea: the Tin Hau Temple. ✉ *Southside.*

Ocean Park

AMUSEMENT PARK/WATER PARK | **FAMILY** | Most Hong Kongers have fond childhood memories of this aquatic theme park. It was built by the omnipresent Hong Kong Jockey Club on 170 hilly acres overlooking the sea just east of Aberdeen. Highlights include the resident pandas, an enormous aquarium, and the

Ocean Theatre, where dolphins and seals perform. Youngsters love thrill rides like the gravity-defying Hair Raiser, as well as the Water World waterpark, added in 2019. The park is accessible by the MTR's South Island Line. From Admiralty Station, the ride takes about four minutes. There are also a number of buses, including the 629; get off at the stop after the Aberdeen tunnel. **■ TIP→ If you have kids, plan to spend a day here. You can even stay the night: Marriott's 471-room hotel has a 52-foot-high, cylindrical aquarium in its lobby.** ✉ *Ocean Park Rd., Aberdeen, Southside* ☎ *3923–2323* 🌐 *www.oceanpark.com.hk* 🎟 *HK$480.*

Repulse Bay

BEACH—SIGHT | The beach in this tranquil neighborhood is large and wide, but be warned: it's the first stop for most visitors to Southside. Two huge statues of Tin Hau—goddess of the sea—at the east end of the beach were built in the 1970s. Worshippers had planned to erect just one statue, but worried she'd be lonely. Look for a famous apartment building with a hole through it—following the principles of feng shui, the opening allows the dragon that lives in the mountains behind to readily drink from the bay. To get here, take Bus 6, 6A, 6X, 66, or 260 from Exchange Square Bus Terminus in Central. **Amenities:** food and drink; lifeguards; parking (HK$50–HK$60 fee for two hours); showers; toilets; water sports. **Best for:** sunset; swimming; walking. ✉ *Beach Rd. at Seaview Promenade, Repulse Bay, Southside* ☎ *2812–2483.*

Shek O

TOWN | **FAMILY** | The seaside locale is Southside's easternmost village. Every shop sells the same inflatable beach toys—the bigger the better, it seems. Cut through town to a windy road that takes you to the "island" of Tai Tau Chau, really a large rock with a lookout over the South China Sea. You can hike through nearby Shek O Country Park, where the bird-watching is great, in less than two hours. To get here from Central, take the MTR to Shau Kei Wan (Exit A3), then take Bus 9 to the last stop (about 30 minutes). ✉ *Southside.*

★ **Stanley**

TOWN | **FAMILY** | This peninsula town lies south of Deep Water and Repulse bays. There's great shopping in the popular Stanley Market, full of casual clothes, cheap souvenirs, and cheerful bric-a-brac. Stanley's popular beach is the site of the Dragon Boat Races every June. To get here from Exchange Square Bus Terminus in Central, take Bus 6, 6A, 6X, 66, or 260. ✉ *Southside.*

Restaurants

The Verandah

$$$$ | **EUROPEAN** | From the well-spaced tables overlooking the bay to the unobtrusive service to the menu of delicious classics (think French onion soup, Dover sole meunière, and tournedos Rossini), this is an unabashedly regal experience that delivers with finesse at every turn. The beautiful colonial setting is also the perfect place to enjoy a traditional English afternoon tea. **Known for:** a reasonably priced wine list; views of Repulse Bay; classic European cuisine. 💲 *Average main: HK$500* ✉ *The Repulse Bay, 109 Repulse Bay Rd., Repulse Bay, Southside* ☎ *2292–2822* 🌐 *www.therepulsebay.com* 🕘 *Closed Mon. and Tues.*

Shopping

CLOTHING

Sonjia

CLOTHING | Walk past busy garages and funky murals in this industrial Hong Kong area to find the chic atelier of Korean-English ex-lawyer Sonjia Norman. The designer crafts quietly luxurious, one-of-a-kind pieces and modified vintage clothing under the Sonjia label. Her clothes are the epitome of understated wealth, plus the boutique also offers an array of jewelry, scarves, and home accessories. ✉ *12th fl., Shop 12B, Derrick Industrial Building., 49–51 Wong Chuk Hang Rd., Southside* ☎ *2529–6223* 🌐 *www.sonjiaonline.com* Ⓜ *Wong Chuk Hang.*

MARKET

★ Stanley Market

OUTDOOR/FLEA/GREEN MARKETS | This was once Hong Kong's most famed bargain trove for visitors, but its ever-growing popularity means that the market in Stanley Village no longer has the best prices around. Still, you can pick up some good buys in sportswear, casual clothing, textiles, and paintings if you comb through the stalls. Good-value linens—especially appliqué tablecloths—also abound. Dozens and dozens of shops line a main street so narrow that awnings from each side meet in the middle, and on busy days your elbows will come in handy. Weekdays are a little more relaxed. One of the best things about Stanley Market is getting here: the winding bus ride from Central (Routes 6 or 66) or Tsim Sha Tsui (Route 973) takes you over the top of Hong Kong Island, with fabulous views along on the way. ✉ *Stanley, Southside* 🌐 *www.hk-stanley-market.com.*

Lantau Island

Manic development is changing Lantau, but the island is still known as the "lungs of Hong Kong" because of the abundant forests, relative dearth of skyscrapers, and laid-back attractions—beaches, fishing villages, and hiking trails. At Ngong Ping, a minitheme park sits at the base of the island's most famous sight, the Tian Tan Buddha. Hong Kong Disneyland sits on the northeast coast, near the airport. At 147 square km (57 square miles), Lantau is almost twice the size of Hong Kong Island, so there's room for all this development, and the island remains a welcome green getaway.

GETTING HERE AND AROUND

The speediest way to get to Lantau from Central is the MTR's Tung Chung line (HK$26), which takes about 40 minutes. Far more pleasant is the 35-minute fast ferry (HK$26.80–HK$38.80) from Central to Mui Wo (get a window seat for the views).

Sights

Hong Kong Disneyland

AMUSEMENT PARK/WATER PARK | FAMILY | Though Hong Kong's home to Mickey Mouse is tame compared with other Magic Kingdoms, it's fast bringing Mai Kei Lo Su—as the world's most famous mouse is known locally—to a mainland audience. Younger kids will find plenty of amusement at Sleeping Beauty Castle and Toy Story Land, while older siblings and parents will probably gravitate to the more-thrilling Space Mountain. Inside the dedicated Marvel area (to fully open in 2023), daredevils will also enjoy the multisensory, immersive Iron Man Experience and the Ant-Man themed attraction. **■ TIP→ Keen to stay overnight? There are three thematic on-site hotels, including the travel-themed Disney Explorers Lodge.** ✉ *Fantasy Rd., Lantau Island* 🌐 *park.hongkongdisneyland.com* 🎟 *HK$619* Ⓜ *Disneyland Resort.*

Lantau Peak

VIEWPOINT | The most glorious views of Lantau—and beyond—are from atop Lantau Peak, but at 3,064 feet, the mountaintop experience is not for the fainthearted. The ascent up the mountain that locals call Fung Wong Shan requires a strenuous 7½-mile hike west from Mui Wo, or you can begin at the Po Lin Monastery—still a demanding two hours. You can also take Bus 23 to a trail that is closer to the summit, and climb from Stage 3 of the Lantau Trail. The most striking views are at sunrise, particularly between December and February, when the air is dry and the sky is clear. ✉ *Lantau Island.*

★ **Tian Tan Buddha**

PUBLIC ART | Hong Kongers love superlatives, even if making them true requires strings of qualifiers. So the Tian Tan Buddha, also known as the Big Buddha, is the world's largest Buddha—that's seated, located outdoors, and made of bronze. Just know the vast silhouette is impressive. A set of 268 steep stairs lead to the lower podium, essentially forcing you to stare up at all 202 tons of Buddha as you ascend. At the top, cool breezes and fantastic views over Lantau Island await. The Wisdom path runs beside 38 halved tree trunks arranged in an infinity shape on a hillside. Each is carved with Chinese characters that make up the Heart Sutra, a 5th-century Buddhist prayer that expresses the doctrine of emptiness. The idea is to walk around the path—which takes five minutes—and reflect. Follow the signposted trail to the left of the Buddha. ✉ *Ngong Ping, Lantau Island* ☎ *2985–5248* 🌐 *www.plm.org.hk* 🎫 *Monastery and path free; walking with Buddha: HK$40* Ⓜ *Tung Chung, Exit B.*

The New Territories

With rustic villages, incense-filled temples, green hiking trails, and pristine beaches, the New Territories are a favorite Hong Kong getaway. Sha Tin, Tuen Mun, and other "new towns" house more than half a million residents apiece, making them feel like their own cities. Even so, it's still easy to get away from the urban congestion, visit lush parks, and glimpse traditional rural life in restored walled villages and ancestral clan halls.

GETTING HERE AND AROUND

Between the bus and MTR, you can get close to many sights. Set off on the MTR from Central to Tsuen Wan; from there, taxis, buses, and minibuses will take you to places such as the Yuen Yuen Institute and Tai Mo Shan. For Sha Tin and other spots in the east, take the MTR to Kowloon Tong; transfer to the East Rail line and head to Sha Tin station. To reach the Sai Kung Peninsula, take the MTR from Central to Choi Hung, then the green Minibus 1A to Sai Kung Town.

Sights

The Chinese University of Hong Kong Art Museum

MUSEUM | Located in the Institute of Chinese Studies building, the museum is home to more than 15,000 historical objects, including well-respected collections of bronze seals, classical paintings, calligraphy, Yixing earthenware, and Lingnan school paintings. **■ TIP→ Take the East Rail line to University station, then hop on the free campus shuttle bus (1A on weekdays; H on weekends) to reach the museum.** ✉ *Institute of Chinese Studies, The Chinese University of Hong Kong, Tai Po Rd., Sha Tin, New Territories* ☎ *3943–7416* 🌐 *www.artmuseum.cuhk.edu.hk* 🎫 *Free* 🕓 *Closed Thurs.* Ⓜ *University, Exit D.*

Ching Chung Koon Taoist Temple

RELIGIOUS SITE | This temple has room after room of altars filled with the heady scent of incense. On one side of the main entrance is a cast-iron bell with a circumference of about 5 feet—all large monasteries in ancient China rang such bells at daybreak to wake the monks and nuns for a day of work in the rice fields. On the other side of the entrance is a huge drum that was used to call the workers back in the evening. Inside, some rooms are papered with small pictures; the faithful pay to have these photos displayed so they can see their dearly departed as they pray. Hundreds of dwarf shrubs, ornamental fishponds, and pagodas bedeck the grounds. The temple sits adjacent to the Ching Chung MTR Light Rail station near the town of Tuen Mun. The entrance isn't obvious, so ask for directions. ✉ *Tsing Chung*

Did You Know?

The Tian Tan Buddha is surrounded by six smaller bronze statues known as "The Offering of the Six Devas." They represent flowers, incense, lamp, ointment, fruit, and music, and symbolize charity, morality, patience, zeal, meditation, and wisdom—all necessary traits if one wishes to reach Nirvana.

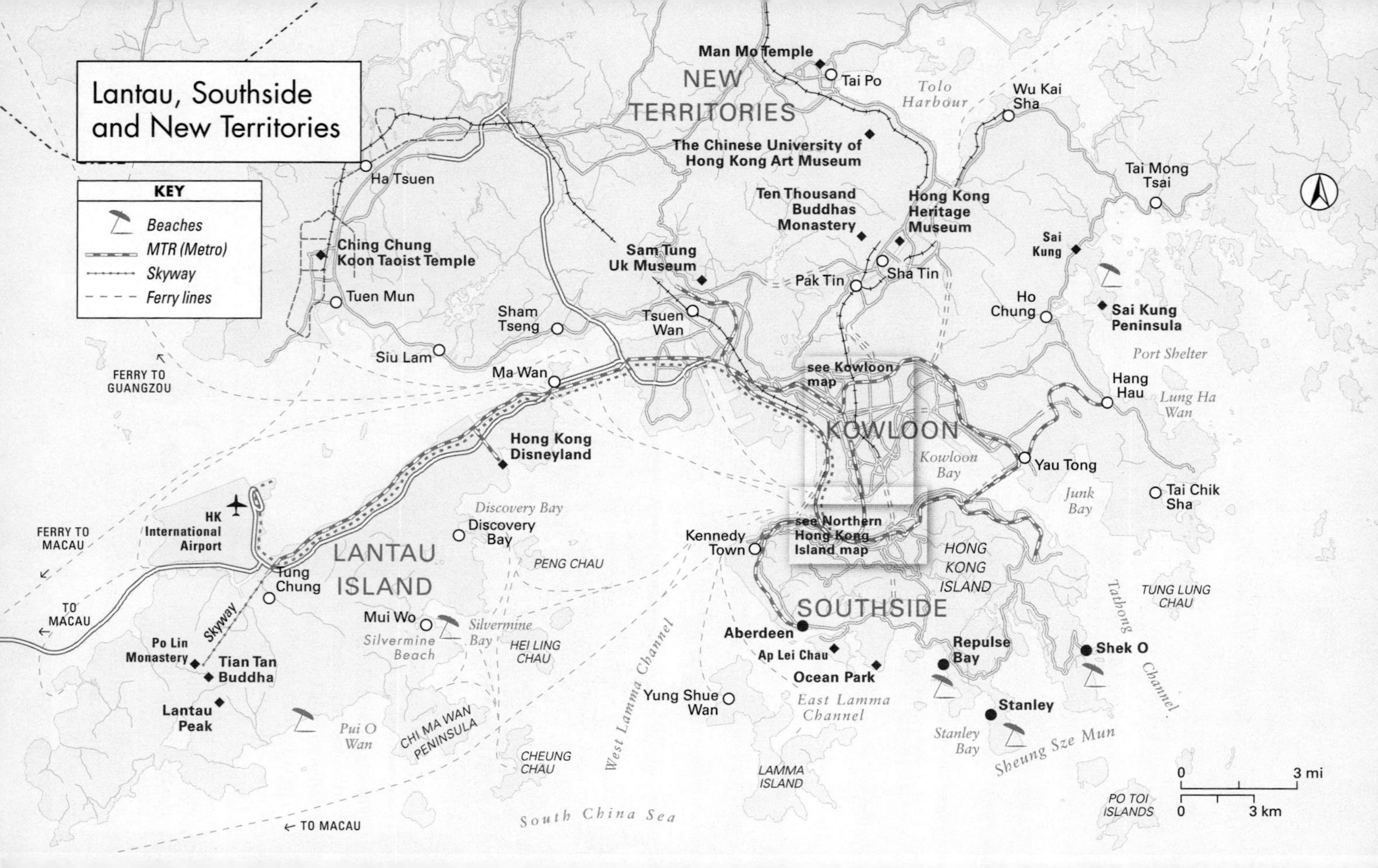

Lantau, Southside and New Territories
KEY
Beaches
MTR (Metro)
Skyway
Ferry lines
NEW TERRITORIES
Man Mo Temple
Tai Po
Tolo Harbour
Wu Kai Sha
The Chinese University of Hong Kong Art Museum
Tai Mong Tsai
Ha Tsuen
Ten Thousand Buddhas Monastery
Hong Kong Heritage Museum
Sai Kung
Ching Chung Koon Taoist Temple
Sam Tung Uk Museum
Pak Tin
Sha Tin
Tuen Mun
Sham Tseng
Tsuen Wan
Ho Chung
Sai Kung Peninsula
Siu Lam
Port Shelter
FERRY TO GUANGZOU
Ma Wan
see Kowloon map
Hang Hau
Lung Ha Wan
KOWLOON
Hong Kong Disneyland
Kowloon Bay
Yau Tong
Junk Bay
Tai Chik Sha
HK International Airport
Discovery Bay
FERRY TO MACAU
see Northern Hong Kong Island map
Kennedy Town
LANTAU ISLAND
PENG CHAU
HONG KONG ISLAND
Tung Chung
TO MACAU
Tathong Channel
TUNG LUNG CHAU
SOUTHSIDE
Skyway
Mui Wo
Silvermine Beach
Silvermine Bay
HEI LING CHAU
West Lamma Channel
Aberdeen
Po Lin Monastery
Tian Tan Buddha
Ap Lei Chau
Repulse Bay
Shek O
Ocean Park
Lantau Peak
Yung Shue Wan
East Lamma Channel
Stanley
Pui O Wan
CHI MA WAN PENINSULA
Stanley Bay
Sheung Sze Mun
CHEUNG CHAU
LAMMA ISLAND
0
3 mi
0
3 km
PO TOI ISLANDS
South China Sea
← TO MACAU

Koon Rd., Tuen Mun, New Territories ☎ 2462–1507 🌐 www.daoist.org Ⓜ Siu Hong, Exit B.

★ Hong Kong Heritage Museum

MUSEUM | This fabulous museum is Hong Kong's largest, yet it still seems a well-kept secret: chances are you'll have most of its 11 massive galleries to yourself. They ring an inner courtyard, which pours light into the lofty entrance hall. Although many of the halls focus on ancient Chinese art and heritage, the museum recently energized its offerings with an exhibition that covers Hong Kong's pop culture. The T.T. Tsui Gallery of Chinese Art, exquisite antique Chinese glass, ceramics, and bronzes, fill hushed second-floor rooms. The curators have gone for quality over quantity. Look for the 3½-foot-tall terra-cotta *Horse and Rider,* a beautiful example of the figures enclosed in tombs in the Han Dynasty (206 BC–AD 220). The Cantonese Opera Heritage Hall is all singing, all dancing, and utterly hands-on. The symbolic costumes, tradition-bound stories, and stylized acting of Cantonese opera can be impenetrable: the museum provides simple explanations and stacks of artifacts, including century-old sequined costumes that put Vegas to shame. Don't miss the virtual makeup display, where you get your on-screen face painted like an opera character. ✉ *1 Man Lam Rd., Sha Tin, New Territories ☎ 2180–8188 🌐 www.heritagemuseum.gov.hk 🎫 Permanent exhibitions, free; special exhibitions, HK$10 ⏲ Closed Tues. Ⓜ Che Kung, Exit A; Sha Tin, Exit A.*

★ Man Mo Temple

RELIGIOUS SITE | No one knows exactly when Hong Kong Island's oldest temple was built—but the consensus is sometime between 1847 and 1862. The temple is dedicated to the Taoist gods of literature and of war: Man, who wears green, and Mo, dressed in red. The temple bell, cast in Canton in 1847, and the drum next to it are sounded to attract the gods' attention when a prayer is being offered. ✉ *124 Hollywood Rd., Sheung Wan, Western 🌐 www.man-mo-temple.hk Ⓜ Sheung Wan.*

Sai Kung Peninsula

NATURE PRESERVE | To the east of Sha Tin, the Sai Kung Peninsula is home to one of Hong Kong's most beloved nature preserves, Sai Kung Country Park. It has several hiking trails that wind through majestic hills overlooking the water. The hikes through the hills surrounding High Island Reservoir are also spectacular. Seafood restaurants dot the waterfront in Sai Kung Town as well as the tiny fishing village of Po Toi O in Clear Water Bay. At Sai Kung Town you can rent a sampan that will take you to one of the many islands in the area for a day at the beach. Take the MTR to Diamond Hill (Exit C2) and take Bus 92 to Sai Kung Town. Alternatively, catch a taxi along Clearwater Bay Road, which runs through forested areas and land that's only partially developed, with Spanish-style villas overlooking the sea. This excursion will take a full day, and you should only go if it's sunny. ✉ *Sai Kung Peninsula, Kowloon.*

Sam Tung Uk Museum

MUSEUM VILLAGE | A walled Hakka village from 1786 was saved from demolition to create this museum. It's in the middle of industrial Tsuen Wan, in the western New Territories, and its quiet courtyards and small interlocking chambers contrast with the nearby residential towers. It looks more like a large home than a village—not surprisingly, the name translates as "Three Beam House." Rigid symmetry dictated the construction: the ancestral hall and two common chambers form a central axis flanked by private areas. Traditional furniture and farm tools are on display. **■ TIP→ Head through the courtyards and start your visit in the exhibition hall at the back, where a display gives helpful background on Hakka culture and**

pre-industrial Tsuen Wan—explanations are sparse elsewhere. You can also try on a Hakka hat. ✉ *2 Kwu Uk La., Tsuen Wan, New Territories* ☎ *2411–2001* 🌐 *www.heritagemuseum.gov.hk* 🎫 *Free* Ⓜ *Tsuen Wan, Exit B3.*

★ **Ten Thousand Buddhas Monastery**

RELIGIOUS SITE | You climb some 400 steps to reach this temple, but look on the bright side: for each step you get about 32 Buddhas. The uphill path through dense vegetation is lined with 500 life-size golden Buddhas in all kinds of positions. Be sure to bring along water and insect repellent. Prepare to be dazzled inside the main temple, where walls are stacked with gilded ceramic statuettes. There are actually nearly 13,000 here, made by Shanghai artisans and donated by worshippers over the decades. Kwun Yam, goddess of mercy, is one of several deities honored in the crimson-walled courtyard.

Look southwest on a clear day and you can see nearby **Amah Rock,** which resembles a woman with a child on her back. Legend has it that this formation was once a faithful fisherman's wife who climbed the mountain every day to wait for her husband's return, not knowing he'd drowned. Tin Hau, goddess of the sea, took pity on her and turned her to stone.

The temple is in the foothills of Sha Tin, in the central New Territories. Take Exit B out of Sha Tin station, walk down the pedestrian ramp, and take the first left onto Pai Tau Street. Keep to the right-hand side of the road and follow it around to the gate where the signposted path starts. ■ **TIP→ Don't be confused by the big white buildings on the left of Pai Tau Road. They are ancestral halls, not the temple.** ✉ *221 Pai Tau Village, Sha Tin, New Territories* 🎫 *Free* Ⓜ *Sha Tin, Exit B.*

Side Trip to Macau

Enter the desperate, smoky atmosphere of a Chinese casino, where annual gaming revenues are three times more than those in Vegas. Sit down next to unassuming grandmothers playing baccarat—the local game of choice—elbow-to-elbow with visiting high rollers. Then step out of the climate-controlled chill and into tropical air that embraces you like a warm, balmy hug. Welcome to Macau.

The many contrasts in this tiny enclave of 650,000 people serve as reminders of how different cultures have embraced one another's traditions for hundreds of years. Though Macau's population is 95% ethnic Chinese, there are still vibrant pockets of Portuguese and Filipino expats. And some of the thousands of Eurasians—who consider themselves neither Portuguese nor Chinese, but something in between—can trace the intermarriage of their ancestors back a century or two.

Macau's Old Town, while dominated by the buildings, squares, and cobblestone alleyways of colonial Portugal, is tinged with Eastern influences as well. In Macau you can spend an afternoon exploring Buddhist temples before feasting on a dinner of *bacalhau com natas* (dried codfish with a cream sauce), grilled African chicken (spicy chicken in a coconut-peanut broth—a classic Macanese dish), Chinese lobster with scallions, or fiery prawns infused with Indian and Malaysian flavors. Wash everything down with *vinho verde,* the crisp young wine from northern Portugal, and top it all off with a traditional Portuguese *pastel de nata* (egg-custard tart) and dark, thick espresso.

GETTING HERE AND AROUND

Ferries travel between Hong Kong and Macau every 15 minutes with a reduced schedule from midnight to 7 am.

Weekday traffic is usually light, so you can buy tickets right before departure. Weekend tickets often sell out, so make reservations. You must pick up tickets at the terminal at least a half hour before departure. The cost of one-way economy tickets ranges from HK$160 to HK$211, depending on the time of sailing. Evening and weekend trips tend to be more expensive.

Most ferries leave from Hong Kong's Shun Tak Centre (which is connected to the Sheung Wan MTR station), though limited service is available at Kowloon's Hong Kong China Ferry Terminal in Tsim Sha Tsui. In Macau most ferries disembark from the main Macau Ferry Terminal, but Cotai Water Jet services the terminal on Taipa. The trip takes about one hour each way. Buses, taxis, and free shuttles to most casinos and hotels await on the Macau side.

Public buses are clean and affordable. Trips cost MOP$6 around Macau Peninsula, Taipa, and Coloane. Buses run from 6:30 am to midnight and require exact change upon boarding unless you have a MACAUPass (www.macaupass.com) smartcard, which you can purchase for MOP$130 (MOP$30 deposit; MOP$100 minimum value added) at any 7-Eleven, Circle K, or supermarket. All that said, you also can get downtown for free, via hotel or casino shuttles that run from the official Border Gate crossing just outside mainland China, from the airport, and from the Macau Ferry Terminal.

Taxis are inexpensive but not plentiful in Macau. The best places to catch a cab are the major casinos—the Wynn Macau, the Lisboas, the Sands Macao, and the Venetian Macao. Carry a bilingual map, or ask the concierge at your hotel to write the name of your destination in Chinese. All taxis are metered, air-conditioned, and reasonably comfortable. The base charge is MOP$19 for the first 1.6 km (1 mile) and MOP$2 per additional 240 meters (787 feet). Trips between Coloane and either the Macau Peninsula or Taipa incur respective surcharges of MOP$5 and MOP$2. Drivers don't expect a tip.

The Macau Light Rapid Transit (LRT) opened in 2019 as the territory's first train system. The first phase includes 21 stops across the main peninsula and Taipa, including the airport and ferry terminals.

CASINOS

Gambling is lightly regulated, so there are only a few things to remember. No visitor under age 18 is allowed into casinos. Most casinos use Hong Kong dollars in their gaming and not Macau patacas, but you can easily exchange currencies at cashiers. High- and no-limit VIP rooms, where minimum bets range from HK$50,000 to HK$100,000 per hand, are available on request. You can get cash from credit cards and ATMs 24 hours a day, and every casino has a program to extend additional credit to frequent visitors. Most casinos don't have strict dress codes outside of their VIP rooms, but men are better off not wearing shorts or sleeveless shirts. Minimum bets for most tables are higher than those in Las Vegas, but there are lower limits for slots and video gambling.

VISITOR INFORMATION

To enter Macau, Americans and Canadians need only a valid passport for stays of up to 30 days; EU citizens likewise need only a valid passport but can stay for up to 90 days. The Macau Government Tourist Office has all the information you need.

Downtown Macau

Chances are you'll arrive at the Macau Ferry Terminal after sailing from Hong Kong. There's not much to see around the terminal itself, so hop into one of the many waiting casino or hotel shuttles and head straight downtown, less than 10 minutes away. From there it's a short walk to the city's historic center, along the short stretch of road named Avenida de Almeida Ribeiro, more commonly known as San Ma Lo, which is Macau's commercial and cultural heart.

Sights

Camões Garden
GARDEN | Macau's most popular park is frequented from dawn to dusk by tai chi enthusiasts, palm readers, lovers, students, and men huddled over Chinese chess boards with their caged songbirds nearby. The gardens, which were developed in the 18th century, are named after Luís de Camões, Portugal's greatest poet, who was banished to Macau for several years during the 16th century. A rocky niche shelters a bronze bust of him in the park's most famous and picturesque spot, Camões Grotto. At the grotto's entrance a bronze sculpture honors the friendship between Portugal and China. A wall of stone slabs is inscribed with poems by various contemporary writers, praising Camões and Macau. In **Casa Garden,** a smaller park alongside Camões Garden, the grounds of a merchant's estate are lovingly landscaped with a variety of flora and bordered with a brick pathway. A central pond is stocked with lily pads and lotus flowers. ✉ *13 Praça Luis de Camões, Downtown.*

★ **Fortaleza da Guia** (*Guia Fortress*)
MILITARY SITE | This fort, built between 1622 and 1638 on Macau's highest hill, was key to protecting the Portuguese from invaders. You can walk the steep, winding road up to it or take a five-minute cable-car ride from the entrance of Flora Garden on Avenida Sidónio Pais. From the drop-off point, follow the signs for the **Guia Lighthouse**—you can't go in, but you can get a good look at the gleaming white exterior that's lit every night. Next to it is the **Guia Chapel,** built by Clarist nuns to provide soldiers with religious services. Restoration work in 1996 uncovered elaborate frescoes mixing western and Chinese themes. They're best seen when the morning or afternoon sun floods the chapel, which is no longer used for services. The views from here are among the best, sweeping across all of Macau. ✉ *Guia Hill, Downtown* ☎ *853/8399–6699* 🎟 *Free.*

Fortaleza do Monte (*Mount Fortress*)
MILITARY SITE | On the hill overlooking the ruins of São Paulo and affording great peninsular views, this renovated fort was built by the Jesuits in the early 17th century. In 1622 it was the site of Macau's most legendary battle, when a priest's lucky cannon shot hit an invading Dutch ship's powder supply, saving the day. The interior buildings were destroyed by fire in 1835, but the outer walls remain, along with several large cannons and artillery pieces. Exhibits at the adjoining **Macau Museum** (daily 10–6, MOP$15) take you through the territory's history, from its origins to modern development. ✉ *Monte Hill, Downtown* ☎ *853/2835–7911* 🌐 *www.macaumuseum.gov.mo* 🎟 *Free.*

Igreja de São Domingos (*St. Dominic's Church*)
RELIGIOUS SITE | The cream-and-white interior of one of Macau's most beautiful churches takes on a heavenly golden glow when illuminated for services. St. Dominic's was originally a convent founded by Spanish Dominican friars in 1587. In 1822 China's first Portuguese newspaper, *The China Bee,* was published here, and the church became a repository for sacred art in 1834 when convents were banned in Portugal. ■ **TIP→ Admission to all churches and temples is free, though donations are suggested.** ✉ *Largo de São Domingos, Downtown* ☎ *853/2836–7706.*

Igreja de São Lourenço (*Church of St. Lawrence*)
RELIGIOUS SITE | One of Macau's three oldest churches, the Church of St. Lawrence was founded by Jesuits in 1560 and has been lovingly rebuilt several times. Its present appearance dates from 1846. It overlooks the South China Sea amid pleasant, palm-shaded gardens. Families of Portuguese sailors used to gather on the front steps to pray for the sailors' safe return; hence its Chinese name, Feng Shun Tang (Hall of the Soothing Winds). Focal points of its breathtaking interior are the elegant wood carvings, striking stained glass windows, a baroque altar, and crystal chandeliers. ✉ *Rua de São Lourenço, Downtown* ☎ *8399–6699.*

Largo de Santo Agostinho
PLAZA | Built in the pattern of traditional Portuguese squares, St. Augustine Square is paved with black-and-white tiles laid out in mosaic wave patterns and lined with leafy overhanging trees and lots of wooden benches. It's easy to feel as if you're in a European village, far from South China. One of the square's main structures is the **Teatro Dom Pedro V,** a European-style hall with an inviting green-and-white facade built in 1859. It's an important cultural landmark for the Macanese and was regularly used until World War II, when it fell into disrepair. The 300-seat venue once again hosts concerts and recitals—especially during the annual Macau International Music Festival—as well as important public events, the only times you can go inside. It does, however, have a garden that's open daily, and admission is free. **Igreja de Santo Agostinho (Church of St. Augustine),** to one side of the square, dates from 1591, and has a grand, weathered exterior and a drafty interior with a high turquoise-colored wood-beam ceiling (open daily 10–6). There's a magnificent stone altar with a statue of Christ on his knees, bearing the cross, with small crucifixes in silhouette on the hill behind him. The statue, called Our Lord of Passos, is carried in a procession through the streets of downtown on the first day of Lent. ✉ *Off R. Central, Downtown.*

★ **Largo do Senado** (*Senado Square*)
PLAZA | Open only to pedestrians and paved in shiny black-and-white tiles, this has been the charming hub of Macau for centuries. Largo do Senado is lined with neoclassical-style colonial buildings painted in bright pastels. The **Edifício do Leal Senado** (Senate Building), which gives the square its name, was built in 1784 as a municipal chamber and continues to be used by the government today. An elegant meeting room on the first floor opens onto a magnificent library based on one in the Mafra Convent in Portugal, with books neatly stacked on two levels of shelves reaching to the ceiling; art and historical exhibitions are frequently hosted in the beautiful foyer and garden. Alleys adjacent to the square are packed with restaurants and shops. ■ **TIP→ Visit on a weekday to avoid the crowds, and try to come back at night, when locals of all ages gather to chat and the square is beautifully lit.** ✉ *Downtown.*

Lin Fung Miu
RELIGIOUS SITE | Built in 1592, the Temple of the Lotus honors several Buddhist and Taoist deities, including Tin Hau (goddess of the sea), Kun Iam (goddess of mercy), and Kwan Tai (god of war and wealth). The front of the temple is embellished with magnificent clay bas-reliefs of renowned figures from Chinese history and mythology. Inside are several halls, shrines, and courtyards. The temple is best known as a lodging place for Mandarins traveling from Guangdong Province. Its most famous guest was Commissioner Lin Zexu, whose confiscation and destruction of British opium in 1839 was largely responsible for the First Opium War. ✉ *Av. do Almirante Lacerda, Downtown.*

Lou Lim Ieoc Gardens

GARDEN | These beautiful gardens were built in the 19th century by a Chinese merchant named Lou Kau. Rock formations, water, vegetation, pavilions, and sunlight were all carefully considered, and the balanced landscapes are the hallmark of Suzhou garden style. The government took possession and restored the grounds in the mid 1970s, so that today you can enjoy tranquil walks among delicate flowering bushes framed with bamboo groves and artificial hills. A large auditorium frequently hosts concerts and other events, most notably recitals during the annual Macau International Music Festival. Adjacent to the gardens, a European-style edifice contains the **Macau Tea Culture House,** a small museum with exhibits on the tea culture of Macau and China (Closed Mon.). ✉ *10 Estrada de Adolfo Loureiro, at Av. do Conselheiro Ferreira de Almeida, Downtown* ☎ *853/2882–7103* 🌐 *www.icm.gov.mo* 🎟 *Free.*

Macau Fisherman's Wharf

NEIGHBORHOOD | **FAMILY** | This sprawling complex of rides, games, and other minor attractions has a Disney-esque vibe. The centerpiece is the Roman Amphitheatre, which hosts outdoor performances, but the main draws are the lively themed restaurants on the west side. Come for the food, and stay after dark, as Fisherman's Wharf is most active at night. ✉ *Av. da Amizade, at Av. Dr. Sun Yat-Sen, Outer Harbour* ☎ *853/8299–3300* 🌐 *www.fishermanswharf.com.mo* 🎟 *Admission free; games from MOP$1.*

Macao Museum of Art

MUSEUM | The large, boxy museum is as well-known for its curving, rectangular framed roof as it is for its calligraphy, painting, ceramics, and photography exhibitions. It's Macau's only fully dedicated art museum, with five floors of eastern and western works, plus international partnerships with museums in China, including Beijing's Palace Museum and the Shanghai Museum. ✉ *Macao Cultural Centre, Av. Xian Xing Hai, Outer Harbour* ☎ *853/8791–9814* 🌐 *www.mam.gov.mo* 🎟 *Free* 🕒 *Closed Mon.*

★ **Macau Tower Convention & Entertainment Centre**

SPORTS VENUE | Rising above peaceful San Van Lake, this 338-meter (1,109-foot) freestanding tower recalls Sky Tower, a similar structure in New Zealand—and it should, as both were designed by New Zealand architect Gordon Moller. The Macau Tower offers a variety of thrills, including the Tower Climb, which challenges the strong of heart and body with a two-hour ascent on steel rungs 100 meters (328 feet) up the tower's mast for incomparable views of Macau and China. Other thrills include Skywalk X, an open-air stroll around the tower's exterior—without handrails; SkyJump, an assisted, decelerated 233-meter (765-foot) descent; and the world's highest bungee jump. More subdued attractions inside the tower include a mainstream movie theater and a revolving restaurant (the 360° Café) serving lunch, high tea, and a dinner buffet. ✉ *Largo da Torre de Macau, Downtown* ☎ *853/2893–3339* 🌐 *www.macautower.com.mo* 🎟 *MOP$788 Skywalk X; MOP$1888 Tower Climb; MOP$3488 bungee jump; photos extra.*

★ **Ruínas de São Paulo** (*Ruins of St. Paul's Cathedral*)

RELIGIOUS SITE | Only the magnificent, towering facade, with its intricate carvings and bronze statues, remains from the original Church of Mater Dei, built between 1602 and 1640 and destroyed by fire in 1835. The sanctuary, an adjacent college, and Mount Fortress—all Jesuit constructions—once formed East Asia's first western-style university. Now a tourist attraction, the ruins are the widely adopted symbol of Macau. Snack bars and shops are clustered at

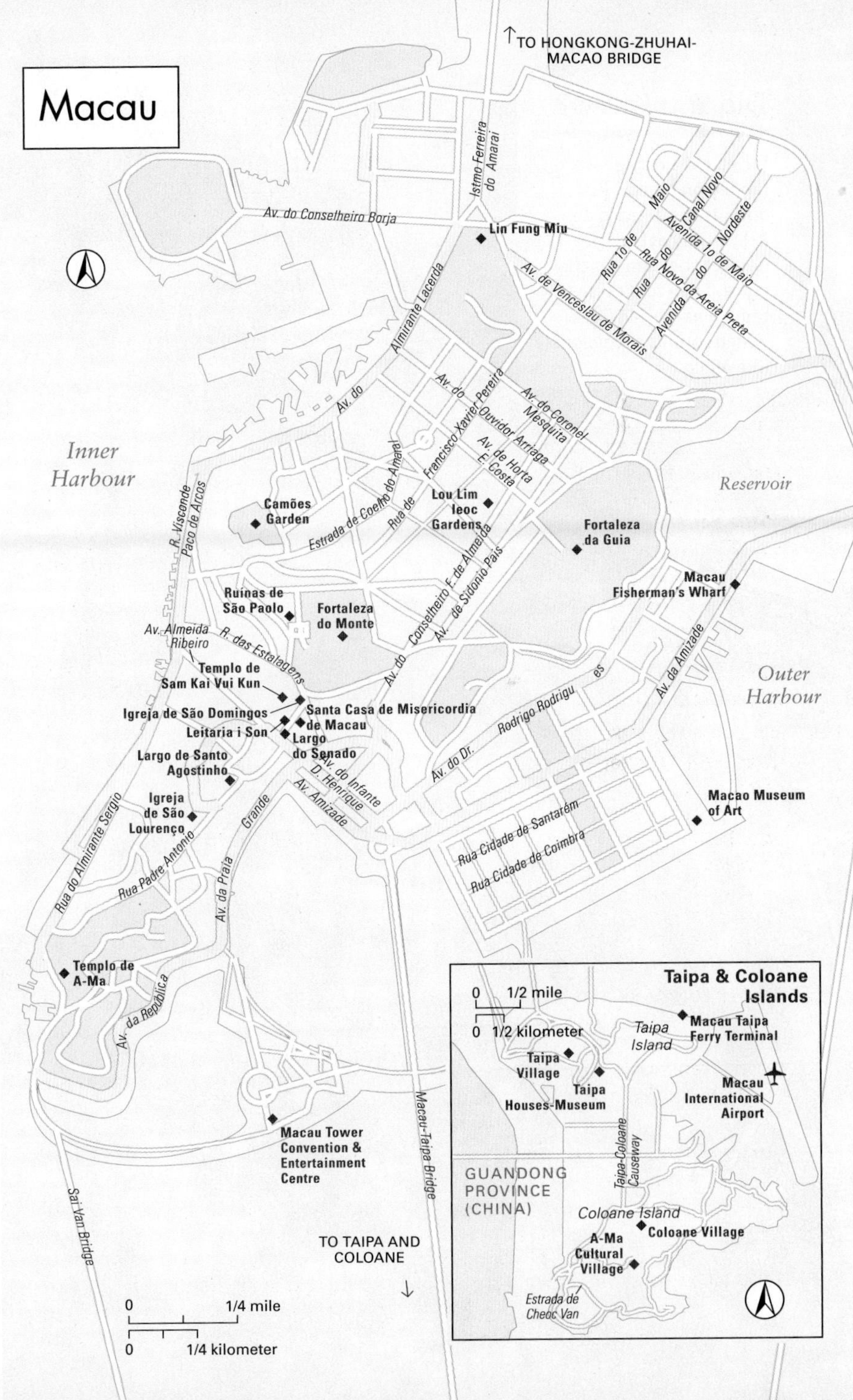

Macau
TO HONGKONG-ZHUHAI-MACAO BRIDGE
Istmo Ferreira do Amaral
Av. do Conselheiro Borja
Lin Fung Miu
Rua 1o de Maio
Canal Novo
Avenida 1o de Maio
Nordeste
Rua do
Rua Novo da Areia Preta
Avenida do
Av. de Venceslau de Morais
Almirante Lacerda
Av. do
Av. do Francisco Xavier Pereira
Av. do Ouvidor Arriaga
Av. do Coronel Mesquita
Av. de Horta E. Costa
Inner Harbour
Reservoir
Rua de
Estrada de Coelho do Amaral
R. Visconde Paco de Arcos
Camões Garden
Lou Lim Ieoc Gardens
Fortaleza da Guia
Av. do Conselheiro F. de Almeida
Av. de Sidonio Pais
Ruínas de São Paolo
Fortaleza do Monte
Macau Fisherman's Wharf
Av. Almeida Ribeiro
R. das Estalagens
Templo de Sam Kai Vui Kun
Outer Harbour
Av. da Amizade
Igreja de São Domingos
Santa Casa de Misericordia de Macau
Leitaria i Son
Largo do Senado
Av. do Dr. Rodrigo Rodrigues
Largo de Santo Agostinho
Av. do Infante D. Henrique
Av. Amizade
Igreja de São Lourenço
Rua do Almirante Sergio
Rua Padre Antonio
Av. da Praia Grande
Macao Museum of Art
Rua Cidade de Santarém
Rua Cidade de Coimbra
Templo de A-Ma
Av. da Republica
Macau Tower Convention & Entertainment Centre
Macau-Taipa Bridge
Sai Van Bridge
TO TAIPA AND COLOANE
0 1/4 mile
0 1/4 kilometer
Taipa & Coloane Islands
0 1/2 mile
0 1/2 kilometer
Macau Taipa Ferry Terminal
Taipa Island
Taipa Village
Taipa Houses-Museum
Macau International Airport
Taipa-Coloane Causeway
GUANDONG PROVINCE (CHINA)
Coloane Island
Coloane Village
A-Ma Cultural Village
Estrada de Cheoc Van

Did You Know?

When the Portuguese landed on Macau, just outside the Templo de A-Ma, they asked the natives the name of the place. They told them the temple name, *Mā Gé Miào,* which sounds suspiciously like *Macau*.

the foot of the site. Tucked behind the facade of São Paulo is the small **Museum of Sacred Art and Crypt,** which contains statues, crucifixes, and the bones of Japanese and Vietnamese martyrs. There are also some intriguing Asian interpretations of Christian images, including samurai angels and a Chinese Virgin and Child. Note that admission to the site isn't allowed after 5:30 pm. ✉ *Top end of Rua de São Paulo, Downtown* ☎ *853/8399–6699* 🌐 *www.icm.gov.mo/en/StPaul* 🎫 *Free.*

Santa Casa da Misericordia de Macau
(*The Holy House of Mercy*)
BUILDING | Founded in 1569 by Dom Belchior Carneiro, Macau's first bishop, the Macau Holy House of Mercy is the China coast's oldest Christian charity, and it continues to take care of the underprivileged with a welfare shop and low-rent housing. It also operates a nursery, a house for the elderly and a center for the blind. The exterior of the heritage-listed building is neoclassical, but the interior is done in a contrasting opulent, modern style. The second floor houses a museum of Roman Catholic relics and also displays portraits of its earliest benefactors, including Martha Merop. ✉ *2 Travessa da Misericordia, Downtown* ☎ *853/2857–3938* 🌐 *www.scmm.mo* 🎫 *MOP$5.*

★ **Templo de A-Ma**
RELIGIOUS SITE | The tiered A-Ma Temple is one of Macau's oldest and most picturesque buildings. Properly Ma Kok Temple but known to locals as simply A-Ma, the structure originated during the Ming Dynasty (1368–1644) and was influenced by Confucianism, Taoism, and Buddhism, as well as local religions. Vivid red calligraphy on large boulders tells the story of the goddess A-Ma (also known as Tin Hau), the patron of fishermen. A small gate opens onto prayer halls, pavilions, and caves carved directly into the hillside. ✉ *Rua de São Tiago da Barra, Largo da Barra, Downtown.*

Templo de Sam Kai Vui Kun
RELIGIOUS SITE | Built in 1750, this temple is dedicated to Kuan Tai, the bearded, fierce-looking god of war and wealth in Chinese mythology. Statues of him and his two sons sit on an altar. A steady stream of people comes to pray and ask for support before they go wage battle in the casinos. May and June see festivals honoring Kuan Tai throughout Macau. ✉ *10 Rua Sui do Mercado de São Domingos, Downtown.*

Restaurants

★ **Dom Galo**
$$ | **PORTUGUESE** | "Quirky" springs to mind when describing the colorful decor, with plastic monkey puppets and funky chicken toys hanging from the ceilings. The eclectic clientele includes graphic designers, gambling-compliance lawyers, and 10-year-old Cantonese kids celebrating birthdays. **Known for:** insalada de polvo (octopus salad), king prawns, and steak fries served in a tangy mushroom sauce; giant pitchers of sangria; reservations are essential. 💲 *Average main: MOP$100* ✉ *Av. Sir Andars Ljung Stedt, Downtown* ☎ *853/2875–1383.*

Leitaria i Son
$ | **CANTONESE** | **FAMILY** | Look for the small cow sign marking the out-of-the-ordinary Leitaria i Son milk bar. The decor is cafeteria-style and spartan, but the bar whips up frothy glasses of fresh milk from its dairy and blends them with all manner of juices: papaya, coconut, apricot, and more. 💲 *Average main: MOP$35* ✉ *Largo do Senado 7, Downtown* ☎ *853/2857–3638.*

Margaret's Café e Nata
$ | **INTERNATIONAL** | **FAMILY** | Not far off the main drag but somewhat hidden down an alleyway, Margaret's Café e Nata offers a cool—albeit increasingly crowded—place to sit, outside under fans and awnings, with some of the best

custard tarts in town, plus fresh juices, sandwiches, homemade tea blends, and pizza slices. **Known for:** crispy, creamy egg tarts; big-as-your-face sandwiches; fresh juices and teas. [$] *Average main: MOP$45* ✉ *Rua Comandante Mata e Oliveira, Downtown* ☎ *853/2871–0032* ▭ *No credit cards* ⏲ *Closed Wednesday.*

Pastelaria Koi Kei

$ | **MACANESE** | Walking toward the Ruins of St. Paul's, you will likely be accosted by salespeople forcing Macanese snacks into your hands and enticing you to enter one of the street's *pastelarias.* Competition is fierce, but Pastelaria Koi Kei is one of the oldest and best. **Known for:** distinctive tan bags, often carried by Hongkongers back home; Portuguese custards; almond cakes, ginger candy, beef jerky, and egg rolls. [$] *Average main: MOP$20* ✉ *70–72 Rua Felicidade, Downtown* ☎ *853/2893–8102* 🌐 *www.koikei.com* ☞ *Cash is preferred.*

Robuchon Au Dome

$$$$ | **FRENCH** | Situated in the dome of the Grand Lisboa Hotel, Robuchon au Dome has been awarded three Michelin stars for 10 consecutive years. It's easy to see why: from the dazzling 131,500-piece Swarovski-crystal chandelier to the live piano music, marathon set menus, and jaw-dropping dessert cart, this restaurant makes you feel like King Louis XIV. **Known for:** Asia's most extensive wine cellar (over 16,800 labels); views across Macau from its 43rd-floor perch; signature dishes like Le Caviar (impérial caviar and king crab). [$] *Average main: MOP$550* ✉ *Grand Lisboa Hotel, Av. de Lisboa, 43rd fl., Downtown* ☎ *853/8803–7878* 🌐 *www.joel-robuchon.com.*

Wing Lei

$$$$ | **CANTONESE** | A Michelin star–spangled Chinese restaurant inside the Wynn Macau, Wing Lei dazzles with rich mustard decor and an enormous Swarovski-crystal dragon sculpture flying overhead. The chef mixes up the menu with each changing season and reservations are recommended. **Known for:** signature tea-smoked crispy chicken and steamed Macau sole; refined dim sum menu; effortless wine pairings with the Chinese cuisine. [$] *Average main: MOP$400* ✉ *Wynn Macau, Rua Cidade de Sintra, NAPE, Downtown* ☎ *853/8986–3663* 🌐 *www.wynnmacau.com.*

Nightlife

★ MacauSoul

BARS/PUBS | Housed in a bright pink building with pine-green shutters, this lively wine bar is just steps away from the Ruins of St. Paul's Cathedral. The two British expats who manage the place have assembled a wine list that includes more than 430 Portuguese varieties, and there's a fine selection of whiskeys available as well. On the food front, look for British cheese plates, charcuterie boards, and many homemade offerings (desserts among them). Live after-dinner music plays on select dates—particularly Fridays, depending on the season. It's best to call ahead for details. ✉ *31A Rua de Sao Paulo, Travessa da Paixao, Downtown* ☎ *853/2836–5182* 🌐 *www.macausoul.com* ⏲ *Closed Tues. and Wed.*

Whisky Bar

BARS/PUBS | Depending on the time of day or night, this bar on the 16th floor of the StarWorld Hotel provides either upbeat cabaret entertainment or a cool moment of respite from the clinking casinos all around. Happy hour is daily from 5 to 9, and the Star Band – EVOII starts playing nightly at 10. In addition to a full selection of the usual hard stuff, the bar has 100 whisky varieties, including the ultrarare Macallan 1946. ✉ *StarWorld Hotel, Av. da Amizade, Downtown* ☎ *853/8290–8698* 🌐 *www.starworldmacau.com.*

CASINOS

Casino Lisboa

CASINO—SIGHT | Opened in 1970 by Dr. Stanley Ho, this iconic Macau gaming den is replete with ancient jade ships in the halls, gilded staircases, and more baccarat tables than you can shake a craps stick at. It's great for a few rounds of *dai-siu*—dice bets over cups of iced green tea. Most of the gamblers are from neighboring Guangdong province, and Cantonese is the lingua franca. Other popular pastimes at this storied casino revolve around international fine-dining venues and colorful coffee shops, if you care to wander around a maze of marbled floors and low ceilings. ✉ *Av. de Lisboa, Downtown* ☎ *853/2888–3888* 🌐 *www.hotelisboa.com.*

Grand Lisboa

CASINO—SIGHT | The main gaming floor, notable for its glowing egg statue, features more than 430 tables, about 800 slot machines, and a sexy Paris cabaret show that runs every 15 minutes. The second floor has additional gambling opportunities as well as a great bar. The Grand Lisboa has a variety of dining choices, too, from the baroque Casa Don Alfonso 1890 to the Round-the-Clock Coffee Shop. If the slots have been kind, celebrate by having a divine dinner on-site at Robuchon au Dôme or The Eight: both have earned three Michelin stars. ✉ *2–4 Av. de Lisboa, Downtown* ☎ *853/2838–2828* 🌐 *www.grandlisboahotels.com.*

MGM Macau

CASINO—SIGHT | A stylish part of Macau's gambling scene offers lavish lounges, Dale Chihuly glass sculptures, Portuguese-inspired architecture, and fine dining. The gambling floor itself is popular with high rollers from Hong Kong, including business tycoons who are just in for a few days. One of the owners, Pansy Ho, is the daughter of Macau's "gambling godfather," Dr. Stanley Ho; she is a high-octane business professional in her own right and a woman's classy touch shows up in this place's glitz-and-glam energy and high-society appeal. ✉ *Av. Dr. Sun Yat Sen, Downtown* ☎ *853/8802–8888* 🌐 *www.mgmmacau.com.*

StarWorld Hotel, Macau

CASINO—SIGHT | As you enter the StarWorld empire you're greeted by tall girls in high heels, while a mariachi band serenades you from across the lobby. The gaming floors are small and have a couple of Chinese-style diners if you get peckish, but the cool Whisky Bar on the 16th floor of the adjacent hotel is an atmospheric place to either begin or end your evening. The neon-blue building is just across from the Wynn Macau and down the block from the MGM Macau. Live lobby entertainment and local holiday attractions add a kitschy, friendly feel. ✉ *Av. da Amizade, Downtown* ☎ *853/2838–3838* 🌐 *www.starworldmacau.com.*

★ **Wynn Macau**

CASINO—SIGHT | Listen for theme songs such as "Diamonds are Forever," "Luck Be a Lady," or "Money, Money" as Wynn's outdoor Performance Lake dazzles you with flames and fountain jets of whipping water every 15 minutes from 11 am to midnight. Inside the "open hand" structure of Steve Wynn's Macau resort, the indoor Rotunda Tree of Prosperity also wows guests with feng shui glitz. Wynn's expansive, brightly lit gaming floor, fine dining, buffet meals, luxury shops, deluxe spa, and trendy suites make this one of the more swish resorts in Macau. ✉ *Rua Cidade de Sintra, Downtown* ☎ *853/2888–9966* 🌐 *www.wynnmacau.com.*

Shopping

DEPARTMENT STORE

New Yaohan

DEPARTMENT STORES | Originally a Japanese-owned department store, this failing facility was taken over by Macau entrepreneur Dr. Stanley Ho 20 years ago and transformed into a popular shopping destination for locals. "Macau's only department store" offers a good mix of shops selling household goods, clothing, jewelry, sports equipment, gadgets, and beauty products. It also has an extensive food court, a well-stocked supermarket, and a large bakery. ✉ *90 Av. Doutor Mário Soares, Downtown* ☎ *853/2872–5338* 🌐 *www.newyaohan.com.*

Macau Outer Harbour

Restaurants

Aux Beaux Arts

$$$ | **FRENCH** | This 1930s-style Parisian brasserie in the MGM Macau is one of the trendiest restaurants around. Diners are particularly fond of its catch-of-the-day seafood, French mains, and chic decor. **Known for:** French Concession Shanghai-esque decor with tan wood booths and a terrace; steak Parisien with french fries; sommeliers who pair the latest wines with dishes. $ *Average main: MOP$210* ✉ *MGM Macau, Av. Dr. Sun Yat Sen, NAPE, Outer Harbour* ☎ *853/8802–2319* 🌐 *www.mgmmacau.com* ⏲ *Closed Mon.*

Hotels

★ **MGM Macau**

$$$ | **HOTEL** | The chic accommodations—with their muted cream palette, picture windows, standalone tubs, and spacious seating areas—have all the luxuries and comforts you'd expect from a luxury brand; a Portuguese-theme further distinguishes this hotel from the rest. **Pros:** tasteful architecture; fine art collections; refined restaurants and lounges. **Cons:** inseparable from the casino, which can get loud; high-traffic location; lots of young children, possibly a deterrent for couples or business types. $ *Rooms from: MOP$2688* ✉ *Av. Dr. Sun Yat Sen, NAPE, Outer Harbour* ☎ *853/8802–8888* 🌐 *www.mgmmacau.com* *582 rooms* *No meals.*

Nightlife

CASINOS

★ **Sands Macao**

CASINO—SIGHT | This was one of the largest casinos in the territory until its sibling, The Venetian Macao, stole the spotlight. It's also the first casino you'll see on the peninsula even before disembarking from the ferry. Past the sparkling 50-ton chandelier over the entrance, the grand gaming floor is anchored by a live cabaret stage above an open bar and under a giant screen. Several tiers are tastefully linked with escalators leading to the high-stakes tables upstairs. The friendly atmosphere and handy location, just across from Fisherman's Wharf and near the bar street in NAPE, make this a good place to warm up for your big night out. ✉ *203 Largo de Monte Carlo, Outer Harbour* ☎ *853/2888–3330* 🌐 *www.sands.com.mo.*

Inner Harbour

Restaurants

★ **A Lorcha**

$$ | **PORTUGUESE** | Vastly popular A Lorcha (the name means "wooden ship") celebrates the heritage of Macau as an important port with a maritime-theme menu. Save room for *serradura* (Macau sawdust pudding, made with biscuits and whipped cream). **Known for:** signature Lorcha-style clams; seafood paella and fire-roasted chicken; luring racers during the Grand Prix (the Macanese owner is a fervent Formula fan). $ *Average main: MOP$140* ✉ *289 Rua do Almirante Sérgio, Inner Harbour* ☎ *853/2831–3193* ⏲ *Closed Tues.*

Rickshaws await the gamblers leaving the Casino Lisboa, the gambling den that started it all.

★ Henri's Galley

$$ | **MACANESE** | **FAMILY** | A tiny spot overlooking Sai Van Lake, Henri's Galley has been serving up home-style Macanese cuisine since 1976. The place is cozy and unpretentious, with a few tables outside should the weather decide to play nice. **Known for:** friendly staff; famous African chicken and signature sangria; tasty sharing plates (spicy prawns, roast pigeon, chili crab). *Average main: MOP$150* ✉ *4G–H Av. da Republica, Inner Harbour* ☎ *853/2831–3193* 🌐 *www.henrisgalley.com.mo.*

Litoral

$$ | **MACANESE** | In a tasteful setting, with whitewashed walls and dark-wood beams, one of the most popular local restaurants offers authentic Macanese dishes that are simple, straightforward, and deliciously satisfying. **Known for:** must-tries such as tamarind pork with shrimp paste or Portuguese vegetable cream soup; bebinca de leite (coconut-milk custard) for dessert; a line out the door on weekends, when reservations are highly recommended. *Average main: MOP$180* ✉ *261 Rua do Almirante Sergio, Inner Harbour* ☎ *853/2896–7878.*

Taipa

The island directly south of peninsular Macau was once two small islands that were, over time, joined by deposits from the Pearl River Delta. It's connected to peninsular Macau by three long bridges. The region's horse-racing track, quiet villages, scenic hiking trails, and international airport are all here.

Like downtown Macau, Taipa has been greatly developed in the past few years, yet it retains a visual balance between old Macau charm and modern sleekness. If you don't mind crowds, visit on a weekend, so you can shop for clothing and crafts in the traditional flea market that's held every Sunday from morning to evening in Taipa Village. Otherwise, visit midweek for better hotel rates and a slower pace.

Sights

Taipa Houses-Museum

BUILDING | These five sea-green buildings are interesting examples of Porto-Chinese architecture and were originally residences of wealthy local merchants. They now house changing art exhibitions. Paths lead into the beautiful adjoining **Carmel Garden,** where palm trees provide welcome shade. Within the garden stands the brilliant white-and-yellow **Nossa Senhora do Carmo** (Church of Our Lady of Carmel), built in 1885 and featuring a handsome single-belfry tower. ✉ *Av. da Praia, Carmo Zone, Taipa* ☎ *853/2882–7103* 🌐 *www.taipavillagemacau.com/directory/taipa-houses-museum* 🎫 *Free* 🕒 *Closed Mon.*

★ Taipa Village

TOWN | The narrow, winding streets are packed with restaurants, bakeries, shops, temples, and other buildings with traditional South Chinese and Portuguese design elements. The aptly named Rua do Cunha (Food Street) has many great Chinese, Macanese, Portuguese, and Thai restaurants. Several shops sell homemade Macanese snacks, including steamed milk pudding, almond cakes, beef jerky, durian ice cream, coconut candy, and the famous Lord Stow's egg tarts. ✉ *Taipa* 🌐 *www.taipavillagemacau.com.*

Hotels

★ Altira Macau

$$$ | **HOTEL** | Towering over Taipa, the award-winning Altira provides stunning sea views of the Macau Peninsula from all of its 200 villas, suites and rooms, each of which also comes with a dedicated lounge, walk-in wardrobe, warm brown hues, wraparound windows, and circular stone bath. **Pros:** world-class spa and dining options; open-air rooftop bar; infinity-edge swimming pool. **Cons:** sometimes noisy from nearby construction; a taxi ride from the peninsula; rates vary wildly throughout the year. [$] *Rooms from: MOP$2500* ✉ *Av. de Kwong Tung, Taipa* ☎ *853/2886–8888* 🌐 *www.altiramacau.com* 🛏 *210 rooms* 🍴 *No meals.*

Nightlife

CASINOS

Mocha at The Altira Macau

CASINO—SIGHT | Not only is the hotel run by Altira, a homegrown luxury brand, a stellar place to rest your head, but its on-site Mocha gaming parlor is one of Taipa's classiest. Facing the glow of casinos to the peninsula's north, it offers swank, '70s-style gaming floors decked out in browns and taupes with mod chandeliers. Though you can find a broad selection of games in the Altira's own casino, Mocha is devoted to slot machines. VIP resort suites, fine-dining, and the rooftop 38 Lounge add to the overall ambience. ✉ *Av. de Kwong Tung, Taipa* ☎ *853/2886–8888* 🌐 *www.altiramacau.com.*

★ Venetian Macao

CASINO—SIGHT | Twice the size of its namesake in Las Vegas, The Venetian Macao Resort Hotel offers ample opportunities for gaming, shopping, dining, and sleeping. Expect faux-Renaissance decoration, built-in canals plied by crooning gondoliers, live carnival acts, plenty of sheer spectacle, and more than a touch of pretension. The 374,000 square feet of gaming areas have more than 1,500 slot machines and around 600 tables of casino favorites. The sprawling property also includes nearly 3,000 suites, plus performance venues like the 1,800-seat Venetian Theatre and 15,000-seat Cotai Arena. It's no wonder the Venetian Macao is the must-see megacomplex that everyone's talking about. ✉ *Estrada da Baía de N. Senhora* *da Esperança, Cotai ☎ 853/2882–8888 ⊕ www.venetianmacao.com.*

Shopping

★ Quarter Square

CERAMICS/GLASSWARE | A blend of a gallery, showroom, and coffee bar, Quarter Square sits in a charming pedestrian square in the heart of Old Taipa Village. The boutique curates a design-savvy selection—much of which is Scandinavian or European—that includes eco-friendly steel straws, contemporary wine decanters, coffee accessories, bags, blankets, and more. Grab a coffee or mocha, made with locally roasted beans, to sip while you shop. ✉ *89 Largo Maia de Magalhaes, Taipa ☎ 853/2857–6914 ⊕ www.quartersquare.co.*

Cotai

Restaurants

★ Dynasty 8

$$ | **CANTONESE** | **FAMILY** | Don't let this restaurant's mall location or dynastic Chinese decor turn you off. Kitschy setting aside, Dynasty 8 serves some of the best—and most photogenic—dim sum in town. **Known for:** contemporary dim sum (lobster soup dumplings, salted lemon puffs); popular so reservations are recommened; great sharing dishes, including crispy fried crab claws. $ *Average main: MOP$200* ✉ *Conrad Hotel, Estrada do Istmo, Cotai ☎ 853/8113–8920 ⊕ conradhotels3.hilton.com.*

★ Lai Heen

$$$ | **CANTONESE** | Michelin-starred Lai Heen showcases haute Chinese cuisine in a sky-high dining room at The Ritz-Carlton, Macau. The menu might focus on fine Cantonese dishes, but the decor weaves together Macau's east-meets-west heritage with Portuguese-style mosaics, wood-carved partitions, eye-catching artwork, and plush furniture. **Known for:** excellent views from the 51st floor; melt-in-your-mouth Iberico pork char siu (barbecue pork) and crab claw in creamy lobster bisque; fantastic service start to finish. $ *Average main: MOP$300* ✉ *Ritz-Carlton Macao, Galaxy Macau, Nossa Senhora da Esperanca, 51st fl., Cotai ☎ 852/8886–6706 ⊕ www.ritzcarlton.com.*

Hotels

Conrad Macao

$$ | **HOTEL** | Stylish and sophisticated, the Conrad Macao offers a subdued brand of luxury—a refreshing break from all the over-the-top thematic hotels on the Cotai Strip. **Pros:** award-winning Bodhi spa; gorgeous pool deck with waterfall, whirlpools, and free cabanas; sprawling mall (Shoppes at Cotai Central). **Cons:** many rooms don't have open views; taxi line can be long at peak hours; hotel's restaurants are in the adjacent mall, detracting from their atmosphere. $ *Rooms from: MOP$1698* ✉ *Estrada do Istmo, Cotai ☎ 853/2882–9000 ⊕ www.conradmacao.com* *654 rooms* *No meals.*

Morpheus

$$$$ | **HOTEL** | A haven for art and design lovers, the Zaha Hadid–designed Morpheus is the world's first free-form, exoskeleton-bound, high-rise architectural composition—a mouthful of a superlative that essentially means the hotel's facade looks straight out of a science fiction film. **Pros:** incredible art and design features; smart in-room touches (Japanese toilets and tablet room-controllers); two Alain Ducasse restaurants. **Cons:** rooms are on the pricier side; tends to book out months in advance; part of large, busy City of Dreams hotel-and-entertainment complex. $ *Rooms from: MOP$3200* ✉ *Estrada do Istmo, City of Dreams, Cotai ☎ 853/8868–8888 ⊕ www.cityofdreamsmacau.com* *770 rooms* *No meals.*

★ **Wynn Palace Cotai**

$$$ | **HOTEL** | This hotel has taken Macau's luxury scene to new heights, with stylish mustard-toned rooms and suites, 14 restaurants and bars, a mind-boggling art collection, and an opulent spa that's designed to feel like a Chinese palace. **Pros:** standard rooms are the biggest in town; free snacks and drinks by the pool; all-around stellar service. **Cons:** no children's club; getting around the massive resort complex can be tiring; long check-in lines at times. *$ Rooms from: MOP$2588* ✉ *Av. Da Nave Desportiva, Cotai* ☎ *853/8889–8889* 🌐 *www.wynnpalace.com* *1,706 rooms* *No meals.*

★ **The Ritz-Carlton Bar & Lounge**

PIANO BARS/LOUNGES | On the 51st floor of its namesake hotel, this classy spot is a restaurant by day and a sultry jazz bar, often with live music, at night. If the choices on the enormous menu of specialty cocktails and hard-to-find spirits leaves you paralyzed, order a signature gin and tonic. The bar has more than 150 types of gin, including an edited selection on an old-fashioned trolley that can be wheeled right to your table. ✉ *The Ritz-Carlton Macau, Galaxy Macau, Estrada da Baía da Nossa Senhora da Esperança, 51st fl., Cotai* ☎ *853/8886–6706* 🌐 *www.ritzcarlton.com.*

Shoppes at Cotai Central

SHOPPING CENTERS/MALLS | **FAMILY** | Decked out in faux jungle foliage and cascading waterfalls, Shoppes at Cotai Central is wedged between the Conrad and Sheraton hotels. The hub of international designers and lifestyle brands covers 620,000 square feet and 200 shops, including the largest duty-free shopping area in Macau. Around the mall, look for flashy names like Gucci, Prada, Zegna, Tom Ford, Ferragamo, Bvlgari, Dior, and Burberry, plus some more affordable spots like Zara. **■ TIP→ Traveling with little ones? Take them to the live-action role play Planet J attraction or Qube 2 Kid's Play Zone for an action-packed afternoon.** ✉ *Estrada da Baía de N. Senhora da Esperança, Cotai* ☎ *852/8118–3643* 🌐 *www.sandscotai-central.com.*

Shoppes at Venetian

SHOPPING CENTERS/MALLS | **FAMILY** | The Venetian Macao's vision of a gentrified megamall comes complete with cobblestone walkways, arched bridges, and working canals manned by singing gondoliers (rides are MOP$128). Its 350-plus retailers include all the big-name brands and luxury labels in fashion, accessories, gifts, services, and sporting goods. You'll also find more than 30 restaurants and an international food court. Don't be surprised to see wandering stilt walkers, violinists, and juggling jesters, especially around St. Mark's Square, which hosts two to three daily live performances. The mall connects with the Shoppes at Four Seasons, Shoppes at Parisian, and Shoppes at Cotai Central, further adding to the number of upscale retail options. ✉ *The Venetian Macao, Estrada da Baía de N. Senhora da Esperança, Cotai* ☎ *853/2882–8888* 🌐 *www.venetianmacao.com/shopping.html.*

Coloane

Centuries ago, Coloane was a wild place, where pirates hid in rocky caves and coves, awaiting their chance to strike at cargo ships on the Pearl River. Early in the 20th century the local government sponsored a huge planting program to transform Coloane from a barren place to a verdant one. Today this island is idyllic, with green hills and clean sandy beaches.

Sights

★ A-Ma Cultural Village

TOWN | FAMILY | A huge complex built in a traditional Qing Dynasty style pays homage to Macau's namesake, the goddess of the sea. The vibrancy and color of the details in the bell and drum towers, the tiled roofs, and the carved marble altars are truly awe-inspiring. It's as if you've been transported back to the height of the Qing Empire and can now see temples in their true state of greatness. Other remarkable details include the striking rows of stairs leading to Tian Hou Palace at the entrance. Each row features painstakingly detailed marble and stone carvings of auspicious Chinese symbols: a roaring tiger, double lions, five cranes, the double phoenix, and a splendid imperial dragon. The grounds here also have a recreational fishing zone and an arboretum with more than 100 species of local and exotic flora.

Behind A-Ma Cultural Village, **Coloane Hill** rises 170 meters (560 feet); it is crowned by a gleaming white-marble statue of A-Ma that's 21 meters (68 feet) tall and visible from miles away. You can make the short hike up to the top or take one of the shuttle buses that leave from the base of the hill every 30 minutes. ⊠ *Off Estrada de Seac Pai Van, Coloane Island South.*

★ Coloane Village

TOWN | Quiet, relaxed Coloane Village is home to traditional Mediterranean-style houses painted in pastels, as well as the baroque-style Chapel of St. Francis Xavier and the Taoist Tam Kung Temple. The narrow alleys reveal surprises at every turn; you may well encounter fishermen repairing their junks or a baptism at the chapel. At the village's heart is a small square adorned with a fountain with a bronze Cupid. The surrounding Macanese and Chinese open-air restaurants are among the region's best; some are the unheralded favorites of chefs visiting from Hong Kong and elsewhere in Asia. ⊠ *Coloane Island West.*

Restaurants

★ Restaurante Espaço Lisboa

$$ | PORTUGUESE | Occupying a converted two-story house with a small but pleasant balcony overlooking Coloane Village, this restaurant is Portuguese owned and has a Portuguese chef—so it's no surprise that it is a favorite of Portuguese residents. **Known for:** codfish cakes, savory duck rice, boiled bacalhau; an extensive list of hearty Portuguese wines; house-made desserts (rice pudding or flan). [$] *Average main: MOP$180* ⊠ *8 Rua das Gaivotas, Coloane Island West* ☎ *853/2888–2226* ⊙ *Closed Wed.*

★ Restaurante Fernando

$$ | PORTUGUESE | Everyone in Hong Kong and Macau knows about Fernando's, but the vine-covered entrance close to Hác-Sá Beach is difficult to spot. The open-air dining pavilion and bar have attracted beachgoers for years now, and the enterprising Fernando has built a legendary reputation for his Portuguese fare. **Known for:** home-style grilled fish, baked chicken, and huge bowls of spicy clams; beloved sangria and long list of Portuguese wines; informal, boisterous atmosphere. [$] *Average main: MOP$150* ⊠ *9 Praia de Hác-Sá Beach, Coloane Island South* ☎ *853/2888–2531* 🌐 *www.fernando-restaurant.com* ▭ *No credit cards.*

Hotels

Grand Coloane Resort

$$ | RESORT | FAMILY | This is where you can truly get away from it all: it's built into the side of a cliff, and each of its rooms has an ocean view. **Pros:** green surroundings on Hác-Sá Beach; golf-club access; fun for kids. **Cons:** isolated location; beach can be dirty after a storm; free shuttles to Cotai only run on weekends. 💲 *Rooms from: MOP$1300* ✉ *1918 Estrada de Hác Sá, Coloane Island South* ☎ *853/2887–1111* 🌐 *www.grandcoloane.com* 🛏 *208 rooms* 🍽 *No meals.*

★ **Pousada de Coloane**

$ | **HOTEL** | Set in a former manor house on quiet Cheoc-Van Beach, at the southernmost tip of Coloane, this *pousada* makes the most of its quiet, natural setting and 1930s architecture. **Pros:** intimate coastal location with an on-site pool; sea-view balconies; excellent Portuguese restaurant. **Cons:** tile rooms feel chilly in winter; limited facilities; far-flung address. 💲 *Rooms from: MOP$800* ✉ *Praia de Cheoc-Van, Cheoc-Van Beach, Coloane Island South* ☎ *853/2888–2143* 🌐 *www.hotelp-coloane.com.mo* 🛏 *28 rooms* 🍽 *Free Breakfast.*

Chapter 8

THE SOUTHWEST

Updated by
Clarissa Wei

Sights ★★★★★ | Restaurants ★★★★☆ | Hotels ★★★☆☆ | Shopping ★★☆☆☆ | Nightlife ★☆☆☆☆

WELCOME TO THE SOUTHWEST

TOP REASONS TO GO

★ **Lose yourself in Lijiang:** Treasured by the Chinese and home to a UNESCO World Heritage Site, the winding cobblestone lanes of Lijiang beckon to all.

★ **Lush Xishuangbanna rain forests:** Hugging the borders of Laos and Myanmar, this small city in Yunnan is home to the Dai ethnic group, who make you feel far from the rest of China.

★ **Trek Tiger Leaping Gorge:** Explore the deepest gorge in the world, and one of the most scenic spots in all of Yunnan, and possibly China.

★ **Guizhou's eye-popping Huangguoshu Falls:** Travel to the Baishui River in Guizhou, where the largest waterfall in China plummets 230 feet.

★ **Cycling around Yangshuo:** Snake your way through this strange lunar landscape of limestone karsts.

1 **Guilin.** Karst mountains and rivers have attracted travelers for centuries.

2 **Heping District.** The gateway to the Longsheng terraced rice fields.

3 **Yangshuo.** On the backpacker circuit since the '70s.

4 **Nanning.** Jumping off point for Vietnam.

5 **Guiyang.** A famous Buddhist temple, hundreds of monkeys, and amazing views.

6 **Kaili.** Visit the regions minority villages

7 **Kunming.** Yunnan's capital city is a great base for exploring the rest of the province.

8 **Stone Forest.** These twisted limestone formations are a great side trip from Kunming.

9 **Dali.** Perched on the edge of Erhai Lake, this rustic town is a major tourism draw.

10 **Lijang.** The Old Town here is a UNESCO World Heritage Site.

11 **Tiger Leaping Gorge.** Come here and hike this beautiful gorge.

12 **Xishuangbanna Region.** Bordering Laos and Myanmar, this region attracts well-heeled Chinese.

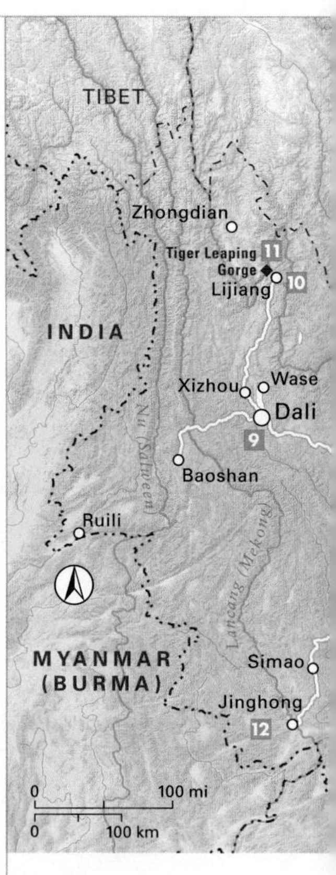

CHONGQING
Chongqing
SICHUAN
Jinsha Jiang (Yangzi)
Zunyi
GUIZHOU
HUNAN
Zhaotong
6
Guiyang
5
Kaili
Huangguoshu Falls
Huize
Duyun
Anshun
Longsheng
Qujing
2
Zhanyi
Guilin
1
Kunming
7
8
Xingyi
Stone Forest
Chuxiong
Shilin
3
Yangshuo
Dian Lake
Yishan
Yuxi
YUNNAN
Liuzhou
Baise
Kaiyuan
GUANGXI
Gejiu
Wenshan
Hechi
Mengzi
Yuan (Red)
4
Yulin
Nanning
GUANGDONG
Qinzhou
VIETNAM
Fangcheng
Beihai
Gulf of Tonkin
LAOS

The southwestern provinces are among the most alluring destinations in the country. This region lays claim to some of the most breathtaking scenery in all of China—from the moonscape limestone karsts and river scenery of Yangshuo, to China's mightiest waterfall in Guizhou, to Yunnan's tropical rain forests and spectacular Tiger Leaping Gorge.

Yunnan is home to almost a third of China's ethnic minorities. In 1958 Guangxi became an autonomous region in an attempt to quell the friction between the Zhuang minority and the ethnic Han majority. Yunnan, Guangxi, and Guizhou represent the complex tapestry of China's ethnic groups.

In Kunming, Dali, and villages around Yunnan, the Yi and Bai peoples hold their Torch Festivals on the 24th day of the sixth lunar month. They throw handfuls of pine resin into bonfires, lighting the night sky with clouds of sparks. The Dai Water Splashing Festival in the rain forests of Xishuangbanna on the 22nd day of the third lunar month is liquid pandemonium. Its purpose is to wash away the sorrow of the old year and refresh you for the new.

Dali has two festivals of note: the Third Moon Fair (middle of third lunar month) during which people from all around Yunnan come to Dali to sell their wares; and the Three Temples Festival (usually May). The Sister's Meal Festival, celebrated in the middle of the third lunar month by Miao people throughout Guizhou, is dedicated to unmarried women. During the great rice harvest, special brightly colored dishes are made, and at nightfall there's much ado about courtship, dancing, and old-fashioned flirting. The Zhuang Singing Festival turns Guangxi's countryside into an ocean of song. On the third day of the third lunar month, the Zhuang gather and sing to honor Liu Sanjie ("Third Sister Liu"), the goddess of song. Singing "battles" ensue between groups who sing—often improvising—at each other until one group concedes.

MAJOR REGIONS

Southwest China can be summed up in one word: diversity. The regions of Guangxi, Guizhou, and Yunnan offer some of China's most singular travel opportunities. Having inspired countless paintings and poems in the past, the spectacular karst scenery of **Guilin** and **Yangshuo** today inspires travelers who are in search of an unforgettable Chinese experience. Capital city **Nanning** is being groomed as China's gateway to Vietnam while the **Heping District** is the gateway to the Longshen Rice Terraces. Off the beaten path **Guiyang** and **Kaili** are fascinating places known for their undulating mountains and terraced fields. **Kunming** is the capital of Yunnan and the **Stone Forest** just east of the city. The ancient towns of **Lijiang** and **Dali** offer glimpses into the centuries-old traditions of the Naxi and Bai ethnic groups. For a more rugged experience, hike through the breathtaking **Tiger Leaping Gorge.** If a slow boat on the Mekong appeals, head south to the **Xishuangbanna Region** and chill out in the tropics.

Planning

When to Go

When you are packing for travel in Southwest China, think of the region as three distinct zones separated by altitude. Steamy tropical lowlands spread across the southern halves of Yunnan and Guangxi. The mountainous highlands of central and northwest Yunnan are characterized by intense sun, long rainy seasons, and cold winters. Somewhere in between are the cloudy mountain scenes found throughout Guizhou and northern Guangxi. Each zone requires a different packing strategy.

In summer the monsoon rains can be heavy, so keep abreast of weather reports as you travel. Temperatures don't get as hot as the tropics or as cold as the highlands, but summers can be quite hot in Guilin and Yangshuo, and winters in Guiyang can be cold enough for snow. The best time of year is spring, in April or early May. Winter months can be surprisingly cold (except in southern Guangxi and Yunnan), and the summertime heat is stifling. Mid-September can also be a comfortable time to travel. The falls at Huangguoshu are at their best in the rainy season from May through October.

Getting Here and Around

With new roads, faster trains, and more airports every year, traveling around Southwest China is becoming increasingly convenient. If you're short on time, flying within the region is the best option, with most flights taking an hour or less. If you're not in a hurry, trains and buses are a cheap and scenic option.

AIR TRAVEL

Southwest China's air network is constantly expanding, with most popular travel destinations served by their own airports. China Eastern Airlines is the dominant carrier in the region. Kunming, Guilin, Nanning, Jinghong, and Guiyang all have international airports, and cities such as Lijiang and Dali are reachable by air.

BUS TRAVEL

Traveling around Southwest China by bus is a good way to cover the shorter distances in your travels. The regional bus network is efficient and is primarily served by luxury coaches. Keep in mind that in general there is no English spoken on buses here.

CAR TRAVEL

Ridesharing apps are all the rage these days. Didi is the Uber of China and a good alternative to taxi or bus if you have a smartphone.

Restaurants

In addition to great Chinese food, usually on the spicier side, Southwest China is home to a rainbow of ethnic cuisines, with Dai, Bai, and Tibetan being some of the most notable. Yunnan has the most diverse culinary offerings, which even include some breads and cheeses. Wild mushrooms are available every May through September.

What It Costs in Yuan			
$	$$	$$$	$$$$
RESTAURANTS			
under Y50	Y50–Y99	Y100–Y165	over Y165

Hotels

Locally run hotels in Southwest China's larger cities offer adequate service and amenities for a reasonable price, but don't expect an English-speaking staff. There is a growing number of international luxury hotels in Kunming, Guiyang, and Nanning that offer personal service and well-regarded restaurants. Cities like Dali, Lijiang, and Yangshuo have plenty of comfortable and cheap small hotels and guesthouses where you can get home-cooked local meals. *Hotel reviews have been shortened. For full information, visit Fodors.com.*

What It Costs in Yuan			
$	$$	$$$	$$$$
HOTELS			
under Y1,100	Y1,100–Y1,399	Y1,400–Y1,800	over Y1,800

Tours

Although they can be cheaper, Chinese package tours tend to be noisy, crowded, and aimed at getting you to buy junk. In Southwest China's larger cities, hotels are the most convenient places to make transportation arrangements. In travel hot spots such as Yangshuo, Lijiang, and Dali there are plenty of English-speaking travel agents.

China Minority Travel
GUIDED TOURS | One of the oldest travel agencies in Southwest China, China Minority Travel offers tours exploring virtually every corner of Southwest China. 🌐 *www.china-minority-travel.com* 🎫 *From Y1800 for 2–4 people.*

WildChina Travel
GUIDED TOURS | This company specializes in unique itineraries in Yunnan, Guizhou, and Guangxi, and can create journeys tailored to specific interests. Prices vary greatly depending on number of days, destination, and options. About $3,000 per person for a 10-day custom tour with driver is a good estimate. ✉ *Oriental Place, 9 Dongfang Dong Lu, Room 801, Chaoyang* ☎ *010/6465–6602* 🌐 *www.wildchina.com* 🎫 *From Y2100.*

Visitor Information

This part of China has virtually nothing in the way of useful English-language tourist information. Cafés and guesthouses are usually good places to ask about travel in the region.

Guilin

500 km (310 miles; 11 hrs by train) northwest of Guangzhou; 1,675 km (1,039 miles; 11 hrs by high-speed train) southwest of Beijing.

Guilin has the good fortune of being situated in the middle of some of the world's most beautiful landscapes. This region of limestone karst hills and mountains, rising almost vertically from the earth, has a dreamy, hypnotic quality. They were formed 200 million years ago, when the area was under the sea. As the land beneath began to push upward, the sea receded, and the effects of the ensuing erosion over thousands of years produced this sublime scenery.

Architecturally, the city lacks charm, having been heavily bombed during the Second Sino-Japanese War and rebuilt in the utilitarian style popular in the 1950s. Still, the river city is replete with beautiful parks and bridges, and has a number of historic sites that make it worthy of exploration. It's also a good base from which to explore northern Guangxi.

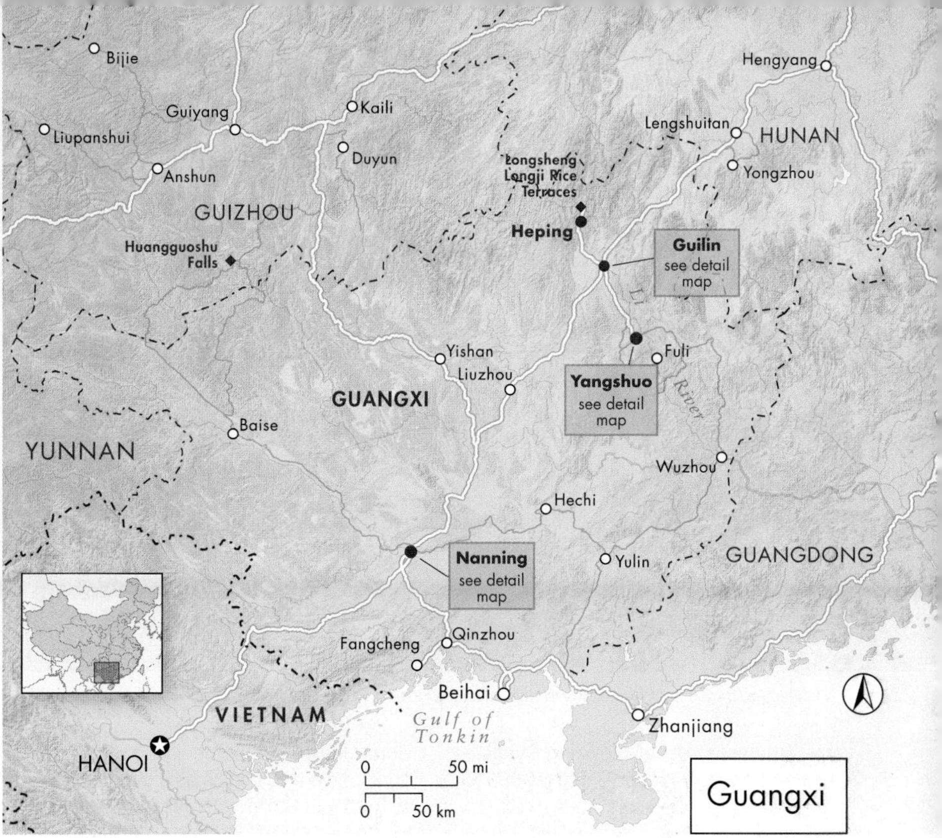

GETTING HERE AND AROUND

About 28 km (17 miles) southwest of the city center, Guilin Liangjiang International Airport has flights to cities throughout China as well as throughout Asia. An airport shuttle bus, which operates daily from 6:30 am to 8 pm, runs between the airport and the Aviation Building at 18 Shanghai Lu, across from the main bus station. The cost is Y20 per person.

The main bus station in Guilin is just north of the train station on Zhongshan Nan Lu. Short- and long-distance buses connect Guilin to nearby cities, including Yangshuo, Liuzhou, and Nanning. For Longsheng, you need the Qingtan Bus Station. Long-distance sleeper coaches travel to cities throughout the Pearl River delta.

Guilin is linked by daily rail service with most major cities in China. Most long-distance trains arrive at Guilin's South Railway Station.

TIMING

Although it is increasingly overshadowed by nearby Yangshuo, Guilin is a pleasant city that's well worth a stop. Most of the sights can be taken in within a couple of days.

Sights

Elephant Trunk Hill (象鼻山 *Xiàngbí shān*)
NATURE SITE | On the banks of the river in the southern part of the city, Elephant Trunk Hill takes its name from a rock formation arching into the water like the trunk of an elephant. Nearby is a grotto covered in poetic inscriptions inspired by the beauty of the place, some by

Watching a Dragon Boat race at the Water Splashing Festival in Xishuangbanna

the greatest poets of the Song Dynasty. ✉ *Xiangshan Rd.* ☎ *0773/258–6602* 🎫 *Y60.*

Ming Tomb (Guilin Jingjiang King Tomb) (靖江王陵 *Jìngjiāngwáng líng*)
MEMORIAL | East of downtown is the tomb of Zhu Shouqian, the nephew of the first Ming emperor, who founded a principality here. It makes a pleasant excursion by bicycle, and its gates combine with the surrounding hills to make for good photo opportunities. To get here, take Jiefang Dong Lu east about 9 km (5 miles). ✉ *Jiefang Dong Lu* ☎ *0773/589–7276* 🎫 *Y20.*

Peak of Solitary Beauty (独秀峰 *Dúxiù fēng*)
VIEWPOINT | The 492-foot Peak of Solitary Beauty, with carved stone stairs leading to the top, offers an unparalleled view of Guilin—and a short but intense workout for your legs. It's one of the attractions of the **Prince City Solitary Beauty Park** (*Jing Jiang Wang Cheng*). Surrounded by an ancient wall, outside of which vendors hawk their wares, sits the heart of Old Guilin. Inside are the decaying remains of an ancient Ming Dynasty palace built in 1393 and Guilin's Confucius temple. Sun Yat-sen lived here for a few months in the winter of 1921 (a fact duly noted on the wall by the outside gate). Cixi, the former empress dowager of China, inscribed the character for "longevity" on a rock within these walls. ✉ *Donghua Rd.* ✥ *2 blocks north of Zhengyang Lu Pedestrian Mall* 🎫 *Y120.*

Seven Star Park (七星公园 *Qīxīng gōngyuán*)
CITY PARK | This park gets its name from the arrangement of its hills, said to resemble the Big Dipper. At the center of this huge park is **Putuo Mountain** (Putuoshan), atop which sits a lovely pavilion housing a number of famous examples of Tang calligraphy. Indeed, calligraphy abounds on the side of this hill, mostly the work of Ming Dynasty Taoist philosopher Pan Changjing. Nearby is **Seven Star Cliff** (Qixing Dong), with several large caves open for exploration. The largest contains rock formations

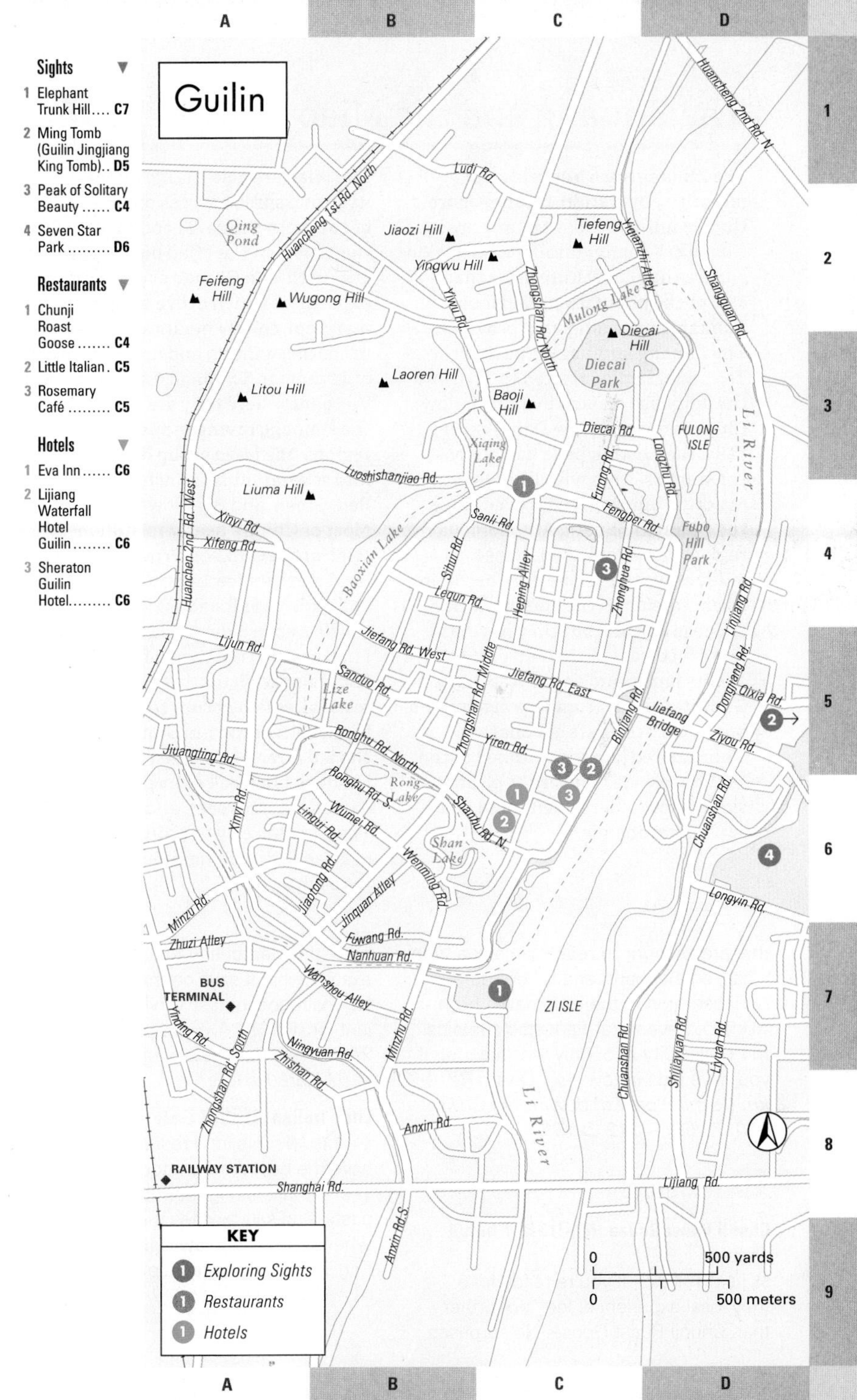
Guilin
Sights
1 Elephant Trunk Hill.... C7
2 Ming Tomb (Guilin Jingjiang King Tomb).. D5
3 Peak of Solitary Beauty C4
4 Seven Star Park D6
Restaurants
1 Chunji Roast Goose C4
2 Little Italian . C5
3 Rosemary Café C5
Hotels
1 Eva Inn C6
2 Lijiang Waterfall Hotel Guilin C6
3 Sheraton Guilin Hotel......... C6
A
B
C
D
1
2
3
4
5
6
7
8
9
Huancheng 2nd Rd. N.
Ludi Rd.
Qing Pond
Huancheng 1st Rd. North
Jiaozi Hill
Tiefeng Hill
Yiqianzhi Alley
Yingwu Hill
Feifeng Hill
Wugong Hill
Zhongshan Rd. North
Yiwu Rd.
Mulong Lake
Shangguan Rd.
Diecai Hill
Diecai Park
Laoren Hill
Litou Hill
Baoji Hill
Diecai Rd.
FULONG ISLE
Li River
Xiqing Lake
Furong Rd.
Longzhu Rd.
Luoshishanjiao Rd.
Liuma Hill
Sanli Rd.
Fengbei Rd.
Fubo Hill Park
Xinyi Rd.
Xifeng Rd.
Huanchen 2nd Rd. West
Baoxian Lake
Sihui Rd.
Heping Alley
Zhonghua Rd.
Lequn Rd.
Linjiang Rd.
Lijun Rd.
Jiefang Rd. West
Zhongshan Rd. Middle
Sanduo Rd.
Jiefang Rd. East
Dongjiang Rd.
Lize Lake
Binjiang Rd.
Qixia Rd.
Jiefang Bridge
Ziyou Rd.
Yiren Rd.
Ronghu Rd. North
Jiuangling Rd.
Ronghu Rd. S.
Rong Lake
Shanhu Rd. N.
Chuanshan Rd.
Xinyi Rd.
Lingui Rd.
Wumei Rd.
Shan Lake
Jiaotong Rd.
Jinquan Alley
Wenming Rd.
Longyin Rd.
Minzu Rd.
Zhuzi Alley
Fuwang Rd.
Nanhuan Rd.
BUS TERMINAL
Wanshou Alley
ZI ISLE
Yinding Rd.
Minzhu Rd.
Ningyuan Rd.
Zhishan Rd.
Chuanshan Rd.
Shijiayuan Rd.
Liyuan Rd.
Zhongshan Rd. South
Li River
Anxin Rd.
RAILWAY STATION
Shanghai Rd.
Lijiang Rd.
Anxin Rd.S.
KEY
Exploring Sights
Restaurants
Hotels
0
500 yards
0
500 meters

The Zhuang and the Miao

The Zhuang are China's largest minority population, totaling more than 18 million. Most Zhuang are in Guangxi Zhuang Autonomous Region (where they constitute more than 85% of the population), Guizhou, Yunnan, and Guangdong provinces. The Zhuang language is part of the Tai-Kadai family, related to Thai and the language spoken by their fellow Chinese minority the Dai. Historically, the Zhuang have had almost constant friction with China's Han majority, but that's improved since the Guangxi Zhuang Autonomous region was established in 1958. In many ways the Zhuang are becoming assimilated into the dominant Han Chinese culture, but they have still preserved part of their strong culture and its music and dance traditions. Clothing varies from region to region, but mostly consists of collarless embroidered jackets buttoned to the left, loose wide trousers or pleated skirts, embroidered belts, and black square headbands.

The Miao are also a large minority group spread across much of southern China. Throughout their history, the Miao have had to deal with Han China's southward expansion, which drove them into marginal, chiefly mountainous areas in southern China and northern areas of Myanmar, Thailand, Laos, and Vietnam (where they are known as the Hmong). Living in such isolated regions, the Miao group developed into several subsets, including Black, Red, Green, and Big Flowery Miao. Most of China's nearly 10 million Miao are in Guizhou Province, where local markets feature their intricate and expert craftsmanship, especially jewelry, embroidery, and batik. The Miao are also renowned for their festivals, particularly the Lusheng festival, which occurs from the 11th to the 18th of the first lunar month. Named after a Miao reed instrument, Lusheng is a week of lively music, dancing, horse races, and bullfights. The Guizhou city of Kaili is the center of Miao festivals, hosting more than 120 each year.

that are thought to resemble a lion with a ball, an elephant, and other figures. An inscription in the cave dates from AD 590. Seven Star Park also contains the Guilin City Zoo, only worth a stop if you have kids in tow. ✉ *1 Qixing Rd.* ✢ *1 km (½ mile) east of downtown Guilin* ☎ *0773/581–4342* 🎫 *Y99.*

Restaurants

Chunji Roast Goose (**椿记烧鹅** *Chūn jì shāo é*)

$$ | **CANTONESE** | If you're ready for a truly local experience, look no further than Chunji Roast Goose. No surprises here: this Cantonese restaurant serves exactly what it says on the facade. **Known for:** roast goose; fast service; convenient location. $ *Average main: Y60* ✉ *2 Zhongshan Rd., inside Zhongshan Hotel* ☎ *0773/280–6188.*

Little Italian (**唐纳德** *Café Tángnàdé Café*)

$ | **ITALIAN** | This little restaurant may have the best Western food in Guilin. The menu is straightforward: pizza, pasta, and sandwiches that are made when you order. **Known for:** great coffee; English-speaking staff; cozy atmosphere. $ *Average main: Y45* ✉ *1–4, 18 Binjiang Lu* ☎ *0773/311–1068.*

Miao girls wear hairpieces woven from the hair of their ancestors on special occasions.

Rosemary Cafe (迷迭香 *Mídiéxiāng*)
$ | **INTERNATIONAL** | Just a hop, skip, and a jump away from the Sheraton Hotel, the Rosemary Cafe has outside seating in the middle of a calm pedestrian street, making it a nice place to while away an evening. It may not have the most inspired decor, but don't let that deceive you: the Western menu includes delicious burritos and salads, which you can wash down with a glass of freshly pressed pineapple juice. **Known for:** wine; pizza; vegetarian options. *$ Average main: Y45 ✉ 1–3 Yiren Lu ☎ 0773/281–0063.*

Hotels

★ **Eva Inn** (四季春天酒店 *Sìjì chūntiān jiǔdiàn*)
$ | **HOTEL** | At what's the best budget hotel in town, the room are modern, with all the necessities. **Pros:** great location; good value; pleasant views. **Cons:** rooms could be a bit bigger; limited English; old carpets. *$ Rooms from: Y400 ✉ 66 Binjiang Lu, on west bank of Li River ☎ 0773/283–0666 ⇨ 113 rooms 🍴 No meals.*

Lijiang Waterfall Hotel Guilin (漓江大瀑布酒店 *Líjiāng dàpùbù jiǔdiàn*)
$ | **HOTEL** | With a privileged perch overlooking the river, this luxury hotel has breathtaking views of Elephant Trunk Hill and Seven Star Park. **Pros:** reasonable rooms for reasonable rates; 13 restaurants; staff speaks great English. **Cons:** occasionally chaotic due to conferences; air-conditioning is spotty; a lot of tourists. *$ Rooms from: Y600 ✉ 1 Shanhu Bei Lu, southern end of Zhengyang Lu Pedestrian St. ☎ 0773/282–2881 ⇨ 674 rooms 🍴 No meals.*

Sheraton Guilin Hotel (贵林喜来登饭店 *Guìlín xǐláidēng fàndiàn*)
$$ | **HOTEL** | Easily the most elegant hotel in town, the Sheraton Guilin welcomes you with a chic lobby with a sunny atrium and glass elevators that whisk you upstairs. **Pros:** plenty of creature comforts; good restaurants; English-speaking staff. **Cons:** slightly overpriced; furniture is dated; mediocre breakfast. *$ Rooms*

Did You Know?

Most of the magnificent Longji terraced fields were built about 500 years ago, during the Ming Dynasty. They're called Dragon's Backbone because the peaks of the mountain range resemble the backbone of the dragon, and the water-filled terraces shimmer like a dragon's scales. If you stand at the summit, you can see the dragon's backbone curving off to the horizon.

Guangxi's Silver-Toothed Touts

Aggressive touts are a fact of life for Western travelers in modern-day China. Guangxi Province is known for the tenacity of its touts—mostly older tribal women with silver teeth (as is the local custom). To these wandering merchants a Western traveler is a coin purse with legs.

It's not uncommon for half a dozen of these women to surround you at any given site, shouting "water" and "postcard." They'll follow you around until you buy something from each of them.

It's hard for travelers to maintain equilibrium when confronted with a gaggle of old women who seem doggedly intent on turning a hiking trip around, say, the Longsheng Rice Terraces into a no-win trinket-buying binge. Polite "no, thank you's" can soon escalate into expletive-laden tirades, possibly leading to remorse for cursing a poverty-stricken old woman.

What's worse, it accomplishes nothing. No sooner will the last bitter word leave your lips than someone will thrust a pack of commemorative postcards at you and shout "10 yuan!"

Consider the purchasing of minor souvenirs or unwanted sodas as part of the experience; keep a few yuan handy for just that, and deal with it smilingly. Failing that, you can always run. But remember, these old women know all the shortcuts, and you'll tire out and need to buy a beverage anyway. And maybe some postcards as well.

from: Y600 ✉ *15 Binjiang Lu, on west bank of Li River* ☎ *0773/282–5588* 🌐 *www.sheraton.com/guilin* *408 rooms* *No meals.*

Nightlife

Guilin Back Garden Irish Pub (后园爱尔兰酒吧 *Hòu yuán Ài'ěrlán jiǔbā*)
BARS/PUBS | Refurbished in mid-2014, this bar offers occasional live music, a well-stocked bar, and a friendly owner. Guinness is available in bottles, but not on tap—yet. It's the only bar in Guilin worth visiting. ✉ *Mingcheng Hotel, Zhengyang Lu* ☎ *773/280–3869.*

Heping District

120 km (74 miles; 3 hrs by bus) northwest of Guilin.

The town of Heping, which administrates the villages and surrounding area, is the gateway to Longsheng's terraced rice fields. Ping'an, about 10 km (6 miles) northeast of Heping, up a winding drive along a river and up a mountain, is where the most impressive scenery is, although the entire area makes for a great visit.

GETTING HERE AND AROUND

Buses are the best way to get to Heping town. The only alternative to a bus is to pay a premium to retain a taxi's services for the day, which will set you back at least Y500.

Buses heading to Heping from Guilin's Qintan Bus Station leave every 15 minutes and take about two hours (Y20). The express bus back to Guilin departs from Longsheng every two hours.

TIMING

The Longsheng (aka Longji) Rice Terraces make for a fulfilling day trip from Guilin, but shutterbugs may want to catch the terraces at sunrise and sunset over the course of two or three days to maximize the chance of getting that perfect shot.

TOURS

Travel plans in Longsheng are best arranged in Guilin, because Longsheng doesn't have many suitable tour companies. The stretch of Binjiang Lu south of the Sheraton has several English-speaking travel agencies.

Sights

Longsheng Longji Rice Terraces (**龙胜龙脊梯田** *Lóngshèng lóngjí tītián*)
FARM/RANCH | These terraced rice fields cut into the hills make a mesmerizing pattern of undulating color. Amazing for their scale as well as their beauty, they're called the "Dragon's Backbone" because the peaks of the mountain range resemble the backbone of the dragon, and the water-filled terraces shimmer like a dragon's scales. They've been worked for generations, by rice farmers from the local Yao, Dong, Zhuang, and Miao communities, who build their houses in villages on the hills. ✉ *Longsheng* 🎫 *Y100.*

Restaurants

Li Qing Restaurant (**丽晴饭店** *Lìqíng fàndiàn*)
$ | **CHINESE** | In addition to well-known Chinese dishes, this extremely popular restaurant serves a number of less-common dishes, such as bamboo stuffed with sticky rice, or stir-fried mountain vegetables. **Known for:** cheap; fresh vegetables; seasonal. $ *Average main: Y25* ✉ *Ji Lu, Ping'an* ☎ *0773/758–3048* 💳 *No credit cards.*

Hotels

★ **Li'an Lodge** (**理安山庄** *Lǐ'ān shānzhuāng*)
$$$$ | **B&B/INN** | Perched atop a mountain and peeking through the morning mist, a stay at Li'an Lodge is the ultimate way to immerse yourself in stylish Chinese style without sliding into kitsch. **Pros:** absolutely unique; magnificent location; English-speaking staff. **Cons:** food geared toward a Western palate; only accessible on foot (but sedan chair and porters are available); pricey. $ *Rooms from: Y1850* ✉ *Ping'an* ☎ *0773/758–3318* 🌐 *www.guilinboutiquelodge.cn/* *16 rooms* 🍽 *No meals.*

Yangshuo

70 km (43 miles; 90 mins by bus) south of Guilin.

Yangshuo has taken center stage as Guangxi's top tourist destination. At the heart of the city is West Street, a pedestrian mall extending to the Li River. Many visitors are content to spend a few days eating, drinking, and gazing over the low-slung traditional structures facing toward the fang-shaped peaks that surround the town. Yangshuo is a major destination for adventure travel, and the countryside is filled with opportunities for biking, hiking, rock climbing, and caving.

Keep in mind that Yangshuo is part and parcel of the Southeast Asia backpacker circuit that was forged in the 1970s, and remains well trodden to this day. The main drag throbs with the cacophony of Hong Kong canto-pop, reggae, hip-hop, and classic rock. In restaurants competing for the tourist trade you can order everything from lasagna to enchiladas to pad Thai.

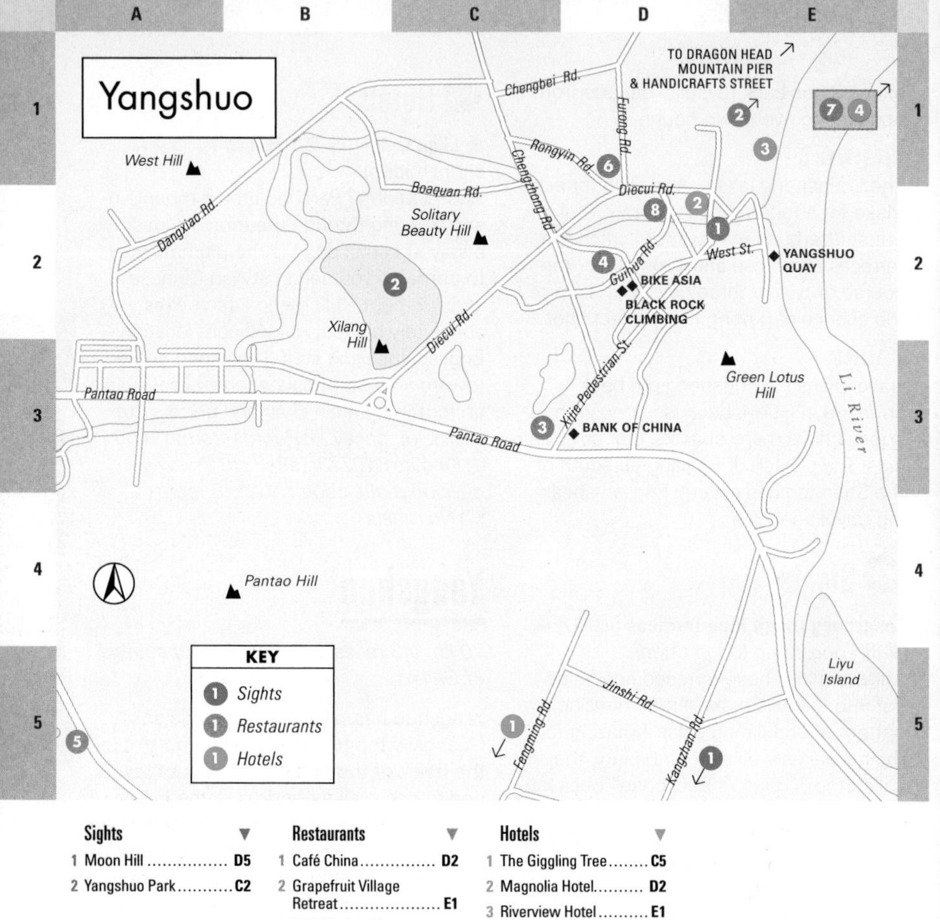

Sights

1 Moon Hill **D5**

2 Yangshuo Park........... **C2**

Restaurants

1 Café China............... **D2**

2 Grapefruit Village Retreat..................... **E1**

3 Kali Mirch Indian Cuisine (Black Pepper Indian Restaurant)....... **C3**

4 Kelly's Place............. **D2**

5 Man De Guai **A4**

6 Mood Food Energy Café **D1**

7 Pomelo Garden **E1**

8 Pure Lotus............... **D2**

Hotels

1 The Giggling Tree........ **C5**

2 Magnolia Hotel.......... **D2**

3 Riverview Hotel.......... **E1**

4 Yangshuo Mountain Retreat.................... **E1**

Li River and the limestone karsts of Yangshuo

GETTING HERE AND AROUND

Arriving via train or airplane means traveling via Guilin. You can also get from Guilin to Yangshuo by bus or minibus, or via a costly but pleasant boat trip.

The boat from Guilin takes approximately four hours. At Y533 for a round-trip ticket, it's much costlier than other modes of travel, but the trip is pleasant and scenic. Tickets are available from any of the countless travel agents in Guilin.

Departing from the Guilin Train Station, express luxury buses travel between Guilin and Yangshuo every half hour between 7 am and 8 pm. The trip in air-conditioned and smoke-free buses takes just under two hours and cost Y25.

TIMING

Two or three days is enough time to take in Yangshuo's town and surrounding areas.

TOURS

If getting wet and muddy underground is your idea of a good time, look no farther than Water Cave, the deepest and largest underground grotto in the area. Accessible only by flat-bottom boat, it includes a mud bath and a number of crystal clear pools perfect for washing off. Tours can be arranged through any of the travel agencies in the Xi Jie area. There are also several Chinese locals walking the streets with pictures of tour suggestions. While their quality cannot be guaranteed, some of them actually have interesting tour ideas which may include a visit to local homes. Most tours start at Y150.

Sights

Moon Hill (**月亮山** *Yuèliàng shān*)
VIEWPOINT | Probably the most popular destination in Yangshuo, Moon Hill is named after the large hole through the center of this karst peak. Amazing vistas are at the top of the several trails that snake up the hill's side. This is a favorite for rock climbers. ⊠ *Yangshuo–Gaotian Lu* 🎫 *Y15.*

Yangshuo Park (阳朔 *Yángshuò gōngyuán*)
CITY PARK | In the center of town, Yangshuo Park is where older people come to play chess while children scamper about in small playgrounds. The park has a number of statues and ponds worth seeing, and Yangshuo Park Peak has a small pagoda offering excellent views of the surrounding town. For a more intense climb with even better views, ascend the television tower across the street from the park's entrance. ✉ *Diecui Lu, at Pantao Lu* 🎫 *Free.*

Restaurants

Café China (原始人 *Yuánshǐ rén*)
$ | **ECLECTIC** | On a cozy corner on bustling West Street, Café China serves addictive rotisserie chicken made from a highly guarded local recipe. The kitchen roasts between 12 and 18 chickens each night, so in-the-know diners call at least an hour in advance. **Known for:** cheesecake; espresso machine; vegetarian options. $ *Average main: Y35* ✉ *34 Xi Jie* ☎ *0773/882–7744* 💳 *No credit cards.*

Grapefruit Village Retreat (罗马假日柚子山庄 *luómǎ yòuzi shānzhuāng*)
$ | **INTERNATIONAL** | A 20-minute walk from Yangshuo's center, the Village Retreat is an excellent place to enjoy a healthy breakfast, filling lunch, or a romantic dinner with views of the surrounding scenery. Trained by European masters, the chef clearly understands how Western food ought to taste—without neglecting the Chinese menu. **Known for:** outdoor dining; tasty Western dishes; romantic. $ *Average main: Y200* ✉ *Village Retreat, 36 Shi Ban Qiao Village* ☎ *073/888–8766* 🌐 *www.yangshuo-village-retreat.com.*

Kali Mirch Indian Cuisine (Black Pepper Indian Restaurant) (黑胡椒印度餐厅 *Hēihújiāo yìndù cāntīng*)
$$ | **INDIAN** | Kali Mirch's spices and chefs come directly from India, and it's a delicious option if you're looking to take a break from Chinese food and approximations of Western food. The tandoori chicken, curry mutton, palak paneer, and pulao rice are but a few of the solid dishes here; the outdoor tables are a good place for people-watching. **Known for:** English-speaking waitstaff; fresh ingredients; cozy atmosphere. $ *Average main: Y60* ✉ *15 Binjiang St.* ☎ *137/3739–6451* 💳 *No credit cards.*

Kelly's Place (灯笼风味馆 *Dēnglóng fēngwèiguǎn*)
$ | **ECLECTIC** | Beloved by expats, this closet-size café is an escape from the hustle and bustle of West Street. On any given night, English teachers can be found sampling tasty Chinese-style dumpling soups and drinking beer in the cobblestone pavilion. **Known for:** burgers; great coffee; Western breakfast. $ *Average main: Y35* ✉ *43 Guihua Lu, 1 block north of Xi Jie* ☎ *0773/881–3233* 💳 *No credit cards.*

Man De Guai (满得拐 *Mǎn de guǎi*)
$ | **CHINESE** | Popular with locals but unknown to most travelers, this family-owned restaurant serves an amazing array of local dishes, with a focus on fish from the Li river. There are no English menus, but the owners will bring you into the kitchen and let you pick out what you want. **Known for:** fresh fish; casual atmosphere; family-style meals. $ *Average main: Y25* ✉ *40 Jingfeng Lu* ☎ *0773/881–1456* 💳 *No credit cards.*

Mood Food Energy Café
$ | **VEGETARIAN** | Whether you believe in good karma or not, Mood Food Energy Café is a great destination for excellent vegetarian and vegan food, as well as juices. The cuisine is eclectic, with Mexican wraps and Indian soups sharing the same menu. **Known for:** gluten-free options; vegetarian food; sauna. $ *Average main: Y40* ✉ *8 Furong Rd.* ☎ *189/7868–6637.*

Pure Lotus (暗香疏影素菜馆 *Ànxiāng-shūyǐng sùcàiguǎn*)
$ | **CHINESE** | This vegetarian restaurant serves a variety of mouthwatering creations, including almond rolls, crispy tofu skin in a spicy sauce, and a vegetarian version of the famous Shanghainese *shizi tou* (meatballs). The Zen-like interior adds to the calm atmosphere, helping diners forget about the hubbub outside. **Known for:** veggies; fresh juice; fantastic view. *Average main: Y45 ✉ 26 West St. ☎ 0773/882–7744 No credit cards.*

Hotels

★ **The Giggling Tree**
$ | **B&B/INN** | **FAMILY** | Among the karst mountains outside of Yangshuo, the Giggling Tree is one of China's coolest guesthouses. **Pros:** beautiful views; quiet countryside; good food. **Cons:** a bit remote; can get busy; bathrooms need upgrading. *Rooms from: Y250 ✉ Aishanmen Village ☎ 136/6786–6154 🌐 www.gigglingtree.com No credit cards 23 rooms No meals.*

Magnolia Hotel (白玉兰酒店 *Báiyùlán jiǔdiàn*)
$ | **HOTEL** | Built around a traditional courtyard, the Magnolia welcomes you with a glass-roofed lobby overlooking a lovely carp pond. **Pros:** comfortable rooms; lovely views; good value. **Cons:** uninspiring decor; noisy area of town; weak Wi-Fi. *Rooms from: Y200 ✉ 1 Diecui Lu ☎ 0773/881–9288 🌐 http://magnolia.hotel-yangshuo.com/en/ 30 rooms No meals.*

Riverview Hotel (望江楼客栈 *Wàng-jiānglóu kèzhàn*)
$ | **HOTEL** | With its curvaceous tile roof and balconies with stunning views of the Li River, this is one of the town's nicest budget hotels. **Pros:** comfortable rooms; tasty restaurant; river views. **Cons:** slightly isolated from the rest of town; rooms a bit outdated; spotty Wi-Fi. *Rooms from: Y400 ✉ 25 Binjiang Lu ☎ 0773/882–2688 🌐 www.riverview.com.cn 52 rooms Breakfast.*

Yangshuo Mountain Retreat (阳朔胜地渡假山庄 *Yángshuò shèngdì dù jiǎ shānzhuāng*)
$ | **RESORT** | **FAMILY** | Far away from the hubbub of Yangshuo, the Yangshuo Mountain Retreat is one of the area's most relaxing places to stay. **Pros:** quiet atmosphere; some of the best views around; novel experience. **Cons:** too remote for some; hard beds; average facilities. *Rooms from: Y350 ✉ Yulong River Road ✣ Gaotian Town ☎ 773/877–7091 🌐 www.yangshuomountainretreat.com 29 rooms No meals.*

Nightlife

The Brew (阿里酒吧 *Ālǐ jiǔbā*)
BARS/PUBS | With its impressive selection of beers and spirits, The Brew also happens to serve excellent bar food, including steak, burgers, and pizza. Open until late, it's an excellent place for those seeking a quiet hangout. *✉ Guihua Lu ☎ 0136/678–66922.*

Activities

BIKING

Bike Asia
BICYCLING | Cheaply made mountain bikes are available all over Yangshuo for about Y10 per day. For a better-quality ride, Bike Asia rents all sizes for Y70 per day. The company also leads short trips to the villages along the Li River that start at Y340, including lunch by the river. *✉ 5 Furong Rd. ☎ 0773/882–6521 🌐 www.bikeasia.com.*

BOATING

Starting as a humble spring at the top of Mao'er Mountain, the majestic Li River snakes through Guangxi, connecting Yangshuo to many other towns along the way. One of the country's most scenic—and less polluted—rivers, its banks are lined with stone embankments where people practice tai chi. Several local companies offer rides on bamboo rafts along the river. You can bargain with them at the stone quay at the end of West Street.

ROCK CLIMBING

Black Rock Climbing

CLIMBING/MOUNTAINEERING | Yangshuo is the undisputed rock-climbing capital of China. Run by an American-Chinese couple, Black Rock is the go-to place for guided climbs suited for all skill levels. The crew are among the most experienced in China and will take care of all necessary equipment and transportation. Half-day climbs are Y260 per person; a full day will set you back Y500. ✉ *19 Guihua Lu* ☎ *137/3773–4124* 🎟 *From Y260.*

Nanning

350 km (217 miles; 2½ hrs by train) southwest of Guilin; 440 km (273 miles; 13 hrs by train) southeast of Guiyang; 600 km (372 miles; 12 hrs by train) west of Guangzhou.

Built along the banks of the Yong River, Nanning is the capital of Guangxi Zhuang Autonomous Region. The city isn't a major tourist draw, but it is a pleasant place to stop for a day or two. Many travelers come here for a visa before continuing into Vietnam.

GETTING HERE AND AROUND

Nanning is most accessible by bus if you're are already in Guangxi. For anything beyond, it's a flight or an overnight train.

Nanning Wuxu International Airport is 31 km (19 miles) southwest of the city and has flights throughout China, including to Guilin.

There are frequent buses between Nanning and Guilin, taking at least four hours. There is no direct service from Yangshuo. Nanning's train station is at the northwestern edge of town, and offers frequent service to Guilin. The fastest routes take five hours.

TIMING

Nanning doesn't have much going on tourism-wise, but is an otherwise pleasant city with nice parks.

Sights

Guangxi Zhuang Autonomous Region Museum (**广西壮族自治区博物馆** *Guǎngxi zhuàngzú zìzhìqū bówùguǎn*)

MUSEUM | This museum focuses on Guangxi's numerous ethnic minorities. In the back are magnificent full-size reconstructions of houses, pagodas, and drum towers set among attractive pools and bridges. A collection of more than 300 bronze drums made by local people is also on display. ✉ *34 Minzu Dadao* ☎ *0771/281–0907* 🌐 *www.gxmuseum.com* 🎟 *Free.*

People's Park (**人民公园** *Rénmín gōngyuán*)

CITY PARK | This park surrounding White Dragon Lake has some 200 species of rare trees and flowers. Here you'll find the remains of fortifications built by a warlord in the early part of the 20th century. ✉ *1 Renmin Dong Lu* 🎟 *Free.*

South Lake (**南湖** *Nánhú*)

CITY PARK | South Lake covers more than 200 acres. A bonsai exhibit and an orchid garden are in the surrounding park, which is encircled by a wide path that's ideal for strolling or jogging. ✉ *Gucheng Lu* 🎟 *Free.*

Restaurants

Beifang Renjia (**北方人家** *Běifāng rénjiā*)

$ | **CHINESE** | Tired of the local rice noodles? This is where many transplants from northeastern China come to dine on traditional *dongbei cai.* A large dumpling menu is complemented by a full range of northeastern favorites, such as moo shu

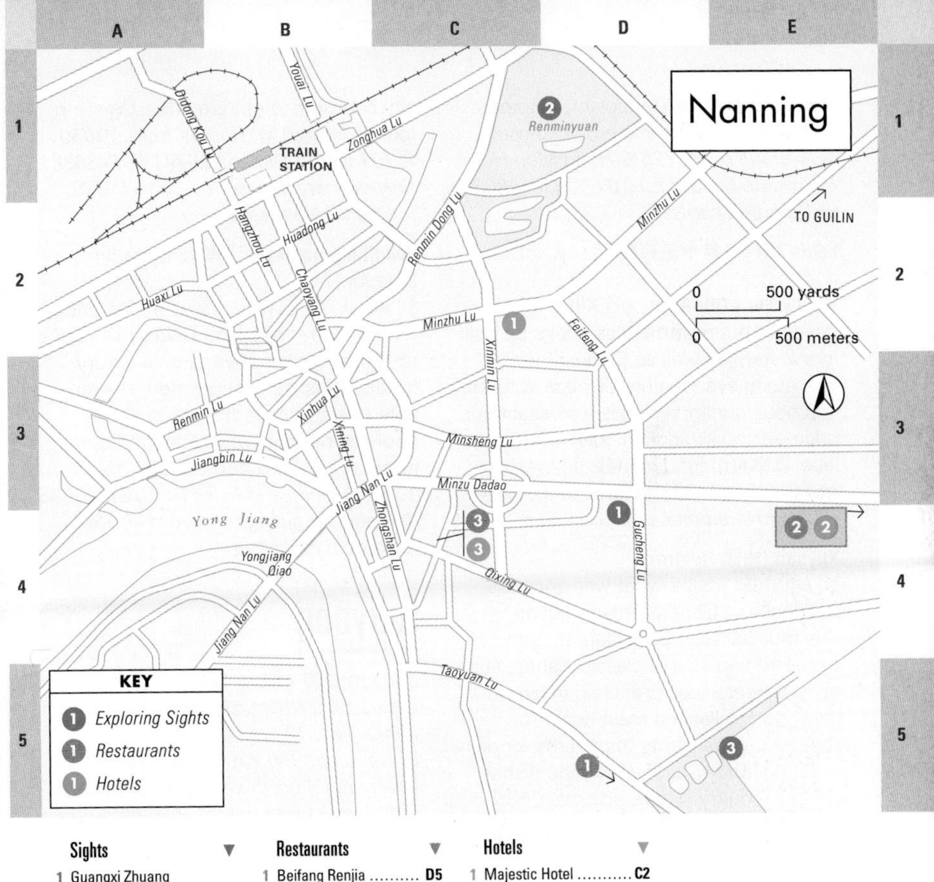

Sights	
1 Guangxi Zhuang Autonomous Region Museum	D4
2 People's Park	D1
3 South Lake	E5

Restaurants	
1 Beifang Renjia	D5
2 Louis XIII	E4
3 Xuyuan	C4

Hotels	
1 Majestic Hotel	C2
2 Nanning Marriott	E4
3 Yongjiang Hotel	C4

pork and *disanxian* (eggplant, potatoes, and green peppers in a brown sauce). *Average main: Y25 Hong Men Hotel, 6 Huichun Lu, 3rd fl. 0771/530–4263 No credit cards.*

Louis XIII (路易十三西餐厅 *Lùyì shísān xī cāntīng*)

$$ | **INTERNATIONAL** | Louis XIII is Chinese-run but nevertheless cooks up quality Western as well as Chinese dishes. The menu even features a pizza with the infamous durian, which is a pleasant surprise—if you like durian. **Known for:** cozy vibe; Western food; coffee. *Average main: Y50 1 Yuanhu Lu 0771/570–0278 No credit cards.*

Xuyuan (旭园 *Xùyuán*)

$ | **CHINESE** | Inside what was once the residence of General Huang Xuchu, this much-acclaimed restaurant serves excellent versions of classic dishes, such as cold beef slices drenched in lemon juice, pork rolls, and roast duck. The menu includes plenty of pictures for easy ordering. **Known for:** family-style dishes; privacy; poultry. *Average main: Y30 53 Mingde Jie, next to Yongjiang Hotel 0771/280–8228.*

Hotels

★ **Majestic Hotel** (明园新都酒店 *Míngyuán xīndū jiǔdiàn*)

$ | **HOTEL** | Close to the main square, this luxury hotel is efficiently run. **Pros:** professional staff; well-outfitted gym; pleasant pool. **Cons:** in a tough place to catch a cab; not much of interest in the immediate vicinity; worn interior. *Rooms from: Y450 38 Xinmin Lu 0771/211–8988 290 rooms Breakfast.*

Nanning Marriott (鑫伟万豪酒店 *Xīnwěi-wànháo jiǔdiàn*)

$ | **HOTEL** | This Marriott is in an eye-catching cylindrical tower, in the city's northeastern reaches, and close to the local convention center. **Pros:** good service; high-tech touches; good for business travelers. **Cons:** far from the city center; can get crowded; Western food is limited. *Rooms from: Y1050 131 Minzu Dadao 0771/536–6688 www.nanningmarriott.com 328 rooms No meals.*

Yongjiang Hotel (邕江宾馆 *Yōngjiāng bīnguǎn*)

$ | **HOTEL** | With nice views of the bridge crossing the Yongjiang River, this is one of Nanning's most venerable luxury hotels. **Pros:** central location; reasonable rates; excellent service. **Cons:** pool not open all year-round; a little impersonal; hard beds. *Rooms from: Y385 1 Linjiang Lu 0771/218–0888 www.yongjianghotel.com 130 rooms No meals.*

Guiyang

350 km (217 miles; 11½ hrs by the fastest train) northwest of Guilin; 425 km (264 miles; 12 hrs by train) northwest of Nanning; 850 km (527 miles; 19½ hrs by train) northwest of Guangzhou; 1,650 km (1,023 miles; 26½ hrs by train) southwest of Beijing.

The capital is a pleasant place to begin an exploration of the province. Like most cities in China, Guiyang is fast losing its older buildings, but even in the heart of downtown enough remain to make a short stay here worthwhile. The main streets of the sprawling city are Zunyi Lu, Ruijin Lu, Zhonghua Lu, and Yan'an Lu.

GETTING HERE AND AROUND

Guiyang Airport lies 15 km (9 miles) to the southeast of the city. There are direct flights between Guiyang and most of China's main cities.

Guiyang East Passenger Terminal, the city's main long-distance bus station, has been relocated to the remote airport district southeast of the city. Luckily, the smaller bus station on Jiefang Lu just north of Guiyang's train station

Continued on page 408

FOR ALL THE TEA IN CHINA

Legend has it that the first cup dates from 2737 BC, when *Camellia sinensis* leaves fell into water being boiled for Emperor Shennong. He loved the result, tea was born, and so were many traditions.

Historically, when a girl accepted a marriage proposal she drank tea, a gesture symbolizing fidelity. Betrothal gifts were known as "tea gifts," engagements as "accepting tea," and marriages as "eating tea." Today the bride and groom kneel before their parents, offering cups of tea in thanks.

Serving tea is a sign of respect. Young people proffer it to their parents or grandparents; subordinates do the same for their bosses. Pouring tea also signifies submission, so it's a way to say you're sorry. When you're served tea, show your thanks by tapping the table with your index and middle fingers.

And forget about adding milk or sugar. Not only is most Chinese tea best without it, but why dilute and sweeten a beverage long known by herbalists to be good for you? Even modern medicine acknowledges that tea's powerful antioxidants reduce the risk of cancer and heart disease. It's also thought to be such a good source of fluoride that Mao Zedong eschewed toothpaste for a green-tea rinse. Smiles, everyone.

In China, tea was first discovered by the Emporer Shennong.

HISTORICAL BREW

Tea preparation is a careful affair.

THE RISE AND FALL OF EMPIRES

Tea has a long and tumultuous history, making and breaking empires in both the East and the West. Bricks of tea were used as currency, and Chinese statesmen kept rebellious northern nomads in check by refusing to sell it to them.

Rumor has it that tea caused the downfall of the Song Empire. Apparently, tea-whisking was Emperor Huizong's favorite pastime: he was so obsessed with court tea culture that he forgot all about trivial little matters like defense. The country became vulnerable to invasion and fell to the Mongols in 1279.

Genghis preferred *airag* (fermented mare's milk), but after the Mongol's defeat, the drink of kings returned with a vengeance to the court of the Ming Dynasty (1368–1644). Tea as we know it today dates to this period: the first Ming emperor, Hongwu, set the trend of using loose-leaf tea by refusing to accept tea tribute gifts in any other form.

TEA GOES INTERNATIONAL

The first Europeans to encounter the beverage were navigators and missionaries who visited China in the mid-16th century. In 1610, Dutch traders began importing tea from China into Europe, with the Portuguese hot on their heels. It was initially marketed as a health drink and took a while to catch on. By the 1640s, tea had become popular among both the Dutch and Portuguese aristocracy, initially the only ones who could afford it.

Although we think of tea as a quintessentially British drink, it actually arrived in America two years before it appeared in Britain. When the British acquired New Amsterdam (later New York) in 1664, the colony consumed more tea than all the British isles put together.

Tea was available in Britain from about 1554 onward, but Brits were wary of the stuff at first. What tipped the scales in tea's favor was nothing less than celebrity product endorsement.

All types of tea come from one plant.

King Charles II married the Portuguese princess Catherine of Braganza in 1662. She arrived in England with tea and fine porcelain tea ware in her dowry and a healthy addiction to the stuff. Members of the royalty were the 16th century's trendsetters: tea became the thing to drink at court; pretty soon the general public was hooked, too.

TEMPEST IN A TEAPOT

Tea quickly became a very important—and troublemaking—commodity. Religious leaders thought the drink sinful and doctors declared it a health risk. In Britain, ale brewers were losing profits, and pressure groups successfully persuaded the government to tax tea at 119%. On top of all this, the immensely powerful British East India Company held the monopoly on tea importation.

Tea's value skyrocketed: by 1706, the retail price of green tea in London was equivalent to $300 for 100 g (3.5 oz), far beyond the reach of normal people. Tea smuggling quickly became a massive—and often cutthroat—business. To make sought-after tea supplies stretch even further, they were routinely mixed with twigs, leaves, animal dung, and even poisonous chemicals.

Back in the New World, Americans were fed up with paying taxes that went straight back to Britain. Things came to a head when a group of patriots dressed as Native Americans peacefully boarded British ships in Boston harbor and emptied 342 chests of tea into the water. The act came to be known as the Boston Tea Party and was a vital catalyst in starting the American Revolution.

The War of Independence wasn't the only war sparked by tea. In Britain, taxes were axed and, as tea was suddenly affordable for everyone, demand grew exponentially. But China remained the world's only supplier, so that by the mid-19th century, tea was causing a massive trade deficit. The British started exporting opium into China in exchange for tea, provoking two Opium Wars. In the 1880s, attempts to grow tea in India were finally successful and Indian tea began to overtake Chinese tea on the market.

These days, over 3.2 million metric tons of tea are produced annually worldwide. After water, tea is the world's favorite drink. Though Britain and Ireland now consume far more tea per capita than China, tea is still a regular presence at the Chinese table and is inextricably bound to Chinese culture.

ANCIENT TRADE ROUTES

The Ancient Tea and Horse Caravan Road, also known as the Southern Silk Road, is a trade corridor dating back to the Tang Dynasty (618–907). The 4,000-km route emerged more than 1,200 years ago and was actually still in use until recently.

Back in the heyday of the Caravan Road, Xishuangbanna, Dali, Lijiang, and many other parts of Yunnan were important outposts on the route. Tea, horses, salt, medicinal herbs, and Indian spices all featured prominently in this massive network.

During World War II, the route was used to smuggle supplies from India into the interior of Japanese-occupied China.

DRINKING IN THE CULTURE

The way tea was prepared historically bears little resemblance to the steep-a-teabag method many westerners employ today. Tea originally came in bricks of compressed leaves bound with sheep's blood or manure. Chunks were broken, ground into a powder, and whisked into hot water. In the first tea manual, *Cha Jing (The Way of Tea)*, Tang-dynasty writer Lu Yu describes preparing powdered tea using 28 pieces of teaware, including big brewing pans and shallow drinking bowls.

The potters of Yixing (near Shanghai) gradually transformed wine vessels into small pots for steeping tea. Yixing pottery is ideal for brewing: its fine unglazed clay is highly porous, and if you always use the same kind of tea, the pot will take on its flavor.

Today the most elaborate Chinese tea service—which requires only two pots and enough cups for all involved—is called *gong fu cha* (skilled tea method). Although you can experience it at many teahouses, most people consider it too involved for every day. They simply brew their leaf tea in three-piece lidded cups, called *gaiwan*, tilting the lid as they drink so that it acts as a strainer.

Green Tea leaves in a Chinese gaiwan

THE CEREMONY

1. Rinse teapot with hot water.
2. Fill with black or oolong to one third of its height.
3. Half-fill teapot with hot water and empty immediately to rinse leaves.
4. Fill pot with hot water, let leaves steep for a minute; no bubbles should form.
5. Pour tea into small cups, moving the spout continuously over each, so all have the same strength of tea.
6. Pour the excess into a second teapot.
7. Using the same leaves, repeat the process up to five times, extending the steeping time slightly.

TEA TIMELINE

Japanese tea ceremony

350 AD	"Tea" appears in Chinese dictionary.
618–1644	Tea falls into and out of favor at Chinese court.
7th c.	Tea introduced to Japan.
1610–1650	Dutch and Portuguese traders bring tea to Europe.
1662	British King Charles II marries Portugal's Catherine of Braganza, a tea addict. Tea craze sweeps the court.

HOW TEA IS MADE

Chinese tea is grown on large plantations and nearly always picked by hand. Pluckers remove only the top two leaves. A skilled plucker can collect up to 35 kg (77 lbs) of leaves in a day; that's 9 kg (almost 20 lbs) of tea, or 3,500 cups. After a week, new top leaves will have grown, and bushes can be plucked again. Climate and soil play an important role on a tea plantation, much as they do in a vineyard. But what really differentiates black, green, and oolong teas is the way leaves are processed.

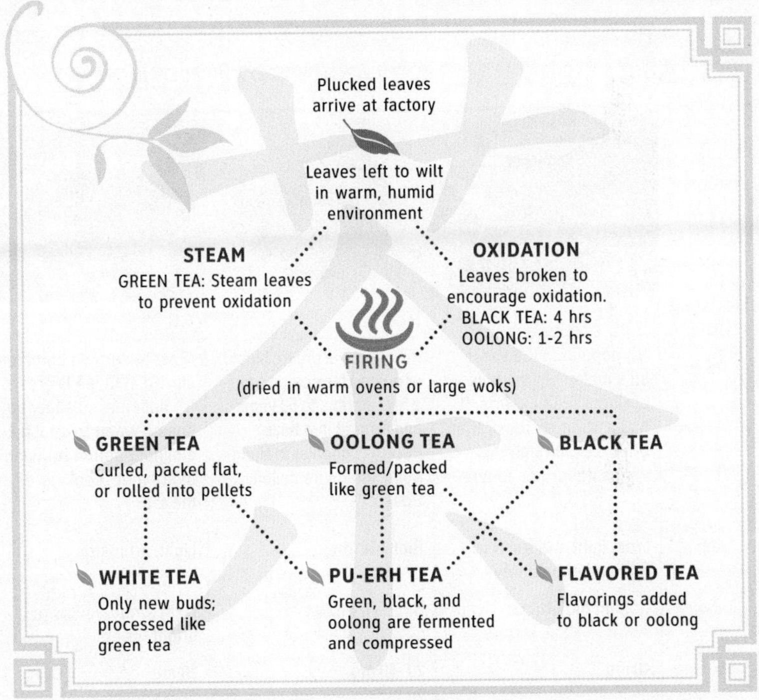

Plucked leaves arrive at factory

Leaves left to wilt in warm, humid environment

STEAM
GREEN TEA: Steam leaves to prevent oxidation

OXIDATION
Leaves broken to encourage oxidation.
BLACK TEA: 4 hrs
OOLONG: 1-2 hrs

FIRING
(dried in warm ovens or large woks)

GREEN TEA
Curled, packed flat, or rolled into pellets

OOLONG TEA
Formed/packed like green tea

BLACK TEA

WHITE TEA
Only new buds; processed like green tea

PU-ERH TEA
Green, black, and oolong are fermented and compressed

FLAVORED TEA
Flavorings added to black or oolong

1689	Tea taxation starts in Britain; peaks at 119%.
1773	Boston Tea Party: Americans dump 342 chests of tea into Boston Harbor, protesting British taxes.
1784	British tea taxes slashed; consumption soars.
1835	Tea cultivation starts in Assam, India.
1880s	India and Ceylon produce more tea than China.
1904	Englishman Richard Blechynden creates iced tea at St. Louis World's Fair.
1908	New York importer Thomas Sullivan sends clients samples in silk bags—the first tea bags.
2004	Chinese tea exports overtake India's for the first time since the 1880s.

Boston Tea Party

TYPES OF TEA

The universal word for tea comes from a single Chinese character, pronounced "te" (Xiamen dialect) or "cha" (Cantonese and Mandarin). Some teas are simply named for the region that produces them (Yunnan or Assam); others are evocatively named to reflect a particular blend. Some are transliterated (like Keemun); others translated (Iron Goddess of Mercy).

	BLACK	PU-ERH	GREEN
Overview	It's popular in the West so it makes up the bulk of China's tea exports. It has a stronger flavor than green tea, though this varies according to type.	Pu-erh tea is green, black, or oolong fermented from a few months to 50 years and formed into balls. Pu-erh is popular in Hong Kong, where it's called Bo Le.	Most tea grown and consumed in China is green. It's delicate, so allow the boiling water to cool for a minute before brewing to prevent "cooking" the tea.
Flavor	From light and fresh to rich and chocolatey	Rich, earthy	Light, aromatic
Color	Golden dark brown	Reddish brown	Light straw-yellow to bright green
Caffeine per Serving	40 mg	20–40 mg	20 mg
Ideal Water Temperature	203°F	203°F	160°F
Steeping Time	3–5 mins.	3–5 mins.	1–2 mins.
Examples	Dian Hong (chocolatey aftertaste; unlike other Chinese teas, can take milk). Keemun (Qi Men; mild, smoky; once used in English breakfast blends). Lapsang Souchong (dried over smoking pine; strong flavor). Yunnan Golden (full bodied, malty).	Buying Pu-erh is like buying wine: there are different producers and different vintages, and prices vary greatly.	Bi Luo Chun (Green Snail Spring; rich, fragrant). Chun Mee (Eyebrow; pale yellow; floral). Hou Kui (Monkey Tea; nutty, sweet; floral aftertaste). Long Ding (Dragon Mountain; sweet, minty). Long Jing (Dragon's Well; bright green; nutty).

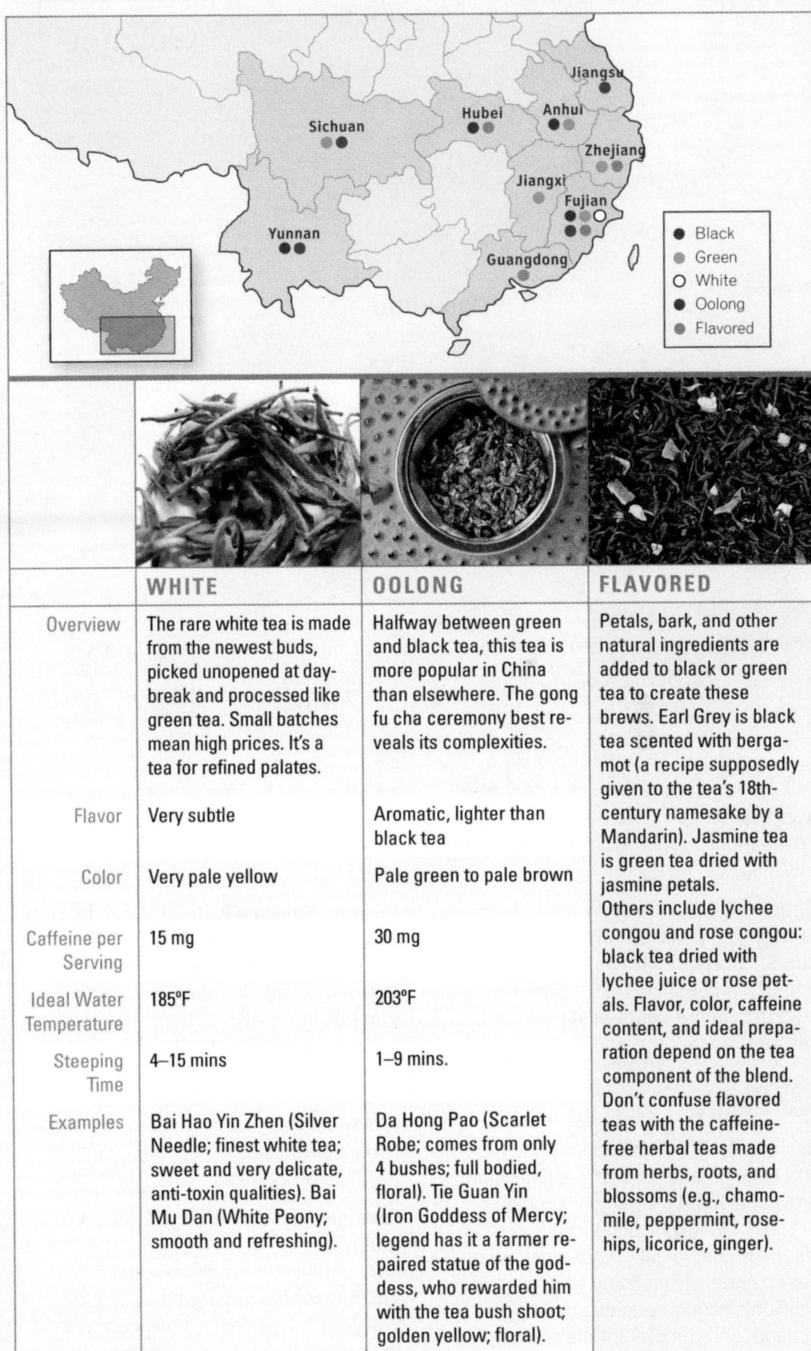

	WHITE	OOLONG	FLAVORED
Overview	The rare white tea is made from the newest buds, picked unopened at daybreak and processed like green tea. Small batches mean high prices. It's a tea for refined palates.	Halfway between green and black tea, this tea is more popular in China than elsewhere. The gong fu cha ceremony best reveals its complexities.	Petals, bark, and other natural ingredients are added to black or green tea to create these brews. Earl Grey is black tea scented with bergamot (a recipe supposedly given to the tea's 18th-century namesake by a Mandarin). Jasmine tea is green tea dried with jasmine petals. Others include lychee congou and rose congou: black tea dried with lychee juice or rose petals. Flavor, color, caffeine content, and ideal preparation depend on the tea component of the blend. Don't confuse flavored teas with the caffeine-free herbal teas made from herbs, roots, and blossoms (e.g., chamomile, peppermint, rosehips, licorice, ginger).
Flavor	Very subtle	Aromatic, lighter than black tea	
Color	Very pale yellow	Pale green to pale brown	
Caffeine per Serving	15 mg	30 mg	
Ideal Water Temperature	185°F	203°F	
Steeping Time	4–15 mins	1–9 mins.	
Examples	Bai Hao Yin Zhen (Silver Needle; finest white tea; sweet and very delicate, anti-toxin qualities). Bai Mu Dan (White Peony; smooth and refreshing).	Da Hong Pao (Scarlet Robe; comes from only 4 bushes; full bodied, floral). Tie Guan Yin (Iron Goddess of Mercy; legend has it a farmer repaired statue of the goddess, who rewarded him with the tea bush shoot; golden yellow; floral).	

Guizhou

CHONGQING
Luzhou
River
SICHUAN
Yangzi
Zunyi
Zhaotong
Bijie
GUIZHOU
Kaili
Guiyang
Liupanshui
Duyun
Huize
Anshun
YUNNAN
Qujing
Zhanyi
Huangguoshu Falls
Xingyi
GUANGXI
0 50 mi
0 50 km

still has regular bus service to Anshun (two hours), Kaili (two hours), and other destinations around Guizhou and the rest of China.

Direct trains link Guiyang with Chongqing (9 hours), Guilin (12 hours), Kunming (10 hours), Liuzhou (8 hours), Nanning (12 hours), and Shanghai (26 hours). The train station is at the southwest edge of the city, at the southern end of Zunyi Lu.

Sights

Hebin Park (河滨公园 *Hébīn gōngyuán*)
CITY PARK | **FAMILY** | Filled with bamboo groves, Hebin Park sits on the banks of the Nanming River. In many ways it's the archetypical Chinese park, with senior citizens practicing tai chi in the pavilions, young couples strolling hand in hand, and the omnipresent sound of music and public announcements playing from loudspeakers. For children, there's a Ferris wheel and other rides. ✉ *Ruijin Nan Lu* 🎫 *Free.*

Qianling Mountain Park (黔灵山公园 *Qiánlíngshān gōngyuán*)
CITY PARK | **FAMILY** | Dominating this 740-acre park is a 4,265-foot-high mountain that has fine views of the town from its western peak. The park itself has a bit of everything, including thousands of plants and a collection of birds and monkeys (many of which roam freely through the park). ✉ *187 Zaoshan Lu, 2½ km (1 mile) northwest of city* 🎫 *Y5.*

Underground Gardens (地下公园 *Dìxià gōngyuán*)
CAVE | In this poetically named cave, 1,925 feet below the ground, a path weaves its way past the various rock formations, which are lit up to emphasize

Guizhou reveals even more of its natural splendor with Huangguoshu fall, on of the tallest waterfalls in East Asia.

their similarity with animals, fruits, and other living things. *187 Zaoshan Rd., 25 km (15 miles) south of Guiyang* *0851/511–4014* *Free.*

Unicorn Cave (**麒麟洞** *Qílín dòng*)
CAVE | Discovered in 1531, Unicorn Cave was used as a prison for the two Nationalist generals, Yang Hucheng and Chang Xueliang, who were accused of collaborating with the Communists when Chiang Kai-shek was captured at Xi'an in 1937. The cave is known for its unicorn-shape stalactite and used to host a nunnery. *187 Zaoshan Rd.* *Y5.*

Restaurants

Highlands Coffee (**高原咖啡** *Gāoyuán kāfēi*)
$ | **CAFÉ** | Understated decor, comfy seating, and high-quality imported coffee turned into tasty beverages by skilled baristas are the highlights here. There are also savory panini on homemade bread, as well as a wide selection of teas, smoothies, and desserts. **Known for:** designated smoking area; English-speaking service; great beverages. *Average main: Y30* *1 Liudong St., Bo'ai Lu* *0851/582–6222* *www.highlands-coffee.com.*

★ **Old Kaili Sour Fish Restaurant** (**老凯俚酸汤鱼** *Lǎo kǎilǐ suāntāngyú*)
$$$ | **SEAFOOD** | Sour fish soup, Guiyang's signature dish, is the specialty at this venerated local joint. Choose a fish from the tanks, select your other ingredients, and mix your own sauce. **Known for:** fresh fish; spicy cuisine; photogenic. *Average main: Y150* *55 Shengfu Lu* *0851/584–3665* *No credit cards* *No lunch.*

Hotels

Nenghui Hotel (**能辉酒店** *Nénghuī jiǔdiàn*)
$ | **HOTEL** | With a central location, cozy accommodations, and reasonable prices, this handsome, modern hotel offers lot of bang for the yuan. **Pros:** close to the sights; firm beds; bargain rates. **Cons:** noisy part of town; shortage of

English-speaking staff; outdated rooms. $ *Rooms from: Y450* ✉ *36 Ruijin Nan Lu* ☎ *0851/589–8888* *125 rooms* *Breakfast.*

Sheraton Guiyang Hotel (喜来登贵阳酒店 *Xĭláidēng guìyáng jiŭdiàn*)
$$ | **HOTEL** | Among the city's best lodgings, this chain hotel has everything a high-end traveler needs, and more: a full-service spa, a bar with amazing city views, great international dining, and an attentive staff. **Pros:** excellent city views; near a pretty park; soothing spa. **Cons:** a bit impersonal; slightly tired rooms; breakfast is subpar. $ *Rooms from: Y855* ✉ *49 Zhonghua Nan Lu* ☎ *0851/588–8888* 🌐 *www.sheraton.com/guiyang* *376 rooms* *Breakfast.*

Side Trip to Huangguoshu Falls

These falls are at their best from May through October and are set in lush countryside, where you'll find numerous villages. To avoid switching buses en route at the city of Anshu, book a tour with a local agency or at your hotel.

Sights

★ **Huangguoshu Falls** (黄果树瀑布 *Huángguŏshù pùbù*)
BODY OF WATER | The Baishui River tumbles over nine sets of rocks, creating nine waterfalls over a course of 2 km (1 mile). At the highest point, Huangguoshu Falls drops an eye-popping 230 feet, making it the tallest in China. You can enjoy them from afar or by wading across the Rhinoceros Pool (Xiniu Jian) to the Water Curtain Cave (Shuilian Dong) hidden behind the main falls. Seven km (4½ miles) downstream is the **Star Bridge Falls** (*Xingqiao Pu*). ✉ *160 km (99 miles) southwest of Guiyang* ☎ *400/683–3333* 🌐 *www.hgscn.com* *Y180.*

Kaili

200 km (124 miles; 3 hrs by train) east of Guiyang.

The capital of the Qian Dongnan Miao and Dong Autonomous Region, Kaili serves as the starting point for a journey to the Miao and Dong villages that dominate eastern Guizhou. More than two-thirds of the population is Miao, and their villages are along the eastern and northeastern outskirts of Kaili. The Dong communities are to the southeast.

Outside town the local villages are of great interest. To the north is the Wuyang River, which passes by many mountains, caves, and Miao villages. At **Shibing** you can take boat rides through spectacular limestone gorges and arrange stops at these towns. South of Kaili are the Dong villages of **Leishan, Rongjiang,** and **Zhaoxing.** The latter village, set in a beautiful landscape, is known for its five drum towers.

GETTING HERE AND AROUND

The fastest way to get from Guiyang to Kaili is often by bus, which can take as little as two hours. The train takes about three hours.

From the long-distance bus station just north of the Guiyang Train Station, Kaili-bound buses depart every 20 minutes or so. Buses usually don't leave until they're full. Tickets are about Y60.

Kaili's small train station is three hours from Guiyang. Trains passing through Kaili connect to Guilin, Kunming, Beijing, Shanghai, and much of the rest of China.

TIMING

Though the sites in Kaili could conceivably occupy a day's time, the city is better viewed as a stepping-off point for multiday tours of the surrounding countryside and its scenic ethnic villages.

Did You Know?

During the Sisters' Meal festival, Miao women express interest (or rejection) by giving parcels of brightly colored sticky rice labeled with one of three images, each with a meaning. A pair of chopsticks says "let's get married now!" A single chopstick means "maybe." And an image of a chili means "get lost."

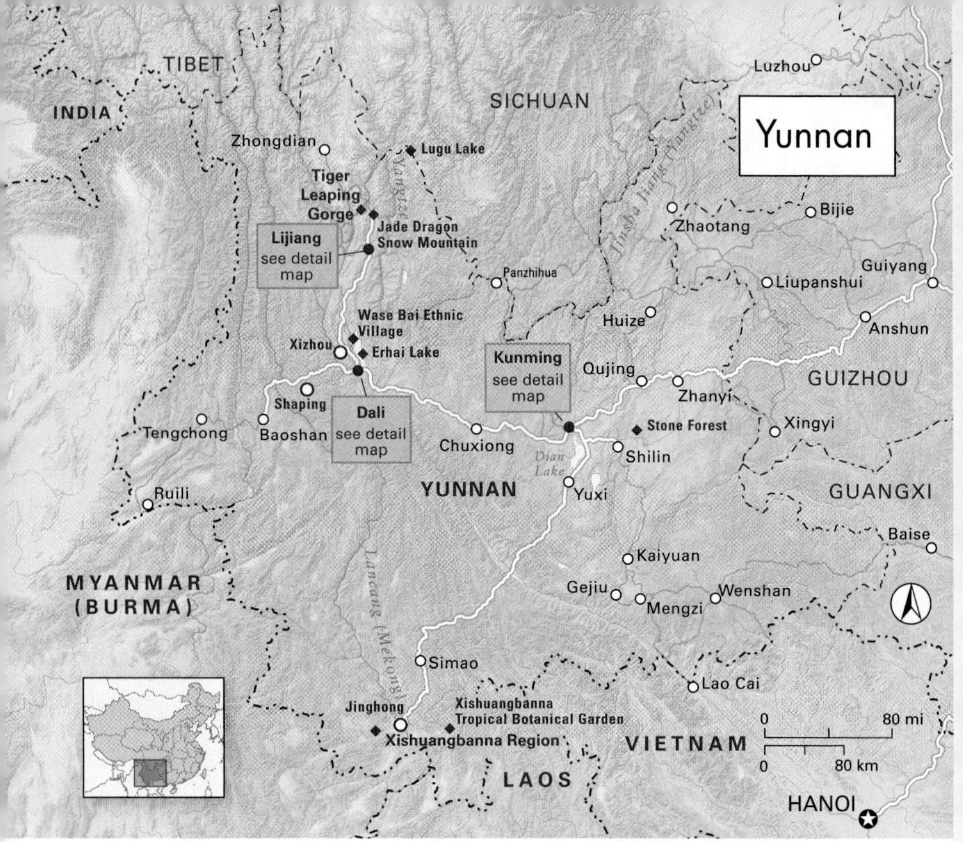

TOURS

Tour operator WildChina offers trips that take travelers from Guiyang to Kaili via several minority villages. Guizhou can sometimes be difficult for tourists to navigate, particularly for non-Chinese speakers: this tour offers a hassle-free and off-the-beaten-path look at Guizhou minority culture, with English-speaking guides.

Sights

Drum Tower (鼓楼 *Gǔlóu*)
BUILDING | This tower in Jinquanhu Park is the Dong people's gathering place for celebrations. ✉ *Jinquanhu Park.*

Minorities Museum (州民族博物馆 *Zhōu mínzú bówùguǎn*)
MUSEUM | This museum displays arts, crafts, and relics of the local indigenous peoples. ✉ *5 Guangchang Lu* 🎫 *Y10.*

Hotels

Guotai Dajiudian (国泰大酒店 *Guótài dàjiǔdiàn*)
$ | **HOTEL** | With a downtown location and comfortable guest rooms, the Guotai Dajiudian compares favorably with flashier options that have appeared on the outskirts of town. **Pros:** ideal location; reasonable rates; cozy rooms. **Cons:** restaurant service can be slow; shortage of English-speaking staff; noisy. *Rooms from: Y250* ✉ *6 Beijing Dong Lu* ☎ *0855/826–9818* *No credit cards* *73 rooms* *No meals.*

Kunming

400 km (248 miles; 7 hrs by train) southwest of Guiyang; 650 km (403 miles; 17½ hrs by train) southwest of Chengdu; 1,200 km (744 miles; 24 hrs by train) west of Guangzhou.

With its cool mountain air and laid-back locals, Kunming is one of China's most comfortable big cities, and is an ideal base for Yunnan travels. It's one of the few cities in the country that regularly has blue skies, and is nicknamed the "Spring City." Despite this moniker, weather can be gray and soggy during the summer monsoon season and chilly in January and February.

Kunming is changing rapidly as the city is transforming into China's gateway to Southeast Asia. But despite the disappearance of the Old City and increasingly congested traffic, Kunming remains a relaxed and somewhat idiosyncratic metropolis.

GETTING HERE AND AROUND

An architectural highlight of the city, the new international airport is about 30 km (19 miles) east of the city center. Taxis take 30 to 40 minutes and cost Y120 to Y180, depending on traffic. Kunming is a busy air hub, with flight links all over China, as well as direct routes to Southeast Asia, Nepal, India, and the United Arab Emirates, among other areas.

Kunming has five long-distance bus stations: the north, east, south, west, and northwest stations. All buses bound for Dali, Lijiang and Shangri-la depart from the west station; buses to Laos depart from the south station; and buses to Guangxi Province and the Yunnan-Vietnam border crossing at Hekou depart from the east station.

If you need a car and driver while you're in Kunming, make arrangements through your hotel.

In 2014 metro Lines 1 and 2 began service. They act as one line, connecting southern University City in the district of Chenggong to the northern bus station. Line 3, running east–west, is supposed to open in 2015, although that date may change. The shorter Line 6 links the eastern bus station to the airport; this will eventually connect to Line 3.

TIMING

A day or two in Kunming should suffice for most travelers.

 Sights

★ **Green Lake Park** (翠湖公园 *Cuìhú gōngyuán*)
CITY PARK | Filled with willow- and bamboo-covered islands connected by stone bridges, Green Lake Park is a favorite gathering place for Kunming's older residents, who begin to congregate in the park for singing and dancing in the late morning and stay until the gates close at 11 pm. In summer the lake is filled with pink and white lotus blossoms. In winter the park fills with migrating seagulls from Siberia, attracting large crowds. The lake was once part of Dianchi Lake, but it was severed from that larger body of water in the 1970s. ✉ *Cuihu Nan Lu* 🎫 *Free.*

Yuantong Temple (圆通寺 *Yuántōng sì*)
RELIGIOUS SITE | The largest temple in the city, Yuantong Temple dates back some 1,200 years to the Tang Dynasty. The compound consists of a series of gates leading to the inner temple, which is surrounded by a pond brimming with fish and turtles. The chanting of worshippers in the serene environment makes it hard to believe you're in the middle of a big city. In the back of the compound a temple houses a statue of Sakyamuni (the Buddha), a gift from the king of Thailand. ✉ *30 Yuantong Jie* 🎫 *Y6.*

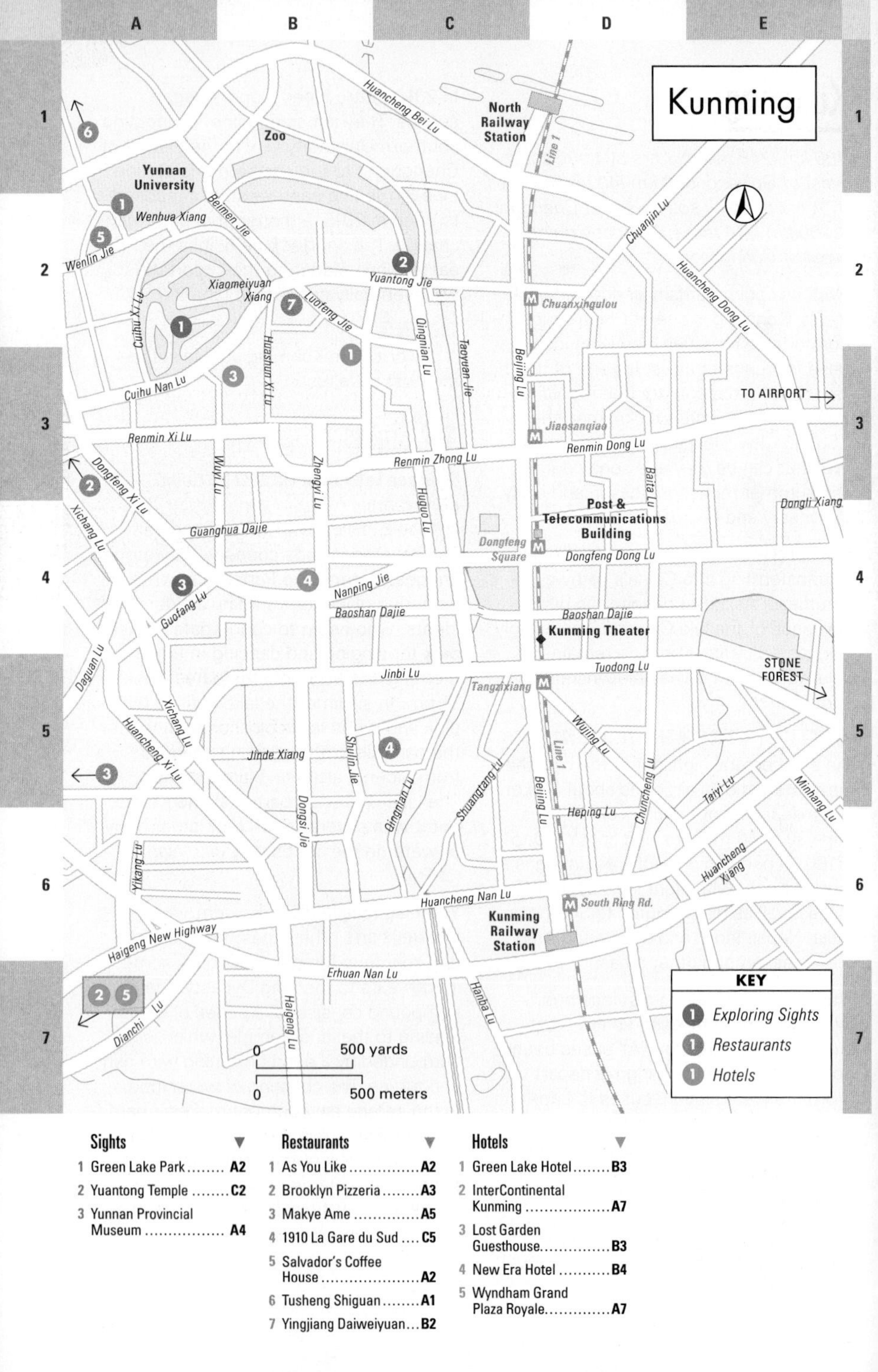

Kunming
A
B
C
D
E
1
2
3
4
5
6
7
North Railway Station
Zoo
Yunnan University
Wenhua Xiang
Beimen Jie
Huancheng Bei Lu
Line 1
Chuanjin Lu
Huancheng Dong Lu
Wenlin Jie
Xiaomeiyuan Xiang
Yuantong Jie
Luofeng Jie
Cuihu Xi Lu
Huashun Xi Lu
Qingnian Lu
Taoyuan Jie
Beijing Lu
Chuanxingulou
Cuihu Nan Lu
TO AIRPORT
Renmin Xi Lu
Jiaosanqiao
Renmin Zhong Lu
Renmin Dong Lu
Dongfeng Xi Lu
Wuyi Lu
Zhengyi Lu
Huguo Lu
Baita Lu
Dongli Xiang
Xichang Lu
Guanghua Dajie
Post & Telecommunications Building
Dongfeng Square
Dongfeng Dong Lu
Nanping Jie
Guofang Lu
Baoshan Dajie
Baoshan Dajie
Kunming Theater
Daguan Lu
Jinbi Lu
Tuodong Lu
Tangzixiang
STONE FOREST
Xichang Lu
Huancheng Xi Lu
Jinde Xiang
Shulin Jie
Wujing Lu
Line 1
Chuncheng Lu
Taiyi Lu
Minhang Lu
Dongsi Jie
Qingnian Lu
Shuangtang Lu
Beijing Lu
Heping Lu
Yikang Lu
Huancheng Xiang
Huancheng Nan Lu
South Ring Rd.
Haigeng New Highway
Kunming Railway Station
Erhuan Nan Lu
Haigeng Lu
Hanba Lu
Dianchi Lu
0 500 yards
0 500 meters
KEY
Exploring Sights
Restaurants
Hotels
Sights
1 Green Lake Park........ A2
2 Yuantong Temple C2
3 Yunnan Provincial Museum A4
Restaurants
1 As You Like A2
2 Brooklyn Pizzeria........ A3
3 Makye Ame A5
4 1910 La Gare du Sud C5
5 Salvador's Coffee House A2
6 Tusheng Shiguan........ A1
7 Yingjiang Daiweiyuan... B2
Hotels
1 Green Lake Hotel........ B3
2 InterContinental Kunming A7
3 Lost Garden Guesthouse............... B3
4 New Era Hotel B4
5 Wyndham Grand Plaza Royale.............. A7

The Yuantong Temple is the largest temple in Kunming.

Yunnan Provincial Museum (云南省博物馆 *Yúnnánshěng bówùguǎn*)
MUSEUM | The museum focuses primarily on the Dian Kingdom, which ruled much of Yunnan from 1000 BC to 1 BC. Most of what you'll see here is more than 2,000 years old. Exhibits have good English captions. *118 Wuyi Lu* *0871/6362–9328* *www.ynbwg.cn* *Free.*

Restaurants

As You Like (有佳面包店 *Yǒujiā miànbāo diàn*)
$ | **VEGETARIAN** | Tucked away in an alley off bustling Wenlin Jie, As You Like is a quaint vegetarian restaurant and deli. The freshly baked bread, healthy salads, and all kinds of pastries will make your mouth water, and the pizzas are some of the best around. **Known for:** Western food; quaint atmosphere; veggies. *Average main: Y45* *5 Tianjundian Xiang, up alley next to Dune Cafe* *0871/6541–1715* *No credit cards.*

Brooklyn Pizzeria (布鲁克林披萨店 *Bùlǔkèlín pīsàdiàn*)
$$ | **PIZZA** | **FAMILY** | Popular with locals and expats alike, this place stands for quality pizza and other American-style snacks and fast food, such as meatball sandwiches and a range of salads. Pizza can be ordered per slice or as a whole, with massive sizes for groups. **Known for:** American cuisine; craft beers; homemade desserts. *Average main: Y60* *11 Hongshan Dong Lu, Backstreet Block, Bldg. 12–6/8, a bit down road from McDonald's* *0871/6533–3243* *No credit cards* *Closed Wed.*

Makye Ame (玛吉阿米 *Mǎjí āmǐ*)
$$ | **TIBETAN** | As much a cultural experience as a culinary adventure, Makye Ame is known for its Tibetan and Indian song-and-dance performances. The shows are enjoyable, but can be hard on the eardrums. **Known for:** entertainment; Tibetan culture; English menu. *Average main: Y60* *Huapu Rd., 2nd fl., behind Yimen Hotel* *0871/6833–6300* *No credit cards* *No lunch.*

★ **1910 La Gare du Sud** (1910火车南站 *Yījiǔyī líng huǒchē nánzhàn*)

$$ | **YUNNAN** | Inside a renovated railroad station, this restaurant has outdoor seating and a historic atmosphere that are just as appealing as the menu full of tasty Yunnan dishes. The structure was built in the early 20th century by French colonists, and was once the terminus of the 535-mile railroad linking Hanoi to Kunming. **Known for:** cheese; authentic Yunnanese cuisine; historic atmosphere. *Average main: Y60* *8 Houxin Jie* *0871/6316–9486* *No credit cards.*

★ **Salvador's Coffee House** (萨尔瓦多咖啡馆 *Sà'ěrwǎduō kāfēi guǎn*)

$ | **CAFÉ** | **FAMILY** | Regularly packed to capacity and brewing some of Kunming's best coffee using a custom blend of Yunnan beans, Salvador's also has an extensive food menu. About half of its ingredients are organic, and more are being added regularly, with the goal of becoming one of the few entirely organic eateries in China. **Known for:** people-watching; great breakfast; sense of community. *Average main: Y45* *76 Wenhua Xiang* *0871/6536–3525* *www.salvadors.cn* *No credit cards.*

★ **Tusheng Shiguan** (土生食馆 *Tǔshēng shíguǎn*)

$ | **YUNNAN** | Without a doubt the best organic Chinese restaurant in town, Tusheng Shiguan is a must for anyone who wants to try the finest Yunnan cuisine. Don't miss the *erkuai* (rice pancakes), the *fuzhu* (a tofu-skin dish whose misleading name translates to "rotten bamboo") or the ginger beef dish, and ask which vegetables are in season. **Known for:** meticulous sourcing; wheat buns; fresh vegetables. *Average main: Y35* *Loft Jinding 1919 Complex, 15 Jindingshan Lu* *0871/6542–0010* *No credit cards.*

★ **Yingjiang Daiweiyuan** (盈江傣味园 *Yíngjiāng dǎiwèiyuán*)

$ | **YUNNAN** | This often hectic eatery may be the best place in Kunming to enjoy Dai cuisine, which is known for its liberal use of chili peppers. If you want to go straight for the heat, try the *gui ji* or "ghost chicken," a cold salad that is slightly sour and extremely spicy. **Known for:** extremely spicy; cultural diversity; unique atmosphere. *Average main: Y40* *Cuihu North Rd., Xiansheng Po Intersection* *0871/512–2251* *No credit cards.*

Biking Kunming

Traffic may seem a bit daunting, but Kunming is one of the best cities in China for biking. Small brown signs point to historical and cultural sights. The signs are in Chinese, but just follow the arrows. Explore the winding lanes at Green Lake Park; heading south, you'll find pockets of Old Kunming, including parks, temples, and pagodas.

Xiong Brothers Bike Shop Decent rental bikes are available here for about Y40 per day. *51 Beimen Jie* *Unit 5* *0871/6519–1520.*

Hotels

Green Lake Hotel (翠湖宾馆 *Cuìhú bīnguǎn*)

$$$$ | **HOTEL** | Adjacent to Green Lake Park, this is one of Kunming's most elegant lodgings, with comfortably furnished guest rooms that are a pleasant blend of traditional design and modern style. **Pros:** solid breakfast buffet; good service; comfortable rooms. **Cons:** many staff members speak little or no English; no restaurants around; pricey. *Rooms from: Y2277* *6 Cuihu Nan Lu* *0871/6515–8888* *www.greenlakehotelkunming.com* *307 rooms* *Breakfast.*

Yunnan Cuisine

Dian cuisine is the term for Han Chinese cuisine found in Yunnan, especially around Kunming. Dian-style dishes are similar to Sichuan dishes and tend to favor spicy and sour flavors. Rice is a staple here, as is a type of rice noodle called *mixian.* A favorite dish is *guoqiao mixian*, a boiling broth served with raw pork and vegetables that all cook in the bowl. *Qiguo ji* (steampot chicken), another trademark Dian-style dish, uses a special earthenware pot to steam chicken and vegetables into a savory soup.

One thing that sets Dian cuisine apart from that of the rest of China is its use of dairy products. *Rubing* is a mildly flavored cheese made from goat's milk, and is typically fried and served with dried chili peppers or sugar. It is a little drier and less pungent than most other goat cheese. *Rushan*, or "milk fan," is a long strip of a cheese that is spread with a salty or sweet sauce. Wrapped around a chopstick, it makes a handy snack.

Street barbecue is a major part of the Yunnan culinary experience. Every kind of meat and vegetable is on offer, as well as quail eggs, *chou doufu* (stinky tofu), and *ou* (lotus root filled with sticky rice). Most restaurants in Yunnan close early, but barbecue stands stay open until the wee hours, making them a good place for a late-night snack. As for the morning after, a Yunnan breakfast is incomplete without *shao erkuai* (grilled rice pancakes with sweet or savory fillings and optional *youtiao*, a fried dough stick), often sold at mobile grills.

★ **InterContinental Kunming** (昆明洲际酒店 *Kūnmíng zhōujì jiǔdiàn*)
$ | **HOTEL** | If you're in Kunming only to relax, and noisy streets and busy traffic hold little appeal, then the international chain hotel is an exceptional option. **Pros:** absolutely beautiful; quiet location; luxurious. **Cons:** remote; hard to find; staff doesn't speak much English. *Rooms from: Y980* ✉ *5 Yijing Rd., near Dianchi Lake* ☎ *400/886–2255* 🌐 *www.ihg.com/intercontinental* *541 rooms* 🍴 *Breakfast.*

Lost Garden Guesthouse (一丘田七号客栈 *Yīqiūtián qī hào kèzhàn*)
$ | **B&B/INN** | If you manage to book a room in this always-packed guesthouse, you'll find yourself a stone's throw from Green Lake. **Pros:** close to Green Lake; personal service; cozy touch. **Cons:** basic furnishings; common areas shared with diners from outside; noisy. *Rooms from: Y160* ✉ *7 Yi Qiu Tian* ☎ *0871/6511–1127* 🌐 *www.lostgardenguesthouse.com* *14 rooms* 🍴 *No meals.*

New Era Hotel (新纪元大酒店 *Xīnjìyuán dàjiǔdiàn*)
$ | **HOTEL** | Conveniently located on Kunming's central pedestrian area, the New Era Hotel has well-furnished rooms with views on the west mountains and the crawling crowd below. **Pros:** great location; excellent value; sensational breakfast. **Cons:** impersonal; busy area; staff struggles with English. *Rooms from: Y520* ✉ *1 Dongfeng West Rd., on Nanping square* ☎ *0871/6362–4999* 🌐 *www.erahotel.com* *315 rooms* 🍴 *Breakfast.*

Kunming's Flying Tigers

Despite being in the hinterland of Southwest China, Kunming played a crucial role in World War II by preventing Japanese forces from taking control of all of China. At the center of this role was the American Volunteer Group, best known by its local nickname *feihu*, or the Flying Tigers, because of the shark faces painted on their fuselages.

The group of around 300 American servicemen was led by the mysterious Claire L. Chennault. A retired captain in the U.S. Air Force, Chennault first came to Kunming in 1938, when Madame Chiang Kai-shek, wife of the country's leader, asked him to organize a Chinese air force to counter the relentless attacks from the Japanese, who were busily bombing much of China with little opposition.

Supply routes to China's capital were being taken out one after another, leaving just one road. Chennault argued that a group of American pilots could defend this crucial supply artery, as well as push the Japanese out of the region.

The Flying Tigers were tenacious fighters. They swept through much of China to combat the constant bombing by Japanese forces. Their record was second to none in World War II. They had more than 50 enemy encounters and were never defeated.

★ **Wyndham Grand Plaza Royale** (昆明七彩云南温德姆至尊豪廷大酒店 *Kūnmíng qīcǎi yúnnán wēndémǔ zhìzūn háo tíng dà jiǔdiàn*)
$$$ | **HOTEL** | Without a doubt the city's most luxurious hotel, the Wyndham Grand Plaza Royale brings taste and style to everything from the grand lobby to the soothing spa to the selection of six globe-trotting restaurants. **Pros:** attentive staff; excellent restaurants; tasteful touch to everything. **Cons:** far from the city center; water pressure can be low; pricey. *Rooms from: Y1600* ✉ *569 Dianchi Lu* ☎ *0871/6817–7777* 🌐 *www.wyndham.com* *374 rooms* *Breakfast.*

Nightlife

Chapter One
BARS/PUBS | This Western-style bar attracts a largely Chinese clientele and offers a decent selection of drinks and snacks at very acceptable prices. It's very popular with locals in the evenings, when the outdoor terrace is packed to the brim. And there's an all-you-can-eat brunch buffet for Y40 every day at 11 am; although the Western food's quality can vary, as the cooks are still finding their way, the Chinese food is impeccable. ✉ *20 Wenlin Jie* ☎ *0871/6533–1151.*

Moondog (月亮狗 *Yuèliàng gǒu*)
BARS/PUBS | Open until the wee hours, this bar on a side street from bustling Kundu has Kunming's widest selection of whiskeys. It's a favorite with expats for foosball, cards, and other games. ✉ *138–5 Wacang Nan Lu* ☎ *0158/8714–6080.*

O'Reilly's Irish Pub (O′ Reilly′ s爱尔兰酒吧 *O'Reilly's ài'ěrlán jiǔbā*)
BARS/PUBS | Run by a trio who claims never to have set foot on Irish soil, O'Reilly's Irish Pub has cold Guinness on tap, as well as a remarkable selection of Belgian ales. The obligatory pub grub is very good. The northern bar, at 13 Beichen Pedestrian Street, is quieter than the southern one, which can get quite rowdy when the local rugby team is in. ✉ *119 Beimen St.* ☎ *0871/6561–5661.*

The Stone Forest in Yunnan is a UNESCO World Heritage Site.

Performing Arts

Dynamic Yunnan (云南映象 *Yúnnán yìngxiàng*)

DANCE | Chinese dance legend Yang Liping has retired, but the Yunnan native's award-winning dance and musical production, Dynamic Yunnan, still plays to full-capacity crowds, nightly at 8:30. It's an impressive fusion of the storytelling, songs, and dances of local indigenous groups. ✉ *Kunming Arts Theatre, 81 Dongfeng Xi Lu, near Xiao Xi Men* ☎ *087/6313–0033* *From Y180.*

Shopping

If you're looking for a good deal on tea, look no further than the wholesale tea market at the southeast corner of Beijing Lu and Wujing Lu. Within the market you'll find an amazing variety of green teas, black teas, flower teas, and herbal teas. It's a wholesale market, but vendors will sell you small quantities.

Qianju Jie, near the intersection of Wenlin Jie and Wenhua Xiang, is one of the more popular shopping streets in the city.

Bird and Flower Market (花鸟市场 *Huāniǎo shìchǎng*)

OUTDOOR/FLEA/GREEN MARKETS | For all kinds of trinkets and oddities, head to the Bird and Flower Market. Consisting of a bunch of street stalls along Jingxing Jie, this market is the ultimate place to sharpen your haggling skills—and perhaps find that one special gift for the folks back home. ✉ *Jingxing Jie, off Zhengyi Lu, nearby Nanping square.*

Mandarin Books (漫林书苑 *Mànlín shūyuàn*)

BOOKS/STATIONERY | One of the best foreign-language bookstores in all of Yunnan. ✉ *52 Wenhua Xiang 9–10* ☎ *0871/6551–6579* 🌐 *www.mandarin-books.cn.*

Stone Forest (Shilin)

125 km (78 miles) southeast of Kunming.

This cluster of dark-gray limestone formations, twisted into odd shapes, makes a memorable side trip—it's one of the most interesting sites near Kunming.

GETTING HERE AND AROUND

There are several ways to get here, the best being a car and driver. One can be arranged through your hotel and should cost between Y500 and Y600. Stone Forest–bound buses depart every 15 to 30 minutes from Kunming's East Bus Station, and cost about Y25 round-trip. This trip takes at least four hours, as the driver makes numerous stops at souvenir stands and junk stores along the way.

Sights

★ **Stone Forest** (石林 *Shílín*)

NATURE SITE | The forest's groups of karst, first formed 270 million years ago, have been given names to describe their resemblance to creatures real (turtles) or mythological (phoenixes). Walking through the park you'll find plenty of Sani women eager to act as guides and sell you their handicrafts. The main trail has become rather commercialized, but there are plenty of similar formations in other parts of the park. ⊠ *Shilin, Kunming* *Y175.*

Dali

250 km (155 miles; 5 hrs by bus; 6 hrs by train) northwest of Kunming; 140 km (87 miles; 3 hrs by bus; 2 hrs by train) south of Lijiang.

This rustic town is one of those rare places that feel completely cut off from the rest of the world but still has high-speed Internet access. It's perched at the foot of the towering Cangshan Mountains and overlooks lovely Erhai Lake. The typically sunny weather, sleepy artistic atmosphere, and gorgeous sunsets have made it one of Yunnan's most popular destinations

Home to the Bai people, Dali has been inhabited for more than 4,000 years, serving as a major rice-production base for the region. Today tourism is rejuvenating the town. The upside of its building boom is a greater variety of restaurants and hotels; the downside is that the Old Town is constantly being demolished and reconstructed. A planned high-speed rail link with Kunming means now is the time to see Dali before it changes even more.

GETTING HERE AND AROUND

There are multiple daily flights from Kunming to Dali. Dali's airport is at the southern tip of Erhai Lake. Taxis between the airport and the Old Town cost Y90 and take just under an hour.

Buses from Kunming to Dali take five hours and cost Y110. Most drop you off in "New Dali," the nondescript city of Xiaguan. From there, a 25-minute cab ride gets you to the Old Town. It should cost Y40 to Y60, depending on the time of day and your haggling skills.

Trains between Kunming and Dali cost around Y100, but the trip takes six hours, about one hour longer than taking a bus. However, there's an overnight train from Kunming that drops you in Dali at 6 am, so it can be a good way to save on time as well as on lodging.

TIMING

Most of the major sites in and around Dali can be enjoyed within two or three days. Many travelers find themselves arriving in Dali with ambitious itineraries, but end up staying to enjoy the town's lazy vibe.

Dali and the Nanzhao Kingdom

The idyllic scenery belies Dali's importance as the center of power for the Nanzhao Kingdom. The easily defensible area around Erhai Lake was the kingdom's birthplace, which began as the Bai- and Yi-dominated Damengguo in 649. Almost a century later, Damengguo was expanded to include the six surrounding kingdoms ruled by powerful Bai families. This expansion was supported by the ruling Chinese Tang Dynasty, and the kingdom was renamed Nanzhao.

The primarily Buddhist Nanzhao Kingdom was essentially a vassal state of the Tang Dynasty until AD 750, when it rebelled. Tang armies were sent in 751 and 754 to suppress the insurgents, but they suffered humiliating defeats. Emboldened by their victories, Nanzhao troops helped the kingdom acquire a significant amount of territory. Before reaching its high point with the capture of Chengdu and Sichuan in 829, the Nanzhao Kingdom had expanded to include all of present-day Yunnan, as well as parts of present-day Burma, Laos, and Thailand.

Although the capture of Chengdu was a major victory for Nanzhao, it appears to have led directly to its decline. The Tang Dynasty couldn't stand for such an incursion and sent large numbers of troops to the area. They eventually evicted Nanzhao forces from Sichuan by 873. About 30 years later the Nanzhao leaders were finally overthrown, ending the story of their meteoric rise and fall.

Sights

Three Pagodas (三塔寺 *Sān tă sì*)
RELIGIOUS SITE | The most famous landmark in Dali, the Three Pagodas appear on just about every calendar of Chinese scenery. The largest, 215 feet high, dates from AD 836 and is decorated on each of its 16 stories with Buddhas carved from local marble. The other two pagodas, also richly decorated, are even more elegant. When the water is still, you can ponder their reflection in a nearby pool. A massive Chan Buddhist Temple has been built behind the pagodas. The pagodas are a 20-minute walk from the Old Town. ✉ *1 km (½ mile) north of Dali Gucheng* 🎫 *Y128.*

Restaurants

The Bakery No. 88 (88号西点店 *Bābāhào xīdiăndiàn*)
$ | CAFÉ | The dessert counter here has some of Dali's best cakes, which can be enjoyed with a coffee and a book on the second floor if you're after somewhere quiet. It's one of the best places in town for good Western food and take-away stuffed baguettes. **Known for:** homemade cakes; pleasant environment; mulled wine. [$] *Average main: Y30* ✉ *17 Renmin Rd.* ✣ *Next to mosque* ☎ *0872/267–9129.*

Bird Bar (鸟吧 *Niăo bā*)
$ | CAFÉ | For a taste of one of Yunnan's major cash crops, head to the Bird Bar, which grows, roasts and grinds its own coffee beans. The owner's love for antique buildings clearly shines through in the coffeehouse's cozy, old-fashioned interior. **Known for:** cozy; fresh coffee; Western menu. [$] *Average main: Y38* ✉ *21 Renmin Lu* ☎ *0872/266–1843* 🌐 *www.birdbardali.com.*

Café de Jack (樱花园西餐厅 *Yīnghuā yuán xīcāntīng*)
$ | ECLECTIC | A longtime favorite specializing in Western and Chinese classics

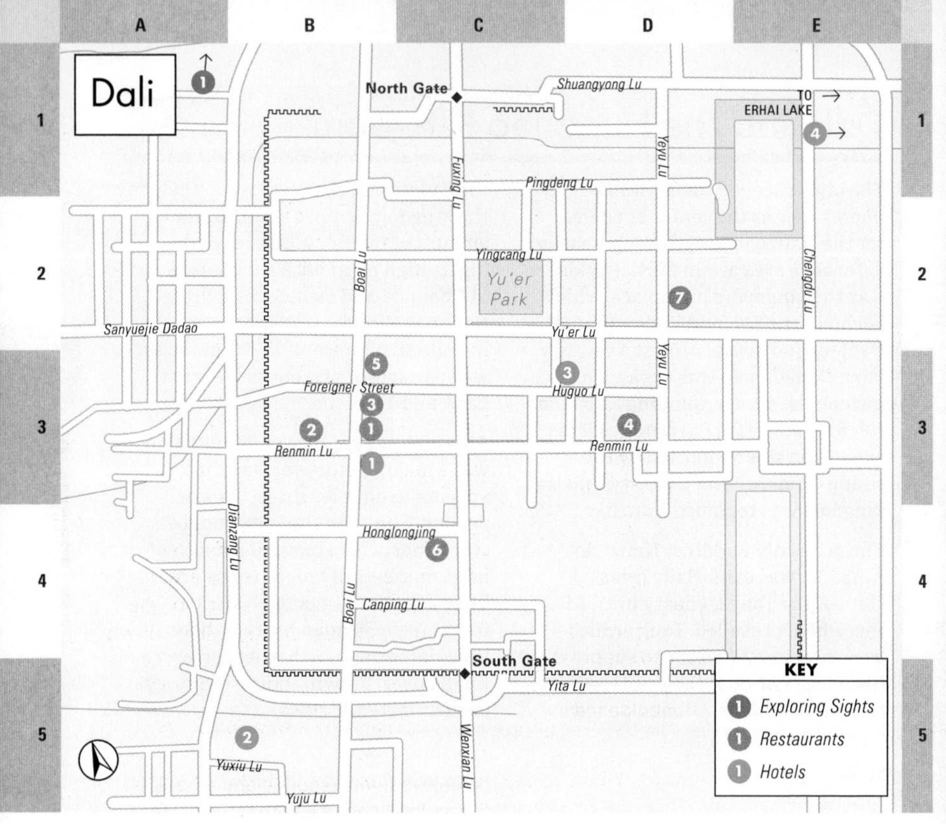

Sights

1 Three Pagodas.......... **A1**

Restaurants

1 The Bakery No. 88...... **B3**
2 Bird Bar.................. **B3**
3 Café de Jack............ **B3**
4 Duyichu Fanzhuang **D3**
5 The Sweet Tooth........ **B3**
6 Waffle Wizard............ **C4**
7 Xinghua Cun............. **D2**

Hotels

1 Dali Gurong Hotel........ **B3**
2 Jim's Tibetan Hotel **B5**
3 Landscape Hotel......... **C3**
4 Regent Hotel **E1**

as well as some local Bai specialties, Café de Jack serves good breakfast, lunch, and dinner—and the strongest cup of coffee in Yunnan. All three floors are a bit different: the first floor feels like a bar, the second floor is more like a restaurant, and the rooftop is a perfect place to kick back with a beer. **Known for:** historical; variety of options; fireplace. *Average main: Y45 ✉ 82 Bo'ai Lu ☎ 0872/267–1572.*

Duyichu Fanzhuang (独一处饭庄 *Dúyīchù fànzhuāng*)
$ | **NORTHERN CHINESE** | Hidden inside a leaning shack, this little dumpling palace wraps the best *jiaozi* in Dali and the surrounding region. Other dishes are on offer, depending on what's available in the local markets. **Known for:** cozy; small bites; variety of dumplings. *Average main: Y15 ✉ Renmin Lu, across from Mayana Restaurant No credit cards.*

The Sweet Tooth (甜点屋 *Tiāndiǎnwū*)
$ | **MEXICAN** | Dali's expat community indulges in its love of pastries at this low-profile little eatery. Surprisingly enough, it also cooks up some of the best Mexican food in town. **Known for:** blueberry cheesecake; coffee; excellent savory mains. *Average main: Y35 ✉ 52 Bo'ai Lu ☎ 0872/266–3830.*

Waffle Wizard (比利时挖福饼 *Bǐlìshí wā fú bǐng*)
$ | **CAFÉ** | Here you'll find authentic Belgian waffles topped with whipped cream, ice cream, or just a dusting of powdered sugar. If you don't have a sweet tooth, sip a cold Belgian ale while you watch the people stroll past. **Known for:** sugary treats; English-speaking staff; cozy. *Average main: Y20 ✉ Corner of Honglongjing Lu and Fuxing Lu ☎ 137/0060–6575.*

Xinghua Cun (杏花村 *Xìnghuā cūn*)
$ | **YUNNAN** | In business for decades, Xinghua Cun is a no-nonsense Chinese restaurant with the usual revolving-top tables and a counter filled with all kinds of homemade liquor. If you look past the spartan decor, you'll notice what this place does best: tasty Yunnanese and local Bai dishes, all served with a smile. **Known for:** soups; cultural diversity; cozy. *Average main: Y35 ✉ 165 Ye'er Lu ☎ 0872/267–0082.*

Hotels

★ **Dali Gurong Hotel** (古榕会馆 *Gǔ róng huìguǎn*)
$ | **HOTEL** | One of the most pleasant hotels in Dali's Old Town, the upscale Dali Gurong offers spacious and well-furnished rooms in a cluster of villas in a park-like setting. **Pros:** luxurious feel; helpful staff; central location. **Cons:** somewhat expensive for the area; not many Western food options; lack of English-speaking staff. *Rooms from: Y880 ✉ 59 Bo'ai Lu ☎ 0872/268–5999 🌐 www.guronghoteldali.com/ 61 rooms Breakfast.*

Jim's Tibetan Hotel (吉姆藏式酒店 *Jímǔ zàng shì jiǔdiàn*)
$ | **B&B/INN** | **FAMILY** | Outside the south gate, this quiet lodging is ideal if you want to avoid the hubbub of Dali's Old Town. **Pros:** kid-friendly vibe; unique interior. **Cons:** a bit dusty; a little far from the sights; outdated furniture. *Rooms from: Y300 ✉ 4 Yuyuan Alley ☎ 0872/267–7824 15 rooms Breakfast.*

Landscape Hotel (兰林阁酒店 *Lánlíngé jiǔdiàn*)
$ | **HOTEL** | With exits on both Huguo and Yu'er Roads, the Landscape Hotel is probably the most centrally located place to stay in town. **Pros:** doesn't get any more central; great courtyards; rustic. **Cons:** average rooms; average breakfast; confusing to get around. *Rooms from: Y880 ✉ 96 Yu'er Lu ☎ 0872/266–6188 🌐 www.landscapehoteldali.com/ 206 rooms No meals.*

Regent Hotel (风花雪月大酒店 *Fēnghuāxuěyuè dà jiǔdiàn*)
$ | **HOTEL** | Littered with luxury artifacts, the Regent might seem a little

unnecessary when compared to the highly affordable options in the Old Town. **Pros:** good quality; excellent service; open layout. **Cons:** feels isolated from the Old Town; average facilities; outdated rooms. *Rooms from: Y754 ✉ Yu'er Lu and Da-Li 1st Class intersection ☎ 0872/266–6666 599 rooms Breakfast.*

Nightlife

Bad Monkey (坏猴子 *Huàihóuzi*)
BARS/PUBS | One of the town's oldest establishments, this is Dali's most popular watering hole. In addition to an extensive bar, Bad Monkey brews its own beer, with every batch selling out quickly. Drinks aside, the kitchen stays open until early morning and cooks up decent fish-and-chips and pizzas. There's live music almost every night. *✉ 59 Renmin Lu ⊕ www.badmonkey-bar.com.*

Kaki Cafe (柿子树咖啡馆 *Shìzǐshù kāfēi guǎn*)
CAFES—NIGHTLIFE | Tucked away in an alley off busy Renmin Lu, this is a café by day that gets a bit more lively at night, when the bottles come out. There's a standard selection of drinks, completed with the obligatory Belgian ales. This is an excellent place if you are after a quiet spot. *✉ 164 Huguo Lu, off Renmin Lu ☎ 0872/536–5688.*

Sun Island (太阳岛 *Tàiyáng dǎo*)
BARS/PUBS | One of Old Town's most pleasant bars, the civilized Sun Island draws a crowd that's young, alternative, and mostly Chinese. Grab a seat at the wooden bar and strike up a conversation with the friendly staffers. **■ TIP→ For a local specialty, ask for the plum wine—it's actually plum liquor—on the rocks.** *✉ 324 Renmin Lu.*

Did You Know?

The cormorants used by fishermen on Erhai Lake have a collar around their necks that prevents them from swallowing the fish they have caught.

Shopping

Foreigner Street is lined with Bai women who have been selling the same jewelry, fabrics, and Communist kitsch for two decades. Don't be afraid to walk away when bargaining; vendors will often drop their prices at the last minute.

Bo'ai Lu and Renmin Lu are peppered with a variety of shops featuring outdoor clothing and equipment; handicrafts from India, Nepal, and Southeast Asia; as well as Chinese antiques. Fuxing Lu, aimed primarily at Chinese tourists, is where you'll find local teas, specialty foods, and, most prominently, jade. Much of it is of low quality, so buy only if you know something about jade.

Side Trips from Dali

Sights

★ **Cangshan** (苍山 *Cāngshān*)
MOUNTAIN—SIGHT | With a peak that rises to more than 4,500 meters (14,765 feet), "Green Mountain" can be seen from just about anywhere in Dali. A 16-km (10-mile) path carved into the side of the mountain offers spectacular views of Dali and the surrounding villages. There are also several temples, grottoes, and waterfalls just off the main trail. To get to the footpath, follow Yu'er Lu to the foot of the mountain. If you don't want to climb,

The Old Town in Lijiang at dusk

there are two cable cars to take you up the mountain. ✉ *Dali.*

Erhai Lake (洱海湖 *Ěrhǎi hú*)
BODY OF WATER | Almost any street off Fuxing Lu will bring you to the shore of Erhai Lake. from which you can marvel at the looming Cangshan peaks. You may catch a glimpse of fishermen with teams of cormorants tied to their boats. In good weather, ferries are a wonderful way to see the lake and the surrounding mountains. The ferries cost between Y30 and Y70 (depending on your ability to bargain). More interesting—and cheaper—is hiring fishermen to paddle you wherever you want to go. Boats depart from the village of Zhoucheng. ✉ *Dali.*

Shaping
TOWN | This town sits on the lake's northern shore, and can be most easily reached by boat or by hiring a car and driver. Its market, held every Monday morning, is the most popular in the area. ✉ *Dali.*

Wase Bai Ethnic Village
TOWN | Wase has a popular area market featuring Bai clothing. The town is on the opposite side of the lake from Dali and can be reached by car or boat. Wase also has some inexpensive places to stay if you want to spend the night in a lake village. ✉ *Dali.*

Xizhou (喜洲 *Xǐ zhōu*)
TOWN | Among the prettiest towns in the area is Xizhou, about 20 km (12 miles) north of Dali. It has managed to preserve a fair amount of its Bai architecture. The daily morning market and occasional festivals of traditional music attract a fair number of tourists from Dali. Minibuses leave from Dali's west gate and cost Y7. ✉ *Dali.*

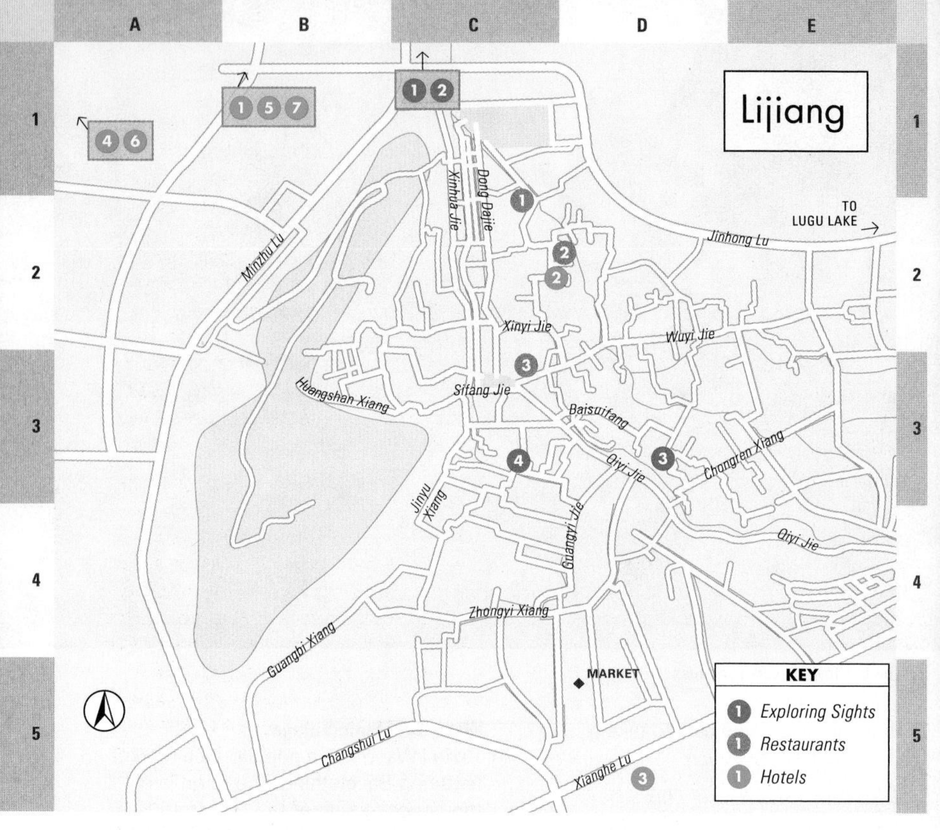

Sights

1 Black Dragon Pool Park C1

2 Jade Dragon Snow Mountain.......... C1

3 Puxian Temple D3

4 Visitor Center for Nature and Culture in Northwest Yunnan....... C3

Restaurants

1 Lamu's House of Tibet... C2

2 N's Kitchen D2

3 Prague Café.............. C3

Hotels

1 Banyan Tree Lijiang B1

2 East River Hotel.......... C2

3 Lijiang InterContinental Resort...................... D5

4 New Huifeng Resort Hotel.............. A1

5 Pullmann Lijiang Resort & Spa............. B1

6 Wenhai Ecolodge......... A1

7 Wuer Inn.................. B1

Lijiang

150 km (93 miles; 3 hrs by bus; 2 hrs by train) north of Dali; 320 km (198 miles; 7 hrs by bus; 8 hrs by train) northwest of Kunming; 550 km (341 miles; 20 hrs by bus) southwest of Chengdu.

Lijiang is probably the most famous travel destination in Yunnan, as its Old Town is a UNESCO World Heritage Site. At the base of majestic Jade Dragon Snow Mountain, Lijiang is home to the Naxi people, who are related to Tibetans but have their own language and culture.

Lijiang's Old Town is a labyrinth of winding alleys, fish-filled streams, and old Naxi houses with tile rooftops. Traditional Naxi singing and dancing are on display nightly at Sifang Jie, the square in Old Town's center.

GETTING HERE AND AROUND

There are multiple daily flights from Kunming. The airport is 48 km (30 miles) south of Lijiang. A Y20 bus from the airport takes you to the edge of the Old Town. A taxi to the Old Town will run you Y80.

Lijiang's main bus station is on Xianggelila Dadao. Trips from Kunming take just more than eight hours.

There are day and night trains from Kunming. The ride takes eight hours and costs about Y150 for a berth. A train from Dali takes two hours and costs Y34. Don't expect much in the way of views, as most of the route goes through tunnels.

TIMING

Lijiang is good for two or three days of taking in the Old Town and surrounding areas. If you're feeling active, head to Tiger Leaping Gorge or Lugu lake for two to three days.

Sights

Black Dragon Pool Park (黑龙潭公园 *Hēilóngtán gōngyuán*)
CITY PARK | Outside the Old Town, Black Dragon Pool Park has a tranquil pavilion where locals come to play cards and drink tea. The park is one of the most popular places to photograph nearby Jade Dragon Snow Mountain. The park is home to the Dongba Research Institute Museum (*Dōngba wénhuà bówùguǎn*), devoted to Naxi Dongba culture. ✉ *Xinde Lu* 🎫 *Y80.*

Jade Dragon Snow Mountain (玉龙雪山风景区 *Yùlóng xuěshān fēngjǐng qū*)
MOUNTAIN—SIGHT | Towering majestically over Lijiang, the 18,360-foot Jade Dragon Snow Mountain is one of China's most spectacular peaks. The mountain's jagged, snow-covered face is one of the defining sights of a trip to Lijiang. The well-maintained road to the scenic area passes numerous villages and has fine views of the valley. The park entrance is about a 30-minute drive from Old Town. Taxis should cost around Y40 one way, or Y100 or more if you want the driver to wait for you. ✉ *Lijiang* 🎫 *Y130.*

Puxian Temple (普贤寺 *Pǔxián sì*)
RELIGIOUS SITE | If you can find it, the Puxian Temple is a tranquil place to get away from the crowds. At the temple's vegetarian restaurant, try the *jidoufen,* a bean concoction that can be eaten hot as a porridge or cold and cut up like noodles. The ubiquitous *baba* bread is also quite good. Wash it all down with a pot of Tibetan tea, made with yak butter. ✉ *76 Qi Yi Jie* 🎫 *Free.*

Visitor Center for Nature and Culture in Northwest Yunnan (滇西北自然与文化之窗暨绿色旅游推广中心 *Diān xīběi zìrán yǔ wénhuà zhī chuāng jì lùsè lǚyóu tuīguǎng zhōngxīn*)
MUSEUM | This small but fascinating museum highlights the region's cultural and biological diversity. Exhibits include one in which villagers were given

Naxi Music of Lijiang

The Naxi culture is rich in artistic elements—the Naxi pictographs, architecture, Dongba shamans, and, not least of all, the music. It is a complex and intricate musical blending of Han and Naxi musical traditions that has commonly served as entertainment, as well as a measuring stick for Confucian social relationships. Naxi musicians and members of social clubs related to the music were considered to be of a higher status than the average Naxi villager.

Today Naxi music, with its 500 years of history, is a sonic time capsule, giving us the opportunity to hear songs dating as far back as the Tang, Song, and Yuan Dynasties. Most of the Naxi-inhabited counties around Lijiang feature their own orchestras specializing in the two extant versions of Naxi music: Baisha fine music and Dongjing music. A third type, Huangjing music, fell out of practice over the centuries and has since been lost.

The Roots of Rhythm

Legend has it that Baisha fine music developed as a result of Kublai Khan's gratitude for Naxi assistance during his conquest of Yunnan during the Yuan Dynasty. The Khan is believed to have left a group of his best musicians and their musical canon with the Naxi in Lijiang. Baisha fine music is one of the grander Chinese musical styles, with large orchestras including the Chinese flute, the lute, and the zither.

Dongjing music came to this region from central China during the Ming and Qing dynasties, and is based on Taoist classics. It is the better preserved of the two musical styles, most likely because the Naxi incorporated more of their indigenous music into it.

Beauty Is in the Ear of the Beholder

Naxi orchestras have their own standards for what makes for a quality Naxi musical experience, the key factor being age. In the eyes of the Naxi, the older the musicians, the better. Perhaps this is because fewer and fewer are learning the traditional styles. The musicians' instruments are also old, often much older than the septuagenarians playing the music—the craftsmanship 100 years ago was better than today. Naxi orchestras refuse to play any modern music. They only jam to centuries-old tunes.

For many travelers, Naxi music is an aural step back in time. Others find it screechy and grating. You can catch a show at a number of venues in Lijiang's Old Town and the new city. The most famous groups are the Baihua and Dayan orchestras. Tickets can typically be purchased starting at Y120 at most hotels and guesthouses.

cameras to document their daily lives. Another compares photos taken in the 1920s with those taken more recently. The museum is funded by the Nature Conservancy. ✉ *42 Xianwen Xiang, at Guangyi Jie* ☎ *0888/511–5969* 🎫 *Free.*

Restaurants

Lamu's House of Tibet (西藏屋西餐厅 *Xīzàngwū xīcāntīng*)

$$ | CHINESE | The traditional Tibetan decor, pleasant atmosphere, and helpful staff make this one of Lijiang's better dining options. The kitchen serves Tibetan,

Chinese, and Naxi cuisine, as well as familiar dishes like lasagna and French fries. **Known for:** Western dishes; yak meat; English-speaking staff. $ *Average main: Y50* ✉ *56 Jishan Xiang, Xinyi Jie* ☎ *0888/511–5776* ▭ *No credit cards.*

N's Kitchen (二楼小厨 *Èrlóu xiǎochú*)
$$ | **ECLECTIC** | Norman's Kitchen, or simply N's Kitchen, serves a classic selection of Western food at reasonable prices. Diners eat on the second floor, from which vantage point they can watch tourists leisurely stroll by. **Known for:** coffee; hearty sandwiches; breakfast. $ *Average main: Y55* ✉ *17 Jishan Xiang, 2nd fl.* ☎ *0888/512–0060.*

Prague Café (布拉格咖啡馆 *Bùlāgé kāfēiguǎn*)
$$ | **CAFÉ** | A favorite with expats, this bright, sunny eatery serves international favorites like Japanese-style *katsu don* (pork cutlets in a savory sauce). This is also the town's top choice for fresh bread, good coffee, and, especially, American-style breakfasts. **Known for:** quiet atmosphere; coffee; vegetarian options. $ *Average main: Y50* ✉ *80 Mishi Xiang, at Xinyi Jie* ☎ *0888/512–3757* ▭ *No credit cards.*

Hotels

Banyan Tree Lijiang (悦榕庄 *Yuèrōng zhuāng*)
$$$ | **RESORT** | The area's only luxury resort, the Banyan Tree is made up of villas designed to resemble traditional courtyard houses. **Pros:** nearly perfect service; upscale accommodations; breathtaking scenery. **Cons:** very expensive for the area; confusing to get to; poor gym facilities. $ *Rooms from: Y1500* ✉ *Yuerong Lu, Shuhe* ☎ *0888/533–1111* 🌐 *www.banyantree.com* *55 villas* *No meals.*

East River Hotel (东河客栈 *Dōnghé kèzhàn*)
$ | **HOTEL** | Well hidden in the maze of streets in Old Town, the East River Hotel offers some of the area's most comfortable rooms. **Pros:** quiet atmosphere; idyllic courtyard; quaint. **Cons:** hard to find; dearth of English-speaking staff; rooms are slightly worn. $ *Rooms from: Y400* ✉ *44 Mishi Xiang, off Xinyi Jie* ☎ *0888/515–1668* ▭ *No credit cards* *40 rooms* *No meals.*

Lijiang InterContinental Resort (丽江和府皇冠度假酒店 *Lìjiāng héfǔ huángguàn dùjià jiǔdiàn*)
$$ | **RESORT** | **FAMILY** | Filling the gap between the small hotels and guesthouses in the Old Town and the ultraluxurious Banyan Tree, the Lijiang InterContinental was the beginning of a wave of international five-stars moving into Lijiang. **Pros:** comfortable; high level of service; great views. **Cons:** a bit removed from the Old Town; reception understaffed; mediocre food. $ *Rooms from: Y1280* ✉ *276 Xianghe Lu* ☎ *888/558–8888* 🌐 *www.ichotelsgroup.com* *270 rooms* *Breakfast.*

★ **New Huifeng Resort Hotel** (新回峰度假酒店 *Xīn huífēng dùjià jiǔdiàn*)
$ | **B&B/INN** | Although calling it a "resort" may be a bit misleading, the New Huifeng offers plenty of peace and quiet. **Pros:** great views; swimming pool; unique architecture. **Cons:** some low ceilings, so mind your head; can get cold; mediocre breakfast. $ *Rooms from: Y780* ✉ *31 Zhonghe Cun, Shuhe* ☎ *131/506–75155* *34 rooms* *Breakfast.*

★ **Pullman Lijiang Resort & Spa** (丽江铂尔曼度假酒店 *Lìjiāng bó ěr màn dùjià jiǔdiàn*)
$$$$ | **RESORT** | With a hard-to-beat location, the Pullman Lijiang Resort offers views of the Jade Dragon Snow Mountain so beautiful that it has a dedicated viewing area. **Pros:** stupefying views; ultimate comfort; efficient service. **Cons:** expensive; almost clinically perfect; cocktails are average. $ *Rooms from: Y1880* ✉ *Entrance to Shuhe Old Town* ☎ *0888/530–0111* 🌐 *www.pullmanhotels.com/7231* *130 villas* *Breakfast.*

Black Dragon Pool Park with Jade Dragon Snow Mountain in the distance

Wenhai Ecolodge (文海生态旅馆 *Wénhǎi shēngtài lǚguǎn*)
$ | **B&B/INN** | One of the country's first "green" resorts, Wenhai Ecolodge is in the mountain valley that is home to Lake Wenhai, a seasonal lake that appears between July and March. **Pros:** fascinating for nature lovers; gorgeous setting; great tour recommendations. **Cons:** remote location; rougher than some travelers can handle; no private bathrooms. *Rooms from: Y120* *Lake Wenhai* *139/888–26672* *www.northwest-yunnan.com/wenhai_ecolodge.htm* *No credit cards* *12 rooms* *All meals.*

Wuer Inn (回峰客栈 *Huífēng kèzhàn*)
$ | **B&B/INN** | With each room uniquely decorated to represent one of Yunnan's many different ethnic minorities, the Huifeng Inn is one of the most remarkable hotels in Lijiang. **Pros:** splendid interior design; nice swimming pool; tour desk. **Cons:** low ceilings; gets cold in winter; can get noisy. *Rooms from: Y680* *56 Jiewei Alley, near to Old Sifang Sq., Shuhe* *0888/511–7879* *16 rooms* *No meals.*

Nightlife

Stone The Crows (乌鸦飞了酒吧 *Wūyā fēile jiǔbā*)
BARS/PUBS | Run by an eccentric Irishman, Stone The Crows offers some interesting cocktails and a selection of imported beer. Pub grub is also available, if the staff is in the mood. *134–2 Wenzhi Alley* *0131/5066–2289.*

Performing Arts

Lijiang Impression (印象丽江 *Yìnxiàng Lìjiāng*)
DANCE | The city's most impressive cultural event is Lijiang Impression, a music and dance performance that makes full use of the spectacular location. There are four performances a day, and admission is Y190 to Y260, depending on how close you want to be to the front. *Ganhaizi Scenic District* *0888/888–8888.*

Mountain Spirit Show (丽水金沙 *Lìshuǐ jīnshā*)
THEATER | At the Meeting Hall of Lijiang, the Mountain Spirit Show offers fire eating and other extraordinary feats. The 8 pm performances cost around Y280. ✉ *211 Minzu Lu.*

Tiger Leaping Gorge

91 km (57 miles; 2½ hrs by car) north of Lijiang.

Above a river that winds along for about 16 km (10 miles), this gorge is home to some of China's most breathtaking mountain scenery. The best time to visit is the dry season, from October through May.

GETTING HERE AND AROUND

The easiest way to get to the Gorge is by hiring a car. If you're interested in hiking the gorge, the easiest way to get started is to take the 8:30 am or 9 am bus on Xianggelila Avenue to Qiaotou and hike toward Daju. The trip takes about two hours.

Sights

Lugu Lake (泸沽湖 *Lúgū hú*)
SCENIC DRIVE | If you have a few days to spare, Lugu Lake is a great getaway from Lijiang. The lake straddles the border of Sichuan and Yunnan provinces and is dotted with dreamy little towns belonging mostly to the Mosuo, a matriarchal subgroup of the ubiquitous Naxi. Exploring the Lake's 80 km (50 miles) of stunning lake and mountain scenery is possible by bus, but biking and hiking provide better views.

Buses taking about five hours depart each morning from Lijiang. Tickets that grant entrance to the area are Y80, and a car ticket can set you back another Y30 for one day. There's an airport with flights from Chengdu and Kunming. ✉ *Lugu Lake, Lijiang.*

★ **Tiger Leaping Gorge** (虎跳峡 *Hǔtiàoxiá*)
NATURE SITE | The deepest gorge in the world is hard to forget once you've seen it in person, and it makes an excellent trekking destination. If you're hiking along the upper trail, the 40-km (25-mile) route can be finished in a day or two. The upper trail connects the towns of Qiaotou in the west and Daju in the east, and there is a ferry across the river near Daju. The easiest way to tackle the walk from Lijiang is to take the 8:30 am or 9 am bus on Xianggelila Ave to Qiaotou and hike toward Daju.

There are several guesthouses in the gorge, scattered at distances to accommodate hikers at any stage of their trek. All offer food, hot showers, and beds for Y20 to more than Y100, depending on season and weather. Many of the guesthouses have expanded and upgraded accommodations in the past couple of years, so there is more selection and even some higher-end rooms for Y150. The guesthouses have put up signs and arrows to let hikers know how much farther until the next lodging. If you don't mind not hiking the whole gorge, stop in Walnut Garden, where you can take one of the regular buses back to Lijiang. If you continue to Daju, there are only two buses a day to Lijiang, at 8:30 am and 1 pm. Also remember that the road connecting Daju to Lijiang goes through the Jade Dragon Park and tickets cost around Y220 per person just to go through. Daju is a very pleasant—though quiet, because of the road fee—town that offers basic rooms for around Y50 a night.

For those only interested in seeing the point that gives the gorge its name, the river's narrowest point, which a tiger is supposed to have leaped across to evade a hunter, there are two options: the prettier one is on the Lijiang side of the gorge, includes a nice 4-km (3-mile) walk along a path cut out of the cliffside, and costs Y50 to enter; the Shangri-La side can be reached directly by minivan but will include a few hundred steps down to where the water rages most fiercely. The entrance fee costs Y70, which also includes the rest of the gorge. Most hotels will also gladly arrange tours in minivans—expect to pay more than Y140 per person each way. ⊠ *Lijiang* 🎫 *Y70.*

Xishuangbanna Region

380 km (238 miles; 8 hrs by bus, 10 at night) southwest of Kunming; 400 km (250 miles; 12 hrs by bus) south of Dali.

Jinghong is the capital of southern Yunnan's Xishuangbanna Dai Autonomous Region, which borders Laos and Myanmar. Xishuangbanna is home to the Dai, a people related to the Thai and the Lao. Like their cousins to the south, they love very spicy food.

The city sits on the banks of the muddy Mekong, although this stretch of the legendary river is known locally as the Lancang. This is where China meets Southeast Asia; it looks and feels more and more like Laos or Thailand the farther you travel from Jinghong. Even inside the city the architecture, the clothing, and the barbecue seem much more like what you'd find in Vientiane or Chiang Mai.

Jinghong has experienced a tourism explosion, with the city completely filling up with visitors from all over China and hotel prices skyrocketing during the holidays. Thousands of apartments have been constructed to accommodate China's rich, who head here in winter. It has its own international airport, connecting it to Kunming and other major cities. But despite the increase in economic activity, the pace of life in Jinghong still moves about as fast as the Mekong.

GETTING HERE AND AROUND

Jinghong's international airport has service to and from Kunming, Chengdu, Beijing, and-Shanghai, as well as destinations in Thailand. The international terminal is about 15 minutes west of the city center. From the airport, take the Number 1 bus into town for Y2, or opt for a taxi for Y30.

Jinghong's three main bus stations are Jinghong Bus Station, north of Zhuanghong Lu on Mengle Avenue; Banna Bus Station, just north of the intersection of Mengle Avenue and Xuanwei Avenue; and the Jinghong South Bus Station, at the intersection of Mengle Avenue and Menghai Road. The former two both have services to Kunming and Dali. For shorter routes, head to Banna Bus Station. The South Station has connections to Laos and the Thai border.

TIMING

Spend a day exploring downtown Jinghong, and add an extra day or two if you plan to tour out to the surrounding countryside.

TOURS

Tours organized by Sara Lai and Stone Chen from Forest Café are your best bet for a tailored English-language tour of Xishuangbanna.

Sights

Lancang River (澜沧江 *Láncāngjiāng*)
BODY OF WATER | The Lancang River is the name of the Mekong River in China, where it originates before flowing through Southeast Asia. It is easiest to access the river from Jinghong at the Xishuangbanna Bridge. The southern bank is lined with bars and really livens up at night. ⊠ *Jinghong.*

Manting Park (曼听公园 *Màntīng gōngyuán*)
CITY PARK | On the southeastern edge of Jinghong is Manting Park, where you can have a closer look at some of the area's indigenous plants. Also worth exploring is the large peacock aviary. The park is especially lively around mid-April, when people gather to celebrate the Water

Naxi and Bai Ethnic Minorities

Naxi

Living primarily in the area around Lijiang and neighboring Sichuan, the Naxi culture is unique, even when compared with other minority groups in China. The society is traditionally matriarchal, with women dominating relationships, keeping custody of children, and essentially running the show. Some Naxis practice Buddhism or Taoism, but it is the shamanistic culture of the Dongba and Samba that set their spiritualism apart from other groups. The Dongba (male shamans) and Samba (female shamans) serve their communities as mediators, entering trancelike states and communicating with the spirit world in order to solve problems on earth. Naxi script, like Chinese script, is made up of ideograms. These pictographs are vivid representations of body parts, animals, and geography used to express concrete and abstract concepts. Despite numbering fewer than 300,000, the Naxi are one of the better-known ethnic groups in China.

Bai

The Bai, also known as the Minjia, are one of the more prominent minorities in Yunnan, although they are also found in Guizhou and Hunan provinces. Primarily centered around Dali prefecture, the Bai are known for their agricultural skills and unique architecture style. The Bai also have some of the most colorful costumes, particularly the rainbow-colored hats worn by women. The Bai, along with the Yi people, were part of the Nanzhao Kingdom, which briefly rose to regional dominance in Southwest China and Southeast Asia during the Tang Dynasty, before giving way to the Kingdom of Dali. The Dali region and the Bai have essentially been a part of the Chinese sphere of influence since the Yuan Dynasty, during which the Yuan's Mongolian armies conquered the area in the 13th century. The Bais' highly productive rice paddies were seen as an asset by the Yuan, who let them operate under relative autonomy. Today the Bai and their festivals, including the Third Moon Festival and Torch Festival, are major attractions for domestic and international tourists.

Splashing Festival. ✉ *35 Manting Lu, Jinghong* ☎ *0691/216–1061* 🎫 *Y40.*

Xishuangbanna Tropical Flower and Plant Garden (西双版纳热带花卉园 *Xishuāngbǎnnà rèdài huāhuì yuán*)
GARDEN | With a well-designed layout, this is one of China's finest gardens, and an interesting place to spend several hours among fragrant frangipani, massive lily pads, drooping jackfruit, and thousands of other colorful and peculiar plants. Don't walk through too fast, or you'll miss out on some of the more unique plants, such as *tiaowu cao*, or "dancing grass," which actually stands up if you sing at it. Each plant's placard features English and Latin names. ✉ *99 Xuanwei Dadao, Jinghong* 🎫 *Y40.*

Restaurants

Foguang Yuan (佛光园 *Fóguāng yuán*)
$$ | **YUNNAN** | Behind a school and a police station, Foguang Yuan is a true oasis of peace and quiet. The restaurant is actually several dining areas built around a patch of jungle. **Known for:**

The future leaders of the Naxi people.

veggie options; great atmosphere; quirky. *Average main: Y50* *2 Jiaotong Xiang, near Yiwu Lu, Jinghong* *0691/213–8608* *No credit cards.*

Meimei Café (美美咖啡厅 *Měiměi kāfēitīng*)

$ | **INTERNATIONAL** | This is a good place to compare notes with other travelers, as many people come here to buy tickets, book tours, or get travel information. One of the few places in Jinghong with an English-speaking staff, Meimei Café serves Western and Chinese favorites, as well as great coffee and juices. **Known for:** burgers; coffee; nice atmosphere. *Average main: Y45* *2 Menglong Lu, Jinghong* *0691/216–1221* *No credit cards.*

Mekong Café (湄公咖啡馆 *Méigōng kāfēiguǎn*)

$ | **FRENCH** | Opened by a Frenchman who was once a hotel chef and his Chinese wife, Mekong Café is a favorite with all sorts of travelers. Backpackers, expats, couples as well as locals gather on its large front and back patios to enjoy afternoon dessert, delicious French cuisine, Chinese classics, or simply a drink to recover from the Jinghong heat. **Known for:** view; pizza; offers travel advice. *Average main: Y30* *F1–104 Kingland International, Menglong Lu, Jinghong* *0691/216–2395* *www.mekongcafe.cn.*

Hotels

Anantara Xishuangbanna Resort & Spa (西双版纳安纳塔拉度假酒店 *Xīshuāngbǎnnà ānnàtǎlā dùjia jiǔdiàn*)

$$$$ | **RESORT** | **FAMILY** | On the banks of the Luosuo River, this luxury resort is in Menglun, about 60 km (37 miles) from Jinghong. **Pros:** perfect service; great views; sparkling pool. **Cons:** expensive; service is inconsistent; remote. *Rooms from: Y2000* *Country Road 009, Menglun* *691/893–6666* *xishuangbanna.anantara.com* *80 rooms, 23 villas* *Breakfast.*

Dai and Yi Ethnic Minorities

Dai

Related to Thais and speakers of languages belonging to the Tai-Kadai family, the Dai seem much more Southeast Asian than Chinese. In China they are primarily located in the Xishuangbanna, Dehong, and Jingpo regions of southern Yunnan, but can also be found in Myanmar, Laos, and Thailand. They practice Theravada Buddhism, the dominant form of Buddhism in Southeast Asia. The linguistic, cultural, and religious connections with Southeast Asia give Dai-inhabited regions a decidedly un-Chinese feel. Within China, they are most famous for their spicy and flavorful food and their Water Splashing Festival (water is used to wash away demons and sins of the past and bless the future). Many grow rice and produce such crops as pineapples, so villages are concentrated near the Mekong (Lancang) and Red (Honghe) rivers. The Dai population here has ebbed and flowed with China's political tide, and many are now returning after the turmoil of the 1960s and '70s.

Yi

Descendants of the Qiang people of northwestern China, the Yi (aka Sani) are scattered across southwestern China in Yunnan, Sichuan, and Guizhou provinces as well as Guangxi Zhuang Autonomous Region. The largest concentration of the more than 6½ million Qiang descendants are in Sichuan's Liangshan region. They live in isolated, mountainous regions and are known for being fierce warriors. Notable traits include their syllabic writing system, ancient literature, and traditional medicine—all of which are still being used today. The Yi also sport extravagant costumes that vary according to geographical region. Massive black mortarboard-style hats, blue turbans, ornate red headdresses, and other headwear complement brilliantly colored vests and pants. Their language is part of the Tibeto-Burman language family and similar to Burmese. Some Yi also live in Vietnam, where they are called the Lolo.

Crown Hotel (皇冠大酒店 *Huángguàn dà jiǔdiàn*)
$ | **HOTEL** | In the heart of Jinghong, the Crown Hotel has several low-slung buildings in a parklike setting with a lily-leaf-shape swimming pool. **Pros:** central location; night market nearby; good value. **Cons:** tired rooms; too few English-speaking staff; noisy. *Rooms from: Y350 70 Mengle Dadao, Jinghong 0691/219–9888 121 rooms No meals.*

★ **Yourantai** (悠然台 *Yōurán tái*)
$$ | **RESORT** | The "Terrace of Serenity" more than lives up to its name. **Pros:** excellent atmosphere; gorgeous setting; amazing mattresses. **Cons:** minimum stay required; steps to climb; remote. *Rooms from: Y1280 2 Galan North Rd., Jinghong 138/8793–4096 www.yourantai.com No credit cards 6 rooms Breakfast.*

Shopping

On Zhuanghong Lu in the northern part of town, there's a handicrafts market filled with Burmese jade jewelry and goods from Vietnam and Thailand. Assume that much of it is counterfeit. There is a small but vibrant night market on Mengla Lu outside the Crown Hotel. Genuine Pu'er tea can be safely bought from the tea shop in the Golden Zone hotel.

Side Trips from Jinghong

Sights

Ganlan Basin (橄榄坝 *Gănlăn bà*)
FOREST | One of the more scenic areas of Xishuangbanna is this valley 37 km (23 miles) from Jinghong. Locals still live in bamboo huts in the beautiful rain forest. The area is famous in Yunnan for its tropical flowers and its millions of butterflies. ✉ *Jinghong.*

Sanchahe Nature Reserve
NATURE PRESERVE | One of China's first serious attempts at ecotourism, the 900-acre Sanchahe Nature Reserve is home to wild elephants. Two hours north of Jinghong, the park also features a butterfly farm and a cable car that offers breathtaking views. Lodging is in "tree houses" about 25 feet above ground—a unique place to spend a night. ✉ *Jinghong.*

Xishuangbanna Tropical Botanical Garden (西双版纳热带植物园 *Xishuāngbănnà rèdài zhíwùyuán*)
FOREST | The nearest large town in the area, Menglun, is the location of China's largest botanical garden. With a gorgeous setting on a peninsula in the Luosuo River, the garden holds more than 13,000 tropical and subtropical plant species and a section of dense, unspoiled tropical rain forest. A museum tells about the local flora and fauna, as well as the humans that have inhabited the region. Families enjoy the humid and fragrant air of the tropics, picnicking in pavilions, and observing rare plants and animals. Visits can take anywhere from a few hours to an entire day (there are restaurants and places to stay overnight). Electric buses help you explore, and hop-on, hop-off tickets are available for Y100. ■ **TIP→ Buses only run until 6 pm, so start at the eastern park and make your way back toward the entrance.** Menglun is about 60 km (37 miles) east of Jinghong, a trip that takes about 90 minutes by bus. Or you can take a cab. ✉ *Menglun* 🎫 *Y100.*

Yiwu (易武 *Yì wŭ*)
TOWN | Once one of the starting points of the ancient tea and horses trade route to Tibet, this village has an Old Town featuring the houses of the "tea lords" of yesteryear. The Old Town is hidden away behind the school on a hill and makes for very pleasant investigation for an hour or two. Yiwu's higher altitude also means that it's a great way to get away from the Jinghong heat. All around the area are tea plantations you can stroll in. Several buses to Yiwu leave from Jinghong daily. ✉ *Yiwu.*

Chapter 9

SICHUAN AND CHONGQING

Updated by
Clarissa Wei

Sights ★★★★☆ | Restaurants ★★★★★ | Hotels ★★★☆☆ | Shopping ★★☆☆☆ | Nightlife ★☆☆☆☆

WELCOME TO SICHUAN AND CHONGQING

TOP REASONS TO GO

★ **Emeishan:** Hike 10,000 feet to the top of one of China's holy mountains and a UNESCO World Heritage Site.

★ **Giant Panda Breeding Research Base:** Stroll through the bamboo groves, bone up on the latest in genetic biology and ecological preservation, and check out cute baby pandas.

★ **Horseback riding in Songpan:** Marvel at the raw beauty of northern Sichuan's pristine mountain forests and emerald-green lakes from the backs of these gentle beasts.

★ **Liquid fire:** Savor some of the spiciest food on the planet in Chongqing's many hotpot restaurants.

★ **An engineering miracle or madness:** Enjoy a lazy riverboat ride through the surreal Three Gorges, and stand in awe of one of China's latest engineering feats, the mighty Three Gorges Dam.

1 **Chengdu.** Sichuan's financial capital and culinary hub is home to more than 16 million people. While bent on modernizing and no longer the laid-back character she once was, the capital city still retains small pockets of tranquillity if you know where to look.

2 **Emeishan.** One of China's holy mountains, it has almost 50 km (31 miles) of paths leading to the summit.

3 **Leshan.** Leshan is the home of the Giant Buddha, the world's largest Buddhist sculpture, carved into a mountainside.

4 **Songpan.** This historical town, surrounded by rolling grasslands, is known for its diversity, with Tibetan, Qiang, and Hui communities.

5 **Chongqing.** Chongqing is an exploding municipality with more than 30 million residents. Chongqing's meandering alleys will appeal to those who love getting lost in crowded, hilly, and twisting streets.

6 **The Three Gorges.** Riverboat cruises along the Yangtze between narrow cliffs from Fengjie to Yichang offer spectacular scenery.

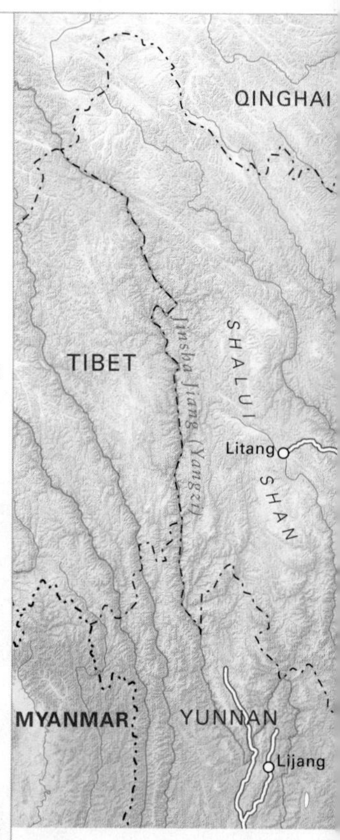

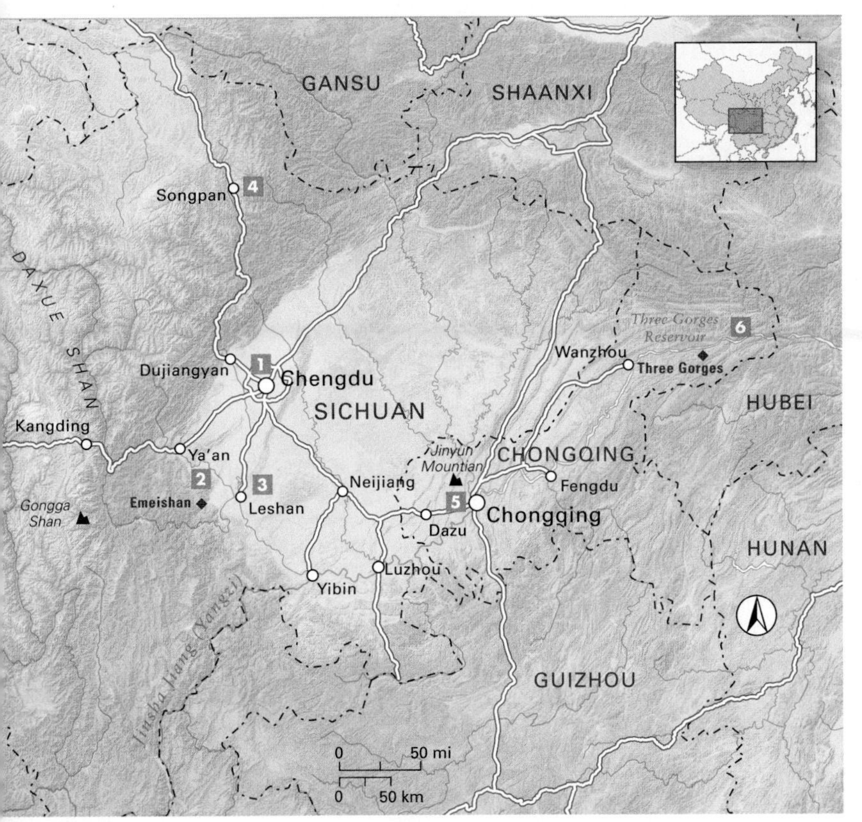
GANSU
SHAANXI
Songpan
4
DAXUE SHAN
Dujiangyan
1
Chengdu
SICHUAN
Kangding
Ya'an
2
Emeishan
3
Leshan
Gongga Shan
Neijiang
Jinyun Mountian
5
Chongqing
Dazu
Yibin
Luzhou
Jinsha Jiang (Yangzi)
CHONGQING
Fengdu
Wanzhou
Three Gorges Reservoir
6
Three Gorges
HUBEI
HUNAN
GUIZHOU
0
50 mi
0
50 km

Renowned for spicy, mouth-numbing cuisine, giant pandas, and subtropical rainforests, Sichuan is one of China's most interesting and influential provinces. Chongqing is known as China's "mountain city." Vast and modern, while still retaining many of its old buildings—for now—Chongqing features a fascinating balance of modern Chinese dynamism and Sichuan spice.

With a population of more than 83 million, Sichuan is known for its people's commitment to leisure. The Sichuan basin, flanked by mountains on all sides, has historically shielded the area from considerable war and conflict. And the soil, some of the most fertile in the country, has created a culture of agriculture that locals are immensely proud of.

Sichuan's cuisine is famous in China for its liberal use of the chili pepper as well as the numbing flavor of the *huajiao*, also known as the Sichuan peppercorn. Popular dishes such as mapo tofu, rabbit head, and the ubiquitous hotpot originated in this part of the country.

The variety of ingredients found in Sichuan cooking are a reflection of the province's diverse topography. The eastern half of Sichuan is dominated by the Sichuan Basin, an area of high agricultural output that in dynastic times was fought over by rival kingdoms. Heading westward, the basin gives way to mountains that become increasingly awe-inspiring as Han Sichuan yields to the province's Tibetan regions.

Sichuan's capital of Chengdu is currently one of the country's most evolving cities. During the day, leisure-loving residents sip on tea and crack sunflower seeds while chatting or playing mahjong. When the sun goes down, there is plenty of amazing food to sample along with one of China's best live music scenes waiting afterward.

Once the capital of Sichuan—and China—the megacity of Chongqing sits to the east of the province and now answers directly to Beijing. With the completion of the Three Gorges Dam, which allows seagoing barges to make it all the way to Chongqing, the city is now changing faster than ever in its new role as Western China's seaport.

MAJOR REGIONS

Chengdu is Sichuan's capital city and famous for it's and culinary scene. The spectacular **Emeishan** is a great place for hiking buffs and **Leshan's** Giant

Buddha is not to be missed. The historic village of **Songpan** is famous for it's diverse communities. The metropolis of **Chongqing** is crowded and hilly, and incredibly charming. **The Three Gorges** riverboat cruises should be on everyone's bucket list.

Planning

When to Go

Chengdu and eastern Sichuan are hot and humid, with temperatures of 35°F to 50°F in winter and 75°F to 85°F in summer. Chongqing, known as one of China's Three Furnaces, is infamous for its broiling summer temperatures—sometimes over 100°F. The western plateau is cold but intensely sunny (bring sunscreen and sunglasses). In winter temperatures drop to –15°F. Summers are around 65°F.

Getting Here and Around

Traveling in and out of Sichuan and Chongqing has never been more convenient. The rapid modernization of the two cities and their surrounding rural areas has changed what was once a difficult area for traveling into a corridor of connectivity within and without the region.

Chengdu and Chongqing are both modern cities with international airports serving regional, national, and international destinations. Since the launch of a high-speed rail link, the two cities are no longer connected by flights. Sichuan Airlines is the largest local airline and serves smaller destinations throughout the province, including Jiuzhaigou. New international routes are constantly being added to Chengdu including direct flights to Bangkok (Thai Airlines), Amsterdam (KLM), Abu Dhabi (Etihad), and Vancouver (Sichuan Airlines).

Taking buses around Sichuan is a convenient and economical option for short-distance travel, including Leshan. It is worth keeping abreast of the weather situation in western Sichuan, as heavy rains in the area can cause large—occasionally fatal—landslides that can close roads for days.

Chengdu and Chongqing are both major hubs in China's national rail network. The two cities are connected by a bullet train that takes about two hours. It's usually possible to buy tickets at the station on the day you want to travel if you don't mind a bit of pushing and long lines. Reserve at least two weeks in advance if you plan to travel during major Chinese holidays. It is highly recommended to avoid travel during the Chinese New Year, usually celebrated each year around late January/early February, as the spectacular crush of people make all forms of travel (planes, trains, and especially buses) difficult and unpleasant.

Restaurants

Eating out in Sichuan and Chongqing can be a boisterous affair, with the tables surrounding you filled with loud, animated diners. Almost anything in these parts comes with some serious spice, so if you can't take the heat it's worthwhile to learn the phrase *bu lade* (boo-lah-duh, meaning "not spicy"). In addition to great Sichuan cuisine, Chengdu and Chongqing also have a growing number of international restaurants.

What It Costs in Yuan

	$	$$	$$$	$$$$
RESTAURANTS				
	under Y50	Y50–Y99	Y100–Y165	over Y165

Hotels

Chinese-run hotels in Sichuan and Chongqing offer adequate accommodations at a reasonable price, but the staff usually won't speak English. There are more and more international five-star hotels in Chengdu and Chongqing. In destinations such as Jiuzhaigou and Ciqikou, guesthouses are also an option. *Hotel reviews have been shortened. For full information, visit Fodors.com.*

What It Costs in Yuan

$	$$	$$$	$$$$
HOTELS			
under Y1,100	Y1,100–Y1,399	Y1,400–Y1,800	over Y1,800

Chengdu

240 km (149 miles; 2 hrs by train) northwest of Chongqing; 1,450 km (900 miles; 25 hrs by train) southwest of Beijing; 1,300 km (806 miles; 27 hrs by train) northwest of Hong Kong.

Home to more than 14 million people, Chengdu is what you want it to be: while some visitors seek out the pulsating nightlife, others are happy to while away the days strolling through the city's many parks or sipping tea and cracking sunflower seeds in one of its multitude of tea gardens.

Upon arrival, you may be a bit disappointed. Much of the traditional architecture of the charming Old Town has been razed to make room for uninspired, communist-era apartment blocks and modern high-rises. The city has been torn in half, literally, for the last several years as new expressways, additional subways lines, a modern airport, and gleaming office towers push locals' tolerance and pollution levels sky-high.

Chuan Chuan Guo

Chuan chuan guo, which translates to skewer hotpot, is a method of hotpot that's unique to Sichuan and Chongqing. Meat, vegetable, and fungi are skewered then boiled tableside in a spicy cauldron. The price of the meal is calculated based on the cumulative weight of the empty skewers.

Despite the rush to modernize, there is still much to see in terms of history and culture. Temples and memorials demonstrate Chengdu's position as the cosmopolitan capital of Western China. The city is also the world's great center for Sichuan cooking, famous for its spicy, mouth-numbing peppers, which many believe to be the best in China. Chengdu has too many good restaurants to list, and the hole-in-the-wall around the corner may serve the tastiest Sichuan dishes you'll eat.

All roads into Southwest China lead through Chengdu. As the gateway to Tibet, this city is the place to secure the permits and supplies needed for your trip there. Journeys south to Yunnan or north to Xi'an pass through here as well. Lying in the middle of Sichuan Province, Chengdu is also a good base for excursions to the scenic spots dotting Sichuan. **■TIP→ Like many big cities in China, Chengdu suffers from pollution. Bring eyedrops, antibacterial wipes, and possibly even a face mask.**

GETTING HERE AND AROUND

Chengdu is the transportation hub of Western China. Bus, train, and plane connections are as convenient as they get in China.

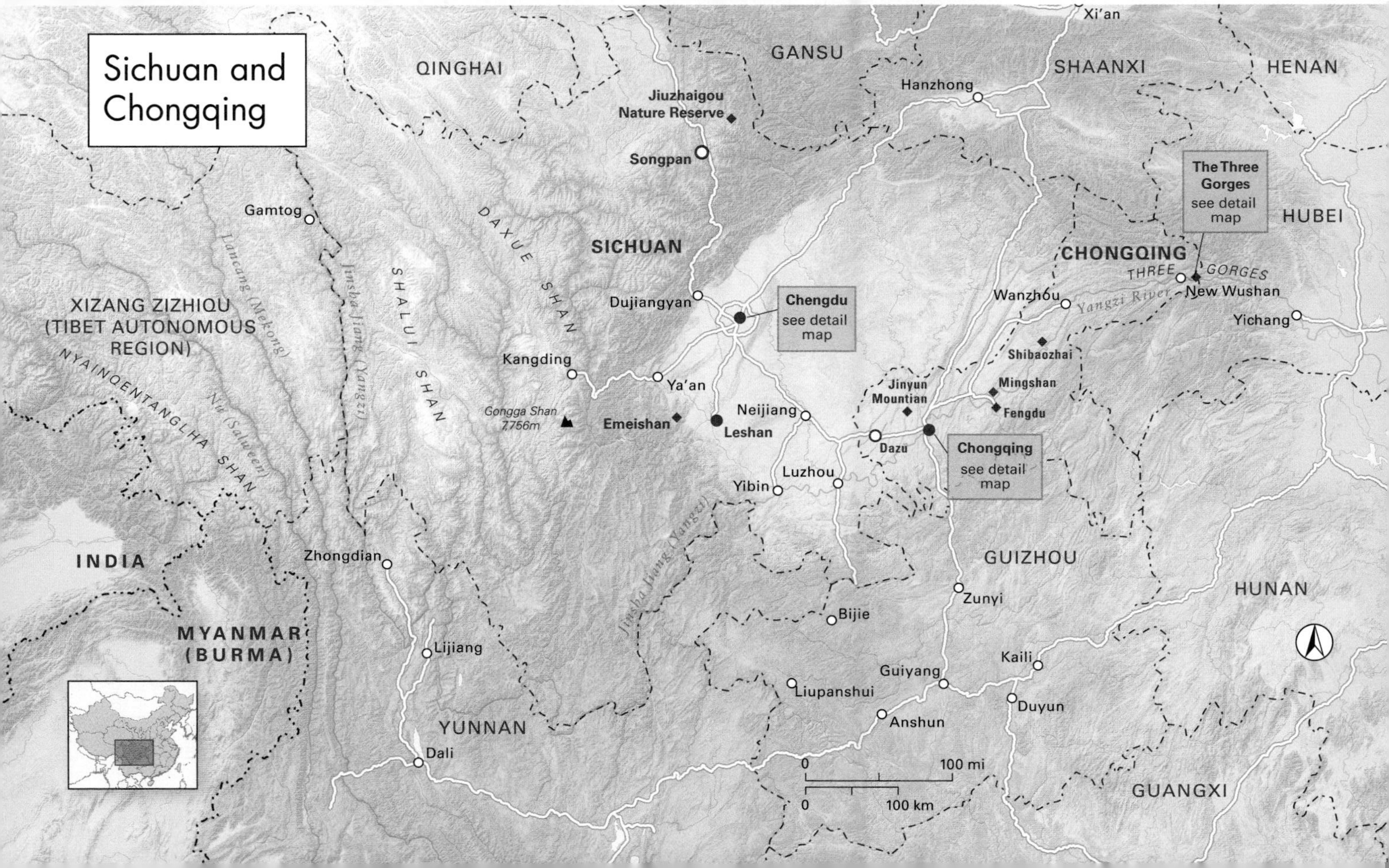

Sichuan and Chongqing
QINGHAI
GANSU
SHAANXI
HENAN
Xi'an
Hanzhong
Jiuzhaigou Nature Reserve
Songpan
Gamtog
DAXUE SHAN
SICHUAN
The Three Gorges see detail map
HUBEI
CHONGQING
THREE GORGES
New Wushan
Yichang
Wanzhou
Yangzi River
XIZANG ZIZHIQU (TIBET AUTONOMOUS REGION)
Lancang (Mekong)
Jinsha Jiang (Yangzi)
SHALUI SHAN
Dujiangyan
Chengdu see detail map
Shibaozhai
Kangding
Ya'an
NYAINQENTANGLHA SHAN
Nu (Salween)
Jinyun Mountian
Mingshan
Fengdu
Gongga Shan 7,756m
Emeishan
Leshan
Neijiang
Dazu
Chongqing see detail map
Luzhou
Yibin
INDIA
Zhongdian
Jinsha Jiang (Yangzi)
GUIZHOU
Zunyi
HUNAN
Bijie
MYANMAR (BURMA)
Lijiang
Kaili
Guiyang
Liupanshui
Duyun
Anshun
YUNNAN
Dali
0
100 mi
0
100 km
GUANGXI

Plight of the Panda

Mysterious, endangered, and cuddly are a few of the monikers typically associated with China's best-known symbol. Given China's recent economic reforms, pandas face a mixed future. On the one hand, economic growth and overpopulation along with polluted air and water sources, are increasingly affecting their habitat. On the other hand, more state and international resources are pouring into special research institutes like Sichuan's Panda Breeding Research Base, which has recently had success in regard to breeding. In addition, China's pandas are now used as political capital through what's being called "Panda Diplomacy" as certain foreign countries preferential to Beijing are being rewarded with a giant panda. What will be the ultimate fate of these stoic creatures? It's hard to say. One thing is certain though: those who visit ecological panda preserves are part of the solution.

Chengdu Shuangliu International Airport (CTU) is about 16 km (10 miles) southwest of the city. From here you can fly to Beijing (2½ hours), Guangzhou (2 hours), Kunming (1 hour), Shanghai (2½ hours), and practically every major domestic destination. Keep in mind Chinese airports, including CTU, has one of the world's worst on-time performance rating records, so it is advised to double-check delays online before heading to the airport. There is an expanding list of international connections.

Bus service links the airport terminal and downtown Chengdu, with Bus 303 traveling to the center of town. Taxis should cost about Y55.

There are three main bus stations in Chengdu. The Xinnanmen Bus Station, in the city center, has buses to almost every town in Sichuan. The Wuguiqiao Bus Station, east of the city, is used mainly for travelers to Chongqing or Yibin. The Chadianzi Bus Station, in the northwestern part of the city, has buses to destinations in the mountains to the north and west (including Jiuzhaigou and Songpan).

Chengdu sits on the Kunming–Beijing railway line, and connections are reliable. A high-speed railway runs between Shanghai and Chengdu, traveling through Nanjing and Wuhan and reaching speeds of 350 kph (217 mph). The Chengdu Railway Station is in the northern part of the city. The Chengdu East Railway Station, accessible by subway Line 2, is where all the bullet trains arrive and depart. It's a Y20 cab ride from Tianfu Plaza.

Chengdu is built along a main north–south artery and surrounded by three ring roads. Cheap taxis (flag fall starts at Y9, or Y10 from 10 pm until 6 am) and the ever-expanding subway system are the best ways to get around (fares range depending on distance traveled, starting at Y2). If you are on foot, many of the city's sights are within walking distance of Tian Fu Plaza.

TIMING

Chengdu deserves at least a few days, but travelers coming from remote areas of China may wish to stay longer to take a break in the city's increasingly cosmopolitan atmosphere.

TOURS

A good resource for package and individual food-focused tours in Chengdu and throughout Sichuan is Chengdu Food Tours.

Sights

Du Fu's Thatched Cottage Museum (杜甫草堂 *Dùfǔ Cǎotáng*)
FOREST | This museum is named for the famous poet Du Fu (AD 712–770) of the Tang Dynasty, whose poetry continues to be read today. A Manchurian, he came to Chengdu from Xi'an and built a small hut overlooking the bamboo and plum tree–lined Huanhua River. During the four years he spent here he wrote more than 240 poems. After his death the area became a garden; a temple was then added during the Northern Song Dynasty (960–1126). A replica of his cottage now stands among several other structures, all built during the Qing Dynasty. Some of Du Fu's calligraphy and poems are on display here. ✉ *37 Qinghua Rd.* ☎ *028/8731–9258* 🎫 *Y60.*

Giant Panda Breeding Research Base (大熊猫博物馆 *Dàxióngmào Fánzhí Yánjiū Zhōngxīn*)
ZOO | **FAMILY** | The Giant Panda Breeding Research Base is worth the 45-minute drive (from the center of Chengdu) to walk the peaceful bamboo groves, snap pictures of the lolling pandas, and catch a glimpse of the tiny baby pandas that are born with startling regularity. Crews of scientists help pandas breed and care for the young in a safe, controlled environment. ■ **TIP→ Visit early in the morning, when the pandas are most active.** To get here, book a driver through your hotel for Y300 to Y400 round-trip. A taxi will cost about Y80 each way depending how well you bargain. ✉ *26 Jiefang Rd.* ☎ *028/8351–0033* 🌐 *www.panda.org.cn/english* 🎫 *Y58.*

Qingyang Gong (青羊宫 *Qīngyáng gōng*)
RELIGIOUS SITE | Built during the Tang Dynasty, Qingyang Gong is the oldest Taoist temple in the city, and one of the most famous in China. Six courtyards open out onto each other before arriving at the sculptures of two goats, which represent one of the earthly incarnations of Lao Tzu (the legendary founder of Taoism). If you arrive midmorning, you can watch the day's first worshippers before the stampede of afternoon pilgrims. The temple grounds are filled with nuns and monks training at the Two Immortals Monastery, the only such facility in Southwest China. A small teahouse is on the premises. ✉ *37 Qinghua Rd.* ☎ *028/6892–1800* 🌐 *www.cddfct.com/* 🎫 *Y5.*

★ **Tibetan Quarter** (小拉萨 *Xiǎolásà*)
MARKET | Chengdu's tiny Tibetan Quarter is a fascinating place to explore. Shop for colorful Tibetan clothing and art, including religious objects such wooden beads, Buddhist prayer flags, and Tibetan scrolls. Make sure to bargain hard. If you can't make it to Tibet, stop for a cup of salty butter yak milk tea at one of the many restaurants lining the main drag. ✉ *Wuhuoci Heng St., Wu Hou Ci.*

★ **Wangjianglou Pavilion Park (Bamboo Park)** (望江楼公园 *Wàngjiāng Lóu Gōngyuán*)
VIEWPOINT | The four-story wooden pavilion in Wangjianglou Pavilion Park, dating from the Qing Dynasty, offers splendid views of the Fu River. The poet Xue Tao, who lived in Chengdu during the Tang Dynasty, was said to have spent time near the river, from which she apparently drew water to make paper for her poems. The pavilion stands amid more than 200 species of bamboo, a plant revered by the poet. ■ **TIP→ A perfect place to stroll early mornings while the older population practice tai chi and the "Chinese yo-yo."** Don't rush out before enjoying a cup of inexpensive, Y10, Mao Feng green tea (a local specialty grown in the nearby mountains). It is the perfect escape to the messy city! ✉ *30 Wangjiang Rd.* ☎ *028/8522–3389* 🌐 *www.wangjianglou.com* 🎫 *Y20.*

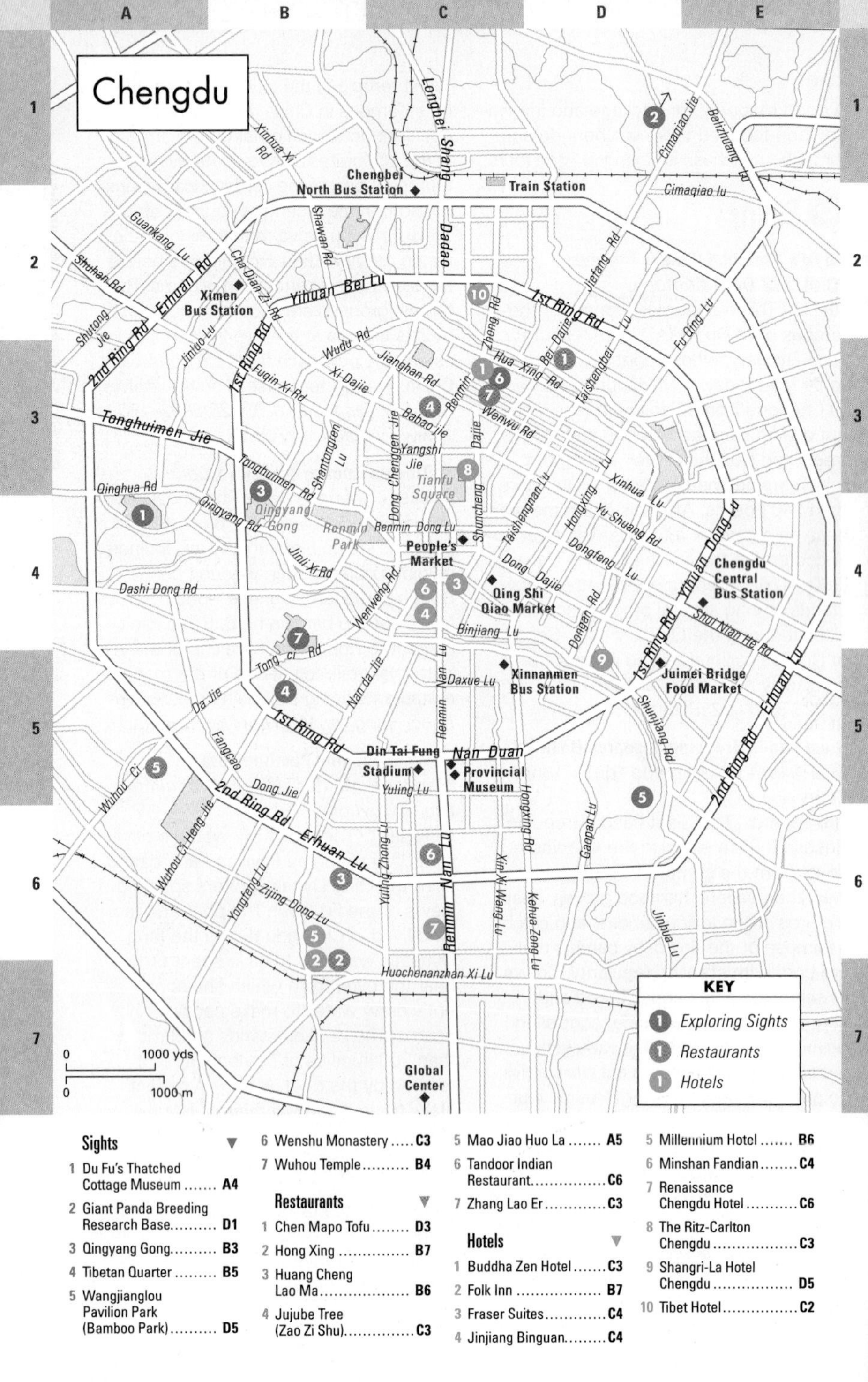

Chengdu
A
B
C
D
E
1
2
3
4
5
6
7
Chengbei North Bus Station
Train Station
Ximen Bus Station
People's Market
Qing Shi Qiao Market
Chengdu Central Bus Station
Xinnanmen Bus Station
Juimei Bridge Food Market
Din Tai Fung
Stadium
Provincial Museum
Global Center
Tianfu Square
Renmin Park
Qingyang Gong
Longbei Shang Dadao
Yihuan Bei Lu
1st Ring Rd
2nd Ring Rd Erhuan Rd
2nd Ring Rd Erhuan Lu
Renmin Nan Lu
Nan Duan
Tonghuimen Jie
Huochenanzhan Xi Lu
Cimaqiao Jie
Cimaqiao lu
Xinhua Lu
Dong Dajie
Binjiang Lu
Daxue Lu
KEY
Exploring Sights
Restaurants
Hotels
0 1000 yds
0 1000 m
Sights
1 Du Fu's Thatched Cottage Museum A4
2 Giant Panda Breeding Research Base.......... D1
3 Qingyang Gong.......... B3
4 Tibetan Quarter B5
5 Wangjianglou Pavilion Park (Bamboo Park).......... D5
6 Wenshu Monastery..... C3
7 Wuhou Temple.......... B4
Restaurants
1 Chen Mapo Tofu........ D3
2 Hong Xing B7
3 Huang Cheng Lao Ma.................. B6
4 Jujube Tree (Zao Zi Shu)............... C3
5 Mao Jiao Huo La A5
6 Tandoor Indian Restaurant................ C6
7 Zhang Lao Er............ C3
Hotels
1 Buddha Zen Hotel....... C3
2 Folk Inn B7
3 Fraser Suites............ C4
4 Jinjiang Binguan......... C4
5 Millennium Hotel B6
6 Minshan Fandian........ C4
7 Renaissance Chengdu Hotel........... C6
8 The Ritz-Carlton Chengdu C3
9 Shangri-La Hotel Chengdu D5
10 Tibet Hotel............... C2

The Wenshu Monastery in Chengdu

★ Wenshu Monastery (文殊院 *Wénshū Yuàn*)

RELIGIOUS SITE | Named after Manjusri, the bodhisattva of transcendent wisdom, Wenshu Monastery is one of the most important (and well-preserved) Zen Buddhist monasteries in China, and has been around almost as long as the religion itself. It was originally constructed during the Sui Dynasty, around the same time as Zen Buddhism's emergence in China. The monastery and accompanying temples have since been destroyed several times, most notably during the Ming Dynasty, after which the monks are said to have continued sitting among the ruins chanting sutras. It is notable for hundreds of antique statues crafted from a variety of materials that have survived upheavals of times past better than the actual buildings. The attractive 11-tiered Thousand Buddha Peace Pagoda is actually a rather late addition—it was built in 1988 based off an original Sui Dynasty pagoda. The on-site tea garden is a great place to relax in the afternoon. ✉ *15 Wenshu Yuan St., off Renmin Middle Rd.* 🎫 *Free.*

Wuhou Temple (武侯祠 *Wǔhòu cí*)

MUSEUM | The Temple complex houses the **Zhuge Liang Memorial Hall Museum,** a shrine to the heroes that made the Shu Kingdom legendary during the Three Kingdoms Period. The temple here was constructed in AD 221 to entomb the earthly remains of Shu Emperor Liu Bei. During the Ming Dynasty, Liu Bei's subjects were also housed here, most notably Zhuge Liang. Liu Bei's most trusted adviser during the Three Kingdoms Period, Zhuge Liang is a legendary figure in Sichuan, and in some respects more honored than his master. The temple burned during the wars that toppled the Ming Dynasty and was rebuilt in 1671–72 during the Qing Dynasty. The main shrine, Zhaolie Temple, is dedicated to Liu Bei; the rear shrine, Wu Hou Temple, to Zhuge Liang. There is also the Sworn Brotherhood Shrine, which commemorates Liu Bei, Zhang Fei, and Guan Yu's "Oath in the Peach Garden." The Sichuan Opera performs here nightly from 7:30 to 10. The Y180 ticket is expensive, but the face-changing, fire-breathing, lyre-playing ensemble may help justify the price tag. ✉ *231 Wuhou Ci Da St.* ☎ *028/8555–2397* 🌐 *www.wuhouci.net.cn* 🎫 *Y60.*

Restaurants

Chen Mapo Tofu (陈麻婆豆腐 *Chén má pó dòufu*)
$ | CHINESE | This is the original mapo tofu shop, first invented by a lady whose surname was Chen. Mapo tofu is a classic Sichuanese dish, which features cubes of silken tofu topped with spicy ground pork and fermented fava bean paste. **Known for:** history; family-style dishes; fast casual vibes. $ *Average main: Y10* ✉ *179 Yulong Rd.* ☎ *028/8675–4512.*

Hong Xing (红杏酒家 *Hǒngxìng jiǔ jià*)
$$ | SICHUAN | Eat like a local at Hong Xing, where Sichuan cuisine is done consistently well. Favorites on offer include eggplant with garlic and ginger, pork with peanuts and peppers, or the house signature dish called Hong Xing Ji, which is tender bits of chicken floating in a sea of sesame oil topped with peanuts and mouth-numbing pebbles of Sichuan peppercorns. **Known for:** spicy cuisine; lots of veggies; poultry dishes. $ *Average main: Y80* ✉ *137 Ziwei Dong Lu* ☎ *028/8517–5388* 💳 *No credit cards.*

Huang Cheng Lao Ma (皇城老妈 *Huàng chéng lǎo mǎ*)
$$$ | SICHUAN | Run by artists, this amazing restaurant occupies a massive brick-and-stone building with sculpted pillars flanking either side and a facade depicting scenes from old Chengdu. The hotpot comes in the traditional spicy varieties, as well as a *qing tang,* or "soft soup," style without the spices. **Known for:** tongue-numbing spice; decor; artsy vibes. $ *Average main: Y100* ✉ *20 3rd Section, 2nd Ring Rd., Wu Hou Ci* ☎ *028/8513–9999* 🌐 *www.hclm.net* 💳 *No credit cards.*

Jujube Tree (Zao Zi Shu) (枣子树 *Zǎo zǐ shù*)
$$$ | CHINESE | All famous Chinese dishes can be found on this restaurant's user-friendly picture menu, from Peking duck to Sichuan numbing peppercorns and chicken. Well, mock chicken, but it tastes so close to real chicken, and sometimes better, even the biggest carnivore would enjoy dining here. **Known for:** diverse dishes; spicy cuisine; impeccable interior. $ *Average main: Y120* ✉ *27 Qinglong St., Qingyang District* ☎ *028/8628–2848* 💳 *No credit cards.*

Mao Jiao Huo La (冒椒火辣 *Mào jiāo huǒ là*)
$$ | CHINESE | This is a chuan chuan restaurant, which is meat on skewers cooked in a hotpot. It's a family-style affair with everyone boiling their food tableside in a cauldron of spicy chili oil. **Known for:** superspicy; cheap; fun vibe. $ *Average main: Y80* ✉ *33 Kuixinglou St.* ☎ *028/8005–5358* 🌐 *www.mjhl1986.com* 💳 *No credit cards.*

Tandoor Indian Restaurant (天都里印度餐厅 *tiǎndù lǐ índù cǎi*)
$$$ | INDIAN | Just a couple of blocks southwest from the American Consulate and across the street from the Bookworm Cafe, this northern Indian restaurant serves Chengdu's best Indian fare. The decor, a sophisticated combination of wood and mirrors, makes a meal here seem like a special occasion. **Known for:** great roti; meat platters; unique interior. $ *Average main: Y100* ✉ *34 S. Renmin Rd., 4th Section, behind Sunjoy Inn, Wu Hou Ci* ☎ *028/8555–1958.*

Zhang Lao Er (张老二 *Zhāng lǎo èr*)
$ | CHINESE | Located next to the Wenshu Monastery, Chengshi Liangfen has been doling out street snacks since 1944. Their claim to fame is the tian shui mian, or sweet water noodles. **Known for:** historical vibes; noodles; quick service. $ *Average main: Y6* ✉ *39 Wenshuyuan St.* 💳 *No credit cards.*

Chengdu's Green Tea

Not many people know that some of the best green tea comes from the mountains of western Sichuan. In Chengdu, the art of drinking tea is taken very seriously and almost every local is passionate about their chosen favorite leaf.

Chengdu's most celebrated green tea, grown row upon row on Sichuan's Emei Mountain (Emeishan), is called Zhuye qing (Bamboo Leaf Green). Slightly bitter, crisp, and earthy in flavor, Zhu Ye Qing is also the name of a ritzy tea franchise with several outlets in Chengdu and generous sample tastings.

If you want to sample some good tea, head to People's Park, Wenshu Temple, or the recently redeveloped *kuan xiangzi* and *zhai xiangzi* (wide and narrow alley) area. Another interesting experience is to wander the fragrant alleys of Chengdu's Northside Tea Market (五块石茶叶市场 Wǔkuàishí cháyè shìchǎng), a wholesale tea market featuring tea from all over China along with an incredible selection of tea utensils including teapots, pickers, boilers, scoopers, and patterned glasses. You'll no doubt be invited to sample a variety of different teas. Remember that buying is optional, and bargaining is expected and part of the fun.

Hotels

Buddha Zen Hotel (成都圆和圆佛禅文化酒店 *fóshēnwénhuà jiǔdiàn*)
$ | **HOTEL** | Drawing inspiration from the nearby Wenshu Zen Buddhist monastery, this boutique hotel has carefully designed antique wooden decorations, a peaceful courtyard, wonderful staff, and good food. **Pros:** good location; crisp service; reasonable prices. **Cons:** street can be noisy; hard beds; difficult to find. *Rooms from: Y700 ✉ B6–6 Wenshu Fang, near Wenshu Temple ☎ 028/8692–9898 🌐 www.buddhazenhotel.com 35 rooms No meals.*

Folk Inn (同档次酒店)
$ | **HOTEL** | In the southern part of Chengdu near leafy Shen Xi'an Shu Park, this boutique hotel has temple-style architecture and antique wooden furniture that give it plenty of character. **Pros:** plenty of charm; reasonable rates; near a pretty park. **Cons:** staff doesn't speak English; hard beds; far from downtown. *Rooms from: Y400 ✉ 63 Shenxianshu South Rd. ☎ 028/8123–8888 110 rooms No meals.*

Fraser Suites (成都仁恒辉盛阁国际公寓 *Rèn héng huī shèng gé guǒ jī góng yǔ*)
$$$ | **HOTEL** | This ritzy hotel has all of the amenities of a service apartment complete with plush sofas and wide balconies. **Pros:** great location; luxe rooms; English-speaking staff. **Cons:** expensive rates; lack of dining options; balconies have to be unlocked to use. *Rooms from: Y1500 ✉ 111 Zhihui St. ☎ 028/8516–6999 🌐 chengdu.frasershospitality.com 360 rooms Breakfast.*

Jinjiang Binguan (锦江宾馆 *Jǐnjiāng bīngguǎn*)
$ | **HOTEL** | For years this was the city's best hotel—foreign dignitaries and bigwigs from Beijing could always be found milling around the lobby. **Pros:** great riverside location; large rooms; next to subway. **Cons:** no longer the best in town; near heavy traffic; pricey. *Rooms from: Y900 ✉ 80 Renmin Nan Rd., 2nd Section ☎ 028/8550–6666 🌐 www.jjhotel.com 456 rooms No meals.*

Millennium Hotel (新东万千喜大酒店 *Xín dǒng wān qián huàn dàjiǔdiàn*)
$$ | **HOTEL** | Located south of the city center in the Tongzilin residential district, this hotel faces a slender park that's a great place to watch elderly couples practice tai chi while their grandchildren fly homemade kites. **Pros:** great amenities; adjoining multilevel Starbucks Coffee; peaceful location. **Cons:** disappointing breakfast buffet; long waits for taxis; small rooms. *Rooms from: Y1100 ✉ 41 Shenxianshu Rd. ☎ 028/8512–7777 🌐 www.millenniumhotels.com.cn 359 rooms All meals.*

Minshan Fandian (岷山饭店 *Mĭnshānfàndiàn*)
$ | **HOTEL** | This elegant hotel seems out to prove a point: a locally owned lodging can match and even outdo the international chains. **Pros:** great value; excellent service; city center. **Cons:** noisy streets outside; staff has minimal English; mediocre breakfast. *Rooms from: Y800 ✉ 55 Renmin South Rd., 2nd Section ☎ 028/8558–3333 🌐 www.minshan.com.cn 383 rooms No meals.*

Renaissance Chengdu Hotel (万丽酒店)
$ | **HOTEL** | Located in close proximity to the airport, this hotel is a solid option for business travelers. **Pros:** location; English-speaking staff; spa amenities. **Cons:** worn facilities; not near temples and other tourist attractions; spotty service at times. *Rooms from: Y1000 ✉ 48 S. Renmin Rd., 4th Section, Wu Hou Ci ☎ 028/8887–8888 🌐 www.marriott.com 368 rooms Breakfast.*

The Ritz-Carlton Chengdu (成都富力丽思卡尔顿酒店)
$$$ | **HOTEL** | Conveniently located right next to Tianfu Square, the Ritz is one of the poshest hotels in the city and has great dining options, spacious rooms, and a luxurious spa. **Pros:** great dining options; very comfortable rooms; luxe. **Cons:** loud; not located near any other "foreign" friendly dining; expensive. *Rooms from: Y1800 ✉ 269 Shuncheng Ave., Qingyang District ☎ 28/8358–8888 🌐 www.ritzcarlton.com 353 rooms Breakfast; All meals.*

★ **Shangri-La Hotel Chengdu** (香格里拉大酒店 *xiāng gē lí là dàjiǔdiàn*)
$$$ | **HOTEL** | Opulent style and exceptional service are hallmarks of the Singapore-based Shangri-La chain, and the Chengdu property delivers both. **Pros:** great service; good restaurants; soothing spa. **Cons:** slightly inconvenient location; aging a bit; breakfast service is spotty. *Rooms from: Y1400 ✉ 9 Binjiang Dong Rd. ☎ 028/8888–9999 🌐 www.shangri-la.com 593 rooms All-inclusive.*

Tibet Hotel (成都西藏饭店)
$ | **HOTEL** | Located near the train station, this inexpensive Tibet-themed hotel is a good option for those planning trips to Tibet. **Pros:** good value; handy travel office; convenient location. **Cons:** far from many dining and nightlife areas; no Tibetan food; minimal English. *Rooms from: Y380 ✉ 10 Renmin North Rd. ☎ 028/8318–3388, 800/886–5333 🌐 www.tibet-hotel.com 260 rooms No meals.*

Nightlife

Bookworm (老书虫咖啡 *Lǎoshùchóng*)
BARS/PUBS | South of the U.S. Consulate you'll find the Bookworm, a relaxed haven for thousands of the city's expats to drink, eat, and browse through more than 1,000 books. It doubles as a library, bar, and café. An annual literary festival (usually held in March) draws famous authors like humorist David Sedaris. The Worm is also a great place to enjoy a pint of Guinness or decent imported wine as well as decent Western and Asian dishes. *✉ Yujie Dong Jie 2–7, off Renmin South Rd. ☎ 028/8552–0117 🌐 www.chengdubookworm.com.*

Kuan Zhai Xiang Zi (Wide and Narrow Alleys) (宽窄巷子)
BARS/PUBS | The gentrified ancient alleys of the Qing Dynasty is now a walking street packed with restaurants, bars, shops, and one of the city's many Starbucks outlets—all built in a traditional Chinese style. It is popular among tourists and locals alike. Chengdu has an increasingly chic and sophisticated bar scene, with more Western-style establishments serving high-quality beer, wine, and mixed drinks. Although the priciest drinks in the city, it is all set in a beautiful setting. ✉ *Kuan Zhai Xiang Zi.*

Underground Pub (随到酒吧 *Suì dǎo*)
BARS/PUBS | Tucked away in Jiu Yan Qiao, one of the city's biggest areas for nightclubs, this small and smoky British-owned bar draws in a good mix of young locals and expats. The beer list is constantly expanding, and offers Chengdu's largest selection of Belgian beers. The place is also gay friendly. ✉ *Tai Ping Nan Xin Jie, Jiu Yan Qiao* ☎ *028/135–4022–1774* 🌐 *www.undergroundchengdu.com.*

Shopping

New Century Global Centre (世界纪的全球中心)
SHOPPING CENTERS/MALLS | Nothing says modern China quite like this gigantic superstructure currently holding the "biggest free-standing building in the world" title. China is no stranger to superlatives and this stands as a reminder by the government of just how economically powerful China, and particularly Chengdu, has become. One can shop, sleep, swim, and ice skate without leaving. The Paradise Island Water Park even provides artificial sunlight. The massive structure designed by a British-Iraqi architect has also become a huge embarrassment to the Communist Party due to reminders of the widespread corruption, as the billionaire financier was convicted of embezzlement and since vanished. ✉ *1700 Tianfu Ave. N.*

Emeishan's Tea 

Emeishan is part of a range that stretches from Ya'an in the north to Xichang in the south. These mountains produce some of the world's best green tea. Emei's local tea is called Zhu Ye Qing (Jade Bamboo Leaf), and there are several types and grades. It's possible to buy organic Zhu Ye Qing around the mountain and in more than a dozen ultrasleek shops in Chengdu.

Song Xian Qiao Antique and Art Market (送仙桥 *Sóng xiān qiǎo*)
ANTIQUES/COLLECTIBLES | A good place to shop for souvenirs is Song Xian Qiao Antique City, the country's second-largest antiques market, with more than 500 separate stalls selling everything from Mao-era currency to fake Buddha statues to wonderful watercolor paintings. It's near Du Fu's Cottage and Wu Hou Temple. The market does not get into full swing until late morning. There are several noodle shops and teahouses surrounding the market and river. **Always counter offer with less than half the asking price and proceed from there.** ✉ *416 Qingyang Shang Jie.*

Emeishan

100 km (62 miles) southwest of Chengdu.

This 10,000-foot mountain is a famous Buddhist pilgrimage site, dotted with temples. You can hike the 25 miles of stone staircase to the Golden Summit of Emeishan in two to three days. It's a difficult climb—the stairs up the mountain somehow make it seem more arduous. On the first day, hike until a bit before nightfall and walk into one of the temples along the way to sleep for Y20 to Y40 per person. Most hikers can reach the summit by nightfall of the second day or sometime on the third day. Stay a night near the top of the mountain and rise early: the clouds that often obscure views during the day are bathed in a breathtaking amber color at sunrise.

The most common route to the top is past Long Life Monastery. This route takes you past the Elephant Bathing Pool, once used by Bodhisattva Puxian to wash the grime off his white elephant. Once you ascend from here you will be mostly free of the madding crowd. A recommended route down is the long shoulder of the mountain past Magic Peak Monastery, where the scenery is beyond compare. Sharing a simple meal with monks in the courtyard and then staying the night in the monastery is magical.

For an easier pilgrimage, take advantage of the Y40 minibus service from the Mount Emeishan Tourist Transportation Center below Declare Nation Temple up to the Leidong Terraces, from where your climb will take about two hours. To avoid climbing altogether, ride the cable car (Y120 round-trip) to the summit from Jieyin Dian.

Regardless how you ascend, the best times to climb are in the spring or fall. Bring a change of clothes for the sweaty part of the journey and a warm jacket for the summit. Water and food are available on the mountain, carried by pipe-puffing porters to the stalls along the way.

GETTING HERE AND AROUND

Most people get to Emeishan Town via a shuttle bus from Chengdu or Leshan, but you can also take the train. The trip from Chengdu takes about two to three hours by bus or a little bit more than an hour by high-speed train. Inexpensive public buses travel between destinations, but schedules vary and stops are often unmarked.

There are departures from Chengdu's Xinnanmen station every half hour and from Leshan every hour on the hour between 7 am and 6 pm. One-way tickets cost between Y35 and Y45, and the trip takes two hours. Also departing from Leshan are buses that travel directly to Emeishan's Baoguo Si. They depart every half hour between 9 and 5 for about Y10.

Most buses coming from Chengdu and Leshan bypass Emei altogether and head directly for the base of the mountain.

You can take a high-speed train from Chengdu East or Chengdu South Station to Emeishan; it takes a little bit over an hour and is around Y65.

TIMING

Climbing the mountain from base to peak and back again can take anywhere from three to six days, depending on your fitness level. A day of relaxation and recovery for tender joints and muscles will likely be in order afterward. Taking a shuttle bus most of the way and then transferring to a chairlift requires as little as a day.

Sights

Emeishan (峨眉山 *Éméi shān*)
FOREST | The 10,000-foot-high Emeishan (literally translated as Lofty Eyebrow Mountain) in southern Sichuan is one of China's holiest Buddhist pilgrimage sites. The temples here survived the Cultural Revolution better than most others in China, due in part to courageous monks. Still, of the hundreds of temples that once were found here, only 20 remain. Today it is one of the better-known tourist attractions in the country. ■ **TIP→ A bamboo walking stick is very useful when ascending the mountain. It's also a good way to scare off the fearless gangs of Tibetan macaques that inhabit the area.** ✣ *4 miles from Emeishan City.*

The Wannian monastery at Emeishan

Restaurants

Emei Kaoyu (峨眉烤鱼 *Éméi kăo yú*)
$ | **SICHUAN** | Set among several other decent restaurants on "Good Eats Street," Emei Kaoyu lays out a variety of fresh dishes every day, including fiddlehead ferns fried with local bacon. Simply choose your vegetable and protein of choice, and the cooks will turn them into delicious stir-fries. **Known for:** cheap prices; fresh vegetables; grilled fish. *Average main: Y35* *Haochi Jie* *138/0813–5338* *No credit cards.*

Hotels

Baoguo Monastery (报国寺 *Bàoguó sì*)
$ | **HOTEL** | This monastery at the foot of the mountain is one of the many accommodations available to those journeying to the Golden Summit. **Pros:** monastic experience; handy location; reasonable rates. **Cons:** pretty basic; rooms can get a bit chilly; limited English. *Rooms from: Y75* *Baoguo Si* *No credit cards* *30 rooms* *No meals.*

Teddy Bear Hotel (小熊咖啡 *Xiăoxióng kāfēi*)
$ | **HOTEL** | The Teddy Bear is one of the few hotels in town with an English-speaking staff. **Pros:** free maps and information; congenial owners; photogenic. **Cons:** hard beds; no-smoking areas are not enforced; bathrooms are slightly dirty. *Rooms from: Y250* *43 Baoguosi Lu* *0833/559–0135* *No credit cards* *40 rooms* *No meals.*

Leshan

165 km (102 miles; 3 hrs by bus) south of Chengdu.

Leshan is famous for the Great Buddha, carved into the mountainside at the confluence of the Dadu, Qingyi, and Min rivers. The Great Buddha—a UNESCO World Heritage Site—was initiated by the monk Haitong in 713, but he didn't live to see its completion in 803. The statue, blissfully reclining, has overlooked the swirling, choppy waters for 1,200 years and is the world's largest Buddhist sculpture.

Did You Know?

The Giant Buddha of Leshan has a sophisticated, built-in drainage system of hidden gutters and channels embedded on the head, arms, behind the ears, and in the clothes. This helps displace rainwater and cut back on erosion.

GETTING HERE AND AROUND

Leshan-bound buses leave from Chengdu's Xinnanmen station every 30 minutes between 7:30 and 7:30. Buses from Chongqing leave every hour from 6:30 to 6:30. From Leshan's Xiao Ba Bus Station, take public bus Line 13 directly to the Great Buddha's main gate.

The high speed train trip between Chengdu and Leshan takes between 46 minutes to 1½ hours and costs around Y54.

TIMING

One day is sufficient to see the Buddha and the surrounding park and pavilions.

Sights

Giant Buddha (乐山大佛极 *Dàfó*)
PUBLIC ART | Rising 233 feet, this is the tallest stone Buddha and among the tallest sculptures in the world. The big toes are each 28 feet long. A monk who wished to placate the rivers that habitually took local fishermen's lives started the construction of the Giant Buddha in AD 713. The project took more than 90 years to complete, and it had no noticeable effect on the waters. It's possible to clamber, via a stairway hewn out of rock, down to the platform where the feet rest. ✉ *Leshan* ☎ *0833/230–2121* 🎫 *Y90.*

Wu You Temple (乌尤寺 *Wūyóu Sì*)
RELIGIOUS SITE | There are several temples and pagodas in the park that houses the Giant Buddha, including this Ming Dynasty structure with a commanding view of the city. You might find yourself staring at the lifelike figures and wondering about the people who served as the models. ✉ *Leshan* 🎫 *Y90, includes Giant Buddha.*

Restaurants

Deng Qiang (邓强饭店 *Dèngqiǎng fàndiàn*)
$$ | **SICHUAN** | **FAMILY** | This always-packed family-run restaurant near the river is only a five-minute walk from the Giant Buddha. Local Sichuan dishes, including Leshan's famous cold chicken in a spicy sauce can be sampled here. **Known for:** convenient location; poultry dishes; spicy food. $ *Average main: Y50* ✉ *158 Binjiang Lu Xia Duan* ☎ *0833/212–5110* 💳 *No credit cards.*

Songpan

350 km (217 miles; 8–10 hrs by bus) northwest of Chengdu.

Songpan has experienced quite a mini-construction boom over the past decade, with better transport connections and more accommodation options offering travelers a bit of comfort along with plenty of fresh mountain air. The ancient village of Songpan was once an important military post built during the Tang Dynasty (AD 618–907). Although horseback riding through the surrounding countryside is the major draw, Songpan's unique mix of Tibetan, Qiang, Han, and Hui cultures provides plenty of local color. The charming Old Town features ornate gates, bridges, and old wooden buildings and is the perfect place to stock up on Tibetan-inspired souvenirs such as carved knives, turquoise-beaded jewelry, leather bridles, and handmade woolen blankets.

GETTING HERE AND AROUND

Don't be fooled by the name of Songpan's Jiuzhaigou Huanglong Airport—it's about 88 km (55 miles) from Jiuzhaigou. Aggressive cabbies compete to take you on the 60-minute trip to Songpan (Y100).

Buses from Chengdu's Chadianzi bus station shuttle passengers daily (eight hours), with several buses departing between 6:30 am and 9:30 am. Tickets cost Y123. From Songpan to Jiuzhaigou it's another two to three hours. Tickets cost Y28.

Restaurants

Emma's Kitchen
$ | **CHINESE** | On the main drag not far from the bus station, Emma's Kitchen serves both Western and Chinese fare. The prices are reasonable, and the very friendly staff speaks English. **Known for:** Western food; English-speaking staff; coffee. *Average main: Y40* *Main road, near bus station* *0837/723–1088* *No credit cards.*

Old House Hotel (古韻客棧 *Gŭyùnkèzhàn*)
$ | **B&B/INN** | Also known as the Guyun Inn, this guesthouse has a café with good coffee and online access. **Pros:** convenient location; helpful staff. **Cons:** small rooms. *Rooms from: Y130* *Shunjiang North Rd., near bus station* *0837/723–1368* *No credit cards* *15 rooms* *No meals.*

Chongqing

240 km (149 miles; 4 hrs by bus) southeast of Chengdu; 1,800 km (1,116 miles; 3 hrs by plane) southwest of Beijing; 1,025 km (636 miles; 34 hrs by train) northwest of Hong Kong.

With a layout reminiscent of Hong Kong and a distinct Sichuanese vibe, Chongqing is one of the most interesting and dynamic cities in Western China. The "Mountain City," as it is known, is much more three-dimensional than your average Chinese metropolis, so prepare for plenty of hills and stairs. By Western standards, Chongqing is not a sophisticated place, and this is precisely the reason it is so captivating. Wander off the main pedestrian and shopping drags, get lost in its alleys and local neighborhoods, and dive right in. One of the world's most massive cities, Chongqing is raw and unforgiving. If you want a taste of the real modern China, skip dressed-up Shanghai and sanitized Beijing and head directly into the beating heart of the dragon.

Did You Know?

Chongqing is the heart of the Ba Yu Culture—vibrant, colorful, and proud—with its own version of Sichuan Opera, its own cuisine, and a history of rebelliousness. The Chongqingese are known for their directness and fiery tempers.

The central peninsula area of Yuzhong District, between the Jialing River to the north and the Yangtze River to the south, is the most interesting and dynamic area of Chongqing. Within Yuzhong, most of the action is centered around the Jiefang Bei (Liberation Monument) area, where you will find the bulk of Chongqing's top hotels, restaurants, bars, and clubs. It is essential to wander off Jiefang Bei to immerse yourself in this thriving metropolis.

GETTING HERE AND AROUND

Chongqing is smack-dab in the middle of China, connected by rail, bus, and plane to every major city in the country. Chongqing's Jiangbei International Airport is among the busiest in the region, with daily flights to all major cities in China. For trips to Chengdu, the high-speed rail link is the best bet.

Chongqing's light-rail line from the city center to the zoo in the south is worth the Y10 round-trip ticket price. The two stations in the city center (Jiao Chang Kou and Lin Jiang Men) are easily accessible from Jiefang Bei. The line curves north to the Jialing River—above ground—and goes through six riverside stations before it heads south to the terminal station at the zoo.

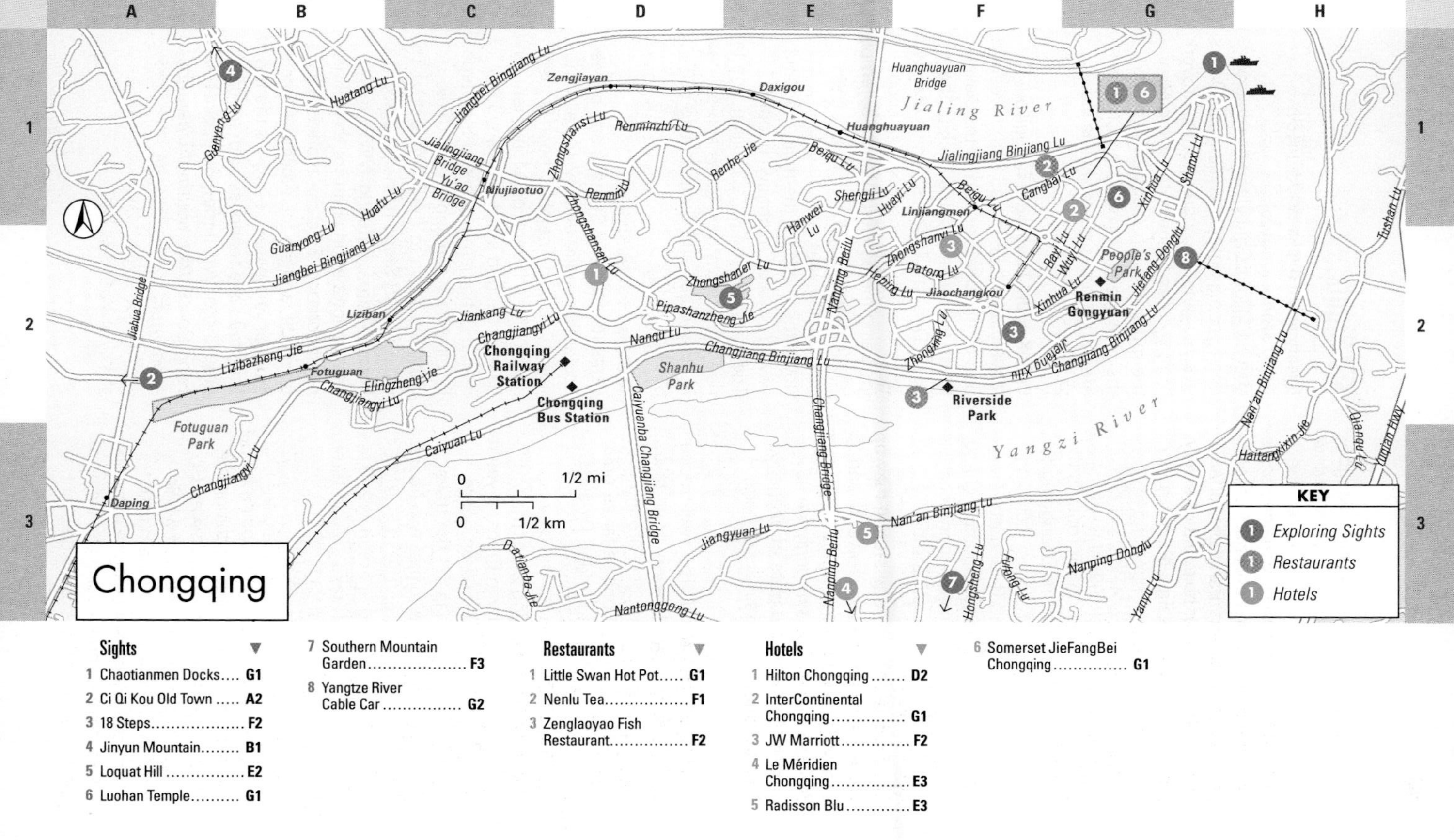

Sights

1 Chaotianmen Docks.... G1
2 Ci Qi Kou Old Town A2
3 18 Steps.................... F2
4 Jinyun Mountain......... B1
5 Loquat Hill E2
6 Luohan Temple.......... G1
7 Southern Mountain Garden.................... F3
8 Yangtze River Cable Car G2

Restaurants

1 Little Swan Hot Pot..... G1
2 Nenlu Tea................. F1
3 Zenglaoyao Fish Restaurant................ F2

Hotels

1 Hilton Chongqing D2
2 InterContinental Chongqing............... G1
3 JW Marriott.............. F2
4 Le Méridien Chongqing................ E3
5 Radisson Blu............. E3
6 Somerset JieFangBei Chongqing.............. G1

Traffic permitting, Chongqing's Jiangbei International Airport is a 40-minute drive north by taxi from the city center. The airport has flights to every major domestic, and some international hubs, mostly within Asia, including Bangkok (Air Asia) and Doha (Qatar Air). It is also connected to Europe via Helsinki (Finn Air).

Boats go on the Yangtze from Chongqing all the way to Shanghai (seven days), but the most popular route is the cruise downstream from Chongqing to Yichang. Most major sights, including the Three Gorges and Three Little Gorges, lie between Chongqing and Yichang. Tourist boats offer air-conditioned cabins with a television and private bath.

The shared train and bus station may be the most inconvenient, crowded, and annoying station in the world. Once your taxi has maneuvered through the corrugated tin walls and piles of baggage, finding your bus or train is not hard, however.

Chongqing to Chengdu is a well-trodden path. The bus departs every hour, takes five to six hours, and costs around Y100. Buses are viable options as far as Yibin, but trains are recommended for all other destinations.

Trains leave Chongqing every minute for every conceivable city in China. If you're going to Chengdu, the ultramodern high-speed rail link has cut the travel time from four hours to just two hours. A second class seat on the train is Y154 and first class averages around Y246. Regular trains, which take around three to four hours, start at Y47.

TIMING

You could easily stay in Chongqing for a week without seeing everything, but most of the sights of interest in and around the city can be visited within three or four days. Avoid the brutal summers when Chongqing morphs into a furnace and come visit in the spring or the fall when the climate is pleasant.

Sights

Chaotianmen Docks (朝天门码头 *Cháotiānmén mǎtóu*)
MARINA | Not as busy and bustling as once upon a time, Chaotianmen Docks lets you get a glimpse of China at work. Here you can witness the merging of the muddy-brown Yangtze River and the blue-green Jialing River. Chaotianmen Square has great skyline views. ✉ *Shaanxi Rd.*

Ci Qi Kou Old Town (磁器口 *Cíqìkǒu*)
NEIGHBORHOOD | Perched in the western part of the city overlooking the Jialing River, this district dates back to the late Ming Dynasty. There is a main drag with dozens of souvenir and snack shops, including the peaceful Baolun Si Temple, which dates back 1,500 years. If you do stay until late into the evening, head down the alleys off the main drag and have a bowl of "night owl noodles." They're spicy, meaty, and filling. The taxi ride from downtown takes approximately 30 minutes and costs around Y30. ✉ *Chongqing.*

18 Steps (十八梯 *Shíbātī*)
NEIGHBORHOOD | 18 Steps is one of the coolest places in the city, literally and figuratively. The neighborhood is just south of the Liberation Monument, and hasn't changed since the early 20th century. The name refers to the steps leading from the upper level of Jie Fang Bei down to the slums below. The infamous 18 Steps tunnel, the scene of horrible carnage during WWII, serves as a congregation point for the whole neighborhood. Find the tunnel, pull up a mat, and sip tea while the locals stare at you incredulously. At the top of the steps is a teahouse with a treasure trove of WWII memorabilia. ✉ *Jie Fang Bei District, south of Liberation Monument.*

Continued on page 465

A CULINARY TOUR OF CHINA

For centuries the collective culinary fragrances of China have drifted far beyond its borders and tantalized the entire world. Now with China's arms open to the world, a vast variety of Chinese flavors—from the North, South, East, and West—are more accessible than ever.

Four corners of the Middle Kingdom

In dynasties gone by, a visitor to China might have to undertake a journey of a thousand li just to feel the burn of an authentic Sichuanese hotpot, and another to savor the crispy skin and juicy flesh of a genuine Beijing roast duck. Luckily for us, the vast majority of regional Chinese cuisines have made successful internal migrations. As a result, Sichuanese cuisine can be found in Guangzhou, Cantonese dim sum in Urumuqi, and the cumin-spiced lamb-on-a-stick, for which the Uigher people of Xinjiang are famous, is now grilled all over China.

Before you begin your journey, remember, a true scholar of Middle Kingdom cuisine should first eliminate the very term "Chinese food" from their vocabulary. It hardly encompasses the variety of provincial cuisines and regional dishes that China has to offer, from succulent Shanghainese dumplings to fiery Sichuanese hotpots.

To guide you on your gastronomic journey, we've divided the country's gourmet map along the points of the compass—North, South, East, and West. Bon voyage and bon appétit!

Following the revolution, it was hard to find authentic Chinese cuisine.

NORTH

THE BASICS

Cuisine from China's Northeast is called dongbei cai, and it's more wheat than rice based. Vegetables like kale, cabbage, and potatoes are combined with robust, thick soy sauces, garlic (often raw), and scallions.

Even though many Han Chinese from southern climates find mutton too gamey, up north it's a regular staple. In many northern cities, you can't walk more than a block without coming across a small sidewalk grill with yang rou chua'r, or lamb-on-a-stick.

NOT TO BE MISSED

The most famous of all the northern dishes is Peking duck, and if you've ever had it well prepared, you'll know why Beijingers are proud of the dish named for their city.

As far back as the 15th century it was an Imperial dish, reserved for royalty. Like many such delicacies, it's likely the recipe was smuggled out of the Forbidden City by cooks or servants, eventually finding its way into restaurants.

Peking duck sliced table-side.

A bit different from the "crispy duck" eaten in Cantonese-style restaurants around the globe, proper Peking duck should have skin that's both brittle and yielding. Getting there is a meticulous, multi-day process, but the real key is the date-infused liquid poured into the duck cavity, which is sealed, and the bird is then hung over the fire. Full of fruity juice, the meat will steam gently from the inside as the flames in the oven lick and crackle the skin.

THE CAPITAL CITY'S NAMESAKE DISH

SOUTH

(left) Preparing for the feast. (top right) Dim sum as art. (bottom right) Place your order.

THE BASICS

The dish most associated with Southern Chinese cuisine is dim sum, which is found in great variety and abundance in Guangdong province, as well as Hong Kong and Macau. Bite-size dim sum is usually eaten early in the day. Any good dim sum place should have dozens of varieties. Some of the most popular dishes are *har gao,* a shrimp dumpling with a rice-flour skin, *siu maai,* a pork dumpling with a wrapping made of wheat flour, and *chaa-habao,* a steamed or baked bun filled with sweetened pork and onions. Adventerous eaters should order the chicken claws. Trust us, they taste better than they look.

> The Cantonese saying *"fei qin zou shou"* roughly translates to "if it flies, swims or runs, it's food."

For our money, the best southern food comes from Chaozhou (Chiuchow), a coastal city only a few hours' drive north of its larger neighbors. Unlike dim sum, Chaozuo cuisine is extremely light and understated. Deep-fried bean curd is also a remarkably fresh Chaozuo dish.

NOT TO BE MISSED

One Chaozuo dish that appeals equally to the eye and the palate is the plain-sounding mashed vegetable with minced chicken soup. The dish is served in a large bowl, and resembles a green-and-white yin-yang. As befitting a dish resembling a Buddhist symbol, a vegetarian version substituting rice gruel for chicken broth is usually offered.

SOUTHWEST AND FAR WEST

Southwest

THE BASICS

When a person from the Southwest asks you if you like spicy food, consider your answer well. Natives of Sichuan and Hunan take the use of chilies, wild pepper, and garlic to blistering new heights. These two areas have been competing for the "spiciest province in China" title for centuries. The penchant for fiery food is likely due to the weather—hot and humid in the summer and harshly cold in the winter. But no matter what the temperature, if you're eating Sichuan or Hunan dishes, be prepared to sweat.

Sichuan pepper creates a tingly numbness.

Southwest China shares some culinary traits with both Southeast Asia and India. This is likely due to the influences of travelers from both regions in centuries past. Traditional Chinese medicine also makes itself felt in the regional cuisine. Theory has it that sweating expels toxins and equalizes body temperature.

As Chairman Mao's province, Hunan has a number of dishes with revolutionary names. The most popular are red-cooked Hunan fish *(hongshao wuchangyu)* and red-cooked pork *(hongshao rou),* which was said to have been a personal favorite of the Great Helmsman.

NOT TO BE MISSED

One dish you won't want to miss out on in Sichuan is *mala zigi*, or "peppery and hot chicken." It's one part chicken meat and three parts fried chilies and a Sichuanese wild pepper called *huajiao* that's so spicy it effectively numbs the tongue. At first it feels like eating Tiger Balm, but the hot-cool-numb sensation produced by crunching on the pepper is oddly addictive.

KUNG PAO CHICKEN

One of the most famous Chinese dishes, Kung Pao chicken (or gongbao jiding), enjoys a legend of its own. Though shrouded in myth, its origin exemplifies the improvisational skills found in any good Chinese chef. The story of Kung Pao chicken has to do with a certain Qing Dynasty era (1644–1911) provincial governor named Ding Baozhen, who arrived home unexpectedly one day with a group of friends in tow. His cook, caught in between shopping trips, had only the chicken breast and a few vegetables he was planning to cook for his own dinner. The crafty chef diced the chicken into tiny bits and fried it up with everything he could find in the cupboard—some peanuts, sugar, onion, garlic, bits of ginger, and a few handfuls of dried red peppers—and hoped for the best.

(top left) Tibetan dumplings. (center left) Uyghur-style pilaf. (bottom left) Monk stirring tsampa barley. (right) Juggling hot noodles in the Xinjiang province.

Far West

THE BASICS

Religion is the primary shaper of culinary tradition in China's Far West. Being a primarily Muslim province, chefs in Xinjiang don't use pork products of any kind. Instead, meals are likely to be heavy on spiced lamb. Baked flat breads coated in sesame seeds are a specialty. Whole lamb roasted on a spit, fine spicy tomato salads, and lightly spiced mutton and vegetable soups are also favorites.

NOT TO BE MISSED

In Tibet, climate is the major factor dictating cuisine. High and dry, the Tibetan plateau is hardly suited for rice cultivation. Whereas a Han meal might include rice, Tibetan cuisine tends to include tsampa, a ground barley usually cooked into a porridge. Another staple that's definitely an acquired taste is yak butter tea. Dumplings, known as *momo,* are wholesome and filling. Of course, if you want to go all out, order the yak penis with caterpillar fungus.

EAST

(top left) Cold tofu with pork and thousand-year-old eggs. (top right) Meaty dumplings. (bottom right) Letting off the steam of Shanghai: soup dumplings. (bottom left) Steamed Shanghai hairy crabs.

THE BASICS

The rice, seafood, and fresh vegetable-based cooking of the southern coastal provinces of Zhejiang and Jiangsu are known collectively as huiyang cai. As the area's biggest city, Shanghai has become a major center of the culinary arts. Some popular dishes in Shanghai are stir-fried freshwater eels and finely ground white pepper, and red-stewed fish—a boiled carp in sweet and sour sauce. Another Shanghai favorite are xiaolong bao, or little steamer dumplings. Similar to Cantonese dim sum, xiaolong bao tend to be more moist. The perfect steamed dumpling is meant to explode in your mouth in a juicy burst of meat.

NOT TO BE MISSED

Drunken anything! Shanghai chefs are known for their love of cooking with wine. Dishes like drunken chicken, drunken pigeon, and drunken crab are all delectable meals cooked with prodigious amounts of Shaoxing wine. People with an aversion to alcohol should definitely avoid these. Another meal not to be missed is hairy freshwater crabs, which only come into season in October. One enthusiast of the dish was 15th-century poet and essayist Li Yu, who wrote of the dish in near-erotic terms. "Meat as white as jade, golden roe . . . to use seasoning to improve its taste is like holding up a torch to brighten the sunshine."

Jinyun Mountain (缙云山 *Jìnyún shān*)
HOT SPRINGS | Just north of the city, Jinyun Mountain has some pretty views and a smattering of pavilions from the Ming and Qing dynasties. Three contain imposing statues: the Giant Buddha, the Amitabha Buddha, and the famous general of the Three Kingdoms period, Guan Yu. The park also has a set of hot springs, where you can swim in a pool or soak in the private cubicles. ✉ *50 km (30 miles) by bus north of city, Beibei* 🎫 *Y15.*

Loquat Hill (枇杷山 *Pípá shān*)
VIEWPOINT | The 804-foot Loquat Hill has great views of the river below. At night, enjoy the city lights. There's also a small park with no entrance fee. ✉ *Zhongshan Er Rd.* 🎫 *Free.*

Luohan Temple (罗汉寺 *Luóhàn sì*)
RELIGIOUS SITE | Originally built about 1,000 years ago, then rebuilt in 1752 and again in 1945, the Luohan Temple is a popular place of worship, and a small community of monks is still active here. One of the main attractions is the 500 lifelike painted clay arhats—Buddhist disciples who have succeeded in freeing themselves from the earthly chains of delusion and material greed. At the back of the temple you can order tea, get a massage, and enjoy a vegetarian lunch. ✉ *Near No. 63 Dongsheng Rd.* 🎫 *Y10.*

Southern Mountain Garden (重庆南山公园 *Chóngqìng Nán shān gōng yuàn*)
GARDEN | Southern Mountain is the highest point in the city, and at 935 feet it's the most popular place from which to view Chongqing. For a thousand years Nan Shan has been the route over which travelers and traders of medicine, tea, spices, and silk entered the city and headed on to Sichuan. The best place to enjoy the views and the feel of the mountain is in this very traditional Chinese garden with oddly shaped rocks and bonsai trees. ✉ *101 Nan Shan Gong Yuan Rd.* 🎫 *Y30.*

★ **Yangtze River Cable Car** (长江索道 *Chángjiāng suǒdào*)
VIEWPOINT | Get a bird's-eye view of Chongqing, one of the world's biggest cities. Ideal for taking photos of the city and the two rivers, it's a good opportunity to rise above it all and get a grip on the massive scale of the metropolis. ✉ *151 Xinhua Rd., YuZhong District* 🎫 *Y20.*

Restaurants

Little Swan Hot Pot (重庆小天鹅 *Chóngqìng xiǎo tián é*)
$$$ | **SICHUAN** | Some of Chongqing's most authentic Sichuanese dishes are served in this restaurant on the bank of the Yangtze. An after-dinner stroll along the banks of the river is a great cap to the meal. **Known for:** iconic restaurant; spicy cuisine; romantic location. $ *Average main: Y100* ✉ *88 Jiabin Rd., 11th fl.* ☎ *023/6303–9958* 💳 *No credit cards.*

Nenlu Tea (嫩绿茶 *Nēn lǜ chá*)
$ | **CAFÉ** | Slick and comfortable, this modern teahouse is the city's answer to Starbucks. With several locations dotted around the city (with the Jiabin Lu branch boasting awesome river views), Nenlu is the perfect place to escape the heat, crowds, and general pandemonium of navigating the hilly streets. **Known for:** diverse tea selection; cheesecake; fantastic views. $ *Average main: Y30* ✉ *88 Jiabin Lu, Hong Ya Cave* ☎ *023/6373–4860* 🌐 *www.nenlu.com.*

Zenglaoyao Fish Restaurant (曾老幺鱼庄 *Céng lǎo yāo yú zhuāng*)
$ | **CHINESE** | Located in a former bomb shelter and open 24 hours a day, this local favorite is popular with everyone and always crowded. They are famous for their spicy carp bathed in chili oil and succulent steamed ribs. **Known for:** quirky location; grilled fish platters; no English language menu. $ *Average main: Y40* ✉ *221 Changjiang Binjiang Rd., YuZhong District* ☎ *023/ 6392–4315.*

Damming the Yangtze

Nearly a century ago, Chinese leader Sun Yat-sen first proposed damming the Three Gorges area of the Yangtze River, a project that subsequently appealed to Chiang Kai-shek and even the invading Japanese, both of whom prepared plans for the project.

Construction and Benefits

It wasn't until the 1990s under the Communist government that China began building the world's largest power generator, the Three Gorges Dam. In addition to power generation, the dam's locks are big enough to handle containerized sea barges, allowing Chongqing to be the world's farthest inland seaport.

Construction of the main body of the Three Gorges Dam was finished in 2006, and the 26th generator was installed in 2008. Eight additional generators bring total power generation capacity to an unmatched 22.5 gigawatts.

Even in China, the sheer scale of this project is staggering. The $26-billion dam is more than 600 feet high and a mile wide. By 2010 it had an installed capacity of 18.2 gigawatts and was able to generate 80,000 gigawatt-hours of power annually.

As with any infrastructure project of its scope, the dam has been controversial from the beginning, with critics focusing on its massive social, cultural, and environmental costs.

Repercussions

The reservoir created by the flooding of the Three Gorges area was preceded by the forced relocation of more than 1.2 million people. Many of these people are now migrant workers in nearby cities.

The rising river levels also resulted in the submerging of many significant and valuable relics and buildings dating back to the beginning of Chinese civilization. Although some artifacts and buildings were moved uphill, it is widely acknowledged that the flooding of the gorges incurred major cultural losses.

It is the environmental impact of the dam project that has attracted the most negative publicity, with serious potential ramifications both upstream and downstream from the dam.

Behind the dam, millions of acres of forest were drowned, and landslides have become a bigger problem than before. The reduced ability of the Yangtze to flush itself clean of wastewater and other pollution has led to the reservoir's containing higher levels of pollution than the river did before damming.

Downstream, it is the lack of sediment that threatens riverbanks, which could become more prone to flooding. The economic dynamo of Shanghai, which is built on the river's floodplain, could also become more vulnerable to inundation after being deprived of normal silt deposits.

While disaster has been averted so far, heavy rains have provided a jittery first major test for the dam, which almost filled to capacity. There are also concerns about cracks already appearing in the dam and its seismological impact.

Hotels

Hilton Chongqing (重庆希尔顿酒店 *Chóngqìng shà ér dùn jiǔdiàn*)
$$ | **HOTEL** | In a leafy, quiet neighborhood near Lianglukou Stadium, the Hilton Chongqing has plush rooms with the firmest beds in town and fabulous bathrooms. **Pros:** modern design; nice views; helpful staff. **Cons:** not very close to shopping; English is sometimes limited; slightly dated. *Rooms from: Y500* *139 Zhongshan San Rd.* *023/8903–9999* *www.hilton.com.cn* *435 rooms* *No meals.*

InterContinental Chongqing (]重庆洲际大酒店 *Chóngqìng zhōu jí dǎ jiǔdiàn*)
$ | **HOTEL** | With one of the city's top breakfast buffets and a trio of top-notch restaurants, the InterContinental is a favorite with locals and visitors. **Pros:** convenient downtown location; lots of amenities; plush rooms. **Cons:** upper-level views tend to be obscured; furniture is a bit outdated; limited English-speaking staff. *Rooms from: Y920* *101 Minzu Rd.* *023/8906–6888* *www.intercontinental.com* *338 rooms* *No meals.*

JW Marriott (重庆JW万豪酒店 *JWwǎnhàojiǔdiàn*)
$ | **HOTEL** | Just off the city's main drag, this gleaming glass tower puts you within walking distance of virtually anywhere near Liberation Monument. **Pros:** great location; elegant rooms; good pool. **Cons:** poor breakfast buffet; some air-conditioning problems; service can be slow. *Rooms from: Y900* *235 Minsheng Road, YuZhong District* *023/6388–8888* *www.marriotthotels.com* *460 rooms* *No meals.*

★ **Le Méridien Chongqing** (艾美大酒店 *Ǎi méi dǎjiǔdiàn*)
$ | **HOTEL** | Successfully blending French hospitality and Chinese architectural flourishes, the upscale Le Méridien Chongqing is truly a gem. **Pros:** spacious rooms; great design; stellar service. **Cons:** not in the center of town; limited English; food quality is lackluster. *Rooms from: Y500* *10 Jiang Nan Rd., Nan An District* *023/8638–8888* *www.lemeridien.com/chongqingnanan* *288 rooms, 31 suites* *No meals.*

Radisson Blu (雷迪森酒店 *Ruīdǐsà jiǔdiàn*)
$ | **HOTEL** | For the price, this is an excellent option in downtown Chongqing. **Pros:** comfortable rooms; great location; good view. **Cons:** predictable design; subpar dining options; lack of English. *Rooms from: Y600* *22 Nan Bin Rd., Nan An District* *023/8866–8888* *www.radissonblu.com* *308 rooms* *No meals.*

Somerset JieFangBei Chongqing (重庆盛捷解放碑服务公寓 *Shèngjiě jiéfàngbēi*)
$ | **HOTEL** | This sleek hotel's prime location makes it easy to see the best of the city. **Pros:** great location; modern feel; memorable river views. **Cons:** often fully booked; mediocre breakfast; spotty Internet. *Rooms from: Y329* *108 Minzu Rd., YuZhong District* *023/8677–6888* *www.somerset.com* *157 rooms* *No meals.*

Performing Arts

★ **Hong Ya Cave** (洪崖洞 *Hóng yá dòng*)
DANCE | This complex overlooks the Jialing River and has a brightly lit waterfall and paved streets built right into the mountainside. The main attraction is the Ba Yu Theater, a rather cheesy performance of Chongqing customs and folklore. The historical aspects of Ba Yu culture have been dumbed down, but the costumes, choreography, and the bit on the Devil Town of Fengdu make it an evening well spent. There are plenty of foot massage places and a sprinkling of Western restaurants, one of the best being Cactus Tex Mex. *56 Changbai Rd., south bank of Jialing River* *023/6303–9968.*

Did You Know?

The Three Gorges has long been famous for their dizzying vertical walls and fortress-like peaks, and even though the river has been tamed with the construction of the dam and the waters raised by 300 feet, the Qutang, Wu and Xiling Gorges remain some of the most spectacular landscapes in China.

Shopping

Carrefour (家乐福超市 *Jiā lé fù chāo shī*) **DEPARTMENT STORES** | Carrefour is the largest foreign-owned department store chain in China. The France-based giant sells everything from congee to caviar, plus there's a decent import section with all the goodies from back home. Carrefour is the best place in Chongqing to stock up on Western food and drink before a Yangtze cruise. ✉ *1 Aoti Rd.* ☎ *023/6808–9847.*

Side Trip to Dazu

Sights

★ **Baoding Shan** (保定山 *Bǎodìng shān*) **PUBLIC ART** | A UNESCO World Heritage site, these Buddhist caves rival those at Datong, Dunhuang, and Luoyang. The sculptures, ranging from teeny-tiny to gigantic, contain unusual domestic details, as well as purely religious works. There are two major sites at Dazu—Bei Shan and Baoding Shan. Work at the caves began in the 9th century during the Song and Tang Dynasties, and continued for more than 250 years.

Baoding Shan is the more impressive of the two sites, where the carvings were completed according to a plan. Here you will find visions of hell reminiscent of similar scenes from medieval Europe; the Wheel of Life; a magnificent 100-foot reclining Buddha; and a gold statue of the 1,000-armed goddess of mercy.

The best way to reach Dazu is to book a tour from Chongqing. ✉ *Dazu* 🎫 *Y130.*

The Three Gorges

The third-longest river in the world after the Amazon and the Nile, the Yangtze cuts across 6,380 km (3,956 miles) and seven provinces before flowing out into the East China Sea. After descending from the mountain ranges of Qinghai and Tibet, the Yangtze crosses through Yunnan to Sichuan, winding its way through the lush countryside between Sichuan and Hubei before flowing northward toward Anhui and Jiangsu. Before the 20th century, many lost their lives trying to pass through the fearsome stretch of water running through what is known as the Three Gorges—the complicated system of narrow cliffs between Fengjie, in Sichuan, and Yichang, in Hubei.

The spectacular scenery of the Three Gorges—Qutang, Wu, and Xiling—has survived the rising waters of the newly dammed Yangtze River. A trip through the Three Gorges offers a glimpse of the new China moving full steam ahead. Almost all of the cities and towns in the area are in the middle of a construction and tourism boom. The Yangtze itself has endless streams of passenger and cargo boats moving up and downstream.

While there is no doubt that much of the charm has been diminished by the flooding of the area, the Gorges are still scenic and fascinating. Sitting on deck and taking in the moon and stars on a clear night while heading downstream is a great way to escape the hustle and bustle of Chinese cities. The scenery is constantly changing, and it only takes an hour outside smog-ridden Chongqing before the sky opens up and the magic begins.

BOAT TOURS

Riverboat rides essentially come in two forms: luxury and domestic. Domestic cruises are much cheaper and have few amenities. No matter which option you choose, book ahead, as berths are limited.

LUXURY CRUISE BOATS

The foreign-owned ships, such as the Victoria Series boats, are big, quadruple-decker liners and by far the most comfortable option. In addition to spacious decks from which to soak up the breathtaking views, many boats

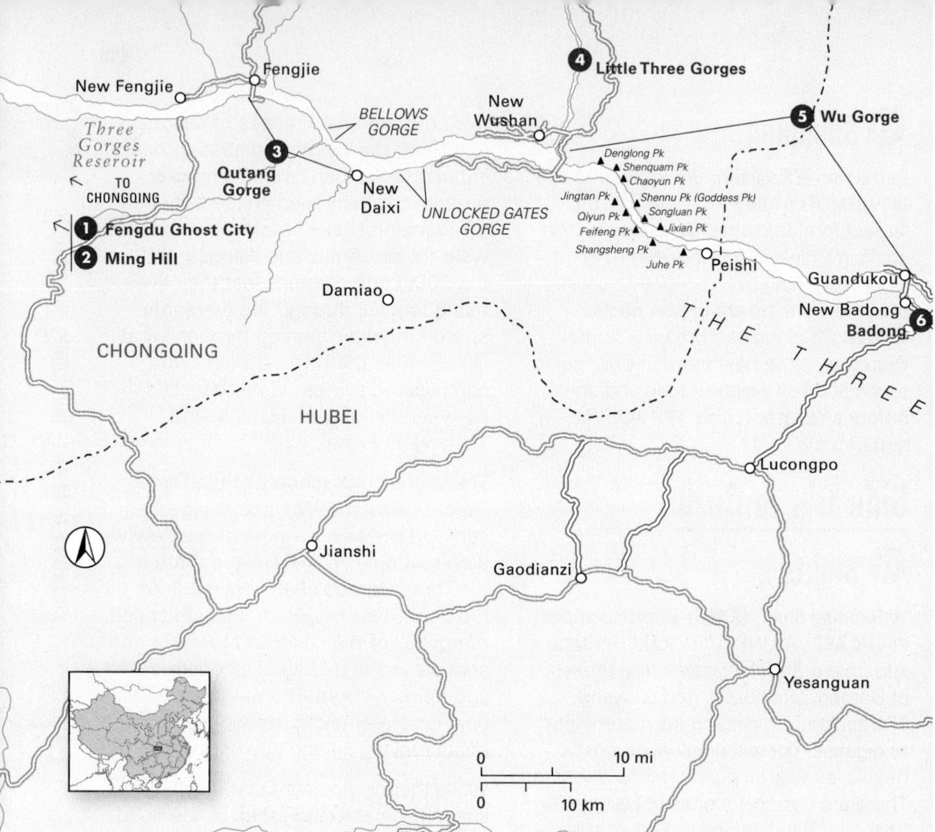

are equipped with a gym, a ballroom, a business center with Internet connection, and bars and restaurants. There are also a few shops in case you run out of film or other necessities. The ticket price includes the admission cost for most of the sites along the way, except the Little Three Gorges. A one-way package tour starts at Y5,363, and the boats themselves are divided into three-, four-, and five-star service.

DOMESTIC BOATS

These less expensive, less luxurious boats are divided into four classes. Suites offer almost all of the amenities of Luxury Cruise Boats and are available for Y2,084 each way. First class sleeps two people and costs Y1,042 each way. Spartan rooms come with two beds, a private bathroom, TV, and air-conditioning. Second and third classes, costing Y503 and Y347 each way, have bunk beds, shared bathrooms that aren't always kept clean, and limited views. The domestic boats usually serve good Chinese food, depending on the class you choose.

HYDROFOIL

This option is used by those returning from Yichang to Chongqing, who don't want to do the whole trip over again in reverse. Prices vary, but currently it is Y280 from Yichang to Chongqing and takes about six hours. You have to get off at Wanxian and take a bus back into Chongqing. This costs Y120 and takes another 3½ hours. If you're pressed for time, an airport in Yichang has daily flights to Chongqing and Chengdu, along with less frequent flights to Beijing, Shanghai, and Guangzhou.

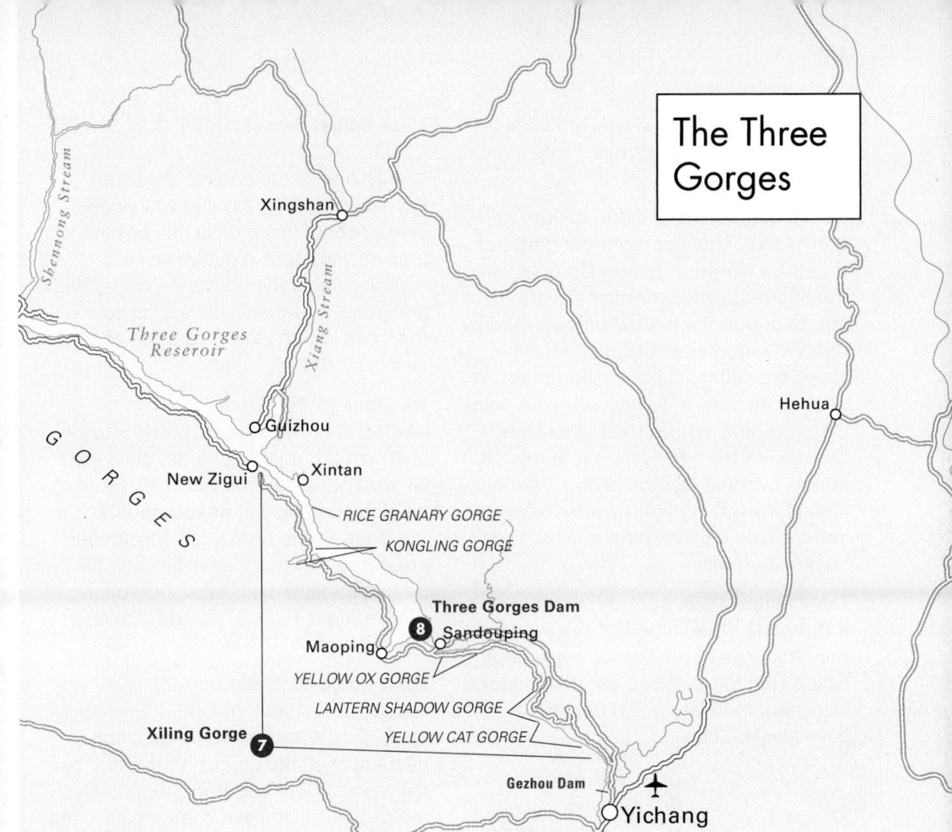

Sights

Badong (巴东 *Bādōng*)
TOWN | At the city of Badong, just outside the eastern end of Wu Gorge, boats leave for Shennongjia on the Shennong River, where you can take in the costumes and traditions of Tujia and Miao ethnic minorities.

★ **Fengdu Ghost City** (丰都魔鬼城 *Fēng dū móguǐ chéng*)
ARCHAEOLOGICAL SITE | Also known as Guicheng or the "city of devils," this city on the banks of the Yangtze is filled with temples, buildings, and statues depicting demons and devils. During the Tang Dynasty, the names of two local princely families, Yin (meaning "hell") and Wang (meaning "king"), were linked through marriage, making them known as Yinwang, or the "king of hell." Part of the old city has been submerged in the Three Gorges Dam project. You can take a series of staircases or a cable car to the top of the mountain. ✉ *160 km (100 miles) east of Chongqing* 🎫 *Y80.*

★ **Little Three Gorges** (小三峡 *Wūyóu Sì*)
NATURE SITE | At the entrance to Wu Gorge, you can take a smaller boat navigated by local boatmen to the Little Three Gorges. These three gorges—Dragon Gate Gorge, Misty Gorge, and Emerald Gorge—are spectacular and not to be missed. They are striking and silent, rising dramatically out of the river. If you have time, take a trip to the old town of Dachang. 🎫 *Y240*

Ming Hill (岷山 *Mǐngshān*)
RELIGIOUS SITE | The bamboo-covered Ming Hill is home to a Buddhist temple, a pavilion, and pagodas with brightly

painted dragons and swans emanating from the eaves. The hill has a nice view of the Yangtze River.

Qutang Gorge (瞿塘峡 *Qūtáng Xiá*)
NATURE SITE | The westernmost gorge of the Three Gorges, Qutang Gorge is also the shortest. The currents here are quite strong due to the natural gate formed by the two mountains, Chijia and Baiyan. There are cliff inscriptions along the way, so be sure to have your guide point them out and explain their significance. Several are from the Warring States period more than 2,000 years ago. Warriors' coffins from that period were discovered in the caves on these mountains, and some still remain.

Three Gorges (三峡 *Sānxiá*)
NATURE SITE | The Three Gorges lie along the fault lines of what once were flourishing kingdoms. Those great kingdoms vanished into history and became, collectively, China.

Three Gorges Dam (长江三峡大坝 *Sān Xiá dă bá*)
DAM | Xiling Gorge ends at the Three Gorges Dam. Nothing that you've seen or read about this project can possibly prepare you for its massive scale. Sit back in awe as the boat approaches this great dam and then slowly slips down the locks into the lower reaches of the river. *Y180*

Wu Gorge (巫峡 *Wūxiá*)
NATURE SITE | The impressive Wu Gorge is 45 km (28 miles) long. Its cliffs are so sheer and narrow that they seem to be closing in on you as you approach in the boat. Some of the cliff formations are noted for their resemblances to people and animals. Most notable is the Goddess Peak, a beautiful pillar of white stone.

Xiling Gorge (西岭峡 *Xīlíngxiá*)
NATURE SITE | About 76 km (47.2 miles) long, Xiling Gorge is the longest and deepest of all the gorges, with cliffs that rise up to 4,000 feet. It is undoubtedly the most peaceful and contemplative leg of the journey.

Chapter 10

XI'AN AND THE SILK ROAD

Updated by
Josh Summers

Sights	Restaurants	Hotels	Shopping	Nightlife
★★★★★	★★★☆☆	★★☆☆☆	★★★☆☆	★☆☆☆☆

WELCOME TO XI'AN AND THE SILK ROAD

TOP REASONS TO GO

★ **Terracotta Warriors:** Take in one of the nation's most haunting and memorable sites—the vast life-size army of soldiers, built to outlast death.

★ **Discover Dunhuang:** Satisfy your inner archaeologist at the magnificent Mogao caves and scale the shifting slopes of Singing Sand Mountain.

★ **Seek Solace at Kumbum Monastery:** Visit one of the six great monasteries of the Tibetan Buddhist sect known as Yellow Hat, reputedly the birthplace of the sect's founder, Tsong Khapa.

★ **Tour Turpan:** Discover the ruins of the ancient city-states Jiaohe and Gaochang, destroyed by Genghis Khan and his unstoppable Mongol hordes.

★ **Kashgar and the Karakorum Highway:** Explore Central Asia's largest and liveliest bazaar before heading south to the snowcapped Pamir Mountains and crystal-clear Karakul Lake.

1 **Xian.** Visit the tomb of China's first emperor and its army of thousands of Terracotta Warriors in Xi'an. Shaanxi is the starting point of the fabled Silk Road that brought silks and spices from China to Rome more than two millennia ago.

2 **Lanzhou.** The jumping-off point for Dunhuang and the remote Labrang Monastery, Lanzhou is one of the most polluted cities in China.

3 **Dunhuang.** Long an important Buddhist destination on the Silk Road, here you'll find the Mogao Grottoes and Singing Sand Mountain.

4 **Xining.** The Kumbum Monastery is located just outside of Xining.

5 **Ürümqi.** The most landlocked city in the world is also Xinjiang's capital.

6 **Turpan.** The hottest place in China, Turpan is located between the ruins of two ancient cities: Jiaohe and Gaochang.

7 **Kashgar.** Closer to Baghdad than Beijing, legendary Kashgar hosts the largest bazaar in Central Asia.

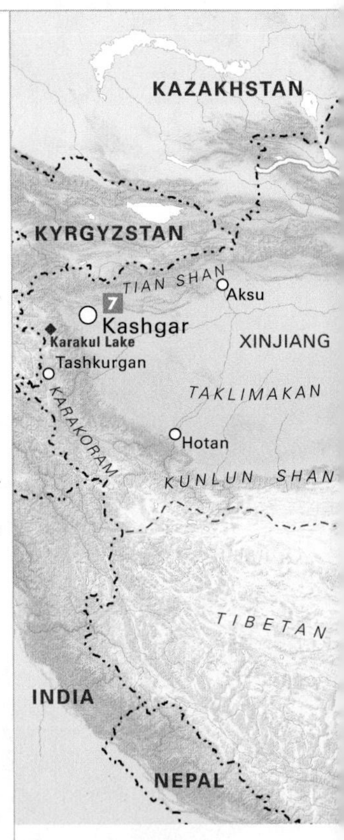

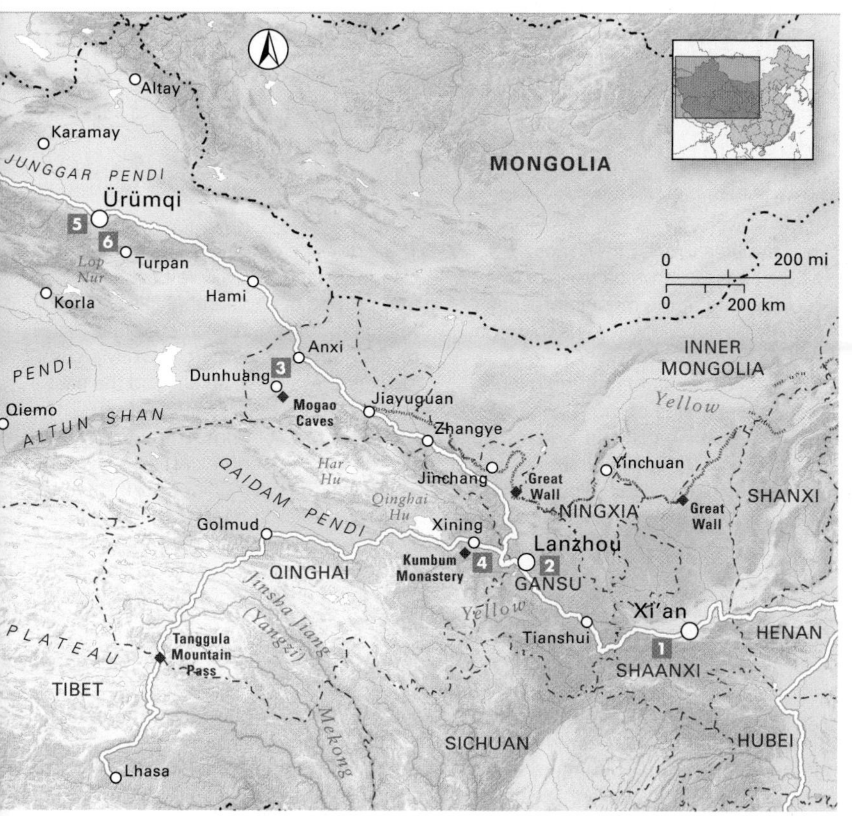
MONGOLIA
INNER MONGOLIA
Altay
Karamay
JUNGGAR PENDI
Ürümqi
Turpan
Lop Nur
Korla
Hami
Anxi
Dunhuang
Mogao Caves
Jiayuguan
Zhangye
Jinchang
Great Wall
Yinchuan
Great Wall
NINGXIA
SHANXI
PENDI
Qiemo
ALTUN SHAN
QAIDAM PENDI
Har Hu
Qinghai Hu
Xining
Kumbum Monastery
Lanzhou
GANSU
Golmud
QINGHAI
Jinsha Jiang (Yangzi)
Yellow
Tianshui
Xi'an
HENAN
SHAANXI
PLATEAU
Tanggula Mountain Pass
TIBET
Mekong
SICHUAN
HUBEI
Lhasa
0 200 mi
0 200 km
1
2
3
4
5
6

The Silk Road spans from far Western China's snowcapped mountains, scorching deserts, and glassy lakes to the thriving metropolis that is Xi'an. It may not be the bustling trade route it once was, but the area still remains alive and kicking.

While the area is one of the most isolated and less-traveled parts of China, it remains one of the most interesting culturally, as a locus where people from Tibet, Kazakhstan, the Han Chinese, and others continue to mix and mingle. There's no shortage of monasteries, mosques, bustling markets, and historical sites to visit, although much of Kashgar's Old City has been and continues to be demolished by Chinese authorities.

The history of the Silk Road starts in 138 BC, when Emperor Wudi of the Han Dynasty sent a caravan of 100 men to the west, attempting to forge a political alliance with the Yuezhi people living beyond the Taklamakan Desert. The mission was a failure, and only two men survived the 13-year return journey, but they brought back with them to Chang'an (present-day Xi'an) tales of previously unknown kingdoms: Samarkand, Ferghana, Parthia, and even Rome. More important, they told stories about the legendary Ferghana horse, a fast and powerful creature said to be bred in heaven. Believing that this horse would give his armies a military advantage over the Huns, Emperor Wudi sent a number of large convoys to Central Asia in order to establish contact with these newly discovered kingdoms—and to bring back as many horses as possible. These envoys of the Han emperor were the first traders on the Silk Road.

The extension of the Silk Road beyond Central Asia to the Middle East and Europe was due to another ill-advised foreign excursion, this time on the part of the Roman Empire. In 55 BC Marcus Licinius Crassus led an army to the east against Parthia, in present-day Syria. The battle was one of Rome's greatest military defeats, but some of the survivors were able to obtain Chinese silk from the Parthians. Back in Rome, wearing silk became the fashion, and for the first time in history a trade route was established covering the 5,000-mile journey between East and West.

It might seem odd today, but the two empires knew very little about the origins of their precious cargo. The reason for this common ignorance was the complicated supply chain that transported goods over the Silk Road. No one merchant made the entire journey, but wares were instead brought from kingdom to kingdom, switching hands in the teeming bazaars of wealthy oasis cities along the way.

Over time, the Silk Road became less important due to the opening of sea routes, and was dealt a death blow by the isolationist tendencies of the Chinese Ming Dynasty in the 14th century. Yet today the Silk Road is being resurrected to transport the modern world's most precious commodity: oil. China's rapid development has created an almost insatiable appetite for energy resources. In the last few years, pipelines have been completed from Kazakhstan and Xinjiang to Shanghai.

MAJOR REGIONS

Xian. Visit the tomb of China's first emperor and its army of thousands of Terracotta Warriors in Xi'an. Shaanxi is the starting point of the fabled Silk Road that brought silks and spices from China to Rome more than two millennia ago.

Lanzhou. The jumping-off point for Dunhuang and the remote Labrang Monastery, Lanzhou is one of the most polluted cities in China.

Dunhuang. Long an important Buddhist destination on the Silk Road, here you'll find the Mogao Grottoes and Singing Sand Mountain.

Xining. The Kumbum Monastery is located just outside of Xining.

Ürümqi. The most landlocked city in the world is also Xinjiang's capital.

Turpan. The hottest place in China, Turpan is located between the ruins of two ancient cities: Jiaohe and Gaochang.

Kashgar. Closer to Baghdad than Beijing, legendary Kashgar hosts the largest bazaar in Central Asia.

In addition to the Terracotta Warriors in **Xi'an**, Shaanxi is the starting point of the fabled Silk Road that brought silks and spices from China to Rome more than two millennia ago. Arid and mountainous, Gansu has served as a corridor to the West for thousands of years.The gateway city of **Lanzhou** leads you to the heralded sites of the Mogao Grottoes, Singing Sand Mountain near **Dunhuang**, and the remote Labrang Monastery. Away from the industrialized cities, on the vast open plains of Qinghai, seminomadic herders clad in brown robes slashed with fluorescent pink sashes still roam the grasslands around **Xining**. Chinese in name only, Xinjiang is a land of vast deserts and ancient Silk Road settlements, including legendary **Kashgar**, **Ürümqi**, and **Turpan**. The region is populated by Uyghurs, China's largest minority group.

Planning

When to Go

The best time to visit is from early May to late October, when it's warm and the land is in bloom with grasses and flowers. It's also high tourist season, when many festivals take place.

In spring, wildflowers make a colorful, riotous appearance on the mountain meadows, rolling grasslands, and lush valleys.

Dry, sunny summers provide blue skies and long days, optimal for exploring and photographing the region. Afternoons, however, can be insufferably hot, and most tourists follow the locals' lead in taking a midday siesta. Clear skies last usually through October, while winter brings subfreezing temperatures and a dearth of travelers. Although solitude may have its charms, a few sights close for the off-season. Note that Xi'an suffers from severe pollution, which is at its worst in winter, when coal is burned for fuel.

Getting Here and Around

Xi'an, the capital of Shaanxi Province, is also the area's main travel hub. You can board trains and buses to most corners of the region and planes to just about anywhere in the country. To avoid long and backbreaking journeys by bus, it's worth flying at least occasionally, and with tickets often heavily discounted there's not always a huge price difference. The train is often more comfortable than buses in addition to being extremely efficient—and with the great scenery, time passes quickly.

AIR TRAVEL

Air China, China Southern, and Hainan Airlines are the main airlines that fly to Xi'an and Lanzhou from major cities in China. From Ürümqi there are daily flights to all cities within Xinjiang and most major airports in China. Tickets are easy to come by, frequently at discounted rates. Daily flights are also available from Hong Kong via Cathay Pacific and Dragonair.

BUS TRAVEL

Spectacular scenery and time for contemplation are the rewards for taking bus journeys. The negatives include long journeys, regular breakdowns, and, often, smoking on board. In Xinjiang, long-distance bus routes crisscross the province, including through the heart of the Taklamakan Desert, and from Ürümqi there are sleeper buses for the 20-hour journey to Kashgar (flying is often a similar price). In addition, there are handy tourist buses from Ürümqi to Heavenly Lake and from Xi'an city out to the Terracotta Warriors.

CAR TRAVEL

It's simple to hire a car and driver in major tourist destinations such as Xi'an, Ürümqi, Kashgar, and Turpan; ask your hotel or contact a local travel agency. It's unlikely that your driver will speak English, so agree on your destination beforehand and whether tolls and other sundry costs are included in the price. Expect to pay around Y900 a day for a modern car.

TRAIN TRAVEL

Shaanxi and Gansu provinces are well connected to major cities in the rest of China, with direct high-speed and standard trains from Beijing and Shanghai to Xi'an, Lanzhou, and Dunhuang. Xinjiang and Qinghai are more isolated, though there are standard trains from all the above cities to Xining and Ürümqi. High-speed rail lines run from Lanzhou to Ürümqi, which cuts total travel time from 22 hours to about 12 hours. From Xining and Lanzhou, there's daily service to Lhasa in Tibet. The trip takes around 24 hours. You must book tickets in advance and secure a Tibet Travel Permit. From Ürümqi there is regular service to Kashgar, Yining, Korla, Hotan, Turpan, and Hami, as well as Almaty in Kazakstan.
■ TIP→ For all train travel, save yourself the hassle and ask your hotel or travel agency to book your ticket.

Women's Wear 

Many places along the Silk Road have large Muslim communities, and it's courteous to dress appropriately when there. Women will feel less conspicuous in Xinjiang if they dress as most locals do and wear long trousers and cover their shoulders. Scarves aren't necessary, but they can be good protection against the sun and dust.

Health and Safety

In an emergency, your first stop should be a good hotel. Even if you are not a guest, or if you don't speak Chinese or have a Chinese friend to call on, get a hotel involved to arrange treatment and provide translation. Emergency services operators do not speak English.

TRAVELING IN THE DESERT

Things change quickly from uncomfortable to dangerous in the intense heat of northwest China's expansive deserts. Temperatures in the summer reach 100°F (37.8°C), with some areas—the depression around Turpan in particular—soaring to 122°F (50°C). Many of the sites you'll be visiting are remote and lack even the most basic facilities.

In conditions like these, it's unwise to travel without abundant water, as well as strong sunscreen, sunglasses, hand sanitizer, a good hat, toilet paper, and some heat-resistant snacks (dried fruit and nuts). Buy frozen plastic bottles of water in the morning and they'll stay cool until lunchtime.

Restaurants

Restaurants vary from street-side stalls to modern restaurants with air-conditioning and English menus, though don't expect cutting-edge style or modern ambience in any of the eateries in this part of the country.

The cuisine in Shaanxi revolves around noodles and *jiaozi* (dumplings) rather than rice; lamb is the meat of choice. A Xi'an Muslim specialty is *yang rou pao mo,* a spicy lamb soup poured over broken pieces of flat bread. Other popular Muslim street foods are *heletiao* (buckwheat noodles marinated in soy sauce and garlic) and *roujiamo* (pita bread filled with beef or pork and topped with cumin and green peppers).

Gansu and Qinghai don't offer many culinary surprises, but in Xinjiang, where temperatures can reach scorching levels, you'll find a variety of local ices, ice cream, and *durap* (a refreshing mix of yogurt, honey, and crushed ice). **■TIP→ While delicious, ices might not be as hygienic as you'd like.** Traditional Uyghur dishes like *bamian* (lamb and vegetables served over noodles), *polo* (local version of rice pilaf) and *kevap* (spicy lamb kebabs) are ubiquitous, and often washed down with fresh pomegranate juice. Grapes from Turpan and melons from the oasis town of Hami are famous throughout China.

What it Costs in Yuan

$	$$	$$$	$$$$
RESTAURANTS			
under Y50	Y50–Y99	Y100–Y165	over Y165

Hotels

Cities that see a regular influx of tourists, such as Xi'an and Ürümqi, offer the full spectrum of lodging options. The more remote the area, the fewer the choices, and standards are lower than you might be used to; also, don't expect your credit cards to be accepted. There are almost no boutique options in the region, though in Kashgar there are some dusty hotels that have historic interest, remnants from when the city was a center for trade between the east and west. *Hotel reviews have been shortened. For full information, visit Fodors.com.*

What it Costs in Yuan

$	$$	$$$	$$$$
HOTELS			
under Y1,100	Y1,100–Y1,399	Y1,400–Y1,800	over Y1,800

Tours

CITS

GUIDED TOURS | The Xi'an branch of the state-run travel service gets good reviews, thanks to the friendliness of its young, well-trained staff. Its tours might be more expensive, but they include nicer cars and smaller groups. Tours head to key Silk Road destinations. ✉ *48 Chang'an Bei Lu, Xian* ☎ *029/6288–9999* 🌐 *www.cits.net* 🎫 *Tours from US$70.*

Xian Travel Service

GUIDED TOURS | Formerly known as the Sino NZ Tourism Group, this tour agency offers walking tours of downtown Xi'an. Price depends on the size of your group and includes all admissions, English-speaking guide, transportation, and lunch. ✉ *Room 906, Saigao Block Plaza, No.150 Weiyang Rd., Xian* ☎ *189/6689–2623 mobile phone (no area code)* 🌐 *www.xiantravelservice.com* 🎫 *From Y300.*

Visitor Information

Travelers should use guidebooks, travel agencies, and online forums like Fodors.com for information. As in the rest of China, official tourist information is hard to come by.

Xi'an

2 hrs by plane or 4–5 hrs by high-speed train southwest of Beijing; 7 hrs by high-speed train west of Shanghai.

Many first-time visitors to Xi'an are seeking the massive terra-cotta army standing guard over the tomb of China's first emperor. Xi'an was known in ancient times as Chang'an (meaning Long Peace), and was one of the largest and most cultured cities in the world. During the Tang Dynasty—considered by many Chinese to be the nation's cultural pinnacle—the city became an important center for the arts. Not surprisingly, this creative explosion coincided with the height of trade on the Silk Road, bringing Turkish fashions to court and foreigners from as far away as Persia and Rome. Although the caravan drivers of yesteryear have long since turned to dust, their memory lives on in the variety of faces seen in Xi'an.

GETTING HERE AND AROUND

Although Xi'an's Xianyang Airport is an inconvenient 47 km (29 miles) northwest of the city center in neighboring Xianyang, it has daily flights to and from Beijing, Shanghai, Hong Kong, Guangzhou, Chengdu, Kunming, Dunhuang, and Ürümqi. International destinations include Japan, South Korea, Singapore, and Thailand. If your hotel doesn't arrange transportation, taxis will try to squeeze every last yuan out of your wallet. Taxis run on a meter, but drivers will often try and charge you a flat fare. Outside of rush hour, expect to pay between Y85 and Y130, depending on the type of vehicle and how far into the city you're going; fuel costs are what accounts for some of the price range. Buses are a far more economical option, costing Y27 and running every 30 minutes. There are six routes to choose from, with Route 1 to the Bell Tower and 2 to the train station the most useful—make sure you have the name of your destination in Chinese.

Just about every bus in Xi'an passes through the traffic circle around the Bell Tower. So long as you have your destinations written out in Chinese and you know what number bus to take and where to get off, riding the bus in Xi'an is not difficult, and is far less expensive than taking taxis.

The long-distance bus station on Jiefang Lu, just past the city wall and west of the train station, has buses to Lanzhou, Xining, and other destinations throughout Shaanxi and Henan. Tourist destinations like the Terracotta Warriors Museum are served from the parking lot between the train station and the Jiefang Hotel.

Because so many of the sights lie outside the city proper, hiring a taxi or a car and driver gives you the freedom to depart when you like instead of waiting for the rest of the tour. Prices start at about Y800 per day, but vary widely based on the type of vehicle and whether you need an English-speaking guide. Every major hotel can arrange car services. Note that during rush hour, finding a taxi may be near impossible. If you're desperate, do what the locals do and hail an already occupied cab. If you're going in the same direction, they'll take you. Expect to pay the amount on the meter minus the amount on the meter when you boarded. Some drivers may charge the full amount.

The train station lies on the same rail line as Lanzhou. Those arriving in Xi'an by train disembark north of the old city walls. The train station is close to most hotels; a taxi should cost less than Y12. The foreigners' ticket window, on the second floor above the main ticket office, is open daily 8:30 to 11:30 and 2:30 to 5:30. It sometimes closes without explanation. You can purchase tickets from other ticket windows, but the foreigners' ticket window has a guaranteed English speaker. For a small booking fee, hotels and travel agencies can get tickets. It's easy enough to get tickets yourself by checking the schedule online and then going to the ticket window armed with the name of your destination in Chinese and what time you want to go. Be prepared to pay in cash.

TIMING

If you're in a rush, you can in two days see the main city and take a day trip to the Warriors. However, Xi'an is one of China's more appealing cities, and a few days' stay will reveal the unique ambience of the city's Muslim quarter and give you an opportunity to taste all the great food.

TOURS

Most hotels offer their own guided tours of the area, usually dividing them into eastern area, western area, and city tours. Most tour operators have English-language tour guides available upon request.

Be sure to check more than one company to confirm that you're being charged the going rate. Bargaining may get you a much better deal. One of the best places to comparison shop is on the second floor of the Bell Tower Hotel, where several tour companies vie for your business. Try Golden Bridge first, but there are other good options.

The Bell Tower in Xi'an

EASTERN TOUR

By far the most popular option from Xi'an, tours that head east of the city usually visit the Tomb of the First Qin Emperor, the Terracotta Warriors Museum, and the Huaqing Hot Springs, all in the town of Lintong. Many tours also stop at the Banpo Matriarchal Clan Village in eastern Xi'an. The China International Travel Service (CITS) offers this tour for around Y550, which includes all admission tickets and an English-speaking guide. The journey takes most of the day; plan on leaving after breakfast and returning in time for dinner. Bring your own snacks and drinks.

If you don't want a guide, you're better off taking Bus 306 (travel Bus No. 5), which leaves constantly from the parking lot between the Xi'an train station and the Jiefang Hotel. The 60-minute journey costs Y8; you can buy tickets on the bus. The Terracotta Warriors are the last stop. To travel between any of the sites in Lintong, a taxi should cost between Y10 and Y15 (although some drivers ask foreigners for Y20). To get back to Xi'an, simply wait along the road for a bus headed to the city.

WESTERN TOUR

Less popular than the eastern tour, this excursion varies wildly from operator to operator. Find out what you're getting for the money. Amateur archaeologists and would-be tomb raiders will hardly be able to tear themselves away from the sites in what's been called China's own Valley of the Kings; others will appreciate some of the relics, but may tire of what appear to be mounds of dirt or holes in the ground. There is no English-language signage.

Of the 18 imperial tombs on the plains west of Xi'an, a list of the best should include the Qianling Mausoleum, resting place of Tang Dynasty Empress Wu Zetian, China's only female sovereign. A number of her relatives—many sentenced to death by her own decree—are entombed in the surrounding area. The tomb of Prince Yi De contains some beautifully restored frescoes. Other stops on the western tour might include the Xianyang

City Museum in Xianyang and the Famen Temple in Famen. Xi'an Travel Services offers a customizable western tour. For an individual traveler, expect to pay around Y1,000 for a one-day tour, inclusive of car, guide, and admissions fees. The larger the group, the lower the price per person. Plan on spending the whole day visiting these sites.

Treasures of Shaanxi

Shaanxi gave birth to 13 major Chinese dynasties. Consider first hitting the Shaanxi History Museum. Once you've steeped yourself in its chronology, local "must-see" destinations like Xi'an's Drum Towers, Muslim Quarter, and Great Goose Pagodas will make much more sense. So, too, will the awe-inspiring army of Terracotta Warriors at the tomb of China's first emperor. True fans of history can even make the trip to China's own Valley of the Kings near Xianyang.

Sights

Banpo Matriarchal Clan Village (半坡博物馆 *Bànpō Bówùguǎn*)

ARCHAEOLOGICAL SITE | About 5 km (3 miles) east of the city are the remains of a 6,000-year-old Yangshao village, including living quarters, a pottery-making center, and a graveyard. The residents of this matriarchal community of 200 to 300 people survived mainly by fishing, hunting, and gathering, although there is ample evidence of attempts at animal domestication and organized agriculture. The small museum contains stone farming and hunting implements, domestic objects, and pottery inscribed with ancient Chinese characters. The archaeological site has captions in English. Unless you're interested in documenting one of China's great tourist oddities, avoid the awful model village that sits in a state of semi-disrepair toward the rear of the property. ✉ *155 Banpo Lu, off Changdong Lu* 🎫 *Mar.–Nov. Y65; Dec.–Feb. Y45.*

Bell Tower (钟楼 *Zhōnglóu*)

BUILDING | Xi'an's most recognizable structure, the Bell Tower was built in the late 14th century in what was then the center of the city. It's still good as a reference point—the tower marks the point where Xi Dajie (West Main Street) becomes Dong Dajie (East Main Street) and Bei Dajie (North Main Street) becomes Nan Dajie (South Main Street). To reach the tower, which stands isolated in the middle of a traffic circle, use any of the eight entrances to the underground passageway. Once inside the building, you'll see Ming Dynasty bells on display. Concerts are given six times daily (9:10, 10:30, 11:30, 2:30, 3:30, and 4:30). For Y5 you can make your own music by ringing a copy of the large iron bell that gives the tower its name. Don't miss the panoramic views of the city from the third-floor balcony. ✉ *Junction of Dong Dajie, Xi Dajie, Bei Dajie, and Nan Dajie* 🌐 *www.xazgl.com/ewzjj.asp* 🎫 *From Y35.*

Big Wild Goose Pagoda (大雁塔 *Dàyàn Tǎ*)

BUILDING | This impressively tall pagoda lies 4 km (2½ miles) southeast of South Gate, on the grounds of the still-active Temple of Thanksgiving (Da Ci'en Si). The pagoda was constructed adjacent to the Tang palace in the 7th century to house scriptures brought back from India by a monk named Xuan Zang. It's been rebuilt numerous times since then, most recently during the Qing Dynasty, in Ming style. A park and huge plaza surround the temple, and locals gather here after work to fly kites, stroll hand in hand, and practice calligraphy. There is a popular water-fountain show synchronized to music at noon and 9 pm. The main entrance gate to the temple is on the plaza's southern edge. ✉ *Yanta Lu* ☎ *029/8552–7958* 🎫 *From Y50.*

Culture Street (Shuyuanmen) (文化街 (书院门) *Wénhuà Jiē (Shūyuàn mén)*)
NEIGHBORHOOD | Take a stroll along this leafy boulevard lined with galleries, shops, and a few cafés. Mostly clear of the city's traffic save for a handful of tuk-tuks or "beng beng che" as the locals call them, the cobbled streets run along the southern end of the old city walls and feature beautifully restored buildings with traditional Ming architecture. Start near Heping Lu and walk towards the South Gate and you'll pass by the Forest of Stone Steles Museum. Not too far after, you'll find the Guanzhong Academy, built in 1609. Take a peek through the gates, as entrance is forbidden. ✉ *1 block north of South Gate.*

Drum Tower (鼓楼 *Gŭlóu*)
BUILDING | Originally built in 1384, this 111-foot-high Ming Dynasty building—which used to hold the alarm drums for the imperial city—marks the southern end of Xi'an's Muslim Quarter. Various ancient drums are on display inside the building, and concerts are given daily at 9:10, 10:30, 11:30, 2:30, 3:30, and 4:30. After passing through the tower's massive base, turn left down a small side street called Huajue Xiang to find everything from shadow puppets to Mao memorabilia—truly a souvenir heaven. After clearing that gauntlet, you'll find yourself deep inside the Muslim Quarter at the entrance to the Great Mosque. ✉ *Beiyuanmen, 1 block west of the Bell Tower* 🎫 *From Y35.*

★ **Forest of Stone Steles Museum** (碑林博物馆 *Bēilín bówùguăn*)
MUSEUM | Head here for a glimpse into what the ancient Chinese deemed important enough to set in stone. As the name suggests, there is no shortage of historical steles, or inscribed stone tablets, with content ranging from descriptions of administrative projects and old maps to artistic renditions of landscape, portraiture, and calligraphy. The garden complex and former Confucian temple house one of the world's first dictionaries and a number of Tang Dynasty classics as well as the epitaphs of nobility. One tablet, known as the Nestorian Stele, dates from AD 781 and records the interaction between the Chinese emperor and a traveling Nestorian priest. After presenting the empire with translated Nestorian Christian texts, the priest was allowed to open a church in Xi'an. Non-Chinese speakers may feel frustrated that they can't read all the tablets, as only a few translations are available, but the complex is well worth the visit for history, anthropology, and culture buffs. ✉ *15 Sanxue Jie at end of Wenhua Jie* ☎ *029/8721–0764* 🎫 *Mar.–Nov. Y75; Dec.–Feb. Y50.*

Great Mosque (西安大清真寺 *Xī'ān Dà Qīngzhēnsì*)
RELIGIOUS SITE | This lushly landscaped mosque with four graceful courtyards may have been established as early as AD 742, during the Tang Dynasty, but the remaining buildings date mostly from the 18th century. Stone tablets mark the various pavilions, often bearing inscriptions in both Chinese and Arabic. Look above the doors and gates: there are some remarkable designs, including three-dimensional Arabic script that makes the stone look as malleable as cake frosting. Non-Muslims are not allowed in the prayer hall, as the mosque is still an active place of worship. The place is a bit hard to find, but wandering the **Muslim Quarter** surrounding the Mosque is a treat, particularly for foodies. The bustling streets are the center of the city's Hui (Chinese Muslim) community. Navigate narrow streets and alleys filled with endless knickknack and food stalls. Step into any well-populated restaurants and try anything from cold sesame noodles to panfried dumplings to yang rou pao mo, the local speciality of crumbled bread in a rich lamb broth. To get to the Mosque, after passing through the Drum Tower, follow a small curving market street called Huajue Xiang on the

left. (You'll see an English sign posted on a brick wall next to the street's entrance reading "Great Mosque.") When you reach a small intersection, the mosque's entrance is on the left. ✉ *30 Huajue Xiang* 🎫 *Y25.*

★ **Shaanxi History Museum** (陕西历史博物馆 *Shǎnxī lìshǐ bówùguǎn*)
MUSEUM | Although museums in China are often underwhelming, this is a notable exception. The works in this imposing two-story structure, built in 1991, range from crude Paleolithic stone tools to gorgeously sculpted ceramics from the Tang Dynasty. Get close to several terra-cotta warriors on display, taken from the tombs outside town. The exhibits, which have English descriptions, leave no doubt that China once had the world's most advanced culture. The museum is free; a limited number of tickets are handed out in the morning and the afternoon. Arrive early, and bring your ID. To avoid crowds, start at the top floor and work your way down. English audio guides are available, and some local companies provide excellent guides who can tell you backstories about the artifacts and the people and places they belonged to. ✉ *91 Xiaozhai Dong Lu* ☎ *029/8525–4727* 🌐 *www.sxhm.com* 🎫 *Free (excluding special exhibitions).*

★ **Small Goose Pagoda** (小雁塔 *Xiǎoyàn Tǎ*)
RELIGIOUS SITE | Once part of the 7th-century Jianfu Temple, this 13-tier pagoda was built by Empress Wu Zetian in 707 to honor her predecessor, Emperor Gao Zong. Much less imposing than the Big Goose Pagoda, the smaller pagoda housed Buddhist texts brought back from India by the pilgrim Yiqing in the 8th century. A tremendous earthquake in 1555 lopped off the top two stories of what was originally a 15-story structure; climbing to the top lets you examine the damage. The Xian Museum (free admission, ID required) is part of the same complex, and shows how the ancient capital changed over the centuries. On the grounds there is also a giant bell visitors can ring for good luck—for a price. The whole park offers good people-watching opportunities, and is very peaceful compared to other Xi'an attractions, making it a good place to take a break. ✉ *72 Youyi Xi Lu, west of Nanguan Zhengjie* ☎ *029/8523–8032* 🌐 *www.xabwy.com* 🎫 *Y30 to climb pagoda.*

South Gate and City Walls (南门 (永宁门) *Nán mén (yǒngníng mén))*
BUILDING | Also known as Yongning Gate, this is the most impressive of the 13 gates leading through Xi'an's 39-foot-high city walls. This was the original site of Tang Dynasty fortifications; the walls you see today were built at the beginning of the Ming Dynasty, and they include the country's only remaining example of a complete wall dating to this dynasty. Head up top to watch the sunset, or even a bike ride around the city fortifications. Biking the entire 13.7-km (8½-mile) route atop the walls takes about 90 minutes. Rental bikes are Y45 for a single and Y90 for a tandem lasting 100 minutes, and you must put down a Y200 deposit. Open-air electric cars cost Y80. ✉ *Nan Dajie near Yongningmen metro station* 🎫 *Y54.*

AROUND XI'AN

Famen Temple (法门寺 *Fǎmén Sì*)
RELIGIOUS SITE | Originally built in the 3rd century AD, the temple was the site of an amazing find during renovations in 1981. A sacred crypt housing four of Sakyamuni Buddha's finger bones was discovered to hold more than 25,000 coins and 1,000 sacrificial objects of jade, gold, and silver. Many of these objects are now on display in the on-site museum. The temple is in Famen, 125 km (80 miles) west of Xi'an. ✉ *Famen* ☎ *0917/525–4002* 🌐 *www.famensi.com* 🎫 *Y120.*

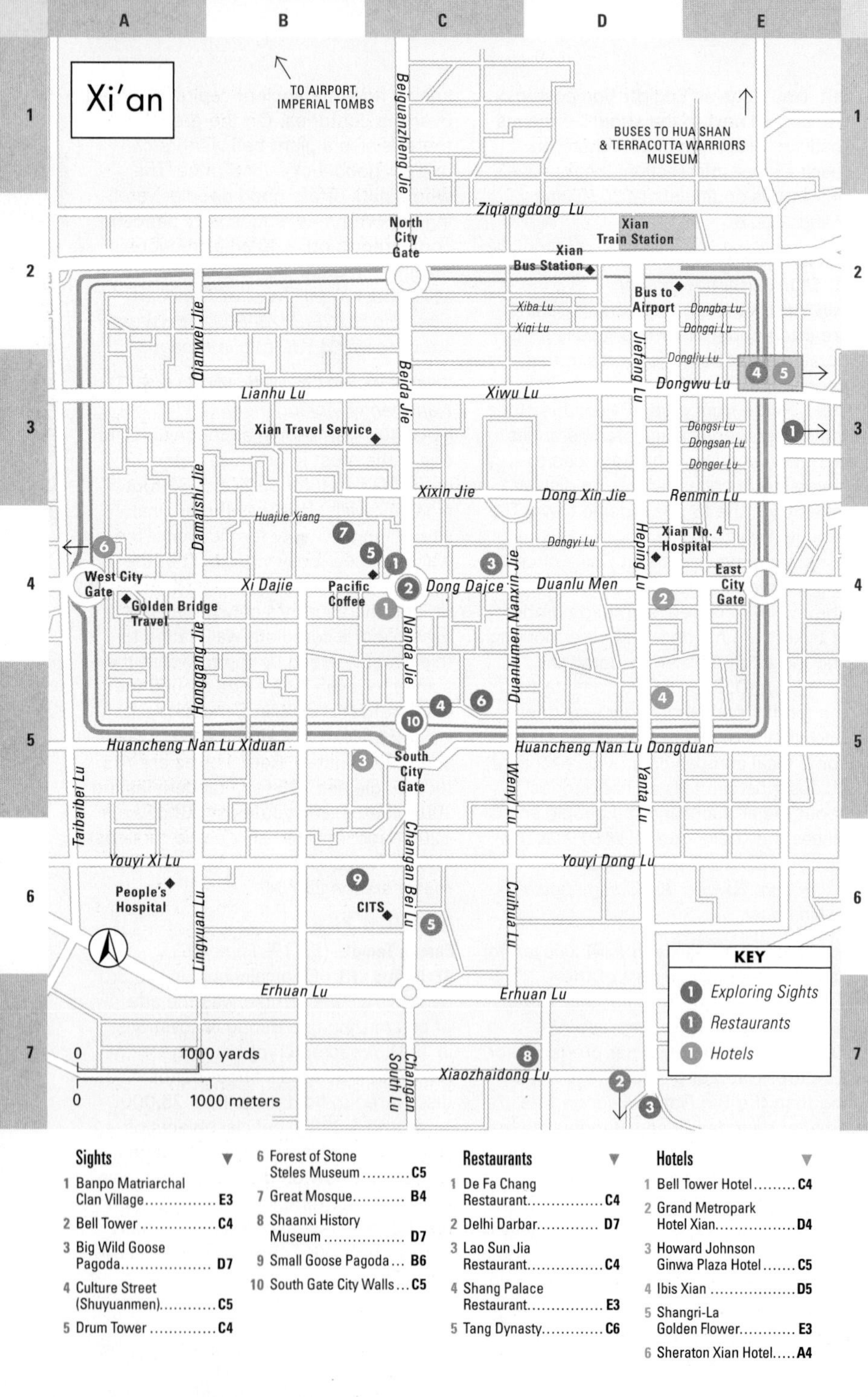

A
B
C
D
E
1
2
3
4
5
6
7
Xi'an
TO AIRPORT, IMPERIAL TOMBS
BUSES TO HUA SHAN & TERRACOTTA WARRIORS MUSEUM
Beiguanzheng Jie
Ziqiangdong Lu
North City Gate
Xian Train Station
Xian Bus Station
Bus to Airport
Xiba Lu
Xiqi Lu
Dongba Lu
Dongqi Lu
Dongliu Lu
Dongwu Lu
Qianwei Jie
Beida Jie
Jiefang Lu
Lianhu Lu
Xiwu Lu
Xian Travel Service
Dongsi Lu
Dongsan Lu
Donger Lu
Damaishi Jie
Xixin Jie
Dong Xin Jie
Renmin Lu
Huajue Xiang
Dongyi Lu
Heping Lu
Xian No. 4 Hospital
West City Gate
Golden Bridge Travel
Xi Dajie
Pacific Coffee
Dong Dajce
Duanlu Men
East City Gate
Honggang Jie
Nanda Jie
Dunlumen Nanxin Jie
Huancheng Nan Lu Xiduan
South City Gate
Huancheng Nan Lu Dongduan
Taibaibei Lu
Wenyi Lu
Yanta Lu
Changan Bei Lu
Youyi Xi Lu
Youyi Dong Lu
People's Hospital
CITS
Lingyuan Lu
Cuihua Lu
Erhuan Lu
Erhuan Lu
Changan South Lu
Xiaozhaidong Lu
0
1000 yards
0
1000 meters
KEY
Exploring Sights
Restaurants
Hotels
Sights
1 Banpo Matriarchal Clan Village E3
2 Bell Tower C4
3 Big Wild Goose Pagoda D7
4 Culture Street (Shuyuanmen) C5
5 Drum Tower C4
6 Forest of Stone Steles Museum C5
7 Great Mosque B4
8 Shaanxi History Museum D7
9 Small Goose Pagoda ... B6
10 South Gate City Walls ... C5
Restaurants
1 De Fa Chang Restaurant C4
2 Delhi Darbar D7
3 Lao Sun Jia Restaurant C4
4 Shang Palace Restaurant E3
5 Tang Dynasty C6
Hotels
1 Bell Tower Hotel C4
2 Grand Metropark Hotel Xian D4
3 Howard Johnson Ginwa Plaza Hotel C5
4 Ibis Xian D5
5 Shangri-La Golden Flower E3
6 Sheraton Xian Hotel A4

Huaqing Hot Springs (华清池 *Huáqīng Chí*)
HOT SPRINGS | A pleasure palace during the Tang Dynasty and later the living quarters of General Chiang Kai-shek during the Chinese Civil War, this destination gets mixed reviews from visitors. Despite the name, the hot springs are often out of action, leaving visitors to wander around the garden. You'll probably be happier spending your time on **Lishan,** the small mountain directly behind Huaqing Hot Springs. It was on these slopes that Chiang was captured, and it has China's first beacon tower and a number of small temples. It was also thought to be the spot where the Emperor Xuanzong and his consort Yang Guifei came for their romantic escapes. If you are here in the evening (8:30 pm), catch the light-and-sound show that uses the mountain as a backdrop. The attraction is 30 km (19 miles) east of Xi'an. ✉ *38 Huaqing Lu, Lintong* ☎ *029/8381–2003* 🌐 *www.hqc.cn* 🎫 *Dec.–Feb., Y80; Mar.–Nov., Y110.*

★ **Huashan** (华山 *Huáshān*)
MOUNTAIN—SIGHT | A few hours east of Xi'an lies one of China's five sacred mountains, a traditional watercolor come to life. The 7,218-foot mountain has stunning scenery, Taoist temples, pines reminiscent of a Dr. Seuss creation, and sheer granite walls that rise shockingly out of the surrounding plains. The five peaks of Huashan reminded ancient visitors of flower petals, hence the name; translated it means "Flower Mountain." Climbing the mountain is not a trip for the fainthearted: unless you're an Olympic athlete, hiking the main trail to the highest South Peak will take a good seven to nine hours, some of it along narrow passes on sheer cliffs. Thankfully, there are cable-car rides to the North and West Peak that bring you most of the way up the trail. Thrill-seekers can walk the plank path, a narrow wooden ledge built around a cliffside thousands of meters above ground level, dubbed the most dangerous trail in the world. From Xi'an you can take a D train (Y35) or G train (Y55) to Huashan North Station or take one of the coaches that leave hourly every morning from the parking lot in front of the Jiefang Hotel, across from the train station. Tours can be arranged, but it's better to go on your own to have more time on the mountain. **■ TIP→ On a rainy day, bring a raincoat or buy one there, don't bring an umbrella. Gusts of wind can come out of nowhere, and you could be yanked off balance while hiking the narrow trails. The danger is so real that locals go so far as to call them death umbrellas.** ✉ *Xian* 🎫 *Mar.–Nov., Y180; Dec.–Feb., Y100.*

★ **Terracotta Warriors Museum** (兵马俑博物馆 *Bīngmǎyǒng Bówùguǎn*)
MUSEUM | Discovered in 1974 by farmers digging a well, this UNESCO World Heritage site includes more than 7,000 terra-cotta soldiers standing guard over the tomb of Qin Shihuang, the first emperor of a unified China. The warriors, more than 1,000 of which have been painstakingly pieced together, come in various forms: archers, infantry, charioteers, and cavalry. Relics are still being unearthed, and some are being left underground until archaeologists find a way to preserve the painted surface, which as of now disintegrates when it comes in contact with outside air. In 2010, 114 extra warriors were discovered in Pit One. Incredibly, each of the life-size statues is unique, including different mustaches, beards, hairstyles, and even wrinkles. An exhibition hall displays artifacts unearthed from distant sections of the tomb, including two magnificently crafted miniature bronze chariots. Allow yourself at least three hours if you want to study the warriors in detail. The site is 30 km (19 miles) east of Xi'an in the town of Lintong. ✉ *Lintong* ☎ *029/8139–9001* 🌐 *www.bmy.com.cn* 🎫 *Mar.–Nov., Y150; Dec.–Feb., Y120.*

Continued on page 495

THE TERRACOTTA WARRIORS

In 1974, Shaanxi farmers digging a well accidentally unearthed one of the greatest archaeological finds of the 20th century—the Terracotta Warriors of Chinese Emperor Qin Shihuang. Armed with real weapons and accompanied by horses and chariots, the more than 8,000 soldiers buried in Qin's tomb were to be his garrison in the afterlife.

(top) Statues depict different military units. (right) Note how the faces differ. Each one is sculpted to be unique.

Did You Know?

The thousands of life-size soldiers include charioteers, cavalrymen, archers, and infantrymen. They're all arranged according to rank and duty—exactly as they would have been for a real-life battle. Each one has individual facial features, including different mustaches, beards, and hairstyles.

UNCOVERING AN ARMY

WHO WAS QIN SHIHUANG?

After destroying the last of his rivals in 221 BC, Qin Shihuang became the first emperor to rule over a unified China. He established a centralized government headquartered near modern day Xianyang in Shaanxi Province. Unlike the feudal governments of the past under which regional officials developed local bases of power, the new centralized government concentrated all power in the hands of a godlike emperor.

Unfortunately for Qin Shihuang's potential heirs, the emperor's inexhaustible hunger for huge engineering projects created high levels of public unrest. These projects, including a precursor to the Great Wall, his own massive tomb, and numerous roads and canals, required the forced labor of millions of Chinese citizens. In 210 BC, Qin died from mercury poisoning during a failed attempt at making himself immortal. Only four years later, his son was overthrown and killed, bringing an ignominious end to China's first dynasty.

A THANKLESS JOB

The construction of Qin Shihuang's gargantuan tomb complex—which includes the Terracotta Warriors—was completed by more than 700,000 workers over a period of nearly 40 years. The warriors themselves are believed to have been created in an assembly line process in which sets of legs and torsos were fired separately and later combined with individually sculpted heads. Most workers were unskilled laborers; skilled craftsmen completed more delicate work such as the decoration of the tomb and the molding of heads. The soldiers were then painted with colored lacquer to make them both more durable and realistic. It's believed that all of the workers were buried alive inside the tomb (which hasn't yet been excavated) to keep its location and treasures a secret and protect it from grave robbers.

DISCOVERING THE WARRIORS

Only five years after the death of Qin Shihuang, looting soldiers set fire to the thick wooden beams supporting the vaults. As wood burned and the structure became unsound, beams and earthen walls came crashing down onto the statues, crushing many soldiers and burying all. In many ways, though, the damage to the vaults was a blessing in disguise. The buried Terracotta Warriors were forgotten to history, but the lack of oxygen and sunlight preserved the figures for centuries.

Since its rediscovery, only a part of the massive complex has been excavated, and the process of unearthing more warriors and relics continues. No one is sure just how many warriors there are or how far the figures extend beyond the already excavated 700-foot-by-200-foot section. For the time being, most excavation work has stopped while scientists attempt to develop a method of preserving the figures' colored lacquer, which quickly deteriorates when exposed to oxygen.

(top) Warriors were once painted in bright colors.

VISITING THE WARRIORS

Be sure to walk around to the rear of Vault 1, which contains most of the figures that have already been unearthed. There you can see archaeologists reassembling the smashed sodiers. Vaults 2 and 3 contain unreconstructed warriors and their weapons and give you an idea of how much work went into presenting Vault 1 as we see it today.

CIRCLE VISION THEATER

Before heading to the vaults, stop by this 360-degree movie theater and learn how the army was constructed, destroyed, forgotten, and then rediscovered. Although the film is cheesy, it's nonetheless entertaining and informative. It gives a sense of what the area may have been like 2,200 years ago.

VAULT 1

Here you'll find about 6,000 warriors, although only 1,000 have been painstakingly pieced together by archaeologists. The warriors stand in their original pits and can only be seen from the walkways erected around the digs. Those in the front ranks are well shaped and fully outfitted except for their weapons, whose wooden handles have decayed over the centuries (the chrome-plated bronze blades were still sharp upon excavation). Walk around to the rear of the vault where you can see terracotta warriors in various states of reconstruction.

Archaeologists have puzzled together almost 1,000 statues, including warriors, chariots, horses, officials, acrobats, strongmen, and musicians. The tallest statues are also the highest in rank; they are the generals.

COLORATION

The colored lacquers that were used not only gave the terracotta soldiers a realistic appearance, but also sealed and protected the clay. Unfortunately, upon exposure to oxygen, these thin layers of color become extremely brittle and flake off or crumble to dust. Chinese scientists are devising excavation methods that will preserve the coloration of warriors unearthed in the future.

Ready on one knee with bow in hand, these archers are poised to rise and fire a deadly salvo at a moment's notice.

Every cavalry rider is accompanied by a life-size terracotta horse.

VISITING THE WARRIORS

(top) Statues were made in pieces and then assembled. (right) The statue of an officer. (opposite page) The cavalry horses.

VAULT 2

This vault offers a glimpse of unreconstructed figures as they emerge from the ground. It has remained mostly undisturbed since 1999 when archaeologists found the first tricolor figures—look closely and you can still see pink on the soldiers' faces and patches of dark red on their armor. As with ancient Greek sculptures, the warriors were originally painted in lifelike colors and with red armor. Around the sides of the vault, you can take a close-up look at excellent examples of soldiers and their weaponry in glass cases.

VAULT 3

Sixty-eight soldiers and officers in various states of reconstruction stand in what appears to be a military headquarters. Although the condition of the warriors are similar to those in Vault 2, there is one unique figure: a charioteer standing at the ready, though his wooden chariot has been lost to time.

EXHIBITION HALL

Near Vault 3, an imposing sand-colored pavilion houses two miniature bronze chariots unearthed in the western section of Qin Shihuang's tomb. Found in 1980, these chariots are intricately detailed with ornate gold and silver ornamentation. In the atrium leading to the bronze chariots, look for a massive bronze urn—it's one of the treasures unearthed by archaeologists in their 1999 excavation of an accessory pit near the still-sealed mausoleum. Other artifacts on display including Qin Dynasty tricolor pottery and Qin jade carvings.

How to Visit the Warriors

Getting There

Practically every hotel and tour company in Xi'an arranges bus trips to the Terracotta Warriors as part of an Eastern Tour package. If you aren't interested in having an English-speaking guide for the day, you can save a lot of money by taking one of the cheap buses (Y8 one-way) that leave for the town of Lintong from the parking lot between Xi'an's train station and the Jiefang Hotel. The ride to the Terracotta Warriors Museum should take less than two hours. *Mar.–Nov., daily 8:30–5:30; Dec.–Feb., daily 8:30–5* *Mar.–Nov. Y150, Dec.–Feb. Y120. Price includes movie, access to 3 vaults, and entrance to Exhibition Hall* *029/8139–9001 main office, 029/8139–9126 ticket office.*

Visiting Tips

Cameras: You can shoot photographs and videos inside the vaults, a change from previous years when guards brusquely confiscated film upon seeing your camera. You still can't use a flash or tripod, however.

Souvenirs: You can buy postcards and other souvenirs in the shops outside the vaults and the Circle Vision Theater. Alternatively, you can face the fearsome gauntlet of souvenir hawkers outside the main gates; miniature replica Terracotta Warriors can be found here for as little as Y1 each. If you're intimidated by the aggressive touts, however, there's nothing available here that you can't get back in Xi'an. So be strong, don't look them in the eyes, and most important, never stop walking.

Time: You'll likely end up spending two to three hours touring the vaults and exhibits at the Terracotta Warriors Museum. The time spent here will probably be part of a long day tour visiting a number of sites—the Hauqing Hot Springs and possibly the Banpo Matriachal Clan Village—clustered around the small city of Lintong, east of Xi'an.

Tomb of the First Qin Emperor (秦始皇陵 *Qínshǐhuáng líng*)

MEMORIAL | The tomb—consisting mainly of a large burial mound—may pale in comparison to the Terracotta Warriors Museum, but history buffs will enjoy it. According to ancient records, the underground palace took more than 40 years to build, and many historians believe the tomb contains a wealth of priceless treasures, though perhaps we will never know for sure. You can climb to the top of the burial mound for a view of the surrounding countryside, although most visitors hurry off to see the Terracotta Warriors Museum after watching a mildly amusing ceremony honoring the emperor who united China. The tomb is in Lintong, 30 km (19 miles) east of Xi'an, by the Terracotta Warriors Museum. ✉ *Lintong* *Nov.–Mar., Y150; Apr.–Oct., Y120; includes admission to Terracotta Warriors Museum.*

Restaurants

De Fa Chang Restaurant (德发长饺子馆 *Dé fā chǎng jiǎozi guǎn*)

$$ | **CHINESE** | **FAMILY** | As one of Xi'an's most famous restaurants, De Fa Chang offers a buffet of Chinese dumplings that will satisfy even the hungriest of travelers. The restaurant can be a bit tricky to find; walk along the front of the building facing Xi Dajie, past the shops selling trinkets and antiques to the end of the

Raiders of the Lost Tomb

Qin started construction on his enormous, richly endowed tomb, said to be booby-trapped with automatic crossbows, almost as soon as he took the throne. According to ancient records, this underground palace contained 100 rivers of flowing mercury as well as ceilings inlaid with precious stones and pearls representing the stars and planets. Interestingly enough, mercury levels in the area's soil are much higher than normal, indicating that there may be truth to those records. Though the site of the tomb was rediscovered to the east of Xi'an in 1974 (soon after the Terracotta Warriors were unearthed), the government didn't touch it because it lacked the sophisticated machinery needed to excavate safely. Authorities also executed any locals foolish enough to attempt a treasure-seeking foray. In 1999, archaeologists finally began excavations of the area around the tomb and unearthed some fabulous treasures. They've only scratched the surface, however. Most of the tomb still lies buried. In fact, no one is even certain where its main entrance—reportedly sealed with molten copper—is located. Authorities have delayed further excavations until the tomb can be properly preserved rather than risk damaging what may be China's greatest archaeological site.

row. **Known for:** delicious dumpling soup; dumplings made into shapes of animals; both meat and vegetarian options. $ *Average main: Y60 ✉ 3 Xi Dajie, north side of Bell Tower Sq. ☏ 029/8721–4060 ▭ No credit cards.*

Delhi Darbar (新德里餐厅 *Xīndélǐ cāntīng*)
$$ | INDIAN | For a break from Chinese food, try this authentic Indian restaurant that combines fragrant curries with oven-fresh naan bread. Although the service needs some polishing, the staff are good at handling requests for vegetarian dishes, of which there are also enough on the menu to ensure everyone leaves satisfied. **Known for:** authentic Indian curries; chhach, a yogurt-based drink; being vegan-friendly. $ *Average main: Y80 ✉ 3 Yanta Xi Lu, near Big Wild Goose Pagoda ☏ 029/8525–5157 ▭ No credit cards.*

Lao Sun Jia Restaurant (孙老家饭庄 *Lǎo sūn jiā fàn zhuāng*)
$ | NORTHERN CHINESE | This traditional, family-run affair has been serving some of the best local Islamic lamb and beef specialties since 1898; it's become so popular that it's grown into a small Xi'an chain. A few famous offerings, such as the roasted leg of lamb or the spicy mutton spareribs, are pricey, but most dishes are inexpensive. **Known for:** mouthwatering yang rou pao mo; juicy lamb dumplings; hot-off-the-grill lamb kebabs. $ *Average main: Y30 ✉ 364 Dong Dajie, near corner of Duanlu Men ☏ 029/8742–1858 ▭ No credit cards.*

Shang Palace Restaurant (香宫 *Xiāng gōng*)
$$$ | CANTONESE | All of Xi'an's top hotels have elegant eateries, but Shang Palace deserves special mention for its Cantonese and Sichuan dishes, which are authentic and approachable. Classics like honey-barbecued pork and stir-fried chili chicken compliment their specialty noodle dishes. **Known for:** classic roasted duck with Shaanxi spices; elegant decor and often live music; extensive wine menu. $ *Average main: Y150 ✉ Shangri-La Golden Flower Hotel, 8 Changle Xi Lu ☏ 029/8323–2981.*

★ **Tang Dynasty** (西安唐乐宫 *Xī'ān táng lè gōng*)
$$$$ | CHINESE | Although it's better known for the affiliated theater, this separate restaurant specializes in the imperial cuisine of its namesake, a taste you're not likely to find back home at your local Chinese restaurant. You can eat at the restaurant separately or reserve tickets for dinner and the show (Y500). **Known for:** entertaining and colorful show; excellent seafood dishes; ornate Tang-era decoration. *Average main: Y180 ✉ 75 Changan Bei Lu ☎ 155/5258–9030 ⊕ www.xiantangdynastyshow.com.*

Hotels

Bell Tower Hotel (钟楼饭店 *Zhōnglóu fàndiàn*)
$ | HOTEL | Directly across from the Bell Tower, this comfortable and centrally located hotel puts you within walking distance of many of the city's most popular tourist sights. **Pros:** excellent location near public transport; clean rooms; some rooms with view of Bell Tower. **Cons:** absence of character; rooms dated and showing wear; hotel restaurants are mediocre. *Rooms from: Y548 ✉ 110 Nan Da Jie ☎ 029/8760–0000 ⊕ www.belltowerhotelxian.cn 311 rooms No Free Breakfast.*

Grand Metropark Hotel Xian (阿房宫维景国际大酒店 *Āfáng gōng wéi jǐng guójì dà jiǔdiàn*)
$ | HOTEL | Although there are newer luxury properties, people return to the Grand Metropark because of its friendly staff, most of whom speak some English, and its central location. **Pros:** walking distance to the city's sights; ample breakfast spread; several restaurant options inside and nearby. **Cons:** breakfast overpriced if not included in room rate; music in the atrium lobby can be annoying; rooms show signs of age. *Rooms from: Y599 ✉ 158 Dong Dajie ☎ 029/8723–1234 337 rooms No meals.*

Howard Johnson Ginwa Plaza Hotel (金花豪生国际大酒店 *Jīnhuā háoshēng guójì dà jiǔdiàn*)
$ | HOTEL | Though dated, this HoJo offers good value for money in a hotel that sits just outside the city walls near the south gate and the Yongningmen metro station. **Pros:** convenient to city wall; breakfast buffet has plenty of Western options; caters to the Western comfort standard. **Cons:** nothing individual about this place; language barriers with staff; located outside the old city. *Rooms from: Y538 ✉ 18 Huancheng Nan Lu (Xi Duan) ☎ 029/8818–1111 198 rooms No meals.*

Ibis Xian (西安宜必思酒店 *Xī'ān yíbìsī jiǔdiàn*)
$ | HOTEL | The best bargain in Xi'an's Old City is part of the French budget hotel chain Ibis. **Pros:** great location; friendly service; excellent value for the comfort. **Cons:** unappealing breakfast; roadside rooms can be a bit noisy at night; far walk from the subway stop. *Rooms from: Y303 ✉ 59 Heping Lu ☎ 029/8727–5555 ⊕ www.accorhotels.com 220 rooms Breakfast.*

★ **Shangri-La Golden Flower** (西安金花大酒店 *Xī'ān jīn huā dà jiǔdiàn*)
$ | HOTEL | The older of the two Shangri-La's in Xi'an, this remains one of the city's most luxurious hotels with English-speaking staff, an indoor swimming pool and gym facilities. **Pros:** spacious rooms; large indoor swimming pool; quick access to the subway. **Cons:** layout is confusing; rooms beginning to show age; bathrooms are in need of updating. *Rooms from: Y550 ✉ 8 Changle Xi Lu ☎ 029/8323–2981, 800/8942–5050 in U.S. ⊕ www.goldenflowerhotel.com/en 415 rooms No meals.*

Sheraton Xian Hotel (喜来登西安大酒店 *Xǐláidēng Xī'ān dà jiǔdiàn*)
$ | HOTEL | Expect high-quality standards in this name-brand hotel, among them truly comfortably beds and front desk staff who speak English well. **Pros:** glitzy

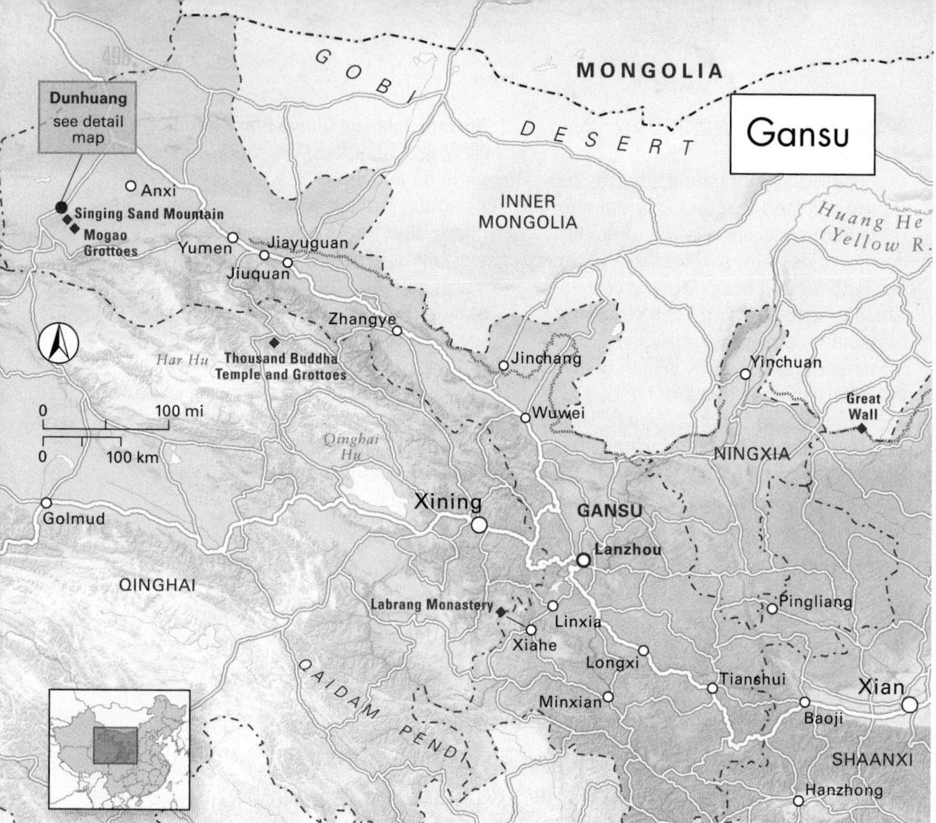

and well-fitted bathrooms; excellent buffet breakfast; Sheraton-level service. **Cons:** located in an uninteresting commercial part of town; lack of guest control over a/c. $ *Rooms from: Y558* ✉ *262 Fenghao Dong Lu* ☎ *029/8426–1888* 🌐 *www.starwoodhotels.com* 🛏 *426 rooms* 🍽 *No meals.*

Performing Arts

Tang Dynasty (唐代 *Táng dài*)

DANCE | In a city where the list of nightlife options isn't terribly long, the song and dance performance at Tang Dynasty makes for a fun if slightly cheesy evening. Dinner starts at 7 pm, shows begin at 8:30 pm, and for the meal you have a choice between the dumpling banquet (Y400) and the Tang Dynasty Dinner (Y500). You may be able to get a better deal through travel agencies that often have offices in hotel lobbies. ✉ *75 Chang'an Bei Lu* ☎ *029/8782–2222* 🌐 *www.xiantangdynastyshow.com.*

Shopping

Huajue Xiang Market (化觉巷市场 *Huàjué xiàng shìchǎng*)

GIFTS/SOUVENIRS | In the alley leading to the Great Mosque, the Hua Jue Xiang Market is one of the best places to find souvenirs. From embroidered bags and trinkets to lamps and musical wooden frogs, all kinds of wares are available for sale. Expect the antique you're eyeing to be fake, no matter how vehemently the vendor insists that your find is "genuine Ming Dynasty." ✉ *Huajue Xiang right by Great Mosque, Lian Hu district.*

The Great Prayer Festival at the Labrang Monastery

Lanzhou

3 hrs by high-speed train northwest of Xi'an; 12 hrs by high-speed train southeast of Ürümqi; 1½ hrs by train east of Xining; 9 hours by high-speed train from Beijing.

Built on the banks of the Yellow River, the capital of Gansu extends along the base of a narrow gorge whose walls rise to 5,000 feet. A city with a long history, Lanzhou has been nearly ruined by rampant industrialization, and is now one of the world's most polluted urban areas. Though air quality is getting better, in winter the city can be filled with smog.

The ethnic mix of the city's population makes the place interesting for a few hours, but plan to stay here only as long as it takes to arrange transportation to somewhere more pleasant, like Xiahe or Dunhuang.

GETTING HERE AND AROUND

The city's Zhongchuan Airport is 67 km (42 miles) north of town, which translates to about an hour's drive in a taxi. From Lanzhou there are daily flights to Dunhuang, Beijing, Guangzhou, Shanghai, Chengdu, Ürümqi, and Xi'an. A public bus costing Y30 per person takes almost two hours to reach the airport from the China Northwest Airlines office at 512 Donggang Xi Lu.

Long-distance buses arrive at the East Station (汽车东站 Qìchē dōng zhàn) on Pingliang Lu, north of the train station. Leaving the city can be a bit more complicated. Buses to major destinations like Xi'an, Xining, Jiayuguan, and Dunhuang usually leave from the East Station, while smaller destinations are served by the West Station (汽车西站 Qìchē xī zhàn). Buses to Xiahe depart from the South Station (汽车南站 Qìchē nán zhàn).

Buses originating in Lanzhou often require foreigners to show proof of travel insurance bought from the Chinese company PICC (The People's Insurance

Company of China—a monstrously large insurance company) before purchasing tickets. It's unclear why this regulation exists, or why there's usually at least one daily bus to each destination that doesn't require the paperwork. You should be able to purchase insurance with your bus ticket, but this is often not the case. For peace of mind, head straight to the main PICC office on the north side of Qingyang Lu, just east of Jingning Lu. They'll know why you're there. A two-week policy costs Y40. At this writing, you were required to show two photocopies of your visa and passport details.

The train station (兰州火车站 Lánzhōu huǒchē zhàn) is at the southern end of Tianshui Lu, 1 km (½ mile) south of the city's main hotels. With few trains originating here, buying sleeper tickets in Lanzhou can be difficult; your best bet is to buy tickets early, or hope for an upgrade once onboard.

TIMING

Lanzhou's appeal is limited; stay only as long as you need to arrange transportation to the province's other worthier attractions.

TOURS

Gansu China Travel Service offers a day trip to Thousand Buddha Temple and Grottoes that includes all transportation for Y380 with a group. The company also has tours to Xiahe, including a five-day trip that visits the spectacularly beautiful Tibetan temples at Langmusi on the border with Sichuan. A basic two-day tour from Lanzhou costs between Y700 and Y850 per person, including hotel.

Sights

Five Springs Mountain Park (五泉山公园 *Wǔ quánshān gōngyuán*)
CITY PARK | Sip tea among ancient temples and take in impressive views of the city from this pretty park. The five springs that gave the place its name, unfortunately, have dwindled to a trickle. ✉ *103 Wuquan Dong Lu* ☎ *0931/824–3247.*

★ **Gansu Provincial Museum** (甘肃省博物馆 *Gānsù shěng bówùguǎn*)
MUSEUM | The most famous item in this excellent museum's collection is the elegant bronze "Flying Horse," considered a masterpiece of ancient Chinese art that you'll find replicated all across China. Other notable objects include a silver plate documenting contact between China and Rome more than 2,200 years ago, and wooden tablets used to send messages along the Silk Road. Not all exhibits have information in English. Admission is free but you'll need your passport. ✉ *3 Xijin Xi Lu, near Lanzhou west train station* ☎ *0931/233–9131* 🌐 *www.gansumuseum.com* *Free* *Closed Mon.*

White Pagoda Mountain Park (白塔山公园 *Báitǎshān gōngyuán*)
CITY PARK | Laid out in 1958, the park covers the slopes on the Yellow River's north bank. Beautiful views of Lanzhou and the river are a leisurely walk or cable car away. It's more of a carnival than a place to relax, but it's a great place for people-watching. ✉ *Enter at Zhongshan Qiao, bridge extending over Yellow River* ☎ *0931/836–0800* *Free.*

Restaurants

Chuanwei Wang (川味王 *Chuān wèi wáng*)
$ | **SICHUAN** | You can often tell a good restaurant by the lack of empty tables; at mealtimes, this Sichuanese eatery is always packed. The picture menu makes ordering dishes very simple, but if you're stuck, order *gongbao jiding* (aka authentic kung pao chicken), a slightly spicy dish of chicken stir-fried with peanuts. **Known for:** authentic kung pao chicken; spicy tofu; dandan noodles. $ *Average main: Y40* ✉ *16 Nongmin Xiang* ☎ *0931/887–9879* *No credit cards.*

Ma Zilu Beef Noodles (马子禄牛肉面 *măzilù niúròumiàn*)
$ | **CHINESE** | This lively canteen opens at the crack of dawn and has some of the most fragrant, toothsome beef noodles in Lanzhou, among other excellent dishes. The downstairs is set up like a cafeteria, where you can take what you want and grab a seat, while the upstairs is a dining room with air-conditioning and table service. **Known for:** delicious beef noodles; lively atmosphere; a quick, cheap meal. *Average main: Y15 86 Da Zhong Xiang 931/845–0505 No credit cards Closed after 2 pm.*

Xinhai Restaurant (鑫海大酒店 *Xīnhăi dà jiŭdiàn*)
$$ | **CHINESE** | Xinhai is surprisingly affordable and offers Cantonese and Sichuan dishes in addition to Lanzhou specialties such as braised beef and hand-pulled noodles. There's a picture menu in Chinese only and one without pictures in English. **Known for:** hand-pulled noodles; good location; comfortable seating and relaxing atmosphere. *Average main: Y80 69 Jinchang Bei Lu 0931/886–1678 No credit cards.*

Hotels

Crowne Plaza Lanzhou (皇冠假日酒店 *Huángguàn jiàrì jiŭdiàn*)
$$ | **HOTEL** | Located close to the Gansu International Convention and Exhibition Center, this modern hotel is a little removed from the city center but offers solid service and good views of the neighboring Yellow River. **Pros:** attentive staff; good breakfast buffet; generous room size. **Cons:** difficult to get a taxi back to the hotel; staff don't speak much English; small gym. *Rooms from: Y1125 1 Beibinhe Dong Lu 0931/871–1111 www.ihg.com 440 rooms Breakfast.*

Don't Miss

A highlight of a visit to the Labrang Monastery is the daily gathering of monks for religious debate in the liveliest fashion. The monks charge at each other in groups, hissing good-naturedly, as older monks supervise with a benevolent air. The debate takes place on a lawn in the afternoon; ask at the ticket office for times. Another interesting daily event is the gathering of hundreds of chanting monks on the steps of the main prayer hall, beginning around 11:30 am.

Jinjiang Sun Hotel (锦江阳光酒店 *Jĭnjiāng yángguāng jiŭdiàn*)
$ | **HOTEL** | From the marble floors in the lobby to the plush furnishings, this 25-story tower houses one of Lanzhou's top hotels. **Pros:** excellent value; reception staff speak English; good Chinese/Western breakfast options. **Cons:** Wi-Fi is free but very slow; business-center facilities are sparse; in a commercial part of town. *Rooms from: Y549 589 Donggang Xi Lu 0931/880–5511 236 rooms No meals.*

Lanzhou Hotel (兰州饭店 *Lánzhōu fàndiàn*)
$ | **HOTEL** | Built in 1956, this concrete behemoth's Sino-Stalinist exterior hides a modern if drab interior. **Pros:** a local landmark that's easy to find; great value rooms; good on-site Chinese restaurant. **Cons:** even the no-smoking rooms smell smoky; rooms lack any character; few staff speak English. *Rooms from: Y349 486 Donggang Xi Lu at corner of Tianshui Zhong Lu 0931/841–6321 www.lanzhouhotel.com 468 rooms No meals.*

Side Trips from Lanzhou

★ Labrang Monastery (拉卜楞寺 *Lābŭléng sì*)

RELIGIOUS SITE | In the remote town of Xiahe, the monastery is a little piece of Tibet along the Gansu-Qinghai border. A world away from Lanzhou, Xiahe has experienced a dizzying rise in the number of travelers over the past decade. Despite the encroaching modernity, Xiahe is still a wonderful place, attracting large numbers of pilgrims who come to study and to spin the 1,147 prayer wheels of the monastery daily, swathed in their distinctive costume of heavy woolen robes tied with brightly colored sashes.

The Labrang Monastery is the largest Tibetan lamasery outside Tibet. Founded in 1710, it once had as many as 4,000 monks, a number much depleted due in large part to the Cultural Revolution, when monks were forced to return home and temples were destroyed. Though the monastery reopened in 1980, the government's continued policy of restricted enrollment has kept the number of monks down to about 1,500. There are guided tours daily at 10:15 am and 3:15 pm.

There are two ways to reach Xiahe: by public bus or by private tour. Buses for Xiahe leave from Lanzhou's South Station (汽车南站, Qìchē nán zhàn) in the morning (6:30 and 7:30) and afternoon (2 and 3) and take about four hours. Make sure to purchase tickets in advance, as some departures require travel insurance. Have two photocopies of your visa and passport information on hand in case they are required. **■ TIP→ As of this writing, the monastery is open to tourists. However, it has been closed in the recent past due to political uprisings, so as you plan your trip, keep tabs on the news.** ✉ *2 km (1 mile) west of long-distance bus station, Xiahe* 🎫 *Y40.*

★ Thousand Buddha Temple and Grottoes (炳灵寺 *Bĭng líng sì*)

RELIGIOUS SITE | One of the best day trips is the Thousand Buddha Temple and Grottoes, about 80 km (50 miles) from Lanzhou. More commonly known by its Chinese name *Bingling Si,* it's filled with Buddhist paintings and statuary, including an impressive 89-foot-tall Buddha carved into a cliff face.

The canyon that holds the Thousand Buddha Temple runs along one side of the Yellow River. The journey through a gorge lined by water-sculpted rocks is spectacular. When the canyon is dry you can travel 2½ km (1½ miles) on foot or by four-wheel-drive vehicle to see the small community of Tibetan lamas at the Upper Temple of Bingling. However, it's much easier to book a tour. Gansu Western Travel Service offers a popular day trip that includes all transportation, insurance, and entrance fee (Y1,300 for a one-person tour; Y340 if you join a group tour of 14 people). ✉ *Lanzhou* 🎫 *Y50.*

Dunhuang

17 hrs by bus or 14 hrs by train northwest of Lanzhou; 6 hrs by bus west of Jiayuguan.

A small oasis town, Dunhuang was for many centuries the most important Buddhist destination on the Silk Road. Just outside of town, beyond the towering dunes of Singing Sand Mountain, you can see the extraordinary caves of the Mogao Grottoes, considered the world's richest repository of Buddhist art.

Buddhism entered China via the Silk Road, and as Dunhuang was the point of entry to the Chinese world, it was not long before a temple was established here. By AD 366, the first caves were being carved and painted at the Mogao oasis. Work continued until the 10th century, after which they were left undisturbed for nearly 1,000 years.

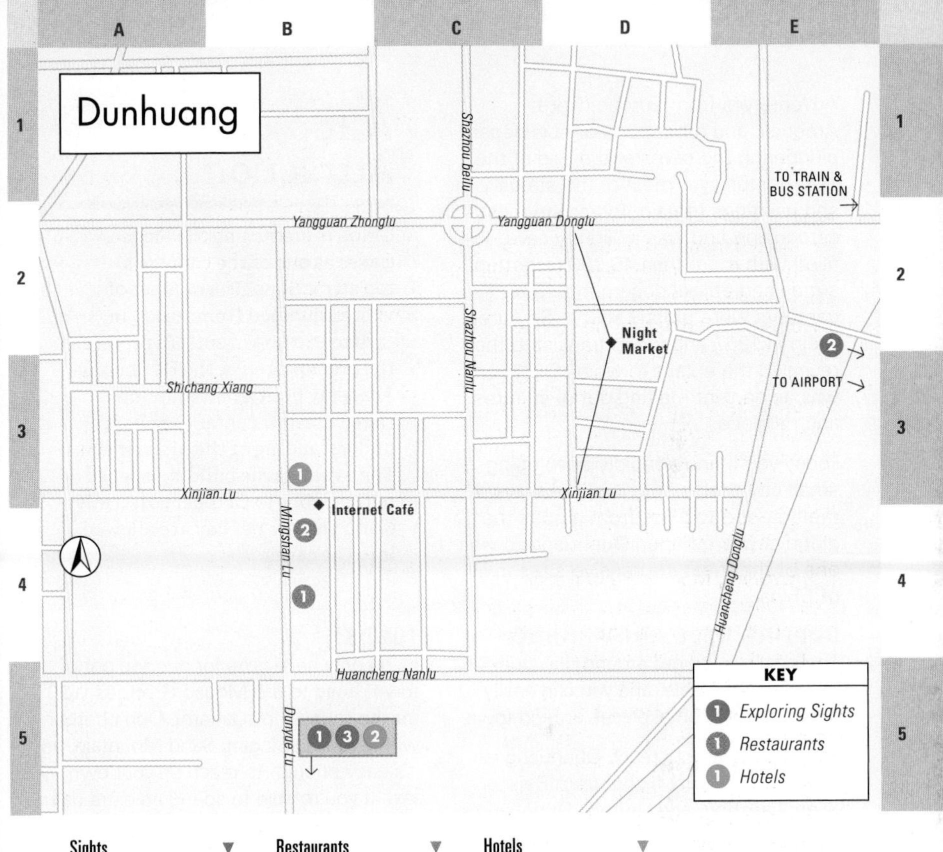

Sights

1 Dunhuang Museum **B5**

2 Mogao Grottoes **E2**

3 Singing Sand Mountain **B5**

Restaurants

1 John's Information Café **B4**

2 Sichuan Restaurant............... **B4**

Hotels

1 Dunhuang Fandian **B3**

2 Dunhuang Silk Road Hotel................**B5**

Adventurers from Europe, North America, and other parts of Asia began plundering the caves at the end of the 19th century, yet most of the statuary and paintings remain. By far the most astounding find was a "library cave" filled with more than 45,000 forgotten sutras and official documents. The contents were mostly sold to Sir Aurel Stein in 1907, and when translated they revealed the extent to which Dunhuang was an ancient melting pot of cultures and religions.

Today you'll find a rapidly developing small city that is still, in some ways, a melting pot; tourists from across the globe converge upon Dunhuang to visit one of the most impressive sites in all of China.

GETTING HERE AND AROUND

The best way to get around tiny Dunhuang is by bicycle, and you can easily hire one from rental places around town.

The easiest way to reach Dunhuang is by air, with regular flights from Beijing, Xi'an, Lanzhou, and Ürümqi. Dunhuang's airport is 13 km (8 miles) east of town, on the road to the Mogao Grottoes. A taxi ride from the airport costs Y20 to Y30.

Buses from Lanzhou, Turpan, and Jiayuguan depart frequently for Dunhuang.

Dunhuang's train station is 13 km (8 miles) northeast of the town and serves Lanzhou, Xi'an, and Jiayuguan. A better-connected station, with services to Beijing and Shanghai, is in the small town of Liuyuan, 120 km (74 miles) away. Taxis from Liuyuan to Dunhuang cost Y120, or you can hop aboard one of the buses that leave hourly for Y15 from the main bus station.

TIMING

Aim to spend at least two days in Dunhuang: one day to see the Mogao Caves and Singing Sand Mountain, and the other to spend time in the town itself.

A Top Attraction

China is promoting the Mogao Caves as one of the country's top attractions. The number of visitors jumped from 26,000 in 1979 to 680,000 in 2011. To protect the precious relics, the Dunhuang Academy built a new state-of-the-art visitor center to enhance understanding of the historic site. The avant-garde building opened to the public in October 2014. Only 6,000 visitors per day are allowed into the caves.

TOURS

If you only have time for one trip out of town, head to the Mogao Grottoes (Y20 for the round-trip bus fare). Don't bother with a tour to Singing Sand Mountain, as it's easy enough to reach on your own by taxi. If you're able to spend an extra day in town, take a tour of sites relating to ancient Dunhuang.

Sights

Dunhuang Museum (敦煌博物馆 *Dūnhuáng bówùguǎn*)
MUSEUM | The museum, which got shiny new digs in late 2013, displays objects recovered from nearby Silk Road fortifications such as reclining Buddhas, sumptuous wall paintings, and sculptures. If you've visited the Jade Gate or Yangguan Pass, you may enjoy seeing the treasures that were once hidden within their walls. ✉ *1390 Mingshan Bei Lu* *Free.*

★ **Mogao Grottoes** (莫高窟 *Mò gāo kū*)
CAVE | The magnificent Buddhist grottoes, considered by some to be the most famous in China, lie southeast of Dunhuang. At least 40 of the 700 caves—dating from the Northern Wei Dynasty in the 4th century AD to the

The dramatic landscape of Qinghai

Five Dynasties in the 10th century AD—are open to the public. Which caves are open on a given day depends on the whim of local authorities, but you shouldn't worry too much about missing something. Everything here is stunning. You'll almost certainly visit the giant seated Buddhas in caves 96 and 130, the Tang Dynasty sleeping Buddha in cave 148, and the famous "library" in caves 16 and 17, where 45,000 religious and political documents were uncovered at the turn of the 20th century. A flashlight is a useful item for your visit. Note that photographs are not allowed.

This is one site where you should hire an English-speaking guide. At a cost of Y20, your understanding of the different imagery used in each cave will increase immeasurably. Tours in English take place about three times a day in high season, so you may have to wait to join one. After the tour, you'll have time to wander around and revisit any unlocked caves. A fine museum contains reproductions of eight caves not usually visited on the public tour. A smaller museum near the Library Cave details the removal of artifacts by foreign plunderers. If you have a deep interest in the cave art, you may be able to pay extra to visit other caves that are sealed off to the general public. Ask at the ticket office.

To get here, take a taxi (Y60–Y80 round-trip) or take the half-hour bus ride that departs from Xinjian Lu, near the corner with Minshan Lu. The bus runs from 8:30 am to 7 pm, and tickets cost Y8 each way. The CITS branch at the Feitan Hotel offers a daily bus service, leaving Dunhuang at 8 am and returning at noon. A round-trip costs Y20. ✉ *25 km (17 miles) southeast of Dunhuang* ☎ *0937/882–5000* 🎫 *May–Oct., Y180 with guided tour; Nov.–Apr., Y100 with guide.*

Singing Sand Mountain (鸣沙山 *Míng shā shān*)
MOUNTAIN—SIGHT | South of Dunhuang, where the oasis gives way to desert, you'll find a gorgeous sweep of sand dunes named for the light rattling sound

that the sand makes when wind blows across the surface. At 5,600 feet above sea level, the half-hour climb to the summit is difficult but worth it for the views, particularly at sunset. Nestled in the sand is **Crescent Moon Lake** (月牙泉, *Yuèyá quán*), a lovely pool that by some freak of the prevailing winds never silts up. Camels, sleds, and various flying contraptions are available at steep prices; try your bargaining skills. ✉ *Mingshan Lu, 5 km (3 miles) south of town* 🎫 *Y120.*

John's Information Café
$$ | **AMERICAN** | Cool off after a full day of sightseeing on this trellised patio with an ice-cold beer and plate of noodles. In addition to an array of familiar foods, the restaurant can arrange overnight camel rides for Y700 per person, as well as trips to Yadan National Park and other destinations. **Known for:** good coffee brews; familiar Western foods; popular travel tour options. $ *Average main: Y60* ✉ *21 Mingshan Lu* ☎ *0998/258–1186* 🌐 *www.johncafe.net* 💳 *No credit cards.*

Sichuan Restaurant (四川餐厅 *Sìchuān cāntīng*)
$ | **SICHUAN** | Delicious Sichuanese classics like chicken with peanuts, sweet-and-sour pork, and spicy fried potato strips are available here at very cheap prices. There's an English menu, but prices are much higher than on the Chinese menu. **Known for:** extra spicy flavors; familiar classics like kung pao chicken; location in the lively part of town. $ *Average main: Y30* ✉ *21 Mingshan Lu* 💳 *No credit cards.*

Dunhuang Fandian (敦煌饭店 *Dūnhuáng fàndiàn*)
$ | **HOTEL** | If you're looking for something mildly luxurious, this lodging in the center of town will fit the bill. **Pros:** central location near plenty of restaurants; excellent value; well-appointed rooms. **Cons:** some noise from a local nightclub if you're on a low floor; Chinese breakfast options only; no elevator. $ *Rooms from: Y200* ✉ *373 Mingshan Lu, Xiyu Rd.* ☎ *0937/885–2999* *98 rooms* *No meals.*

★ **Dunhuang Silk Road Hotel** (敦煌山庄 *Dūnhuáng shānzhuāng*)
$ | **HOTEL** | This cross between a Chinese fortress and an alpine lodge is the most interesting place to stay in Dunhuang, and possibly in the whole of the province. **Pros:** rooftop terrace; good hotel food; walking distance from the sand dunes. **Cons:** touts approach guests all the time; far from the night market; comparatively expensive. $ *Rooms from: Y960* ✉ *Dunyue Lu near Wenchang Nan Lu* ☎ *0937/888–2088* 🌐 *www.dunhuangshanzhuang.com* *266 rooms* *Breakfast.*

Xining

3 hrs by train or bus west of Lanzhou; 24 hrs by train northeast of Lhasa.

Its name means "peace in the west," so it's no surprise that Xining started out as a military garrison in the 16th century, guarding the empire's western borders. It was also an important center for trade between China and Tibet. A small city by Chinese standards, with a population slightly more than 2.3 million, Xining is no longer cut off from the rest of China, but the city still feels remote. A far-flung metropolis wedged between dramatic sandstone cliffs, Xining is populated largely by Tibetan and Hui peoples.

For travelers, Xining is a convenient base for visits to the important Kumbum Monastery, which sits just outside the city, and the stunning avian sanctuary of Bird Island, 350 km (217 miles) away on the shores of China's largest saltwater

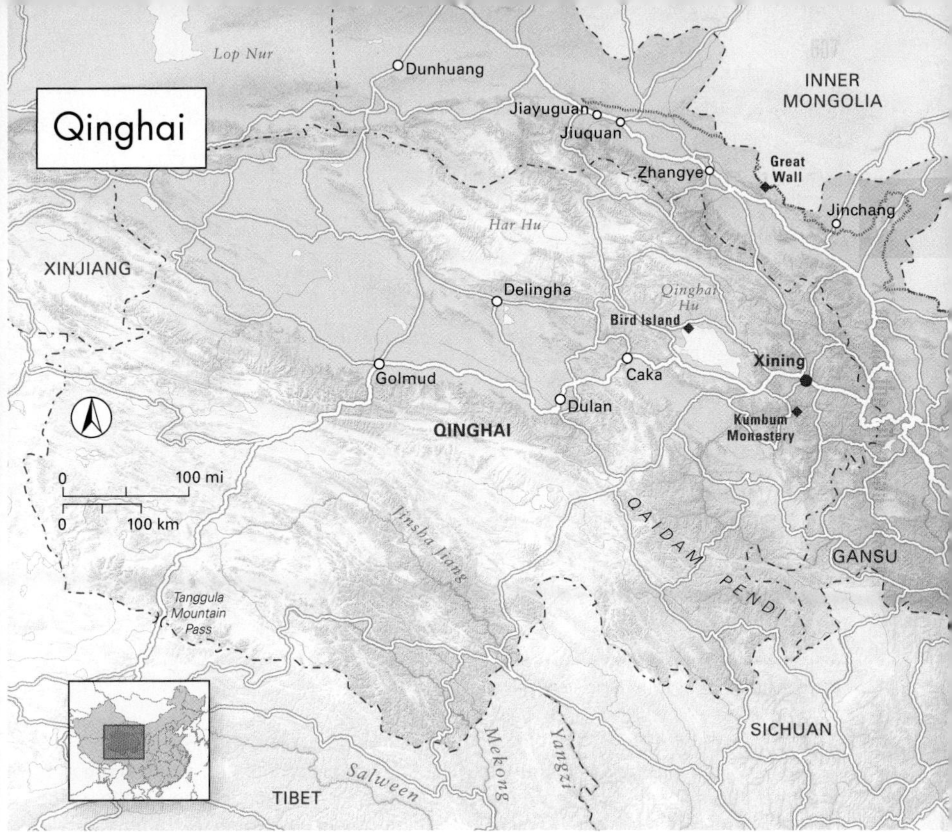

lake. Tibet-bound trains stop in Xining, so this could be a good place to acclimatize to the high altitude.

GETTING HERE AND AROUND

Xining Caojiabao Airport is 30 km (19 miles) east of the city. Shuttle buses costing Y25 per person can get you to or from the airport in about 40 minutes. If you're traveling with someone else, a taxi (Y80–Y100) is a better option. If you arrive by train or bus, a taxi should be around Y10.

Daily flights link Xining with Beijing, Shanghai, Chengdu, Guangzhou, Xi'an, Shenzhen and many other Chinese cities. There is less frequent service to Lhasa, Ürümqi, Qingdao, and Golmud.

Tickets for the long, bumpy bus ride to Lhasa can be purchased from any travel agent. Tickets for the journey to Lanzhou (3 hours) and Xi'an (15 hours) are available at the long-distance bus station, a few minutes north of the train station. If your next stop is Dunhuang, but you don't want to backpedal to Lanzhou, take the bus to Jiuquan in Gansu and get a connection farther west; the mountain scenery and small Tibetan villages along the way are spectacular.

The train to Lhasa runs every day, but foreign travelers need to arrange permits and book a tour before they can buy train tickets for the 24-hour journey. You can also travel by train east to Beijing, Shanghai, Lanzhou, Guangzhou, and Chengdu or venture west on the high-speed train to the western Xinjiang region.

Wenshu Hall in the Kumbum Monastery

TIMING

Xining is not a place to linger, as there are other, more appealing cities in the region. Spending a night here to explore and see the city's sights is enough.

TOURS

Xining's more upscale hotels have travel offices that can help you arrange expensive private tours with English-speaking guides to Kumbum Monastery or Bird Island. For less expensive tours, contact Tibetan Connections or consider the services of an enterprising individual like Niu Xiaojun, who speaks good English and has been leading foreigners to off-the-beaten-path destinations for years.

Sights

Dongguan Mosque (东关清真大寺 *Dōngguān qīngzhēn dàsì*)
RELIGIOUS SITE | This is one of the largest mosques in all of China and illustrates the ethnic diversity of Xining. Built in the 14th century, its green and white dome and two tall minarets see some 40,000 to 50,000 people for Friday prayers. The streets around the mosque are a great place to wander and people-watch should you have some extra time.
⊠ *Dongguan Jie near Ledu Lu* 🎫 *Y30*
⏲ *Closed to tourists Fri. 10–noon.*

Tulou Temple (土楼寺 *Tǔlóu sì*)
RELIGIOUS SITE | Xining's most important site is the Taoist Tulou Temple or North Monastery, at the northwest end of town. Construction on this series of mountainside cloisters and pavilions began more than 1,700 years ago during the Northern Wei Dynasty. Climbing the stairs to the white pagoda at the top gives you a view of the entire city sprawled out beneath you. Unfortunately, at the time of publication, many of the cliffside temples have been closed to visitors, leaving only a few temples at the bottom of the hill and views from adjacent hills for you to enjoy. To get here, take a taxi. ⊠ *Beichan Lu* 🎫 *Y10.*

AROUND XINING

★ Kumbum Monastery (塔尔寺 *Tă ĕr sì*)
RELIGIOUS SITE | The magnificent Kumbum Monastery lies 25 km (15 miles) southwest of Xining. One of the six great monasteries of the Tibetan Buddhist sect known as Yellow Hat—and reputedly the birthplace of the sect's founder, Tsong Khapa—construction began in 1560. A great reformer who lived in the early 1400s, Tsong Khapa formulated a new doctrine that stressed a return to monastic discipline, strict celibacy, and moral and philosophical thought over magic and mysticism. Tsong's followers have controlled Tibetan politics since the 17th century. Still a magnet for Tibetan pilgrims and, more recently, waves of tourists, Kumbum boasts a dozen prayer halls, an exhibition hall, and monks' quarters (look out for the yak butter sculptures), each one a beautiful demonstration of Tibetan architectural style. No photos are allowed. Public buses (Y6) to Huangzhong depart frequently from Zifang Jie Bus Station. Get off at the last stop and walk 2 km (1 mile) uphill, or take the shuttles (Y2) to the monastery's gates. Taxis from Xining will run you around Y35. ✉ *Huangzhong* ☎ *0971/223–2357* 🌐 *www.kumbum.org* 🎫 *Y80.*

Restaurants

Black Tent (黑帐篷藏吧 *Hēi zhàngpéng cáng ba*)
$$ | **INTERNATIONAL** | This place serves great Tibetan, Indian, and Nepali food. The friendly Tibetan waitstaff all hail from Anmo and add to the already-warm atmosphere. **Known for:** international cuisine; momo dumplings; friendly Tibetan staff. 💲 *Average main: Y50* ✉ *Wenmiao Square, Wenhua Jie near Xingwang Hotel, 3rd fl.* ☎ *187/9715–2326 mobile phone (no area code)* 💳 *No credit cards.*

Elite's Bar and Grill
$$ | **AMERICAN** | Like manna from heaven, Jesse Hoffman's café serves proper American fare, like juicy steaks, best washed down with Belgian beer, and pizzas that'll make anyone who's been on the Silk Road for awhile dive in with joy. If you're interested in meeting other foreigners, Elite's is the place to go. **Known for:** Belgian beer; delicious pizzas; proper steaks. 💲 *Average main: Y75* ✉ *Bldg. 2, 37 Xiguan Da Dao* ☎ *971/881–6683* 💳 *No credit cards.*

Did You Know? 

In the 1980s, archaeologists discovered dozens of tombs in various parts of Xinjiang, with bodies that had been buried for about 3,000 years yet remained remarkably preserved thanks to the arid desert climate. Many of the mummies, believed to be forefathers of the Uyghurs, had northern European features, including fair hair and skin.

Greenhouse Coffee (古林房咖啡 *Gŭlínfáng kāfēi*)
$$ | **CAFÉ** | With free Wi-Fi and waitstaff who speak English, this is a great place to hunker down and plan your next steps on the Silk Road. The coffee here is better than at most of Xining's hotels, and the menu appeals to Westerners with panini, pizza, soups, and desserts such as carrot cake with proper cream cheese icing. **Known for:** excellent coffee; delicious cheesecakes; free Wi-Fi. 💲 *Average main: Y50* ✉ *222–22 Banshan Huayuan, Xiadu Dajie* ☎ *0971/820–2710* 💳 *No credit cards.*

Jianyin Revolving Restaurant (建银宾馆旋转餐厅 *Jiànyín bīnguăn xuánzhuăn cāntīng*)
$$ | **ASIAN** | Perched atop the 28-story Jianyin Hotel, this slowly revolving restaurant may not serve the finest Asian cuisine, but the food isn't the biggest draw. People come here for the spectacular views of the city, where

The Xinjiang Uyghur Autonomous Region

you can sip a cup of tea while enjoying the scenery or playing cards. **Known for:** panoramic city views; cheap scenic rest stop; selection of teas. *Average main: Y60* *Jianyin Hotel, 55 Xida Jie near southeast corner of central square* *0971/826–1885* *No credit cards.*

Snow Mountain Creamery (雪山冰淇淋 *Xuěshān bīngqílín*)

$ | **AMERICAN** | Those who visit share glowing reviews of Snow Mountain Creamery as not just the best ice cream in Xining, but perhaps in all of China. While ice cream is the draw, this small café also offers plenty of meal options and an English menu to make it easy to choose. **Known for:** China's best ice cream; Yak burgers; clean, friendly environment. *Average main: Y40* *18–184 Bandao Buxing Jie* *971/827–8334* *No credit cards.*

Hotels

Qinghai Hotel (青海宾馆 *Qīnghǎi bīnguǎn*)

$ | **HOTEL** | Although the outside looks drab, this hotel's lobby is decked out in tapered columns, fountains, marble sculptures, and ornate wall decor to go with simple yet sophisticated rooms. **Pros:** central location; large, clean rooms; good restaurant options. **Cons:** staff speak limited English; the temperature in the rooms cannot be adjusted; caters to business people, not tourists. *Rooms from: Y900* *158 Huanghe Lu* *0971/614–8999* *www.qhhotel.com* *396 rooms* *Breakfast.*

Yinlong Hotel (银龙酒店 *Yínlóng jiǔdiàn*)

$ | **HOTEL** | This ultramodern hotel is considered the finest lodging between Xi'an and Ürümqi, with exceptionally comfortable rooms and a quiet location. **Pros:** central location; good-quality hotel restaurants; Wi-Fi in rooms. **Cons:** expensive buffet breakfast; small gym; dearth of English-speakers. *Rooms from: Y850*

38 Huanghe Lu *0971/616–6666* *316 rooms* *No meals.*

Shopping

Jianguo Lu Wholesale Market (建国路批发市场 *Jiànguó lù pīfā shìchǎng*)
CLOTHING | This market sells everything from traditional Tibetan clothing to favorite local foods. *Jianguo Lu, opposite main bus station, near Binhe Dong Lu.*

Side Trip from Xining

★ **Bird Island** (鸟岛 *Niǎo dǎo*)
NATURE PRESERVE | Bird Island is the main draw at Qinghai Hu, China's largest inland saltwater lake. The name Bird Island is a misnomer: it was an island until the lake receded, connecting it to the shore. The electric-blue lake is surrounded by rolling hills covered with yellow rapeseed flowers. Tibetan shepherds graze their flocks here as wild yaks roam nearby. Beyond the hills are snowcapped mountains. An estimated nearly 100,000 birds breed at Bird Island, including egrets, speckle-headed geese, and black-neck cranes; sadly, the numbers have been much depleted because of the country's efforts to suppress the spread of avian flu. There are two viewing sites: spend as little time as possible at Egg Island in favor of the much better Common Cormorant Island, where you can see birds flying at eye-level from the top of a cliff. The best months to see birds are May and June.

To get to Bird Island, either contact a tour agency or catch a tourist bus from Xining Railway Station for Y35 each way.

If you opt for a tour, make sure that you're not headed to the much closer tourist trap known as Qinghai Hu 151. ⊠ *350 km (215 miles) northwest of Xining* *Mid-Apr.–mid-Aug. Y100; mid-Aug.–mid-Apr. Y60; Y15 for eco-sightseeing bus.*

Ürümqi

32 hrs by train, 4 hrs by plane from Beijing.

Xinjiang's capital and largest city, Ürümqi is at the geographic center of Asia, and has the distinction of being the most landlocked city in the world. It's a new city by Chinese standards, little more than barracks for Qing Dynasty troops when it was built in 1763. Once a sleepy trading post, Ürümqi has grown to be a sprawling city, with more than 3.35 million inhabitants. Yet despite this modernization, Ürümqi manages to conjure up the past, especially in the Uyghur-populated area near the International Grand Bazaar.

GETTING HERE AND AROUND

Many people fly to Ürümqi from Beijing, Shanghai, Hong Kong, or Xi'an to begin a journey on the Silk Road. The airport is 20 km (12 miles) north of the downtown area, and can be reached in about 30 minutes by taxi (Y50–Y60) or 45 minutes by shuttle bus (Y20). Construction is almost complete on a subway line that links the airport with downtown Ürümqi, set to be open in mid-2019.

Long-distance buses are often the only way to travel in Xinjiang if you don't want to wait a day or two for the next available train. Every city in the region is served at least daily by buses from Ürümqi. There's even bus service to Almaty, Kazakhstan.

It's usually a straightforward affair buying tickets from the only station in town, but Ürümqi is more complicated. Destinations in northern Xinjiang, such as Yili and Altai are served by the Nianzigou Station (**碾子沟客运站** Niǎnzi gōu kèyùn zhàn) not far from the train station. If your destination is located in southern Xinjiang, such as Turpan, Kashgar or Hotan, you'll need to head to the South Station (**南郊客运站** Nánjiāo kèyùn zhàn).

Buses (Y25 each way) leave for Heavenly Lake (Tianchi Hu) at 9 am from the north gate of Renmin Park. They usually leave the lake at 6 pm and arrive back in Ürümqi at 7:30 pm. Be careful to get on a regular bus rather than a tour bus that will take you to minor attractions on the way, limiting your time at the lake.

Those arriving by train will find themselves either at Ürümqi's older South Station (**火车南站** huǒchē nán zhàn) on the southwest corner of the city or at the newer high-speed rail hub known as the Ürümqi High Speed Station (**乌鲁木齐高铁站** Wūlǔmùqí gāotiě zhàn).

TIMING

While there is plenty to see in Ürümqi, it's fair to say that Xinjiang's best attractions are outside of the capital. If the clock is ticking, spend no more than two days enjoying Ürümqi's sights before heading farther afield.

Sights

International Grand Bazaar (**国际大巴扎** *Guójì dàbā zhā*)

MARKET | The streets around the bazaar were once full of donkey carts and flocks of sheep. Men in embroidered skullcaps and women in heavy brown wool veils remain, preserving this bustling Central Asian street market. You can bargain for Uyghur crafts, such as decorated knives, colorful silks, and carved jade. Small shops are tucked into every nook and cranny. The international bazaar itself has been heavily expanded, and now includes a newly built minaret, which you can experience for Y50. The stalls, while interesting enough, are aimed firmly

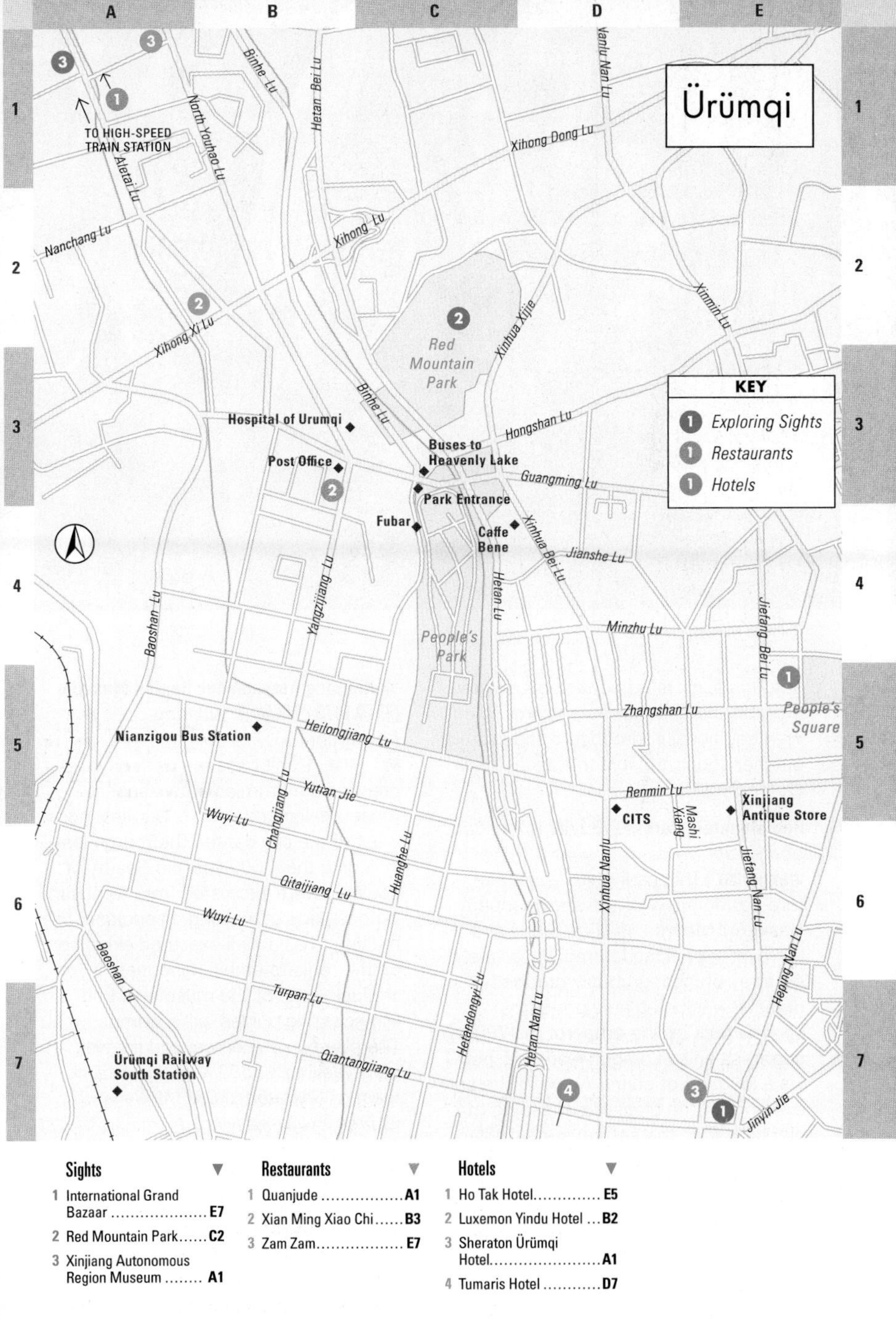

Sights

1 International Grand Bazaar **E7**

2 Red Mountain Park...... **C2**

3 Xinjiang Autonomous Region Museum **A1**

Restaurants

1 Quanjude **A1**

2 Xian Ming Xiao Chi...... **B3**

3 Zam Zam.................. **E7**

Hotels

1 Ho Tak Hotel.............. **E5**

2 Luxemon Yindu Hotel ... **B2**

3 Sheraton Ürümqi Hotel....................... **A1**

4 Tumaris Hotel **D7**

Chinese Muslim children

at tourists; more authentic options are available along the streets nearby, filled with traditional ironmongers and Islamic butcher shops. ✉ *Jiefang Nan Lu, near Outer Ring Rd.*

Red Mountain Park (红山公园 *Hóngshān gōngyuán*)
VIEWPOINT | This park gives you a picture-perfect view of the snowcapped Heavenly Mountains (*Tian Shan*) and the ever-expanding Ürümqi cityscape. An array of incongruously grouped objects—including an eight-story pagoda built by the emperor in 1788 to suppress an evil dragon—are reached via a long set of stairs. Arrive in the early evening for the pleasure of seeing the city bathed in the setting sun's golden light. Ignore the cheap carnival rides near the entrance. The park entrance is hard to find, and few tourists venture here, so take a taxi. ✉ *Enter on Ximin Xi Jie, across from athletic complex* ☎ *0991/885–5671* *Free.*

★ **Xinjiang Autonomous Region Museum** (新疆自治区博物馆 *Xīnjiāng zìzhìqū bówùguǎn*)
MUSEUM | Don't miss the perfectly preserved mummies at this superb museum, located 4 km (2½ miles) northwest of the city center. The mummies—including the 4,000-year-old Beauty of Loulan—were excavated from tombs in various parts of Xinjiang. In addition, the museum has a well-executed exhibition on the region's ethnic minorities. If you are lucky, one of the museum's English-speaking guides will accompany you. There's no extra charge, and it's well worth asking. ✉ *585 Xibei Lu, 1 block west of Sheraton* ☎ *0991/453–4453* *Free* ⏲ *Closed Mon.*

Restaurants

Quanjude (全聚德 *Quánjùdé*)
$$$ | **NORTHERN CHINESE** | This outpost of the famous Beijing Peking duck restaurant serves up a variety of food from that capital and Northeastern China. The menu differs a little from the Beijing

The Jade Road

The residents of Xinjiang are apt to point out that the Silk Road isn't the first road they knew. That honor goes to the "Jade Road," which was established nearly 7,000 years ago. Running from Hotan into today's Qinghai and Gansu provinces, the Jade Road was the artery for Xinjiang's legendary white jade trade. Primarily mined from the Hotan River, Xinjiang jade comes in a number of hues, although small white stones with a reddish-brown exterior are the most highly valued. Sensuous and smooth to the touch, this "mutton fat jade" is cloudy with translucent qualities. Chinese emperors have craved it for centuries. Good places to hunt around for all manner of jade in Ürümqi include the swirling International Grand Bazaar and the Xinjiang Antique Store.

Visitors who wish to know more about this region's heady history of jade, silk, and more should visit the Xinjiang Autonomous Region Museum.

branches, which includes crispy, juicy panfried dumplings, spicy meat stews, thick cut noodles, and steamed root vegetables, but the duck is the same. **Known for:** perfectly cooked duck meat; well-decorated interior; always busy and lively. *$ Average main: Y110 ✉ 338 Beijing Nan Lu ☎ 991/366–1066, 991/382–2523 ▭ No credit cards.*

Xian Ming Xiao Chi (西安名小吃 *Xī'ān míng xiǎochī*)
$ | **CHINESE** | If you need a change from Uyghur fare, this cheap and cheerful fast-food joint offers tasty Xi'an-style snacks, from famous noodle dishes to specialty meat sandwiches. There are a number of these chain restaurants throughout the city, which are a cheap option and whose cold dishes are particularly popular during the warmer months. **Known for:** burger-style pork sandwiches called roujiamo; liang pi, a cold noodle dish; fast and cheap. *$ Average main: Y30 ✉ 61 Yangzijiang Lu ☎ 0991/451–5668 ▭ No credit cards.*

Zam Zam
$ | **NORTHERN CHINESE** | Located just east of the International Bazaar, this restaurant offers excellent Uyghur cuisine within an authentic atmosphere. The ornate room is outfitted with carved wood and Arabic-style arches, and there's even a helpful picture menu. **Known for:** Uyghur rice pilaf (polo); ornate decorations; walking distance from the bazaar. *$ Average main: Y30 ✉ 423 Heping Nan Lu ☎ 0991/853–0555 ▭ No credit cards.*

Hotels

★ **Hoi Tak Hotel** (海德酒店 *Hǎidé jiǔdiàn*)
$ | **HOTEL** | Overlooking People's Square in bustling downtown Ürümqi, this hotel offers tastefully appointed rooms that would satisfy those seeking a higher level of comfort. **Pros:** the staff speak English; rooms are good value; free Wi-Fi. **Cons:** removed from main attractions; disappointing breakfast buffet; limited selection of restaurants nearby. *$ Rooms from: Y700 ✉ 1 Dongfeng Lu, west side of People's Square ☎ 0991/232–2828 🌐 www.hoitakhotel.com 356 rooms No meals.*

Luxemon Yindu Hotel (银都酒店 *Yíndū jiǔdiàn*)
$ | **HOTEL** | Situated between the city center and the Xinjiang Museum, this

hotel has long catered to foreign tourists and visiting diplomats. **Pros:** comfortable rooms; staff speak enough English to communicate; breakfast buffet offers enough Western options. **Cons:** bad location for exploring the sights; no convenient bus stops nearby; awkward bathroom window. *Rooms from: Y700* *179 Xihong Xi Lu* *0991/453–6688* *www.luxemonyindu.com/en* *308 rooms* *Breakfast.*

Sheraton Ürümqi Hotel (喜来登酒店 *Xǐláidēng jiǔdiàn*)
$ | **HOTEL** | Very popular with both well-heeled business and leisure travelers, this luxury hotel pampers you with an indoor pool illuminated with skylights and one of the better hotel gyms you'll find in Ürümqi. **Pros:** near the museum; plenty of shopping; proper pool and gym. **Cons:** most staff don't speak English; not the Sheraton service you expect; slightly overpriced. *Rooms from: Y850* *669 Youhao Bei Lu* *0991/699–9999* *www.starwoodhotels.com* *398 rooms* *No meals.*

Tumaris Hotel (突玛丽斯大饭店 *Tūmǎlìsī Dàfàndiàn*)
$ | **HOTEL** | This Uyghur-style hotel provides thoughtful interior design and comfortable rooms at an ideal location near the International Grand Bazaar. **Pros:** near the International Bazaar; beautiful local architecture and decoration; excellent value. **Cons:** shows signs of age; next to a noisy highway; no English-speaking staff. *Rooms from: Y250* *618 S. Xinhua Rd.* *0991/852–5555* *152 rooms* *No meals.*

Nightlife

Fubar (福吧 *Fúba*)
BARS/PUBS | Formerly owned and operated by two foreign gentlemen, Fubar still retains that real tavern feel complete with imported beer, pool tables and authentic pub grub. The pizza is especially noteworthy, as are the fish-and-chips. This is the best place in Ürümqi to relax and watch some international sports matches after a tiring day exploring the city. *40 Gongyuan Bei Jie* *0991/581–4698.*

What Time Is It?

A constant source of confusion for travelers in Xinjiang is figuring out the time. Uyghurs often refer to unofficial Xinjiang time, whereas Han Chinese use standard Beijing time (which applies to all of China and doesn't follow daylight saving time). If in doubt, ask. No matter what time is spoken, you can count on everything in Xinjiang starting two hours later than in Beijing. That is, lunch in Kashgar is usually eaten at 2 pm Beijing time.

★ **International Grand Bazaar Banquet Performance** (国际大巴扎宴会演出 *Guójì dàbāzhā yànhuì yǎnchū*)
DANCE | This entertaining song-and-dance performance is preceded by a ho-hum buffet that unsuccessfully tries to capture the delights of Uyghur cuisine. Never mind the food, as this is your best chance to see Uyghur, Uzbek, Kazakh, Tajik, Tartar, and even Irish dancing all in one eye-popping evening. Make reservations through your hotel or at the banquet hall. *Jiefang Lu, near Heping Nan Lu* *0991/855–6000* *From Y260.*

Shopping

Xinjiang Antique Store (新疆古玩店 *Xīnjiāng gǔwàn diàn*)
ANTIQUES/COLLECTIBLES | This shop has a good selection of Chinese bric-a-brac, including jade, jewelry, carpets, and porcelain. As all items come with a state-certified export certificate, you won't have to worry about getting your

purchase through customs. There is a smaller branch inside the Xinjiang Autonomous Region Museum. ✉ *39 Jiefang Nan Lu, south of Renmin Lu* ☎ *0991/282–5161.*

Side Trip from Ürümqi

★ **Heavenly Lake** (**天池** *Tiānchí*)
MOUNTAIN—SIGHT | After a three-hour ride from Ürümqi you'll reach what is quite possibly the prettiest lake in China, surrounded by snow-sprinkled mountains. The water is crystal clear with a sapphire tint. In summer, white flowers dot the hillsides. Unfortunately, tourism is leaving its ugly footprint. The lake's northern shore is crowded with tour groups posing for snapshots with Mount Bogda in the background. To better appreciate the lake's natural beauty, arrive before the hordes, or stay until after the last bus has departed.

Kazakh families still set up traditional felt tents along the shores of Heavenly Lake from early May to late October, bringing their horses, sheep, and cashmere goats. The Kazakh people have a long history as horse breeders and are known to be skilled riders.

From Ürümqi, day-tour buses to Heavenly Lake leave at 9 am from a small street beside the north gate of People's Park (Heilongjiang Lu near Gongyuan Bei Ji). Expect to pay Y25 each way plus the Y215 entrance fee to the lake. You'll have from about noon to 6 pm to explore the lake, arriving back in the city at 8 pm. Tickets—usually available up until the bus leaves—can be purchased near the buses. ✉ *Ürümqi* 🎫 *Y215, including mandatory shuttle from tourist center to lake.*

Turpan

1 hr by high-speed train southeast of Ürümqi.

Turpan, which means "the lowest place" in Uyghur, lies in a desert basin at the southern foot of the Heavenly Mountains. Part of the basin lies 505 feet below sea level, the hottest spot in China and the second-lowest point in the world after the Dead Sea. In summer, temperatures can soar to more than 122°F (50°C), so come prepared with lots of water and sunscreen.

Turpan's claim to fame is its location between the ruins of two spectacular ancient cities: Jiaohe and Gaochang. Thanks to the high-speed train, Turpan is an easy day trip from Ürümqi, but there's enough to see here to occupy two or three days of touring. Surrounded by some of the richest farmland in Xinjiang, Turpan's vineyards are famous for producing several varieties of candy-sweet raisins popular throughout China.

GETTING HERE AND AROUND

While the tiny town of Turpan does have its own airport, it's usually faster and more comfortable to take a high-speed train from Ürümqi. When traveling by train, travelers should pay careful attention to the train destination on the ticket they are purchasing. The older train station, referred to as Turpan Station (**吐鲁番站** Tǔlǔfān zhàn) is inconveniently located 60 km (30 miles) northwest of downtown Turpan in a village called Daheyan. Taxis from here to the city center can take an hour and run upward of Y100 depending on your bargaining skills. The newer train station, which serves all the high-speed trains running between Ürümqi and Lanzhou, is much more convenient. This station, named Turpan North Station (**吐鲁番北站** Tǔlǔfān běi zhàn), is only 10 minutes away from the city center by taxi or bus. If at all possible, it's best to arrive and depart from the Turpan North Station near the city.

China's Muslims

Uyghur

The Muslim Turkic people known as Uyghurs (pronounced "WEE-grs") are one of China's largest—and in the eyes of Beijing, most troublesome—minority groups. Uyghurs mostly live in northwest China's Xinjiang, an "autonomous region" that is one of the most tightly controlled parts of the country after Tibet. Uyghurs are descendants of nomadic Turkic Central Asian tribes. Their language, food, music, dance, clothing, and other customs have little or no relation to those found elsewhere in China. Yet despite a population of more than 10 million people, most foreigners have never heard of them or their troubled independence movement. Protests and occasional violence in the region during the late 1990s brought a severe crackdown from Beijing; limits were placed on religious education and hundreds of suspected Uyghur separatists were executed. The attacks of September 11, 2001, gave the Chinese government further leverage to oppress Uyghurs in the name of fighting terrorism.

Hui

Identifiable by their brimless white caps and head scarves, the Hui are descendants of Middle Eastern traders who came to China via the Silk Road, settling down with Chinese wives after their conversion to Islam. Over a thousand years' time, the Middle Eastern influence on the Hui appearance became diluted, but it is still very easy to distinguish between the different facial features of the Hui and Han Chinese. Because of cultural differences associated with their Islamic faith, the Hui tend to associate with others in their largely Muslim neighborhoods. The Hui reject eating several kinds of meat that can be popular with Han Chinese, including pork, horse, dog, and several types of birds. In what could be seen as a form of respect by the business-savvy Han Chinese, the Hui are generally considered to be shrewd businesspeople, perhaps a nod to their being descendants of foreign traders.

When traveling by bus, you'll need to purchase tickets at the regional bus station south of the local bazaar. Daily buses run all throughout southern Xinjiang to places like Korla, Aksu, Kashgar and Hotan among others. For destinations in northern Xinjiang, you'll have to head back to Ürümqi on one of the hourly buses to the capital.

TIMING

The high-speed train has made day trips from Ürümqi possible for those who are short on time. To see all the sights that lie on the outskirts of town, one or two nights should be more than enough.

Sights

Emin Minaret (苏公塔 *Sū gōng tǎ*)
MEMORIAL | Emin Minaret is Turpan's most recognizable image, often featured in tourist brochures. Built in 1777, it commemorates a military commander who suppressed a rebellion by a group of aristocrats. The 141-foot conical tower is elegantly spare, with bricks arranged in 15 patterns. A spiral staircase leads to the top of the minaret, but has been closed to tourists for safety reasons since the 1990s. This complex lies 4 km (2½ miles) from the city center at the southeast end of town. To get here, head east on

The Thousand Buddha Caves outside Turpan

Laocheng Xi Lu and follow the signs to turn right outside of town. ✉ *South side of Munar Village* 🎫 *Y45.*

Karez Irrigation System (坎儿进民俗园 *Kǎnerjìn Mínsúyuán*)

HISTORIC SITE | This remarkable 2,000-year-old underground irrigation system allowed the desert cities of the Silk Road to flourish despite an unrelentingly arid environment. In the oasis cities of Turpan and Hami, 1,600 km (990 miles) of tunnels brought water—moved only by gravity—from melting snow at the base of the Heavenly Mountains. You can view the tunnels at several sites around the city. Most tour guides take visitors to the largely educational Karez Irrigation Museum. Although the karez are widely regarded as the greatest Uyghur engineering achievement, most visitors are completely underwhelmed by what are essentially narrow dirt tunnels. ✉ *888 Xincheng Lu, on city's western outskirts* 🎫 *Y40.*

AROUND TURPAN

★ **Ancient City of Jiaohe** (交河故城 *Jiāohé gù chéng*)

ARCHAEOLOGICAL SITE | On a plateau at the confluence of two rivers, these impressive ruins lie in the Yarnaz Valley west of Turpan. The city, established as a garrison during the Han Dynasty, was built on the natural fortification of cliffs rising 100 feet above the rivers. Jiaohe was governed from the 2nd to the 7th century by the kingdom of Gaochang, and occupied later by Tibetans. Despite destruction in the 14th century by Mongol hordes, large fragments of actual streets and buildings remain, including a Buddhist monastery and Buddhist statues, a row of bleached pagodas, a 29-foot observation tower, and government offices. Guards and cameras will make sure you stay on the designated boardwalk. As at the Ruins of Gaochang, there's almost no shade, so arrive early with an umbrella and plenty of water in tow. ✉ *8 km (5 miles) west of Turpan, within Yaer village* 🎫 *Y70.*

Bezeklik Thousand Buddha Caves (**柏孜克里克千佛洞** *Bǎizīkèlǐkè qiānfúdòng*)
RELIGIOUS SITE | In a breathtaking valley inside the Flaming Mountains is this ancient temple complex, built between the 5th and 7th century by slaves whose entire lives went into the construction. Many of the fine examples of Buddhist sculpture and wall frescoes were destroyed after Islam came to the region in the 13th century. Other sculptures and frescoes, including several whole murals of Buddhist monks, were removed by 20th-century archaeologists like German Albert von Le Coq, who shipped his finds back to Berlin. Although they remain a feat of early engineering, the caves are in atrocious condition. Go just to see the site itself and the surrounding valley, which is magnificent. The views of the scorched, lunar landscape leading up to the site, which clings to one flank of a steep, scenic valley, make the trip worth the effort. Avoid the nearby Buddha Cave constructed in 1980 by a local artist; it isn't worth an additional Y20. ✉ *35 km (22 miles) northeast of Turpan* 🎫 *Y40.*

★ **The Ruins of Gaochang** (**高昌故城** *Gāochāng gù chéng*)
ARCHAEOLOGICAL SITE | These fascinating city ruins lie in a valley south of the Flaming Mountains. Legend has it that a group of soldiers stopped here in the 1st century BC on their way to Afghanistan, found that water was plentiful, and decided to stay. By the 7th century the city was the capital of the kingdom of Gaochang, which ruled more than 21 other towns, and by the 9th century the Uyghurs had moved into the area from Mongolia, establishing the kingdom of Kharakhoja. In the 14th century Mongols destroyed the kingdom, leaving only the ruins seen today. Only the city walls and a partially preserved monastery surrounded by muted, almost unrecognizable crumbling buildings remain, an eerie and haunting excursion into the pages of history. Over the years, archaeologists have uncovered buried ancient texts written in Uyghur, Sanskrit, Chinese, and Tibetan, a testament to the changing demographic of the city throughout its history. Entering the city from the south, you'll want to visit the temple complex in the southwest corner of the city. Because of the sheer size of the ruins, any further exploration requires renting an electric cart or bicycle. There is little shade, so go early and bring an umbrella. ✉ *30 km (19 miles) east of Turpan* 🎫 *Y70.*

Restaurants

Herembag (**海尔巴格** *Hǎi'ěr bā gé*)
$$ | **TURKISH** | Located down the road behind the Turpan Museum, this restaurant features elegant decoration, an exotic ambience and a selection of tasty Uyghur cuisine that may settle better in your stomach than most of the street food you'll find. Their selection of coffee and Turkish tea in addition to functioning air-conditioning make this a great place to rest during the often unbearable heat of a Turpan summer. **Known for:** elegant decoration; tasty Uyghur kebabs; location near the museum and local park. [$] *Average main: Y50* ✉ *21 Shahezi Rd., 100 meters behind Turpan Museum* ☎ *0995/855–5111* 🌐 *http://herembag.com/* 💳 *No credit cards.*

John's Information Café
$$ | **AMERICAN** | Part of a small, family-run chain that operates in destinations along the Silk Road, this popular tourist hangout is far from authentic, but people flock here for the familiar Western fare and rock-solid travel advice. The café is only operational during the summer tourist season, so if you visit in the winter you'll find the area locked up. **Known for:** familiar Western cuisine; quiet and comfortable outdoor atmosphere; bike rentals. [$] *Average main: Y50* ✉ *Qingnian Lu, rear of Turpan Hotel* ☎ *0998/258–1186* 🌐 *www.johncafe.net* 💳 *No credit cards.*

Hotels

Turpan Hotel (**吐鲁番宾馆** *Tǔlǔfān bīnguǎn*)
$ | **HOTEL** | This study in basic geometry has definitely seen better days, but rooms are relatively clean and large, the restaurant is good, and the gift shops are handy. **Pros:** offers good discounts; friendly staff; swimming pool. **Cons:** if you can't get a discount, better values are available elsewhere; Chinese breakfast options only; aging rooms. *Rooms from: Y280 ✉ 1695 Qingnian Nan Lu, south of Laocheng Lu, near Royal Garden ☎ 0995/856–8888 204 rooms No meals.*

Turpan Jiaotong Hotel (**交通宾馆** *Jiāotōng bīnguǎn*)
$ | **HOTEL** | This budget option, whose rooms have been renovated, isn't a bad place to stay, despite noise from the busy street and bazaar across the street. **Pros:** bargain rates; located near the bazaar; plenty of convenient transportation. **Cons:** bad water pressure; occasional power outages; constant street noise. *Rooms from: Y260 ✉ 230 Laocheng Xi Lu, across from bazaar ☎ 0995/625–8666 No credit cards 100 rooms Free Breakfast.*

Turpan Silk Road Lodge (**丝绸之路公寓** *Sīchóuzhīlù Gōngyù*)
$ | **B&B/INN** | Nestled among quiet rows of a grape vineyard, the Silk Road Lodge is one of the few boutique hotels in all of Xinjiang. **Pros:** friendly staff; serene location surrounded by a vineyard; tasty breakfast with real coffee. **Cons:** signs of poor construction; more expensive lodging option; far from the city center. *Rooms from: Y600 ✉ Munar village 4 km east of Turpan, just north of Emin Minaret ☎ 0995/856–8333 www.silkroadlodges.com 15 rooms Free Breakfast.*

Kashgar

20 hrs by train or 1½ hours by plane southwest of Ürümqi.

Kashgar, the westernmost city in China, is closer to Baghdad than Beijing. More than 3,400 km (2,100 miles) west of the capital, the city has been a center of trade between China and the outside world for at least 2,000 years. Today, Kashgar is a hub for merchants coming in over the Khunjerab Pass from Pakistan and the Torugart Pass from Kyrgyzstan. When these two treacherous mountain passes are open from May to October, Kashgar becomes a particularly colorful city, abuzz not only with curious Western tourists but also with visitors from every corner of Central Asia.

Despite an increasing Han presence in central Kashgar (symbolized by one of the largest Mao statues in the country), the city is still overwhelmingly Uyghur. A great deal of modernization has taken place here since the railway from Ürümqi arrived in 1999. Beijing is showering the city with attention and money to boost the local economy and placate Kashgar's Uyghur population. There are still clashes, which has led to a heavy security presence, but the area is safe enough for foreigners.

Much of the city's Uyghur architecture has been demolished, but there are still some traditional houses with ornately painted balconies, as well as a few remaining sections of the Old City. Most visitors come to Kashgar for the amazing Sunday Market, the largest bazaar in Central Asia and one of the best photo ops in all of China.

GETTING HERE AND AROUND

Daunted by the long train journey from Ürümqi, many tourists opt for quicker transportation to Kashgar by air. The airport is 13 km (8 miles) north of the city center; a taxi to your hotel shouldn't cost more than Y35, and shuttle buses

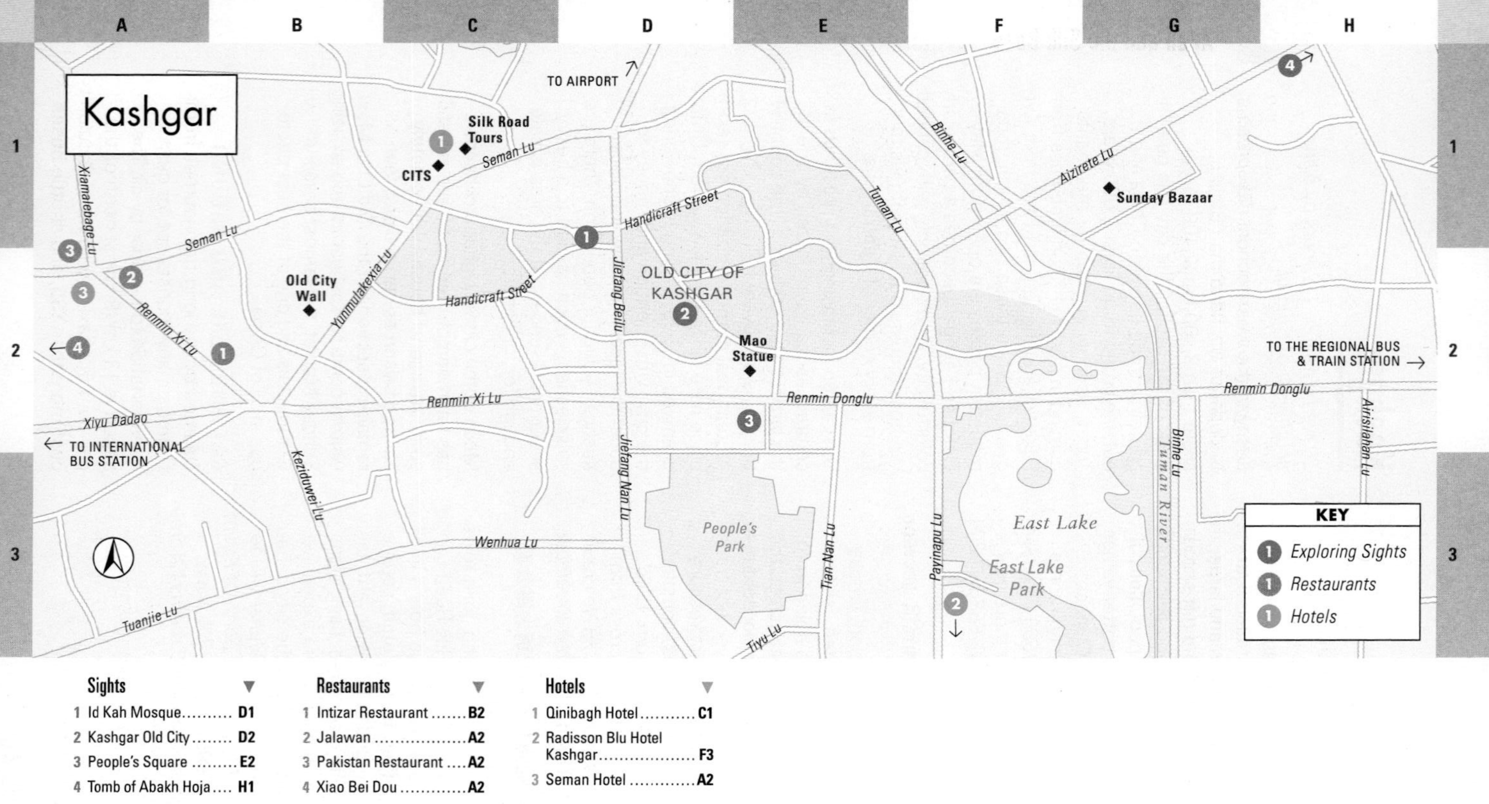

Sights

1 Id Kah Mosque **D1**
2 Kashgar Old City **D2**
3 People's Square **E2**
4 Tomb of Abakh Hoja **H1**

Restaurants

1 Intizar Restaurant **B2**
2 Jalawan **A2**
3 Pakistan Restaurant **A2**
4 Xiao Bei Dou **A2**

Hotels

1 Qinibagh Hotel **C1**
2 Radisson Blu Hotel Kashgar **F3**
3 Seman Hotel **A2**

are Y15. Trains between Ürümqi and Kashgar (18 to 22 hours) depart multiple times a day; the slow train is half the price of the fast train, but you'll have to do without air-conditioning. The train station is 10 km (6 miles) east of town, next to the regional bus station. Taxis from here cost about Y15. International buses and those heading to Tashkorgan depart from a different bus station 12 km southwest of Kashgar.

TIMING

Allow two or three days if possible, and try to time your stay to include the famous Sunday Market. If you're able to nail down the date of Eid al-Fitr, the roaming Islamic holiday marking the end of Ramadan, it's a treat to watch tens of thousands of Uyghur gather for prayers at the Id Kah Mosque.

Sights

Id Kah Mosque (艾提尕尔清真寺 *Àitígǎěr qīngzhēnsì*)
RELIGIOUS SITE | Start your tour of the city with a visit to the center of Muslim life in Kashgar. One of the largest mosques in China, the ornate structure of yellow bricks is the result of many extensions and renovations to the original mosque, built in 1442 as a prayer hall for the ruler of Kashgar. The main hall has a ceiling with fine wooden carvings and precisely 100 carved wooden columns. When services aren't being held, you are free to wander the quiet shaded grounds and even to enter the prayer hall. Women are permitted to enter but as this is an active site of worship, dress modestly. ✉ *Just off Jiefang Bei Lu, near Nuo'er Beixi Lu* *Y20.*

Kashgar Old City (喀什老城 *KāshiS lǎo chéng*)
BUILDING | Once the heart of Uyghur culture in Kashgar, the well-known "old city" has undergone serious renovation since 2009. What you'll see around the reconstructed portion of the Old City is almost nothing like it was before: wider streets, tourist shops and plenty of police security. Despite these changes, wandering the streets of the Old City offers a picturesque look at Uyghur culture and plenty of good food options. ✉ *Spread throughout city center.*

People's Square (人民广场 *Rénmín guǎngchǎng*)
PLAZA | If you happen to forget which country Kashgar is in, chances are you aren't standing in this square. A statue of Mao Zedong—one of the largest in China—stands with his back to Kashgar's Old City and his right arm raised in perpetual salute. The statue is evidence of an unspoken rule in China that directly relates the size of a Mao tribute to its distance from Beijing; the only Mao statue larger than this one is in Tibet. ✉ *Renmin Lu, between Jiefang Nan Lu and Tian Lu.*

★ **Tomb of Abakh Hoja** (香妃墓 *Xiāng fēi mù*)
MEMORIAL | About 5 km (3 miles) northeast of the city lies one of the most sacred sites in Xinjiang. The sea-green tiled hall that houses the tomb—actually about two dozen tombs—is part of a massive complex of sacred Islamic structures built around 1640. Uyghurs named the tomb and surrounding complex after Abakh Hoja, an Islamic missionary believed to be a descendant of Mohammed, who ruled Kashgar and outlying regions in the 17th century. Excavations of the glazed-brick tombs indicate that the first occupant was Abakh Hoja's father, who is buried here along with Abakh Hoja and many of their descendants.

The Han, who prefer to emphasize the site's historical connection to their dynastic empire, call it the Tomb of the Fragrant Concubine. When the grandniece of Abakh Hoja was chosen as concubine by the Qing ruler Qianlong in Beijing, Uyghur legend holds that she committed suicide rather than submit to the emperor. In the Han story, she dutifully went to Beijing and spent 30 years in the emperor's palace, then asked to be buried in her homeland. Either way, her alleged tomb was excavated in the 1980s and found to be empty. The tomb is a bit difficult to navigate via bus, so take a taxi. ⊠ *Aizirete Lu* 🎫 *Y30.*

Restaurants

★ **Intizar Restaurant** (银提扎尔快餐厅 *Yíntízhāěr kuài cāntīng)*

$ | **NORTHERN CHINESE** | Frequented by locals and outfitted with wooden paneling and chandeliers, Intizar is the most formal of Kashgar's Uyghur restaurants. It offers a range of Uyghur cuisine, and the menu is translated into English, including helpful descriptions of each dish. **Known for:** delicious kebabs; baked jiaozi (samsa); Uyghur-style atmosphere. [$] *Average main: Y30* ⊠ *33 Renmin Xi Lu, near Wenzhou Hotel* ▭ *No credit cards.*

Jalawan (吉乌兰美食 *Jíwūlán měishí)*

$ | **MIDDLE EASTERN** | It's very easy to join the crowds of locals relaxing at this local Uyghur restaurant, especially underneath the (admittedly) fake trellises of grapes around a fountain. The staff will hand you an English-language menu whose prices are a few yuan higher than on the Chinese-language menu, but when it's all so cheap, you can't complain too much. **Known for:** Uyghur polo (rice pilaf); tiger salad; local kawas drink. [$] *Average main: Y30* ⊠ *Seman Lu, on roundabout opposite Seman Hotel* ▭ *No credit cards.*

Pakistan Restaurant (巴基斯坦西餐厅 *Bājīsītǎn xī cāntīng)*

$ | **MIDDLE EASTERN** | Foreign restaurants are rare in Kashgar, so this dirt-cheap curry joint with its delicious roti (flat bread) is a welcome addition. This restaurant's sign is covered by a large tree, but it's directly opposite the Seman Hotel's rear entrance. **Known for:** variety of delicious curries; English menu; hot chai tea served with milk. [$] *Average main: Y40* ⊠ *Seman Lu, opposite Seman Hotel's rear entrance* ▭ *No credit cards.*

Xiao Bei Dou (小北斗 *Xiǎo běidǒu)*

$ | **SICHUAN** | When you've grown tired of mutton, head here for the best Sichuan-style dishes in Kashgar. There's plenty of cold beer in the refrigerator, and the second-floor covered terrace is perfect on a warm summer evening. **Known for:** gongbao jiding (kung pao chicken); tangcu liji (sweet-and-sour pork); relaxing outdoor atmosphere. [$] *Average main: Y20* ⊠ *285 Seman Lu, east of Seman Hotel* ▭ *No credit cards.*

Hotels

★ **Qinibagh Hotel** (其尼瓦克宾馆 *Qíníwǎkè bīnguǎn)*

$ | **HOTEL** | Located on the site of the former British consulate, the Qinibagh combines an interesting history with one of Kashgar's largest and most popular hotels. **Pros:** free Wi-Fi; excellent location; free Chinese breakfast. **Cons:** windows between the bathroom and main room; decorations lack any Uyghur style; elevators are too few and too slow. [$] *Rooms from: Y220* ⊠ *93 Seman Lu, northwest of Id Kah Mosque* ☎ *0998/298–2103* ⇨ *338 rooms* 🍽 *Free Breakfast.*

Radisson Blu Hotel Kashgar (喀什深业丽笙酒店 *Kāshi shēn yè lì shēng jiǔdiàn)*

$ | **HOTEL** | Located 10 minutes by cab from the city center, this stylish and modern hotel in Kashgar is a bit of luxury in the far western reaches of China. **Pros:** some staff speak English; free Wi-Fi in rooms; indoor pool. **Cons:** not walking distance from downtown; breakfast not included; comparatively high rates for Kashgar. [$] *Rooms from: Y788* ⊠ *2 Duolaite Bage Lu* ☎ *0998/268–8888* 🌐 *www.radissonblu.com/hotel-kashgar* ⇨ *261 rooms* 🍽 *Free Breakfast.*

Seman Hotel (色满宾馆 *Sèmǎn bīnguǎn*)
$ | **HOTEL** | Built in 1890 as the Russian consulate, this edifice served as a center of political intrigue for many years until it was transformed into a hotel in the 1950s. **Pros:** near some excellent restaurants; competitive prices from the lobby tour agencies; attractive Uyghur-style decoration. **Cons:** musty bathrooms in the cheaper rooms and dorms; many rooms in need of updating; a long walk from the city center. *Rooms from: Y120 ✉ 170 Seman Lu, at Renmin Lu ☎ 0998/258–2129 168 rooms No meals.*

Shopping

Handicraft Street (手工艺品街 *Shǒu gōngyìpǐn jiē*)
SHOPPING NEIGHBORHOODS | Running alongside the Id Kah Mosque is a narrow lane known as Handicraft Street. In either direction you'll find merchants selling everything from bright copper kettles and wedding chests to Uyghur instruments and wood carvings. ✉ *Wusitang Boyi Lu near Jiefang Bei Lu.*

Sunday Market (星期天大巴扎 *Xīngqítiān dàbā zhā*)
OUTDOOR/FLEA/GREEN MARKETS | Kashgar's famous Sunday Market consists of two bazaars with a distance of almost 10 km (6 miles) between them. The **Yengi Bazaar** on Aizilaiti Lu (Aizerete Road), about 1½ km (1 mile) northeast of the city center, is open every day, but on Sunday the surrounding streets overflow with vendors hawking everything from boiled sheep's heads to sunglasses. In the covered section you can bargain for decorative knives, embroidered fabrics, and all sorts of Uyghur-themed souvenirs. Behind the bazaar, rows of sleepy donkeys nod off in the bright sunlight, their carts lined up neatly beside them. For the best photos, however, you'll need to head over to the **Livestock Market,** a 20-minute taxi ride northwest of town. Every Sunday, farmers here tug recalcitrant sheep off their trucks, scarf-shrouded women preside over heaps of red eggs, and old Uyghur men squat over baskets of chickens, haggling over the virtues and vices of each hapless hen. In the market for a camel? You can buy one here. In the small shops surrounding the market you can get an Old World–style straight-razor shave from a Uyghur barber or grab a bowl of *laghman* noodles, knowing that it's flavored with meat that is very, very fresh. ✉ *Kashgar.*

Uyghur Musical Instruments Workshop (维吾尔民族乐器制作销售店 *Wéiwú'ěr mínzú yuèqì zhìzuò xiāoshòu diàn*)
MUSIC STORES | At this shop you can watch the owner or his apprentice working on Uyghur string instruments—stretching snakeskin or inlaying tiny bits of shell to make a Uyghur guitar called a *ravap.* ✉ *272 Kumudai'erwazha* ☎ *133/6488–8194.*

Side Trips from Kashgar

★ **Karakorum Highway** (喀喇昆仑公路 *Kā lǎ kūnlún gōnglù*)
BODY OF WATER | The Karakorum Highway (KKH), a spectacular road winding across some of the most dramatic and inhospitable terrain on Earth, traces one of the major ancient silk routes, from Kashgar south for 2,100 km (1,300 miles) through three great mountain ranges over the Khunjerab Pass (the highest border crossing in the world) into Pakistan. The journey can be hair-raising in part because of rock- and mudslides and in part because of daredevil driving. Modern highways have taken away most of the risk—and some of the fun—of taking this incredible journey.

At an altitude of 3,600 meters (11,800 feet), **Karakul Lake** is surrounded by mountains covered in beautiful glaciers and dominated by the 7,800-meter (25,600-foot) peak of **Muztagata,** the "Father of the Ice Mountains." Tourism has ebbed and flowed around the lake but restrictions over the past couple

Did You Know?

Karakul Lake is the highest body of water on the Pamir plateau. Snow-covered mountains, with the three highest peaks visible from the lake, surround it. Muztagh Ata (shown here) is 24,757 feet (7,546 meters) high.

years on overnight visitors has taken its toll on the local tourism economy. It's possible and recommended to eat a meal in one of the lakeside yurts but without an expensive permit from officials in Kashgar, you'll need to continue on to Tashkorgan or return to Kashgar. Toilet facilities in this area are some of the worst in China, but the area's beauty makes it worthwhile. Tour the lake via camel, horse, or motorbike, or just walk around, which will take about three hours. Bring warm clothing even in the summer, as it can be downright chilly: during our visit in July, we were applying sunscreen in the morning and battling sleet in the afternoon.

Any travel agent can arrange tours to Karakul Lake, but most people make the breathtaking journey by public bus on their way to Tashkorgan. Along the way you'll be stopped by at least four different police checkpoints, so have your passport handy. Buses headed for Tashkurgan, two hours south of the lake, leave Kashgar's International Bus Station every morning at 9:30 Beijing Time (the bus station operates on Xinjiang time, off by two hours). You'll have to pay the full price of Y51 for your ticket even though you're not traveling the full distance. Buses reach the lake in about four hours. To catch the bus back, wait by the side of the highway and flag it down—the bus returning to Kashgar from Tashkurgan passes the lake between 11 am and 1 pm. A seat should only cost Y40, but enterprising drivers may demand Y50. Either way, the bus is much cheaper than private tours, which will set you back about Y600 per day. ✉ *Kashgar*.

Index

A

B

C

P

Q

R

S

T

Z

Photo Credits

Front Cover: Aurora Photos, USA [Description: Rear view of man wearing traditional straw hat standing on Great Wall of China.] Back cover, from left to right: Shutterstock / Hung Chung Chih; fenghui/Shutterstock; leungchopan/Shutterstock. Spine: Nicha/Shutterstock. Interior, from left to right: Fedor Selivanov/Shutterstock (1). ssguy/Shutterstock (2-3). Alvaro Leiva / age fotostock (5). **Chapter 1**: Experience China: Jose Fuste Raga / age fotostock (6-7). 4045/Shutterstock (8-9). Meiqianbao/Shutterstock (9). Hung Chung Chih/Shutterstock (9). Philippians44 | Dreamstime.com (10). martinho Smart/Shutterstock (10). Leonid Andronov/Shutteerstock (10). Chuyu | Dreamstime.com (10). Decha Kiatlatch-anon/Shutterstock (11). Fedor Selivanov/Shutterstock (11). DoublePHOTO studio/Shutterstock (12). Eastphoto | Dreamstime.com (12). Toa55/ Shutterstock (12). wonderfoolphoto/Shutterstock (12). hidear/Shutterstock (13). Patrick Foto/Shutterstock (14). Calvin Chan/Shutterstock (14). GuoZhongHua/Shutterstock (14). Vassamon Anansukkasem/Shutterstock (14). dttmstock/Shutterstock (15). Sean Pavone/Shutterstock (15). Weixing | Dreamstime.com (16). pratan/Shutterstock (16). Tang Yan Song/Shutterstock (16). Hung Chung Chih/Shutterstock (17). R Scapinello/Shutterstock (17). inewsfoto/Shutterstock (20). Carla Nichiata/Shutterstock (20). YSK1/Shutterstock (20). Lisovskaya Natalia/Shutterstock (21). BTPhoto/Shutterstock (21). Curiosopl | Dreamstime.com (22). Taolmor | Dreamstime.com (22). Creativefire | Dreamstime.com (22). Maocheng | Dreamstime.com (22). Heinteh | Dreamstime.com (23). Mypokcik | Dreamstime.com (23). Ingehogenbijl | Dreamstime.com (23). 5 second Studio/Shutterstock (23). badboydt7/Shutterstock (24). Hungchungchih | Dreamstime.com (24). Hungchungchih | Dreamstime.com (24). Etherled | Dreamstime.com (25). Zenglegato | Dreamstime.com (25). zhu difeng/Shutterstock (26). Dmitri Ometsinsky/Shutterstock (26). Kolf/Shutterstock (26). PixHound/Shutterstock (26). chuyuss/Shutterstock (26). Mark Brandon/Shutterstock (27). ebenart/Shutterstock (27). Meiqianbao/Shutterstock (27). Efired/Shutterstock (27). dfrauchiger/Shutterstock (27). qingqing/Shutterstock (35). Kowloonese/Wikimedia Commons (36). Daniel Shichman & Yael Tauger/Wikimedia Commons (36). wikipedia.org (36). Hung Chung Chih/Shutterstock (37). rodho/Shutterstock (37). Chinneeb/Wikimedia Commons (38). B_cool/Wikimedia Commons (38). Imperial Painter/Wikimedia Commons (38). Wikimedia Commons (39). Joe Brandt/iStockphoto (39). Wikipedia.org (39). Wikimedia Commons (40). Wikipedia.org (40). Wikipedia.org (40). K.T. Thompson/wikipedia.org (40). Wikipedia.org (41). Wikipedia.org (41). tomislav domes/Flickr, [CC BY-ND 2.0] (41). **Chapter 3**: Beijing: Tao Images / age fotostock (55). lu linsheng/iStockphoto (76). Tao Images / age fotostock (77). Bob Balestri/iStockphoto (77). Lance Lee | AsiaPhoto.com/iStockphoto (78). Jiping Lai/iStockphoto (79). May Wong/Flickr (79). William Perry/iStockphoto (79). bing liu/iStockphoto (79). William Perry/iStockphoto (79). Wikipedia (80). Helena Lovincic/iStockphoto (80). Wikipedia (80). Wikipedia (81). rehoboth foto/Shutterstock (81). Wikipedia (81). P. Narayan / age fotostock (85). Tao Images / age fotostock (87). Admin270 | Dreamstime.com (97). Lim Yong Hian/ Shutterstock (98). Sylvain Grandadam / age fotostock (102-103). patrick frilet / age fotostock (110). Werner Bachmeier / age fotostock (117). Tao Images / age fotostock (123). Tao Images / age fotostock (125). Christian Kober / age fotostock (126). feiyuezhangjie/Shutterstock (128). Wikipedia (129). Liu Jianmin / age fotostock (130-131). Alan Crawford/iStockphoto (132). Eugenia Kim/iStockphoto (132). Chris Ronneseth/ iStockphoto (133). JTB Photo / age fotostock (141). **Chapter 4**: Beijing to Shanghai: P. Narayan / age fotostock (143). richliy/Shutterstock (151). View Stock / age fotostock (156). David Lyons / age fotostock (161). Karl Johaentges / age fotostock (163). Zhanglianxun | Dreamstime.com (170). nozomiiqel/Flickr, [CC BY-ND 2.0] (178). Charles Bowman / age fotostock (183). White Star Spierenb / age fotostock (191). suecan1/Flickr, [CC BY-ND 2.0] (195). Karl Johaentges / age fotostock (200). Philippe Michel / age fotostock (203). **Chapter 5**: Shanghai: Patrick Foto/Shutterstock (207). Gaby Wojciech / age fotostock (217). Karl Johaentges / age fotostock (221). claudio zaccherini/Shutterstock (222). ESB Professional/Shutterstock (227). JTB Photo / age fotostock (228). Pixattitude | Dreamstime.com (234-235). Saldari / age fotostock (263). **Chapter 6**: Eastern China: Bjmcse | Dreamstime.com (269). SuperStock / age fotostock (277). JTB Photo / age fotostock (282). Tao Images / age fotostock (284). JTB Photo / age fotostock (287). SuperStock / age fotostock (298). Tao Images / age fotostock (299). Mark52/Shutterstock (299). Shigeki Tanaka / age fotostock (300). Yuan yanwu - Imaginechina (301). Huiping Zhu/iStockphoto (301). richliy/Shutterstock (301). Christian Kober / age fotostock (304). **Chapter 7**: Hong Kong: chuyuss/Shutterstock (309). Amanda Hall / age fotostock (317). JayneRussell-Photography/Shutterstock (324). BrokenSphere/wikipedia.org (339). TungCheung/Shutterstock (342). Raga Jose Fuste / age fotostock (359). Steve Vidler / age fotostock (368). Christian Goupi / age fotostock (373). **Chapter 8**: The Southwest: Philippe Michel / age fotostock (379). Christian Kober / age fotostock (386). Li Xin/age fotostock (389). KingWu/iStockphoto (390-391). EcoPrint/Shutterstock (395). Huang jinguo - Imaginechina (401). discpicture/Shutterstock (401). Bartruff Dave / age fotostock (402). YinYang/iStockphoto (403). Natallia Yaumenenka/ iStockphoto (404). Wikimol/Wikipedia (404). Christopher Noble/iStockphoto (404). Wikimedia Commons (405). Christine gonsalves/iStockphoto (406). dem10/iStockphoto (406). Jason Fasi/Wikimedia Commons (406). jacus/iStockphoto (406). lateasquirrel/Wikimedia Commons (407). Juanmonino/iStockphoto (407). annastock/Shutterstock (407). 4045/Shutterstock (409). Seux Paule / age fotostock (411). Cintract Romain / age fotostock (415). Stefan Auth / age fotostock (419). Andrea Pistolesi / age fotostock (425). Michele Falzone / age fotostock (430). Angelo Cavallii / age fotostock (434). **Chapter 9**: Sichuan and Chongqing: clkraus/Shutterstock (437). Jose Fuste Raga / age fotostock (447). Manfred Bail / age fotostock (453). Jose Fuste Raga / age fotostock (454). Fotosearch RM / age fotostock (459). FotoosVanRobin/Wikimedia Commons (460). Chubykin Arkady/Shutterstock (460). ImagineChina (461). hywit dimyadi/iStockphoto (461). Maria Ly/Flickr (461). Hannamariah/Shutterstock (462). zkruger/iStockphoto (462). Ritesh Man Tamrakar/Wikimedia Commons (463). Rjanag/Wikimedia Commons (463). Craig Lovell / Eagle Visions Photography / Alamy (463). Cephas Picture Library / Alamy (463). Eneri LLC/iStockphoto (464). Man Haan Chung/iStockphoto (464). Holger Gogolin/iStockphoto (464). Eneri LLC/iStockphoto (464). WeiShen/Shutterstock (468) **Chapter 10**: Xi'an and The Silk Road: Rick Wang/Shutterstock (473). William Fawcett fotoVoyager.com/iStockphoto (482). John Goulter / age fotostock (488). Greg Knudsen, Fodors.com member (488-489). hanhanpeggy/iStockphoto (490). Wikimedia.org (491). André Viegas/Shutterstock (491). zhuda/Shutterstock (492). Amy Nichole Harris/Shutterstock (492). Martin Puddy / age fotostock (493-494). Yan Vugenfirer/Shutterstock (493). Ke Wang/Shutterstock (493). Lukas Hlavac/Shutterstock (494). Olaf Schubert / age fotostock (494). vito arcomano / age fotostock (499). Aldo Pavan / age fotostock (505). TAO IMAGES / age fotostock (508). Raga Jose Fuste / age fotostock (510). Mark Henley / age fotostock (514). JTB Photo / age fotostock (519). Philippe Michel / age fotostock (526-527). About Our Writers: All photos are courtesy of the writers.

Notes

Notes

Notes

Notes

Fodor's ESSENTIAL CHINA

Editorial: Douglas Stallings, *Editorial Director*, Margaret Kelly, Jacinta O'Halloran, *Senior Editors*; Kayla Becker, Alexis Kelly, Amanda Sadlowski, *Editors*; Teddy Minford, *Content Editor*, Rachael Roth, *Content Manager*

Design: Tina Malaney, *Design and Production Director*, Jessica Gonzalez, *Production Designer*

Photography: Jill Krueger, *Senior Photo Editor*

Maps: Rebecca Baer, *Senior Map Editor*, David Lindroth, Mark Stroud (Moon Street Cartography), *Cartographers*

Production: Jennifer DePrima, *Editorial Production Manager*, Carrie Parker, *Senior Production Editor*, Elyse Rozelle, *Production Editor*

Business & Operations: Chuck Hoover, *Chief Marketing Officer*, Robert Ames, *General Manager*, Stephen Horowitz, *Director of Business Development and Revenue Operations*; Tara McCrillis, *Director of Publishing Operations*

Public Relations and Marketing: Joe Ewaskiw, *Manager*, Esther Su, *Marketing Manager*

Writers: Jamie Fullerton, Julie Grundvig, Amy Hawkins, Cat Nelson, Kate Springer, Josh Summers, Clarissa Wei, Crystal Wilde

Editor: Margaret Kelly

Editoral Contributors: Linda Cabasin and Laura Kidder

Production Editor: Carrie Parker

Production Design: Liliana Guia

1st Edition

ISBN 978-1-64097-129-5

ISSN 2639-4987

Library of Congress Control Number 2018958615

SPECIAL SALES

This book is available at special discounts for bulk purchases for sales promotions or premiums. For more information, e-mail SpecialMarkets@fodors.com.

PRINTED IN THE UNITED STATES OF AMERICA

10 9 8 7 6 5 4 3 2 1

About Our Writers

Jamie Fullerton updated the Eastern China Chapter.

Julie Grundvig is a professional writer, editor, and arts consultant, with a specialty in Chinese arts and cultural heritage. Julie has over 20 years' experience living, working, and traveling in the greater China region and across Asia. She holds an MA from the University of British Columbia in Asian Studies (China) and an MA in Museum Studies (Heritage and Interpretation) from the University of Leicester, UK. Julie has been editor of *Yishu: Journal of Contemporary Chinese Art* since 2002 and sits on the Board of Directors for the Canadian Society of Asian Arts. She is founder and director of Different Mountain, a Chinese arts consultancy based in Vancouver, British Columbia. Julie updated our Travel Smart chapter.

Amy Hawkins is a freelance journalist based in Beijing. She is the former Deputy Editor and Food & Drink Editor of *Time Out Beijing* and has spent more than two years getting to know and love the city. As well as *Fodors*, she has written for the *Guardian, Foreign Policy, Dazed and Confused, WIRED, New Statesman*, the *Times Literary Supplement*, the *Sunday Times* and others. You can follow her on Twitter @XLHawkins. This year Amy updated the Beijing chapter.

Former editor-in-chief of *Time Out Shanghai*, **Cat Nelson** moved to China nearly a decade ago to research rural development and sustainable agriculture before setting out on her current path, writing about food, culture, travel and lifestyle. She enjoys eating at hole-in-the-wall noodle joints, Michelin-starred establishments, and everywhere in between. You can find her at www.cat-nelson.com or on Instagram at @_catnelson

Kate Springer is a Hong Kong-based freelance journalist who covers travel, food, culture, and architecture. Her work has been published by *Condé Nast Traveler, CNN, BBC Travel, Travel & Leisure, Food & Wine, Forbes Travel Guide, Fodor's, Vice, The Independent*, and more. She holds a master's degree from Northwestern University's Medill School of Journalism. While ambling around Asia, Kate dabbles in photography and devours *xiaolongbao* dumplings at every chance. Kate is our Hong Kong updater.

Josh Summers and his wife first moved to China in 2006 and spent over 10 years living and traveling around the country. Most of their time was spent in the gorgeous western region of Xinjiang, which Josh has photographed and written about extensively. He loves sharing his experience in China through travel writing and on his website, TravelChina-Cheaper.com. Josh updated the Silk Road chapter.

About Our Writers

Clarissa Wei is an American journalist who has traveled extensively throughout the greater China area. She has backpacked and written about over a dozen Chinese provinces for various outlets, including *VICE* and *National Geographic.*

Crystal Wilde is a British journalist and travel writer who has lived in Asia for more than 10 years. After earning her journalism stripes in London, she spent four years running a team of travel writers in Thailand before moving on to work for websites and print publications in Hong Kong and finally Beijing. As well as *Fodors*, she has written for *CNN Travel, New York Magazine, The Times of London, The Daily Telegraph* and several leading inflight magazines.